Dùthchas nan Gàidheal

Dùthchas nan Gàidheal

Selected Essays of John MacInnes

Edited by Michael Newton

BIRLINN

First published in 2006 by
Birlinn Limited
West Newington House
10 Newington Road
Edinburgh
EH9 1QS

www.birlinn.co.uk

ISBN10: 1 84158 316 2
ISBN13: 978 1 84158 316 7

British Library Cataloguing-in-Publication Data
A catalogue record for this book is available from the British Library

The Publisher acknowledges subsidy from The Scotland Inheritance Fund and

towards the publication of this book

Typeset by Hewer Text UK, Edinburgh
Printed and bound by Antony Rowe Ltd, Chippenham

Table of Contents

Acknowledgments

I had wondered for some time what I could do to bring the work of Dr John MacInnes to a wider audience, and was glad to accept the invitations from Margaret Bennett, and Hugh Andrew of Birlinn to do this volume.

We are grateful to those who have provided permission to reprint original work: the Gaelic Society of Inverness for granting us permission to reprint so many of the articles from their indispensable journal; Loraine MacLean and the Inverness Field Club for permission to reprint 'Gaelic Poetry and Historical Tradition'; Cathal Ó Luain for permission to reprint 'Sùil air Bàrdachd na Gàidhlig'; Seosamh Watson for permission to reprint 'Baird is Bleidirean'; Raymond Ross and Joy Hendry for permission to reprint 'Language, Metre and Diction in the Poetry of Sorley MacLean'; William Gillies for permission to reprint 'The Gaelic Perception of the Lowlands'; Hilda Davidson for permission to reprint 'The Seer in Gaelic Tradition'; Douglas Gifford for permission to reprint 'Gaelic Poetry in the Nineteenth Century'; Norman Gillies for permission to reprint 'Cainnt is Cànan'; Lindisfarne Books for permission to reprint the new introduction to their edition of the *Carmina Gadelica*; Dornach Studio for permission to reprint both English and Gaelic versions of the essays on Highland droving; Wilson McLeod and Máire Ni Annracháin, for permission to reprint 'Am Fàsach ann an Dùthchas nan Gàidheal'.

A number of people have been generous in providing references to relevant articles and materials, particularly Margaret Bennett, Ronald Black and Wilson McLeod. Cathlin Macaulay compiled information from the indices of the archives of the School of Scottish Studies regarding MacInnes' fieldwork.

I wish to acknowledge my debt to the University of Edinburgh for providing me access to the main library and to the libraries of the School of Scottish Studies and the Department of Celtic, and also to the Edinburgh Central Library and the National Library of Scotland for the privilege of utilising their resources.

The dedication of Andrew Simmons of Birlinn was crucial in completing this undertaking. Wendy MacInnes was always generous and kind during our efforts, and Rhiannon Giddens has been a welcome source of support and encouragement. A travel grant from the Carnegie Trust for the Universities of Scotland made my work on this project possible.

Michael Newton
Richmond, Virginia
May 2006

Foreword

Many of us have waited a very long time for this book and at last, like the Claymore coming in shining from way beyond Calvay, here it is. And in much the same way in which the MacBrayne's steamer brought friends and family and food as well as expectation and lights and excitement, this book brings a precious cultural cargo to the bare pier on which we find ourselves standing at the beginning of the 21st century.

On reflection, perhaps the pier is not bare at all. Perhaps, in fact, it is filled to overflowing. In a world where the miraculous (sending an e-mail, for instance) has become commonplace, the commonplace – such as the arrival of a ferry – has become miraculous. As she sails in, through the darkness, red to port and green to starboard, we are amazed: once more, the expected has been made marvellous.

This book is of that precious sort: one of our own, bringing our own marvels to our own land. Not coming as a stranger or a visitor or a trader or a salesman with alien goods sparkling from a foreign land but as one of ourselves, revealing to us that – all along – the miracles were always at our own doorsteps, in our own tongue in our own land, right in front of our very eyes.

I suppose the marvel of the indigenous is always difficult to grasp or understand or appreciate, but that fundamental responsibility will now be made that bit easier for all of us because of the publication of these essays. They will give us a window through which we can not only view but frame the very complex Gaelic world which has far too often been over-simplified, ridiculed, lampooned, distorted and abused by lesser men and lesser scholars and lesser writers than Dr John MacInnes.

What we have here, instead, is not just an exploration of but a terrific manifestation of the complexity and richness and vitality and depth and reach and range of Gaelic culture. The picture that emerges is not one of a backward-looking, depressed culture under threat of extinction but rather the very opposite: of a language and culture that was internationalist in outlook, universal in sympathy, trans-national in ideology, outward-looking and expansive in trade, travel, commerce, education, exchange and fellowship.

That is not to say that Dr MacInnes is not aware and has nothing to say about the way in which this same Gaelic culture also became increasingly inward-looking, introverted, paranoid and besieged. Among many first-class modern Gaelic scholars he has been as willing as anyone to patiently explain and re-explain the reasons for this ideological, political, cultural and linguistic collapse: not least, the marriage of Malcolm Canmore to the Saxon Queen Margaret (later St Margaret) in 1070 which, in Dr MacInnes's view was the very beginning of a by now 1000-year-long assault on all things Celtic. He was also, as far as I am aware, the first Gaelic scholar to convincingly use the word 'ethnocide' as the correct description for what the state, under various educational and military and other guises, has consistently done to the Gaelic language and its associated culture ever since.

Not once throughout this book does Dr John MacInnes use the largely defensive terms *mion-chànan* or 'minority language'. It's not, of course, as I have already suggested, that he is not fully aware of the demographic and geographic as well as cultural and linguistic diminution of the language – that's exactly why he calls it 'ethnocide' – but because, both as a scholar and as a Gael, he is more aware than most of the largeness of the intellectual spatial territory which Gaelic has occupied in European civilization. To put it simply, I think that his underlying belief is that Gaelic is right up there alongside Greek and Latin and German and French and Russian and Italian and Spanish and Welsh – and English for that matter – as being one of the chief corner-stones as well as artistic banners of classical European civilisation.

The overall effect of that argument is to gladden the heart and to revive these peculiarly old-fashioned virtues called faith, hope and charity. It is to realise afresh that Gaelic is nothing to be ashamed of or embarrassed about, despite what our educational history told many of us: on the contrary, it is to realise with fresh astonishment just how versatile and vivacious and vital the Gaelic language has been, in a pan-European context. Which is, of course – and not just because of the Clearances – equally true in a world context.

The other striking thing about this collection is its sheer range –

from Poetry to Protestantism, from Droving to Divination. And not just for the sake of mentioning topics, whether alliterative or not, in the passing but for this simple reason – that each of the many subjects covered by Dr MacInnes in these essays are necessary explorations of his central theme of *Dùthchas*, the focal web of belief and kinship which is at the cosmological centre of MacInnes's world.

Like the spokes of a bicycle wheel – or perhaps more appropriately of a cart – issues and topics such as 'The Gaelic Perception of the Lowlands' or 'Dròbhaireachd' or 'Gaelic Song and Dance' – or indeed any of the essays in this book – are but the necessary shafts which connect the central cosmology to the rims which go round in front of our eyes. Whether we agree or not with any or all of his insights or arguments is probably secondary: what matters is that we take them seriously, as authentic versions of a Gaelic-centred ontology – and therefore epistemology – of what it was like to have been a Gael in a complete if simultaneously expanding and diminishing world.

He has important things to say about the central significance of having Gaelic-language scholarship in a global world and crucially draws our attention to the imperial agenda which has dominated and filtered through our consciousnesses. As with the late Edward Said, he serves us well by reminding us that our culture needs to be measured and enjoyed from other than the imperial standard.

Perhaps his prize essay in this book is his seminal address origin-ally given to the Gaelic Society of Inverness in 1978 under the title 'The Panegyric Code in Gaelic Poetry and its Historical Background'. As with all the other talks in this book it is scholarly, elegant, entertaining and opinionated in the best sense of the word, which is to say that – unlike some scholars – Dr John has always been courageous enough to give an informed opinion when asked. Many of our Gaelic singers owe their knowledge of the songs they sing – who wrote that song and when and why and under what circum-stances and exactly what does that word or phrase mean? – to him. In this of course, Dr MacInnes is but one of a great thread of innumer-able scholars – perhaps most importantly the late Reverend William Matheson – who have crucially bridged the gap between the modern interpreter and the original material. That itself has been one of the great under-valued services offered by our universities and scholars and, without wishing to harp on about it, one we would ignore at our peril. There is enough ignorance in the general media already about things Gaelic: treasuring the academic custodians of our great cultural treasures is at least one small bulwark against increasing globalization, if not barbarism.

The 'Panegyric Code' broke new and important literary ground in the Gaelic world by framing a structural and historical context in which to position a good deal of our major literature. In analysing the rhetoric of praise in traditional *bardachd*, MacInnes unveils a complex and fascinating hinterland which is crucial to understand before one can begin to adequately comment upon some of our greatest works of literature. And it is important to stress that this hinterland is not merely or even mainly literary, but rather historical and political – there are critical insights into the notion of Gaelic and Scottish nationhood in this essay which ought to be fundamentally understood by anyone interested in questions of identity or of political and civic (as well as cultural and linguistic) nationhood. He has extremely important things to say about the dialectical relationship between the Campbells and the MacDonalds: a relationship – or a rivalry – of huge ideological and therefore political and cultural significance to the country which has (or hasn't) become Scotland.

And above all, this essay has really important things to say about the function of poetry – which is to say the function of all art – in shaping kinships, allegiances, ideas, rivalries, communities and nations. And lest anyone believe that MacInnes's essay merely addresses some ancient bardic phenomena I would argue that his essential thesis is as valid for the modern as for the old media: I have no doubts that a very modern (or post-modernist) panegyric code applies to the daily messages we receive through our 21st-century bards via live satellite from the set of Big Brother or Baghdad.

The vibrant connections that MacInnes makes between poetry and religion, for example, or between the supernatural and the subconscious, run throughout all the essays in the book. It's perfectly evident and perfectly obvious that he is a Gael: otherwise he wouldn't speak with such assurance of *Dùthchas nan Gàidheal*. It's an assurance that comes from having experienced a thousand real (as opposed to artificial) céilidhs in real people's houses in real places at a time when Gaelic really was the language of the heart and hearth. MacInnes's essay are in many places only manifestations of what the late Iain Crichton Smith eloquently described in an essay as 'Real People in Real Places'.

It is equally perfectly evident and obvious that MacInnes is a son of the manse: his fascination with and his knowledge of religion is not just textual, but contextual. What he has to say about it (and it is almost completely sympathetic) comes from not just having read about it, but from having seen it and experienced it throughout his life. Dr John has sat with too many authentic believers to be cynical about any of them, or about their beliefs. In a civic Scotland which has often ignorantly condemned religious belief – whether that be Calvinism or Catholicism or any a hundred variations in between – it is refreshing to read the thoughts of a humanist who gives due dignity and reverence – I would go as far as to say a sacredness – to beliefs that he does not himself perhaps necessarily share.

And it is equally evident and obvious that this is a man who loves words. He picks and places words like a stonemason, and part of the delight of this book is the way in which his arguments are constructed, like a stone wall – sometimes it runs up hill, sometimes across a bare moor, sometimes down the bottom of the garden. Knowledge balances insight and speculation is wedged between fact or quote, so that the wall is never either or – never just a concrete wall of facts or just a higgledy-piggledy juggle of notions, but a fine balance of the two. If you don't agree with the speculation, trust the fact; and if you don't trust the fact, just agree with the speculation.

He has very fine essays on Sorley MacLean and his public discourses perhaps especially on the poem 'Hallaig' over the years have done much to elevate modern Gaelic poetry in the national consciousness. In fact, it is only a matter of weeks since I quoted his comment about 'Hallaig' – the place and the poem – at Hallaig itself, on the east side of Raasay, when the Nobel Laureate Seumas Heaney read MacLean's translation after I'd read the original Gaelic, on site.

'Such a sense of completion at the symbolic level', MacInnes says of the poem, 'and such a sense of incompletion at the level of history.'

On a professional level, as a journalist and writer, I would also wish to say this: that Dr John MacInnes has for very many years been an articulate and willing contributor to the often much-maligned world of the media. He has been willing to share the stories and knowledge he has gathered over very many years at the great School of Scottish Studies at the University of Edinburgh and I think the Gaelic community owe him – and indeed to all his many colleagues at the School and at the universities – a great debt. Our perceptions have been widened, our linguistic registers enriched and our language and culture ennobled by all their work.

As a journalist and writer, I would wish that anyone who dares to write anything about Gaelic Scotland should read this book first. Not only will they be enlightened and informed but they might be challenged to enter through the gates of *dùthchas* itself which is to say – in this instance at least – to learn and use Gaelic so that they would know what they're talking, or at least writing, about. For any student of Gaelic, this volume ought to a be a standard, oft-read text.

It is an honour and a privilege to commend this book that comes from the heart of our great articulate tradition.

Angus Peter Campbell
Isle of Skye
2006

Roimh-Ràdh

'S fhad' on a bha an fheadhainn againn a tha eòlach air an Ollamh Iain MacAonghuis air a bhith a' feitheamh gu mi-fhoighidneach ris an leabhar seo – cruinneachadh de chuid dhe na sgrìobhaidhean 's na h-aistean 's na léirmheasan 's na h-òraidean a tha Iain air toirt seachad ann an iomadh àite airson iomadh bliadhna.

'S a-nis tha an leabhar againn 's tha e brèagha 's tomadach is prìseil is ealanta, mar bu dual dhan duine 's mar a bha dùil is dòchas againn a bhitheadh e. Tha sinn an comain an Dotair Mìcheal Newton airson an obair mhór ionmholta a rinn e ann a bhith a' cruinneachadh nan ulaidhean seo, 's tha e gu math follaiseach cuideachd nach e obair fhuar sgoileireil a bha fainear dha, ach obair bhlàth a chridhe, a bheireadh urram an dà chuid do dh'Iain còir agus dha smuaintean agus fhiosrachadh 's a bheachdan.

Ach chan eil an sin ach a' bheag dheth, oir tha an t-urram as motha, saoilidh mise co-dhiù, anns an leabhar seo a' dol gu na Gàidheil fhéin air a bheil Iain air a bhith an dà chuid cho eòlach agus cho miosail.

Tha sgoilearachd ann a bheir fiosrachadh seachad agus tha sgoi-learachd ann a bheir am fiosrachadh sin seachad le tlachd agus le gràdh, agus chan eil teagamh sam bith nach ann dhan dara treubh sin a bhuineas an leabhar seo. Tha e a' dèanamh uaislean dhe na Gàidheil agus dhe an cuid cànain agus cultar agus ann an saoghal far am bheil iad air an cur gu tric ann an suarachas 's e rud mór a tha sin ann fhéin. Nuair leughas tu na tha aig Iain MacAonghuis ri ràdh anns an leabhar seo tha e gad fhàgail le grunn rudan, agus iad uile uasal.

Anns a' phrìomh àite, saoilidh mi, tha sinn a' faighinn dealbh mhionaideach air cho fìor ealanta agus urramach 's bha (agus aig a sin 's a tha) dualchas nan Gàidheal. Chan e dealbh bheag chumhang de mhion-chànain air a phronnadh ann an oisean a tha ag éirigh a-mach às na duilleagan seo ach an dearbh chaochladh: dealbh de chànan mór Eòrpach a bha 'na chlach-oisne ann an sìobhaltas na Roinn Eòrpa 's bha 'na bhratach mhór dhathach nuair a labhras sinn air na rudan móra mar litreachas is creideamh is modhan is beusan.

Anns na h-aistean 's anns na h-òraidean seo chì sinn cho eadar-nàiseanta an dà chuid ann am brìgh agus ann an cliù 's a bha a' Ghàidhlig, agus tuigidh sinn cuideachd cho fìor shuarach agus cho fìor bhrùideil 's a bha an dìmeas agus an suarachas a rinn ionnstramaidean na stàite air ar cànan agus air ar dualchas. Bha e mar gun cuireadh tu ban-righinn a-mach air an t-sitig no rudeigin naomh dhan teine.

Aig cridhe na tha aig MacAonghuis ri ràdh tha tiotal an leabhair fhéin – 's sin *Dùthchas nan Gàidheal*. Tha am facal sin – 'dùthchas' – saoilidh mise cho ceangailte ri MacAonghuis 's a tha gathan ris a' ghréin. 'S gann gun urrainn dhomh smaoineachadh air Iain a' labhairt seantans gun am facal sin – 'dùthchas' – a bhith 'na lùib an àiteigin.

Tha e a' ciallachadh grunn rudan ann an diofar sheaghan, ach aig cridhe a' ghnothaich tha e a' ciallachadh am pòsadh iongantach sin – am pòsadh dualach sin – eadar cànan agus àite agus dualchas, ceangailte – no co-cheangailte – ri treubh is cinneadh is eachdraidh is cairdeas is creideamh is sgeulachd is eile. Tha e mar aiseal na rotha air am bheil spògan na cairte uile a' crochadh. Mar nach biodh na spògan ann gun an cridhe, ciamar a bhios Gàidhlig fhéin ann gun dùthchas?

Tha am facal 'dùthchas' cuideachd doirbh a mhìneachadh – mar an Cuilthionn fhéin tha e nas fhasa fhaicinn no aithneachadh na tha e a mhìneachadh no fiùs a mholadh. Ach anns an leabhar seo tha sinn a' tighinn cho faisg air dùthchas nan Gàidheal – chan ann a mhìneachadh ach fhoillseachadh – 's a gheibh sinn.

Tha am foillseachadh sin farsaing agus fradharcach, agus gad fhàgail moiteil (seach nàireach) a bhith 'nad Ghàidheal. Tha Iain a' toirt dùthchas nan Gàidheal beò agus gu slàn far comhair ann an iomadh seagh agus ann an iomadh raon, eadar pìobaireachd is dannsa, bho chreideamh gu bardachd.

Tha na tha aige ri ràdh mu iomadach cuspair fiosrachail, beòthail, ealanta agus inntinneach agus saoilidh mi gur e seo an rud as fhearr buileach – mar a tha e a' ceangail nan cuspairean dlùth ri chéile, mar gum biodh e a' fighe plaide no còta ioma-dhathach chan e a-mhàin a chumas blàth thu ach a bhios brèagha mu do bhroilleach. Mar ann am fighe, chan eil aon snàithlein, mar gum bitheadh, 'na seasamh leatha fhéin: dé math a bhith mach air dannsa, mar eisimpleir, mur a bheil thu mothachail gu bheil e cho ceangailte ri ceòl; no, dé math a bhith mach air creideamh, mar eisimpleir, mur a bheil thu cuideachd mothachail gun robh buaidh iongantach aig a-sin air poileataics is eile, mar a bha cuideachd air an dearbh chaochladh.

Tha Iain a' dealbh dhuinn saoghal iomadh-fhillteach agus iomadh-dhaite far am faigh leughadair sam bith as d'fhiach tuigse air-leth gun robh agus gu bheil a h-uile mac màthar rud ann an saoghal nan Gàidheal ('s chan ann a-mhàin ann an saoghal nan Gàidheal) a' suathadh air 's a' gluasad 's a' toirt buaidh air choireigin air a h-uile mac màthar rud eile.

Agus is e rud mór a tha anns an leasan sin fhéin, ged nach ionnsaicheadh sinn ach sin fhéin bhon leabhar iongantach seo. Oir ann an saoghal a tha sìor fhàs beag agus cumhang, ann an astar agus ann an tìm agus ann am feallsanachd agus ann an dreuchd, 's e rud mór a tha ann cuimhneachadh cho faisg agus cho farsaing 's a tha a h-uile rud ri chéile agus bho chéile.

Tha rudan aige ri ràdh mu Ìmpireileis, mar eisimpleir, a tha air leth cudromach dhuinn mar Ghàidheil. An siud 's an seo tron leabhar tha e a' cur nar cuimhne gun robh ar dualchas agus ar dòighean daonnan (cha mhór) air an tomhas no air am faicinn tro ghloinne Ìmpirileis an àite bho ar sealladh fhéin no ar cànan fhéin le ar slatan-tomhais fhéin. Anns na làithean a th'ann tha beagan atharrachaidh air tighinn air a sin, ach mar a bha Eideard Said nach maireann cuideachd a' cur nar cuimhne, bu chòir dhuinn daonnan a bhith nas mothachaile air na diofar slatan-tomhais chultarach is eile a tha ann airson ar dualchas fhéin, chan e a-mhàin a thomhas ach a leasachadh.

Tha na h-aistean anns an leabhar seo a' cur nar cuimhne ann an dòigh gu math beòthail, nach math dhuinn a bhith ceangailte gu teann ri beachdan nach eil air am bonntachadh air fiosrachadh mionaideach, agus nach math dhuinn a bharrachd a bhith luma làn fiosrachaidh mionaideach nach urrainn dhuinn a chleachdadh gu h-éifeachdail agus gu saoirsneachail ann an còir ar co-chreutairean. Ma tha òran againn seinneamaid e; 's ma tha sinn a' cluinntinn òran nach eil sinn a' tuigsinn, ionnsaicheamaid mu dheidhinn.

'S tha sin fhéin a' cur nar cuimhne gu bheil oilthighean agus sgoilearan na h-Alba 'nan stòras phrìseil a bu chòir dhuinn a dhìon gu faiceallach le ar n-uile neart. Gu ìre mhath 's iadsan na drochaidean eadar ar n-eachdraidh agus sinn fhìn, 's le bhith a' geàrd nan sgoilearan tha fhios cuideachd gu bheil sinn a' geàrd nan òran 's nan làmh-sgrìobhaidhean 's na beul-aithris is eile a dh'innseas dhuinn chan e a-mhàin mar a bha sinn, ach cuideachd gu ìre ciamar a tha sinn a-nis mar a tha sin, gun ghuth a ràdh air ciamar a dh'fhaodamaid a bhith na b'fhearr. Tha dòighean eile ar n-eachdraidh is ar beusan 's ar dòighean a thuigsinn, ceart gu leòr, ach na diochuimhnicheamaid gu

bheil ar n-oilthighean (no co-dhiù gum bu chòir dhar n-oilthighean a
bhith) – coltach ri eaglaisean is eile – a bhith 'nan raon saor eadar
sìobhaltas agus brùidealas. Chan e nach eil deagh fheum againn air a
leithid 's na làithean teann a th'ann.

Tha grunn dhe na h-aistean anns an leabhar seo air leth ann an
stoidhle agus ann an susbaint. Tha na h-òraidean mu litreachas gar
toirt a-steach gu h-ealanta chan ann a-mhàin a-steach dha na dàin 's
dha na h-òrain fhéin ach – a cheart cho cudromach – dha na h-
amannan 's na modhan 's na beusan 's na h-iarrtasan sòisealta is eile a
bha a' teannadh air na baird a rinn na h-òrain.

Tha na sgrìobh MacAonghuis timcheall Shomhairle MhicGhill-
Eain agus mu 'Hallaig' 'nan deagh eisimpleirean dhen dòigh Mharc-
sach seo air coimhead air eachdraidh: gun aon lide a thoirt air falbh
bho shàr-chomasan Shomhairle mar dhuine 's mar bhard, tha Mac-
Aonghuis a' cur nar cuimhne cuideachd cho fìor chudromach 's a bha
an suidheachadh 's an togail a fhuair MacGill-Eain. Chan e nach
b'urrainn do Shomhairle an corr a dhèanamh ach a bhith 'na shàr-
bhard (nach iomadh bard is eile a thilg an cothrom), ach tha Mac-
Aonghuis a' mìneachadh dhuinn cho dathach 's cho làidir 's cho
beairteach 's a bha am *palette* a chaidh a bhuileachadh air Somhairle
òg: beairteas cànain agus coimhearsnachd agus creideamh ann an
Ratharsair aig toiseach na ficheadamh linn a bha mar charraig am
measg na luaithre.

Tha an aon seòrsa de choluadar sparrach – an comhstri no an
cairdeas eadar uachdar is ìochdar, no eadar briathran is brìgh, no
eadar an rud a tha an dàn ag ràdh agus ag ràdh – ri fhaicinn gu soilleir
anns an aiste as ainmeil a tha aig Iain – 's e sin an òraid a thug e do
Chomunn Gàidhlig Inbhir Nis ann an 1978 fon tiotal 'The Panegyric
Code in Gaelic Poetry and its Historical Background'.

Chan e a-mhàin gum faic sinn cho soilleir anns an òraid seo cho fìor
ealdhanta 's a bha bardachd Ghàidhlig ach mhìnich Iain dhuinn ann
an dòigh a tha cho reusanta agus cho sgoileireil agus cho soilleir agus
cho ealanta mar a bha a' bhardachd fhéin co-cheangailte ri, agus ag
éirigh às, ach cuideachd ag ath-nuadhachadh, siostam shòisealta-
phoilitigeach an àma.

Chan eil teagamh sam bith agamsa nach e mìneachadh a tha seo a
dh'fhaodamaid a chleachdadh chan ann a-mhàin airson tuigse a thoirt
dhuinn air bardachd Chlaiseagach na Gàidhlig, ach air gach dòigh eile
a tha na meadhanan, fiùs anns an latha th'ann, a' mìneachadh an t-
saoghail dhuinn. Chan e a-mhàin gu bheil am 'Panegyric Code' a' toirt

iuchair dhuinn a-steach dhan bhardachd aig A' Chlàrsair Dhall, can, ach cuideachd dha na còdaichean a tha a leithid CNN a' toirt dhuinn anns an linn a tha againn.

Tha an t-Ollamh Iain MacAonghuis air a bhith 'na charactar cliùiteach ann an saoghal nan Gàidheal o chionn iomadh bliadhna a-nis. Tha e air iomadh neach a mhisneachadh le a bhriathran 's le a chuid eòlais iongantach thairis nam bliadhnachan sin, 's chan eil àm nach éisd mi ris air an rèidio no nach fhaic mi e air an teilidh no nach leugh mi a bhriathran toinisgeil air duilleig nach eil mi air mo nàrachadh le cho truagh 's a tha mo chuid Ghàidhlig agus m' eòlas agus m' fhiosrachadh mu ghnothaichean Gàidhealach an coimeas ris.

Tha a eòlas farsaing agus domhainn agus tha liut labhairt aige anns a' chànan nach deach a bhuileachadh air móran: gach uair a labhras e, tha a Ghàidhlig fhéin mar gum bitheadh a' fàs nas uaisle agus nas uaisle le mar a tha e ga labhairt, cho grinn agus cho nàdarra. Tha an sgrìobhadh aige anns an leabhar seo a cheart cho uasal, agus chan eil teagamh sam bith agam nach e ulaidh air leth a tha againn an seo a bhios glé phrìseil do dh'iomadach oileanach is sgoilear is leughadair is eile anns na bliadhnachan móra a tha romhainn.

Agus – bhon a tha deagh chuid dhen leabhar anns a' Bheurla – b'e mo mhiann gun leughadh gach neach aig a bheil beachd sam bith mun Ghàidhlig agus mu na Gàidheil an leabhar uasal seo mus fosgladh iad am beul no mus sgrìobhadh iad aon lide mur deidhinn ann am paipear-naidheachd no ann am meadhan sam bith eile.

'S mura h-ionnsaich iad bhuaithe seo, mo thruaighe oirnn, oir mar a tha Iain fhéin ga chur: 'Tha a cheart uiread de "shaobh-chreideamh" ann am beachdan foghlaimte ar latha-ne is a tha ann an uirsgeulan na Gàidhlig.'

Ach aon rud cinnteach – cha bu chòir leisgeul sam bith a bhith aca os déidh an leabhar seo a leughadh.

Taing airson sin, agus iomadach rud eile.

Aonghas Pàdraig Caimbeul
An t-Eilean Sgitheanach,
An Cèitean, 2006

Introduction

Dr John MacInnes has produced scholarship both prolific and profound during his career with the University of Edinburgh. His is the work of a polymath who has applied his extensive academic training to an inherited tradition, giving us a perspective on the Highlands which is both intimate and analysed with intellectual rigour. His articles have been seminal re-examinations of Gaelic tradition; his influence on scholarship, through his writing, his lectures, and his personal mentorship and encouragement to countless students, cannot be overstated. Ronald Black has recently commented that his article on the 'Gaelic Panegyric Code' – surely his most admired contribution – 'represents an act not of discovery but of recovery', and this could be said of his work on the history, culture, and literature of the Highlands as a whole.

A cursory glance at his extensive list of publications reveals that his labour has not been confined to the narrow halls of academia, and even this list is inevitably incomplete. Nor have I been able to collate a list of the many programmes he has done for the BBC and the lectures he has given for many distinguished institutions. Through these many platforms, his influence has been pervasive wherever the Scottish Highlands are studied.

I have also tried to underline the importance of his legacy in preserving Scotland's precious oral traditions by drawing attention to the decades of fieldwork he conducted throughout the Gàidhealtachd (Gaelic-speaking areas). His writings are all the more authoritative because they draw upon his experiences with tradition-bearers, and MacInnes's interests in the margins of the Gàidhealtachd – eastern Perthshire, Aberdeenshire, Sutherland, Arran and Cape Breton, for example – allowed him to draw from these ancient and neglected sources before they disappeared forever.

His passion for Highland tradition did not start with employment or with his university training: as his biographical sketch demonstrates, MacInnes was heir to a wealth of tradition from his family, and from an early age he absorbed the linguistic and literary riches all around him. The topics that he pursued as a scholar, featured in this volume, were already captivating his attention as a child.

My goal has to been to gather a selection of his written work and present it as a cohesive volume. MacInnes has worked with me to update and sometimes augment his articles. I have imposed a consistent reference and spelling system upon the texts, and where possible I have also changed the references to point to more recent editions and have cited subsequent research. Although these articles reach back to the 1960s, they are still just as pertinent and vital to the modern student attempting to gain an authentic understanding of the Scottish Highlands.

Gaelic cosmology places a heavy emphasis on hereditary traits, characteristics transmitted through family lines. The terms *dùthchas* and *dualchas* are commonly used to discuss issues of heritage. *Dualchas* means most specifically one's genetic inheritance; *dùthchas* has much wider connotations, such as hereditary territory and customs. The translation of English 'heritage' and 'culture' to the Gaelic *dualchas*, the common practice at the present, is inadequate given that a minor aspect of *dualchas* been extended to mean 'tradition', to the exclusion of the genetic implications of the term and the more appropriate term *dùthchas*. Hence the title of this book.

Dr John MacInnes is one of the few scholars daring enough to write scholarship about Gaelic matters in Gaelic and one of the few whose command of Gaelic is powerful enough for him to do so without relying on English calques or awkward neologisms. The late Reverend William Matheson praised him as the best Gaelic writer that he had met. I hope, therefore, that his essays in Gaelic will not just be records of the past but signposts for the future as a new generation of writers struggles to develop Gaelic to discuss complex issues in the contemporary world, including the survival of this marvellous cultural inheritance.

Michael Newton

Biographical Sketch

(Based on recorded interviews)

A native speaker of Gaelic, John MacInnes was born in Uig, Lewis in 1930, but came to the island of Raasay before he was eight. Childhood memories in Lewis included hearing stories about the clan feuds between MacLeods and MacAulays, a genre of historical legends to which he later gave the name 'Clan Sagas'.

After primary school in Raasay he spent six years as a boarder in Portree Secondary School in Skye. The English language dominated education there. Gaelic was taught to native speakers only but through the medium of English and as an option to French or Greek. Literacy was gained, nevertheless, by thousands of children in Gaelic Presbyterian areas through church services and family worship.

> Almost every day after school, I used to visit a kind and generous lady, Mrs Beaton, in whose house my sister had lodged while attending Portree school. Mrs Beaton spoke Gaelic to me all the time. Her friendship and hospitality made an enormous difference throughout these years of secondary schooling, for her house was truly home from home for me.

During his childhood and youth, there was everywhere an abundance of stories and legends about portents and omens and other preternatural phenomena. These were quite freely discussed but stories about witches and witchcraft, though all that was well established in popular belief, were told in a rather more circumspect way.

> Few people by that time actually believed in the existence of fairies but there are plenty of tales that had come down in tradition about encounters with *sìdhichean*. Almost everyone, though, believed in second sight; and that is probably true to the present day.

There were place names that preserved other memories.

> My paternal grandmother's family came from Torrin in Skye. In that township, you have one of the seven beds on Skye of the *Glas Ghoibhleann*,

the supernatural cow of Gaelic lore. At the other end of the Strath, there is the Sìdhean, the Fairy Knoll, beside which Uilleam Ros, the poet, was born. His mother's father was the celebrated piper and poet *Am Pìobaire Dall*. In all Gaelic communities there were individuals who specialised in genealogy and their lists of lineages and anecdotal information about people of the past and about places with immemorial associations gave a view of history that had little to do with book-learning as we knew it.

As a child I heard about Gaelic in Kintyre and Arran and Perthshire. Argyll was famous for 'having the best Gaelic'. We knew people from Ross-shire and Sutherland who spoke Gaelic. Because of that we had a sense of the Gàidhealtachd as an unbroken cultural and linguistic area; and even as late as the 1950s we were told that there was far more Gaelic spoken in Nova Scotia than in Scotland.

Although none of this was accurate information, for only the older generation in many of those parts were by then fluent speakers, it gave us the sense of belonging to a much wider community and strengthened our Gaelic identity in the face of the Anglicising policies of formal education.

During those same years Gaelic songs were to be heard at concerts throughout the Highlands and Islands, with 'star singers' (usually formally trained and accompanied by pianists) who made their circuits from one village or town to another. Enormously popular, their natural gifts, their repertoires (including arrangements by Marjory Kennedy-Fraser) and their singing styles gave them a status denied to most local, traditional singers.

In his late teens, John MacInnes discovered that older relatives (especially his paternal granduncles) had preserved an astonishingly rich store of song, music and legend. The poetry of these songs seemed utterly different from what he had previously known. While he stresses the fact that hundreds of other Gaelic-speaking families kept alive the same kind of traditional material, often more abundantly, it is obvious that his own interest was first kindled by relatives who were born from the 1850s to 1870. A much younger man, the Rev. Dr Donald MacKinnon of the Free Church of Scotland, himself related to the family, had learnt much from the same sources.

> The Rev. Donald MacKinnon was an authority on Highland history and genealogy and in many conversations with him I was able to clarify and add to what I had learnt in my teens. Another relative, Dr Allan MacDonald, GP in the Isle of Skye for many years, was a good piper, a beautiful singer, and a devotee of traditional Gaelic music. He did not regard 'tradition' as a static or unchanging thing. For instance, it was he who arranged – or perhaps

indeed re-created – the melody of the flyting or verse-debate between a Barra woman and a Uist woman, 'An Spaidsearachd Bharrach' (known under the English title of 'The Barra Boasting').[1] Dr MacDonald's ideas about Gaelic singing – styles and interpretation – were always stimulating and enriching.

But by far the most important element in my background was the fact that at home we spoke Gaelic all the time. My parents, from Uist and Skye, both of them equally, had a wonderful command of rich, idiomatic Gaelic. To the present day, my sister and myself, like a great number of our relatives, would never dream of conversing in any other language than Gaelic.

In 1948, MacInnes came to study at the University of Edinburgh and met two people from Barra: the piper and singer Calum Johnston, and Flora MacNeil, both of whom lived there at the time.

Their repertoires of music and song were extraordinarily extensive. Calum and his sister Annie had recorded for Kennedy-Fraser. Flora, now internationally famous, was at the beginning of her career. In some instances they had versions and variants of songs I had learnt in the family, but invariably they knew longer texts.

The historical folktales which he first heard early in life were of particularly engrossing interest to him for they had a prominent part in family tradition:

These stories were generally accepted as authentic accounts of historical events but it later became clear that, although they are founded on history and use the names of places and historical personages, they were best treated as naturalistic fictions in which motifs move from one tale to another. (In this context, it may be said, 'naturalistic' covers a wide range of preternatural phenomena!) The stories may of course preserve details of actual events; they certainly reflect motives and attitudes. But overall it is their narrative power, with vivid and often laconic exchanges of dialogue, that makes them so arresting. Because these qualities frequently remind one of the Icelandic sagas, I refer to them as the Gaelic 'Clan Sagas'.

John MacInnes points out that several generations may be bridged in oral transmission of information in quite remarkable fashion.

For instance, my grandfather's brothers remembered their own grandfather – my great-great-grandfather, Niall mac Mhaol-Mhoire – and one of them actually remembered Niall's uncle, Niall mac Iain mhic Mhaol Chaluim. I heard that Maol Caluim had fought on the Jacobite side at Sliabh an t-Siorraim, which I later realised was called 'Sheriffmuir' in the history textbooks. Both of these men (the two called 'Niall') were born towards the end of the eighteenth century and they in turn knew men who had fought at the Battle of Culloden in 1746.

Through such sources we were able to add a whole dimension to our experiences as Gaels. Legend and song, music and poetry, opened up a perspective on Gaelic history that was denied to generations of us in our formal schooling.

After initially intending to go to Art College, MacInnes studied English at Edinburgh, with one session (quite separate from the English literature and language curricula) devoted to Philosophy and Psychology. 'Behaviourist psychology, I must say, held little interest for me but John MacMurray's lectures on Moral Philosophy were to me, as to so many, of seminal importance.'

At this juncture he was awarded a competitive scholarship in Gaelic established by the Church of Scotland. Returning to English, he found the teaching of literature 'excessively dull' and opted to specialise in language: Old and Middle English primarily and Old Norse; with Old High German and Gothic for philological purposes, and phonetics as a special subject. The last was taught by a brilliant lecturer, David Abercrombie.

> His ideas on rhythm and metrics are the entire basis for any understanding I have of the prosody of Gaelic verse and song-poetry.
>
> Being able to read the Icelandic sagas – Hermann Pálsson and O. K. Schram were our teachers – undoubtedly gave me the hint that our orally composed and transmitted 'historical folktales' might in some way be connected with a cultural heritage that derives from the centuries-long settlement of North-west Scotland by the Norse.
>
> In 1953 I made my earliest recordings for the School of Scottish Studies, founded by the University in 1951. These were mostly from relatives, supplemented over the next couple of years by contributions from others. In 1953, too, I received my first formal instruction in Gaelic by enrolling in the Department of Celtic Studies where the teachers were Professor K. H. Jackson and the Reverend William Matheson. Eventually I sat an Intermediate Honours examination and in subsequent years I attended many of Professor Jackson's lectures and tutorials in an informal capacity.

Although MacInnes has always insisted that, apart from study in the Celtic Department, work among the tradition-bearers of the Gàidhealtachd had much greater reality for him than formal education. He none the less distinguished himself in more than one field. In literature he was awarded the J. Logie Robertson Prize; in Moral Philosophy the class medal and James Seth Prize; and after Finals in English was the recipient of the Gatty Scholarship, which enabled him to spend two years in postgraduate research.

Compulsory military service followed. During this period he was posted to Cyprus.

> Those of us who had 'desk-jobs' enjoyed a great deal of free time. I took advantage of that to get to know members of the community and learn Modern Greek. Learning a people's language always opens doors and I was offered the warmest of hospitality, being invited to weddings, baptisms and all sorts of social gatherings.
>
> I used to hear songs of the *Klephts* – the Greeks who fought in the mountains against the Ottoman Empire – and ballads of the great *Digenes Akritas*. There were some fascinating parallels between these songs and Gaelic panegyrics, and between the balladry and *Duain na Fèinne* (the Fenian or 'Ossianic' ballads).

He remembers vividly that when he was ten years of age he heard a Fenian ballad (recited, not sung) by a Free Church minister, the Rev. Roderick MacCowan, a native of Skye who had retired to the island of Raasay. The ballad was *Laoidh Dhiarmaid*, and the Rev. MacCowan gave it as he had heard it in his boyhood in Braes in Skye, opposite Raasay.

In 1958, MacInnes was appointed to a Junior Research Fellowship in the School of Scottish Studies; and shortly afterwards as tutor in Old and Middle English in that department, a post which he held until 1963. After years focused primarily on fieldwork, he wrote a doctoral thesis on Gaelic poetry. After he retired as a senior lecturer, he was given an Endowment Fellowship of the University of Edinburgh.

Scots Gaelic for MacInnes has the dimensions of a major language and is flexible enough to cope with a range of situations in the modern world (see, for example, his translation from English to Gaelic of the constitution of the Gaelic Society of Inverness printed in volumes of the society's *Transactions*). At the same time he has written that 'The hostile forces of history [. . .] have left Gaelic essentially a medieval European language.'[2]

His own work is founded directly on the actions and beliefs of his native community. For this reason the late Rev. William Matheson referred to him as 'the last of the native scholars'. But he himself adds:

From time to time I have also drawn conclusions that are rather speculative. However, these might or might not stimulate further study and perhaps encourage people to formulate antithetical arguments with at least the possibility of synthesis. I have tried to draw attention to beliefs that, I believe, have not hitherto been given proper acknowledgement, for example, the importance of the 'messianic' theme in Gaelic history. Then in song there is the custom of audience participation in refrains, so well attested in Gaelic Scotland. There are at least fragments of evidence that suggest there may be a connection between that and an ancient art-form in which dance and song were combined.

His work in this field led in 1964 to the award of a scholarship by the Faroese government to study the danced ballad in the Faroe Islands.

On another point altogether, what I have called the 'Panegyric Code' of Gaelic poetry is not something whose existence is capable of proof. That praise-poetry is abundant and pervasive in Gaelic is of course obvious: that it operates as an aesthetic code is an autonomous value judgment. There are other possible approaches.

A notion that I find absorbing is the belief, apparently much more securely established in our Gàidhealtachd than in the sister culture of Ireland, that every person has an alter ego, which may appear to anyone in certain circumstances. (It wasn't just people with second sight who saw this *samhla* or *co-choisiche*.) This is not exactly a doppelgänger, except of course in physical characteristics. Sometimes it represents a darker or more sinister aspect of the personality, a sort of baser 'self'. The comparison with Jekyll and Hyde is surely quite arresting.

Anyway, these various speculations may merit the attention of psychologists, musicologists and students of dance, as well as literary critics, in order to qualify, refute or endorse them.

John MacInnes retired from the School of Scottish Studies in 1993, but has, since that time, continued to conduct research, write and contribute to books, conferences, and programmes.

Published Works of Dr John MacInnes

Gaelic texts marked with *

1960, Translations in *More West Highland Tales* vol. 2 (Edinburgh: Birlinn, 1994).

1960, Transcriptions, translations and notes in *Scottish Gaelic Folk Tales* (Edinburgh: School of Scottish Studies).

1961, 'A Traditional Song from Skye', *Scottish Studies* 5, 106–8.

1961, 'A Folktale from St. Kilda', *Scottish Studies* 5, 215–9.

1961, Review of *Tales of Barra Told By The Coddy*, *The Scottish Historical Review* 40 (no. 129), 79.

1962, 'Two Poems Ascribed to Duncan Ban McIntyre (1724–1812)', *Scottish Studies* 6, 99–105.

1962, 'Personal Names in a Gaelic Song', *Scottish Studies* 6, 235–43.

1963, 'Sgeulachd Mhìcheil Scot', *Scottish Studies* 7, 106–14.

1963, 'Tàladh Choinnich Òig', *Scottish Studies* 7, 226–30.

1963, 'Farquhar son of Alasdair' in Bødker (ed.) *European Folktales* (Copenhagen: Council of Europe), 131–4.

1964, 'A Gaelic Song of the Sutherland Clearances', *Scottish Studies* 8, 104–6.

1965, 'A Variant of a Poem Ascribed to Duncan Ban McIntyre', *Scottish Studies* 9, 117–9.

1965, 'Òran nan Dròbhairean', *Scottish Studies* 9, 189–203.

1966, 'The Choral Tradition in Scottish Gaelic Songs', *Transactions of the Gaelic Society of Inverness* 46, 44–65.

1966, 'MacMhuirich and the Old Woman from Harris', *Scottish Studies* 10, 104–8.

1966, 'Notes on Mary MacLeod', *Scottish Gaelic Studies* 11, 3–23.

1966, 'Dugald Buchanan', 'Eachdraidh a' Phrionnsa' and 'Ossian' in *Kindlers Lexikon* (Munich).

1967, 'Òran Mór Sgor[a]breac', *Scottish Studies* 11, 100.

1968, Review of *Seòbhrach às a' Chlaich*, *Scottish International* 3, 59–60.

1968, 'The Oral Tradition in Scottish Gaelic Poetry', *Scottish Studies* 12, 29–44.

1970, 'Poetry, passion and political consciousness', *Scottish International* 10, 10.

1971, 'Gannet Catching in the Hebrides', *Frókaparit* 18, 151–8.

1971, 'Death of a Language', *The Listener* Vol. 86, No. 2214 (2 September).

* 1971, Review of *Scottish Gaelic Studies* 12, *Gairm* 77, 92–6.

1971, 'Gaels in Glasgow', *Stornoway Gazette and West Coast Advertiser* (18 September).

1971, Text of *Music from the Western Isles*, Scottish Tradition Series (Edinburgh: Greentrax).

1972, Text of *Waulking Songs from Barra*, Scottish Tradition Series (Edinburgh: Greentrax).

1972, Review of *An Rathad Cian*, *Scottish International* 5 (no. 20), 36–37.

* 1973, Review of *The Far Road*, *Gairm* 82, 188–92.

1973, Review of *Barran agus Asbhuain: Somhairle MacGill-eain a' leughadh cuid de a dhàin fhéin*, *Scottish International* 6, 38.

1974, 'Alexander MacDonald of the Forty-Five: the man and his poetry', *Rosc* May, 3–10 and July, 7–15.
* 1974, Review of *Aitealan Dlù is Cian*, *Gairm* 86, 185–91.
1975, 'Sorley Maclean's "Hallaig": A Note', *Calgacus* 1 (no. 2), 29–32
1975, 'Scotland (Highlands)' in R. M. Dorson (ed.), *Folktales told around the World* (Chicago and London: University of Chicago Press), 45–52.
* 1975, (with Prof. John MacQueen) 'Gàidhlig air Gall[d]achd Alba', *The Scotsman* (December 6).
* 1975, 'Dùn Éideann is a' Ghàidhlig o chionn dà cheud bliadhna', *The Scotsman* (December 20).
1976, 'The Cultural Background to the Eighteenth-Century Collections of Gaelic Poetry', *Papers Presented To Kenneth Jackson By Some Of His Pupils And Colleagues In July 1976 On The Occasion Of His Completing Twenty-Five Years In The Chair of Celtic At Edinburgh* (privately published).
1976, 'Eathar caol na h-inntinn / The slender ship of the mind', *Akros* 11 (no. 31), 26.
* 1976, 'Dùn Éideann is a' Ghàidhlig o chionn dà cheud bliadhna', *The Scotsman* (January 10).
* 1976, '. . . mas dàinig an Soisgeul', *The Scotsman* (August 7).
* 1976, 'Prìomh-athraichean luchd-siubhail na Gàidhealtachd', *The Scotsman* (August 21).
1976, 'The Gaelic Literary Tradition', in *Scottish Literature in the Secondary School* (Edinburgh: HMSO), 56–67.
* 1977, 'Dé cho Gàidhealach 's a tha Gallaibh?', *Gairm* 98, 141–5; Review of *Scottish Gaelic Studies* 12, 184–9.
* 1977, Review of *Bith-eòlas: A' Chealla, Gintinneachd is Mean-fhàs*, *Gairm* 100, 377–9; Review of *Bards and Makars*, 381–3.
1977, 'Some Gaelic Words and Usages', *Transactions of the Gaelic Society of Inverness* 49, 428–55.
1977, Review of *Gaelic in Scotland* and *An t-Aonaran*, *Scottish Review* 7, 52–4.
* 1978, Review of *Màiri Mhór nan Òran*, *Gairm* 102, 188.
1978, Review of *River, River*, *Lines Review* 67, 45–6.
1978, 'The Panegyric Code in Gaelic Poetry and its Historical Background', *Transactions of the Gaelic Society of Inverness* 50, 435–98.
* 1978–9, Review of *Saorsa agus an Iolaire*, *Gairm* 105, 89–92.
* 1979, Review of *Leth-cheud Bliadhna*, *Gairm* 106, 177–79.
* 1979, 'Tolg an "Carmina Gadelica"?', *The Scotsman* (3 March).
* 1979, 'Eachdraidh is Fàisneachd', *The Scotsman* (29 September).
* 1979, (edited) *Eachann nan Cath*, Allan Fraser (Glasgow: Gairm).
* 1981, Review of *Eileanan* and *A' Mheanbhchuileag*, *Gairm* 115, 279–83.
1981, 'Gaelic Poetry and Historical Tradition', in Loraine MacLean (ed.), *The Middle Ages in the Highlands* (Inverness: Inverness Field Club), 142–63.
1981, 'The Gaelic Continuum in Scotland', in Robert O'Driscoll (ed.), *The Celtic Consciousness* (New York: George Braziller Inc), 269–88.
1981, Review of *Poetry Australia* 78, *Lines Review* 63, 10–16.
* 1981–2, Review of *Oighreachd agus Gabhaltas*, *Gairm* 117, 91–3.
1981–2, 'A Radically Traditional Voice: Sorley MacLean and the Evangelical Background', *Cencrastus* 7, 14–17.
1982 'Religion in Gaelic Society', *Transactions of the Gaelic Society of Inverness* 52, 222–42.
* 1983, 'Samhla na Craoibhe', in *Sàr-Ghàidheal* (Inverness: An Comunn Gàidhealach), 64–9.

1983, 'The World Through Gaelic-Scots Eyes' (Review of *Creachadh na Clàrsaich*), *Lines Review* 85, 11–20.

1983, 'Sorley Maclean', in Alan Bullock and R. B. Woodings (eds.), *The Fontana Biographical Companion to Modern Thought* (London: Fontana Paperbacks).

* 1983, 'Sùil air Bàrdachd na Gàidhlig' in Cathal Ó Luain (ed.), *For a Celtic Future: A Tribute to Alan Heusaff* (Dublin: Celtic League), 4–24.

* 1984, (Participant in debate) 'Am Mòd Nàiseanta', *Gairm* 129, 13–22.

1984, Text of *James Campbell of Kintail*, Scottish Tradition Series (Edinburgh: Greentrax).

1985, 'Gleanings from Raasay Tradition', *Transactions of the Gaelic Society of Inverness* 56: 1–20.

* 1986, 'Baird is Bleidirean', in Seosamh Watson (ed.), *Féilscríbhinn Thomáis de Bhaldraithe*, (Dublin: Coiste Féilscríbhinn Thomáis de Bhaldraithe, An Coláiste Ollscoile), 94–110.

1986, 'Language, Metre and Diction in the Poetry of Sorley MacLean' in Raymond Ross and Joy Hendry (eds.), *Sorley MacLean: Critical Essays* (Edinburgh: Scottish Academic Press), 137–53.

1986, Introduction in Stanley Simpson (ed.), *Callum Macdonald: Scottish literary publisher* (Edinburgh: National Library of Scotland).

1986–7, 'Sorley MacLean at Seventy-five' (Review of *Sorley MacLean: Critical Essays* and *Ris a' Bhruthaich: The Criticism and Prose Writings of Sorley MacLean*), *Planet* 60, 103–7.

1987, English translations of 'A Pair for the Prince' and 'The Drunkard and the Thistle', *Margin* 3, 25–31, 32–8.

1987, 'Twentieth-Century Recordings of Scottish Gaelic Heroic Ballads', in Bo Almqvist (ed.), *Fiannaiocht : Essays on the Fenian Traditions of Ireland and Scotland* (Dublin: The Folklore of Ireland Society), 101–30.

1987, 'MacLean's "Hallaig" ' and 'The Tunes of His Own Mind', in *Sorley MacLean: Poems 1932–82* (Philadelphia: Iona Foundation), 6–9.

1988, 'Family Tradition In The Isle of Skye: Clann Aonghuis – The MacInneses', in Gordan W. MacLennan (ed.), *Proceedings of the First North American Congress of Celtic Studies* (Ottawa: The University of Ottawa), 407–15.

1989, 'The Gaelic Perception of the Lowlands', in William Gillies (ed.), *Gaelic and Scotland / Alba agus a' Ghàidhlig* (Edinburgh: Edinburgh University Press), 89–100.

1989, 'The Seer in Gaelic Tradition' in Hilda Davidson (ed.), *The Seer in Celtic and Other Traditions* (Edinburgh: John Donald), 10–24.

1989, 'Gaelic Poetry in the Nineteenth Century', in Douglas Gifford (ed.), *The History of Scottish Literature* Volume 3 (Aberdeen : Aberdeen University Press), 377–95.

1989, Afterword in Margaret Bennett, *The Last Stronghold* (Edinburgh: Canongate Publishing).

* 1989, Review of *Seachd Luinneagan le Shakespeare*, *Gairm* 148, 381–2; Review of *Clann a' Phroifeasair*, 382.

1990, 'MacCaig and Gaeldom', in Joy Hendry and Raymond Ross (eds.), *Norman MacCaig: Critical Essays* (Edinburgh: Edinburgh University Press), 22–37.

1990, Review of *O Choille gu Bearradh/From Wood to Ridge*, *Lines Review* 112, 40–5.

1990, Review of *Gaelic Scotland: The Transformation of a Culture Region*, *Journal of Historical Geography* 16, 234–76.

* 1990, 'Cainnt is Cànan', *An Tarbh* 1, 23–5.

1991, (interview with Jim Wilkie) 'The fox that ate the bagpipes', *West Highland Free Press* (12th April).

1991, 'Clan Sagas and Historical Legends', *Transactions of the Gaelic Society of Inverness* 58, 377–94.

1991, 'The voice of an entire people', *Lines Review* 117, 10–11.

1992, New Introduction to *Carmina Gadelica* (Herndon: Lindisfarne Books).

* 1992, Review of *Uirsgeul/Myth*, *Gairm* 158, 181–3.

* 1992, Review of *Brigh nam Facal*, *Gairm* 159, 274–6.

1992 'The Scottish Gaelic Language', in Glanville Price (ed.), *The Celtic Connection* (Dublin: Gerrard's Cross), 101–30.

1992, 'Looking at Legends of the Supernatural', *Transactions of the Gaelic Society of Inverness* 59, 1–20.

1993, 'Scottish-Gaelic Poetry', in Alex Preminger and T. V. F. Brogan (eds.), *The New Princeton Encyclopedia of Poetry and Poetics* (Princeton: Princeton University Press).

* 1993, 'Eachdraidh Each', *Gairm* 162, 107–12.

* 1993, Review of *The MacDiarmid MS Anthology*, *Gairm* 164, 373–4.

1993, 'The Celtic World' in Roy Willis (ed.), *World Mythology* (Richmond Hill: Duncan Baird), 176–89.

1993, 'Gaelic Folksong', 'Gaelic Short Story', in David Daiches (ed.), *The New Companion to Scottish Culture* (Edinburgh: Polygon), 120–1.

1994, Contributions (originally published in *Tocher*) to A. J. Bruford and D. A. MacDonald (eds.), *Scottish Traditional Tales* (Edinburgh: Polygon). (no. 32 'The Poor Man's Clever Daughter' and no. 49 'The Man Who Stopped Going to Church', and translations for no. 57 'MacPhail of Uisinnis' and no. 62a 'Àirigh an t-Sluic')

1994, Reviews of *Rè na h-Oidhche* and *Gaelic Poetry in the Eighteenth Century*, *Scottish Book Collector* 4 (no. 4), 31.

1994, Review of *Gaelic Bards and Minstrels*, *Scottish Book Collector* 4 (no. 5), 31.

1994, Review of *Gàir nan Clàrsach*, *Scottish Book Collector* 4 (no. 6), 29.

1994, Reviews of *Popular Tales of the West Highlands*, *More West Highland Tales* and *One Road*, *Scottish Book Collector* 4 (no. 7), 29.

* 1994, Review of *Siud an t-Eilean*, *Gairm* 166, 175–6.

1994, Review of *Kalevala Mythology*, *Cosmos* 10, 108–11.

1994, 'Aos-dána', 'Caraid nan Gàidheal', 'Dance in Gaelic Society', 'Dòmhnall nan Òran', 'Later Folksong (1645–1800)', 'Dòmhnall MacAmhlaigh', 'Mairearad Nighean Lachlainn', 'Màiri Nighean Alasdair Ruaidh', 'Pòl Crùbach', 'James Ross', 'Neil Ross', 'Metres of Waulking Songs', 'Alexander Stewart', 'Donald Stewart', 'Short Stories', 'Panegyric Verse', 'Political Verse (Twentieth Century)' in Derick Thomson (ed.), *The Companion to Gaelic Scotland* (Glasgow: Gairm).

1994–5, Reviews of *The Celtic Place-Names of Scotland* and *A Description of the Western Isles of Scotland circa 1695*, *Scottish Book Collector* 4 (no. 8), 29.

1995, Review of *The Companion to Gaelic Scotland*, *Scottish Book Collector* 4 (no. 9), 29.

1995, Reviews of *A' Gabhail Ris* and *Scottish Traditional Tales*, *Scottish Book Collector* 4 (no. 10), 29.

* 1995, Review of *A' Gabhail Ris*, *Gairm* 171, 280–1.

1995, Reviews of *Iain Dubh* and *Domhnall Ruadh Chorùna*, *Scottish Book Collector* 4 (no. 11), 28.

1995, Review of *A Hundred Years in the Highlands*, *Scottish Book Collector* 4 (no. 12), 29.

1995, Review of *History of Skye*, *Scottish Book Collector* 5 (no. 1), 30.

1995–6, Review of *Hiort: Far na laigh a' ghrian*, *Scottish Book Collector* 5 (no. 2), 30.

* 1995–6, 'Sgrìob liath an Earraich', *Gairm* 173, 72; Review of *Meall Garbh*, 87–9.

1996, Review of *The Welsh Fairy Book*, *Folklore* 107, 121–2.

1996, Reviews of *Iona: The Earliest Poetry of a Celtic Monastery* and *Columba's Island*, *Scottish Book Collector* 5 (no. 3), 30.

* 1996, 'Sgeulachd', *Scottish Gaelic Studies* 17, 181–92.

* 1996, Review of *Alasdair Mac Mhaighstir Alasdair, Selected Poems*, *Gairm* 176, 373–6.

* 1996, 'Sgrìob Chlann Uisnich', *Gairm* 175, 269–70; Review of *Tuath is Tighearna*, 279–82.

1996, Review of *Rob Roy MacGregor: His Life and Times*, *Scottish Book Collector* 5 (no. 4), 29.

1996, Review of *The Democratic Muse*, *Scottish Book Collector* 5 (no. 5), 28.

1996, Reviews of *The Poetry of Scotland* and *Alasdair Mac Mhaighstir Alasdair*, *Scottish Book Collector* 5 (no. 6), 29.

1996, 'Gaelic Song and the Dance', *Transactions of the Gaelic Society of Inverness* 60, 56–73.

1996, with Roibeard Ó Maolalaigh, *Gaelic in Three Months* (Hugo).

1996–7, Contributions to Dolina MacLennan, *OK Ma Tha* (Perth and Kinross Council).

1996–7, Reviews of *Tocher* 50 and 51, *Scottish Book Collector* 5 (no. 7), 29.

1997, Contributions to Angela Cran and James Robertson (eds.), *Dictionary of Scottish Quotations* (Edinburgh: Mainstream).

1997, Obituary for Sorley MacLean, *Scottish Book Collector* 5 (no. 8), 32; Reviews of *The Poems of Ossian and Related Works* and *Hebridean Odyssey*, 36.

1997, Review of *The Oxford Companion to Irish Literature*, *Scottish Book Collector* 5 (no. 9), 36.

1997, Reviews of *Bogha-frois san Oidhche / Rainbow in the Night* and *Ainmeil an Eachdraidh*, *Scottish Book Collector* 5 (no. 10), 36.

1997–8, Review of *Hebridean Song Maker*, *Scottish Book Collector* 5 (no. 11), 36.

* 1998, 'Dròbhaireachd', in *Bho Dhròbhadh Gàidhealach gu Fàsaichean Astrailia* (Dornoch: No. 19 Dornach Studio), 10–31.

* 1998, Review of *Ainmeil an Eachdraidh*, *Gairm* 182, 179–81; Review of *General Robertson's Gaelic Manuscript*, 183–4.

1998, Review of *A History of Scottish Women's Writing*, *Scottish Book Collector* 5 (no. 12), 36.

1998, Review of *Dictionary of Celtic Mythology*, *Scottish Book Collector* 6 (no. 1), 39.

1998, Review of *The Bardic Source Book*, *Scottish Book Collector* 6 (no. 2), 38.

1998, Reviews of *Fax agus dàin eile* and *All my Braided Colours*, *Aberdeen University Review* 58, 342–3.

* 1998, Review of *Scottish Gaelic Studies* 18, *Gairm* 185, 89–91.

1999, 'The Bard Through History', in Timothy Neat, *The Voice of the Bard: Living Poets and Ancient Tradition in the Highlands and Islands of Scotland* (Edinburgh: Canongate), 321–52.

1999, Reviews of *Scottish Tradition 18: Clò Dubh, Clò Donn, Òrain Red, Bardachd Leòdhais* and *Nis Aosmhor*, *Scottish Book Collector* 6 (no. 3), 38.

1999, Reviews of *The Gesto Collection of Highland Music* and *One Hundred and Five Songs of Occupation from the Western Isles of Scotland*, *Scottish Book Collector* 6 (no. 4), 38.

1999, Review of *Oatmeal and the Catechism*, *Scottish Book Collector* 6 (no. 5), 38.

1999, Reviews of *Chì Mi* and *The Voice of the Bard*, *Scottish Book Collector* 6 (no. 6), 38.

* 2000, Preface in Michael Newton, *Bho Chluaidh gu Calasraid / From the Clyde to Callander* (Stornoway: Acair).

* 2000, Review of *An Tuil*, Gairm 190, 185–7.
2000, Review of *Eimhir*, Scottish Book Collector 6 (no. 7), 38.
2000, Review of *Scottish Studies 32*, Scottish Book Collector 6 (no. 8), 38.
2000, Review of *Tron Bhogha-Froise*, Scottish Book Collector 6 (no. 9), 38.
* 2000, Preface in Michael Newton, *A Handbook of the Scottish Gaelic World* (Dublin: Four Courts Press).
2000, Review of *A Handbook of the Scottish Gaelic World*, Scottish Book Collector 6 (no. 10), 38.
2000–1, Reviews of *When I was Young* and *The Islands*, Scottish Book Collector 6 (no. 11), 38.
2001, Contributions to Stanley Sadie (ed.), *The New Grove Dictionary of Music and Musicians*, 2nd edition (New York: Macmillan Publishing).
2001, Review of *The Quest for Celtic Christianity*, Scottish Book Collector 6 (no. 12), 42.
2001, Reviews of *Reportage Scotland*, *An Lasair*, *An Tuil* and *Smuaintean fo Éiseabhal*, Scottish Book Collector 7 (no. 1), 40.
2001, Reviews of *The Gaelic of Islay*, Scottish Life and Society and *Scottish Gaelic Studies 19* and 20, Scottish Book Collector 7 (no. 2), 40.
2001, 'Mod, Royal National' in Michael Lynch (ed.), *The Oxford Companion to Scottish History* (Oxford: Oxford University Press).
* 2002, 'Dìoghlam á Dùthchas Ratharsair', in *Duanagan, Dàin is Dualchas à Eilean Ratharsair* (Raasay Heritage Trust), 131–40.
2002, Reviews of *We're Indians Sure Enough* and *Scottish Studies 33*, Scottish Book Collector 7 (no. 3), 42.
2002, Review of *Sàr-Obair nam Bard Gaelach / The Beauties of Gaelic Poetry*, Scottish Book Collector 7 (no. 4), 39.
2002, Reviews of *The Occult Laboratory* and *Scottish Fairy Belief*, Scottish Book Collector 7 (no. 5), 40.
2002, Introduction to *Bardachd le Ruaraidh MacThòmais / Poetry by Derick Thomson* (Glasgow: Scotsoun).
2002, 'A Notional Unity', *The Drouth* 8, 54–7.
* 2003, 'Am Fàsach ann an Dùthchas nan Gàidheal', in Wilson McLeod and Máire Ní Annracháin (eds.), *Cruth na Tíre* (Dublin: Coiscéim), 166–79.
2003, Reviews of *Plants of Mystery and Magic*, *The Green Mantle* and *A Pleasure in Scottish Trees*, Scottish Book Collector 7 (no. 6), 40.
2003, Review of *A Different Country*, Scottish Book Collector 7 (no. 7), 40.
2004, Review of *Raasay: the Island and its People*, Scottish Book Collector 7 (no. 9), 40.
2004, Review of *Scottish Place-name Papers*, Scottish Book Collector 7 (no. 10), 40.
2004, Notes in *From Battle Lines to Bar Lines* (Edinburgh: Edinburgh International Festival).
2004, 'Adhamh MacFhearghuis, Seumas MacMhuirich agus Literati Dhùn Éideann', *Fras* 1, 38–43.
(forthcoming), Entries in Elizabeth Ewan (ed.), *Scottish Women*.
(forthcoming), 'The Church and Traditional Beliefs in the Gàidhealtachd' in Lizanne Henderson (ed.), *Fantastical Imaginations*.
(forthcoming), 'Comhachaig na Sròine', *Festschrift for Colm Ó Baoill*.
*'Glac nan Daoine ann an Rathasair'.

Archival Recordings

In addition to trips for the purpose of formal recording, John MacInnes has travelled extensively over many years getting to know Gaelic-speaking communities throughout Scotland and Canada, and gleaning all manner of oral history and tradition from those he has met.

The following is a partial list of the recordings in which he was involved and which are stored in the archives of the University of Edinburgh, some of which were done with colleagues. 'Locations' generally refers to the place where the recordings were done, although it sometimes refers to the origin of the person recorded. In addition to the items on this list, John MacInnes also visited and recorded native Gaelic speakers from Perthshire, and along with Iain Crawford, he recorded native St Kildans living in Glasgow.

In the archives of the Place Names Survey:

Year	Locations
1961	*Ross and Cromarty*: Coigach, Reiff, Alltan Dubh, Poll Bàn [Polbain]
1968	*Ross and Cromarty*: Tain, Inver, Gairloch
	Inverness-shire: Glenuig, Samalaman, Onich
1969	*Argyll*: Inverary, Tayvallich, Auchindrain, Lochgair

In the archives of the School of Scottish Studies:

Year	Locations
1953	*Inverness-shire*: Barra, Raasay, Skye
	Lothians: Edinburgh
1954	*Inverness-shire*: Barra, North Uist, Scalpay
	Ross and Cromarty
1955	*Inverness-shire*: North Uist, Skye
1958	*Inverness-shire*: Berneray, North Uist, Skye
	Sutherland: Durness
1959	*Aberdeenshire*: Braemar
	Inverness-shire: Scalpay
	Moray: Elgin, Forres
1960	*Aberdeenshire*: Cults, Fyvie
	Argyll: Tiree
	Inverness-shire: Barra, Berneray, North Uist, Skye, Vatersay

Perthshire: Comrie
Ross and Cromarty: Achiltibuie, Coigeach, Dundonnel, Inverasdale, Loch Broom, Strath Canaird, Ullapool
Shetland: Yell
Sutherland: Lochinver
1961 *Argyll*: Oban
Dunbarton: Dumbarton
Inverness-shire: Lochaber, Skye, South Uist, St Kilda
Moray: Elgin
Ross and Cromarty: Coigeach, Loch Broom
1962 *Inverness-shire*: Skye, South Uist
Renfrew: Paisley
Ross and Cromarty: Applecross, Diabaig, Gairloch, Kinlochewe, Lewis, Torridon
1963 *Argyll*
Inverness-shire: Grimsay, Nethy Bridge, North Uist, Skye, South Uist
Perthshire: Strathtay
Ross and Cromarty: Lewis
Sutherland: Kirtomy, Lairg
1964 *Argyll*: Tiree
Inverness-shire: Lochaber, North Uist, Skye
Ross and Cromarty: Lewis
1965 *Argyll*: Arran
Ross and Cromarty: Lewis
1966 *Argyll*: Tiree
Inverness-shire: North Uist, South Uist
Ross and Cromarty: Lewis
1967 *Argyll*: Morvern
Inverness-shire: North Uist, Scalpay, Skye
Ross and Cromarty: Aultbea
1968 *Argyll*: Tiree
Canada: Nova Scotia
Inverness-shire: North Uist, Onich, Skye, South Uist
Ross and Cromarty: Balintore, Easter Ross, Edderton
1969 *Argyll*: Ardgour
Inverness-shire: Fort Augustus, Fort William, Glenelg, Harris, Lochaber, Roy Bridge, Skye, Spean Bridge
Ross and Cromarty: Keppoch, Lewis
Sutherland
1970 *Argyll*: Islay, Mull, Tiree
Inverness-shire: North Uist
1972 *Inverness-shire*: North Uist
Ross and Cromarty: Kessock
1975 *Argyll*: Oban
Canada: Cape Breton
Inverness-shire: St Kilda
1980 *Canada*: Cape Breton
Inverness-shire: Skye
Ross and Cromarty: Kintail, Lewis
1983 *Inverness-shire*: North Uist
1985 *Canada*: Quebec
1986 *Inverness-shire*: Skye

Essays on History, and Local and Family Tradition

Gaelic Poetry and Historical Tradition

Poetry is not perhaps the most obvious area of Gaelic literature in which to look for direct evidence of an historical kind. At first sight it might seem a more profitable undertaking to study the considerable body of historical tales that have been recorded from oral tradition over the last two centuries and the oldest of which go back to Somerled's campaign against the Norsemen. But important as these stories are, their primary value is as literature. They are in general short dramatic narratives whose laconic style is often reminiscent of the Icelandic sagas, with which perhaps they share some degree of common ancestry. In the Gaelic stories interest focuses on personal relationships and individual feats, and events are depicted on a local rather than a national scale. Yet it is important to emphasise that the Gaelic sense of identity is conditioned and sometimes actually shaped by information that emanates from these historical legends as well as from other, less formally organised categories of tradition. Poetry and legend combine in tradition to create a native view of history. Even in the diminished traditional lore of our own times we can still find a surprising unanimity of opinion as to what constitutes the salient features of Gaelic history and the history of Scotland, which we still call 'Alba'.

In certain ways poetry stands in contrast to the prose narratives. Poets are the spokesmen of Gaelic society; in all ages and at a variety of social levels poetry is the traditional medium for the expression of society's customary expectations. It is not a different awareness so much as a difference in artistic convention that makes the Gaelic poet concern himself with the national dimensions of a given issue. But it is also a matter of artistic lineage. A contemporary bard in a crofting township is the distant heir of the poets who once enjoyed the patronage of the kings of Scotland and the great magnates of the kingdom, and will make songs, as of right, on issues of national and international import.

I shall try to indicate some of the main perspectives which poets have adopted down to the eighteenth century. This involves some consideration of the fascinating, and neglected, theme of prophetic tradition. I shall also discuss some aspects of the hostility between Clan Donald and the Campbells if only for the reason that it occupies a central place in Gaelic historical lore. Finally, I shall give a brief outline of the rhetorical strategy which Gaelic poets employed (and in some of its reaches employed unconsciously) in order that at least a conceptual unity of the Gaelic nation in Scotland should be preserved.

I am conscious of the fact that it may seem anomalous that much of the verse cited in this essay is drawn from the vernacular poetry of the seventeenth and eighteenth centuries, the bulk of which is oral, rather than from the written record of Classical Gaelic, which stretches back much farther in time. But as some of the examples may show, Gaelic poetry retained a peculiarly medieval quality long after what we normally think of as the Middle Ages had passed. This is certainly true of the rhetoric. There are, too, extraordinary survivals such as the following statement implies: 'I would drink a drink in spite of my kinsfolk: not of the red wine of Spain but the blood of your body, to me a better drink.'[1] This reference, one of half a dozen or so of its kind,[2] is from an eighteenth-century lament by the daughter of the Laird of Scalpay to her lover. The image may be no more than an expression of distraught grief. There is, however, a tale of the death of Martin of Bealach in Skye in the same century which suggests that the actual practice survived until then though in a greatly attenuated form. It is also a motif of certain Irish keens. Readers of Spenser's *A View of the Present State of Ireland* will remember:

> the Gauls used to drink their enemies' blood and to paint themselves therewith, so also they write that the old Irish were wont; and so have I seen some of the Irish do but not their enemies' but friends' blood, as namely at the execution of a notable traitor at Limerick called Murrogh O'Brien, I saw an old woman which was his foster mother took up his head whilst he was quartered and sucked up all the blood running there out, saying that the earth was not worthy to drink it, and therewith also steeped her face and breast, and tore her hair, crying and shrieking out most terribly.[3]

In the Middle Ages such practices were already old. There are also ancient survivals of belief. For instance, Donald MacDonald of Eriskay, the victorious hero of the Battle of Carinish in North Uist, which was fought in 1601 against the Macleods, is described as having routed the 'Seed of the Mare',[4] a totemistic allusion which is presumably to be linked with names like *Arcaibh* (Orkney) 'among the

Pig-Folk', or *Cataibh* 'Cat-Folk' – the south and south-east of Sutherland according to local usage; the County of Sutherland in general
usage elsewhere. Watson argues that in *Inse Chat* we have the pre-
Norse name of the Shetlands; the first element in Caithness is from the
same source.[5] We may compare Clann Chatain or MacGilleChatain.
According to tradition to dream of a cat is designative of a Mac-
Pherson or a Macintosh, both members of Clann Chatain. Apparently
we have traces here of a system of dream interpretation which can be
linked with these ancient totemistic names. To dream of a horse or
mare signifies that a MacLeod is involved, and so on for a number of
other kindred-groups. We may have a survival of a different kind in
another paean to the same victorious MacDonald warrior in 1601.[6]
This triumphal song seems to be a late example of the same kind of
welcome as was performed three hundred years earlier when seven
women of Strathearn 'came out to meet the King [Edward I . . .] and
sang before him, as they used to do according to the custom of the time
of the Lord Alexander, late King of Scotland'.[7]

There are thus certain areas of Gaelic tradition in which elements of
great antiquity co-exist with those that reflect the history of more
recent times. This is seen even in the name of 'Alba'. In the oldest
Gaelic literature it denotes the whole of mainland Britain but it
appears also to have been used, perhaps anachronistically, in the
restricted sense of 'Gaelic Britain' as opposed to Pictland, before
coming to denote the Gaelic kingdom of Scone.[8] It is now in Gaelic
simply the equivalent of Scotland, from Shetland to the Borders.
Behind the modern Gaelic usage, however, there probably lie various
developments and adjustments which we cannot now reconstruct in
any detail. Iain Lom of Keppoch in the seventeenth century talks of
'Orkney to Tweed'[9] and in the previous century not all Hebridean
poets thought of the Isles as part of Alba.[10] And what, for instance, is
the precise significance of the name 'Drumalban' in Lanarkshire? It is
surely very significant that the men of Galloway at the Battle of the
Standard in 1138 'cried out the war-cry of their fathers – and the
shouts rose, even to the skies – *Albani, Albani*'.[11] This indicates that at
that date the same 'Alba' had cultural and ethnic affiliations which
transcended the merely geographical limits of Scotia – Scotland north
of Forth. The plain inference would seem to be that wherever the
Gaelic language had penetrated, that area was part of Alba. Yet the
men of *Innse Gall* 'the Hebrides' may have had a different perspective.
The *Gall* are of course the Norsemen; the connotation is the same in

our name for Caithness, *Gallaibh*. But although we still call a Caithness man *Gallach* the simplex *Gall* in all Gaelic dialects means 'Lowland Scot' and *Galldachd* 'the Lowlands'.

Writing about the Highlands in the lifetime of Robert the Bruce, Professor Barrow has this to say:

> Neither in the chronicle nor in the record of the twelfth and thirteenth centuries do we hear of anything equivalent to the 'Highland Line' of later time. Indeed, the very terms 'Highlands' and 'Lowlands' have no place in the considerable body of written evidence surviving from the period before 1300. 'Ye hielans and ye lawlans, oh whaur hae ye been?' The plain answer is that they do not seem to have been anywhere: in those terms, they had simply not entered the minds of men. We commonly think of this highland-lowland dichotomy as being rooted deep in the history of Scotland, as being, indeed, imposed upon that history by the mere facts of physical geography. Yet it seems to have left no trace in the reasonably plentiful record of two formative centuries [. . . In the thirteenth century] the Gaelic language must have been perfectly familiar up and down the east coast from the Ord of Caithness to Queensferry. It must, moreover, still have been the ordinary working language of Carrick and the rest of Galloway. [. . . But after the partial retreat of Gaelic] one great historic divide between Highlands and Lowlands had established itself before the end of the middle ages. The Highlands and Islands were now synonymous, as they had not previously been, with the Gàidhealtachd, the Gaelic speakers and their culture, while the Lowlands [. . .] became the country of the Sasunnach, the people who (whatever their racial origins) spoke and wrote a variant of the English tongue. Lowlanders, for their part, recognised the same division, though they thought in significantly different terms. They were not Sasunnach either to themselves or to the English south of the Border. They were Scots.[12]

To the Gael, too, they are Scots. A Lowlander is unequivocally an Albannach and it would be a contradiction in terms to speak of an 'Albannach Sasunnach'. And although Gaels recognise more or less the same division of the country into Highland and Lowland, there are certain subtle differences in that division which we are perhaps prone to ignore. It is not the fact of a geographical divide that the Gaelic names emphasise. 'Gàidhealtachd' and 'Galldachd' are abstract terms, not ordinary place names, and the areas they designate are not drawn with precise boundaries. The perspective here is cultural. Some tradition-bearers indeed extend the Gàidhealtachd vaguely beyond the Highland Line. This may suggest some faint reflection of the limits of Gaelic speech, as described by Professor Barrow, before c. 1350.[13]

The creation of what we may call the Gàidhealtachd proper does not imply that the mandarin class of poets and seanchaidhs deserted their memories of former greatness. In a Classical Gaelic poem addressed to the chief of Clan Gregor (1461–1519) the poet, brother of the Dean of Lismore, says:

Here is a quatrain I have found [. . .]
Such is thy history aright,
up to Fergus son of Erc the warlike.

In thy line, not niggard to help,
the number who assumed a crown
hath been kings two score and three:
in the high enumeration knowledge of them is meet.

Three in the north, three in the south were there,
after Malcolm Canmore;
twice five crowns is the tale
from Malcolm to Ailpín.

From Malcolm upwards their number known
is fourteen men to Fergus.
To what number then doth thy lineage extend?
Reckoning may be made up to Fergus.[14]

This 'high enumeration' is essentially the same as we find in the 'Duan Albanach' ('The Scottish Poem'), composed during, or immediately after, the reign of Malcolm Canmore.[15] From such sources also the seanchaidhs who recited in Gaelic the lineage of Alexander III at his inauguration in 1249 drew his information. Given the nature of Gaelic society and the immense importance of oral tradition at so many social levels, it would be strange if that information was restricted entirely to one social or professional class. Over three centuries after the date of the poem to the chief of the MacGregors, and from the same area of Perthshire, we have an interesting testimony to the state and content of oral tradition. It comes from Duncan Campbell, who was born in 1828 at Kerrumore in Glenlyon. He depicts a society of small tenants, farmers, and minor gentry, who were all Gaelic-speaking. He tells us, and demonstrates his claim, that 'Our Glenlyon men of age [. . .] were wise and deep in traditional lore.' In one vignette concerning the coronation of Queen Victoria, in 1838, he describes his own aged grandmother discussing that event and adds:

> She and others of her generation enjoyed the liberty this occasion gave them for going [. . .] to the history of Scottish kings as far as Kenneth Macalpin, *which had come down by oral tradition* [my italics]. Long afterwards when I read the 'Duan Albanach', I was much surprised to discover that the substance of it was retained to a remarkable extent in the oral and local traditions which our aged people recalled and told [. . .] As for the later kings from the time of Wallace and Bruce, as Glenlyon was visited by so many of them for hunting purposes until the Union of the English and Scottish Crowns, there was nothing very strange in the fact that the traditions were fairly strong and unbroken.[16]

We need not take it at face value that there was an unbroken continuity of oral tradition in the transmission of these facts. Oral tradition was probably reinforced throughout the ages from other sources, clerical and lay, including the parish school. It may be remarked that in modern Gaelic oral tradition Bruce and Wallace are both represented as being Gaelic speakers; and although this is sometimes demonstrably based upon (or reinforced by) English-language sources, tradition bearers will cite it as evidence of the predominance of Gaelic at one time in Scottish history and, by implication, of the reality of a Gaelic Scotland. Except at that 'dynastic' level, however, Gaelic poets are not in general concerned with the earlier distribution of Gaelic culture or speech beyond the Highland Line. Around 1730 Edmund Burt has this to say of the Gaels:

> they have an adherence to one another as Highlanders, in opposition to the people of the Low-Country, whom they despise as inferior to them in courage, and believe they have a right to plunder them whenever it is in their power. This last arises from a tradition, that the Lowlands, in old times were the possession of their ancestors [. . .] When I mentioned this tradition, I had only in view the middling and ordinary Highlanders, who are very tenacious of old customs and opinions; and [now] I would be understood that it is very probable such a notion was formerly entertained by some, at least, amongst those of the highest rank.[17]

As to the first part of this, much the same sentiments could be heard expressed in the twentieth century. They also find expression in poetry though not over conspicuously and on the whole confined to a popular level of song. But as regards Burt's conjecture about 'the highest Rank', the only qualification to be made is that there must have been men of high rank still alive at that time who subscribed to the same principle. On the evidence of the poetry of that age some of them were MacDonalds.

The importance of Clan Donald in the history of Gaelic poetry cannot be over-estimated. This stems directly from their status in the Lordship of the Isles and from their continuing influence on the Gàidhealtachd after the Lordship was forfeited. In the twelfth century the Lordship emerges as a new focus of Gaelic culture and loyalty in Scotland. In terms of political and military organisation no less than cultural patronage and diversity it is as if Gaelic Alba had been reaffirmed and re-created within narrower territorial limits. The cultural inheritance of Somerled's heirs was a rich complex which on the one hand drew on ancient traditions of the Cenél nGabhráin,[18] going back to the foundation of the Scoto-Pictish kingdom; on the other upon those of the Gallghaidheal and the Norse kingdom of the Isles.

The role played by the *Gall* of the North in the formation of this 'Nova Scotia' is not neglected by the poets. In their claims to Norse ancestry the MacLeods are outstanding, as when Mary MacLeod celebrates these descendants of a 'line of kings who laid the Isle of Man under tribute [. . .] stately race, seed of Olver and Ochraidh; from the city of Bergen did your first title spring'.[19] But there were lesser kindreds also who remembered their Norse origin and in the sixteenth century a MacDonald song, the famous 'Lullaby' to Domhnall Gorm of Sleat contains the phrase 'Nuair théid mac mo Rìgh-sa dh'Alba' ('when my King's son goes to Scotland').[20] There may well have been atavistic longings, of which we have now little trace, to be found among the Gaelicised Norsemen comparable with those that are still fostered by the Scotticised Shetlanders. But this is not the norm.[21] Even Mary MacLeod, in her elegy for Sir Norman of Berneray, is careful to state, 'One half of your kinship was with the race of Coll [. . .] from the province of Connacht.'[22] In the eighteenth century John MacCodrum says of Clan Donald: 'They came from Egypt in the days of Gathelus and Scota [. . .] Alba, though it is much to say, they divided from sea to moor, many great nobles were there who received their right from the hand of Clan Donald.'[23]

MacCodrum was illiterate. So was Eachann Bacach, a warrior poet of the Macleans. Yet he too shows his knowledge of the learning that was primarily cultivated and transmitted by the Gaelic *literati*, among whom the great literary dynasty of the MacMhuirichs was outstanding. Eachann's elegy for Sir Lachlan Maclean opens with the words: 'Your origins went back to Pharaoh.'[24] In the context of vernacular poetry as a whole such allusions may be no more than stray items, or decorative asides, from the 'Milesian Legend' – one of the constructions of medieval Gaelic pseudo-history (it features also, of course, in the 'Declaration of Arbroath') in which Gàidheal Glas (Gathelus), son of Scota daughter of Pharaoh, is the eponymous ancestor of the Gaels. But the references serve to illustrate two things. One is the deep consciousness of Gaelic identity and continuity of history, particularly within the Lordship. At the beginning of the seventeenth century Sir James MacDonald of Islay claims that 'My race hes bene tenne hundreth yeeris kyndlie Scottis men, under the Kinges of Scotland.'[25] Dr John Bannerman sums up the developments that sustained such a claim: 'Indeed, it could be argued that the ultimate origin of the Lordship of the Isles lay in the erstwhile political fact of the Kingdom of Dalriada itself.'[26] The other point to be made about learned allusions in oral poetry is that they show the connection between vernacular and Classical Gaelic poets, of which more later.

Sir James MacDonald's phrase 'under the Kinges of Scotland' may seem to stand in contrast to the line in Domhnall Gorm's 'Lullaby': 'When my king's son goes to Scotland'. This king is of course MacDonald. The Lord of the Isles is in modern Gaelic often referred to as 'Tighearna nan Eilean', but genuine tradition-bearers do not use it. To them he is known simply by the cognomen 'MacDonald'; in literary sources his usual title is *Rí* ('King').[27] The *Clanranald History*, for example, has 'John, son of Angus Òg who was called MacDonald and Mormaer of the Isles and King of Fionnghall'.[28] 'Am Mormhaire' ('The Mormaer') is the normal and still current style of MacDonald of Sleat; otherwise 'Am Mormhaire Domhnallach' or less commonly 'Am Mormhaire Sléiteach' (the Gaelic adjectival forms of 'MacDonald' and 'Sleat'). The Gaelic *literati*, then, continue to use the title reflected in *Rex Insularum*. Thus Raghnall son of Somerled is in the *Clanranald History* 'Raghnall King of the Isles of the Norsemen and the Coastland of the Gaels; foremost of all Gaels and Norsemen'.[29] But there is never, so far as I know, any suggestion in poetry or elsewhere that the Gaels do not owe allegiance to the true line of Malcolm III no matter how much their loyalty might become obscured in the turbulence of history or how much hostility the policies of an individual monarch and the attitudes of the central authorities might provoke. In poetry the rhetorical topic of *rìoghalachd* – loyalty to the king and participation in the kingly virtues – is constantly reiterated.

Much of the rhetorical structure of Gaelic verse took shape in the work of the poets who wrote in what we know as Classical Gaelic, a standard language evolved sometime toward the end of the twelfth century. It remained the standard for the whole Gaelic-speaking area, up to the middle of the seventeenth century in Ireland, and nearly a hundred years later in Scotland, where it came to an end with the death of the last representative of the hereditary bardic family of the MacMhuirichs.[30] A considerable amount of what has survived, though by no means all, of the work of this Bardic Order is praise-poetry. One of the earliest, if not *the* earliest, examples of the genre is a poem to Raghnall King of Man and the Isles from 1188 to 1226.[31] It has been ascribed to Muireadhach Albanach, ancestor of this same MacMhuirich family who for well over five hundred years held literary office first, apparently, under the patronage of the Lordship of the Isles in Kintyre and for over two centuries under that of Clanranald in South Uist. The MacMhuirichs have a fair claim to be regarded as the most illustrious family of learned poets and historians in Gaelic Scotland but there were, of course, others. The great early sixteenth-century manuscript known as *The Book of the Dean of Lismore* is in part a collection of bardic poetry. Dr Bannerman observes that:

> It has been noted before that the poetry of Scottish provenance, in both authorship and content, belongs overwhelmingly to a limited area of Scotland. Except for the earldom of Ross, whose links with the Lordship seem to have been at best tenuous and not of long duration, it is now possible to equate that sphere with the sphere of influence of the Lords of the Isles [. . .] Indeed, considering that the compilers were natives of Fortingall, the distribution pattern of the Scottish poetry, beginning, as it does, at Fortingall and proceeding west from there along a narrow corridor as far as Loch Awe, and then opening out dramatically to include a poem addressed to MacLeod of Lewis at one end of the Lordship and another to MacNeill of Gigha at the other end, would be an extraordinary one seen in any light other than that of the Lordship of the Isles.
>
> The only Scottish poet [. . .] who was certainly not a native of the area dominated by the Lords of the Isles is the only one for whom the compilers saw fit to record his place of origin, namely, Donnchadh Mór from Lennox.[32]

W. J. Watson was of the opinion that 'there must have been, all over the north and north-east from Sutherland southwards, and eastwards by Aberdeen, to say nothing of Galloway, a very large amount of early Gaelic poetry, by trained professional bards and others, of which we have no record.'[33] But this does not necessarily follow. Even if we allow that there must have been poetry and song of one kind or another everywhere throughout the Gàidhealtachd, our classical bardic poetry, a special development of the high Middle Ages, dependent equally on a rigorous scholastic training and the availability of patronage, might well have failed to penetrate or failed to flourish in the greater part of the Gàidhealtachd outside the sphere of the Lordship's influence. In fact, the later distribution of some other forms of poetry tends to support this view.[34]

Dr Bannerman's delimitation of the bounds of the Lordship is based among other evidence on the so-called 'MS. 1467', whose 'form and content leave no doubt that its compiler's intention was to set down the pedigrees of the chiefs of important clans who, in his opinion, recognised the authority of the Lord of the Isles at that time'.[35] The time was c. 1400, when the Campbells had not yet become conspicuous in the role in which later tradition has made them famous. *The Book of the Dean*, incidentally, contains a considerable number of poems of Campbell provenance. Poem I in W. J. Watson's edition contains the verse 'Write expertly, learnedly [. . .] bring unto Mac-Cailein no poem lacking artistry to be read.'[36] It is by the chief of Macnab and appears to project an anthology, which Watson takes to be the manuscript actually compiled by the Dean of Lismore. Watson comments:

> The reference in the poem to MacCailéin, the Earl of Argyll, as a shrewd and competent critic of poetry is specially interesting; and incidentally suggests that hostile relations between the MacGregors and the Campbells did not preclude friendly intercourse between Dugall MacGregor and the Campbell chief.[37]

The MacDonald-Campbell 'feud', with the Campbells cast in the role of villain, is part of Scottish folklore. It is also deeply rooted in genuine Gaelic oral tradition. That it should have these sources and this distribution is itself a token of the importance of MacDonald influence in forming popular views. There is nowadays a salutary tendency on the part of historians to de-mythologise such accounts but this should not tempt us to set aside the facts that traditional Gaelic society accepted: an important element in all history is what people believe to have happened. To convert these traditions, for the sake of brevity, into modern terminology, we find the hostility between Clan Donald and the Campbells presented as if it were a dialectical opposition of resistance to and collaboration with the central authorities. (In documentary sources the concept of resistance is summarily expressed in the often quoted statement made by the commissioners of the Lordship in 1545.[38]) There is no traditional memory of a time when the Campbells were under the sway of the Lordship. Throughout the wide area which the Lords of the Isles dominated, the custodians of tradition emphasise one point. That is, that the Campbells, being as truly Gaelic as any other *fine* ('kindred'), nevertheless took the side of the *Gall* of Scotland. There is a cultural dimension to this: an awareness of the encroachment of the *Galldachd* on the *Gàidhealtachd*. In the last quarter of the fifteenth century when the Lordship was under heavy attack by the central authorities and about to be forfeited by the Crown, Giolla Coluim mac an Ollaimh wrote a sad elegant poem 'It is no joy without Clan Donald':

Alas for those who have lost that company;
alas for those who have parted from their society;
for no race is as Clan Donald,
a noble race, strong of courage.

There was no counting of their bounty;
there was no reckoning of their gifts;
their nobles knew no bound,
no beginning, no end of generosity.

In the van of Clan Donald
learning was commanded,
and in their rear
were service of honour and self-respect.

For sorrow and for sadness
I have forsaken wisdom and learning:
on their account I have forsaken all things:
it is no joy without Clan Donald.[39]

The apprehension expressed here must have been greatly increased in 1609 when the Statutes of Icolmkill threatened among other things to suppress the bardic order itself. In the eighteenth century Alexander

MacDonald was to coin or use a phrase that sums up the reaction to these ethnocidal policies: 'Mìorun mór nan Gall' ('the great ill-will and hostility of the Lowlanders'). The traditions of the Campbell lands do indeed reflect the separate identities of Gàidheal and Gall but explicit statements of that nature are not to be found.

The Campbell and MacDonald poet-spokesmen each make a unique and identical claim on behalf of their respective clans: to each of them belongs *ceannas nan Gàidheal*, the 'headship', leadership and supremacy, of the Gaels. This formal attempt to wrest from Clan Donald their proud, ancient title raises the struggle above the level of any other vendetta in Gaelic history. The MacDonald claim in fact goes back beyond the eponymous Donald: 'The headship of the Gaels (belongs) to the Seed of Coll'; the genealogy of John of Islay is then traced by this poet through Somerled to Colla Uais, the mythical fourth-century ancestor to whose descendants properly belong 'the headship of Ireland and Scotland'.[40] The counter-claim is couched in similar terms: to the Campbells belongs the headship of the Gaels: 'A good charter is the headship of the Gael'; 'The headship of the Gael of the island of Alba'; 'Lord of the Gaels is Gilleasbuig'.[41] In the 1550s Maclean's poet reflects Campbell claims when he says in elegant diplomatic verse that he comes 'with my finished poem to the King of the Gaels'.[42] Viewed against the background of events from the 1490s onwards the precise words of this Campbell poetry make an illuminating comment:

> A good charter is the headship of the Gael,
> whoever it be that has a grip of it;
> a people's might at this time it has exalted;
> it is the noblest title in Alba. [. . .]

> Gilleasbuig, earl of the Gael
> has grasped the charter of the headship of the people;
> in his charter it has ever been of right
> to rule a willing people without self-seeking.[43]

The use of 'charter' reminds us of a *locus classicus* in Clan Donald poetry: 'The broadsword's charter is the birthright of that bold people; often without seal's impression do they (the Campbells) impose tax and tribute.'[44] It recalls also the bitter and often quoted words of Iain Lom in 1678: 'The sharp stroke of short pens protects Argyll [. . .] By falsehoods you deprived us (MacDonalds) of Islay green and lovely, and Kintyre with its verdant plains.'[45]

Hostility to Crown charters by those who suffered under the policies they endorsed was real enough and the Campbells were justifiably regarded as masters of such 'un-Gaelic activities'. The point to note, however, is that Campbell military and political ambitions are here backed by explicit claims at the diplomatic level of Classical Gaelic bardic exchanges. Mr Ronald Black has shown that this particular Campbell poem was well known to the poets of Clan Donald. He adds: 'it exists in two manuscripts [. . .] To find a Scottish bardic poem in more than one manuscript is unusual; to find a poem in praise of MacCailein Mór written by two different MacMhuirichs seems on the face of it little short of amazing.'[46]

Whatever the MacMhuirichs' reasons for preserving the poem so carefully, the implications of this Campbell *démarche* would certainly not elude them nor could its language fail to distinguish Campbell policy from that of others whose acceptance of the leadership of Clan Donald might well be less than total. Consequently, even the MacKenzies, who frequently played a part in the north comparable to that of the Campbells elsewhere (and who may have begun to pursue a distinctive course as far back as Harlaw)[47] never achieved a commensurate notoriety in the general tradition of the Gaels. It is frequently observed that no feud is as bitter as that between kinsmen. Yet tradition has preserved no memory of the consistently treacherous behaviour, from the Clan Donald point of view, of MacIan of Ardnamurchan who from 1494 until his death c.1518 'never failed to oppose the restoration of the Lordship by MacDonald claimants and throughout [. . .] was in close association with the Campbell earls of Argyll'.[48] Except at a private and local level the custodians of MacDonald tradition could not deal with this without making a fundamental shift in historical perspective. A larger ideological framework was required. It is a curious irony in view of the Campbell reputation for double-dealing that their notoriety should have been built up not so much perhaps by Campbell involvement in Scottish state affairs as, at the cultural level, by the plain speaking of the Campbells' poets with regard to the Headship of the Gael.

This interpretation may seem to put too much weight on the evidence of a few poems. My own view is that in Gaelic society one single composition of the kind I have quoted would be sufficient. We hear in tradition, often enough, how one taunt or one satire was registered, and recalled at the proper moment. It is quite likely that among the manuscripts that have perished through destructiveness and neglect there were other poems to rouse Clan Donald to an awareness of the Campbells' ultimate aim. At the same time we can only make an informed guess at what values might have been expressed in the lost poetry of Gaelic Scotland.

There is a well-known poem of incitement to battle addressed to Archibald, 2nd Earl of Argyll and Chancellor of Scotland, possibly on the eve of the Battle of Flodden, where, along with other Campbells, he lost his life. It begins: 'The race of the Gael from the land of Greece', and draws upon Gaelic legendary history and mythology. Within the conventional form the author articulates his message:

Meet it is to rise against Saxons [. . .]
ere they have taken our country from us;
let us not yield up our native country,
let us make no gentle warfare;
let us, after the pattern of the Gael of Banbha [i.e. Ireland]
watch over our fatherland. [. . .]

Saxons for a space
raised tribute from our country:
[it was so done] through each man's fear;
such is our mistrust. [. . .]

Send thy summons east and west
for the Gael from [Ireland];
drive the Saxons westwards over the high sea,
that Alba may suffer no division.[49]

The references to fear, mistrust and division may well reflect an underlying concern with the unity of the realm of Scotland, not just the Gàidhealtachd. Nevertheless the poem as a whole is very much a composition from the world of the 'sea-divided Gael'. Watson remarks on 'its fierce national spirit' and observes: 'there must no doubt have been many such poems, now lost to us, in connection with the Wars of Independence; one other, composed in 1310 [. . .] is found in the Dean's book.'[50] As a matter of fact this other poem, a panegyric to Eoin mac Suibhne of Knapdale, is by no means an unequivocal example of pan-Scottish propaganda: as it happens, it is from the Balliol or, as Watson puts it, 'from the English' side.[51]

The MacDonalds were of course deeply involved in the Wars of Independence but there is no evidence to suggest that the poets would have celebrated the Scottish rather than the Gaelic cause. In this connection it is of some interest that the tone of the *Clanranald History* (although perhaps affected by later events) in dealing with these stirring times is markedly detached. The writer merely notes that the MacDougalls took Balliol's side and the line of Raghnall son of Somhairle took that of Bruce.[52] By the sixteenth century Campbell participation in the affairs of state would naturally have brought something of the 'Scottish dimension' into their poetry, even if the poets still express themselves in figures of traditional rhetoric. But by the eighteenth century, under the pressures of Jacobitism, some MacDonald poetry, as we shall see later, is quite explicitly Scottish, not merely Gaelic.

It was established some years ago by Mr W. D. H. Sellar that the genealogy of Somerled's line is almost certainly authentic back to Gofraid son of Fergus, contemporary with Kenneth mac Alpin.[53] We have already noticed briefly how we can find even in oral, vernacular poetry occasional references to the Gathelus story and other learned lore, showing the sense of continuity of Gaelic history. In a pioneering study of Classical Gaelic poetry W. J. Watson drew attention to the fact

> that while the MacDonalds vaunted descent from Conn Cétchathach [. . .] and Colla Uais [. . .] MacCailin's bards disclaimed Irish connection, and traced the line of MacCailin up to Arthur of the Round Table, emphasising the British origin [. . .] 'Thy pure descent, Giolla-easbuig, I could recount to Arthur every step [. . .] Ten generations from thee in the heroic warrior-host comes wondrous Cailin of lasting feats [. . .] eleven steps from wondrous Cailin to Arthur comely and pure of the Round Table, the best king throughout the world.'[54]

Elsewhere MacCailein is the 'heir of Arthur', 'of the blood of Arthur and Béine Briot'. Watson implies that this pedigree is to be taken as part of the rival claim that Campbell poets urge against MacDonald pretensions. In fact, as Professor Gillies has shown, the Campbells did not exactly disclaim Irish connection; rather they used different lines of descent as political or other needs dictated.[55] The MacDonald poets were aware of the Campbell pedigree:

> Brutus son of Silvius [. . .] Descended from that Brutus are the British and MacCailin of Scotland and the whole race of Arthur son of Uther. It is that Brutus that used to be called Brutus the Repugnant, and the reason he was so called is that his mother died in bearing him and that he killed his own father

with an arrowshot so that he could have the kingdom after him; his brother Silvius therefore banished him from Rome to the isle of Britain, hence the British are named after him.[56]

From the Campbell viewpoint the connection with Brutus the Trojan, grandson of Aeneas and eponymous hero of Britain, has psychological as well as political advantages connecting them as it does with the 'Matter of Britain' and the great cosmopolitan world of Arthurian romance and pseudo-history which enjoyed such a prodigious vogue in Western Christendom throughout the Middle Ages. In the eighteenth century, however, the MacDonalds would over-trump this Campbell ace.

Nearer home there were other advantageous connections to be made. The obvious one is with the British of Strathclyde whose capital of Dumbarton lay just beyond the limit of the modern Gàidhealtachd. The Campbells' claim to British ancestry however is not merely propaganda but does appear to have a basis in fact. Alexander MacBain suggested, somewhat tentatively, that their origins lay 'on the borderland of the Strathclyde Briton and the Gael'.[57] Mr Sellar's brilliant unravelling of Campbell genealogies strongly endorses a British origin and directs our attention to the Lennox and to one of the leading families of that part of Strathclyde.[58] The family is the Galbraiths: *Clann a' Bhreatunnaich* 'The Children of the Briton'. Sellar quotes a Gaelic saying associated with them: 'The Briton from the Red Hall, the noblest race in Scotland.' In medieval Gaelic romantic tales the 'Fortress of the Red Hall' is King Arthur's capital. Smeirbi or Merevie or Mervin, 'a son of King Arthur [. . .] was born at Dumbarton Castle on the south side of the fort, in the place called the Red Hall [. . .] He was called to by his by-name, The Fool of the Forest; he was a wild and undaunted person.'[59]

Scholars of Gaelic and Welsh literature are well aware of the complex of relationships and correspondences that lie behind the Merlin of post-Geoffrey of Monmouth tradition. Among other elements, characters and places these involve the primitive theme of the Wild Man of the Woods, the madman who lives in the forest and possesses the gift of prophecy, and the court of Rhydderch Hael of Dumbarton around the end of the sixth century.[60] Mr Sellar surmises that the diverse forms of the name 'Smeirbi' are all variants of 'Myrddin' (Merlin). In the poem 'Maith an chairt ceannas na nGaoidheal' ('A good charter is the headship of the Gael') it is said: 'The

headship of the Gael [. . .] will be in the possession of one man of the
nobility of Britain.' This recalls the prophecy of the one monarch who
is to unite Scotland and England, attributed to Merlin in the form of
the old rhyme 'When Tweed and Pausayl join at Merlin's grave |
Scotland and England shall one monarch have',[61] and invoked in
connection with the crowning of James VI as James I of England.
However that may be, the sententious nature of the statement in the
Gaelic poem does suggest the formulas of popular prophecy and the
use of 'Britain' fits into the Campbell scheme of things.

In the poem, also, MacCailein is 'high judge over Scotland': in 1483
the first Earl of Argyll was appointed Lord High Chancellor of
Scotland. Two years later Henry Tudor ascended the throne of
England. As Kendrick puts it:

> The prophecy made to Cadwallader, last King of the Britons, that his people
> would once again possess the land of their fathers seemed to be fulfilled
> when, after a dramatic dynastic upheaval, a man whom Wales could call her
> son became King of England. The British History, in other words, had
> suddenly proved to be true, and we find that it was not considered
> inappropriate to include in fanciful designs for Tudor Royal Arms the
> quarterings Brutus, Belinus, and King Arthur.[62]

The new lease of life which Henry Tudor's accession to the throne
gave the British History could not go unnoticed among men of
learning everywhere; we know in fact that Campbell poets drew upon
English sources from the form of the name 'Cing Artur' which appears
in Gaelic poetry.

The One Monarch prophecy is also attributed to Thomas the
Rhymer: 'The lands of the north sall a' be free | And ae king rule
owre kingdoms three.' Thomas was as well known in Gaelic tradition
as he was elsewhere. 'When Thomas comes with his horses, there will
be a day of great havoc on the Clyde; nine thousand good men will be
slain, and a young King will take the crown.'[63] The Clyde is the
boundary between the Gàidheal and the Gall. In this prophecy, which
is still current, Thomas has taken the place of 'the deliverer whose
appearance precipitates terrible battles but who finally establishes a
rule of peace'.[64]

Thomas's name, as Dr Emily Lyle points out, has obviously become
associated with the Legend of the Sleeping Warrior, the story which is
probably most widely known in connection with the return of King
Arthur.[65] Elsewhere in Gaelic tradition it is Fionn mac Cumhaill

('Finn mac Coul') who is cast as the warrior who will one day return to save his people. Fionn is no doubt the earlier, though probably not the original, deliverer and has not been entirely displaced in popular lore by Thomas, originally only the prophet of the return. And in political poetry of the seventeenth and eighteenth centuries there is no mention of a specific saviour figure, only references to Thomas's prophecy of the ultimate triumph of the Gaels.

In the tradition of the northern Gàidhealtachd Fionn and Thomas, in separate versions of the legend, both sleep with the ancestral dead in the fairy mound of Tom na h-Iubhraich, near Inverness. In a variant account, apparently centred on the southern Gàidhealtachd, Thomas is in Dunbuck Hill, which brings us back yet again to Dumbarton and Strathclyde. Here, presumably, Thomas has displaced Fionn or some other deliverer, perhaps King Arthur himself. Indeed, J. F. Campbell guessed as much when he comments on a saying current in Islay which makes Dumbarton the location: it 'joins true Thomas to a common British legend'.[66] In Lowland tradition Thomas and Arthur are both associated with the Eildon Hills. It is therefore not impossible that British beliefs in the prophesied saviour, coming through Strathclyde, provide the link between Thomas the Rhymer and Gaelic tradition. Whether this is so or not, the messianic theme is old in Gaelic: certainly older than the early fourteenth century, when Thomas was already known as a prophet, and older even than the thirteenth century, when the historical Thomas of Erceldoune lived.

In Ireland the birth of a child of destiny who would restore former glories is at least as old as the twelfth century[67] when it appears in the prophetic poem ascribed to St Berchan; and from the thirteenth century on references to him are common in professional verse. Among the numerous references to Scottish Kings in the 'Prophecy of Berchan' there occurs:

Welcome! welcome! if he it is,
who has long been prophesied:
a King of the Kings [. . .]

Scotland will be full from his day.
This will be a fair, long reign [. . .]
for seven and two score years:

with fruit upon slender branches,
with ale, with music, with good cheer;

with corn, with milk, with nimble cattle;
with pride, with fortune.

Battles will not stand against his face [. . .]
God, the son of man, is faithful to him.[68]

It seems reasonable to assume a connection between the still current Gaelic prophecy and that of St Berchan. Like prophetic utterances elsewhere it could be adapted or changed to fit changing circumstances, coming into prominence at various points of crisis in Gaelic history. The initial crisis was of course the anglicisation brought about by the marriage of Malcolm III and Margaret. The hostile reaction of the Gaels is well known. It would be remarkable if such a profound setback did not produce some formal expression of hope that the former state would be restored. However gradual the process, curtailment and ultimately withdrawal of court patronage of the *filidh* – the highest caste of poets and historians – would lead us to expect the first articulation to be made at that cultural level. Some time might elapse before a messianic hope became diffused throughout society. And there it would remain, merged with related popular beliefs, a prophecy on behalf of all the Gaelic nation, though doubtless given focus by the achievements and aspirations of Clan Donald.

In the seventeenth century the Civil War, which for the first time drew the Gaels into a major British military and political struggle, gave the prophecy a new dynamic. In a song of greeting to Montrose, Iain Lom refers to it: 'Were Montrose to come to Ireland to join forces with us [. . .] with King Charles's command, the fulfilment of that prophecy would bring us to life, as Thomas the Rhymer foretold.' He uses almost identical words in his lament for the Marquis of Huntly.[69] Quite clearly the prophecy is an established part of Gaelic tradition: the poet does not require further elaboration. In the eighteenth century John MacCodrum alludes to the prophecy in his 'Praise of Clan Donald': 'Our friends and faithful kinsfolk would rise to fight with us [. . .] when the men of the Yew-wood awakened, who would come first but Thomas?'[70]

Just after Sheriffmuir Sìleas MacDonald of Keppoch observes: 'Justice has gone and injustice has come [. . .] Thomas says in his prophecy that it is the Gaels who will win the victory; every brow shall sweat blood, fighting the battle at the river Clyde.'[71]

Just before the 1715 Rising another Macdonald poet rallies the Gaels with the opening words 'This is the hour in which we will prove the Prophecy to be true'. Here, in 'Òran nam Fineachan' ('The Song of the Clans'), the messianic hope is identified with the Jacobite cause.[72] Another poem by the same author 'Am Bruadar' ('The Dream about the State of the Kingdom in the year 1715') is a vision of foreboding.[73] Nonetheless the poet is reassured that the final outcome will be in accord with the 'Prophecy of the Kingdom'.

The words which are used for 'prophecy' in these poems contain the same root as in the normal generic term for the Otherworld in medieval Irish mythology and literature. The Otherworld is represented 'locally' in the *sìdhein* ('Fairy Hill') of which Tomnahurich and Dunbuck are both examples. To the present day certain seanchaidhs will recall that the Fairy Hill is the source of prophecy as well as other, sometime ambivalent or even dangerous, gifts.

The association of saviour figure, prophet and fairy hill is given an added significance by the ideology of kingship in ancient Gaelic tradition.[74] The king is the centre of the cosmos: kingship has an Otherworld dimension and legitimate kingship has its source in the Otherworld; the true and righteous king (whose rule, in some of the narratives, is sanctioned by Otherworld personages) mediates between his people and the powers of the Otherworld, thereby conferring peace and fertility upon his realm as we have seen described in the 'Prophecy of St Berchan' concerning the King who has long been foretold. There is a reflection of the Otherworld dimension of Gaelic nobility in a panegyric to Alasdair mac Colla: 'Not alike are trees of lineage from fairy hills and (?) domesticated Saxon knights.'[75]

Although my quotations have been from poets of Clan Donald it should be noted that the authors do not use the prophecy to press specifically MacDonald claims. Sìleas of Keppoch in fact continues, after the reference to the battle at the River Clyde: 'England shall submit, however great her cunning, seeking peace from the king who is away from us'; and elsewhere: 'But arise, Scotland, as one, before the English cut your throats.' 'Òran nam Fineachan' ('The Song of the Clans') is not only a muster-roll of the Gaels; the nobility of the Lowlands are also numbered (though not by individual kindreds) among the Men of Scotland. Even before 1715 Scottish nationalism finds expression in 'Òran an Aghaidh an Aonaidh' ('Song against the Union of 1707').[76] The author is Iain Lom, than whom no poet was ever more conscious of the status and dignity of Clan Donald. In a song to Sir Donald of Sleat[77] he emphasises the old obligations of vassals of the Lordship, which are all the greater, he implies, seeing that those clans owe their position now (in the last quarter of the seventeenth century) to the reckless generosity of the Lords of the Isles. This he puts as a sequel to his announcement of their unique right.

The specific claim of Clan Donald is expressed in the curious formula that they have a right to a 'House and half of Scotland'. This phrase, which occurs in a number of poems, is in certain respects difficult to interpret. Iain Lom and John MacCodrum introduce it in the same stanza with Harlaw, which may suggest that they associated the claim with that campaign. Another song links it with Domhnall Ballach, son of John Mór of Dunivaig, who along with Alasdair Carrach defeated the Earl of Mar at Inverlochy in 1431: 'Domhnall Ballach of the Rough Bounds who made a boundary of the House of the Harp-strings, at the half-way point of Scotland.'[78] This particular house – *Taigh nan Teud* – near Pitlochry, is well known in local tradition as marking the exact centre of Scotland.

If this is in fact the place which symbolises the territorial claim, the formula may be very significant indeed. The concept of the sacral centre is known the world over; it is known in Gaelic tradition also and is associated with the sacred site of kingship. Thus, even if MacDonald and the centre of Scotland were only linked by popular tradition in relatively recent times, a good deal of interest would still attach to the interpretation. For one thing the site does not lie within the confines of the Lordship of the Isles at all but in the heartland of the ancient Scoto-Pictish kingdom. For another, since possession of the sacral centre confers a title to the whole territory, we should still have to assume there was at least a popular belief that assigned that right to the leader of Clan Donald. There is, however, one poem which appears to make an even larger claim. Writing soon after 1645, in Classical Gaelic, the poet observes: 'Tax and tribute over Alba's greater half once again those folk shall have as right, or else the old division.'[79] The implication would seem to be that the Gaels, represented and headed by Clan Donald, will share Scotland with the Gall, provided their *de jure* right to the whole is acknowledged. Otherwise, they lay claim *de facto* to Alba. There is no reason to suppose that 'Alba' here does not correspond to Scotland, at least 'from Orkney to Tweed'. It may be worth noting, especially if poets associated these claims with Harlaw, that the attitudes expressed may have a bearing upon the intentions of Donald Lord of the Isles towards the crown of Scotland.

In the same poem occurs the stanza: 'The Gael of Alba and Éire long ago were the same in origin and in blood, as our schools relate.'[80] No seanchaidh, to the present day, would deny that commonplace. Yet in the eighteenth century we can detect in certain quarters a shift of emphasis. The Gaels of Ireland and Scotland are still related but what now begins to receive attention is the Caledonian antecedents.

In 1751 Alexander MacDonald published his collection of poetry *Ais-éiridh na Sean Chànoin Albannaich* ('The Resurrection of the Ancient Scottish Language').[81] The title of the book indicates the author's view of his own role as a refurbisher of the tradition in the aftermath of the Jacobite defeat. The Preface is in English, addressed to the English-speaking world in general, but directed in the first place 'to the inhabitants of the Lowlands of Scotland, who have always shared with [the Gaels] the honour of every gallant action, and are now first invited to a participation of their reputation for arts'. MacDonald sees his people as 'a small but precious remain' of

> the Celtic nation [. . . which] once diffused itself over a great part of the globe. From its bosom have issued the conquerors of Rome, the invaders of Gaul, Britain, Ireland [. . .] once great and flourishing in Asia; and peculiarly distinguished, in having one of the holy epistles of the great Apostle of the Gentiles addressed to them.

In 1776 Alexander's son Ranald, also writing in English, puts the matter succinctly in perspective for all Scots: 'The Gaelic language [. . .] was once the mother tongue of the principal states of Europe. It was in particular, and for a considerable length of time, the only language spoken by our ancestors, the ancient Caledonians.'[82]

Into such a scheme could be fitted the British History, the Arthurian descent, and the whole panoply of Campbell pretensions. Although this Caledonian or sometimes Pictish view of Gaelic origins came late and had little effect on traditional poetry it persisted among antiquarians and was subscribed to by one or two scholars into the twentieth century. In the late eighteenth century it helped to obscure important issues of the Ossianic Controversy.

There are two poems of MacDonald's which I shall look at briefly. 'Moladh an ughdair do'n t-seann chànain Ghàidhlig' ('The author's paean to the ancient Gaelic language')[83] contains the first reference to Gaelic as the language of the Garden of Eden. MacDonald, however, does not intend this facetiously: he is in a line of European linguistic speculation which connected Celtic with Hebrew and ultimately produced the fantastic flowering of Celtomania.[84] (Even the Highland

Society Dictionary of 1828 cites 'striking affinities from the Eastern languages'.)

MacDonald observes that Gaelic existed before the Flood and still flourishes in spite of the 'great ill-will of the Gall'. It was the language of Scotland: of Lowlander and Gael, peasant and prince, cleric and layman. Malcolm Canmore spoke it: Gaelic was the language of the Court. There follows a list of the virtues of Gaelic, including its power in satire and flyting, of which MacDonald himself was no mean exponent as his anti-Campbell verse for one thing shows.

The other composition is his 'Òran nam Fineachan' ('Song of the Clans'),[85] a species already noted in connection with 1715. Both these poems of Jacobite propaganda take a convention of panegyric, that of listing the allies, real or ideal, of the kindred that is being celebrated, and develop it to its highest degree so that it becomes a pan-Gaelic roll-call.

Both MacDonald poets include the Campbells; Alexander placing them immediately after Clan Donald and addressing the Duke of Argyll in terms of elaborate praise, in full awareness of what the political and military strategy of the House of Argyll had been and was likely to be, at least in the near future. There were, of course, Campbells on the Jacobite side in both '15 and '45 and Sìleas of Keppoch acknowledges the part played by the Glenorchy branch of the great clan in the first Rising. But she is equally conspicuous in her hostility to the House of Argyll and in her awareness of where 'The Campbells', as if generically speaking, are to be placed.

There are, naturally, different degrees of directness of attitude to be found throughout the poetry. There is the fine denunciatory metaphor of a (seventeenth-century?) song: 'The sickle's stroke on the stubble upon all who live of the Campbells!'[86] Or there is the overt suspicion that the Campbells, although part of the Gàidhealtachd, will not support the '45: 'The whole of the Gàidhealtachd will be brave and bloody in battle; and should the Campbells not come, we don't think much of that pack!'[87] By contrast, the Songs of the Clans are diplomatic overtures.

The diplomatic function, particularly of Classical Gaelic poetry, is well-known. Mr Black suggests that the Campbell composition 'Maith an chairt ceannas na nGaoidheal' ('A good charter is the headship of the Gael') survives in two MacMhuirich manuscripts for the very reason that it 'reflects the poem's usefulness to MacDonald envoys'.[88] Although this can scarcely have been the author's first intention he may well have been aware of the possibility. He is in fact using a sophisticated diplomatic code capable of conveying ambiguities as well as clear information. Here, in a document which asserts the supremacy of the Campbells over all other Gaels, he observes the proprieties and in a list of the allies and supporters of the Campbells places Clan Donald at the top. This of course is far removed from *Real-politik*. The formal approach is much on a level with Alexander MacDonald's address to the Duke of Argyll in 1745, or indeed with his eirenic overtures to the Lowlanders in the introduction, in English, to his collection of 1751, for in the obscure interior of the book, his untranslated poems contain messages of a different kind. If it is true that the book was ordered to be burnt by the common hangman MacDonald obviously succeeded in getting these across!

The rhetoric of Classical Gaelic poetry, in which panegyric with its convention of enumerating friends and allies occupied the most elevated heights, was reproduced to an astonishing degree in the vernacular poetry of Scots Gaelic. But this 'traditional' poetry is by no means composed of a single strand: it draws upon many sources, among them the craft of the simple praise-singer – the original bard. In its registers we can see an ancient and conservative inheritance constantly renewing itself and constantly reflecting the changing circumstances of history. Moreover, the poets whom we regard as its leading practitioners were in some instances scions of aristocratic houses or in others were warrior-bards; in one way or another their involvement in social affairs was intimate and personal. And although they had no more to lose than members of professional orders of *literati*, the conventions of their art makes their propaganda on behalf of society seem less formal and less detached than that of their professional brethren. We have noted that they borrow occasionally from mythical history and the like. But on the whole what we are aware of is the pressure of contemporary events. Yet the expression of this is organised in an inherited panegyric framework.

The earliest dateable Gaelic song (still sung) is 'Pìobaireachd Dhomhnaill Duibh',[89] a panegyric associated with the Battle of Inverlochy of 23rd June 1429. A paean it may be: 'The Macintoshes fled, the MacMhuirichs fled but Clan Donald stayed.' But it also contains the verse: 'Today, today, today has gone against us; today and yesterday and every day has gone against us.' Even if this verse were a later accretion and if it were conceded that the verse expresses only the view of Clan Donald the statement could still be taken as an epitome of the theme that runs through so much of Gaelic tradition.

I leave it to those who know that tradition intimately and in all its manifold variety to judge. It seems to me that there is a strong undercurrent, surfacing occasionally, that expresses the feeling that we are the dispossessed of Scotland. When our poets act as our spokesmen they give evidence of a siege mentality.

I have tried to show elsewhere that panegyric is not only a genre in Gaelic but also a pervasive style.[90] Its mandatory gestures obviously derive from praise of the warrior-aristocrat. There is a persistent myth that what is popularly called 'clan society' was some sort of primitive democracy without distinctions of social class. In reality there was a high degree of economic stratification: the popular conception would at most apply only to the upper stratum. Gaelic poetry, however, does not reflect this as sharply as we might expect, especially when we remember how strictly the main classes were divided in the Isles at least as late as the last quarter of the sixteenth century. Of those who tilled the soil

> nane are chairgit or permittit to gang to ony oisting or weiris in all the haill Isles, but are commandit to remane at hame to labour the ground [. . .] And in raising or furthbringing of thair men (to war) [. . .] na labouris of the ground are permittit [. . .] except only gentlemen quhilk labouris not.[91]

In some areas this class structure may have survived the legislative enactments of the post-'45 period; in others it was perhaps modified much earlier. The growing demand for fighting men, for instance during the Civil War, would tend to have this effect. The parallel process began in Ireland in the second half of the sixteenth century when Seán Ó Néill in Ulster armed the peasantry. The extension of the privileges of a weapon-bearing élite would involve some participation in the aristocratic values of the older warrior class. There may in addition always have been an openness of communication between classes. Moreover a poet might be of low economic status but through family connections of relatively high caste (Mary MacLeod is one instance). At all events, the record of vernacular verse from the seventeenth century onwards shows that the values of the aristocracy had diffused themselves throughout Gaelic poetry.

On internal evidence alone it is often impossible to tell apart the poems of peasants and aristocrats. But occasionally the predilections of the 'gentlemen that labouris not' find overt, clear-cut expression. In the early seventeenth century in Lewis the mother of one of the

MacAulays of Uig, a renowned hunter, says in her elegy to her son: 'Born to roam the cold mountains, you chose the noble life: your fields were unploughed, your cattle-folds untended.'[92] Later in the same century Gilleasbuig, brother of Sir James of Sleat, describes 'the churls whose occupation is the cas-chrom'.[93] But in assessing the value of poetry as evidence of social attitudes we also have to take into account the selectivity of collectors. The gentlemen who compiled the great manuscript collections of the eighteenth century would probably agree with 'Ossian' Macpherson's criticism of Thomas Gray's 'Elegy Written in a Country Church-Yard', as reported by James Boswell: 'Hoots! To write panegyrics upon a parcel of damned rascals that did nothing but plough the land and saw corn!'[94]

The primary function of panegyric, then, is to celebrate the aristocrat and this remains its focal point. Its diction is codified in sets of conventional images most densely concentrated in the heroic elegy composed at the point of crisis brought about by the death of a leader – precisely when it was most necessary to reaffirm the traditional values of society. But the heroic eulogy contains the same topics. These are introduced and re-introduced until a densely woven texture of imagery is produced in which every phrase, every word almost, is charged with significance.

The code uses various forms of address to the subject of the praise poem with patronymic and territorial styles. There are stock descriptions of personal beauty; of the warrior as defender of his kin, as lover, hunter, horseman and seaman. His social roles, his generosity, the magnificence and hospitality of his household are all celebrated in a variety of recurrent impressionistic images. As a hunter of noble game he is accompanied by his hounds, attended by his retinue, and he carries the weapons that are also formally listed in descriptions of war. There are numerous references to the warrior's justice, his mildness to his own people, his piety and loyalty. In descriptions of the household, with its drinking, its blaze of wax candles, dice and chessmen, music of harps and viols, gold and silver vessels, we have vivid scenes of conviviality that remain undimmed after the passage of centuries. There are shipboard scenes also which combine roles of seaman and warrior in vignettes which, like the description of the household, involve conviviality and project indeed a microcosm of society. When this protector dies, his people are likened to motherless lambs, a forest swept bare by storms, a ship at the mercy of the elements, or a hive of bees robbed of its honey.

Territorial styles – of Moidart, Keppoch, and so forth – lead naturally to other names, among them famous fields of battle, of which one of the most important is Harlaw. Such names have an evocative power in other cultures; in Gaelic this has been drawn into the central stream of poetry. Sometimes non-Gaelic warriors are given epithets from the common stock – 'Iain Dubh nan Cath' ('Black John of the Battles'), for instance, is Graham of Claverhouse. The process mediates between an alien or hostile world and an intelligible order, endowing those heroes' names with potency in native terms.

Partly through genealogies, partly through lists of allies, and through place names, there is generated in this poetic tradition a complex sense of territory, not just the territory to which the poet belongs but also a sense of a more extended territory which is at the least potentially friendly; or if it is potentially hostile, according to the circumstances of a given time, its hostility is capable of being subdued by a rehearsal of great deeds enacted in alliance. The poetic 'map' which the bards draw with place names is comparable with the 'map' of political unity; less dominating perhaps, less vividly and precisely drawn, but the function is effectively the same. The native Gael who is instructed in this poetry carries in his imagination not so much a landscape, not a sense of geography alone, nor of history alone, but a formal order of experience in which all these are merged. What is to a stranger an expanse of empty countryside – magnificent or drab according to prevailing notions – to the native sensibility can be a dynamic, perhaps even heroic, territory peopled with figures from history and legend.

Throughout the whole range of the poetry conventional images pass before us like waves on the sea, endlessly recurring, formed in the same creative matrix, each a reflection of others, each one individual. They remind us of those that have passed; they prepare us for those that are to come. The rhetorical systems which contain these elements, inter-locking and lighting up, as it were, in their entirety no matter where we make contact, could not fail to keep alive the unity of the Gaelic nation.

The traditional circuit made by poets from one patron to another reinforced the sense of cultural solidarity. The famous tale of Iain Lom's trip to Inveraray after the Battle of Inverlochy illustrates, even if it is fiction, how poets were held to enjoy diplomatic immunity.[95] At that level there must always have been a good deal of social and artistic communication no matter what hostility might exist at other levels. Alexander MacDonald mentions his friendship with Colin Campbell of Glenure ('The Glen of Yew'). 'I like Colin of Glenure', he declares and then cannot resist adding, 'I wish he *were* yew and not alder.'[96] These are respectively 'noble' and 'base' woods in Gaelic tradition; the significance of Tom na h-Iubhraich ('Knoll of the Yew-wood') has already been noted. In such exchanges the Campbells are disadvantaged in more ways than one. A considerable amount of poetry from Campbell territory has survived but there is a noticeable dearth of vernacular propagandist verse, especially in the ancient declamatory measures which W. J. Watson called 'strophic metre'.[97] (This is the favourite non-classical bardic form for concentrated propaganda.) It is as if the original professional bard (who occupied a relatively lowly position) had not been encouraged to develop his art to the level at which we find it in the work of Mary MacLeod, Eachunn Bacach Maclean or Iain Lom himself.

The growth of that kind of poetry is to be seen as a reaction to the threat of dissolution of a conservative Gaelic society. As we have noted there was still rigid stratification in the Isles in the late sixteenth century – just before the emergence of the 'new' vernacular poetry.[98] By that date Campbell policies had produced a less conservative social order which was more resilient in the face of threats to Gaelic identity. Hence this sort of psychological prop was not so highly valued. But even if the humble praise singers had risen to higher status, their attitudes might occasionally hark back to a time before the *literati* had begun to claim the 'headship of the Gael' for the Campbells.

It is interesting to see how Duncan Ban Macintyre reacted to the Jacobite victory at Falkirk in 1746.[99] Duncan, who was a Campbell panegyrist on numerous occasions, fought with his Campbell masters on the Hanoverian side but his two songs on the event are full of praise of the 'enemy', above all, praise of Clan Donald. The second, composed in the aftermath of Culloden, is whole-heartedly Jacobite, looking forward to the next Rising in terms not unlike that of the 'Song of the Clans'. One verse begins, 'All the Gaels who were in Scotland would drive King George from his place'; the song ends, 'We shall all be of one mind [. . .] in your cause, Charles Stuart, for it is your crowning that will bring us peace.'[100] Rob Donn, among the Whig MacKays, echoes much of what Macintyre says; finally, on the death of the Prince in 1788, William Ross wrote the last genuine Jacobite poem composed in Scotland.[101] The bardic tradition remained Royalist no matter which side the bards' patrons or masters might take.

It is interesting that in current oral tradition Robert the Bruce is the only monarch who is represented as a Gaelic speaker. I suspect that he once played a conspicuous part in Gaelic historical legends. In the traditions of Rathlin (the Gaelic of which is Scottish rather than Irish) he is the Sleeping Warrior, the Saviour King; and the whole background of the story is Scottish.[102] In another context, Bannockburn features in Thomas the Rhymer's non-Gaelic prophecies. According to Barbour's *Brus*, when the Bishop of St Andrews heard that Robert the Bruce had killed the Red Comyn, he expressed the hope that Bruce was the great King prophesied by Thomas.[103] An adage that is still remembered in Gaelic, from the Outer Hebrides to Strathspey, seems like a fragment from that time: 'So long as a sapling grows in the wood there will be treachery in the Comyns.'[104] It was a Douglas who 'saw a dead man win a fight'.[105] The Goodman of Inbhirchadain in Rannoch says: 'I have heard men read from many a prophet in addition to the Rhymer that James has warriors who can perform brave deeds after death.'[106] The lost traditions of Scotland could perhaps have revealed unsuspected connections at that level between Gàidheal and Gall. As it is, what we have in Gaelic tradition is a vision of Alba in which the Galldachd is the country of a people of alien dress – black coats and hats; or they are mere tillers of the soil; or they are gloomy whisky-drinkers instead of high-born topers of red wine.

But Gaelic tradition also is fragmentary and our record of vernacular poetry, in which popular beliefs are most likely to be reflected, almost entirely unknown before the sixteenth century. To take just one of the points raised in this discussion, the dream lore that uses animal symbolism makes the pig the symbol of the Campbells. This suggests immediately the Boar's Head crest but it does not follow that the crest reflects primeval tradition. For in the same system of animal symbolism the deer represents the MacKenzies. If the goat[107] and not the deer was the original MacKenzie totem, it is plain that the interpreters of dreams were quite capable of keeping abreast of new developments. On the other hand it is highly significant that the two great figures of Diarmad and Arthur are both associated with the boar. Diarmad is the boar-slayer; Arthur the hunter of Twrch Trwyth, another magic and venomous boar.[108]

Moreover there may be a lost common background to the Fionn / Arthur figure in his aspect of Saviour of his land, asleep in the fairy mound or with the ancestral dead, and Diarmad's apparent identity with Donn, the god who rules the Otherworld of the dead.[109] The

Otherworld dimension of kingship would be of relevance here. The seanchaidh who drew King Arthur and Diarmad of the Féinn into Campbell genealogies would certainly have access to far richer popular traditions than are available to us. My speculation, admittedly very flimsy, is that a complex of popular beliefs, which probably cannot be unravelled now, underlay the constructions of Campbell seanchaidhs. Political and similar motives would inspire the genealogists but popular belief could point the way and validate the constructs.

It is also to be noted, however, that popular beliefs could be regarded by some genealogists as primitive and odious. According to tradition, the MacLeods, for instance, took any allusion to the horse as a grave insult. In the case of the Campbells, I suggest tentatively that the beliefs they drew upon involved, on the one hand, a boar or swine totem and, on the other, an Otherworld personage who confers legitimacy on the ruler. In the latter connection even the name 'Marbhan' (which to the present day would be immediately understood to mean 'The Dead One') may be significant.[110] Marbhan, incidentally, keeps as a pet a white boar. Swine in general have Otherworld associations, not only in Gaelic mythology. We can at any rate draw attention to the fact that popular genealogical tradition constantly forges links, more or less in that manner, between names.[111] Thus MacCorquodales are held to come from Lewis on the basis of the resemblance between 'Torcadall' and 'Torcall'. The Macleods of Lewis are the Seed of Torquil.

Whatever the truth may be in the present instance, it is pleasant to think that long ago some seanchaidh may have drawn conclusions that in certain respects parallel those of modern scholarship. This sees Arthur as the British counterpart of Fionn and sees Fionn's wife Gráinne, who elopes with Diarmad, as originally one of the manifestations of the loathly hag who turns into a beautiful young woman in the narratives that deal with the Sovereignty of Ireland. Professor MacCana writes:

> It is indeed possible that Arthur was a British leader [. . .] but if he was, it is nonetheless clear that the traditions which subsequently gathered about his name belonged to the same fund of insular mythology which gave rise to the legend of Fionn Mac Cumhaill.[112]

What we have looked at briefly here indicates that tradition has many tiers of information. The survivals of belief are one. At quite another level is the synthesis into which poets resolve the antithetical processes of Gaelic history.

This remained ideal but nonetheless gave a continuity, and what can only be called a national perspective to literature, of such importance that it is impossible to imagine the twentieth century renaissance – in prose as well as in poetry – coming into being without it. It is also worth pointing out that in the Gaelic view the past is not seen in a golden glow. The view has indeed been conditioned by the Clearances, the Evangelical Movement, the Land Agitation, and by the perspectives created by the British Empire. But there is an inherent strain of realism in Gaelic historical tradition as there is in Gaelic poetry. There are historical sagas that show the vices and shortcomings of great men as well as their generosity and valour. A period of the past is known as *Linn nan Creach* ('the Age of Forays and Plundering'). In common usage it refers to a fairly distant past. Its limits, however, are indeterminate. Perhaps a plausible *terminus ante quem* could be set in the mid-eighteenth century. It is very likely that the *terminus a quo* is to be found in the time when the control exercised by the Lordship of the Isles was removed by the actions of the government of Scotland.

The Gaelic Perception of the Lowlands

It would not be difficult to assemble a body of evidence to show that the Gaels of Scotland regarded the people of the Lowlands with something less than love. And it would be just as easy to show that the Lowlanders were perfectly capable of returning the compliment. Relationships between the two were of course much more complicated than such stereotypes would suggest and we have plenty of evidence of cultural interchange at different times and at different social levels: in literature, in folktales, in music, and in language. Still, none of that is incompatible with failure to establish goodwill or even understanding at other possible points of contact, especially perhaps on the political plane.

It may be possible for two communities or two nations to enrich each other's cultures significantly, at several levels, and yet to view each other with mutual hostility. Scholarly analysis apart, once a borrowed item is assimilated to its new cultural environment, its origins are by definition obscured and liable for that reason alone to be ignored. We have Gaelic loan-words in Scots and Scots loan-words in Gaelic: both indicate the range and kinds of contact between the two peoples and their languages. In music there is evidence of considerable affinity between Highlands and Lowlands, even if the precise nature of the relationship is often difficult to interpret. There is evidence also that folktales were carried backwards and forwards across the Highland-Lowland boundary.

But 'perception', in the sense in which I am taking it here, does not deal with that kind of evidence. Nor am I concerned either to confirm or deny the existence of the stereotype to which I alluded in my opening sentence. All I intend to do in the course of this brief and necessarily superficial account is indicate what we have actually said in Gaelic about the Lowlands. At some points this testimony is no doubt ambivalent, but I believe it is none the less possible to disregard most of the problems that arise in that connection and still present a reasonably coherent outline of Gaelic attitudes.

Paradoxically, the first point I have to make is that Gaelic has no word precisely equivalent to 'Lowlands'; nor for that matter does it have a word for 'Highlands'.[1] In this area of nomenclature, as often in other respects, Gaelic is conservative. Professor Barrow, whom I have quoted elsewhere in this connection, makes the comment:

> Neither in the chronicle nor in the record of the twelfth and thirteenth centuries do we hear of anything equivalent to the 'Highland Line' of later time. Indeed, the very terms 'Highlands' and 'Lowlands' have no place in the considerable body of written evidence surviving from before 1300. 'Ye hielans and ye lawlans, oh whaur hae ye been?' The plain answer is that they do not seem to have been anywhere: in those terms, they had simply not entered the minds of men. We commonly think of this highland-lowland dichotomy as being rooted deep in the history of Scotland, as being, indeed, imposed upon that history by the mere facts of physical geography. Yet it seems to have left no trace in the reasonably plentiful record of two formative centuries.[2]

The Gaelic perspective is essentially a cultural one. The Gaelic-speaking area of Scotland is *Gàidhealtachd* and the rest is *Galldachd*; or, with the article, *A' Ghàidhealtachd* and *A' Ghalldachd*. These are not place names in the ordinary sense: there is some degree of vagueness in the way they are used and they carry strong cultural connotations. Some years ago I heard Gaelic speakers in Arran describe the entire stretch of coastland from Galloway to Ayrshire as part of the Gàidhealtachd. They knew some of the place names of that region in their Gaelic form; it was traditional knowledge among them that the Gaelic language had been spoken there in the past; and they assumed that, just as in Arran, it had survived to the present day. Elsewhere, so far as Gaelic usage is concerned, the boundary between Gàidhealtachd and Galldachd corresponds well enough with the Highland Line. Up to about two centuries ago the Line was of course more or less coterminous with the linguistic boundary between Gaelic and Scots/English. After Gaelic began to decline within the 'Highland' area, this usage survived to denote the traditional Gaelic-speaking Highlands. But certain adjustments, perhaps beginning in the nineteenth century, were also made. These naturally affected the use of 'Galldachd' also. Thus in areas like Perthshire or Badenoch and Strathspey, Gaelic speakers have said to me, 'Chan eil an seo ach Galldachd an-diugh' ('This is only a Galldachd nowadays'), though at the same time they would undoubtedly have regarded these regions as part of the traditional Gàidhealtachd. Similar judgments are more and

more to be heard throughout the whole of north and north-western
Scotland as the use of English increases at the expense of Gaelic. In
contemporary usage there is a noticeable tendency among Gaelic
speakers to use 'Gàidhealtachd' not only to denote the geographical
'high land' of Scotland but to denote the communities in which Gaelic
is still an everyday language. The area north and west of the Highland
Line is then sometimes referred to as *An t-Seann Ghàidhealtachd* 'The
old Gàidhealtachd'. Quite clearly then 'Gàidhealtachd' does not
directly translate 'Highlands' nor does 'Galldachd' translate 'Lowlands'.

My friends in Arran did not deny that the Gàidhealtachd of
Ayrshire for instance, was situated in the 'low land', *Machair Alba*
'the Plain of Scotland'. *Machair Alba* or *A' Mhachair Ghallda* is, in a
general sense, the geographical Lowlands. When it is used nowadays –
more commonly, I think, in the plural *Na Machraichean* – it may be
applied equally to, say, lowland Stirlingshire or Fife, Morayshire or
even to the low-lying lands around Beauly; the last, of course, being
within the Highland Line. We might sum all this up by saying that
only in a qualified sense does 'Galldachd' equal 'Lowlands', and
similarly that the much less common term *A' Mhachair Ghallda* or
Machair nan Gall, which geographically denotes the low-lying lands
of Scotland, is not co-extensive physically with what is normally called
the Lowlands.

A glance at one of the Gaelic maps of Scotland produced in recent
years might lead one to think that Gaels know at least the majority of
Lowland names in a Gaelic form. This is not at all the case. *Obar* (or
Abar) *Dheathain, S(t)ruighlea* or *S(t)ruighleidh, Dùn Eideann* and
Glascho or *Glaschu* are known everywhere. To that may be added
Falkirk, *An Eaglais Bhreac*. The Gaelic name of Falkirk persisted
because of its famous tryst, *Féill na h-Eaglaise Brice*, in less conservative dialects *Féill na h-Eaglais Bhreac*. There are many Gaelic
speakers who know 'An Eaglais Bhreac' but who are not aware that
Doune, on one of the main drove-roads from the north, is *An Dùn* or
Baile an Dùin(e). Within living memory, however, there were drovers
who knew names such as *Sliabh an t-Siorra* or *Sliabh an t-Siorraim*
'Sheriffmuir' and others further south through their specialised knowledge. These men carried maps of the droving routes in their heads;
place name collectors working from the 1950s onwards were unfortunately in the main too late in the field to tap their memories.

Sliabh an t-Siorraim or *Cill Saoithe* 'Kilsyth' or *Inbhir Chéitein*

'Inverkeithing' and other names of the sites of battles survive in poetry and most of us have learnt them there. There must have been many more place names, including some that look insignificant today, which were once functionally important to drovers and other travelling people, and hence gained currency in Gaelic, besides those which were involved in wars and achieved the dignity of being enshrined in poetry for that or similar reasons. It is still possible, however, on the periphery of the Gàidhealtachd from Perthshire to Argyll, to recover some of the names of Stirlingshire and Dumbartonshire.

There is one more place name that ought to be mentioned. It is still fairly widely known throughout the Gàidhealtachd, at least by the older generation, and so far as I know it is a unique case. Unlike the other place names I have mentioned or been thinking of, it is not originally Gaelic at all, nor has it been assimilated to the phonology of Gaelic. This is *Loudie* or *Machair Loudie* 'Lothian' or the 'Plain of Lothian'. Clearly it is a Scots form, since its articulation lacks the Gaelic 'dark L' and dental stop. (The occasional spelling 'Lobhdaidh' is misleading.) Yet it has apparently disappeared without trace in spoken Scots; nor is it on record in written Scots, although the form 'Lodian' is known. In the appropriate context, the bare phrase 'A' dol a Loudie' ('going to Lothian') meant going to work in Lothian at harvest-time. Year after year bands of harvesters travelled from all over the Highlands and Islands for this seasonal work, whose beginnings can be traced to the closing decades of the seventeenth century.

The word 'Loudie' itself can be traced back in Gaelic to the same century, when it appears in a Kintail song composed in praise of Coinneach Òg, chief of the MacKenzies: 'Tàladh Choinnich Òig' cannot be dated exactly but it appears unlikely to be much later than the mid-century. If that is so, and if the verse which contains it is not a later accretion (and there is no evidence for that) the name 'Loudie' would seem to have been borrowed before migrant harvest-work became established practice. 'Loudie' may of course have been borrowed more than once, and later borrowings could have displaced a Gaelicised pronunciation or reversed the process of naturalisation we would expect in a case like this. On any other view, unless indeed the song is an exceedingly old-fashioned composition of the eighteenth century, we have to accept that this form of the name of Lothian has remained in Gaelic for over three centuries – obstinately refusing, as it were, to adapt to a Gaelic linguistic environment.

So much for the geographical boundaries of the Lowlands and the

Gaelic perception of where they lie and what they enclose. What does Gaelic tradition have to tell us about the Galldachd in other respects?

The Gaelic for Scotland is *Alba*, and a Scot, no matter which part of Scotland he comes from, is an *Albannach*. The Gaelic for England is *Sasann* or *Sasainn* (slight dialectal variants); an Englishman is a *Sasannach*; 'Scotswoman' is *Ban-Albannach*; 'Englishwoman', *Ban-Sasannach*. This is the regular pattern of nomenclature, as in *Frangach* 'Frenchman'; *Ban-Fhrangach* 'Frenchwoman'; and so forth. No Scot, man or woman, can be 'Sasannach' or 'Ban-Sasannach', and that applies with equal force to Highlanders and Lowlanders alike. A Lowlander (male) is a *Gall*; a Lowlander (female) a *Ban-Ghall*. The adjective is *Gallda*; and 'Galldachd' is formed from it.

The sharpness of the distinction that Gaelic tradition draws between Lowlander and Englishman is not always appreciated to the full by non-Gaels. Their puzzlement may not be altogether surprising. For one thing, as Lowlanders sometimes complain, Gaelic makes no distinction between English and Lowland Scots linguistically. They both speak *Beurla*. But 'beurla' meant originally not 'English' but 'speech': the extended designation *Beurla Shasannach* 'English (speech)' is still to be heard. I must admit that I have never heard this employed to make a contrast with *Beurla Ghallda*, but when I myself use the latter for Scots (in preference to the dreadful neologism *Albais*), all Gaelic speakers understand immediately what is intended. In any event, Lowlanders themselves originally referred to their language as 'Inglis'.

A more important source of misunderstanding, however, exists in the semantic range of the name 'Gall'. Originally denoting a Gaul, the word was applied successively to Norsemen, Anglo-Normans and English, and that does not exhaust its meanings. At an early stage it developed the general connotation of 'foreigner'. Although one cannot say that the adjective 'Gallda' carries this meaning of 'foreign' openly in modern spoken Gaelic, the fact is that most 'foreign' things – food, clothes, artefacts, breeds of domestic animals, language and social customs – came to us through the Lowlands whether or not they originated there. Naturally enough some of that connotation still clings to the word: not perhaps to the noun but certainly to the adjective. To put it in a crude summary way: there is a generic 'gallda' as well as a specific 'Gallda' and in some instances it is very difficult indeed, even for a native Gaelic speaker, to make the proper translation. Privatively the context will suggest 'non-Gaelic'; to find a precise positive equivalent is very much more troublesome. Nevertheless, as a *specific* term 'Gall' means 'Lowland Scot', not 'Englishman' and not 'foreigner'. Of course, there will be occasions when a Lowland Scot is mistaken for an Englishman. In this connection, it is noteworthy that until recent times at least sportsmen who came to the Highlands to stalk deer, shoot grouse and fish for salmon were generally referred to not as *Goill* (plural of 'Gall') but as 'Sasannaich'. If they were in fact Lowlanders, the implication seems to be, they were Lowlanders in English disguise. This perception concerns social class and speech habits.

How old is this distinction between Gall and Sasannach? Was it already part of the Gaelic view before the great historic divide between Highlands and Lowlands had established itself? Or was it drawn at a later date? Whatever the answer may be, the distinction at any rate suggests the importance to the Gaels of the historical boundary between England and Scotland. The people who lived north of that frontier were different from those who lived to the south of it. Hence they had to be given different names.

All we can say from the evidence of Gaelic tradition is that the integrity of Alba, Scotland, is never in question. The inhabitants of the Lowlands are unquestionably Albannaich. But within that framework, there are more detailed perceptions.

Writing around 1730 Edmund Burt had this to say of the Gaels:

> They have an adherence to one another as Highlanders, in opposition to the people of the Low-Country, whom they despise as inferior to them in Courage, and believe they have a right to plunder them whenever it is in their Power. This last arises from a Tradition, that the Lowlands, in old Times were the possession of their Ancestors.[3]

Burt goes on to say that he first gathered this from 'the middling and ordinary Highlanders, who are very tenacious of old Customs and opinions' but he afterwards came to the conclusion that it was also the view of some at least of those 'of the Highest Rank'. So far as I am aware there is no canonical text in Gaelic literature that combines both these ideas: that the Lowlands once belonged to the Gaels and that this gives the Gael a right to plunder the Lowlander. But even in the mid-twentieth century it was still possible to hear somewhat similar ideas expressed by very old people whose traditions were derived from grandparents born at the end of the eighteenth century. And the beautiful Perthshire song 'Bothan Àirigh am Bràigh Raithneach'[4] puts one part of it succinctly:

Cuime am bìomaid gun eudail
Agus spréidh aig na Gallaibh?

Why should we be without stock
Seeing that the Lowlanders have cattle?

Gaelic praise-poetry glorifies the heroic ideal and celebrates the warrior class whose members play the aristocratic game of war. The warriors themselves despise manual labour and the tillers of the earth who are not allowed to carry weapons. The latter are the *bodaich*, not so much 'old men' (the normal modern Gaelic usage) as 'peasants'. The poets equate the Lowland peasant farmers, and by extension all dwellers in the Lowlands, with the 'bodaich' who dig the soil. They are *Gallbhodaich* or *bodaich Ghallda*, 'Lowland peasants' or 'Lowland carles' as the word is sometimes translated. The warrior is taken as the standard of the one society; the peasant as the standard of the other. Seen from this level of Gaelic tradition, peasants of any land are men without pedigree, mere nobodies.

The Gaelic warrior wears the distinctive tartan plaid; the Lowlander wears hodden grey breeches, black cloak and hat. The Gael drinks wine and fights with sword or bow-and-arrow; the Lowlander uses a gun. The Gael eats venison, beef and pork; the Lowlander subsists on kail. This is a crude simplification of the stereotype of the Gall presented in Gaelic poetry but I think it reproduces the essence. The attitudes expressed in this body of heroic song-poetry are not to be dismissed; at the same time it is important to realise that they are couched in terms of the literary conventions of an heroic age. These conventions persisted long after the conditions that allowed a warrior class to flourish had passed. Near the end of the eighteenth century Iain mac Mhurchaidh the Kintail poet, composing his song after emigrating to North Carolina, says:[5]

Gur beag orm féin na daoine seo tha ann
Le an còtaichean dubha, ad mhór air an ceann
Le am briogseanan goirid air an sgoltadh gu am bann
Chan fhaicear an t-osan, is e a' bhochdainn a tha ann.

Little do I care for the folk who live here,
with their black coats and great hats on their heads;
with the short breeches split to the band:
the kilt hose, alas, is not to be seen.

Còta 'coat', *cleòca* 'cloak' and *casag* 'cassock' are all used in descriptions of Lowland dress. They are all, incidentally, loan-words from Scots or English. And they are invariably coloured black. These descriptions may be naturalistic; more important, they are emblematic. The cassock, for instance, was originally a military dress; but from around 1600 it also denoted a dress worn by rustics. The psychological effect of the Disarming Act of 1746 is to be seen in that context.

One of the commonplaces of Gaelic heroic praise-poetry is the carousal of warriors; red wine is the most highly esteemed drink. Considering the close associations of whisky with the Highlands and Islands nowadays it is startling to find in a song of the seventeenth century:

> *Nan robh mise far am bu dual domh [. . .]*
> *Cha b'e mo dheoch bùrn an fhuarain*
> *No uisge-beatha nan Gall gruamach*
> *Ach fìon dearg a' lìonadh chuachan.*[6]

> If I were where I used to be [. . .]
> my drink would not be the water of the spring
> nor the whisky of the gloomy Lowlander,
> but red wine filling the cups.

According to the heroic ideal, personal encounter, in which strength and skill counted, is the centre-piece of battle. Even when our ancestors came to use muskets and other firearms and indeed after guns are listed by the bards as part of the warrior's panoply, we still find statements in poetry that express the old contempt for such an unheroic form of combat. Around 1600 the great MacAulay warrior Domhnall Cam mac Dhubhghaill in Lewis heard about guns and gunpowder. His comment is the epitaph of the heroic age: 'Tha latha a' ghaisgich seachad' ('The day of the hero is gone'). Over a century later Iain Ruadh Stiùbhart's description of the action at Culloden is in the same tradition:

> *Lasair-theine nan Gall,*
> *Frasadh pheilear m'ar ceann,*
> *Mhill sud eireachdas lann 's bu bheud e.*[7]

> The bombardment of the Lowlanders,
> the showering of shot around our heads,
> that destroyed the brilliance of sword-play – more's the pity.

Again, Aonghus mac Alasdair Ruaidh of Glencoe in his song on the battle of Killiecrankie[8] alludes with contempt and outrage to the death of warriors at the hands of peasants with guns:

> *Bhith gan leagail le luaidhe*
> *Is gun tilgeadh buachaillean bhó i.*

> Being felled with lead –
> when even cowherds can throw it.

'We would see who had valour,' he goes on, 'in the exchange of sword-blows':

> *Bodaich Machair a' bhuachair*
> *No sìol uasal nan Garbh Chrìoch*

> The peasants of the Plain of Cow-dung
> or the noble seed of the Rough Bounds.

In the same song, however, Pitchur, who fought alongside the Gaels is celebrated as An Gall Mór 'The Great Lowlander'. Pitchur is not the only Gall who receives his due meed of praise in Gaelic poetry, but such allusions are rare none the less.

The sense of integrity of the kingdom of Scotland, which I have mentioned already, and a perception of the Lowlands as part of that integrated whole, emerges time and time again in Gaelic tradition. And the integrating principle is a sense of the Gaelic basis of Scotland: a realisation, as Dr John Bannerman has put it, of the archetypal role that the Gaels played in the formation of the kingdom. The Clan Donald poets of 1715 have a very secure view of Scotland as a whole; but so, for that matter, has An t-Aos-dàna MacShithich in his poem on the execution of the Earl of Argyll in 1685.[9] The poet is highly critical of the central authorities and much concerned about the state of the realm. This may be the more predictable in a Campbell poem as the Campbells had been involved so closely and for so long at the centre of national affairs. But although the viewpoint is different, MacShithich is no more concerned than the MacDonald poet, Iain Dubh mac Iain mhic Ailein, in his 'Song of the Clans', composed in 1715, where he invokes the unity of all Scots – 'the nobility of the Galldachd' as well as the Gaels – bringing them together in the common cause.[10]

There are perceptions in these and other poems that are really quite different from the derisory judgments of the warrior bards. And this is true even when the perception appears to be that of a hostile critic.

Consummate, all-embracing hostility is the common interpretation of Alasdair mac Mhaighstir Alasdair's resonant phrase 'mìorun mór nan Gall' ('the great ill-will of the Lowlanders'). But this is not the warriors' contempt: it is a reaction, on a different stage, towards the whole attack on Gaelic culture, whether expressed in the Statutes of Icolm-kill of 1609 or in the s.s.p.c.k. schools of the eighteenth century.

'Mìorun mór nan Gall' appears in Alasdair's poem in praise of Gaelic, in which he celebrates Gaelic as the ancient language of Scotland, once spoken by Highlanders and Lowlanders alike, by clerics and laymen, by kings and commons. Whether mac Mhaighstir Alasdair in this phrase refers to Lowlanders only, or whether he intends the word 'Gall' to have a wider reference, is unclear. In a famous poem of incitement to battle, addressed to Archibald, 2nd Earl of Argyll and Chancellor of Scotland, possibly on the eve of the Battle of Flodden in 1513, 'Gall' is used to mean 'English'.[11] Alasdair may be echoing that usage. At all events, he has his own definite view of the Lowlands and a strategy for Highlands and Lowlands working together, as he explains in the Preface (written in English) to his book of poems, published in 1751.[12] The Preface is directed 'to the inhabitants of the Lowlands of Scotland, who have always shared with [the Gaels] the honour of every gallant action, and are now first invited to a participation of their reputation for arts'. Once again, the integrating principle is a sense of the Gaelic basis of Scotland. Alasdair mac Mhaighstir Alasdair is encouraging the Scots of the Lowlands to take an active interest in their Gaelic heritage. If his own poems met with a favourable response he would follow this up with an anthology of Gaelic poetry, ranging from the most ancient compositions to those of his own day. (This anthology in fact only appeared in 1776 when his son published it.)

In some measure Alasdair mac Mhaighstir Alasdair's poem on Gaelic only repeats what the Rev. John Maclean had already said in his poem of 1705 in celebration of Edward Lhuyd. But Alasdair's poem enjoyed a circulation that Maclean's poem did not; indeed it is true to say that in the context of Gaelic culture in Scotland Alasdair mac Mhaighstir Alasdair dominates the eighteenth century. When we find references to the antiquity of Gaelic, as in the work of Màiri Mhór nan Òran in Skye in the nineteenth century, we are probably picking up an echo of mac Mhaighstir Alasdair. Màiri was very much the poet of the Land Agitation Movement. To an unusual degree, I think, among the poets of the Clearances, during which Lowland factors and Lowland shepherds were liable to be in sharp focus, Màiri always makes the distinction between Goill 'Lowlanders' and Sasannaich 'English'. She has about a score of references to Sasannaich and though she is not very complimentary to the Gall, she is quite consistent in her view that the Sasannach is the villain. She does seem to be adopting a definite political stance (some of the leading figures in the Land League Movement were Home Rulers) which involves a particular historical viewpoint. Màiri also uses the very rare term *na Machraich* 'the people of the [Lowland] Plain'. Although in her time Gall meant specifically 'Lowlander', Màiri may have been aware of the older range of meaning and certainly knew the name *Innse Gall* ('the Isles of the Foreigners', i.e. the Norsemen) for the Hebrides. And she may have been aware, too, of the ambivalence that one occasionally finds in the use of 'Gall' in songs composed by her contemporaries. Lady D'Oyly of Raasay, for instance, says that Scotland and Ireland both are in distress, 'is an Gall bho thìr gu tìr' ('and the Gall from land to land', i.e. 'from shore to shore').

A very different aspect of the Gaelic view of the Lowlands is the attitude of the Gaels to the Scottish monarchy. One of the recurrent themes of Gaelic poetry is loyalty to the king. One historian has remarked that it was a 'mystical reverence [. . .] strictly confined to theory'.[13] Politics of individual monarchs and their parliaments have a bearing on the latter part of that judgment. The Gaelic reverence for the monarchy consisted of loyalty to the line of Malcolm III, the true dynastic line that went back to Dál Riata and beyond that to the legendary and mythological kings of Ireland. But it has another dimension also which involves the idea that the Gaels shall be restored to their former place in Scotland.

In common with other peoples who regarded themselves as the dispossessed, we have a distinct messianic theme in Gaelic. In the end the Wheel of Fortune will turn and we shall come into our own again. The prophecy concerning this is still current in oral tradition and the associated legends are variants of the Legend of the Sleeping Warrior, which is probably most widely known in connection with the return of King Arthur. Interestingly enough the prophet of the return of the Gaels to power in Scotland is not himself a Gael – at least in seventeenth century and later tradition – but a Lowlander, Thomas the Rhymer, well known as a prophet in other contexts also. But it is *qua* prophet rather than *qua* Lowlander that he enters Gaelic tradition.

The messianic prophecy which became attached to Thomas the Rhymer's name promises that a young king will inaugurate the age of victory and peace. Given the strong ideological loyalty to the true dynastic line, this 'mystical reverence' of the Gaels for the king, the prophecy could only become prominent if that dynasty were displaced or destroyed. In the Great Civil War, when the ruling monarch was threatened by non-monarchical powers, and later, when James VII was displaced by William of Orange, Thomas's predictions could be invoked. But such points of crisis were comparatively rare. For the rest of the time, or at different times and in different places within the Gàidhealtachd, Fionn mac Cumhaill is the prophesied leader. The difficulty in settling on a kingly figure may be one reason for the strange shift of role that Thomas the Rhymer undergoes in many of the versions of the legend. Instead of being the prophet he himself becomes the messianic leader. With the possible exception of the Wars of Independence, it was only with the Jacobite Risings of the eighteenth century that a properly qualified candidate for the role seemed to emerge: a scion of the true line, appearing to favour the Gaelic nation, and hostile to the powers of the state that the Gaels felt had dispossessed them. Robert the Bruce, associated with Thomas the Rhymer's prophecy in the Lowlands, probably featured in the same role in his time; but the meagre evidence of Gaelic tradition about Bruce does not allow us to draw a firm conclusion. A Jacobite song mentions Thomas, however, and brings the Legend of the Sleeping Warrior and loyalty to the true king together in one equation:[14]

Chuala mi a bhith leughadh
Bharr air Reumair, iomadh fàidh
Gu bheil curaidhean aig Seumas
Nì treubhantas an déidh bhith marbh.

I have heard men read
in many a prophet besides the Rhymer
that James has warriors
who can perform great deeds after their death.

Although the monarch lived in the Lowlands the Gaelic 'mystical reverence' ensured that his influence was seen as beneficent and separate from the hostile policies of the state. (This is in some ways comparable to the loyalty that blamed factors but exonerated the clan chiefs during and after the Clearances.) According to one witness,

> The severest blow which our language has ever received, was the removal of the Royal Family to England, and the attendance of our men of rank and influence at Court; who were carrying back to their country the manners and language of England and of the Lowlands [. . .] And Government exerted its utmost power for the destruction of the Gaelic language, and Highland manners, until by degrees the Highlanders were losing their respect and esteem for the manly and original language of their ancestors.[15]

On the face of it, this would seem to claim that the presence of the monarch in Edinburgh prevented even the imposition of the Lowland tongue on the Gàidhealtachd. But Hugh MacDonald of Cill Pheadair in South Uist, the author of the statement just quoted, was no doubt aware that the Statutes of Icolmkill came six years after the Union of the Crowns.

To sum up, the Gaelic perception of the Lowlands is in essential agreement with that of the medieval Scots writers who regard the Gaels of their time as 'contemporary ancestors', people who preserve the language and culture which were once shared by all. But from the Gaelic point of view, we the Gaels are the disinherited, the dispossessed.

There is sometimes an equivocal attitude, for instance towards the towns. The countryman's attitudes towards the town are in this context made much more complicated by the fact that towns are not only *gallda* but *Gallda*. These include the burghs that were planted in the Highlands by the successors of Malcolm III and which were centres of foreign manners and foreign speech. On the other hand, a sort of local variant of the Seven Wonders of the World, attributed to Gilleasbuig na Ceapaich, begins:[16]

Chunna mi Eaglais Ghlascho
Agus Caisteal Dhùn Éideann

I have seen the Church of Glasgow
and the Castle of Edinburgh

And Glasgow itself is more than once referred to as 'Glascho nam buadh' ('Glasgow of "virtues" ', in the medieval sense), or, in variants, 'nam bùth' ('of the booths'). But 'àileadh nan cladhan' ('the stench of gutters') and 'glagraich nan sràid' ('the din of the streets') are commoner descriptions.

And nothing could be more dismissive than the verse which the late Professor Angus Matheson recorded from his mother:[17]

'An cual' thu rud a chuala mis',
gun bhàthadh Gall an Inbhir Nis?'
'Tiud! tha mi coma dhà,
cha robh cairdeas agam ris.'

'Have you heard what I have heard,
that a Lowlander (foreigner) was drowned in Inverness?'
'Tut! I am quite indifferent,
I had no kinship with him.'

Clan Sagas and Historical Legends

The amount of material that can quite properly be called 'historical' in Gaelic oral tradition is enormous. As anyone who has as much as glanced at one of the volumes of clan history knows, there is an abundance of tales and legends in the traditions of every clan. Some of these are presented by the authors of clan histories as vivid fictions, others are regarded as making a serious contribution to the elucidation of problems in the history of a particular kindred at a particular time.

Less dramatic but unquestionably 'historical' are the mundane narratives that formed a very important part of the storytelling tradition, at least in most areas of Gaelic Scotland in comparatively recent times. Most of these narratives were biographical or autobiographical and might deal with experiences of fishing or shepherding or whatever the audience found interesting. Such experiences were of course often recounted with considerable artistic style. These matters, as well as descriptions of the crafts of a township or a parish all come under the modern rubric of oral history.

Clan legends belong to the past and mention the names of individuals who may or may not be known in written sources. However, there are occasional stories that mention clan chiefs or the like but in which these characters are of secondary importance. They simply fix the tale in a Gaelic setting. For instance, there is a humorous tale about a chief's piper and how he and his wife ran out of whisky. It was told in more than one place with the appropriate chief's name used, whether MacLeod or MacKinnon or, as in this version, MacDonald of Glengarry.

'I'll go to Glengarry', said the piper, 'and I'll say that you have died and that I need whisky for your wake.' He did that and MacDonald gave him a bottle. But the piper and his wife soon drank it all and what could they do then.

'I'll go to the Lady of Glengarry', said the piper's wife, 'and say that you have died and that I need whisky for *your* wake.' She did that and the piper and his wife drank the second bottle.

That afternoon MacDonald of Glengarry came home and said to his wife, 'I have sad news: the piper's wife is dead.'

'No, no', said his wife, 'it's the piper who's dead.'

And Glengarry and his wife began to argue and became quite angry with each other, each of them convinced that the other was wrong.

'There's only one thing for it', said Glengarry, 'we'll have to go to the piper's house and see which of them is dead.'

The piper and his wife saw them coming. 'What shall we do? What shall we do?' they said. 'Let's go and lie on the bed', said the wife, 'and we'll both pretend to be dead.'

Glengarry and his lady came in. 'Oh, this is a tragic house', Glengarry said. 'The two of them are dead!' But then he added: 'And now we'll never know which of them died first. I must say I'd give a bottle of the best to anyone who'd tell me that.'

'Me', shouted the piper's wife. 'I died first!'

And MacDonald of Glengarry had to give her another bottle.

A story of a very different kind tells of MacDonald of Clanranald's pet seal which came and went as it pleased, going to sea and sometimes disappearing for a couple of days or more at a time. On one occasion it was away for over a week and when it came home it was severely wounded, with a harpoon still embedded in one of its flippers. Clanranald's men took the harpoon out of the wound and the seal recovered. The harpoon had certain initials carved in it and Clanranald kept it hanging above the fireplace.

Some years after that a Dutch ship put in at one of the harbours in South Uist and Clanranald invited the captain to dinner. The captain kept staring at the harpoon and at last asked Clanranald where he had found it. Clanranald told him. 'These are my initials', said the captain, 'and I'm the man who threw that harpoon at a seal off the River Bann in Ireland.'

It was then Clanranald and all who heard the story realised how far a seal may travel.

Another story, which I heard in Nova Scotia, tells how MacDonald of Clanranald's grooms had instructions to watch how the fillies drank water. Those that did not have to pause often for breath were selected as brood mares.

Such stories, whether they preserve interesting details of a perfectly realistic kind, or whether they survive simply because they are humorous anecdotes, or for some other reason are rather different from the clan legends. But, as we shall see, the difference is one of degree. It is, indeed, partly a matter of classification. The main group can be called 'Clan Sagas'. These are all fairly short but there are also sequences or cycles of stories that give a more extended narrative, the portions of which are linked by the biographies of individuals or by the vicissitudes of the history of a clan.

The stories in question were described in summary fashion, but with characteristic clarity, by the late Professor Kenneth Jackson in his paper on 'The Folktale in Gaelic Scotland':

> Another important body of Gaelic folktale, and a large one, is the stories about known historical characters and events, particularly about clan chiefs and the relations between the clans. These may sometimes contain fragments of real history unknown to conventional historical sources. The clan tales are a type of folklore very much more developed in Scotland than in Ireland, where the upheavals of the sixteenth and seventeenth centuries and the English rule of the eighteenth and nineteenth seem to have wiped almost all memory of the local aristocracy from the popular mind. Here in Scotland one may gather traditions about the battle of Inverlochy, the Keppoch murders, Culloden, the massacre of Glencoe, and much else, and endless tales of the feuds and battles and adventures of the clan chiefs, often involving some element of the marvellous or supernatural.[1]

Even in that summary Jackson touches on some of the problems that invite analysis: for example 'fragments of real history' juxtaposed with 'elements of the supernatural'. And there are other, larger structural and stylistic problems.

Some modern historians will dismiss clan sagas as fiction but accept later (sometimes not very much later) traditions – of the Clearances, for instance – as fact, even when both are indistinguishable in their sober and restrained narrative. But as we all know, if we have listened to Gaelic storytellers at all, such stylistic criteria are no guarantee of historical veracity.

Perhaps it is worth saying that Jackson's claim that the upheavals of Irish history 'have wiped almost all memory of the local aristocracy from the popular mind' seems to me to be rather strong. It would, however, be true to say, I think, that the Scottish Gaelic tales that I call 'sagas' are more numerous than their Irish counterparts.

Although the problem of historicity is of course of the greatest importance, I am primarily concerned with the historical stories as narrative fictions rather than reflections of Gaelic history. The stories are 'Heroic' and deal with a warrior society and that alone isolates them within the much wider spectrum of tradition which as I said at the beginning of this essay can properly be called 'historical'.

It is perfectly acceptable to call them legends but 'legend' alone does not perhaps have quite the right connotation. Moreover, there are many episodes in clan legends that remind us of the Icelandic sagas. And not just episodes: there is a general stylistic tone that connects both. But although there are numerous historical and cultural links between Iceland and Gaelic Scotland, especially the north-western areas of Gaelic Scotland, I do not insist that the literary resemblances are genetic.

Interestingly enough though the oldest clan sagas centre on the actions of a man with a name of Norse origin: the Gaelic *Somhairle* is from Norse *Sumarlidhi* and *Somerled*, as he is known in English-language accounts, was no doubt of mixed Norse and Gaelic ancestry.

There are two small groups of sagas about him that tell 1) how he came to be a leader of the Gaels and 2) about some of the battles in which he defeated the Norsemen.

The first involves Clann Aonghuis (the clan MacInnes), and there may be a fragment of historical motivation to be discerned in them. Clann Aonghuis were then in Morvern, and apparently not very numerous. According to the version I have known from childhood, Somerled asked the MacInneses for their support, which they gave; according to Clan Donald sources (their eponymous ancestor being a grandson of Somerled), the MacInneses asked Somerled to lead them.

According to a story I heard in our family, Clann Aonghuis once fought a great battle against the Norsemen in Islay. I was very small when I heard this and cannot remember whether the Norsemen had been defeated or not; there was probably a suggestion that they had lost. But if in fact the Norsemen were victorious, and if we are dealing with a real historical event, this great battle may have marked the loss of Islay to the Norsemen. Islay was the territory of Cinéal nOenghusa, one of the three divisions of the original Dalriadic settlement. If my speculation has any validity at all, the Clann Aonghuis of Morvern were a remnant of the Cinéal nOenghusa and Somerled's appeal to them (or their support of Somerled) was connected with the Gaelic leader's attempt to establish his own Dalriadic credentials. This alliance would strengthen that as much on psychological as on military grounds.

But our Gaelic sagas also conceal historical events and processes. Although the great Clan Campbell was at one time associated with the confederation of the Lordship of the Isles and the Coastland of the Gael, there are no accounts of that, even in the stories that come from

MacDonald sources, which might be expected to make a propaganda point about the Campbells having been at one time under the hegemony of the kindred of Somerled. In some respects at least clan sagas have in contrast with political poetry rather a limited horizon. They are concerned with individuals and focus on individual relationships, with only an occasional passing reference to a wider historical framework.

J. F. Campbell, in the nineteenth century, was of the opinion that the makers, or the transmitters, of clan tales saw the deeds of great men from a lower level of society.[2] Some of them do, and some of them depict clan chiefs as grasping and tyrannical. But I believe, though I cannot go into the matter here, that they come from a variety of social levels. In a qualitative sense, however, they are rarely parochial and it could be argued that the bards and the makers of sagas are simply working according to different aesthetic principles.

While the Lordship of the Isles lasted, it was strong enough to maintain a general peace (even if that term is relative) over a wide area of the Highlands and Islands. When its power was broken by the King and Parliament of Scotland, latent rivalries were released and anarchy broke out as Gaelic society was reduced to a multiplicity of warring units. The great mass of clan sagas come from that background and from this period of c.1500 to c.1745. If we use the concept of a 'Heroic Age', we might say that this was perhaps a late manifestation of it. Certainly some of the constants of 'Heroic Ages' are present in the stories: war as a sort of aristocratic game; the figure of the young warrior; stress on single combat; death in battle and the praise of the bards.

It is reported that around 1600, when a great warrior of the MacAulays in Lewis, Domhnall Cam mac Dhubhghaill, heard of the invention of gunpowder he remarked: 'Tha latha a' ghaisgich seachad. Tha an duine lag a nis cho math ris an duine làidir' ('The day of the hero is over. Now the weakling is as good as the strong man'). *Gaisgeach* can be translated 'hero' or 'warrior' and certainly the day of the warrior in Gaelic society was not over by 1600. But contempt for this non-heroic form of combat and hostility to the use of fire-arms is reflected in poetry as late as the eighteenth century: in, for instance, Colonel John Roy Stuart's songs about Culloden, where he himself fought on the side of the Prince.

The Forty-Five is commonly seen as the terminus of this age of anarchy. Whether it began with the destruction of the Lordship of the

Isles or whether its terminus a quo aught to be placed earlier, it is known in Gaelic as *Linn nan Creach* 'the Age of the Forays', although the ideas of plunder and ruin are involved in the term also. Specifically *creach* is cattle taken in a raid. Such raids – *togail creach* – known in other cultures too were an institution of great antiquity and functioned as part of the initiation of young warriors.

The warrior class, as we may call it for convenience, has not yet been sufficiently studied from an anthropological point of view. It had important privileges and to it belonged by right of birth all those who counted themselves *uasal* 'noble'. What was originally a serf class, who tilled the soil and whose menfolk were not only not expected to go to war but were not even allowed to carry weapons, had largely disappeared by about 1600. This did not mean of course that when the men of that class were armed all distinctions between high and low disappeared. We have here and there in the clan sagas incidental references to those processes and social attributes. From time to time young men of the *tuath* 'the commonalty' were recruited into the warrior class because of their unusual strength, stature or agility. In a few sagas we find an emphasis on the high-handed behaviour and the depredations of the privileged warriors. In some areas these warriors, or those of them that formed a comitatus or bodyguard for a chief, were known as *buannaichean*, the best known of whom were *Buannaichean MhicLeòid*. The general Gaelic term for them is *Léine-chneas* or *Léine-chnios* and their leader is a *ceann-feadhna*, the head of a *feadhan* 'troop'. Such bands of young warriors – the 'braves' of the clan – enjoyed a high degree of eligibility as prospective suitors: the term *fear dhe m'fheadhain* 'one of my beaux' is probably not unconnected with that. This is in fact one of a number of interesting semantic developments in Gaelic that seem to reflect the importance of the warriors in society. Another is *sluagh* 'an (armed) host', which comes to mean simply 'populace' as in *sluagh an àite*, though it has of course more specific meanings as well.

The characteristic dress of the warrior is the *breacan* 'tartan' which, as I have pointed out elsewhere, was recognised as such by the Disarming Act of 1746. In a very different context, its function in the imagery of women's love-songs is as a marker of the lover's social status as warrior. The significance of the epithet *na Plaide Bàine* in the story of *Fionnlagh na Plaide Bàine* in Skye, who overcame *Buannaichean MhicLeòid*, is that as a non-warrior he does not wear the colourful 'uniform' of these privileged young braves.

A relatively small group of stories contain what is apparently no more than a naturalistic motif. A band of young warriors, often said to be three, chance to come, usually late at night, to a humble dwelling in a lonely part of the moor. An old woman and her daughter – a red-haired girl in a number of variants – live there. The men ask for shelter until morning and are told they are welcome provided one of them can defeat the girl in wrestling. Only one of them succeeds; they are given hospitality; and in most variants the victor and the girl become lovers. (There is a sequel in some versions in which the son born to the girl later meets his father.) It is at least possible that this group of stories is influenced, no matter at how many removes, by the theme of the goddess of sovereignty and the rightful king, so closely linked to the idea of kingship in Irish tradition. The goddess who personifies the kingdom appears as an ugly hag but is transformed when she meets and is embraced by the rightful claimant.

For example, in the story of Niall Noíghiallach, Niall and his four brothers lose their way while out hunting and rest in order to cook part of their kill. They find a well guarded by a hideous crone who will give them water only in return for a kiss. Three of them simply refuse her request, the fourth gives her no more than a token kiss, while Niall agrees not only to kiss her but to become her lover. When he embraces her, the dreadful crone is transformed into a radiantly beautiful girl. She then explains who she really is and foretells that Niall and his descendants will hold the kingship in perpetuity except for two kings of the line of the brother who gave her a token kiss. If there is indeed a trace of influence from this myth on the Scottish Gaelic folktale, it might be that the roles of crone and beautiful girl, the appearance of the goddess before and after the embrace, are redistributed. This is all a very flimsy speculation but there is something strange and unexplained in at least a number of the versions of this tale.

There is a sub-category of stories that deal with bowmen. In the Isle of Skye the most renowned family of bowmen were the MacInneses who were hereditary bowmen to MacKinnon of Strath. They were descended, according to tradition, from one Niall a' Bhogha who was born (or so it was said in our family: I have no independent corroboration from any other tradition) in Duisdale in Sleat. Some said that the head of the house in every generation was named Niall. This may however be a rationalisation. Stories about the MacMhuirich poets in Uist refer simply to 'MacMhuirich' without forename and stories about 'Niall a' Bhogha' who cannot be the same individual may use a comparable convention. The first Niall a' Bhogha is supposed to have been a man of great strength and of at least ordinary stature. But many of the famous bowmen of Gaelic tradition were small, insignificant and even misshapen men. These are generally speaking not represented as members of a *comitatus* but as men who lead solitary lives, living in isolated borderlands and entering into temporary service with a clan chief or called upon in times of need. This emphasis on their solitariness may be realistic enough in some cases but probably the storyteller's art has in certain instances at least heightened this aspect for dramatic purposes.

One of the most famous bowmen in island sagas is Dubh Sìdh from Jura who fought for Sir James MacDonald in the Battle of Gruinneart in 1598 in Islay, against Sir Lachlan Maclean, Lachann Mór Dhubhairg.

Dubh Sìdh is a sinister figure in the saga of that battle: 'isean a ghuir an Diabhal ann an Diùraidh' ('an imp hatched by the Devil in Jura'). In some versions of the tale Dubh Sìdh is depicted as an undersized man, practically a dwarf, of exceedingly unprepossessing features. In others, while Dubh Sìdh does not undergo the *riastradh* which distinguishes Cú Chulainn's frenzy, his face became horribly distorted before battle. There may be no connection but it would be unsafe to discount it entirely.

In most versions Dubh Sìdh approaches Lachann Mór first and offers his services. Sir Lachlan orders the ugly grinning dwarfish creature out of his sight. Dubh Sìdh then goes to Sir James MacDonald: 'Will you have me?' he says. 'Indeed, I will', says MacDonald, 'and twenty more of your kind if I could get them.' 'Then I'll see to Lachann Mór', said Dubh Sìdh, 'and you see to his men.' 'Honey on your lips!' said MacDonald. 'Blood on my hand!' said Dubh Sìdh. The saga goes on to tell how Dubh Sidh got his wish.

Sir James MacDonald, the last of Clann Eoin Mhóir, bore the title of 'MacDonald', head of all Clan Donald. In tradition this is not 'MacDhomhnaill' but 'Màg ònaill'. The change of 'c' to 'g' in 'mac' is not uncommon (cf. MagUidhir, MagAoidh; and in English forms such as Maguinness; or, in pronunciation, Magloud). It may have been a high-register pronunciation and had an honorific force. Some of the storytellers who used it did not realise it was 'MacDonald' at all; and neither did some eighteenth-century writers, who reproduced it as 'Matha Conail[l]', which represents the pronunciation – 'th' being merely a syllable divider – accurately enough.

The man of insignificant appearance or stature who compensates for that by developing special skills is realistic. In the sagas, this functions as a narrative device. In story after story these formidable archers win because their enemies invariably underestimate them. So in the stories about Little John mac Andrew whom the storytellers often placed on the borders of Keppoch – a liminal setting in the disputed territory between MacDonalds and Macintoshes – although he is known to have lived in Dail na h-Aitnich in the parish of Duthil.[3]

So, too, in the stories set in Aberdeenshire and between Atholl and the Braes of Angus about An Crom Ruadh or, on the southern Perthshire boundary, in the stories about Domhnall Beag nan Saighdean.

The William Tell story is told about a number of bowmen: Iain Buidhe nan Saighead in Kintail, for instance, and in Uist, where the target is not an apple but an egg and the archer is Gille Padara Dubh. Migratory legends of various kinds became attached to the names of such renowned warriors and a variety of motifs move from saga to saga.

One such motif is particularly brutal and violent. I mention it only to draw a possible parallel with an episode in the old Irish story *Scéla Muicce Meicc Da Thó*. In the Irish story the hero Cet mac Mágach is about to receive the champion's portion of the pig at the feast when the great Conall Cernach comes in and claims the portion. Cet reluctantly acknowledges that Conall is the greater hero but adds that if a certain Anluan were present he would contest the claim. 'But he is', said Conall, taking Anluan's head from his belt. And he hurled it at Cet's chest so that blood flowed from the mouth.

In more than one Scottish story the severed head of a man is suddenly set on the table in front of his wife who does not know until that moment that her husband is dead. In two variants at least the mouth is stuffed with cheese.

There may be no connection between old and new here but it does raise the question of whether we are dealing with a continuous tradition, constantly renewing itself of course, of common Gaelic storytelling. A certain Iain Gallach was born on a flat stone – in some versions his head was flattened as his mother delayed the birth of her child – and Leac Iain Ghallaich is still known. Similar details may be found in earlier literature but there is no way of proving a direct connection. These may all be no more than migratory motifs. Yet in some sense there must be continuity of Gaelic storytelling with perhaps Norse influences, particularly in northern and north-western areas in particular, playing a part.

There is one vignette which is worth looking at briefly. It comes from the Icelandic saga of Grettir the Strong: *Grettis Saga*. Grettir is haunted by Glámr, who is one of the walking dead of Icelandic tradition, an *aptrgöngumadhr*. When Glámr was alive he was a morose, difficult man, and strong; after death he was stronger still. In the saga, he tries to get Grettir to come outside and fight him and develops the habit of riding on the roof-tree of Grettir's house, kicking the sides with his heels while he issues his challenge. When at last they do fight, Glámr falls on his back outside the doorway; it is night-time and there is a sudden break in the clouds and the moon appears. Glámr glares at the moon and Grettir sees his eyes. And although Grettir was a strong man and very brave, that sight gave him, as he always said afterwards, the most terrible fright he had ever had.

There is a short anecdote in Gaelic in which these events are replicated. A man named Domhnall Bàn is haunted by a *bòcan* 'bogle' who had once, when he was alive, been a neighbour. The bòcan rides on the roof-tree and kicks the sides of the house with his heels. In contrast to Glámr the bòcan is harmless and only wants to show where he had buried certain objects which are to be returned to their owner. He does this eventually. It is night-time; the moon appears; and Domhnall Bàn sees the eyes of the bòcan in the moonlight. Domhnall Bàn is a brave man too but, just like Grettir, he always said afterwards that that was the most terrible fright he had every had. The words are in fact almost identical in Gaelic and Icelandic.

The Gaelic tale is a mere anecdote; the Icelandic saga a much more complex and sophisticated work which then develops the haunting of Grettir by the memory of the eyes. (The name 'Glámr', as Professor Hermann Pálsson has pointed out, is cognate with English 'gleam', and related to one of the poetical names for the moon.) Our little Gaelic story on the other hand ends at the point I have indicated when the bòcan shows Domhnall Bàn where the buried objects lie.

That is probably the closest parallel that we have between Gaelic and Icelandic storytelling but in much more general terms there is that common stylistic tone I have already referred to.

The style of Gaelic clan sagas is always bare and economical. Dialogue is laconic and acts as a narrative device to further and explain the action. In stories of violent events, dialogue also is frequently sharp and violent – which sometimes leads translators to modify or even omit the crucial words. There are English versions in print of a story in which young MacLeod of Assynt has been refused the hand of MacKenzie's daughter; he and his men in their birlinn pass the ship of one Fionnlagh Dubh nan Saighead as MacLeod returns from his unsuccessful wooing. Fionnlagh calls across to them and asks for their news and they tell him. In one translation: 'Fionnlagh shouted back an expression so insulting that young MacLeod vowed to be revenged on him sooner or later.' Then the story goes on to tell of how MacLeod got his revenge. It is not difficult to guess the nature of Fionnlagh Dubh's innuendo but the point is that without the dialogue, the whole structure falls apart. Exchange of insult and innuendo is central to the plot in saga after saga; and we may find that otherwise distant variants of a story preserve these crucial exchanges virtually unaltered. Some of the utterances are in more or less rough verse; for example, a couplet linked only by one internal rhyme. But some are in quatrain form. They are often veiled but frequently succeed in conveying a sense of dramatic power. Honour and shame are clearly important in this society and the dialogue, or sometimes monologue, is the vehicle that registers and gives public expression to its values.

An item in the code of honour is how to die properly. This may be in one way or another a human universal but again there are parallels between Icelandic and Gaelic sagas.

In the same saga of Grettir the Strong, Atli, Grettir's brother, is run through the body by a spear. He pulls it out and observes that broad-bladed spears are fashionable now. Then he dies.

In a Gaelic cycle of stories MacIain of Ardnamurchan and his younger brother were in feud with the Camerons.[4] Without asking MacIain's permission, the brother became betrothed to Lochiel's daughter. When MacIain heard about this he lay in wait for his brother in a hill-pass. When the brother saw MacIain, less than fifty yards distant, he raised his hand in greeting. MacIain shot an arrow at him and the arrow struck him in the armpit so that his arms were flung upwards and he spun round and dropped on one knee. MacIain walked over to him. 'You dance well', said he. 'If you dance as well as that on the night of your wedding to that devious, black, luckless daughter of Locheil, no one will have very much to say against you.'[5] And with that the brother died.

The saga then goes on to describe how the Camerons avenged his death.

It was a hot day and MacIain raised his helmet and wiped his brow.

A Cameron bowman took careful aim and the arrow struck Maclain between his two eyes. He reeled back but still upright seized the arrow and tugged it savagely out of the wound. Without looking at it, he flung it on the grass. 'Was that a cleg that bit me?' he said. Then he fell to the ground and died.

Heroic death with memorable words is the ideal. We do occasionally hear of *bàs a' chinn-adhairt* 'pillow death', but on the whole the storytellers appear to take the line that the least said about it the better.

Iain Odhar, a great MacDonald warrior, tried to make his death-bed memorable. As he lay dying, he sent for one of his closest friends. The two old men bade each other farewell and as his friend was about to embrace him, he saw Iain Odhar's hand coming at him with the sgian dubh and he leapt away. 'I have killed twenty men in my time', said Iain Odhar, 'and during my lifetime the River Roy has drowned twenty. If I had got you, I would have beaten the river. Now people will say: Iain Odhar after all was no greater than the River Roy.'

In legends of the supernatural there is a motif of man and river in contest; if the Iain Odhar story is at all connected with that belief in the power of rivers it shows an interesting development. But in these clan sagas in general there is little of the 'supernatural': omens and portents, for instance, are in the Gaelic society which produced the stories regarded as part of the order of nature. Indeed, our use of 'supernatural' there is a little inept. There is one saga in which warriors are seen suddenly to sprout antlers (this is a motif of a wonder-tale kind) but that is highly unusual. They were not, incidentally, MacKenzies and so there is no suggestion of deer symbolism. The men in question were of Clan Donald.

There are traces of what scholars call Heroic Biography in our clan sagas. It has been demonstrated by a number of scholars that there is more or less of a pattern to the biography of 'heroes' in a whole range of cultures. For instance, the hero is born posthumously or supernaturally, the birth attended by mysterious portents, or he is reared in obscurity or suckled by wild animals; there are tokens of his future greatness, though he may be of more or less violent disposition; he slays monsters; takes service in foreign lands; he returns and vanquishes his enemies; the manner of his death is extraordinary.

Not all of these elements are necessarily present in any given Heroic Biography. One may add also that certain features are realistic in a society in which warfare was endemic: flight from the place of birth, for instance, and the return of the hero to seek revenge. It does seem, however, that we are justified in seeing traces of a very widely distributed pattern in many of our clan sagas.

Iain Dubh Seang, progenitor of the House of Bohuntin, was born out of wedlock, suckled by a deerhound bitch, and could outstrip all the warriors of his age. Aonghus Fionn mac Dhomhnaill Hearaich was born posthumously. (His father, according to some versions of the tale, suffered a three-fold death, a motif which may itself be based upon an Indo-European form of ritual killing.) His mother fled from Uist to Skye and brought her infant son up in a hut in the Cuillin. A hind used to visit him as he lay on the sward outside and constantly licked one side of his head, so that the hair on that side became fair: hence the name 'Aonghus Fionn'. In due time he returned to Uist and avenged the death of his father. His name is preserved in 'Dùn Aonghuis' to the present day.

The detail of Aonghus Fionn and the hind is of course reminiscent of the story of Oisein whose mother was a deer: 'Mas tu mo mhàthair gur fiadh thu.' In another saga of the same cycle as that of Aonghus Fionn, one of the killers of Domhnall Hearach, his own half-brother Gilleasbaig Dubh, comes to Dùn Sgàthaich and is shown a longship newly built for still another half-brother Domhnall Gallach. Gilleasbaig draws attention to an alleged flaw low down by the keel; Domhnall Gallach stoops to examine it and gives Gilleasbaig the chance to behead him. In the story of Fionn's youth, Goban Saor made a tree-house for the boy; Luas Lurgann drew his attention to an alleged flaw at the base of the door and Goban Saor dies also. There are other parallels or coincidences to examine in these stories.

Probably the nearest to a full heroic biography is to be found in the cycle of stories about Alasdair mac Colla. His birth was attended by the proper manifestations: 'The night that Alasdair mac Colla was born, the swords leapt out of their scabbards, the shields clanged together on the wall, the mares cast their foals and the midwife said: "Truly this will be a great hero." '[6]

Alasdair is a strange, morose child who has the unpleasant habit of eating live toads. He is of a passionate disposition; he fights not quite with monsters but with a dangerous bull and kills it with his bare hands. He seeks service not exactly in the foreign land of the paradigm of heroic biography but in the hostile and relatively distant territory of the Campbells. His death, prophesied in his boyhood, is not extraordinary but it does happen in a place with an extraordinary name: the unique 'Gocam-Gò'.

As Professor Jackson pointed out in the paper which I have quoted, these tales 'may sometimes contain fragments of real history unknown to conventional historical sources'. It has been suggested that if all the known folktale motifs were removed, we would be left with a core of historical fact. Often enough, however, a clan saga may consist in its entirety of what are patently folktale motifs. Others have a propaganda element in them; these stories have obviously been constructed with a bias in favour of a certain clan or kindred. It would be a fascinating if monumental task to separate fact from fiction in all the historical tales; there is an enormous field for research here.

On a particular point of history a clan saga from the Isle of Lewis has something of interest to tell us. It seems to be assumed, at least in some quarters, that the MacIvers of Lewis are of direct Norse descent and were there before the campaigns led by Somerled. Here is an outline of a Lewis tale which concerns the MacIvers.

In Argyll, a group of warriors on a cattle raid rested for the night. A young man among them dreamt he heard a voice say that they would be overtaken and most of them would lose their lives in that very place where they now were. But he himself would escape and his death would come in *Beirghe Lochlainn*. The pursuit comes upon them before morning; many die; but the youth escapes with his life. Years after that, MacLeod of Lewis married a daughter of Campbell of Argyll and that very same young man was chosen to be a member of her retinue, conveying her to Lewis. He stayed in Lewis and settled at Beirghe in Uig and there he lived and died. He was a MacIver and he is the ancestor of the MacIvers of Lewis.

Lochlann is originally a fabulous land which later came to be associated with the Vikings and their homeland, hence Norway; and *Beirghe* or *Beirbhe* is usually taken to be Bergen. Could it be that at one time Lewis (or perhaps other areas also of the north-west) was regarded by the southern Gaels as a part of the greater 'Lochlann' – a Norwegian empire?

On the question of historicity, there was in fact a marriage between a MacLeod of Lewis and a daughter of Campbell of Argyll in the second half of the fifteenth century and there is a poem in the Book of the Dean of Lismore which celebrates the union: 'Fhuaras mac mar an t-athair'.[7]

The Clan MacIver of Argyll is well known and well known also is their presence on the north-west mainland. Do we have here, then, a 'fragment of real history' with perhaps fictional additions? It may of course have become fashionable after the re-Gaelicisation of the Isles and the north in general to obscure direct Norse ancestry. But this is perhaps unnecessarily sceptical.

There are some clan sagas in which the propaganda is quite palpable. After the MacKenzies overran the MacLeod lands on the mainland, a MacLeod laird and his son return one night to recover their house (now in possession of a MacKenzie) and kill the usurpers. As they look into the house they see the new householder and his son preparing arrows. 'What a splendid night this would be to go out killing MacLeods!' says the young MacKenzie. His father becomes angry and denounces his son's spirit of vengefulness. 'Surely there has been enough killing', he says. 'Let us now have peace.'

The MacLeods, overhearing this conversation, are so impressed by the moral principles of the MacKenzie who has deprived them of house and home, land, stock and possessions, that they turn away and give up their intention of taking revenge.

The moral of this patently MacKenzie saga is that the victor can afford to forget.

There is a splendid cycle of sagas about the MacLeods and the MacAulays in Uig, Lewis. Again, this sequence of stories is patently designed to justify, although quite subtly, the actions of the MacAulays. Some of the stories were known until recently in Lewis tradition but the chief source is the collection made by John Morrison (1787–1834), a native of Harris, and translated into English;[8] a translation which, unfortunately, obscures many of the stylistic virtues of the originals. The story that tells how this great vendetta began explains that old MacLeod of Pabbay's wife was a strong-willed, passionate woman and how, after a certain exchange of insults which MacLeod tried to ignore, incited the sons of the family to exact revenge.

That night old MacLeod saw the sky red over the township of Reef and Valtos while a great surge of lamentation fills the air. Morrison's translation goes on: 'Old MacLeod enquired the cause for the dreadful cries ashore at Reef. His wicked wife replied: "My whelps have now plenty blood about their teeth." '

In Gaelic, as I heard it, she said: 'Fiaclan do chuid chuilean ann an sùilean buidhe Chlann Amhlaigh' ('The teeth of your whelps in the yellow eyes of the MacAulays'), which is much vivider and is constructed as a rhythmical statement with an internal rhyme. The translator also inserts moralising glosses, such as: 'this attempt to wipe out a family was divinely over-ruled by the supreme disposer of every event, to show the good and the bad that there is no device of men, however secretly executed, but he can frustrate and control.'

There is no hint of such moralising in any of the hundreds of historical legends that I have examined. It has no place stylistically in the genre. The controlled detachment of the narrative, the spare descriptive style, and the vivid exchanges of dialogue which we find in these stories make them, to my mind, the most interesting of all Gaelic oral tales.

Gleanings from Raasay Tradition

Although I am not a native of Raasay and did not therefore inherit a family tradition of Raasay lore, I spent some of the most formative years of boyhood on the island. What follows in this essay is a selection of items which were all picked up in the course of going to visit 'air chéilidh' in the houses of various friends in childhood and youth.

The first is an outline of the tale about a battle between the MacLeods of Raasay and the MacKenzies of Gairloch. There are several accounts of this episode in print ranging from direct historiography to naturalistic fiction.[1] This is how I heard the story.

MacKenzie of Gairloch's son was sailing past Raasay and for some reason his ship was forced to anchor in the bay (that is, between Raasay and Skye). There was a feud at the time between the MacKenzies and the MacLeods. Mac Gille Chaluim Òg, MacLeod of Raasay's son, and some others went out to enquire who was on board the strange ship. Because of the hostility between the MacKenzies and the MacLeods, the son of MacKenzie of Gairloch hid below deck while his men offered wine to their Raasay guests. The MacLeods, however, discovered that young MacKenzie was there and laid their plans accordingly. Having bought some wine from the Gairloch men, they returned home and gathered a band of warriors. Shortly afterwards they went out to the ship a second time on the pretext that the new visitors wanted to buy wine too. That was arranged; the MacLeods were invited on board again; and MacKenzies and MacLeods all sat down together to celebrate the occasion. While this was going on, young MacKenzie emerged from hiding and, since the atmosphere seemed so friendly, made himself known. But four of his men were suspicious and decided not to join in the conviviality.

At length, when the Gairloch men had been well plied with wine, young MacLeod seized MacKenzie and tried to take him prisoner. The latter naturally resisted, struck Mac Gille Chaluim, and knocked him down. At this a general fight broke out. MacKenzie drew his sword but as he took a step backwards to get a better advantage his foot caught in the gunwale (*an t-slat-bheòil*) and he went overboard. Meanwhile more of the Raasay men came out to the ship and having disposed of MacKenzie, who was swimming towards Gob na h-Airdeadh on the shore of Skye opposite, joined in the fighting. As each of the Gairloch men, most of whom had gone below after drinking the wine, came up to help their friends, the MacLeods took off their heads, one after another. But the four sober MacKenzies gave such good account of themselves that young Mac Gille Chaluim and his men were all killed. And so the remaining MacKenzies were able to escape and get home safely to Gairloch.

That outline was given to me by the late James Maclean, Osgaig (Seumas Iain Uilleim). He said it was little more that the bare bones of the tale as he had heard it in their own family and added there was something else about MacLeod having his hounds with him and how, at some point in the fight, the hounds had got in the way of the swordsmen. He also remembered that, either in this story or in another similar tale, the MacLeods' hounds attacked those of the MacKenzies and this led to the fight between the men. These details about the hounds are not given in the published variants.

James Maclean is my only source for the story but I gathered from John MacLeod, Clachan, who had much information about the family of Mac Gille Chaluim, that he, too, knew it.

James Maclean also had a version of the well-known 'Àireamh Mhuinntir Fhinn agus Dhubhain'. This puzzle has a wide distribution with variants in other cultures: in medieval Europe it was known as *Ludus Sancti Petri* 'St. Peter's Game'. For comparison with the Raasay variant I give a version published by the Rev. John Gregorson Campbell (1836–91), minister of Tiree, along with part of his explanatory note and English translation:

> Fionn is asked to (Dubhan's) house. A plot was laid to destroy Fionn and his men and on this coming to the knowledge of (Fionn's) daughter, she made an arrangement by which every one of Dubhan's men were got out of the house, and Fionn's men only were let in. The men were set in a circle, and continuously counting, every ninth man was made to rise and go out. This is a curious arithmetical problem [. . .] The numeration is as follows:
>
> Four wild white men, at the beginning,
> And five black next to them,
> Of Duvan's tall fighting men,

Two from Mac Cumal, anew;
One from Duvan of reddish comeliness,
Three from Fionn of fairest appearance,
One from Duvan of secret purposes.
Fionn will not sit in the Fair Fort
Without two black ones on one hand,
And two white ones by his side
Of the family of the King of Alban.
Two black ones about determined Duvan,
One white one in their company,
Two smart black ones near these,
Two from Fionn and one from Duvan.

Ceathrar fear fionn fiadhaich air thùs
Mar chóigear dhubha 'nan dàil
Do dh'fhearaibh ard fir chogaidh Dhubhain,
Dithis o Mhac Cumhail a nuadh,
Fear o Dhubhan dreach ruadh,
Triùir o Fhionn 's àillidh dreach
Fear o Dhubhan diùramach,
Cha suidh Fionn anns a' Bhrugh Bhàn,
Gun dithis dhubh' air a leth làimh,
'S gun dithis fhionna air a leis,
Do theaghlach Rìgh Albainn.
Dithis dhubh' mu Dhubhan dhil,
Aon fhear fionn 'na fhochair sin,
Da lasgair' dhubh 'nan dàil,
Dithis o Fhionn 's fear o Dhubhan.[2]

According to James Maclean, Dubhan was betrothed to Fionn's daughter and the death of Fionn and his men was planned to take place during the wedding feast. The daughter, having discovered the plot, asked to be allowed to arrange the seating at her own wedding. This was granted and the rest follows. Mr Maclean remembered how the game used to be played in their home when he was a boy. As in other places in the Gàidhealtachd, black and white pebbles or small peats and slivers of white wood were used as counters.

The Raasay version is identical with Campbell's so far as the numbers are concerned except that *cóigeamh* 'fifth' is used for 'five'; this may be a slip for *cóig(n)ear* 'fivesome'. One line is defective: James himself thought the word 'geal / geala' might have occurred in it. It should be noted also that the word I print as 'tiùrramach' was pronounced as if it were 'tiùrr a mach'. The text is as follows:

> *Ceathrar fir Féinneadh air tùs*
> *Le'n cóigeamh rùn d'an déidh*
> *Dearbh mhuinntir Dhubhain*
> *Dithis bho mac Cumhail an nuadh*
> *Fear bho Dhubhan tearc an t-sluaigh*
> *Triùr bho Fhionn as àille dreach*
> *Fear bho Dhubhan tiùrramach*
> *Cha shuidh Fionn air a' Bhrugh Bhàn*
> *Gun dithis dhubh' air a làimh chearr*
> *Na gun dithis bhon an Fhionn ad eile*
> *Thoradh a' rìgh [. . .]*
> *Dà laoch dhubh ma Dhubhan dil*
> *Aon fhear fionn 'na fhochar sin*
> *Dà laoch dhubh ma dhùn an àigh*
> *Dithis bho Fhionn is fear bho Dhubhan.*

Many people knew the duan of the wells of Raasay though there was a certain amount of variation in the list, especially in the sequence of names. The one I remember best is:

> *Tobar na Creachain(n) an Osgaig*
> *Tobar an Domhnaich 'sa' Ghleann*
> *Tobar nan Eun air Thotagan*
> *Tobar nam Bioran an Glaic nan Curran*
> *Is an Tobar Mór a Suidhisinis*

Others had Tobar an Fhìon[3] and Tobar a' Bhiorain. Totagan (or Tobhtagan, depending on what the etymology may be; the pronunciation is not affected) was a settlement, near the hill of Meall Damh, said to have been completely cleared of its inhabitants – no one lived there, so far as I know, within living memory – and the water of its well was supposed to be the best in Raasay. Or, according to some, the next best to that of Tobar na Fearna which was ice-cold on a hot summer's day and warm on the coldest day in winter. Tobar na Fearna is not included in any variant of the duan that I have heard. The list in fact covers only the south-west quarter of the island and there may have been similar rhymes, now lost, which applied to other parts of the island.

Tobar an Domhnaich ('the Well of the Lord's Day') lies in the Glen, through which some of the Raasay folk living on the south-eastern side of the island would pass on their way to and from church at Clachan. But, according to tradition, here also men gathered for sport and recreation after worship. This was, of course, common practice throughout the Gàidhealtachd until the emergence of Evangelicalism as a social force.

The name of Baintighearna Dhubh Osgaig was known to most Raasay people, at least those of the older generation. She was Seònaid NicLeòid and became the second wife of Malcolm (as he is known in English-language sources), the ninth chief. She is said to have lived at Craobhan Móra in Osgaig, not in the taigh mór at Clachan. Mac Gille Chaluim and the Baintighearna Dhubh had eight children, the best known by name being Maighstir Calum, Established Church minister of Snizort in Skye and father of the more famous Maighstir Ruairi, minister of Bracadale and then Snizort, and after the Disruption one of the great pillars of the Free Church and a powerful champion of the crofters during the period of the Clearances. As we shall see presently, it is obvious that Mac Gille Chaluim's first family did not approve of the marriage, apparently on grounds of social status. Seònaid was a woman of the common people and her marriage to the chief was probably not calculated to endear her to her own kind any more than to her husband's kinsfolk. That at any rate was the impression given by tradition: the Baintighearna Dhubh was 'dubh' because of her moral character. However, the assertion made without qualification, I think, by everyone in Raasay who knew the story, that she and MacLeod were never married is incorrect. The marriage deed, which was discovered by the late Rev. Dr Donald MacKinnon, is in Dunvegan Castle.[4]

The source of the following story was the late John MacLeod, Baile Mèadhaineach (Seonaidh Dhomhnaill Iain Bhain). Mr MacLeod and his brother Domhnall Ruadh both had a congenitally adducted foot, which, as they themselves used to point out, actually gave them an advantage in climbing in rough terrain. When they were small boys, they were told by Catrìona Uilleim (aunt of James Maclean, mentioned above, and the leading tradition-bearer of Raasay until she died in the late 1920s): 'Tha fuil uasal unnaibh-se: sin dìreach mar a bha Mac Gille Chaluim Camchasach' ('You have noble ancestry: Mac Gille Chaluim was exactly like that'). This Mac Gille Chaluim was in fact the Baintighearna Dhubh's husband and a number of Raasay families claimed descent from the union.

Here now is a resumé in English of the story which Seonaidh Dhomhnaill Iain Bhàin used to tell in Gaelic.

When Seònaid was a girl, probably in her late teens, she went to work in the taigh mór. There she fell in love with a young man, one of Mac Gille Chaluim's servant lads. The lad, however, did not show any sign of interest in her. So she went to the cook to ask for advice and this woman said to her: 'That lad always comes in here for his meal at such and such an hour every evening. You stay here with me and just before he comes in – I'll let you know myself – go and stand behind the door there. As he comes in through the doorway, you jump out and steal a kiss from him. He'll notice you after that!' And so it happened. The cook saw the young man approaching, she told the girl, and the girl went and stood behind the door. But unknown to the cook Mac Gille Chaluim himself was there too and it was Mac Gille Chaluim who came in first. The girl jumped out from behind the door and kissed Mac Gille Chaluim.

And that was how the affair began. Seònaid became Mac Gille Chaluim's mistress and had a large family from him. But Mac Gille Chaluim never married her. That was why she was known as 'A' Bhaintighearna Dhubh'.

James Boswell met her in 1773 during his visit to Raasay with Dr Samuel Johnson. He has this to say:

> We had been met by Mr Charles MacLeod, half-brother to Raasay, a strapping young fellow. Old Raasay had most absurdly married again after the year 1746. His widow, by whom he had several children, lives in a small comfortable house which was built for him just adjoining to the old castle of the family. She has a good farm gratis, and the interest of £400 by way of jointure. Mr Charles took us to her house. She was a stout fresh-looking woman, very plainly dressed, and could not speak a word of English. She treated us with cream and barley-bread. It was not amiss to see the difference between her house-keeping and that of Raasay's. Folly on one side, and probably interested cunning on the other, had produced the second marriage. She was called only Mrs MacLeod now. I know not if ever she was called *Lady*, as her husband had previously given the estate to this gentleman.[5]

'This gentleman' was, of course, Boswell's host, John, the tenth chief. It is worth noting that Boswell omitted the entire description quoted above from the edition of his *Journal* published in 1785. Interesting, too, is the fact that 'she was called only Mrs MacLeod'.

Presumably the family in the taigh mór referred to her as 'Mrs MacLeod', in English, talking to Boswell. Nevertheless, 'Baintighearna' ('Lady'), is her invariable style in the Gaelic tradition of Raasay. The late George Gillies, Baile a' Chùirn (Seòras Iain Iain Raghnaill) informed me that John MacLeod (either the tenth or the twelfth chief) was known in Gaelic as 'Sior Iain' although he was neither knight nor baronet.

James Boswell appears to place the Baintighearna Dhubh's house 'adjoining the old castle of the family', not in Osgaig but in the north of Raasay. This may be due to no more than a lapse of memory: the travellers would have passed Osgaig on their way to the old castle. Oral tradition at any rate is silent about her having lived anywhere else than at Craobhan Móra is Osgaig. (This place name Craobhan Móra is never, incidentally, used with the definite article. The same applies to Creagan Beaga, between Osgaig and the taigh mór.)

The next item is an interesting conundrum which I have never heard elsewhere.[6] The source again is John MacLeod, Baile Mèadhaineach.

> Mo ghaol a' chas
> A shiubhail a fad
> Is tu m'fhear, is tu mo mhac, is tu mo bhràthair
> Is tu mac Mhic Thaidhg
> Is tu ogha Mhic Thaidhg
> Is b'e nighean Mhic Thaidhg do mhàthair.

A husband is addressed as son and brother, told that he is both son and grandson to Mac Thaidhg and that Mac Thaidhg's daughter was his mother. Who is addressing whom? The solution of the riddle is as follows: a male child is born of an incestuous union between a man and his daughter; the child is fostered in a far-away place, returns in manhood to the place of his birth, and innocently marries his own mother. Eventually the woman discovers who her husband really is and takes this way of letting him know.

The conundrum is no more and no less than a genealogical puzzle – incidentally, of the kind the lower orders of itinerant bards were supposed to specialise in – and despite the fact that it adds a dimension to the Oedipus story has no significance from that point of view. As Seonaidh himself used to say: 'Chan eil ann ach tomhaiseachan' ('It's only a riddle').

The name 'Mac Thaidhg' was familiar in the south-western Gàidhealtachd but is unknown, now at any rate, in the north-west. The only instance of 'Tadhg' as a personal name in the genealogies of the latter area that I can think of is Tadhg Mór MacCuinn in Skye, to whom men had recourse in order to get a just decision in difficult disputes. But John MacLeod, who of course knew about Tadhg Mór, had never heard there was any connection between Tadhg and this riddle.

Turning to a different area, the *each-uisge* 'water-horse' is featured in Raasay tradition as in that of so many other places. The fullest version I know of the Raasay story of the each-uisge has been printed: it is taken from the collections of J. F. Campbell of Islay. The main episode of this story at any rate was to be heard quite commonly: namely, that the Gobha Mór had rid the island of the monster at Loch na Mnathadh. Legends such as this are often timeless, not set in any particular age nor attached to any particular individual. Some people said, however, that the Gobha Mór was a Maclean. I give here a slightly modified version of the English translation.[7]

There was once a certain Smith in Raasay. And as it happened, the people of the household themselves acted as herdsmen. But one night the Smith's daughter, who had been looking for the sheep, did not come home, and they went out next day to look for her. There was a loch in the high ground of Raasay where the water-horse used to live; when they came to it they found the heart and lungs of the girl on the shore of the loch. The Smith was deeply distressed, and in his own mind determined he would find a way to kill the water-horse. He and his son began building a smithy by the side of the loch and when they had made the smithy ready the Smith and his son went there during the night. The son took a wether with him and put it on a spit to roast it. In the fire he had great hooks, red-hot and ready should anything come that way.

The door of the smithy faced the loch, and they saw the loch becoming a red blaze of vapour; and the Smith said, 'If anything comes upon us, don't flinch.'

Then they saw coming in at the outer door what seemed to be a year-old horse, shaggy and ugly. The big Smith and his son thrust two hooks in him, red-hot out of the fire. The water-horse began to yell and tried to escape and dragged them near the door. The big Smith dug his heels in and dragged him back to the door again, and there they held him. The Smith told the boy to go and get the big hook out of the fire and thrust it into the water-horse, and the boy did that. And they held him there until they killed him. But when day came there was nothing there but a heap of what looked like star slime.

The ancient belief in the *sìdhichean* – the people of the *sìdh* 'the mountain or hill' – involves a complex of ideas developing dynamically through the ages. One of the strands of belief links them with prehistoric graveyards and burial mounds. There are said to be a number of nameless burial places scattered throughout Raasay, one of them in the vicinity of Dùn Cana, the highest hill, which was itself associated with sìdhichean.

My only example of a story about them – it is a migratory legend known with different detail in other places – was told by the late James Gillies (Seumas Iain Iain Raghnaill), Baile a' Chùirn. The tale concerns the adventure of a certain Eoghain who found the door of the sìdhein open. The sìdhichean welcomed him: 'Fàilte ort Eoghain; thig a-staigh Eoghain; dean do shuidhe Eoghain; deoch ort Eoghain' ('Welcome Eoghain; come inside, Eoghain; have a seat, Eoghain; have a drink, Eoghain'). He was handed a silver cup but, though he pretended to drink from it, he was careful not to let a drop pass his lips, knowing that if he did so he would never reach the outside world again. Eventually, when he saw his opportunity he snatched up the cup and fled. As he ran he could hear the sìdhichean calling their hounds, the *coin-shìdhe*: 'Fear Bheann, Fear Bheann' and 'Fear Charn, Fear Charn'. Soon the hounds were on his trail and gaining fast. Just as he could feel the spurts of water that their paws sent up from the wet ground touching his back, he crossed a boundary stream where the hounds could not pass. Eoghain got home safely and the cup was later taken to Dunvegan Castle.

Stories of this kind that deal with the 'supernatural' are perfectly capable of being analysed in a variety of ways as metaphors of the 'ordinary' or 'natural' world, which includes the imagination.

As I have already implied in connection with the tale about MacKenzie of Gairloch and Mac Gille Chaluim, there were relatively few stories of the 'clan saga' type. The late Bella MacLeod (Beileag an Achaidh) was one of the best sources in my time for this type of tradition. One of her stories (apparently known also to John MacLeod, Clachan) concerned the famous Iain Garbh, the seventh chief, who was drowned in 1671.

Some time after his death, Iain Garbh was seen steering his birlinn between Raasay and Skye and heard chanting an oar-song as he urged on his spectral crew. The refrain of the song was: 'Buille oirre ho ró an ceann': the command 'buille an ceann' is divided by two vocables. Bella could only recall one couplet:

Ged a reidhinn-sa 'na' Chlachan
Chan aithnicheadh iad có bha ann

Buille oirre ho ró an ceann.

Miss MacLeod had an interesting tradition about Clann Mhic Suain who, Raasay tradition strongly asserted, owned the island before the MacLeods. (The latter were of Sìol Torcaill of Lewis and Assynt and invaded Raasay at the end of the fifteenth century or thereabouts.) The gist of it is as follows.

MacSuain Mór lived in Dùn Bhorghadail. He was an expert swordsman who could wield a sword with either hand. Having no heir himself, he sent word to MacLeod of Lewis to send his younger son to Raasay so that he might be fostered in the household of MacSuain Mór and succeed him as chief of Raasay. MacLeod of Lewis sent him his son Gille Caluim; that is how Raasay became MacLeod territory.

As a matter of historical fact, the MacLeods appear to have invaded Raasay and held it by force of arms: in 1549 the Dean of the Isles writes that the land 'perteins to McGyllychallum of Raarsay be the sword'. With the destruction of the Lordship of the Isles at the end of the fifteenth century, the age of anarchy began and this is no doubt the context in which the MacLeods took over the island. In any event, the story that MacSuain had no heir – the implication was that he had no *son* – and therefore asked MacLeod of Lewis to provide a chief is on the face of it highly unlikely. For one thing, succession to the chiefship was not necessarily by primogeniture. The story is of a type that is not uncommon among such clan sagas: a sort of charter-myth that explains and justifies the origins of a family and their possession of place.

The reference to Dùn Bhorghadail – a ruined broch in the south end of Raasay – is intriguing. Was this dùn really occupied by MacSuain about 1500? Was it re-occupied, and presumably repaired for that purpose, because of the anarchy of the times? There are legends such as those of Uisdean mac Gilleasba' Chléirich and Aonghus Fionn and Domhnall Cam and others which link these historical characters with certain dùin in Uist and Lewis, roughly in the century following the destruction of the Lordship. Only the precise investigations of archae-ologists can answer the questions that such stories set in train.

A commoner tradition connects Dùn Bhorghadail with the *Cruith-nich* 'Picts'. Although the name 'Cruithneach', pl. 'Cruithnich', was, and no doubt still is, known to seanchaidhs in other parts, it has always seemed to me that it was a more familiar term in Raasay than elsewhere in the Gàidhealtachd. Some regarded the Cruithnich as people who kept to themselves and were not greatly to be trusted. One can never, of course, discount entirely the influence of book-learning in forming such attitudes, no matter how remote the source may be. At the same time, this assessment of the Cruithnich – who were not, so far as I could make out, firmly identified, by those who knew the name, as the 'Picts' of the school text-books – is remarkably like some of the familiar stereotyped descriptions of 'aboriginal' and 'savage' peoples.

The skills of the MacKay pipers, not to speak of Calum Pìobaire (Malcolm MacPherson) and others, have given Raasay a unique place in the piping world. Tobhta a' Phìobaire in Eyre is still well-known; the names of Iain mac Ruairi and his son Angus rather less so. Beyond that I can recollect only two anecdotes: one from the late Malcolm MacKay (Calum Ruairi) in Fearns, who came from the same family, the other from James Gillies.

The MacKay family story concerned an occasion when the Pìobaire – no personal name was given – was on his way to meet a rival piper where each of them was to play his own composition ('am port aige fhéin') and be judged accordingly. On the journey, other people joined them, one of them being the rival piper whom MacKay had never seen and whom he therefore failed to recognise. At one stage they travelled by boat (whether from Raasay to Skye or somewhere else was not made clear). The Pìobaire sat on a thwart fingering the notes of his port on a staff. The rival piper watched him closely, learnt the tune and, having arranged matters so that he himself played first, gave MacKay's composition as his own – and naturally won.

James Gillies' story told how all the Pìobaire's sons – again no personal names were mentioned – were taught by their father. They were all outstanding pipers. A daughter of the Pìobaire learnt to play, too; not through being formally instructed, however, but simply by watching and listening to her father and brothers. One day the Pìobaire heard her as she played the chanter by herself and realised that she was a better piper than any of them. Shortly after that he asked her to hold a piece of wood for him to chop with an axe. The girl did as she was asked and her father sheared the top joint of one of her fingers off. That ensured that if she ever played again she was in no danger of outshining the MacKay menfolk.

This legend underlines the fact that the pipes were originally a part of a warrior culture and the skills of piping, until recent times, a male preserve. But traditions from other places relate that women could and did learn the *canntaireachd* (oral mnemonics) of pipe-tunes, including ceòl-mór.

I want now to mention briefly the song tradition of the island. The heroic eulogies and elegies, if they were ever abundant in Raasay, had long since disappeared. Raasay was no different in that respect from most other communities of the Gàidhealtachd. The encomiastic songs proper, especially those in the so-called strophic metres, were never 'popular' in the sense that choral songs of various kinds were. Central to the latter tradition were *na h-òrain-luaidh* 'the waulking-songs'. So far as I can make out, the luadh, with its attendant rich poetic culture, had ceased in the nineteenth century, at least as common practice. This meant of course that, as elsewhere, the òrain-luaidh were largely forgotten in the generation immediately following. The only waulking-song (apart from the choral songs given by Dr Calum Maclean[8]) that I heard alluded to was the very widely distributed 'Chunna mise mo leannan | is cha do dh'aithnich e an-dé mi',[9] which was known to the late James Nicolson (Seumas Sheonaidh). His father was a bard and there was a tradition of song in their family although I did not know about that until it was too late. It now appears that Mr Nicolson had a repertory of the older songs. James Gillies knew William Ross's 'Suaithneas Bàn' and Catrìona Montgomery the Gaelic poet learnt a fine version of the song 'Thig an smeòrach as t-earrach' from a Raasay source. No doubt there were others.

The remarkable song which Dr Maclean discusses in his paper and which begins 'Ceud soraidh bhuam fhìn go m'eòlas' apparently celebrates, among other things, a marriage between one of Clann Mhic Neacail of Sgorabreac and a daughter of Mac Gille Chaluim.[10]

In 1955 I recorded a version of this song from the late Mrs Kate Beaton, Woodend, Portree. Mrs Beaton herself mentioned the song first, quoting the opening couplet: she referred to it as 'Òran mór Sgorabreac'. She added that the author was engaged in smuggling liquor, had been captured by the gaugers, tied to the mast and flogged. She was of the opinion that he was either in the service of the family of Sgorabreac or was one of Clann Mhic Neacail himself; he was in any case a companion of Calum mac Dhomhnaill of Sgorabreac. I told her then that the song was known in the MacLean family in Raasay and she asked me to quote it, which I did. She implied that most of it was familiar to her as she had heard it from several people in the Portree area when she was a girl in the 1880s. But she seemed to be less certain about some of the lines that refer to Raasay: for instance, the lines that contain '(Caisteal) Bhròchaill' (which, of course, is a crucial reference) in the Raasay variant.

However, as she did know the lines that contain the personal names of Clann Mhic Gille Chaluim, the existence of a 'Raasay Section' in her variant cannot be doubted. In fact, the names Sìleas, Seònaid and Alasdair – clearly the two sisers of Iain Garbh, the 7th chief of the MacLeods of Raasay, and apparently his younger or youngest brother – occur only in Mrs Beaton's version of the song.

There is another variant, somewhat fragmentary, in K. C. Craig's collection from South Uist which does not mention Raasay or Raasay names at all.[11] Three lines in Craig are identical (except for a verb and a different preposition) with those in the Raasay and Portree variants; one other line is in the Portree but not in the Raasay variant. The refrain of the song as sung by Màiri nighean Alasdair for Craig is 'o ho ao nach till thu, Dhomhnaill?', etc. In J. L. Campbell and Francis Collinson's *Hebridean Folksongs* there is a song which begins 'Dh'éir-ich mise moch Di-Domhnaich'.[12] The refrain, consisting entirely of vocables, 'ì hoireann ò hi ri o ho | ù hoireann ò hi ri rì u | ì hoireann ò hi ri o ho', is remarkably close to that of the Portree and Raasay variants. The Craig and the Campbell and Collinson texts are clearly variants; the latter has a reference to Sgorabreac and, in addition, may preserve some echo of Kate Beaton's text.

The following fourteen lines are those which Mrs Beaton herself was perfectly confident about but she did insist she knew many more if only she could recollect them. Tragically, I only saw her on that one occasion. She was already very frail and died before she could be recorded professionally.[13] Her text contains ten lines that are not known in the Raasay variant.

> *Ceud soraidh bhuam fhìn go m'eòlas*
> *Go Sgorabreac am bi a' chòisir*
> *Far an dean am marcraich tòirleim*
> *Chan ionann sin is mar dh'éirich dhomh-sa*
> *Mi am bothan beag air dhroch comhdhail*
> *Bidh siod aig Calum mac Dhomhnaill*
> *Ciste nan iuchraichean bòidheach*
> *Dhe an umha dhe an airgead dhe an òr ann*

An taigh mór an urlair chomhnaird
Le seuraichean gan cur an ordugh
*   *   *   *   *   *

Iain Mór is Iain Òg dhiubh
Bu dhiubh Sìleas agus Seònaid
Is Alasdair am mac a b'òige
*   *   *   *   *   *

Maighstir Iain is Maighstir Domhnall

I have separated the sections as shown but it was not clear to me where the names of 'Mr John and Mr Donald' were meant to fit. There can be little doubt, however, that these two are Nicolsons of the Sgorabreac family.[14] They only occur in Mrs Beaton's text and the same is true, as already noted, of Sìleas and Seònaid. But the names Sìle and Seònaid appear elsewhere; for instance, in two songs in K. C. Craig's collection.[15] There is nothing in either context there to suggest a connection with Raasay. The fact is that we are dealing here with processes of formulaic composition (which is itself by no means as well understood as some scholars would seem to imply) in which lines and even entire passages can be moved from one song to another. Personal names, too, may sometimes function as formulaic elements.[16]

Nonetheless, it is interesting to find in the song 'Dh'éirich mise moch Di-Domhnaich' some traces that suggest a little more than a coincidental use of formulas. These are:

Thoir mo shoiridh-sa gu m'eòlas
Bhuam do Sgorabreac an eòrna
*   *   *   *   *   *

'S innis dhi mar dh'éirich dhomhsa
*   *   *   *   *   *

Am bothan beag an iomall mòintich
*   *   *   *   *   *

Iain Mhic Chaluim 'ic Dhomhnaill [. . .]
An taigh mór an urlair chomhnaird
Far am bi daoin' uaisle mu bhordaibh.

Some of these correspondences are, of course, very faint indeed. 'Calum mac Dhomhnaill', occurring here only as a kin-name or as part of a patronymic, may have in reality nothing whatsoever to do with Calum mac Dhomhnaill of Sgorabreac. Yet the Nicolsons of Sgorabreac did have an Iain mac Caluim mhic Dhomhnaill. Possibilities such as these serve at least to illustrate the particular problems that may confront us in the Gaelic song tradition when we try to determine the relationships of what are sometimes called 'multiforms'.

Finally, I want to look very briefly at a few place names. One I have mentioned already: Glac nan Curran ('Carrot Hollow'). These are wild carrots and place names with the same element (e.g. Gearraidh nan Curran) are known elsewhere. There is no vestige of tradition in Raasay, so far as I am aware, to connect Glac nan Curran with the celebration of St. Michael's Day, 29th September, as described by Alexander Carmichael,[17] but the possible significance of the Raasay place name in this connection ought not to be overlooked.

Dùn Cana, the highest hill, is usually misspelt 'Caan' or 'Canna' in books and on maps. There is a rhyme which I give here although, curiously enough, I never heard it in Raasay. I think it was reasonably well known in Skye: at any rate, I heard it in our own family tradition. Like most rhymes that are simply a list of place names, followed by a vivid descriptive phrase, or sometimes by a prophetic statement, it has its own strange evocative power.

> *Dùn sin is Dùn Cana*
> *Dùn as aird os cionn na mara*
> *An dùn air a laigheadh na caoraich*
> *Dùn gaolach Mhic Gille Chaluim.*

Some made the last line: 'dùn breac gaolach Mhic Gille Chaluim', which, though a fine image in itself, visually powerful, is less emotive than the bare statement as an expression of *dùthchas*.

Màiri Mhór nan Òran used this old rhyme in a song in which she mentions Raasay and the MacLeods, building it into the structure of her verse in such a way that it adds a whole dimension of resonance and poignancy to her words.

> *Is ged a bha mo chridhe leòinte,*
> *Snighe bho mo shùil a' dòrtadh,*
> *Faicinn Ratharsair gun Leòdach,*
> *Rinn mi sòlas ri Dùn Cana.*
>
> *Cha déid ainm an dùin a chaochladh,*
> *Fhad 's bhios Leòdach beò 'san t-saoghal –*
> *An dùn air a laigheadh na caoraich,*
> *Dùn gaolach Mhic Gille Chaluim.*

Lady D'Oyly thug i gràdh dha –
A shliochd Iain Ghairbh an duine dàicheil –
Thall 'sna h-Innsean rinn i dàn
An dùin as aird os cionn na mara.[18]

What does the name Dùn Cana mean? Among various suggestions by far the most interesting is that put forward by Dr Colm Ó Baoill of Aberdeen University that it preserves the name of one Cano mac Gartnáin, a seventh-century petty king of Skye (or part of Skye) who was born on the island of Inis Moccu Chéin, of which his father was ruler. Dr Ó Baoill argues convincingly that this island of Moccu Chein (or Maic Uchen, depending on how the manuscript is read) is no other than the island of Raasay.[19]

Finally there is a place name given to me in a casual conversation some years ago by the late Alasdair MacRae (Alasdair Mhurchaidh Ghearrloich) of Osgaig and Glasgow. The name is 'Leabaidh na Glas Ghoibhre' ('The Bed of the Grey Goat'). It is at the top of Meall a' Charnain (older 'Meall (n)an Carnan', with the common assimilation of the nasal), above the school park, where the Free Presbyterian church and manse now stand. If the name is what I think it is, another tradition, which I remember hearing from a number of people, that there was an ancient burial ground nearby, may have some bearing on it. The implication is that this whole area had some importance in pagan times as a centre of religious activity.

The name 'Leabaidh na Glas Ghoibhre' is to be compared with 'Leaba(idh) na Bà Bàine' in Gairloch or 'Leaba na Bó Uidhre' (alternatively, 'Leaba na Bà Uidhre' – *bó* is the older genitive – or simply 'Leaba na h-Uidhre') in Strath, Skye. These are mythological cows or cow goddesses. The River Boyne in Ireland is 'cow-white', or at least involves these two elements, 'cow' and 'white'; 'Abhainn Bà Finne' in North Uist is the River of the White Cow. (Rivers and their fertilising waters are frequently conceived of as goddesses in pagan Gaelic, or pre-Gaelic, religion.)

By far the best known of the 'magic cows' of Gaelic tradition is A' Ghlas Ghaibhleann or Ghoibhleann (the name is pronounced with the same sound as in 'oighre', 'goibhre', etc.). In the older literature the form is 'Gaibhneann': this is the cow of Goibhniu, the Divine Smith of Gaelic mythology. The Glas Ghaibhleann is sometimes associated with Fionn and his band of warriors but not in the tradition which I inherited from the Skye side of our family. The Glas Ghaibhleann appeared in times of hardship and famine: she would appear without warning and disappear in the same way after she had brought relief to the district. She had her special 'Beds': large natural hollows in good pasture. It was said that not every place could provide feeding for the Glas Ghaibhleann but any place that she visited, she would provide for it. Her 'leapannan' ('beds') in the Isle of Skye are listed in the following stanza:

> *Gleann Dail an Diùranais*
> *Gleann Ùig an Tròntarnais*
> *Gleann sgiamhach Sgàladail*
> *Gleann àlainn Ròmasdail*
> *Glacagan Beinn Tianabhaig*
> *Is Slaopan mèadhaineach nan Torr.*

There is a quite different Skye list in Rev. J. G. Campbell's *The Fians*. The last Leaba is still a very well known place name in the township of Na Torran (gen. pl. 'nan Torr').

I would suggest then that the Raasay place name is a re-formation. As the significance of 'Gaibhleann' was lost, the more intelligible 'goibhre' was substituted. If this is indeed the case, the name is one of the most fascinating survivals in the traditions of the island.

Family Tradition in the Isle of Skye: Clann Aonghuis – *the MacInneses*

The family whose traditions I am going to talk about is the family in the Isle of Skye to which I myself belong. I cannot, in the short space of this essay, do more than select a few representative items from a considerable range of material which was transmitted orally, in Gaelic, through many generations and some of which I had the good fortune to hear in my boyhood and teens. I use the term 'family' in the sense of extended family, although in fact what I heard derives principally from my grand-uncles – my paternal grandfather's brothers – who were born in the period 1850 to 1870, for active transmission virtually ceased in their generation. I am concerned here only with historical traditions. These, in their mixture of fact and fiction, probably give a fairly representative picture of this class of tradition in Gaelic. I should add that a great wealth of song was preserved in the same family as well as a tradition of piping and dancing and, in earlier generations, charms and heroic ballads. So far as these last two categories are concerned, however, I was too young to have inherited more than the knowledge that they existed.

The family land was in the parish of Sleat, in the south of Skye, which became MacDonald territory in the second half of the fifteenth century when John Lord of the Isles conferred, in 1469, the twenty-four merklands of Sleat on his son, Celestine of Lochalsh, and Celestine transferred these and other lands to his brother Hugh. But Morvern, on the mainland, was the original patrimony. After the downfall of the Lordship of the Isles (it was forfeited to the Crown of Scotland in 1493) widespread anarchy developed in the western Highlands and Islands, and it may have been at some point subsequent to the destruction of the Lordship, probably in the sixteenth century, that the MacInneses came to Skye. The traditional account of their move from Morvern to Sleat is as follows.

The chief of the MacInneses of Morvern had been killed in battle and his nearest kinsman, some say his brother, Maol-Caluim, set sail for Sleat, where the senior line of Clan Donald held sway. Five longships made the journey, each of them carrying a family group: from the heads of these families are descended the five lineages of the name of MacInnes in the Isle of Skye. These five lineages remained distinct and are still traceable.

In the time of the Norsemen, the MacInneses fought a great battle against the Norse in Islay. The MacInneses must have been settled in Islay at that time. When Somhairle (Somerled) was waging his campaign against the Norsemen, it was to the MacInneses he applied for support and that support was readily given. The result was that Somerled promised that so long as he and his descendants were in power, the MacInneses would receive their protection. Centuries later there was a battle in which the MacDonald Lord of the Isles, direct descendent of Somerled, was assisted at a crucial point by MacInnes of Kinlochaline, chief of the clan, and his warriors. After victory was secured, MacDonald turned to MacInnes, thanked him profoundly for his help, without which they would have been defeated, and added, 'Fhad is a bhios MacDhomhnaill a-staigh cha bhi MacAonghuis a-muigh' ('So long as MacDonald is in, MacInnes will not be out'). The statement is enshrined in Gaelic tradition.

Remembering this pledge, Maol-Caluim of Morvern naturally sought the protection of the senior line of Clan Donald. He was given land, free of rent, in Sleat. Successive generations of the family enjoyed the same privileges until the time of the Mormhaire Bàn.

The next traditional story tells of *Niall a' Bhogha* 'Niall of the Bow', who, according to an alternative tradition, was himself the first MacInnes to come to Skye. It would seem that both accounts were known in Sleat. The story goes as follows.

Another branch of MacInneses, related to Maol-Caluim's family, became hereditary bowmen to the MacKinnons of Strath. They were known as *Sliochd Neill a' Bhogha* 'The Lineage of Niall of the Bow' and were descended from Niall, who was born in Sleat some genera-tions after the coming of Maol-Caluim. MacKinnon of Strath took Niall into his employment, at first as a cowherd. MacKinnon had a great bow which only he himself could draw to its farthest extent. Realising that Niall was physically strong, he gave him the bow to draw, as a test, and Niall drew it. No more was said about that at the time.

One day when MacKinnon was entertaining Maclean of Duart and other chiefs, he invited them to draw the great bow. All of them failed.

'What a strange thing is this', said MacKinnon, 'when even my cowherd can draw that bow.' Niall was called in and he drew the bow without any difficulty. It was then that MacKinnon made him his bowman and granted him and his descendants lands free of rent in return for their services as bowmen, generation after generation. From that time forth Niall was known as Niall a' Bhogha.

It is still said, when a difficult task is executed without effort, especially by someone who was not expected to perform it 'Chuireadh Niall a' Bhogha am bogha air lagh' ('Neil of the Bow could draw the bow').

Sliochd Neill a' Bhogha held their lands rent-free until MacAllister became proprietor of Strathaird.

In Sleat, the MacInneses always fought along with the MacDonalds. At the Battle of Coire na Creiche, the men of Sleat were led by a MacInnes, Aonghus Òg, ('Young'; here probably 'Younger') who was a famous warrior.

Domhnall Gorm Mór (the chief of the MacDonalds) married a sister of Ruairi Mór (the chief of the MacLeods). She was very ugly and had only one eye. After a year and a day Domhnall Gorm sent her home on a one-eyed horse, with a one-eyed groom, and a one-eyed dog. She was the Cailleach Cham ('One-eyed Crone'). War broke out then between the MacDonalds and the MacLeods. At this time Aonghus Òg was the 'captain' (*caibtein* < Eng. 'captain') of the men of Sleat.

At the Battle of Coire na Creiche Aonghus Òg fought so well that he went too far ahead of his men and the MacLeods closed round him and took him prisoner. He was taken to Dunvegan and sentenced to be hanged. But MacLeod was reluctant to put such a valiant warrior to death and thought he might get him to become one of his own men. Aonghus Òg was put on the scaffold and MacLeod promised him his life if he would marry his sister. Aonghus Òg asked if he might see her first. The sister was brought out. Aonghus Òg turned to the hangman and said 'Suas a seo mi' ('String me up').

Finally, there is a story about Niall a' Bhogha, who according to this account is a descendant of the original Niall. His son is Niall Òg. In these stories the MacLeods are often referred to as *Na Tormodaich* 'the descendants of Tormod' for the MacLeods of Harris and Skye were known as *Sìol Tormoid* 'the Seed of Tormod', in contrast to the MacLeods of Lewis, Assynt, and Raasay, the Seed of Torcall; Tormod and Torcall being the sons of the eponymous Leod. The designation *Na Tormodaich* is rare, nowadays at least; I have translated it here simply as 'the MacLeods'.

On one occasion the MacLeods raided Strath. They came in their longships and moored them near the shore. As it happened the chief of the MacKinnons at this time was an aged man. The young chief (i.e. the heir) and his men were out hunting in the Cuillins but the old chief, who was too infirm now to go hunting in the mountains, was left at home. Niall a' Bhogha was one of the hunters and he had his son Niall Òg (the younger) with him. Niall was the name of the head of the family in every generation.

The MacLeods began to plunder the place, carrying off food and anything else of value they could find, and rounding up the animals. But unknown to them a dairymaid in MacKinnon's household had seen them coming and set off to tell the men who were hunting in the mountains. She found the hunters and told them. They left off hunting there and then and made for home.

The MacLeods had been at their work for some time and now, as an insult, they drove the old chief out of his house and forced him to carry a load of cheeses down to the longships. One of the MacLeods began to whip him onwards and make him hurry up. He was doing this when the MacKinnons came on the scene. Suddenly and without warning a shower of arrows struck the MacLeods and one would fall here and another there. Niall a' Bhogha aimed at the man who was whipping the old chief; the arrow struck the man in the throat, the blood gushed out and as he fell it spurted on to the cheese. The MacLeods fled and made for the longships.

When they got to the longships the tide had ebbed and the ships were high and dry and the MacKinnons slaughtered those who were left of the MacLeods there on the shore.

Only one ship got away with one MacLeod aboard who was not wounded. This man began to hoist the sail and his two hands were up by the mast. Niall a' Bhogha turned to his son Niall Òg. 'You have that one', said he. Niall Òg shot an arrow and the arrow passed over the mast and fell into the sea beyond the ship. 'Wretch!' said Niall a' Bhogha, 'How you have shamed me!' Then he took aim himself. The arrow struck the MacLeod in the hands and pinned his two hands to the mast. Then the wind caught the sail and the ship rounded the Point of Aird like that, with the man hanging to the mast.

After the battle was over, the young chief of the MacKinnons sat down and sliced some of the cheese from the load his father had been carrying and began to eat it. The dairymaid who had gone out to the mountains to fetch the hunters was standing nearby and saw him. 'For goodness sake', she said, 'don't eat that! Can't you see the brute's blood on it?'

'The best food a man ever got', said he, 'is the cheese of Strath and the blood of the MacLeods.'

I shall now make some brief comments on these traditional tales. The story of Aonghus Òg and MacLeod's ugly sister stands out from the rest. It is in fact the Lowland Scots tale of the Muckle Mou'd Meg transferred to a Gaelic setting. Some of the historical tales in Gaelic are migratory legends and some employ motifs that have an international distribution but overall migratory legends from without the corpus are in a minority. There is, however, a considerable interchange of motifs within it.

Many of the clan legends or sagas are concerned with violent deeds: in that respect the story of Niall a' Bhogha and the MacLeod raid is fairly typical. All are short, vivid, realistic stories told in an unadorned style; the dialogue is naturalistic but almost always contains some memorable phrase. No matter how violent the action or how savage the language may be, there is never any moralising.

The motif of the longships on the ebbing tide appears in similar contexts of forays and battles in other stories; while the archer's feats, here the arrow in the throat, with the doomed man's blood gushing forth on the cheese, and the pinning of the hands to the mast, are reproduced elsewhere in variant form in the corpus of historical legends. But it is worth making the point that practically every story in the corpus has a remarkably individual flavour, some being much more dramatic than the examples I have given here.

MacKinnon of Strath's desire to impress his guests with the strength and skill of his men, so that even his cowherd could draw the great bow, is perhaps faintly reminiscent of the Gaelic variant of the William Tell story, localised in South Uist and Kintail. In the Gaelic story, the archer is ordered to make the famous bowshot in order to impress a chief's guests. The detail of the name 'Niall' being given in every generation is not known, so far as I am aware, outside the story of the MacLeod raid. The name is one of the distinctive MacInnes names, in Morvern as well as in Sleat, but the claim that it was always the name of the head of that particular family is certainly unhistorical. Apart from anything else, Gaelic society has its own ideology of name-giving, and although there is considerable variation in practice, an unbroken sequence, with only the one name, is unknown. There is perhaps a parallel with other families who followed hereditary professions. For instance, Gaelic traditional stories about the MacMhuirichs do not distinguish individual members by name: there is simply one representative 'MacMhuirich' who features throughout. No doubt there were many stories, now lost, about Niall a' Bhogha, set in different generations and it would be natural to argue from that that the name of the head of the family was always Niall.

The flotilla of five longships that brought the MacInneses to Skye merits some comment. The tradition quite probably reflects a historical event: namely, the movement of some of the leading MacInnes families from Morvern to the Isle of Skye after the downfall of the Lordship of the Isles. But of course it may also be the case that there were MacInneses in Skye before that time. Whether that is so or not, the number five is significant. In the Island of Raasay, there are said to be five lineages of MacLeods, unrelated in the male line. In both instances, the number may be symbolic, based perhaps on the five fingers. The hand would then symbolise the complete group. But this is no more than speculation. One of my granduncles, who died when I was a small boy, maintained that he could distinguish all five lineages, each of them still distinct in our own time. There are certainly three lineages of the name of MacInnes in the south of Skye and at least one in the north. It is interesting that such a tradition, whether among the MacInneses or the MacLeods, should exist at all, seeing that each 'clan' is supposed to be descended from an eponymous ancestor. There may be something worth investigating here. Does such a legend serve some function connected with social organisation and structure? Is it relevant that the MacInneses were incomers as the MacLeods were in Raasay? The latter, who came from Lewis, either invaded Raasay or, alternatively, according to their own tradition, were invited to come to the island. But if the matter of ancestry is relevant, the MacLeod traditions name an eponymous ancestor for their clan: there is no record, so far as I am aware, oral or written, as to whom the eponym of the MacInneses might have been.

The story about Somerled and his request for help from the MacInneses of Morvern is in a sense the most interesting tradition of all, taking us back to the first half of the twelfth century. The handful of tales that have survived about Somerled provide us with the *terminus a quo* of this historical lore: the great majority of historical legends, throughout the Gàidhealtachd, belong to a much later era. The connection between Somerled and the MacInneses is not confined to our family tradition: it is also referred to by the so-called 'Sleat historian' in the seventeenth century. Not unpredictably, this account reflects a MacDonald point of view, just as the oral tradition of the family reflects a MacInnes point of view. According to the author, it was the MacInneses who asked Somerled to lead them, not Somerled who asked for MacInnes support. The account is as follows:

> Godfrey Du had possession of the Isles of the north side of Ardnamurchan from the King of Denmark. Olay compelled the inhabitants of some of these Isles to infest Morverin by landing some forces there. The principal surnames in the country were MacInnes's and MacGilvrays, who are the same as the MacInnes's. They being in sight of the enemy could act nothing without one to command them. At length they agreed to make the first person that should appear to them their general. Who came in the meantime but Sommerled, with his bow, quiver, and sword? Upon his appearance they raised a great shout of laughter. Sommerled enquiring the reason, they answered they were rejoiced at his appearance. They told him that they had agreed to make the first that would appear their general. Sommerlid said he would undertake to head them, or serve as a man otherwise. But if they pitched upon him as their commander, they should swear to be obedient to his commands; so, without any delay, they gave him an oath of obedience.[1]

No doubt there is more than one possible interpretation of these traditions of an alliance between Somerled and the MacInneses. It would seem at any rate that the MacInneses, who in Gaelic are *Clann Aonghuis* 'The Children of Angus', were in the twelfth century already a well-established kindred in Morvern. But their antecedents are unknown. The work of David Sellar and John Bannerman has shown how the genealogy of Somerled leads back to the original rulers of Dál Riata and how the cultural authority of the Lordship of the Isles derives from the kingdom of Dál Riata itself.[2] It is, I think, just possible that Clann Aonghuis was connected with, or may have claimed descent from, *Cenél nOenghuso* 'the descendants of Oenghus', one of the three sons of Erc who established a Gaelic kingdom in what became known as Argyll, traditionally in the year 498. If this were the case, it would be natural for Somerled to seek not only a military alliance but also to have his own claim endorsed by representatives of one of the three great divisions of Dál Riata. One objection to this, however, is that the territory of Cenél nOenghuso was not Morvern but the islands of Jura and Islay. In that connection, it might be significant that the MacInneses were said to have fought a great battle against the Norsemen in Islay and that it was implied that

Islay was then MacInnes territory. Is this a faint reflection in oral tradition of the loss of Islay by Cenél nOenghuso? Our information is too meagre and too vague to allow us to answer the question.

In the south of Skye the MacInneses are sometimes represented as 'soldiers'. These traditions are for the most part grouped around the hereditary bowmen of the MacKinnons of Strath, Sliochd Neill a' Bhogha. Indeed, the fame of this branch of the clan may account for the tradition that the first MacInnes to come to Skye was Niall a' Bhogha himself. But in Sleat also there are recurring references to a military role. The battle at which Aonghus Òg was said to have been taken prisoner is a historical event: it was fought c. 1601 and was a great MacDonald victory. It is also remembered as the last clan battle to be fought in Skye. In the present context the point is the role given in tradition to Aonghus Òg who is said to have led the MacDonalds of Sleat. The idea that the MacDonalds were actually led by someone not of their own kindred seems very unlikely but there may be an underlying explanation.

The tradition that the MacInneses were given lands free of rent because of the help their ancestors had given Somerled is perhaps historically possible. But just as Sliochd Neill a' Bhogha held their lands as bowmen to the MacKinnons, the MacInneses in Sleat, too, may have held their lands on somewhat similar conditions. It is possible that at one time they formed a kind of comitatus for MacDonald; but if so, no reference to anything as formal as that has come down in the tradition of the family. The last MacInnes who is said to have been given land in return for military service is Maol-Caluim mac Neill mhic Aonghuis, who is eight generations removed from me. He and an unknown number of his forebears were professional swordsmen and Maol-Caluim himself fought at the battle of Sheriffmuir on the Jacobite side, in 1715. There is indeed a tradition in North Uist that he was one of the three great warriors of Sheriffmuir.[3] Within the family, he was described as an *oifigeach ann an arm a' Mhormhaire* 'an officer in MacDonald's army' and was given the lands of Leitir Fura in Sleat. This area, the sloping land opposite the tidal island of Isleornsay, roughly to the north of it, was also known as *A' Choille* and in English 'Wood' or 'Kinlochwood'; but in older usage, in official documents, the form is 'Letterfure' or 'Letterfure in Slate'. I now turn to the traditional account again.

Leitir Fura got its name from Fura Mhór, a great oak-tree that grew there. At the height of a hot summer day it gave shade for forty (some

said fifty) head of cattle. Maol-Caluim, and later his son and succes-
sor, Iain mac Mhaol-Chaluim, used to send droves of Highland cattle
to the markets of the Lowlands. They were well-off and on one
occasion lent £500 to MacDonald of Sleat. It was never paid back.
In the time of the Mormhaire Bàn, the family lost their lands. Iain mac
Mhaol-Chaluim was allowed to remain in Leitir Fura, and died there,
but his sons did not succeed him. The family were put out of Leitir
Fura on a pretext; and this is how that happened. One summer's day
Iain mac Mhaol-Chaluim's children were playing in the woods and lit
a fire near Fura Mhór. It was a very dry summer and the tree caught
fire and was burnt down.

Some say there was another tree, also an oak, but much smaller,
called Fura Bheag.

The above account contains a number of interesting items. First,
there is the great oak-tree. Did this tree or some tree in the area
originally represent one of the 'sacred trees' of Gaelic tradition? If this
is the case, there is not a vestige of information on that aspect of it in
the traditional account. Nor is there any evidence, such as we have in
some places on the mainland, that coins were embedded in it, or pieces
of cloth hung on it, or that any votive offerings were brought there.
Secondly, there is the name 'Fura', for which I have no parallel
elsewhere. But Leitir Fura is almost certainly the same place as Martin
Martin's 'Lettir-hurr' in the following passage, where he is describing
this part of Skye: 'There are several Coppices of Wood, scatter'd up
and down the Isle; the largest call'd *Lettir-hurr*, exceeds not three
miles in length.'[4]

Am Mormhaire Bàn was Sir Alexander MacDonald, 9th Baronet of
Sleat, whom Johnson and Boswell visited in 1773.[5] He is remembered
as a man who had little sympathy with Gaelic, in language or in
culture: Boswell describes him as an 'English-bred chieftain'. During
his time the rents of the principal tenants were raised to an exorbitant
degree. Whatever agreement there may have been between Mac-
Donald and Maol-Caluim of Leitir Fura, its termination fits into
the general pattern of Sir Alexander's policy. By Iain mac Mhaol-
Chaluim's time, in the 1770s and 1780s, there was no longer any need
for swordsmen such as there had been under an older dispensation.
There is no mention in tradition of a written contract between
MacDonald of Sleat and his tenants in Leitir Fura (although other
documents from 'Letterfure' have survived) but the family who were
regarded in Strath as being direct descendants of Niall a' Bhogha

claimed to have title deeds which were purloined when MacAllister, a nineteenth-century landlord, became proprietor of Strathaird.

Although I have restricted myself to traditions about the MacInneses themselves, there were of course many other tales and legends; a number of these, naturally enough, since Sleat was MacDonald territory, connected with Clan Donald. To the present day, for instance, the exact spot where the Red Hand of Clan Donald touched the foreshore is still pointed out. There were also short novellas, formula-tales, and much else in the way of proverbial lore, genealogy, local tradition (the latter comprising anecdotes, often humorous, attached to local characters) and the lore of place names. In connection with the Jacobite Rising of 1745, two men in particular were talked about: John MacInnes, related to the family through the wife of Iain mac Mhaol-Chaluim of Leitir Fura; and Domhnall Mór Mac-Neacail (Donald Nicolson), my great-grandmother's great-grand-father. The former was one of the crew that rowed Prince Charles Edward Stewart from Strathaird on Friday, 4th July, 1746: he was given five hundred lashes, in instalments of fifty, for his part in the Prince's escape but refused to betray the 'son of the true king'.

Domhnall Mór is said to have been the man who was personally responsible for getting the Prince safely past the Government patrols, from the house of MacKinnon to the boat that conveyed him to the mainland.

Most of the stories that were still being told in my boyhood could be described as historical, using the word in a broad sense. Historical legends have in fact survived better, throughout the Highlands and Islands in general, that any other class of traditional tale. Although everything I have given here was told in Gaelic, it is evident enough that historical tradition passes with relative ease from Gaelic to English. But in that process, even historical legends tend to be reduced to the bare bones of the narrative: the vivid style of the original Gaelic and especially the dramatic exchanges of dialogue rarely survive the transition.

A question that is bound to occur to us is the veracity of what we call 'historical' tradition. These family stories that I have glanced at supply a fairly representative sample; and, as we have seen, they may be migratory legends, both within Gaelic tradition and by borrowing from without. They are often, probably more often than not, concerned with or attached to characters who can be identified from other sources. Where characters cannot be identified, however, we may assume that they are historical, for this particular tradition of story-telling requires a certain verisimilitude. To take the last instances I have given, John MacInnes, a member of the crew that rowed the Prince from Strathaird, Skye, is on record elsewhere (e.g. *The New Statistical Account*, Bishop Forbes' *The Lyon in Mourning*, etc.[6]) but Domhnall Mór, so far as I am aware, is not. There is, however, no reason to doubt the existence of Domhnall Mór: my great-grand-father, Niall mac Mhaol-Mhoire, who had the reputation of being a great seanchaidh, and who taught my grand-uncles, was born at the end of the eighteenth century and knew personally men who had been involved in the Forty-Five. Recently, I had this family account of Domhnall Mór corroborated from a Nicolson source in Australia.

In summary, the kind of oral tradition that purports to describe historical events may be fiction, propaganda, accurate representation, or a mixture of all of these. It ought not to be dismissed; nor, on the other hand, regarded as in any way sacrosanct. Oral tradition is also clearly selective. Let me finish by giving one example. In a letter of 1782, the MacInneses of Leitir Fura are accused of smuggling 'eight or nine hundred casks of Brandy and Rum' every year into the Isle of Skye.[7] Yet not one word of this trade, which must have been the main source of their wealth, came down in family tradition. It seems reasonable to suppose that what applies to family tradition may be extended to bigger social denominations: the unwritten histories do not tell all.

The Scottish Gaelic Language

A simple scenario of what was to become the kingdom of Scotland tells of four peoples, the Scots, the Britons, the Picts and the Angles, each vying with each other for power after the withdrawal of the Roman Empire in these islands. In the end the Scots prevailed; hence the name 'Scotland'. There is never any mention of Gaelic. To the present day, it would appear, most Scots, including those whose native language is Gaelic, are unaware of the role played by the Gaelic people and their language in the formation of the historic kingdom. This is a direct product of Scottish formal education. It is never made clear, so far as I am aware, that these 'Scots' of medieval history were quite simply the Gaels, that their 'Scottish' language was the direct ancestor of modern Gaelic, and that it was the Gaels who established the Border which lasted until 1707. Nor are most people in Scotland aware that before the end of the Middle Ages the term 'Scot' and its congeners were in fact purloined by the speakers of what had in origin been a dialect of northern English. In the processes of political and linguistic change that made this Anglian speech the state language of Scotland (until it was itself eclipsed by southern English) Gaelic was deprived of position and status and finally so reduced that it is now the everyday means of communication only in the adult communities of some of the islands of the Hebrides and by the aged in a few mainland areas of the north-west Highlands. Viewed from the standpoint of the present day, the entire process can be stated in direct terms as the destruction of not one but two Scottish languages, each of which had evolved its own definitive characteristics on Scottish soil, by the encroachment of English and its overwhelming ethnocidal power.

Naturally such fundamental changes were not confined to purely linguistic spheres. As early as 1559, in a letter addressed to certain Scots insurgents by the English Privy Council, the hope is expressed that 'this famous isle may be conjoined in heart as in continent, with uniformity of language, manners and conditions'.[1] And the king who was James VI of Scotland and James I of England, addressing Parliament in 1604 (the year after the Union of the Crowns) states the same sentiment in virtually identical terms, except that he clearly regards this as having already taken place. By 1604 God had 'united these two Kingdomes [. . .] in Language, Religion and similitude of manners'.[2] Yet in 1604 Gaelic was still spoken widely in Scotland. Linguistically the Gaels were non-persons.

In the context of the times religion was one of the most potent means of bringing about a uniformity of culture. Modern analyses of the decline of Gaelic emphasise the importance of the religious factor. Some writers, indeed, see the whole anti-Gaelic campaign merely as the direct consequence of the Reformation. Others, better informed and more specific, single out Presbyterianism and exculpate Protestantism in its Episcopalian variety. These and similar views are open to the criticism that they oversimplify a complex situation and fail to take account of the underlying cultural motives. As we shall see, the displacement of Gaelic at the highest and most influential levels of Scottish society had been completed long before the sixteenth century. And by that century even 'Lowland Scots had long been, in the eyes of nearly all who used it, "English" and not "Scots". The Scotland which mattered politically and economically was consciously Anglo-Saxon, and would have indignantly repudiated the suggestion that it was anything else.'[3] If we accept that judgment at all, and there is ample evidence to back it, the achievement of linguistic unity – sooner or later – was inevitable throughout Scotland. At all events, English for centuries has been the sole language of Scottish administration.

What follows is not a linguistic analysis or description of Gaelic: only incidentally and in connection with other matters are there references to phonology, morphology and syntax. For such information the reader is referred elsewhere, to studies of a specialist nature.[4] A little must be said, however, about such topics as cultural contacts, the extent of dialectal divergence within Gaelic, and the attitudes of Gaelic speakers themselves, past and present, to the language. In general, this essay offers no more than an outline of the fortunes of Gaelic in Scotland during some fifteen hundred years: roughly six centuries of expansion followed by a longer period when the language certainly enjoyed times of creative vigour and renewal but which, overall, marks a relentless decline.

Roman writers refer to the Gaels as Scotti. As early as the third and fourth centuries there are references to Scotti and Hibernici, along with Picti, fighting against the Britons (whose territories lay south of those of the Picti, i.e. south of the two great rivers Forth and Clyde) or against the Romans themselves. The names 'Scotia' and 'Scotti' cannot be traced with certainty to an origin in Gaelic itself, but the term 'Scotia' came to mean 'neither Ireland nor Scotland but "Gaeldom" '.[5] Around AD 500, Fergus king of Dál Riata in Ireland became king of the Scottish Dál Riata, centred on what is now *Arra-Ghàidheal* 'Argyll': in the older language 'Airer / Oirer Goídel' – the Coastland of the Gael. To this foundation, the Gaels of Scotland, and at times all Scots, looked back as to the original establishment which gave a charter, as it were, to the later kingdom of Scotland itself.

In Gaelic, Scotland is *Alba*: a name which once denoted the whole British mainland. The establishment of Scottish Dál Riata and the expansion of Gaelic throughout the land of the Picts, while in southern Britain the Anglo-Saxon invasions brought a new language and culture to that region, naturally restricted the use of the name. To the present day, any Scot, Highland or Lowland, is an *Albannach*.

Gaelic appears to have spread relatively fast, in the end obliterating the language or languages of the Picts. In this linguistic colonisation, the influence of the church of Calum Cille – our vernacular form of Colum Cille, St Columba (521–97) – undoubtedly played a powerful part.[6] In 563 Calum Cille founded the monastery of Iona, leading to the foundation of several daughter monasteries. His later *paruchia* included over fifty Scottish churches. In 574 he consecrated Aedan, grandson of Fergus, king of Dál Riata and thus initiated a partnership which continued after the saint's death and after the embryonic Gaelic kingdom had expanded far beyond its original bounds. According to its own claim, recorded in Gaelic in the twelfth century, no doubt on the basis of oral tradition, the monastery of Deer in Aberdeenshire was founded from Iona; and the Irish record of the death of one of its abbots, in 623, probably derived from the lost chronicle of Iona, endorses the connection. The role of the Gaelic church is summed up by W. J. Watson:

> The widely extended and prolonged activity of the Irish clerics, settled as they usually were, not singly but in communities large or small, must have had a great influence in spreading the language. It must further be conceded, with all due deference to the accomplishments of the Northern Picts, that Gaelic was the language of superior culture.[7]

Around the year 841, Kenneth (Cinaed) mac Alpín became king of Dál Riata and some two years later brought the Picts under his supremacy. This event was evidently the conferment of political sanction on a cultural transformation which had begun long before.[8] There must have been Gaelic colonies deep in Pictland as early as the first part of the eighth century. Thus Atholl, in northern Perthshire, is on record in 740 in the form 'Aithfoithle': this is significant for the name means 'New Ireland'. Somewhat similarly, we find 'Éire' (genitive 'Éireann') early established as a district name far to the east of the Dalriadic border, Strathearn, Lochearn; and north, by the Moray Firth, Auldearn. All contain 'Éire' ('Ireland'). Elements such as 'Fodhla' and 'Éire', originally names of ancient local goddesses, were obviously carried east and north by colonists from the early Gaelic kingdom. Indeed, 'Éire' might well have become the Gaelic name of Scotland as it is that of Ireland. But it was 'Alba' that finally won as the vernacular name while 'Scotia' survived as entirely a literary term.

The essential Scotia lay north of Forth and Clyde. But in the southwest, in Galloway and Ayrshire, there are indications of early Gaelic settlement as well; Gaelic survived there well into the seventeenth century and possibly later. These south-western Gaels were as much men of Alba as the Gaels who lived north of Forth and Clyde. South of the river Forth (itself a Gaelic name) the language was evidently introduced into Lothian well before 973 when the province was ceded to the Gaels of Scotia by the Angles.[9] In 945 the Britons of Strathclyde came under Gaelic overlordship but regained their independence after a generation. There was a certain ebb and flow of war over these British and Anglian territories until the year 1018 and the decisive victory of the Gaels at Carham. That, as well as the fact there is no evidence of general displacement of population, means that the diffusion of Gaelic in those territories is likely to have been intermittent and not a symmetrical growth throughout. None the less, after the Battle of Carham and for most of the eleventh century, Gaelic must have continued to spread steadily over the whole of southern Scotland. In the north and north-west of the country the linguistic situation was different. Norse invasion and settlement had begun in the early ninth century and the Norse language maintained itself there for about five hundred years.

By the early part of the eleventh century the whole of mainland Scotland was under the rule of a Gaelic king – the Duncan of Shakespeare's *Macbeth* – the language of court and administrative deliberations was Gaelic; and, while there must of course have been some degree of bilingualism, or even trilingualism, on both the northern and southern bounds, Gaelic was now clearly the dominating language of the historical kingdom of Scotland.

The first major setback occurred with a simultaneous attack on the language in the two most influential institutions of such a society: court and church. In 1070 Malcolm III (Mael Coluim Ceannmhor) married Margaret, sister of the claimant to the English throne after the Norman Conquest. Under this regime the Gaelic church – which did not repudiate papal authority as such – was 'Romanised'. This in itself is not of great consequence. What is of the utmost importance is that the reorganisation of the clergy, instigated by Queen Margaret, deliberately displaced one language and substituted another. English-speaking clerics were introduced; English-dominated trade was encouraged; there was an influx of English and Anglo-Norman families of high social status; and, in general, there was a replacement of Gaelic personnel in ecclesiastical and judicial positions.

Not all of these changes took place at once or were completed in one generation. Some were only initiated, or consolidated, during the reign of succeeding kings. For example, the policy of planting burghs as centres of trade, predominantly Anglo-Saxon in speech, and loyal to the new dispensation, in purely Gaelic-speaking parts of Scotland was carried out over a lengthy period. It must be said also that the processes of change are often tantalisingly obscure. In the domain of law, to take one important field, there is no evidence of organic continuity between the *judex* (the *breitheamh* 'brehon' of Gaelic law) and the justiciar of the Anglo-Norman system. Yet some Gaelic terminology survived the transformation of the legal order.[10] And it is true, too, that certain of the Anglo-Norman magnates – Frasers, Comyns, Grants, etc. – who were given lands north of Forth and Clyde did become Gaelicised and in Gaelic are still commonly referred to by Gaelicised forms of their names: Frisealaich, Cuimeinich, Granntaich, and so on. But these are only counter-currents that had little perceptible effect on the overall flow of cultural and linguistic change.

The plain fact is that during the reign of Malcolm and Margaret what has been described as a shift to an English way-of-life was deliberately planned and, as far as possible, implemented. The court became English and Norman-French in speech and the loss of status which that entailed for Gaelic in Scotland was profound and permanent. This aggressive Anglicising policy was continued by the sons of Malcolm and Margaret and intensified in response to the fierce Gaelic reaction which followed King Malcolm's death, in 1093, and which flared up intermittently until the early thirteenth century.[11] In Moray, one of the most active centres of Gaelic resistance, there was ruthless displacement of population. In no way can such events be described as 'accidents of history'.

Yet, even at court level, one leading social institution survived for some time. As late as 1249, at Scone, the boy king Alexander the Third was inaugurated as King of Scots according to the traditional Gaelic inauguration ceremony.[12] The reason is clear. Without that age-old ritual by which a Gaelic ruler was 'married' to his land and people, Alexander's kingship would not have been valid in the eyes of his Gaelic subjects. There may have been other survivals, or other compromises, about which history is silent.

Gaelic however was no longer the full *sermo regius* of Scotland and now was fated never to fulfil what had seemed to be its destiny: to become the language of cultured society throughout the kingdom and the medium of expression in its leading institutions. Instead there began the process which ultimately banished it to the remote and inaccessible parts of the land and, although development did not by any means cease, Gaelic was largely cut off, in the high Middle Ages, from the great innovating movements of the later medieval period, and particularly those of post-medieval Europe.

In the Norse-dominated areas of Scotland, the linguistic patterns are not very plain. In the southern Hebrides, for instance, Gaelic was strongly established for centuries before the Norsemen appeared. The same situation presumably obtained in at least part of the north-western mainland, if not in the northern Outer Hebrides. During one period of Norse occupation, it has been suggested, Norse alone was spoken in the Island of Lewis, but that period has not been dated. The received opinion is that, in most areas, Norse and Gaelic communities flourished side by side and that Norse-Gaelic bilingualism must have been prevalent. If so, one would expect Norse to have been the dominant partner where, to the present day, place-names of Norse origin are still dense on the ground. The Hebrides themselves were long known in Gaelic as *Innse Gall* 'The Isles of the Foreigners', and the name still survives, though as a literary rather than as a vernacular term.

In the mid-twelfth century, the process of re-Gaelicising the Norse territories began.[13] The campaign was led by Somerled, whose personal name is of Norse origin but whose descent can be traced back to a leading Dalriadic kindred. In 1266 the Hebrides were formally ceded by Norway to the crown of Scotland. 'The Isles of the Foreigners and Coastland of the Gaels' (the Hebrides and Argyll) became a quasi-

independent state, a Gaelic confederation known in English as the
'Lordship of the Isles'. It was a new centre of Gaelic culture and loyalty
which exerted a powerful influence on most of the north-west mainland of Scotland. In terms of political and military organisation, no
less than cultural patronage and diversity, it is as if Gaelic Alba had
been reaffirmed and recreated within narrower territorial limits. But
although the connection with the older Gaelic kingdom of all Scotland
was not forgotten, the centre of gravity had now moved back into the
Dalriadic area, nearer Ireland, and these two major Gaelic cultures,
both no doubt in process of developing different characteristics,
became strongly linked again. Ireland reassumes a dominant role;
Scotland becomes rather marginalised. This is a view taken from the
heights of Gaelic culture and it does not reveal all. For our part, we
could be in danger of applying too rigorously the canons of linguistic
orthodoxy that we derive from Irish schools of learning.

In the twelfth century, just as the foundations of the Lordship were
being laid in Scotland, a new literary order in Ireland was codifying
the language for poetic and other purposes. Through patronage of
hereditary learned families under the Lordship of the Isles, Scots
participated in these developments: the 'reformed' language which
we call Classical Gaelic was common to the learned orders of Ireland
and Scotland and taught to children of the aristocracy. In Scotland,
that Classical Common Gaelic survived almost to the middle of the
eighteenth century. The literary remains (so much was destroyed, by
accident or design) show an enormous preponderance of material of
Irish provenance. It would seem as if an entire corpus of Scottish-
centred literature – sagas of the early Gaelic kings, for instance – had
been neglected or lost. Anglicisation of the dynasty, the move of Gaelic
power from the east of Scotland back to the west, and the acquisition
by the Lords of the Isles of extensive lands in Ulster must all have
played a part.[14] In the process, we may have lost invaluable linguistic
data, too.

The Classical Gaelic which unites the writers of the 'sea-divided
Gael', simply because it is a standardised language, obscures the
dialectal developments which of course were going on beneath that
linguistic cover. Here and there, departures from the strictest canons
of orthodoxy have been detected. In the mid-twelfth century or a little
earlier, the *notitiae* in the Book of Deer, in addition to 'spellings [. . .]
due to the carelessness and ignorance of the scribes of this remote
monastery' (i.e., remote from *Ireland*), there are a few traces of what

might be vernacular influence. The scribes were not 'in very close touch with the standards of the Irish bardic schools' and consequently did not 'write a high-class literary Common Gaelic'.[15] In sixteenth-century Gaelic prose, in a writer such as Bishop John Carswell, there are some features which are distinctively Scottish. A thorough investigation of the whole canon of Scottish writers of Classical prose will probably show that this is not so very uncommon. Such flexibility, found throughout history in literate societies and traditions, would seem to be natural enough and, indeed, desirable on several grounds, unless we are measuring it all with a somewhat artificial yardstick.

The connection with Ireland and the perspective adopted by the now linguistically English-orientated central powers brought about the use of the term 'Irish' instead of 'Scottis' for Gaelic. 'Ersche' or 'Erse' are dialect variants. The change in nomenclature reflects and symbolises a more complex process of thought with regard to the place of the Gaels and their language in Scotland. In the thirteenth century, Gaelic was still a familiar tongue on the east coast, 'from the Ord of Caithness to Queensferry' on the River Forth. By the middle of the fourteenth century, however, it was being pushed north and west, broadly speaking, of what much later was known as the 'Highland Line' and the Gaelic language and culture became associated with the mountainous regions of the kingdom. The notion of 'Highland versus Lowland', used qualitatively, had come into being.[16]

The basically Anglian dialect of the Lowlands, long known as 'Inglis', was fostered as the national language. It was only in the fifteenth century that the name of 'Scottis' was appropriated by the speakers of Inglis. The Gaels, for their part, did not return the compliment by referring to the Lowlanders as *Sasannaich* 'Saxons': they simply continued to call them by the name of *Gall* (originally a Gaul, then generalised to mean a foreigner; applied to the Norse, as we have seen, and to Anglo-Saxons and Anglo-Normans). This in fact is still the Gaelic for a Lowland Scot and *Galldachd* the Gaelic for the Lowlands: 'Saxons' begin at the Border. The Lowlanders did not regard themselves as Saxons either but as Scots, with a perfect right to the name; even if in the sixteenth century we may read of the Gaels with their 'alde Irishe toung' in contrast to the Lowlanders and their 'auld Saxoune toung'.

It is not a matter of language alone. Writing in the late 1380s, John of Fordun made his celebrated remarks:

> The manners and customs of the Scots vary with the diversity of their speech [. . .]. The people of the coast are of domestic and civilised habits, trusty, patient, and urbane, decent in their attire, affable and peaceful, devout in Divine worship [. . .]. The Highlanders and people of the Islands, on the other hand, are a savage and untamed nation, rude and independent, given to rapine, ease-loving, of a docile and warm disposition, comely in person, but unsightly in dress, hostile to the English people and language, and owing to diversity of speech, even to their own nation, and exceedingly cruel.[17]

This description gives expression to a profoundly significant shift of perception within Scotland. In fact, it is one of the earliest stereotypes of an 'Aboriginal' people. The model selects and focuses on characteristics that are emphasised in similar descriptions of 'Natives' to the present day. It includes latent contradictions of the common stereotyped kind: warmth and docility, on the one hand; hostility and cruelty, on the other; but these are not difficult to reconcile: savages are not predictable. From now on, the Gaels are the 'Wild Scots'.

To some extent, there is a countervailing view, even if it operates with in the same limits of perception, to be found in the historical writings of the sixteenth century. John Major (1521) declares that 'most of us spoke Irish a short time ago'. Hector Boece (1527) endorses this: 'The Hieland hes baith the writingis and language as thay [i.e. the ancestors of all Scots] had afore, more ingenius than ony othir pepill.' Bishop John Leslie (1578) is even more assertive:

> Behaulde now the maneris, wt quilkes the Scottis of ald was induet, bot quhy say I of ald? quhen thay, quha this day wt vs speik the ald scottis toung, planelie haue the selfe sam maneris. For quha this day ar, haue hitherto keipet the institutiounis of thair eldaris sa constantlie, that nocht onlie mair than 2 thowsand yeirs they haue keipet the toung hail vncorrupte; bot lykewyse the maner of cleithing and leiuing.[18]

George Buchanan, the great Humanist, was a pupil of John Major; both of them shared a common interest in the origins and development of the kingdom. Buchanan was a Gael but refers to Gaelic with contempt as a speech of 'barbarous sounds'. Progress towards culture demanded we shed what had 'accrued to us by the infelicity of our birth'.[19] The outstanding Humanist's ideas were of course shaped by his classical learning but though he rejected his native Gaelic he none the less wrote Scots with Ciceronian eloquence. Buchanan had internalised the attitudes of John of Fordun and his successors. It is a process of acculturation which is still vestigially with us.

The historians who acknowledged the place of the Gaelic language in the life of Scotland were principally concerned to maintain a sense of the continuity of Scottish history. Their views, governed by that concern and limited to its own sphere, evidently did not impinge greatly upon the world of contemporary Lowland literature. William Dunbar, a man of Lothian, firmly rejects the entire Gaelic tradition, most vividly in his Flyting (verse debate) with Walter Kennedy. So much is clear, even when full allowance is made for the conventions of the form. Among all writers of Inglis, Kennedy stands out as the stoutest champion of Gaelic. But Kennedy was a native of Ayrshire, then Gaelic-speaking, and himself presumably had some knowledge of the language. Nevertheless, he does not write in it. The centre of the Gaelic world was not in Ayrshire but north of the Clyde where the Lords of the Isles and Coastland of the Gaels held the power.

As the creation of the Lordship of the Isles represents a major triumph in re-grouping the forces of Gaelic after a fall from greatness, so does the destruction of that polity represent a major defeat. The Lordship had preserved peace and stability over a wide area of the Gaelic lands. Its destruction unleashed an anarchy, still remembered in Gaelic tradition, which was then used as an excuse for 'pacification' of the Highlands and Islands. This policy of pacification meant quite simply the destruction of Gaelic political and military power by the Crown and Parliament of Scotland in the interests of an emergent consolidated state. The policy of 'civilising', which meant the deliberate rooting out of all Gaelic, was to come later.

With the forfeiture of the Lordship of the Isles to the Crown in 1493, the second line of defence of Gaelic as a literate culture had been breached, but the world of Gaelic learning was not yet destroyed. Patronage of learned orders was maintained, albeit in diminished circumstances, by various clan chiefs, and enough survived for Classical Gaelic to transform itself, through the poets and through the church, into a written vernacular. The continuity of Gaelic as a *written* language, in its historical circumstances, is the central strand of the present account. It is far too often ignored.

The Protestant Reformation, recognised by the Parliament of Scotland in 1560, affected the whole of the kingdom. The popular idea that the Lowlands at this point became Protestant while the Highlands remained Catholic is superficial: the divisions were much more complicated. The first fruits of the Reformers' policy of giving the people Christian instruction in their own language was a translation of the Book of Common Order, sometimes called John Knox's Liturgy, done by John Carswell, whose name has already been noted, into Classical Gaelic. This is the first printed book (1567) in any Celtic language.[20] The language is vernacular in the sense that it is not Latin but it is scarcely 'the vulgar tongue' through which the Reformation aimed to reach the common people. However, in the Catechism which Carswell added to the Liturgy (based on Calvin's Little Catechism but considerably expanded) the language is simpler and vernacular syntax and vocabulary are in evidence throughout. About 1630, Calvin's Larger Catechism appeared; it too is in Classical Gaelic, with some Scottish Gaelic colouring. The translator was probably the poet Niall MacEoghain; his father Athairne MacEoghain is the putative author of two of the poems prefixed to the Catechism.

This process went on fairly steadily. In 1725 a translation of the Confession of Faith was printed by the Synod of Argyll; it is in vernacular Gaelic, although the orthography is still partly that of the Classical language. After that, other denominations made similar contributions, beginning with the Rev. Robert Menzies' translations of Roman Catholic devotional works: the 'Christian Teaching' (1781) and Thomas à Kempis's *Imitatio Christi* (1785). The Episcopalian Book of Common Prayer was published in Gaelic in 1794.

The watershed between Classical and vernacular, however, lies in a small text completed in 1652 (we only have the second edition, of 1659): the Gaelic translation of the Shorter Catechism of the West-minster Assembly. It has been described as representing

> the spoken language of Scotland with some rather half-hearted attempt at keeping up the fiction of a standard literary language different from the spoken one. The same sort of language appears in the preface to the complete Metrical Psalms in 1694, though in the text itself metrical considerations led to a preference for the older, more compact, constructions. It is also clear that it was the ministers who produced [it] and who must be considered responsible for its language.[21]

Viewed in another perspective, what they achieved was in fact a remarkably skilful transition from Classical Gaelic to vernacular Gaelic and in that lie the origins of Scottish Gaelic literary prose. In particular sections of their catechism, we can see an organic connection with Carswell's translation, mediated by the Gaelic 'Calvin's Catechism', with a further contribution drawn from the Irish Prayer Book. Fragile as these links may be, they indicate both the scope of the writers' awareness and the continuity of Gaelic prose. In verse, there was the stylistic problem of reproducing the 'common metre' of the English psalms in Gaelic. Here the translators had the assistance of one John MacMarquess, as well as that of Mr David Simpson, a minister who had learnt Gaelic under the auspices of the Synod of Argyll. Behind all this, we can sense the co-operation, as well as the disagreements, of a number of men of diverse cultural backgrounds, and glimpse the fascinating confluence of secular and clerical activities. The MacMarquesses are earlier on record as a learned family of poets and John MacMarquess 'able in the Irish language' is clearly a worthy representative; the MacEwens (MacEoghain), to whom Niall and Athairne belonged, were the hereditary poets to the Campbells of Argyll; both of these kindreds, probably, were branches of well-known Irish bardic families who settled in Scotland under the patronage extended by the Lords of the Isles; and the learned Bishop Carswell himself almost certainly derived his learning from them in the first place.

At earlier stages in the history of the language, and perhaps running parallel with ecclesiastical activities, similar transitions were occurring in the vernacularisation of manuscript romances and heroic ballads and the like. These were generally less formal developments. But there were probably more deliberate strategies also. There are poems, for instance, poised linguistically and metrically between Classical and vernacular Gaelic, but part of a process that is ever bringing them nearer common speech, which can hardly be anything other than the work of literate poets modifying the older literary tradition.

As elsewhere, translation of the Bible is crucial. Here the structural organisations under whose auspices the task was carried out were the Church of Scotland and the SSPCK: the Society in Scotland for Propagating Christian Knowledge. The Rev. Robert Kirk's Bible, a Scotticised modification of the Irish Bible of William O'Donnell (New Testament, 1603) and Bishop Bedell (Old Testament, 1686) was published in 1690. Subsequent translations (New Testament, 1767; Old Testament, 1738–1801) were in reality more a transformation of Kirk's Bible than a direct translation from the original languages, as the translators appeared to claim. In other words, the Classical Common Gaelic of the Irish Bible is a dominating presence throughout. A series of revisions designed among other things to demoticise the text weakened the Classical element but not before its stylistic influence had made a profound impression on the Gaelic imagination. The Rev. Fr Ewen MacEachen's Vulgate translation of 1875 is more vernacular in style but the difference is one of degree rather than kind.

Generations of Gaels acquired literacy from reading the Bible, particularly under the great religious movement of the Evangelical Revival. The movement affected most of the *Gàidhealtachd* (the area of Gaelic speech) which was at that time more or less co-extensive with the Highlands and Islands. One of its prime causes was the New Testament of 1767 and as the Revival spread so did Bible reading increase in reciprocal relationship. This was the age of the great preachers, ministers and laymen alike, and in the vehement oratory of their extempore sermons and prayers the Gaelic language was transformed. All this was potentially liberating and stultifying. The intense concentration on religion discouraged or forbade the development of Gaelic in fiction. On the other hand, a vocabulary of theological and philosophical terms became familiar currency, extending into other fields of discussion and analysis. One of the most influential writers, the Rev. Dr Norman MacLeod (*Caraid nan Gàidheal* 'Friend of the Gaels', 1783–1862), in addition to his purely ecclesiastical output, founded and edited periodicals in which his declared aim was to provide his readers with 'every kind of useful information' which had hitherto been 'locked up in English books'. In these sources and in similar works by later authors there are writings on history, geography, the natural sciences, current affairs, and book reviews. The literary essay became a prominent form. Beginning in 1750, translations from English continued to increase in volume throughout the nineteenth century. They are virtually all religious in content and most works of Puritan divinity.[22]

Gaelic prose of the nineteenth and early twentieth centuries developed from pre-existing traditions a formal standard register which, at its best, has a classical lucidity and balance. Its strength is most evident in expository writing; there, the vigour and unpredictability of unrestrained nature are kept at a distance. An inhibitory puritanical code (which still operates) restricts it further but the periodic style, in itself, is inadequate for full 'creative' writing. The immensely rich tradition of oral story-telling had much to offer in this field. There are collections of folktales from 1860 onwards. The mere act of writing, however, and telling at dictation speed, could take away from the vividness of the living voice; in any case, published collections for the most part consist of heroic tales and romances in contrast to the more naturalistic legends and anecdotes. The positive influences on mainstream Gaelic prose from this quarter are not great. Only in the twentieth century, with the founding of the literary periodical *Gairm* (1952) and new opportunities afforded by radio for short-story writing, was Gaelic freed from the rigidity of its older conventions. There is now high promise and a long way still to go.

Over the last two hundred years and more, a great corpus of poetry has been published. From a linguistic point of view, Gaelic verse is remarkable for its idiomatic richness and flexibility even, at times particularly, when it is at its most pedestrian according to some literary criteria. Verse translation does not bulk large; there are curiosities such as the Rev. John Smith's Gaelic Ossian in the 1780s; its linguistic interest is much higher than its literary value. In the 1790s and early 1800s, Ewen MacLachlan translated Books 1-7 and part of Book 8 of the *Iliad*: these were first published together in 1937. John Maclean, the twentieth century translator of the *Odyssey*, pays tribute to MacLachlan's 'facility in Gaelic and his tremendous, and sometimes daring, power in forming compound words. Indeed, his Gaelic vocabulary is far more copious than Homer's Greek one.'[23]

In spite of the significance of ecclesiastical activities to the development of Gaelic and to its modulation from a Classical literary language to a written form of vernacular Gaelic, with its own emergent standards, there is an entrenched belief that the Reformed church has been consistently hostile to Gaelic culture. That view is founded on the following facts.

In 1609 the Scots Parliament, through the Statutes of Icolmkill ('Iona of Columba'), provided for the suppression of bards (the panegyrists of Gaelic society) and the education, in English, of the sons of gentlemen. Previously, the upper classes were educated in Classical Gaelic. In 1616 the Privy Council passed an act (confirmed by Parliament in 1631) in favour of the removal of the 'Irish' language in the Highlands and Islands. These anti-Gaelic attitudes were reinforced by the Civil War of the 1640s, when the ferocity of Alasdair mac Colla's Irish and Highland warriors left vivid and dreadful memories in Lowland minds. Although the campaign was by no means solely religious in motivation, a religious dimension did undoubtedly exist. Alasdair was himself of a Catholic branch of Clan Donald with strong family and military connections with Ireland. In the Lowlands it was well known that an Irish Franciscan mission had been making large-scale conversions among the Gaels of Scotland in the 1620s. The troubled state of Ireland was known to all. In 1626 the powerful chief of Clan Ranald had written to Pope Urban VIII offering to lead a jihad of Irish and Scottish Gaels to restore most of Scotland to the Roman faith. The Civil War, therefore, raised a spectre in Lowland eyes of invasion by the barbarian hordes. From now on, all Gaels, Protestant and Catholic alike, would be under suspicion of being Papists, in sympathy at least, and their 'Irish' language, emblem of their alien manners, was subjected to even more intense persecution.

In 1646 the General Assembly of the Church of Scotland passed a resolution demanding implementation of the Statutes of Icolmkill and the setting up of English schools in every Highland parish. These parochial schools, of which twenty-four had been established in Argyll by 1698, never changed their policy with regard to Gaelic. The shift in political alignment at the Restoration of Charles II, and the restoration of Episcopacy in the Church of Scotland, gave the Gaels (who were in the main royalist: faithful to the descendants of the ancient line of their kings) a brief respite from further extension of English-language schools. But this does not mean that Gaelic was re-instated or given any administrative status in high places. Indeed, some of the Synod of Argyll's work of translation was suspended. Relaxation of English education was paralleled by neglect of Gaelic; and the language, after the Revolution Settlement, was in no stronger position than before to withstand renewed attack. In 1696 the Education Act of 1646 (repealed in 1662) was re-enacted. In 1699 the General Assembly passed an act *Anent Planting in the Highlands* which firmly endorses the establishment of 'English School-Masters [. . .] in all Highland parishes, according to former Acts of Parliament and General Assemblies'.[24] The same act, however, addresses itself to the problems of distributing Gaelic Bibles, the continuance of Gaelic translation of catechisms and psalms in metre, and the provision of a Gaelic-speaking ministry.

We have already noticed the good offices of the SSPCK with regard to the translation of the Bible. That is one side of the story. The declared aim of the Society, founded in 1709, was to root out 'Irish' and 'Papistry' in the Highlands and Islands. To that end, all teaching in its schools was to be in English only and centred on the Bible in English. The policy failed. It was eventually realised that a knowledge of English could only be inculcated through prior literacy in Gaelic and in 1767 the prohibition on the use of Gaelic (previously, and through necessity, often observed in the breach) was officially and finally reversed. In the same year, the New Testament was published in Gaelic. As we have already observed, it was more a modification of earlier Gaelic versions than a translation from first principles and there is a strong Classical element in its diction. But at last, two centuries after the Reformation, the aim of giving the common people the Scriptures in their own tongue was at least in sight of being realised. The fact that the New Testament was in a register of Gaelic only reasonably accessible to all Gaelic speakers is a comment on the cultural attitudes of the Gaels themselves. Classical Gaelic, the dignified language of the learned orders, still commanded respect. The 1767 translation actually strikes an interesting balance between Classical Gaelic and the vulgar tongue. If its language required, as is said, local, extempore glossing from the pulpit, so, too, it may be, as some ecclesiastical tradition avers, that certain ministers were aware of the dangers of the hitherto illiterate faithful becoming too well-versed in the Scriptures. This was not purely on doctrinal grounds. The Gaelic ministers were gentlemen, drawn mainly from the upper ranks of society, and had a position to keep.

There is almost an air of unreality about some of those facts. On the one hand, there is the contribution of the post-Reformation church to translation of the Bible and other religious books; on the other, the hostility of the central authorities of Scotland, often operating through a conjunction of church and state, towards Gaelic and a deliberate policy of rooting it out. A native Gaelic ministry is established; side by side with it, English-language schools are 'planted'. The SSPCK is set up to destroy Gaelic and ends as a staunch ally of the language.

There was, in fact, a genuine ambivalence. The received opinion may be summarised by saying there was a clear-cut divide between secular and sacred. In the former, Gaelic was banned, or at least consistently discouraged; in the latter, it was encouraged, or at least allowed. Thus while the SSPCK eventually supported Gaelic, it was mainly for the purpose of religious instruction; and much the same can be said about other church and voluntary schools. The parochial schools remained anglicised. But, in the reality of the human situation, divisions of that kind are only approximate. People who became literate in the Gaelic Bible and in translations of works of English Puritan divinity and the like went on to extend their activities.

There is an ambivalence also in the attitudes of the Gaelic ministry. The ministers, like the Scottish clergy in general, were men of considerable learning. They were representatives of an established state church and supporters of a conservative social order. But they were also, with a few exceptions, native Gaels who had a deep loyalty to their own language and culture. Tradition depicts them as worldly men: they were devoted to music, the classics, and literature in general; and some of them were even pious. According to the same oral tradition, they never, in Gaelic, spoke against the secular culture, let alone the language, just because it was Gaelic. Yet curiously there is ample evidence in various reports that some of them wrote in *English* of adherence to the anti-Gaelic prejudices of the central authorities. Notable among those who expressed very different opinions, and in English, is the Rev. Donald MacNicol, author of a book, written as a counterblast to Dr Samuel Johnson, in which he defends the continuity of Gaelic literary and linguistic tradition.[25] One cannot but suspect sometimes that writings in English only pay lip-service to the official line. The great Jacobite and Gaelic-nationalist poet of the Forty-Five, Alasdair mac Mhaighstir Alasdair, must have been doing exactly that in his extremely 'proper' reports, written while he was an SSPCK schoolmaster.

It is to Presbyterian ministers of the eighteenth century – the Rev. Alexander Pope, the Rev. James Maclagan and the Rev. MacNicol – that we owe the compilation of those great collections of vernacular poetry from oral tradition on which modern editions of Gaelic poets, from the seventeenth century onwards, are largely based. The orthography they used to put this considerable body of textual material in writing follows essentially the conventions developed by the Synod of Argyll. There are, of course, many local variations and personal idiosyncrasies.

The clerical collectors' great exemplar was mac Mhaighstir Alasdair himself. In 1751 he had his own poems published: the first printed book of secular poetry in Gaelic. In 1776 his son Ranald published an anthology which is at least partly drawn from his father's repository. Alasdair could read Classical Gaelic and collected manuscripts, some from the MacMhuirich family of Classical poets and historians. It is not impossible that Niall MacMhuirich (*c.* 1637–1726), who composed two poems in vernacular Gaelic, wrote these down himself; but Alasdair was a bold innovator (as the language of his poetry for one thing shows). His writing of Gaelic to some degree represents an independent line.

A totally different orthography, based on that of Inglis/Scots, appears in the Book of the Dean of Lismore (*c.* 1530) from Perthshire; the Fernaig MS (*c.* 1690) from Ross-shire, much farther north, employs a roughly similar system. Literacy in Scots relates to provenance (the Gaelic-Scots border) and to social class. In fugitive pieces, e.g. song texts taken down in the nineteenth and early twentieth centuries by writers who were more literate in English than in Gaelic, one may easily detect the influence of English orthography; there are, indeed, evidences of the same influence, or that of Scots, in the manuscripts of the eighteenth century. None the less, these are side-tracks. Throughout the history of Gaelic in Scotland there is a continuity of an 'orthodox' orthographical system which can be traced back, through all its vicissitudes, from the present day to the cultural alliance of the Dalriadic kingdom and the early Gaelic church centred in Iona. The significance of this linguistic and literary continuum had undoubtedly been obscured by an insistence on the *oral* development of the whole Gaelic tradition. This is one of the reasons why Gaelic is occasionally referred to as a 'peasant' language.

A contrast is sometimes drawn between the rather frigid style of the older, mainstream Gaelic prose and the vividness and flexibility of colloquial speech. The two kinds of discourse are, of course, complementary. The real point is that Gaelic, due to the constraints of history, was not allowed to develop its formal registers with anything like the scope that writers of more favoured languages take for granted. Hence, as already noted, there is a 'standard' Gaelic which has an air of remaining aloof from the world of immediate experience with its warmth, its roughness, and its delicateness. This is so even when writers draw upon their own localisms. Gaelic writing of the second half of the twentieth century has wrought a transformation in this respect but there are still unexploited riches in the dialects.

The scientific study of Gaelic dialects belongs to the twentieth century. At the end of the seventeenth century the Welsh polymath Edward Lhuyd made lists of equivalents from an Argyll and an Inverness-shire speaker. Through the orthography used in the Book of the Dean of Lismore and the Fernaig MS, it is possible to glean some information; and there are other, lesser sources. The native pioneer was the Rev. C. M. Robertson, whose descriptive articles, especially those of mainland dialects, are still of great interest and information. Alexander MacBain, of the Etymological Dictionary, wrote about his own eastern Highland dialect. George Henderson (though his work is unequal) and John Fraser both made contributions. Robertson's and Fraser's studies underlie the Scottish element in Thomas O'Rahilly's *Irish Dialects Past and Present*. But after the publication of Dieckhoff's dictionary (1932: it is concerned primarily with phonology) it is the work of the Scandinavian scholars, Borgstrøm, Holmer and Oftedal, that ushers in the scientific age. To these are now to be added the names of Dilworth, Dorian, MacAulay, Ó Murchú, and Ternes.

The Gaelic Linguistic Survey of Scotland, set up by the University of Edinburgh in 1949-50, has covered the whole of the Gaelic-speaking area of Scotland, including parts of the periphery where the language is now dead.[26] The dialects are considered to fall into two major groups: the 'central' and the 'peripheral'. The criteria are principally phonological, positing a central area of innovation, from which change is diffused, and a peripheral area of conservation. According to K.H. Jackson, formerly head of the Survey and the leading authority on its work:

> The central dialect covers the Hebrides as far south as Mull and sometimes further, Ross exclusive of the north-east corner, Assynt, Inverness-shire, western Perthshire, and mainland Argyll roughly north of Loch Awe; while the peripheral dialects comprise Caithness and Sutherland exclusive of Assynt, the north-east corner of Ross, Braemar, eastern Perthshire, the rest of mainland Argyll with Kintyre, and Arran. Moray and the adjacent lower region of the Spey, the wide valley of Strathspey from Rothiemurchus to the Moray border, may go with the peripheral dialects, linking up with Braemar and east Perth.

It is important to emphasise that 'peripheral' dialects may in other respects, e.g. in shedding inflexions, be innovative. Indeed, even on phonological grounds, there are isoglosses that divide the Gàidhealtachd roughly north and south or east and west.

There is some debate about mutual intelligibility of dialects. Native speakers are sometimes rather insensitive about isoglosses and prefer to get on with the conversation. A speaker of north-west Sutherland Gaelic can converse with a speaker from 'distant' Islay for example with consummate ease. To all Gaels regional variation is a question of *blas* – basically articulation and intonation – with word-endings, especially in the verbal noun, ranking next. Over the whole area, syntactical variation is minimal. Mutual comprehension, of course, involves individual skills and confidence. Bilingual speakers can always switch to English. Monoglot Gaels or (nowadays much more likely) those with an indifferent knowledge of English, being denied this option, show more stamina. It is noticeable that individuals vary so much in competence that speakers of closely related varieties of Gaelic may complain of difficulty while speakers of apparently dissimilar dialects find none.

It is interesting that the Classical Gaelic history of the campaign of Alasdair mac Colla tells of a conversation between the son of the chief of Clan Ranald (in the west) and 'an honourable old man' from Angus (in the east and even then on the Gaelic-Scots boundary) who discussed history with the men from the west.[27] This conversation, reported partly in direct speech in Classical Gaelic, may have been in Scots, in the vernacular, or in Classical Gaelic, which the chief's son would know and which the old man would also know, if he was a professional historian. In any case, there is no indication of difficulty in communicating. A knowledge of Classical Gaelic must have been more widely diffused than some scholars allow. There is a received opinion that it was unintelligible to the common people. But this is really a matter of whether, like any other language, the style and content were simple or difficult. We have an excellent example of the former in a letter (a mere chance survival) of Sir James MacDonald of Islay in 1604 to his 'friends and kinsmen'.[28] No Gael now, and *a fortiori* then, literate or not, on hearing it read aloud, could possibly miss its import. More difficult prose is also intelligible, even to those who have no knowledge of, e.g., older Biblical Gaelic, as a radio experiment once demonstrated.

In contrast to Irish, for example, Scottish Gaelic is remarkably uniform. This presumably argues that communities were never for long cut off from contact with each other. A contributing factor here, however slight, may be the circuits of the vernacular bards from one patron's house to another, from Argyll and Perthshire to the Isle of Skye and beyond. They were oral poets but the highest grades enjoyed much social esteem. The poetry itself, even after we discount possible editorial co-operation and emendation in our manuscripts, clearly had a shared diction and offered, as it still does, morphological and lexical options that have probable origins in different dialects. But this could only operate on a superficial level. Clearly there were other contacts, with exogamous marriage at the centre. The mountain passes of the Highlands are scored with ancient tracks which help to explain dialectal patterns as well. Among the maritime and island communities, there was constant travel by sea. The dialects of north-west Skye, for instance, have strikingly more features in common with Uist and Harris, across the Minch, than they have with north-east and south Skye. Lewis shares features not with adjacent Harris, from which it is separated by desolate mountainous terrain, but with Sutherland (particularly Assynt) and Ross-shire on the far opposite mainland. There, we are looking also at old, sea-linked clan territories. Geography and alliances of kindred together affect the very precise and limited distribution of one variety of nasal mutation, found only in Lewis, Assynt, three parishes of Skye, and the island of Raasay.

By way of contrast, the narrow channel between Skye and the mainland, separating two important clan territories, still separates two dissimilar dialects. These differences in Gaelic are all differences of *cainnt* 'speech' as opposed to *càna(i)n* 'language', and a speaker's origins are recognised by *cainnt*.

Gaelic has naturally been affected by the languages and cultures with which it came in contact. One feature has attracted much attention: preaspiration, a term which covers (i) a period of voicelessness between vowel and stop (ii) an /h/ before a stop (iii) voiceless fricative before a stop. The consonants affected are 'p', 't', 'c'. While there is some disagreement about its origin – Holmer called it 'circumpolar' (Icelandic, Faroese, some Norwegian dialects, Finnish, etc.) – Norse is favoured by the majority. Some marginal dialects seem not to have developed preaspiration at all, among them those of the North Sea coastal area where a strong Norse influence might be predicted; whereas west Perthshire in the southern Highlands shows the fullest development. A fresh movement of Gaels from further south in the twelfth century may have been responsible for overlaying the north coast dialects. Preaspiration is said to be confined to Scotland and unknown in Ireland: in fact, it is distinctly perceptible in at least one variety of Donegal Irish.

Published studies of intonation are few. The dialects of Caithness, Sutherland and parts of Ross on the mainland and Lewis were regarded by native speakers, within and without that group, as having qualities of intonation that distinguish them from other varieties of Gaelic. The latest writer to comment on this is Oftedal: 'Tonality is another part of the phonological system where Norse seems to have influenced Gaelic, but only [. . .] on the Isle of Lewis and on the mainland coast opposite Lewis.' It is to be noted that Oftedal (like the native Gaelic-speaking Henderson before him) limits the area to Lewis and Sutherland but adds: 'Methodical investigation of these phenomena is still only at an initial stage.'[29]

Gaelic, as we saw, spread throughout Pictland and into the British areas. It must therefore have been acquired as a second language, with periods of bilingualism, by a large proportion of the population. More than one scholar has seen a reflection of this in the syntax of the verb, both Manx and Gaelic. Greene puts the view succinctly: 'Scottish Gaelic and Manx [. . .] have brought the verbal system inherited from Old Irish into complete conformity with that of modern spoken Welsh [. . .]. The argument for the influence of the substratum seems very strong.'[30]

The cultural influences are, however, best displayed in the loanwords. Out of a larger number which may be Pictish or British, only four seem certain: *monadh/munadh* 'mountainous land, moor'; *preas* 'bush, thicket': *dail* 'field, meadow'; and *pòr* 'crop' which is Pictish. Some two hundred and fifty words are from Latin, almost all of ecclesiastical provenance with a few later medical terms. Norse loans have been estimated at around three hundred and shown not to have penetrated as far towards the semantic centre of Gaelic as Latin and English words. Very many of them are peripheral, i.e. used only in a limited set of situations or by certain groups of speakers. A large number are technical terms of fishing and navigation. Oftedal points out that this is puzzling, since Norse occupation lasted for five centuries, and suggests that the solution 'can only be found by co-ordinate research in several disciplines'.[31] It may be added that the paucity of Pictish/British loanwords is puzzling too. In each case, it would seem, Gaelic, as the dominant culture, was not receptive.

Conversely, English and Scots loanwords are predictably the most numerous and through the contact of many centuries have affected every area of the language. A large number are semantically central, i.e. used by most speakers in everyday speech in relation to everyday objects and activities. Moreover, they are now increasing almost daily. The oldest loans are completely assimilated to the phonology and morphology; a second group, not all of them recent borrowings, are partially assimilated; a third group remain more or less in their original form. The qualification there applies in two areas: initial mutation and verbal noun endings. E.g. 'kink' or 'quota' will undergo lenition from [c] → [ç/x] and, equally, nasalisation (eclipsis), the latter being realised in Scottish Gaelic in basically three ways, according to dialect. In the most vigorous dialects all new loans with initial 'b'/'p';

'g'/'c'; 't' tend to be regularly lenited and nasalised; 'd' is nasalised, more rarely lenited; 'r' and 'm' are lenited. The liquids, nasals and 'r' are not subject to nasalisation in Gaelic nor, in most dialects, are 'f' and 's'. Lenition may affect 's' but is very rare with 'f'. There is, however, a very perceptible degree of difference in treatment, to some extent dialectal but most of all generational.

Practically any borrowed verb can be fitted with an ending in -'adh' or -'igeadh' to form a verbal noun: e.g. 'speileadh'/'speiligeadh' ('spelling'); 'fónadh'/'fónaigeadh' ('phoning'). The simplex -'ig' < English participial ending -'ing' is used in the imperative, e.g. 'speilig e' ('spell it'). The verbal noun ending -'achdain(n)' is largely in complementary distribution with -'adh', but to some extent supplementary: it, too, is productive in this context when it is the dominant form in the dialect. In the North and West the element -'ig' in verbal nouns is associated with the Gaelic of Ross-shire, Sutherland and Lewis.

Preaspiration is sometimes the only phonological feature which indicates a degree of assimilation; morphologically, the plural will then tend to be Gaelic. (If preaspiration is absent, there is a choice between it and the English morph.) 'Clock' is usually borrowed as [klɔhk]. But preaspiration in loanwords is not necessarily as 'developed' as in native words of similar structure in a given dialect. Thus, *tac(an)* 'short time' may be [tahk-] in one dialect, [taxk-] in another: English 'tack' (i.e. a type of nail) will be realised as [tahk] in both. The initial stop here retains the alveolar articulation of English in contrast to the dental articulation of Gaelic initial 't'. Alveolar stops are easily accommodated: many dialects have them in *non*-initial position. 'Title' has been borrowed (not recently: note the vowel) as [tihtǝl] and 'tea' as [ti:] or [te-ǝ]; all with alveolar articulation.

The contrast of palatalised versus velarised is central to Gaelic phonology yet 'clock' does not have the velarised 'l' nor does e.g. [li:hc] 'leak' have the palatalised 'l', each of which would in Gaelic be appropriate (the latter in some dialects only) to its phonetic context. It is perhaps marginally relevant to note that in Gaelic as spoken to very small children, these contrasts of velarised versus palatalised and dental versus alveolar are neutralised. (Traces of this remain in a few words of adult speech in some dialects.) Twentieth-century monoglots treated loanwords, in respect of these points of articulation, in exactly the same way as bilingual speakers. But it has also to be noted that when a word has been borrowed twice, the older borrowing has been fully assimilated: e.g. 'block' (of wood) gives both [pLɔxk] and [blɔhk].

In the spoken language, in monosyllables, the most conspicuously productive plural morph is -'ichean', with some competition from -'achan'; in dissyllables, etc. it is -'an'. As with the presence of pre-aspiration, a dental articulation, which exists in Scots English in some positions (e.g. in association with following 'r') indicates the likelihood of a Gaelic plural morph: thus 'factor': -'an'. This tendency is reinforced by the existence of an agental ending in -'r(e)' in Gaelic. But the English plural morph is common here and elsewhere; and almost invariable if the English word ends with a vowel.

In the written language, the simplex -'an' is a progressive form both in loanwords and in native words; the latter are often reformed, particularly in the Gaelic of younger writers or those who have learnt Gaelic.

Structural remodelling based on English occurs on a large scale in modern spoken Gaelic and to a lesser degree in the written language. So numerous are the calques, indeed, that it is difficult to imagine how Gaelic would function nowadays if the dimension they supply were entirely removed. In the written language, prose has a higher incidence than poetry. Some calques are old and well-established; these escape notice and censure but others evoke strong criticism, particularly when they appear in print.

Switching from Gaelic to English and back is, naturally enough, common in a situation where everyone is bilingual and one language very strongly dominant. While this passes without much comment on some levels of informal speech, it is resented in formal discourse except when it is used in humorous writing and incongruities are being emphasised. There are other aspects of switching which realistic writers have not yet exploited: for instance, the endorsement of something said in Gaelic by a parallel statement in English, the language of authority.

It has to be added that there are still many speakers whose Gaelic has great lexical and idiomatic richness. One of the objectives of the Historical Dictionary of Scottish Gaelic, founded in Glasgow University's Department of Celtic in 1966, is to collect hitherto undocumented oral vocabulary. Between 1967 and 1972, Angus J. Smith visited all the Gaelic-speaking areas of Scotland. He also worked in Nova Scotia where Gaelic, carried there by emigrants in the late eighteenth and early nineteenth centuries, is still spoken by some of the older generation. The Dictionary, which is planned to cover the entire lexicon, is the last in a long series of vocabularies and dictionaries (some English-Gaelic; none purely Gaelic) beginning with Rev. Robert Kirk's vocabulary of 1702. It is a monumental undertaking and the first comprehensive dictionary to be established on scientific lexico-graphical principles throughout.

Finally, there are two events in the history of Gaelic that demand some comment: the Highland Clearances and the Education Act of 1872. The Clearances, extending from the late 1700s to the late 1800s, depleted the Gaelic-speaking population. There had been emigration before the Clearances proper began and the drain continued long after 1886, when the Land Agitation Movement won security of tenure for crofters. The psychological effects were undoubtedly profound; but there is no evidence, unfortunately, that if the Clearances had never happened Gaelic would have been, therefore, spared the effects of a policy which culminated in the Education Act of 1872. This act, by making school attendance compulsory, with no provision for Gaelic, marked the end of Gaelic education in voluntary schools. Education and English became synonymous. Gaelic literacy was now gained, if at all, at home, usually centred on family worship (on the whole, thus, in the stricter Protestant denominations) and in church. The voluntary schools, with all their limitations, had given monoglot Gaels a basic literacy and the confidence to develop the habit of letter-writing in Gaelic. That option was also taken up naturally by bilinguals. But once the effects of the 1872 Act had begun to bite, the idea of correspondence in Gaelic became more and more eccentric. The net result is that now even Gaels who are literate in both languages will converse in Gaelic and correspond with each other in English.

Since 1872 there have been important relaxations and a few encouraging developments, e.g. in 1887 recognition of Gaelic as a specific subject (to be taught through English) in high elementary classes and in some secondary schools; in 1918 the requirement placed on education authorities to make 'adequate provision' in Gaelic-speaking areas; in 1946 the introduction of Gaelic in some schools in Glasgow and elsewhere; in 1962 establishment of a Senior Leaving Certificate for learners; and, from 1959, a commitment to bilingual education, most recently in the Outer Hebrides.

In the earlier years (especially 1872–1918) the teaching profession and the school inspectorate were at best passive and for the most part implacably opposed to Gaelic, even as a subject to be taught in a limited way through the medium of English, whether they themselves were Gaelic speakers or not. It is also claimed – apparently with some justification – that the majority of Gaels were either uninterested in Gaelic in the curriculum or openly in favour of English to the exclusion of Gaelic. The reality would seem to be that while English was unquestionably preferred on grounds of utilitarian value, Gaelic was still warmly cherished as the language of church and home. Moreover, it was regarded by most people as capable of survival in those areas and at that level of society. The dichotomy, of course, however natural in the circumstances, was potentially fatal. Another aspect of the split may be seen in the failure to integrate political, economic and cultural strategies in the later nineteenth century and beyond. On the one hand, the Radical Land Movement secured victories on the economic front. On the other, An Comunn Gàidhealach (1891-) restricted itself to the cultural field, organising publication of textbooks and influencing educational policy in addition to its better known activities symbolised by the annual *Mòd*. This last is essentially a festival of music and song and draws upon similar local mods. Representatives of both movements, cultural and political, were directed by external forces rather than in control of them. In 1828, a pamphleteer by the name of McNish argued that 'until the Highlander gets the language introduced into the courts and other places of business, within the Gaelic districts, it is vain for him to think that he can raise himself.'[32] Over a century and a half later, the status of Gaelic in conspicuous public life and administration remains much as it was. This applies not only to Government institutions but throughout Gaelic society. To take one instance, the Crofters' Unions, obviously an organisation of the highest importance to the survival of a Gaelic community, does not use Gaelic as its official language, whatever may be current linguistic practice at local branch level. Such instances could be multiplied many times over.

An attempt to give Gaelic official status was made in 1981, under a Conservative Administration, when Donald Stewart (Scottish National Party) then MP for the Western Isles, introduced a Private Member's Bill. The measure did not survive its first reading. After several consultations in the 1990s and early twenty-first century about the state of Gaelic and the measures necessary for its survival, the Scottish Executive and the Scottish Parliament have been slow to pass any definitive legislation to protect the rights of Gaelic speakers and enable the unrestricted use of Gaelic in the life of the nation.

By such means Gaelic is reduced in its functioning to the level of a dialect vis-á-vis the language of the state. Gaelic lacks almost all the major social institutions without which no language can survive let alone develop its full potential. The institutional exceptions are the church, where the use of Gaelic is dwindling; education, to a limited degree; and the BBC's Radio nan Gàidheal. This last, though still restricted both in hours of broadcasting and in variety and intellectual scope, none the less makes a contribution of the highest importance. Gaelic TV programmes, small in number and often transmitted after the eleventh hour, literally, can only make a weak impression amidst the constant barrage of English programmes. It is the impact of the latter that is to a very large degree responsible for the wholesale switch to English among children.

On another level, a unique integration of economic and linguistic enterprise is to be seen in the organisation of business on Fearann Eilean Iarmain in the Isle of Skye, where most administration and accounting is carried out in Gaelic. This, like the college of Sabhal Mór Ostaig, which offers full-time diploma courses in business management, computer studies, etc., with instruction entirely in Gaelic, is due to the initiative and vision of Sir Iain Noble, whose own Gaelic was acquired when he came to live in Skye.

The state of Gaelic now exhibits a number of paradoxes. There has been a literary renaissance in this century. All over Scotland there is a greater awareness of and interest in the language: learners of Gaelic, distributed throughout the country, continue to increase in numbers and some of those have gone on to become serious writers. Gaelic publishing, though on a modest scale, is reasonably healthy, partly owing to subsidies mediated by the Gaelic Books Council, set up in 1968 in the Celtic Department of the University of Glasgow. A number of elementary schools have units in which Gaelic is the medium of instruction. Gaelic play-groups (very much due to the dedication of Fionnlagh MacLeòid) have been established. Comhairle nan Eilean (the Western Isles Regional authority) has a policy of bilingualism. Probably more Gaelic is being written now, if we include radio and TV journalism, than at any previous time in the history of the language.

Yet, in its heartland, the evidence of decline is undeniable. In the Lowlands, side by side with goodwill, there is still prejudice and a deep reluctance in certain quarters (as newspaper correspondence columns demonstrate from time to time) to acknowledge that Gaelic has any historical connection with Scotland south of the Highland Line.[33] It is therefore held to be irrelevant to modern, English-speaking Britain. Similar sentiments are expressed occasionally by some who now profess a 'Highland' culture defined to the exclusion of Gaelic. In part, such fixed ideas can be accounted for by ignorance of the historical facts outlined at the beginning of this chapter. But that in turn is due to the selectivity of historians and the effects of that bias in formal education. The primary causes are to be sought in the remarkably consistent hostility to Gaelic which goes back to the great cultural shift of the eleventh century. Relatively speaking, all that follows from that, throughout Scottish history, belongs to the 'surface structure' of events. Sectarian interpretations, whether focused on Romanisation or on Reformation of the church, are clearly not adequate. Neither of those reorganisations of ecclesiastical life was in itself destructive of vernacular language. In fact, as we have seen, the Gaelic clergy maintained a continuity of language and learning; in so doing, they were extending a role in which clerics had participated before the Reformation. There is a parallel in the continuity of English prose from late Old English to Middle English and other parallels can be found farther afield.

This Gaelic continuum has of course literate and non-literate aspects. The former has been emphasised here if only because it tends to be obscured in descriptions of Gaelic life. We ought to see Gaelic linguistic and orthographic tradition in a bold, linear perspective. We should not judge writers of Gaelic in Scotland (whether those are the scribes of the monastery of Deer in the twelfth century or the pioneers of vernacular written Gaelic in the seventeenth and eighteenth centuries) by standards other than their own. They were in command of their language and confident enough to deploy their rules as they saw fit. They were inheritors of the Irish tradition: 'the oldest vernacular literature in western Europe'.[34] They were also men of Alba. It is owing to their achievements that Gaelic is still so vigorous and flexible in its written forms. The hostile forces of history, however, have left it essentially a medieval European language.

Cainnt is Cànan

A dh'ainneoin cnàmh is crìonadh na Gàidhlig, tha an cànan cho beairteach fhathast is gu bheil iomadh cùil is cèal dhi a tha ri an rannsachadh. Tha sin fìor a thaobh cainnt an t-sluaigh is tha e fìor a thaobh tàrmachadh a' chànain sgrìobhte. Anns an ruith thairis a th'agam an seo air puing no dhà, duilgheadas no dhà, agus air ceistean annasach is eile, bidh aon rud co-dhiù soilleir. 'S e sin na tha ann de chuspairean air am faodadh sgoilearan òga an aire a leagail. Tha feadhainn dhe na cuspairean sin gar toirt air ais gu toiseach na Gàidhlig an Alba.

Chan eil sinn cinnteach fhathast cuin a thàinig a' Ghàidhlig a dh'Alba anns a' cheud dol a-mach, ach bha rìoghachd Ghàidhealach air bhonn an Arra-Ghàidheal man bhliadhna 500 AD. Thàinig Calum Cille agus a mhuinntir gu ruige Eilean Idhe ann an 563. Bha creideamh is sgoilearachd is ealain aig na Gàidheil ann an Alba on latha sin a-mach is tha iad aig na Gàidheil ann an Alba fhathast. Tha dùthchas gun bhristeadh, uime sin, ann an eachdraidh na Gàidhlig an Alba a bheir air ais mìle bliadhna gu leth sinn. Tha sin a' toirt leis gu bheil a' Ghàidhlig 'na cànan foghlamaichte sgrìobhte fad an réis a tha an sin.

Nuair a theirear gu bheil faclan a fhuaras air iomall duilleig ann an leabhar air choireigin a bhoineas dhan chóigeamh ceud deug, abair, air cuid dhen Ghàidhlig as sine a lorgadh riamh ann an Alba, chan eil e ciallachadh ach gu bheil na faclan a' nochdadh cainnt shonraichte a tha Albannach seach Éireannach. Ach tha leithid seo de thuaraisgeul a' mealladh dhaoine. Tha feadhainn ann cuideachd nach eil deònach urram sam bith a thoirt dhan Ghàidhlig co-dhiù, is cha mhotha dh'fhuilingeas iad aideachadh gu bheil dùthchas a' chànain sgrìobhte cho urramach no cho aosda. Tha iad sin dhan aon inntinn ris an fheadhainn a bhios a' mionnachadh nach robhar a' bruidhinn Gàidhlig riamh air Machair Alba ged a tha teist eachdraidh agus fianais ainmeannan-àite a' dearbhadh a' chaochlaidh. 'Se an fhìrinn gun do sgaoil a' Ghàidhlig air feadh Alba (ged nach robh i aig aird an t-sùil-mhara aig an aon àm sa h-uile h-àite) suas gu crìch Shasainn. Mara robh i 'na cànan aig Alba gu léir riamh (mar a thogas luchd mì-rùn cho allamh) cha mhotha sin bha aon chànan eile 'na cànan aig Alba gu léir, gos an dànaig Beurla Shasainn 'na tuil chon na Gàidhealtachd o chionn beagan agus ceud bliadhna.

Air taobh a deas na dùthcha, deas air Dùn Éideann, tha cuid de sgoilearan an là-an-diugh a' cumail a-mach nach robh ach grunnan de thighearnan móra fearainn sa chearn sin a bha 'nan Gàidheil; seadh, their iad gu robh an sluagh cumanta an sin dhen t-seann stoc Bhreatannach ach thàinig na h-Anglaich a-staigh air an fhearann aca gu math tràth nar n-eachdraidh is thug iadsan a' Bheurla dhan dùthaich sin. Tha tomhas math dhen fhìrinn an sin ceart gu leòr ach faodaidh sinn a bhith cinnteach cuideachd nach robh na tighearnan-fearainn Gàidhealach 'nan aonar: bhiodh feachd làidir cuide riutha gan cumail tèarainte. Cuimhnicheamaid gur h-ann neart air cheart le faobhar a' chlaidhimh a thug iad a-mach fearann dhaibh féin is cha chumadh iad fada e as aonais làmhachas làidir. Is dòcha nach d'fhàg an luchd-leanmhainn cumanta Gàidhealach lorg domhain no làrach a tha furasda aithneachadh ann an ceann a deas Alba, ach cha ghabh e bhith nach robh iad ann. Cha bhiodh air aon rud Sgìr Pheebles cho làn de ainmeannan Gàidhlig – ainmeannan a mhair chon an là-an-diugh – mura b'e gu robh na Gàidheil pailt san dùthaich sin uair dhe robh saoghal. Saoilidh mi gu bheil feum air sùil eile a thoirt air ainmeannan-àite an ceann a deas na rìoghachd; sùil nas mionaidiche na thugadh orra gu ruige seo.

Tha e dualach dhan a h-uile cànan fon ghréin a bhith roinnte 'na cainntean o sgìr gu sgìr agus o bhaile gu baile. Tha e furasda dhuinn a chreidsinn gum biodh na roinnean sin air an daingneachadh ann an cànan mar a bha a' Ghàidhlig a bha sgaoileadh air feadh Alba is coigrich, Cruithnich is Breatannaich, nach boineadh do shìol nan Gàidheal idir, ga h-ionnsachadh. Tha e aithnichte gu leòr gu bheil cruth air a' Ghàidhlig an Alba a bheir cruth na Cuimrig an cuimhne duine sam bith aig a bheil eòlas air na dhà. (Gu dearbha, tha dreach air a' Bheurla cuideachd a chuir an sluagh Breatannach oirre an déidh dha na Sasannaich tighinn a-nall à tìr-mór na Roinn Eorpa.) Ann an cearnan dhen Ghàidhealtachd, mar is aithne dha na h-uile, dh'fhàg na Lochlannaich an làrach fhéin air a' Ghàidhlig.

Gu dé cho tràth is a nochd na roinnean cainnte an Alba no gu dé cho tràth is a ghabh na Gàidheil fhéin beachd air an sgaradh a bha air tighinn eadar cainnt nan Éireannach agus an cainnt-san? Anns a' bhliadhna 1258, thathar ag innse dhuinn, nuair a thill Domhnall Óg Ó Domhnaill Thìr Chonaill à Alba dhachaigh a dh'Éirinn, bhruidhinn e ri teachdairean Uí Néill anns a' Ghàidhlig Albannaich. Gos o chionn ghoirid, bha sgoilearan dhen bharail gur h-ann man tritheamh ceud deug a thòisich an cànan Éireannach air dol 'na chainntean fa leth agus gu freagradh sin air Gàidhlig Alba cuideachd. Ach ga bè gu dé theirear mu Éirinn is gann a ghabhas e chreidsinn nach robh tàrmachadh cainnte cinneachadh fada roimhe sin an corra chearna de Alba am measg muinntir na tuatha – ga nach biodh 'na adhbhar air sin ach gur h-e coigrich dhan Ghàidhlig air thùs a bh'ann am móran dhiubh. Bhiodh smachd foghlaim air filidhean agus air pearsachan eaglais gan cumail-san air an aon ràmh, ach is cinnteach gum biodh saorsa aig a' chorr dhen t-sluagh mar a gheabhar air feadh an domhain.

Co-dhiù, sa bhliadhna 1258, nuair a bhruidhinn Domhnall Óg 'tria san nGaoidhlicc nAlbanaigh',[1] tha e soilleir gu robh roinn eadar cainnt Alba agus cainnt Éirinn da-rìribh. Ach chan eil iomradh sam bith ann gu robh e doirbh dhaibh a chéile thuigsinn. Fada fada as déidh sin, agus eadar-dhealachadh mór eadar Alba is Éirinn, ann an cuid dhe na cainntean co-dhiù, bhiodh muinntir Arainn an Alba is muinntir Chinn Tìre is Ìle is Dhiùraidh a' dol gu féilltean an ceann a tuath Éirinn is bha e comasach dhaibh seanchas a dhèanamh ri chéile gun mhaill. Mar bu trice cha robh dòigh eile aca air comhradh, a thoradh bha seo man do dh'ionnsaich na Gàidheil móran Beurla. Chuala mi fhìn naidheachdan mu dheidhinn agus chan eil teagamh sam bith 'nam inntinn-sa nach robhar a' tuigsinn a chéile – 's ann ri malairt agus ri reic is ceannach a bha iad!

Bha Gàidhlig Rachlainn, eadar Alba is Éirinn, car eadar an dà chànan cuideachd, a réir an tuaraisgeil as cinntiche. Bhite ràdh roimhe seo nach robh ann an Rachlainn ach Gàidhlig Albannach gun mheasgachadh sam bith. Tha iomradh ann gun do mhurtadh sluagh Rachlainn gu léir ann an 1575 leis na Sasannaich; ma mhurtadh, 's ann on uairsin a thàinig cainnt an àite gu ìre a-rithist. A thaobh cànan nan Gleann an Aontrum, tha fear Robert MacAdam a sgrìobh mun bhliadhna 1870, a' ràdh gur h-ann dhen aon ghnè ri muinntir Arra-Ghàidheal a tha na Gleannaich, mar a tha an cuid sloinnidhean a' deanamh aithnichte. 'Fad nan ceudan bliadhna thathas air a bhith triall a-null is a-nall is muinntir nan Gleann a' tighinn gu faighearaichean an Alba far a faod an dà thaobh conaltradh ri chéile gun strì.' Tha e a' ràdh, 'A chionn is gun do rinn mi fhìn comhradh ri muinntir Arainn is ri Gleannaich is urrainn dhomh fianais a thoirt gu bheil an cainnt co-ionnan.'[2]

'S e aidhbhseachadh a tha ann a ràdh gur h-e cainnt co-ionnan a bha aca, ach chan eil teagamh nach robh a' Ghàidhlig air dà thaobh a' chuain ion is a bhith dhen aon ghnè. Air a shon sin, chan eil e fìor idir, ged a chluinnear aig Goill uaireannan e, gu robh e na b'fhasa do mhuinntir Chinn Tìre na h-Éireannaich a thuigsinn na na Leòdhusaich. Ged a tha a comharradh fhéin air cainnt gach sgìre, 's e aon chànan a th'againn an Alba, eadar Leódhus is Arainn, Gallaibh is Cinn Tìre – eadar Hirt is Peairt, mar a their sinn.

Aig a' cheart àm, bu chòir seo a ràdh: chon an là-an-diugh faodaidh Gàidheil Éirinn agus Gàidheil Alba bruidhinn ri chéile, agus iad a' cumail ris a' Ghàidhlig a tha dùthchasach dhaibh air gach taobh, ach beagan eòlais a bhith aca air cànan a chéile. Sin agus cothrom a thoirt dhan chluais a dhol air ghleus agus togaidh iad brìgh comhraidh riaghailteach furasda.

A thaobh chainntean Alba fhéin, cluinnear an-dràsd is a-rithist nach tuig Leòdhusach Barrach air neo nach tuig Abrach Muileach. Chan fhaca mise riamh dithis à caochladh dhùthchannan, ach iad a bhith fuasgailte ann an Gàidhlig, air an do dh'fhaillich comhradh. Gun teagamh, mar a gheabhar sa h-uile cainnt, tha soirbheachadh na cùise ann an tomhas an crochadh air càileachd nan daoine a tha dol an sàs sa ghnothach. Chan e a h-uile duine a ghearras na faclan leis an aon sgioltachd no chleachdas an aon teibse. Chunnaic is chuala mi fhìn Caoidheach is Ìleach a' comhradh gun duilgheadas: dithis nach do thachair air a chéile go ruige siod; is chuala mi feadhainn eile à caochladh sgìrean a' dèanamh an dearbh nì.

Tha an-diugh Beurla aig na h-uile is ma shaoileas iad cnap-starra a bhith rompa, tionndaidhear ris a' Bheurla air ball. O shean, cha robh an roghainn sin aig a' mhórchuid ann; b'e a bhuil gu robh iad fada na bu togarraiche an uair sin dhol an ceann comhraidh ri coigrich aig a robh Gàidhlig. Tha diofar cuideachd ann eadar na daoine tha ro thàrmasach is ro fhaiceallach ri linn sgoil a bhith aca – tha mi toirt liom an sin luchd-ionnsachaidh a dh'fhaodas a bhith fileanta gu leòr ann an cainnt aon dùthcha – agus na daoine leis an fhearr crac is comhradh na bhith beachdachadh air blas na Gàidhlig a th'aig an duine eile. Uaireannan a bheir iad an aire dha sin is uaireannan nach bi for aca. Nuair a bha luchd-siubhail ann a bhiodh a' dol timcheall corr agus aon sgìr, bha iadsan ainmeil airson cho geur is a bha a' chluas a bh'aca ri claisneachd. Ach mheasadh iad nach robh e modhail cus diù a chur ann na bu lugha na bha e riatanach.

Canaidh cuid de sgoilearan gur h-e slat-tomhais cainnte co-réir cànain: òrdugh is tàthadh nam briathran. Nan gabhte ri sin is gann a tha roinnean cainnte idir sa Ghàidhlig a thuilleadh air rud mar seo: 'Tha mi faicinn e' an coimeas ri 'Tha mi ga / dha fhaicinn'. Bha leithid 'Tha mi faicinn e' aig Caoidhich o chionn corr agus ceud bliadhna; tha e aig na Leódhusaich – ann an cuid de Leódhus co-dhiù – o chionn ùine mhath a-nise is tha e sìor sgapadh.

A réir nan daoine a tha meas cainnte le co-réir a-mhàin, chan eil diofar riatanach eadar 'aithneachadh' is 'aithneachdainn'; eadar 'ràin-ig' is 'ràini'; eadar 'monadh' is 'monag' is 'monu' is 'monav'; agus mar sin air adhart; Chan eil ann ach rud a tha a' ruith air uachdar a' chànain: chan eil e prionnsabalach. A réir sin 's ann a tha a' Ghàidhlig againne faisg air a bhith a dh'aon ghnè an taca ri cuid mhath de chànanan eile air feadh an t-saoghail.

Ga bè air bith dé am beachd a ghabhas sinn, tha diofar gu leòr, agus annas ri linn sin, ann an caitean na cainnte. Tha K. H. Jackson, a bha 'na cheannard air *The Linguistic Survey of Scotland* – cha do chuir iad 'Gàidhlig' air an titeil ann – air an dealbh as coilionta a th'againn gu ruige seo a thoirt dhuinn.[3] B'àbhaist do sgrìobhadairean a bhith ag ainmeachadh roinn eadar tuath agus deas, air a comharrachadh le puing a leithid 'sr' / 'str': 'sròn' / 'stròn'. Tha an diofar a tha sin ann ach gu bheil Tiriodh a' dol leis an roinn a tuath.

Tha Jackson a' daingneachadh dhuinn gu bheil roinn deas-is-tuath ann agus roinn an-ear-is-an-iar ann cuideachd. Ach ma chuirear car an darna taobh iad sin, faodar a' Ghàidhealtachd a roinn 'na dà earrainn-cainnte: *Meadhan* agus *Iomall*. Ach feumaidh sinn a dhèanadh soilleir nach eil an sin ach aon dòigh mìneachaidh agus aon slat-tomhais.

Tha a' chainnt Mheadhain a' toirt leatha na h-Eileannan cho fada deas ri Muile (agus nas fhaide an corra phuing); Siorrachd Rois as aonais oisein san ear-thuath; Asainte; Siorrachd Inbhir Nis; taobh siar Siorrachd Pheairt; agus tìr-mór Arra-Ghàidheal tuath air Loch Obha, no man ìre sin. Tha an t-Iomall a' ruith o Ghallaibh, le Dùthaich MhicAoidh is Cataibh ('s e 'Cataibh' gu h-ionaigeir ceann a deas Siorrachd Chataibh), ceann an ear-thuath Siorrachd Rois, Bràigh Mhàrr an Siorrachd Obar Dheathain, taobh sear Siorrachd Pheairt, an corr de Arra-Ghàidheal air tìr-mór, na h-Eileannan deas air Muile, Cinn Tìre agus Arainn. Faodar Moireabh is ìochdar Srath Spé, an dùthaich o Rata Mhurchais gu crìch Mhoireabh, a cheangal ri cainnt Bhràigh Mhàrr agus taobh sear Siorrachd Pheairt.

Ma ghabhar ris an t-sealladh sin, tha dùthaich fharsaing againn anns an do thòisich fàs is adhartas: 's ann on bhuillsgein seo a sgaoil na h-atharrachaidhean. Mór thimcheall Iomall na Gàidhealtachd gheabhar seann chruthan cainnte nach do dh'atharraich riamh. Is fheudar gun do thòisich an nòs ùr mu thaobh siar Siorrachd Pheairt, dh'obraich e an iar tro na glinn tuath air Loch Obha is tuath tro na glinn is na bealaichean gu ruige an Gleann Mór a tha a' ruigheachd Inbhir Nis.

Gus an suidheachadh a thomhadh nas fhearr, gabhamaid trì faclan mar a tha 'feur', 'fiar' agus 'fìor'; air neo 'seun', 'sian' agus 'sìon'. Air tùs, 's e 'è', 'ia', 'ì' a bh'annta: b'iad sin na 'seann chruthan'. An-diugh, air feadh móran dhan Ghàidhealtachd, tha iad air a dhol a bheag no mhór an lùib a chéile. Ach tha àiteachan fhathast ann far a bheilear gan cumail glan agus dealaichte o chéile. Ma sheallas sinn air Gàidhlig Iomall na Gàidhealtachd, gheabh sinn 'feur' le 'è'; fada mu thuath an Dùthaich MhicAoidh, fada man ear air taobh sear Siorrachd Pheairt agus an Siorrachd Obar Dheathain, agus fada mu dheas an Cinn Tìre is an Arainn. Ma thaghas sinn faclan eile le 'è' – 'feuch' – chì sinn gur h-e 'fiach' a chanas a h-uile duine aig a bheil 'Gàidhlig a' Mheadhain'; ach tha 'feuch' aig muinntir an Iomaill.

Chan eilear a' tagairt, ga tà, gu bheil a h-uile seann chruth riamh ri fhaotainn comhla sa h-uile pàirt dhen Iomall. Seallamaid air eisimpleir eile: faclan de aon lideadh – no aon siollabh – a tha a' crìochnachadh ann an '-NN', '-LL', '-RR', etc. Tha na litrichean sin air an dùblachadh san sgrìobhadh a chionn is gu robh iad fada air tùs sa chainnt. Tha an 'NN' is an 'LL' fada ann an Gàidhlig Ìle, air aon àite, fhathast. Ann an Athall, air taobh eile na dùthcha, tha an 'NN' air an comharrachadh cuideachd; an dearbh rud ann am Bràigh Mhàrr.

Nas mionaidiche, tha 'L', 'N' agus 'R' air an sgrìobhadh dùbailte; dhen aon ghnè, tha 'M' an deireadh facail uaireannan fada ged nach bi sinn ga sgrìobhadh dùbailte ach ainneamh. Eiseimpleir air sin 'cam' agus 'am'. Air tùs, san t-seann Ghàidhlig, 's e lideadh goirid a bha san 'A' agus dh'fhaoite an dearbh nì a ràdh mu 'O' is 'U' agus mu 'I' is 'E', ach a chionn is nach eil an tàrmachadh an sin cho rèidh, tha e nas fhasa an eachdraidh a leantainn a-mach le 'A' fhéin. Ach thig e dhuinn sealltainn air faclan le '-RD' agus '-RN' aig an aon àm: mar a tha 'bard' is 'carn': an-toiseach, bha an 'A' goirid anntasan cuideachd.

Air feadh roinn mhór dhen Ghàidhealtachd, sa chainnt Mheadhain, rinneadh an 'A' ro 'LL' / 'NN' 'na lideadh dà-fhogharach (*diphthong*) agus ghiorraicheadh an 'L' agus 'N': tha faid an fhacail car mar a bha ach dh'atharraicheadh na pàirtean. Le '-RR', rinneadh an 'A' fada agus an 'R' goirid: an-dràsta, *bàrr*, an taca ri 'caul' is 'baunn'. Le 'M' gheabh sinn 'aum' is 'caum' a chionn is gu robh an 'M' sin i fhéin fada

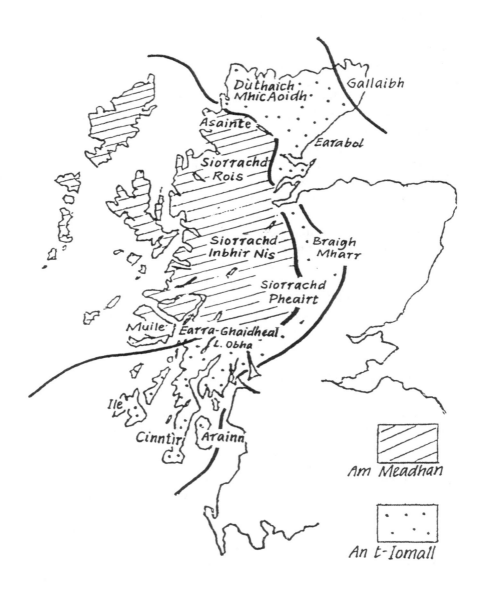

air tùs. Ged nach bithear a' sgrìobhadh 'amm' is 'camm' is a leithid chan eil an sin ach cleachdadh.[4]

Nise, thall is a-bhos an Iomall na Gàidhealtachd, cluinnear an 'L' agus an 'N' dhùbailte agus iad fada ann an gearradh an fhacail. Bhiodh Giobaidh MacPhàil nach maireann a' sealltainn sin anabharrach soilleir san òran 'Cruachan Beann' (a ghabhas cluinntinn fhathast air clàran BBC). Bha sin nàdarrach dhasan oir 's e Ìleach a bh'ann.

Tha an 'M' fada ann an cainntean sonraichte. Mar sin cluinnear 'aMM' is 'caMM' an àite 'AUm' is 'cAUm'. Tha 'loMM' aig daoine ann an cuid de àiteachan; ach cluinnear 'aMM' ann an cearnan far an canar 'lOUm'. Tha an suidheachadh car achrannach. Ma tha an 'M' caol, mar a tha i san fhacal 'druim', faodaidh an lideadh fàs fada air neo dà-fhogharach. 'S e sin as adhbhar gur h-e 'draoim' a their feadhainn agus feadhainn eile 'drìm'.

Air feadh na Gàidhealtachd gu léir 's e 'A' is 'O' fhada a rinneadh dhe na lididhean goirid sin ro 'RR' ('barr' is 'torr'); agus an leithid cheunta, go ìre bhig, a thaobh 'bard' is 'bord', 'carn' is 'dorn' agus mar sin air adhart; sa chumantas an-diugh chanadh tu gum b'e 'bàrr', 'tòrr', 'càrn', 'dòrn' is 'bàrd' a bha annta riamh – agus bidh cuid gan sgrìobhadh mar sin.

Ann an àiteachan, tha iad goirid no eadar goirid is fada fhathast ach air taobh an ear nam Mórbheanna, o Shiorrachd Pheairt gu Bàideanach agus a-null an iar beagan, tha iad dà-fhogharach: 'bAUr', 'bAUrd', 'bOUrd' , 'cAUrn', 'OUrd', 'dOUrn'. Mas ann an Siorrachd Pheairt a thòisich e, dh'obraich an t-atharrachadh seo a-mach a tuath tro bhealach Dhruim Uachdair agus ràinig e a-null cho fada ri Bràighe Loch Abar. (Tha e aig stoc nam Bràghdach ann an Ceap Breatainn chon an latha-an-diugh.)

San iar-thuath cha chluinn thu 'm' romh 'f' idir ged is a bhios sinn ga sgrìobhadh. Boinidh na tha ri tighinn a-nise, uime sin, ri eachdraidh a' chànain sgrìobhte. Ach bidh e nas fhasa ma cheangailear buaidh 'n' / 'm' air 'f' ri buaidh 'n' air 's'. 'S e Gàidhlig an Iomaill a tha seo: airson 's', o Bhràigh Mhàrr agus Siorrachd Pheairt gu beagan an ear air Ceann Loch Gilp agus nas fhaide an iar-dheas an Arra-Ghàidheal, comhla ri sin, airson 'f'. Sna crìochan sin tha buaidh aig 'n' / 'm' air 'f' an gearradh an fhacail mar a tha buaidh aige air 'b' sa h-uile h-àite.

'S e sin, tòisich le 'an barr' is canaidh tu 'am barr'; tha na bilean gu nàdarra a' dlùthadh air 'B' (am Beurla cuideachd 's e sin is adhbhar gu faighear 'Dumbarton' air 'Dùn B(h)reatainn'; tha an rud a tha ann am móran chànanan). Is coltach gu robh gearradh an 'f' dà-bhileach (*bilabial*) is rinn sin 'm' dhen 'n' san alt, agus gu dearbh an àiteachan eile, an teis meadhain na Gàidhealtachd, chan ann air an iomall, ghléidh daoine an 'n': air chor is gun cluinn thu 'an facal' aca. An àiteachan eile a-rithist chailleadh an 'n': 's e 'a facal' a their a' chuid as motha againn an-diugh. 'S ann an Aird Ghobhar is pàirt de Loch Abar agus san Apainn a tha an 'n'. San Apainn cuideachd chuala mi 'Tha mi da faicinn' agus 'dan faicinn' airson 'dha / ga faicinn', aon té agus grunn dhaoine no rudan.

Am Bàideanach is timcheall air gheabhte 'am bear' airson 'am fear'; 'am beur' airson 'am feur'; 'am bàladair' airson 'am fàladair'. An Siorrachd Pheairt agus am Bràigh Mhàrr, chluinnte 'a(m) vear', etc. Am Bràighe Mhàrr agus an Siorrachd Pheairt, tha an 's-' a' toirt 'z' dhuinn ma tha an 's' leathann, agus 'dz' – car coltach ri 'j' am Beurla: 'an dzeo' airson 'an-seo' – ma tha an 's' caol.

Tha an 'm' ro 'f' ann an sgrìobhradh 'na riaghailte dhaingeann a' toirt far comhair gur h-ann anns na cearnan sin (on ear gu deas, agus gu sonraichte an Arra-Ghàidheal) a bha neart agus ughdarras na Gàidhlig san ochdamh ceud deug nuair a thàinig leabhraichean Gàidhlig am follais.

Ged a shaoileas cuid gu bheil leithid 'z' caran coimheach dhan Ghàidhlig, gheabhar 'z' is a leithid fada mu thuath is an iar-thuath ann an seinn. Ach 's e cuspair dha fhéin a tha an sin.

Ged a dh'fhaodadh 'seann chruthan' a bhith mór thimcheall Iomall na Gàidhealtachd, ma tà, agus ged a tha an sealladh sgoilearan a tha gam meas mar sin feumail, chan eil Gàidhlig an Iomaill 'fad air ais' no seann fhasanta. Gu dearbha, 's ann a tha i glé thric nas toiseannaiche na Gàidhlig Meadhain na Gàidhealtachd. Ach cha cheadaich an tìde dhuinn leudachadh seach sin an-dràsda.

Co-dhiù, tha e furasda fhaicinn, agus bidh a dha fhasa nuair a bheirear sùil air an *Linguistic Survey*, gu bheil raointean farsaing ri an treabhadh fhathast ann an sgoilearachd na Gàidhlig – agus a cuid cainnte.

English Summary by the Editor

There is much left to be researched about the historical development of Scottish Gaelic. Although we are not yet sure when or how it first came to Scotland, there appears to have been a Gaelic kingdom established in Argyll in 500 AD. Columba and his followers came to Iona in 563, and Gaelic can claim an unbroken tradition of literature and scholarship since that time.

The Gaelic language was carried throughout Scotland, down to the English border. Even though Gaelic was never the language of the entire nation at any one single time, this was never the case for any language in Scotland until English became dominant in the late nineteenth century. Some scholars assert that we can only recognise a small number of great landholders south of Edinburgh who were Gaels; the commoners were either the original Brythonic stock, or else the Angles who brought an early form of English with them. Gaelic landholders never lived alone, however, especially given the custom of holding and winning land by right of sword, so we can be certain that they brought their Gaelic-speaking dependents with them. While the Gaelic presence in southern Scotland may not have left a large or easily recognised influence, areas such as Peebleshire would not be so full of Gaelic place names if there had not been Gaelic settlements. Much further research is needed on this issue.

It is natural for all languages to develop into a variety of different dialects, and we would expect this for Gaelic, which came to be spoken by people whose first language was Pictish or Brythonic. Indeed, there are features of Gaelic which are reminiscent of Welsh. In some places in the Highlands and Islands, Gaelic was further influenced by the Norse. It was previously asserted by some scholars that Irish Gaelic did not separate into distinct dialects until the thirteenth century, and that that model would suit the divergence of Scottish Gaelic as a separate language as well, but this is only likely to suit the artificial, high-register language of the elite, rather than the common folk. When Donald Óg returned to Ireland in 1258, he was said to have spoken in 'Scottish Gaelic', demonstrating a clear distinction between varieties of Gaelic. Despite the divergences, however, the natives of Argyll and the north of Ireland had no problems in communication even to the late nineteenth century.

Scottish Gaelic is remarkably uniform. While there are apocryphal tales of natives of various parts of Gaelic Scotland not being able to understand one another, communication has always been possible, assuming they are determined not to switch to English (which was not an option for earlier generations). Throughout the entire historically Gaelic-speaking area, syntactical variation is minimal; we must rather look to phonological variation to find and define dialect boundaries.

The area of Gaelic-speaking Scotland which was recorded by the Linguistic Survey of Scotland can be analysed as having two main zones: Centre and Periphery. Many innovations seem to have originated in the centre, and to have sometimes spread outwards. The dialects of the periphery preserve older forms, but also have innovations of their own.

Examples of central innovation include the breaking of long-'e',[5] and the replacement of long consonants '-LL', '-NN', '-RR' in monosyllabic words by diphthongs. The behaviour of the article also varies considerably across dialects.

Dròbhaireachd

Bha an crodh riamh fiachail aig na Gàidheil, mar a bha aig iomadh sluagh eile. Ann an Laideann 's e *pecus* 'crodh', 'spréidh'; 's e *pecunia* 'airgead'. 'S ann anns an spréidh a bha am beairteas. Ann am Beurla 's e *cattle* agus *chattel* an aon fhacal air tùs. Ann an Gàidhlig tha facal bàidheil againn: 'eudail' no 'feudail'. An-diugh, 's e 'gràdh' agus a leithid sin as ciall da; tha e cho cumanta ann an àiteachan is nach eil a bhrìgh ach fann an taca ri 'gaol' no 'gràdh'; car mar a tha 'bròinean' an cleachdadh againn gun ceangal mór sam bith aige ri 'bròn'. Ach seall air an òran 'Bothan Àirigh am Bràigh Raithneach':

> Cuime am biomaid gun eudail
> Agus spréidh aig na Gallaibh?

'S e an 'eudail' an crodh a bhite a' buidhinn nuair a rachte mach a thogail chreach b'e agus an sealbh a bha na Gàidheil a' buannachd an lùib sin.

Ged a bhios daoine a' meas an-diugh nach robh an sin ach goid – agus tha spùilleadh is milleadh gan toirt leotha am brìgh an fhacail 'creach' cuideachd – tha eachdraidh is mìneachadh eile rin cur an céill. Tha Martainn MacGilleMhartainn, aig deireadh an t-seachdamh ceud deug, ag innse sin.

> Bha aig a h-uile h-oighre is ceann-cinnidh òg a thréinead a shealltainn gu follaiseach man gabhte ris 'na thriath is 'na fhear-treòrachaidh air a shluagh is iadsan an sin umhail dha anns gach suidheachadh.

> Bha an triath òg seo is comhlan de dh'fhir òga uasal a' freasgairt air. B'e daoine bh' unntasan nach robh go ruige seo air an gaisge nochdadh is bha iad an geall air an cothrom a ghabhail.

> Bha e 'na chleachdadh aig a' cheannard an toirt a-mach agus ionnsaigh fhiata thoirt air coimhearsnaich sam bith ma bha falachd eatarra.

> Bha e mar fhiachaibh orra an crodh a gheabhadh iad ann an crìochan nan coimhearsnach sin a thoirt leotha le làmhachas-làidir air neo am bàs fhaighinn san oidhirp.

An déidh a' ghnìomh seo bha an ceann-feadhna òg air a mheas tuilleadh 'na thréinfhear a bha toillteannach ann an riaghladh is bha na fir a bha ga leantainn a' cosnadh an dearbh chliù.

Cha robhar a' meas gur e goid a bha ann, oir bha gach fine mu seach ris, ga dhèanamh air a chéile, is bha an call air a chothromachadh nuair a thigeadh ceann-feadhna fine eile gos a chliù fhéin a thoirt a-mach.

Cha chuala mi guth gu robhas ris a' chleachdadh seo o chionn na trì fichead bliadhna sa chaidh.[1]

Chaidh sin a sgrìobhadh timcheall air 1695. Ma ghabhas sinn ri fianais Mhartainn, mar sin, thàinig togail-chreach go crìch sa cheud trian dhen t-seachdamh ceud deug, mu 1635. 'S e Sgitheanach a bha ann am Martainn is bu chòir gu robh fhios aigesan man Eilean co-dhiù. Chì sinn a-rithist ga-ta nach do chuireadh às dha na creachan gu léir, ged a dh'fhaodas e bhith gun do chuireadh casg orra man am a tha e cur air shùilean dhuinn. 'S e as riatanaiche a thomhadh an-dràsta gur ann mu na bliadhnaichean sin a bha an dròbhaireachd, anns an Eilean Sgitheanach air aon àite, a' tòiseachadh.

Tha iomadh adhbhar air sin. A réir cuid, 's e a' bhuaidh a bh' aig Reachdan Idhe Chaluim Chille, ann an 1609 – leis an do rinn Pàrla-maid Alba oidhirp air na fineachan Gàidhealach is air na cinn-chinnidh a cheannsachadh – a chuir grabadh air creachadh is crea-chadairean. A réir sgoilearan eile, 's e gnìomhachas a bhith dol am meud air feadh Bhreatainn bu phrìomh adhbhar. Theagamh gu bheil sin agus corra adhbhar eile is buaidh ann; ach tha e soilleir co-dhiù gu robh an seann saoghal a' dol seachad agus saoghal ùr na malairt a' sìor fhàs làidir.

Bha tìr nam beann is nan gleann a' sìor fhosgladh ri cleachdannan ùra, coimheach. Bha e aithnichte gu robh a' Ghàidhealtachd riamh 'na dùthaich mhath cruidh. Gu dearbh, bha malairt spréidhe a' dol riamh eadar a' Ghàidhealtachd is a' Ghalltachd. San t-seagh sin bha 'dròb-haireachd' ann o thùs, ged nach cainte sin ris a' mhalairt, is dòcha. Ach a-nise, an cois gach atharrachaidh a bha tighinn, thugadh cothrom dhan duine aig an robh an cumhachd, is an t-ealantas a dh'fheumadh e, airgead ceart susbainteach a dhèanamh às na treudan móra. Chaidh féilltean ainmeil a chur air bhonn no chaidh am meudachadh feadh an t-seachdamh ceud deug: Féill Craoibhe an Siorrachd Pheairt air a' chiad té. Agus bha iomadach féill eile air am bithear a' bruidhinn chon an là an-diugh: Féill na Manachainn, cha deach an fhéill sin a shuidheachadh go mu 1820; Féill an Dùin, a chaidh a stéidheachadh beagan ro 1768; Féill Phort-rìgh, a bha ainmeil mar thà san t-seachdamh ceud deug nuair a bha Màrtainn a' sgrìobhadh; agus Am Blàr Dubh, far an do ghluaiseadh Féill na Manachainn, timcheall air mìle go tuath. Ach 'se Féill na h-Eaglaise Brice an fhéill mhór, is an t-ainm sonraichte, a thug buaidh orra uile. An déidh 1770 bha an Eaglais Bhreac air an t-àite aig Craoibh a ghabhail. Ann an 1849 sgrìobh fear cunntas air an Eaglais Bhric: na dròbhairean; na h-ainmhidhean; na seirbheisich; othail is ùpraid dhaoine is bheathaichean; na cainntean Beurla; agus a' Ghàidhlig os cionn nan uile.

'S e saoghal beag dha fhéin a bha an sin, le seinneadairean, cleasaichean, luchd-ciùil, ceannaichean-siubhail is baigearan. Agus creid gu robh òrain is seanchas is naidheachdan gu leòr a' dol.

Mu thuath, bha inbhe fhéin aig a' Bhlàr Dhubh. Ged nach robh i riamh cho mór ri Craoibh no ris an Eaglais Bhric, mhair Féill a' Bhlàir Dhuibh go deireadh an naodhamh ceud deug agus b' i an fhéill bu mhotha a bh' ann airson crodh Chataibh, Rois agus Ghallaibh.

Nise, dé an ceangal a bha eadar togail chreach agus dròbhaireachd? Tha Bhatar Scott a' ràdh: 'Tha na Gàidheil gu sonraichte 'nan sàr-mhaighstirean air an obair dhoirbh seo, ag iomain cruidh: cèaird a tha a' tighinn riutha, a réir coltais, cho math ri cèaird na saighdearachd.'[2]

Chan annas ged a bhitheadh e mar sin. Nuair a bha fir òga, thapaidh cleachdte ri crodh iomain à dùthchannan a bha nàimhdeil riutha, agus sin uaireannan air oidhche dhubh dhorcha, bu shuarach dhaibh treud cruidh iomain air an socair fhéin, ris an latha gheal, à ceann a tuath na Gàidhealtachd go iomall na Galltachd agus suas seachad air sin go ruige crìochan Shasainn. Cha robh ann ach obair fhurasda, shìtheil, a dh'ainneoin mèirlich is feithidich, an taca ri bhith muigh air chreach agus an tòir a' teannadh.

Aig a' cheart àm, bha gnè de chleas anns a' chreach fhéin: lùth chleasach, cunnartach, aoibhneach. Agus tha guth aoibhneach dha réir sin ann an cuid dhe na h-òrain a bhuineas do thogail chreach.

Fios go Eòghainn, fios go Ailean,
Fios go Domhnall Bàn an Caillich
Gu dé an truaighe chum aig bail' iad
'S a' ghealach ag éirigh.[3]

San òran sin 's e an cuspair na ceatharnaich a' dol a-mach air tòir nam mart. Tha cunntas eile againn air Domhnall Bàn Caillich is cho ealanta 's a bha e air an obair. Ach có e, a thuilleadh air sin? Bha, a réir coltais, an duine ris an canadh iad Mac Eòghainn Òig an Sléite san Eilean Sgitheanach. Agus b' esan fear de Chlann MhicGilleMhaoil o Thaobh Loch Arcaig an Loch Abar. Chaill e a bheatha aig Rubha na Caillich, faisg air Caol Reithe, agus b'e sin a' chreach mu dheireadh a thogadh san Eilean Sgitheanach. 'S e an rud a-nise gur h-ann as déidh Bliadhna a' Phrionnsa a bha sin. Is dòcha gun teagamh gu robh a' chreachadaireachd air fàs gu math ainmig, ach mas fìor an seanchas, cha robh Martainn MacGilleMhartainn uile-gu-léir eagarra 'na chunntas.

Eadar-dhà-sheanchas, tha cliù (no urnas) aig Taobh Loch Arcaig ann an naidheachdan mu chreachadairean. Àite math cruidh, is bha tuathanais mhóra air màl an sin a-rithist aig an dròbhair bu mhotha bha riamh an Alba, Camshronach Coire Choinglich. Agus Caol Reithe, far an do mharbhadh an creachadair Abrach: sin far am bite a' snàmh a' chruidh às an Eilean Sgitheanach go Gleann Eilge air tìr-mór – is tha Fuaran nan Sgitheanach an sin fhathast far am biodh daoine is crodh a' leigeil an analach.

Tha fios is cinnt gu robh daoine ann a ghluais o chreachadh go dròbhaireachd; feadhainn eile a bha ri dròbhaireachd gos an do thachair an saoghal riutha – rud a thug orra tionndadh ri creacha-daireachd. Bha Rob Ruadh air fear dhen fheadhainn sin. Agus bha daoine ann a bhiodh ris an dà 'chèaird' mu seach. Ged as ann à Beurla a thàinig na faclan 'dròbh', 'dròbhair', 'dròbhaireachd', chan eil an sin ach rud cumanta: caochladh a' tighinn air seann nì no seann chleach-dadh agus ainm ùr a' tighinn an cois an atharrachaidh. Ach tha an ceangaltas a' ruith fodha agus tha e prionnsabalach.

Tha 'Òran nan Dròbhairean' a' cur an céill cuid dhe na puingean sin.[4] 'S e na Caoidhich a chum beò e agus, mar as dual, chan eil e facal air an fhacal co-ionann aig na seinneadairean. Seo dà sheòrsa dheth: a' chiad fhear o Uisdean MacRath san Eilean Sgitheanach mar a dh'ionnsaich esan e aig Domhnall MacAoidh an Diùranais agus an darna fear mar a bha e aig Domhnall Stiùbhart air an Leathad.

Òran nan Dròbhairean (1)

Nach cianail tha mi fhìn 's mo Dhomhnallan
An Gleann Smeòil mas geamhradh e,
Gun neacha beò bhith tighinn 'nar còir
Mus dig MacCòrn a shealltainn oirnn;

A Rìgh! gur seachdain liom gach latha
Gos an dig blàs an t-samhraidh oirnn,
An uair a bhios na gillean òga
Tighinn air tòir nan gamhnaichean.

Siud far a robh na seòid –
Na dròbhairean nuair ghluaiseadh iad,
Na Bàideanaich bho sliabh gu tràigh
'S an Clàrca 'na dhuine-uasal orr';
Bha MacPhàrlain is MacMhaoilein
'S Mac an t-Saoir à Ruadhainn ann,
'S ma sheasas iad aig tòir na prìs
Chan fhearr a' rìgh na 'n tuathanach.

'S bha iomadh glòir ann an Gleann Smeòil
Nuair thigeadh oirnn a' samhradh ann –
A' ghrian mar òr dol sìos fo sgleò
Is ceòl an crò nan gamhnaichean;
Bhiodh iomadh spòrs aig sean is òg,
'S bu shòlasach bha 'n danns' aca;
Bhiodh iasg is feòil ri dìosgail bhòrd,
Bha sùgh an eòrna 's branndaidh ann.

Siud far a robh na balaich ghasda
Chridheil thapaidh sheannsgeulach,
'S nuair thigeadh iad air tòir nam mart,
Cha bhiodh an achlais gann aca;
'S O! bu toigh liom a' fear fialaidh
A bha riamh mar shamhl' orra –
Le osan gearr is féileadh-beag,
Is daor a chuir e Chaingeis orr'.

Òran nan Dròbhairean (2)

Gur cianail tha mi fhìn 's mo Dhomhnall
An Gleann Smeòil on 's geamhradh e,
Gun duine beò a thig 'nar còir
Mur dig MacCòrn do shealltainn oirnn;
O Rìgh, gur seachdain leinn gach là
Gus an dig blàs an t-samhraidh oirnn,
An uair a bhios na gillean òga
Tighinn air thòir nan gamhnaichean.

'S na gillean òg' tha gleusda, gasd,
Tha tapaidh, sgairteil, luathchoiseach –
Nuair thigeadh sibh air thòir nam mart,
Cha bhiodh bhur n-achlais gann agaibh;
Bu ghasd sibh riamh air siubhal sliabh,
Bu fearail, fialaidh, greannmhor sibh;
Bu gheal ur bian, bu ghasd ur fiamh
Air am biodh miann nam banntighearnan.

'S cha b' i [. . .] Ghallt' a chuireadh stad
Air lùs n-ur cas le banntaichean
Nuair thigeadh sibh air thòir nam mart
Mus tigeadh tart an t-samhraidh orr',
Ach breacan ciatach nam ball fialaidh
A bha riamh mar shamhl' agaibh,
An t-osan gearr 's am féileadh-beag,
'S chan fhaic sibh caitheamh chaingeis aig'.

Ach siud an t-àit' am bi na seòid,
Na dròbhairean nuair ghluaiseas iad –
Na Bàideanaich bho sliabh gu tràigh,
'S bidh 'n Clàrcach 'na dhuin-uasal ac';
Bidh MacPhàrlain ann 's MacM(h)aoilein
'S Mac an t-Saoir à Ruadhainn ann,
'S ma leanas iad air tòir na prìs,
Chan fhearr an rìgh na 'n tuathanach.

Ach nuair thig oirnne tòs a' Mhàigh
'S an crodh air aird na fuarbheannan,
Bidh laoigh gu leòr a' ruith man chrò
'S bidh maighdean òg gam buachailleachd;
Bidh daoine fialaidh 'g inns' na sgeul
'S gun goirinn sè sheann sgeàlaichean;
Bidh mnathan fialaidh dèanamh maitheas
Gu luinneach, subhach, cairdeasach.

Nuair a chuir mi an t-òran sin an clò (is cha robh e riamh an clò roimhe cho fad' 's as aithne dhomh), thug mi tuairmse gur e Murchadh MacCoinnich à Loch Bhraoin a rinn e. 'S e dròbhair ainmeil a bha annsan – Murchadh Ruadh nam Bó, mar a chante ris – a chaochail ann an 1831. Tha e nise dearbhte leam gum b' esan ughdar an òrain da-rìribh.

Chithear mar a tha Murchadh Ruadh a' dèanamh luaidh air éideadh nan dròbhairean. Aig Craoibh an 1723 bha deiseachan nan Gàidheal, uasal is ìosal, a' tarraing shùilean dhaoine. Na h-uaislean 'nan siosacotaichean grinne is 'nam briogaisean de dh'aodach daor leis a' bhreacan air an guailnean is bonaidean gorma air an ceann. Is thathar ag innse gu robh dagaichean is claidheamhnan-móra air chrios aca. Bha an luchd-leanmhainn is breacain orra fhéin agus claidheamh aig gach fear aca. Ceud bliadhna as déidh sin tha iomradh eile orra, ach an àite a' bhreacain 's e plaideachan donna a bha orra – na dròbhairean cumanta co-dhiù. Is faisg air deireadh an naodhamh ceud deug tha R. B. Cunninghame Graham a' tarraing dealbh eile dhiubh ann am briathran boillsgeanta. 'Fir mhóra, mholach, làidir', tha e ràdh, 'le deiseachan clò agus samh na deathcha dheth: aodach cho taisealach is gu saoileadh tu gur e mathain a bha unnta leis a' cheum lunndach a bh' aca.'[5] Cha ghabh e bhith nach e ceum-a'-mhonaidh a bha sin!

Ach 's e daoine sgiobalta a bha sna dròbhairean nuair a gheabhadh iad a-mach air na sléibhtean. Bha iad gu dearbh 'nan eisimpleir dha na Gàidheil fad' is farsaing, gu h-àraid san linn an déidh Chul-fhodair nuair a rinneadh leithid de mheathadh air cultar nan Gaidheal. Bhathar a' faicinn nan dròbhairean mar gum b' eadh 'nan daoine saora a bha leantainn dòighean nan sinnsirean. Tha cuid a' ràdh nach tàinig iad idir fo smachd Achdan Pàrlamaid 1723 agus 1748, nuair a chaidh giùlan arm a thoirmeasg dha na Gàidheil. Agus bhitheadh feum aca air armachd gun teagamh leis cho bitheanta is a bha a' mhèirle agus luchd an ainneirt air gach darnacha bealach. Daoine saora, ruighne nach lùbadh am feòirnean: 's ann mar sin bu dlùithe buileach iad do dh'ìomhaigh a' cheatharnaich mar a bha na baird is na seanchaidhean a' cur sin an céill.

A réir an t-seanchais, 's e fìor cheatharnach a chuir air chois an dròbhaireachd san Eilean Sgitheanach. B' esan Domhnall mac Iain mhic Sheumais, ogha do Shior Seumas a' Chaisteil – Caisteal a' Chamais ann an Sléite. 'S e gaisgeach mór a bh' ann: 's e a chuir Blàr Chàirinis agus Blàr Coire na Creiche an aghaidh nan Leódach (mu 1601). Bha fear-cinnidh dha, Domhnallach eile, an sàs san obair cuideachd: Domhnall a' Chaisteil – an aon Chaisteal an Sléite – ach 'se mac Iain mhic Sheumais am fear air am b' fhearr an robh cuimhne ri ar linn-ne.

Thug a chliamhain, MacLeòid Gheusdo, farainm caran tàireil air: 'Àireach Liath nam Bó' – no, chanadh feadhainn, 'Buachaille Liath nam Bó'. (Cha b' ionann is ainm mar a bha air 'Colla nam Bó', a bha ri creach is a choisinn ainm air sàillibh sin.) 'S e bha ann nach bu diù leis na h-uaislean o shean cromadh ri obair fearainn no buachailleachd no leithid sin ann. Cha bhiodh sna buachaillean ach sgalagan. Ach uasal is gu robh Domhnall mac Iain mhic Sheumais, agus gaisgeil, agus e 'na bhard cuideachd, cha do mheas e gu robh an dròbhaireachd ro shuarach dha. Bha e mar gum b' eadh air thoiseach air a linn fhéin; is fheudar gun do thuig e mar a bha an saoghal ag atharrachadh; is fheudar gu robh rudeigin de chàileachd a' mharsanta ann.

Tha e ri ràdh co-dhiù gur h-e a thug a' chiad dròbh às an Eilean Sgitheanach a dh'ionnsaigh Craoibh agus a dh'ionnsaigh Féill na h-Eaglaise Brice. Bhiodh ceatharnaich làidir cuide ris, chan eil teagamh, ach mas fìor an seanchas, 's e Domhnall mac Iain mhic Sheumais fhéin, gu pearsanta, a bha 'na cheann-feadhna feadh na slighe agus air an fhéill. Faodar a ràdh mar sin gu bheil e 'na bhall-sampaill ann an dùthchas nan Gàidheal air a' ghaisgeach a bha ri togail chreach is eile anns an t-seann saoghal agus 'na dhròbhair ann am freasdal an t-saoghail nodha – agus sin 'na phearsa fhéin. Chuir e air bhonn gnìomhachas a thug móran airgid dhan Eilean agus do dh'iomadach àite eile air feadh na Gàidhealtachd fad suas ri trì ceud bliadhna.

Ma bha daoine-uaisle eile – agus bha – an sàs an obair na dròbhaireachd, tha e nas fhasa sreath ann an òran-luaidh a thuigsinn. 'S e boireannach òg air choireigin gun ainm an-diugh a rinn e do 'Alasdair Òg, mac mhic Neachdain/Neacail'. Tha i a' guidhe nan robh mic aice ris gum biodh inbhe mhór aca:

> Alasdair òig, mhic 'ic Neachdain,
> B' fhearr liom fhìn gum beirinn mac dhut –
> Cóigear no sianar no seachdnar [. . .]
> Bheirinn ciaoird an làimh gach mac dhiubh:
> Fear 'na dhiùc is fear 'na chaiptean,
> Fear 'na cheannard air sluagh feachdach [. . .]
> Fear 'na dhròbhair mór nam martaibh.[6]

Am measg nan daoine iomraiteach eile a bha ri dròbhaireachd foghnaidh dithis gu sonraichte ainmeachadh. Aocoltach is mar a bha iad ri chéile ann an crannchur an saoghail, 's e baird a bha san dithis aca. A' chiad fhear dhiubh am bard Caoidheach Rob Donn (1714–78). Nuair a bha Rob sia no seachd a bhliadhnaichean, thug Iain MacAoidh dhan teaghlach aige am fear beag. Ann an sin 's ann a' buachailleachd laogh a bha e an toiseach. Ach bhiodh MacAoidh ri dròbhaireachd, is nuair a thàinig am bard go ìre thòisich e air falbh cuide ri mhaighstir chon nam féilltean air Galltachd Alba agus ann an Sasainn. Tha a' chiad fhear-deasachaidh aige a' ràdh gun tug na tursan sin farsaingeachd eòlais dha a chuir gu mór ri fhiosrachadh air an t-saoghal, air modhannan dhaoine is an dòighean; feartan a tha cho aithnichte sna dàin aige. Bha Rob Donn tric an Craoibh air an fhéill. 'S ann an sin turas, no air an t-slighe, a rinn e an t-òran 'Ged is Socrach mo Leabaidh' ('Òran mur gum b'ann le dròbhair àraid da leannan').

> 'S mór a b'annsa bhith mar riut
> Ann an gleannan nan laogh
> Na bhith cunntadh nan Sàileach
> Ann am pàirceachan Chraoibh.

'S e na Sàilich an crodh à Cinn t-Sàile MhicAoidh.

'S e an darna fear Murchadh Mór mac mhic Mhurchaidh, Fear Aichealaidh an Siorrachd Rois, a chaochail timcheall air 1689. 'Na òige bha e a' fuireach an Leódhus is nuair a thòisich e air dròbhaireachd nan treudan móra 's ann à Leódhus a bhiodh e toirt àireamh dhen chrodh. 'S ann nuair a bha e an Sasainn turas a rinn e an t-òran iomraiteach 'An Làir Dhonn'.

Bha na dròbhairean a' dèanamh leithid de shiubhal is bha na dròbhan a' tighinn à uimhir de dh'àiteachan, o thuath go deas. Mar a thuirt Donnacha Cuimeanach an Raithneach 'na òran do Pheigi Chamshron, nighean Iain Chamshroin an Taighe-Mhóir an Camghabhran:

> Tarraing suas le d' chuid ghruagach
> Air feadh 'chruidh ruaidh thàin' à Bóid,
> A' chruidh dhuibh thàin' à Ìle
> 'S a' chruidh bhàin thàin' à Leódh's;
> 'S car thu Dhròbhair nan ceudan,
> Fear thionnda lìonmhor nan còrn.[7]

Spréidh às gach àite aig Fear an Taighe-Mhóir agus e fhéin air a mholadh leis an aona seòrsa cliù is a bheirte do cheann-feadhna le na baird.

Tha grunn math òran ann man deidhinn air neo air an dèanamh le dròbhairean. Iain Ruadh Dròbhair, an Raithneach a-rithist, a' ràdh:

> Duine bochd air bheagan mhart,
> Chan fhaigh e meas bho nàbaidh.[8]

Ach gu sonraichte tha 'An Dròbhaireachd' aig Alasdair MacBharrais ann: 'Thogainn fonn 's gun ceannaichinn spréidh'.

Dh'aithnighinn an t-agh dubh no ruadh
Dait air suaicheantas a bhéin,
Speir mholach, leathann, gharbh –
Bhiodh e searbh mar biomaid rèidh.

E bhith leathann os a chionn,
Goirid on dà shùil a bheul,
Fionnadh dualach, tiugh 's e dlùth,
Gun bhith fon a' ghlùn ach réis.

Aisne leoghar, dhomhainn, chrom,
Trusadh 'na chom air an fhéill;
Togail ann a suas gu bharr,
Aigeannach 'na nàdar fhéin.

Thug mi gaol don chèaird cho mór
'S nam biodh mo stòras da réir,
Dh'fhàgadh e mi rithist òg
'G ioman dròbh is iad leam fhéin.[9]

Sin agaibh comhtharraidhean an deagh mhairt Ghàidhealaich agus agalladh an deagh dhròbhair!

Có a-nise a b' ainmeala dhe na dròbhairean air a bheil iomradh againn ann an eachdraidh na Gàidhealtachd? Bha Iain Camshron, aig an robh tuathanas Coire Choinglich ann an Loch Abar. Air feadh na Gàidhealtachd gu léir bha an t-ainm aigesan air bilean an t-sluaigh a h-uile h-uair a bheirte tarraing air spréidh agus air dròbhaireachd. Uaireannan 's e 'Camshronach Coire Choinglich' a theirte ris ach mar bu trice chan fhaigheadh e ach 'Coire Choinglich' fhéin; is bha fhios aig gach aon a chluinneadh an t-ainm sin có bhathar a' ciallachadh. Bha na ficheadan de stòireannan aig daoine mu dheidhinn, feadhainn cho fìrinneach is a ghabhas a bhith; feadhainn eile, is dòcha, a chluinnte fada ro linn a' Chamshronaich ach a chaidh a cheangal ri ainm. Bidh daoine iomraiteach a' tarraing a leithid sin de naidheachdan dhan ionnsaigh fhéin co-dhiù, agus chan ann a-mhàin am measg nan Gàidheal ach air feadh an t-saoghail sa h-uile treubh is cinneach.

Seo ma tà cuid de dh'eachdraidh-beatha Iain Chamshroin.

Rugadh e timcheall air 1780 ann an Cill Mo-Naomhaig an Loch

Abar, far an robh taigh-òsda aig athair. San taigh sin bha Iain eòlach o lathaichean òige air na dròbhairean, oir bhiodh iad daonnan a' tadhal ann, air an t-slighe dh'ionnsaigh Féill na h-Eaglaise Brice. 'S ann an sin a choisinn e a' chiad airgead a rinn e: a' buachailleachd spréidh nan dròbhairean fhad 's a bhiodh iadsan a' gabhail drama san taigh-sheinnse.

Nuair a fhuair e beagan air cùl a chinn cheannaich e grunnan chaorach is ghobhar; reic e iad sin an uair sin air deagh bhuannachd is thuig e gu robh beòthachd mhath, ach duine bhith glic, ann am malairt an stuic. An déidh beagan bhliadhnaichean dh'fhasdaidh e e fhéin 'na sheirbheiseach aig luchd spréidhe is theann e air iomain a' chruidh – is e 'na bhalach casruisgt – go ruige an Eaglais Bhreac. Chanadh cuid gur h-e a' bhochdainn a dh'fhàg gun bhròg e, ach cha b'e. Bha e dh'fhasan aig dròbhairean, mar a bha aig daoine eile, a bhith falbh casruisgt, agus theireadh na seann daoine gu robh an ceum is an giùlan gu mór na b'aodruime as eugmhais caiseirt.

Thuirt Iain mac Dhomhnaill mhic Alasdair, bard Sgitheanach, mu na dròbhairean

> Gum biodh iad tric san Eaglais Bhric
> Ag iomain cruidh tron gharbhchrìoch,
> 'S cha dreidheadh bròg a chur man spòig
> Go ruigt' an Ceò on d'fhalbh iad.[10]

Nuair a bha sùim chuimseach aig Iain Camshron air a chùl ann an seirbheis dhaoine eile, thòisich e fhéin air ceannachd. Bha e ri ràdh gu robh sùil anabarrach sheaghach aige riamh a' taghadh bheathaichean is gun do nochd e sin glé òg. Co-dhiù, theann e nise air gamhna a cheannach is bhiodh e gan toirt leis an lùib a' chruidh a bha an earbsa ris. Cha b'fhada gos an robh e ag obair air a cheann fhéin, is man taca thàinig e go ìre, bha e 'na làn-dhròbhair.

Nuair a thàinig caoraich Ghallta 'nan treudan a dh'ionnsaigh na Gàidhealtachd, chunnaic na h-uachdarain mhóra gu robh airgead ri dhèanamh asta. Ann an Loch Abar bha Loch Iall air fear dhiubh sin. Bha an ceann-feadhna ann an deagh rùn ri fhear-cinnidh is e aith-nichte dha gur e duine comasach, earbasch a bha ann. Nuair a thàinig na caoraich, fhuair Iain Camshron aonta air tuathanas an déidh tuathanais air màl o Loch Iall – ach 's ann o thuathanas Coire Choingligh a thug e ainm. Sa bhliadhna 1834, eadar a h-uile h-àite a bh' aige bha e a' pàigheadh £1,430 de mhàl.

Bha uiread de dh'fhearann aige is gu robh e ri innse gum biodh an crodh a cheannaicheadh e san Eilean Sgitheanach a' cur seachad a h-uile h-oidhche air fear dhe na tuathanais aige go ruigeadh iad an Eaglais Bhreac. Bha cuid dhe na dròbhan aige a' toirt leotha o chóig go seachd mìle rathaid. Agus ma bha an crodh air an iomain timcheall air cóig mìle deug san latha, aig an fhìor chuid a b'fhaide ma bha an rathad garbh, tha sin fhéin ag innse na bha aig Iain Camshron de dh'fhearann Alba air màl. Gu dearbh, tha e air aithris gum biodh e fhéin a' cumail a-mach nach robh fear spréidhe na bu mhotha na e air an t-saoghal ach am Prionnsa Esterhazy – agus, dh'aidicheadh e, bha am Prionnsa sin air thoiseach air leis gu robh am fearann aig an fhear sin saor à grunnd!

Duine beag, aigeannach, dèanta a bha ann anns an robh cruas is fialachd, a réir is mar a bha e fhéin a' meas an t-suidheachaidh. Chaochail e an 1856 is e trì fichead bliadhna agus a cóig deug.

Bha grunnan dhaoine beò fhathast anns an darna leth den fhicheadamh ceud a thug crodh go Féill na h-Eaglaise Brice agus a dh'innis mar a bha cuimhne aca fhéin. Seo a-nis seanchas Dhomhnaill Dhomhnallaich san Lagan am Bàideanach is e an uair sin a' streap ri trì fichead agus a cóig deug.[11]

Bha féilltean gu leòr san àite bho chionn trì fichead bliadhna air ais. Bha iad a' tighinn le crodh. Cha robh caoraich ann ach crodh. Bha féill an Cinn Ghiùthsaich, féill aig Drochaid Charra, féill an uras aig Allt na Frìthe a chuile rathad gu Féill na Manachainn. 'S e féill mhór a bh' ann a Féill na Manachainn. Bha m' athair a' ceannach air Féill na Manachainn. Bha féill an Allt na Frìthe – Freeburn – féill aig Drochaid Charra, féill an Cinn Ghiùthsaich is Féill an t-Sléibh. Bha mise air Féill an t-Sléibh. Cha robh *auctioneers* ann – a chuile duine a' reic is a' ceannach an cuid fhéin. Nuair a dhèanadh iad baragan bha iad a' toirt sgailc air làimh a chéile gun robh am baragan dèante. Nuair nach dèanadh iad baragan, bha iad a' falbh is theagamh gun digeadh iad air ais an ceann fichead mionaid. Bha mi air Féill Dùin is Féill na h-Eaglais Bhreac. Agus bha an t-aon rud a' dol air adhart an sin cuideachd, an t-aon chòrdadh. Bha iad a-mach air *stance* aig an Eaglais Bhreac.

Choisich mi fhìn le spréidh dhan Eaglais Bhreac, nuair nach robh mi ach mu cheithir bliadhn' deug. Bha sinn a' dol a-mach ri Gàdhaig agus a' tighinn a-staigh aig Sruthan dar a rachainn ri Gàdhaig. Dar a bha sinn a' dol ri Druim Uachdar bha sinn a' gearradh dheth aig Dail na Ceàrdaich a-mach ris a' mhonadh. Cha robh sinn a' tighinn a-staigh tuillidh gus an robh sinn a-null faisg air Abar-Pheallaidh. Bha sinn a-rithist a' gearradh cros ri Sliabh an t-

Siorra dar a bha sinn a' dol dhan Eaglais Bhreac – Sheriffmuir – tha mi air call cuimhne air na h-ainmeannan a bha air na h-àitean. 'S ann air na seann rathaidean a bha sinn a' dol fhad 's a b' urra dhuinn an leantainn. Bha sinn an comhnaidh a' dol air na seann rathaid agus a' gearradh thar a' mhonaidh. Air a' rathad bha sinn a' tighinn a-staigh air taighean a-mach ri Gàdhaig. Bhiodh sinn an oidhch' an àite ris an abair iad Coire Bhran. Well, bha geamair a' fuireach urad a sin is bhiodh sinn a' fuireach san taigh aigesan. An ath latha bha sinn a' tighinn a-staigh aig àite ris an abair iad Bruar, far an robh geamair eile. Is bha sinn a' dol a-staigh an sin agus a' fuireach an oidhch' ann. Dar a thigeadh sinn a-mhàn gu Sruthan a-rithist bha *stance* féill ann, *stance* cruidh, is bha sinn a' cur a' chruidh a-staigh an sin agus a' fuireach an sin an oidhche. An uair sin bha sinn a' gearradh a-mach a-null ri Taigh na Fùr. Bhiodh sinn an oidhche sin an Taigh na Fùr. Bhiodh sinn oidhche eile ann an Drochaid – c' ainm seo a theireadh iad rithe? – Drochaid Chonasad a theireadh iad rithe, cha 'reid mi – Tummel Bridge. Is bha sinn a-rithist a' dol air adhart gu Abar-Pheallaidh is a' dol tro Abar-Pheallaidh is a-mach fos a chionn is a' dol air adhart gu rathad Sliabh an t-Siorra. Chan eil cuimhne agam air na h-ainmeannan an déidh sin a' dol chun an Eaglais Bhreac. Dar a bhiodh sinn a' dol gu Féill Dùin a-rithist bha sinn a' cumail a-staigh ro Dùn Blàn is a-rithist a' tionndadh air ais air a' rathad a tha a' dol air ais ris an Òban is ri na h-àitean sin gus an tigeadh sinn gu Dùn. Chan eil Dùn ach mu cheithir mìle air ais o Dùn Blàn. Bha sinn a' fuireach a sin.

Bha sinn a' coiseachd fad a' latha leis a' chrodh. Bha cù againn. Bha cù aig a chuile duine. Bheireadh e tuilleadh is cóig lathaidhean a' dol 'un an Eaglais Bhreac. Bhitheadh – tha mi cinnteach – sia fichead mìle ann co-dhiù na tuillidh. Chan eil an Eaglais Bhreac thar cóig mìle deug na fichead mìle à Glasachu. Cha chreid mi nach biodh sinn seachd na ochd lathaidhean air an rathad. Cha robh sinn a' dèanamh fichead mìle san latha. Cha robh leis a' chrodh uair sam bith. Cha dèanadh sinn ach theagamh dusan mìle san latha na ceithir mìle deug air a' char a b' fhaide. Cha rachadh sinn fos cionn sin. Tha mi a' creidsinn nach robh sinn a' dèanamh sin fhéin.

Nuair a bha an fhéill seachad, bha sinn a' tilleadh dhachaigh. Chan eil beachd agam riamh air a' chrodh a thoirt air ais à siud gun an creic. Bhiodh e tuillidh is cosdail an toirt air ais. 'S ann air an trèan a bhiodh iad a' tighinn air ais ri mo latha-sa an comhnaidh.

Bha m'athair – 'se dròbhair a bh' ann. 'Sann ris an dròbhaireachd a bha eisean. Bha e a' coiseachd dhachaigh dar a bha e na b' òige. Bha neart dhiubh a' coiseachd dhachaigh. Mhaireadh an fhéill aig an Eaglais Bhreac dhà na trì lathachan. An uair ma dheireadh a choisich mise ann, bha sinn a' fuireach an taigh tuathanach [. . .] Sin an t-àite anns an robh sinn a' fuireach. Bha an crodh air an fheirm. Bha mi ochd bliadhn' deug dar a bha mi ma dheireadh ann. Chan eil fhios a'm nach robh mi naodh bliadhn' deug.

Bha dà fhéill Dùn ann co-dhiù. Chan eil cuimhn' a'm. Cha robh mise ach aig aon Eaglais Bhreac anns a' bhliadhn' co-dhiù. Bha mi aig dà Fhéill Dùn ann an aon bhliadhna. 'S e féill mhór a bha ann a Féill Dùn. Bha móran cruidh is eich ann.

Bha dròbhair eile ann, an Arra-Ghàidheal, Dùghall Dùghallach (1866–1957), de theaghlach dhròbhairean, a bha ris a' chèaird o bha e fichead bliadhna dh'aois. Bha an crodh a bha na fir sin a' cur go féill a' tighinn à Muile, à Ìle, à Diùraigh agus cho fada tuath ri Mùideart. Mura faigheadh iad a' phrìs a bha iad ag iarraidh, bheireadh iad an crodh air n-ais. Thug sin deagh chliù dhaibh agus an sin fhuair iad cead a' phrìs a b' fhearr a gheabhadh iad a ghabhail, oir bha fios aig na tuathanaich gu robh iad onarach. 'S ann air dàil a bha na dròbhairean ag obair is tha corra naidheachd ann mu dhròbhairean eas-onarach; ach is dòcha nach robh an leithid-san ach ainmig, oir cha seasadh an dròbhair fada 'na dhreuchd nas lugha na b' urrainn dhan t-sluagh a bhith cinnteach às.

Bha cuimhne aig Dùghall gum biodh crodh Ìle air an aiseag à Port Asgaig do Dhiùraigh agus à sin go tìr-mór. Bha barrach beithe ga chur fon chrodh sa bhàta air chor is nach biodh dochann air an spréidh no milleadh ga dhèanamh air a' bhàta. An sin rathad Taigh a' Bhealaich go Cill Mhìcheil agus an sin go Barr Molach far an robhar gam feurach gon tigeadh an t-àm a chuirte dhan Eaglais Bhric iad.

'S e a' chiad latha air an rathad leis an dròbh bu duilghe, is gun an crodh cleachte ri bhith air an iomain. A thuilleadh air sin bha dìreadh cas aca gos an ruigeadh iad Loch a' Chaorainn, corr is mìle troigh os cionn na mara. Ach mar a bhiodh Dùghall Dùghallach a' ràdh, cha chuireadh an dròbhair math cus deuchainn air spréidh.

Bha a bhlàth orra gun robh iad ann an deagh òrdugh: iad sultmhor agus ann an làn chalg. Nan toireadh tu fallas orra bha an calg a' cromadh is chan éireadh e tuilleadh mar a bha e. Bu chòir an toirt chon na féille a cheart cho eireachdail is a bha iad nuair a dh'fhàg iad an taigh.

Shaoileadh tu nach robh sìon ann ach an iomain is an rotadh le bata, ach cha robh cead sin a dhèanamh. Rachadh iad air adhart gu grinn nuair a leigte leotha fhéin. Bha an duine bha air thoiseach – cha robh iad uile air cùl an dròbh – bheireadh esan is dòcha dusan no mar sin dhen crodh leis, is leanadh càch. Nan rachadh a' chiad fheadhainn tro bheàrna, air neo nam faigheadh iad cachaileith a bha fosgailte, cha robh agad ach dhà dheug fhaighinn a-mach. Ach nam biodh sibh uile air an cùlaibh, bhiodh leth-cheud no trì fichead ann is chosgadh sin ùine gam faighinn a-mach a-rithist.

Bha alt ann, ga dhèanamh ceart, cothromach. Ged a shaoileadh tu gun robh e sìmplidh – bha alt ann ga dhèanamh ceart, cuideachd: gos cothrom a thoirt dhan duine is dhan ainmhidh. Seadh.

Uaireigin bhite a' snàmh a' chruidh à Rubha Eodhnain tarsainn Loch Laomainn. Tha cunntas ann gu robh dà mhart air an cumail an sin a bha eòlach air an t-snàmh: bhathas gan cur air an t-snàmh an toiseach is ghabhadh an corr a-mach as an dèidh gun dragh.

Mu dheireadh, na rothaidean fhéin. Bha seann cheumannan ann – is tha iad ann fhathast – sear is siar, deas is tuath – a' ruith air feadh mhonaidhean is bheanntan na Gàidhealtachd. Tha cuid dhe na bealaichean móra, mar a tha Druim Uachdair, a bhiodh daoine a' leantainn a-mach ro thùs eachdraidh. Agus man do thòisich an dròbhaireachd mhór, cha ghabh e bhith nach robhas ag iomain spréidh, creach is eile, trompa. Shaoilinn co-dhiù gu robh an t-ainm 'Druim Uachdair nam Bó' gu math sean. Agus tha rithist 'Bealach nam Bó' os cionn na Comraich. Nuair a thòisich daoine air treudan móra chur go féilltean bha cuid co-dhiù dhe na rothaidean a' leantainn nan seann cheumannan.

Bha rathad à Sruighleaidh a bha dol tro Chraoibh, Àth Maol Ruibhe, Obar-Pheallaidh, an Uaimh, Drochaid Teimheil agus Trithinn a' Phùir is Dail na Ceàrdaich. Bha rathad eile a' fàgail Pheairt, a' dol a Dhùn Chailleann agus Blàr Athaill. À Blàr Athaill bha e a' ruith go Dail na Ceàrdaich; bha an dà rathad a' comhdha-lachadh an sin.

Bhite a' crùibheadh a' chruidh ma bha an rathad fada, cruaidh, agus 's e Dail na Ceàrdaich fear dhe na h-àiteachan sin. Bha suas ri deich leacan iarainn a' dol air a' chrobhan agus comhdach de leathar. 'S e ceàrdach cruidh a bha aca an sin.

À Dail na Ceàrdaich, seachad air Dail an Spideil, bha an rathad a' dol a dh'ionnsaigh Dail Chuinnidh agus a' dealachadh a-rithist, is a' dol 'na dhà rathad, an dala fear a' gabhail an iar-thuath a-null air a' Gharbhath agus tarsainn Coire Ghearraig go Cille Chuimein is an uair sin go Gleann Moireasdain agus an iar go ruige Gleann Seile agus à sin chon nan Eileanan. Bha an rathad eile a' gabhail mu thuath à Dail

Chuinnidh, a' dol seachad air Ruadhainn am Bàideanach, Drochaid Charra, Sloc Muic agus Dul Mac-Gearraidh, air an t-slighe go Inbhir Nis. Bha rathaidean cuideachd eadar Inbhir Nis agus Cille Chuimein agus an Gearasdan; agus eadar Gearrlochaidh an Loch Abar agus an Lagan. Mu thuath a-rithist bhite a' gabhail na slighe seachad air Aird nan Saor, tron Eilean Dubh do dh'Inbhir Pheotharain agus do Bhaile Dhubhthaich; à sin go Drochaid Bhanna is Brùra agus an t-Ord Gallach, is Taigh Iain Ghròta is Inbhir Ùig.

Ach car mionaideach is gu bheil an t-sreath sin, bha ceudan de rothaidean eile ann, beag is mór, à Dùthaich MhicAoidh is Siorrachd Rois. Chan eil an sin ach Gàidhealtachd Alba; tha a' Ghalltachd làn de rothaidean is de cheumannan cuideachd a bhiodh na dròbhairean a' gabhail air an t-slighe do Shasainn.

Tha eachdraidh cheudan bliadhna tha air a filleadh ann an sgeulachd na dròbhaireachd. Tha an t-ainm 'Féill na h-Eaglaise Brice' 'na shuaicheantas air an eachdraidh, ach nuair a bha an naodhamh ceud deug seachad bha an sgeulachd air tighinn go crìch.

Highland Droving

The Gaels throughout their history valued cattle, as indeed other cultures did also. It is significant that one of the terms of endearment originally meant 'cattle'. In an old song the poet says:

Why should we be without cattle,
Seeing that the Lowlanders have herds of cows?

These cattle that would come from the Lowlands were of course to be taken on a cattle raid. This practice of cattle-raiding is frequently dismissed as mere theft but there is more to it than that. This is what Martin Martin has to say about it in his *A Description of the Western Isles*, written circa 1695.

Every heir or young chieftain of a tribe was obliged in honour to give a public specimen of his valour before he was owned or declared governor or leader of his people, who obeyed him and followed him on all occasions.

This chieftain was usually attended with a retinue of young men of quality, who had not before hand given any proof of their valour, and were ambitious of such an opportunity to signalise themselves.

It was usual for the captain to lead them, to make a desperate incursion upon some neighbour or other that they were in feud with; and they were obliged to bring by open force the cattle they found in the lands they attacked, or to die in the attempt.

After the performance of this achievement, the young chieftain was ever after reputed valiant and worthy of government, and such as were of his retinue acquired the like reputation. This custom being reciprocally used among them, was not reputed robbery; for the damage which one tribe sustained by this essay of the chieftain of another, was repaired when their chieftain came in his turn to make his specimen: but I have not heard an instance of this practice for these sixty years past.[1]

This custom of cattle-raiding by young warriors was in fact an ancient Indo-European institution, as scholars well know. What is interesting is that it should have lasted so long in this corner of Western Europe.

There are other survivals in Gaelic society of a similar nature which we can trace back in history for many centuries.

If we accept Martin's statement, the cattle-raid must have lapsed around 1635. Martin was a native of the Isle of Skye and ought to have known what the situation was, at least in his own island. We shall see later that raiding was not entirely abolished, although it may well be that it was checked about the time he suggests. What is more to the point at the moment is that droving, in the Isle of Skye at any rate, was being established at that very time, and indeed from the earlier part of the 17th century.

There are several reasons for this. Some scholars have found them in the effect of the Statutes of Iona of 1609, whereby the Scots Parliament sought to reduce the power of the Gaelic clans and clan chiefs. According to others the growth of commerce throughout Britain is the primary cause. Probably these and other elements played their parts. At all events it is clear that an old world was passing and a new world of commercial relationships was becoming strong.

The Highlands were from the beginning good cattle country. Driving cattle for sale in the Lowlands was ancient practice and in that sense 'Droving' was always there. But now, with the developments of the seventeenth century, an opportunity arrived to make substantial amounts of money. Trysts for the sale of cattle were established: Crieff Tryst, the Doune Tryst (though the latter was not set up until before 1768) and Portree, which was in operation in Martin Martin's time. The tryst at Muir of Ord, which was a continuation of the Beauly Tryst, was outstanding and there were others less famous.[2]

But it was the Falkirk Tryst which became the supreme cattle fair and its name became synonymous with droving in Gaelic lore. It is described as almost a world of its own: 200 acres filled with animals and drovers; the Scottish drovers mounted on small, shaggy, spirited ponies; tents filled with dealers, auctioneers, pedlars, jugglers, merchants, ballad singers and beggars. Different dialects of Scots and English were to be heard there but over all 'the prevailing Gaelic'. In the North the Muir of Ord Tryst, however, held its position until the nineteenth century and was the largest fair for cattle from Sutherland, Ross-shire and Caithness.

There is a distinct connection between droving and cattle raiding in more than one respect. Young agile men who had been accustomed to driving cattle from hostile territories, sometimes in pitch darkness, thought little of taking droves in broad daylight and in peaceful conditions from the northern Highlands to the far Lowlands and beyond that to the markets of England. That was considerably easier than driving them when the pursuit was drawing near.

At the same time it must be recognised that cattle raiding, with its 'derring-do', was a kind of sport: dangerous and high-spirited. Some of the excitement that went along with it seems to rise out of the songs:

> Word to Ewan, word to Alan,
> Word to Donald Ban in Caillich:
> What the devil keeps you at home
> When the moon is rising?

That was in Lochaber in the central Highlands but further south the Clan MacFarlane were so notorious that the moon was called 'Mac-Farlane's Lantern'! It is said that this Donald Ban (Fair-haired Donald) was one of the MacMillans of Loch Arkaig-side in Lochaber and that he met his death on a cattle raid in Skye, not long after the Battle of Culloden in 1746. This, it was said in Skye, was the last raid to have taken place in that island – over a century later than Martin Martin suggests.

Loch Arkaig-side, was famous (or notorious) in tales about cattle reivers. It was good cattle country and subsequently contained farms which were rented by the greatest drover in Scotland, John Cameron of Corrychoillie. The place where Donald MacMillan was killed was very close to Kylerhea, where the cattle from Skye and other islands were swum across to Glenelg on the mainland. 'The Skyemen's Spring' in Glenelg marks the stance where the cattle rested after their arduous swim.

It is certain that some men who were cattle raiders became drovers. It was, after all, an easy transition. There were others who took up raiding after they had been engaged in legal droving: Rob Roy MacGregor, having fallen 'on evil times and bad markets', is probably the best known of these.

'The Drovers' Song' composed by 'Red-haired Murdoch of the Cows', a MacKenzie from Loch Broom in Ross-shire, celebrates some of the qualities that people admired in clansmen and drovers alike. The song has survived orally in more than one variant. Two of the versions are given here

The Drovers' Song (1)

How sad are we, my little Donald and myself,
in Gleann Smeòil when winter comes:
not a living soul coming near us unless
MacCorn should happen to visit us.
God, every day seems to me like a week
until the warmth of summer arrives,
bringing the young men
who come to gather the farrow cows.

What stout fellows
the drovers were when they got on the move:
the Badenoch men with herds from the moor to the sea's edge,
and Clark a gentleman at their head.
MacFarlane was there and MacMillan,
and Macintyre from Ruthven;
if they stand firm for their price,
the king himself is no better off than the farmer!

It was glorious in Gleann Smeòil
when summer came to us there:
the sun setting in a golden haze
and music in the farrow cows' fold.
Both young and old were amply entertained:
how cheerfully they danced!
Fish and flesh made the tables creak;
there was barley bree and brandy.

Excellent, vigorous, lively lads they were,
and full of ancient stories;
and when they came to seek the cattle,
they would not arrive empty-handed.
Oh, we liked the generous man,
with his kilt and short hose,
who was typical of the best of the kind –
he made it an expensive Whitsuntide for them!

The Drovers' Song (2)

Sad are we, my little Donald and myself,
in Gleann Smeòil since winter's come,
with not a living soul coming near us

unless MacCorn should happen to visit us;
God, every day seems to us like a week
until the warmth of summer arrives,
bringing the young men
who come to gather the farrow cows.

The fine, skilful young men who are brisk
and strong and fleet of foot
would not arrive empty-handed
when they came to seek the cattle.
you were ever expert at walking the moors;
you were manly, generous, and cheerful;
your skin was bright, your appearance was excellent,
you who were the desire of women.

When you appeared, to collect the cows
before the drought of summer
had come upon them,
you wore not the Lowland dress
that curbs the vigour of the leg with its fastenings
but the kilt and short hose and the splendid, ample plaid
that was ever your emblem;
nor would you exchange it for any other habit.

What stout fellows the drovers there are
when they get on the move,
the Badenoch men with herds from the moor to the sea's edge,
and Clark will be a gentleman at their head.
MacFarlane was there and MacMillan,
and MacIntyre from Ruthven,
and if they hold out for their price,
the king himself is no better off than the farmer!

At the beginning of May,
when the cattle are on the high ground of the cold mountains,
calves in plenty will run about the fold,
with young girls herding them.
Generous men will be there telling stories –
I could call on half a dozen reciters of ancient tales –
generous women will be there doing good,
happily, jovially and affectionately.

The poet makes a point of depicting the drovers' Highland dress – 'not the Lowland dress that curbs the vigour of the leg'. At Crieff Tryst in 1723 the Gaels are described in an English-language source as wearing tartan and carrying swords.[3] Acts of Parliament of 1716 and 1746 banned the carrying of arms and after Culloden the belted plaid of tartan (originally very much the warriors' dress) came under the same prohibition.

In both of the variants of the song the kilt is mentioned; the second one in fact gives the impression that the Highland dress was the insignia of the drovers' trade. Whether or not drovers were exempt from the Disarming Acts, as some have stated (they are not specifically mentioned as a class), they may none the less have enjoyed greater freedom than others. Their work, entailing as it did a great deal of walking, often over difficult ground, could in the circumstances be said to demand such a garb. For, as Duncan Forbes of Culloden (although he himself was anti-Jacobite) wrote after the 1745 Rising,

> as the Highlands are circumstanced [. . .] it seems to me, an utter impossibility, without the advantage of this Dress, for the Inhabitants to tend their Cattle, and to go through the other parts of their Business, without which they could not subsist

But the significance is wider than that. After the repeal of the Disarming Act in 1782, tartan was never again universally worn in the Highlands, but its appeal as a symbol of the old order remained. The celebratory references in a large number of Gaelic songs to the 'lads of the kilt', the soldiers of the Highland Regiments, who were exempted from the general prohibition in the Disarming Act, shows this clearly enough. If the drovers did in fact favour Highland dress, they would naturally enough evoke a comparable, though perhaps rather less romantic, response. Moreover, the very nature of the free wandering life must have had an appeal for a people who for centuries regarded cattle raiding as an aristocratic pursuit of young warriors.

According to tradition it was a great aristocratic warrior who established the droving trade in the Isle of Skye. This was Donald MacDonald, grandson of Sir James of Castle Camas. But because of his involvement he was given the somewhat contemptuous nickname of 'The grey-headed cowherd' by his son-in-law. The old warrior aristocrats did not concern themselves with agriculture or tending cattle: these were menial pursuits. Donald clearly did not regard droving as beneath him and in that respect he was ahead of his time.

He obviously read the signs of a changing world and took advantage of the opportunities it afforded. It is said that it was he who took the first drove of cattle to the Trysts of Crieff and Falkirk, and if that is true he was the means of setting up an industry which brought much wealth not only to Skye but to many other parts of the Highlands for some three centuries. There were of course others. Their participation in droving helps to explain why an anonymous girl says in her song to 'Young Alasdair' (a MacNaughton or a MacNicol):

> Young Alasdair MacNaughton,
> How I wish I could bear you a son –
> Five or six or seven sons [. . .]
> I'd give each of them a career,
> One a duke and one a captain,
> One a leader of an armed host,
> One a great drover of cattle

Among the men who were notable in connection with droving, two in particular are worth mentioning, different though they were in social status. The first is the poet of the Land of MacKay, Rob Donn (1714–78). Rob was employed from boyhood with John MacKay of Skerra, a relative of the chief, whose 'principle avocations were those of a grazier and cattle-dealer, the latter a business then followed in the North Highlands comparatively by few, and these few of superior intelligence and attainments'. So Rob Donn's first editor (*Songs and Poems by Robert MacKay*, 1829). From early years Rob accompanied his master to the cattle trysts not only in Scotland but also in the north of England. His first editor is of the opinion that those trips, which gave the young poet an opportunity of meeting and mixing with different sorts of people and seeing a world all far removed from that of his native parish, had a direct bearing on the development of his genius. Behind this lay

> the native sagacity and quick discernment belonging to the Highlander [. . . so] that in the humble capacity of a driver of cattle, knowledge of mankind and the world were to be gained [. . .] in this capacity [. . .] Our bard acquired no small share of that knowledge, discernment of character and of manners, which so strikingly characterise his poetical compositions.

Rob Donn often attended the Crieff Tryst. There, or on the way there, he composed the song 'Although Easy Is My Bed' ('A song as if by a certain drover to his sweetheart'):

> Much more would I rather be with you
> In the little glens of the calves
> Than to be counting the Kintail cows
> In the paddocks of Crieff.

This is 'Kintail of MacKay', the parish of Tongue.

The second is Murdoch MacKenzie, laird of Achility in Ross-shire, who died around 1689. He went far afield with great droves of cattle. He was a poet, as was his son. In his youth he lived in the island of Lewis, and when he began droving on a large scale, it was from Lewis he took many of his cattle. His best known song, 'The Brown Mare', composed to his ship, was made, it is said, when he was detained in England on one occasion after failing to get an immediate sale for his cows at the English markets.

The drovers, then, travelled far and wide and people knew and remarked on the areas where cattle came from. For instance, Duncan Comyn in Rannoch, Perthshire, makes a song, in the late eighteenth century, to Peggy Cameron, daughter of Cameron of the 'Big House' of Camgowan.

> You move with your milkmaids
> Among the red cattle from Bute,
> The black cattle from Islay,
> The white cattle from Lewis –
> You are kin to the Drover of Hundreds,
> He who is generous in dispensing wine.

This is the kind of praise traditionally accorded to the leader of warrior bands; but here the detail of the cattle is added.

Many of the drovers were bards themselves. Some of their songs, orally composed and transmitted, survive in the older anthologies of poetry. Other poems allude to the occupation, always in a celebratory manner. To possess many cows, even to have them temporarily in one's possession, was a symbol of success, and a certain social status went with it. Not to have cattle carried its own sad refrain:

> A poor man with few cows
> Gets no respect from his neighbour.

So a drover bard, Red-haired John the Drover from Rannoch, says in one of his songs. There is another song, one of praise and affection, by an unknown woman to a certain John MacPhail the Drover. But outstanding is a song simply called 'The Droving'. The chorus contains the statement 'I'd raise a song and buy cattle'. The author was Alasdair MacVarish.

> I could tell a heifer, black or red,
> Coloured in the livery of its coat of hair,
> Broad, big-boned, and shaggy hough –
> Harsh would things be if we weren't friends.

That seems straightforward enough but in the original Gaelic the colour is the 'emblem' – *suaicheantas* – a word used for the crest or insignia of a clan or kindred. The significance of it here is that it seems to reflect something from an earlier age, from the world of the warrior caste of Gaelic society. One warrior could identify another by his *suaicheantas*, his insignia, and the colour of his tartan might convey that information. If he came from a hostile kindred or territory, then indeed the encounter might be harsh. The statement is subtle and economical – not unusual qualities in Gaelic poetry.

Then he goes on to detail those points on which a Highland cow is to be judged and which an expert drover ought to know.

> It should be broad above,
> Short between muzzle and eyes,
> Curled coat, dense and thick,
> Beneath the knee no more than a span.
>
> Supple ribs, deep and well-sprung,
> Compact in its form at the fair;
> A lift in it towards the top,
> Full of vigour in its nature.

Drovers always prided themselves on having a good eye for a beast and nothing delighted them more than to get the better of their competitors. MacVarish ends his song:

> I gave such love to the trade
> That, if my wealth were as great,
> It would make me young again
> Driving cattle that were all my own.

Of all these Gaelic-speaking drovers, by far the most renowned was John Cameron of Corrychoillie, born in Kilmonivaig in Lochaber about 1780. He died in 1856. It was he who had farms round Loch Arkaig where the MacMillan free-booter who was killed on a cattle-raid in Skye had lived. His first place on the estate of Cameron of Lochiel (who approved of him and helped him as a young man) was the farm of Caonich and Kenmore, which he began to rent in 1824. As time went on and his business flourished he took farm after farm: Monaquoich, the North side of Glendessary, Crieff, Salachan, Muick, Murlagan, Cailleach, the grazings of Glenkinzie, Glen Pean More, Glen Pean Beg, Coull – in addition to the two first mentioned and Glaickfearn, which he owned himself. The annual rent, in 1834, was £1,430. It was, at that time, an enormous sum of money.

The cattle he bought at the Skye fairs were, as usual, ferried across Kylerhea and driven to the Falkirk Tryst. It is said that these droves were rested each night at a stance at one of his farms and, as their numbers swelled on the way, with additional animals from various parts of the Highlands of Scotland, they took up from five to seven miles of road as they approached Falkirk. Scores of anecdotes are told about him, some of them attached to other names also. One, which is no doubt true, tells that he and a fellow drover were having a drink together and the friend said: 'I think that you are a greater man than the Duke of Wellington!' Cameron of Corrychoille considered this high compliment and said:

> The Duke of Wellington was in no doubt a very able man. He was a good soldier but of course he had reasonable men to deal with: captains and majors and generals who could understand him. But I'm not so sure he could manage twenty thousand sheep and several thousand cattle that couldn't understand one word he said – Gaelic or English – and bring every hoof of them to the Falkirk Tryst. But I have done that often!

In his last years 'Corrychoillie', as he was always known, declared he had attended the three annual meets of the Falkirk Tryst for all of fifty years.

Corrychoillie was a small, brisk, active man of tremendous stamina. As a youth he went barefoot with his drove, which some attribute to the poverty of his early life. But in fact his father kept a toll-house and inn and was by no means in straitened circumstances. Many of the drovers are known to have gone barefoot all their lives, which made them much more agile on moorland and grassy tracks alike.

A Skye bard said about the drovers:

Often did they go to Falkirk
Driving cattle through the rough mountains,
And no shoe went on their feet
Until they returned to the Mist which they had left behind

Skye in Gaelic has a bye-name of 'The Isle of Mist'.

There were still a few people alive in the 1950s who had driven cattle to Falkirk and who described their experiences. The first of two here is a recording made from the late Donald MacDonald in Laggan in Badenoch. He was then (1952) in his seventy-fifth year.[4]

Sixty years ago there were lots of trysts in this place and people used to come with cattle – no sheep, only cattle. There was a tryst in Kingussie, a tryst at Carrbridge, a tryst up at Freeburn – all the roads leading to the Beauly Tryst. My father used to buy at the Beauly Tryst. There was a tryst [. . .] on the Sliabh: I was there myself.

There were no auctioneers: every man buying and selling his own. When they struck a bargain they would shake hands with a slap, signifying that the contract was sealed. When they failed to agree they would separate and probably return in twenty minutes' time.

I was at the Doune Tryst and at the Falkirk Tryst. The same business went on there too – the same kind of bargaining procedure. At the Falkirk Tryst they were on an open stance.

I myself have walked to Falkirk with cattle when I was only about fourteen years old. We used to go out by Gaick and if we went that way we would turn inland at Struan. When we took the Drumochter road we would cut across country at Dalnacardoch and follow the open moor without turning inland any more until we were approaching Aberfeldy. Then we'd take a short cut down towards Sheriffmuir on the way to Falkirk: I've forgotten the names of the places. We always took the old roads, as far as we could follow them. We took the old roads and cut across the moor.

On the way, out by Gaick, we would come upon some houses and we'd spend the night in a place called Coire Bhran. There was a gamekeeper living there in whose house we used to stay.

The following day we came to a place called Bruar where another game-keeper lived. We'd go in there and spend the night there. Then when we came to Struan there was a tryst stance there – a cattle stance – and we put the cattle in there and spent that night there. After that we cut across to Trinafour and we'd be another night in Drochaid – what did they call it again? – Drochaid Chonasad, I think they called it – Tummel Bridge.

Then we went on to Aberfeldy, through Aberfeldy, and out again on the high ground, heading for the Sheriffmuir Road. After that, I don't remember the place names on to Falkirk.

Then, again, when we used to go to the Doune Tryst we kept on through Dunblane [. . .] We stayed at Doune.

We used to walk all day long with the cattle. We had a dog – everyone had a dog. It took more than five days to go to Falkirk: it was a journey of, I suppose, at any rate a hundred and twenty miles or more. Falkirk is no more than fifteen or twenty miles from Glasgow. I think we'd be seven or eight days on the way – we didn't do twenty miles a day. No, never with the cattle: we'd do twelve miles perhaps, or fourteen at the most; but we wouldn't exceed that. I believe we didn't do even that.

When the tryst was over, we returned home. I don't remember ever having brought the cattle back unsold: it would be too expensive to bring them back. In my day it was always by train they came back.

My father was a drover, a professional drover, and when he was a younger man he used to walk home – lots of them did that.

The Falkirk Tryst lasted two or three days. The last time I went to it we stayed at a farmer's house [. . .] The cattle were on that farm. I was eighteen years of age, or perhaps I was nineteen, when I went for the last time. There were at least two trysts at Doune. I don't really remember but I was at only one 'Falkirk' in a single year and I was at two Doune Trysts. Doune Tryst was a big tryst: there were lots of horses and cattle there.

The second account is based on the reminiscences of an Argyll drover, Dugald MacDougall (1866–1957). A native of Lochgilphead, he came from a family of drovers and was engaged in the trade from the age of twenty. The cattle his people dealt with came from the islands of Mull, Islay and Jura and from as far north as Moidart, in Inverness-shire. At first, unless they got the price they asked for (and the owners expected), they would bring the cattle back. This won them a good reputation: people trusted them and left them to accept the best price they could get, for the farmers knew they were honest.

Drovers worked on credit. There are stories about dishonest drovers but probably these were few in number: a drover would not last long in his profession unless people were sure of his honesty.

Dugald remembered that the Islay cattle were ferried from Port Askaig to Jura and from there to mainland Argyll. The bottom of the ferryboat was 'thickly heaped with a protective layer of birch branches'. The cattle were carried to Keills and unloaded on to the jetty.

There was no need for them to swim ashore, as the jetty sloped down to the water, and boats could be discharged in any state of the tide. Its corrugated surface, made of thin slabs of stone set vertically, would offer a ready foothold to the cattle as they scrambled ashore.

The herd made its way by Tayvallich and Bellanoch to Crinan Moss and Kilmichael and up the glen to Barmollach. Here they remained to graze until they were ready to be sold at the Falkirk Tryst.

The Barmollach droves numbered fifty or sixty cattle. They could be handled by two men and their dogs. The seven-day journey of nearly a hundred miles of road and track began early enough to allow the cattle to rest for three days at the end of it before the Tryst commenced. The route they followed was one which had been long used by drovers from Mid-Argyll. First the drove made for the old hilltrack leading from Loch Awe over the high moorland north of Loch Fyne to the farm of Auchindrain near Inveraray. The first day with its unaccustomed fatigues and steep gradients was the hardest on the cattle. The road rises from almost sea level to a loch-strewn terrain a thousand feet higher. It clambers to its summit at Loch a' Chaorainn ('Rowan Tree Loch').

A good drover was careful not to press his cattle too hard, especially at the outset.

> They were in full bloom, and full of flesh and hair. If you sweated them, the hair dropped down and never got up again into the same condition. The great secret was to take them there as good-looking as they were when they left home. One would think there was nothing but drive and force them on with a stick, but that wasn't allowed at all. They'd go quite nicely when they were left alone.
>
> The man that was in front – they didn't all stay behind – he took maybe twelve or so of the first cattle on, and the rest followed; and if these went into a gap, or found an open gate, and went in, you had only to get twelve out, whereas if you were all behind, you would have the whole fifty or sixty, and that took time to get them back out again. There was an art in doing it right, properly; even suppose one would think it was a simple thing. There was an art in doing it properly too, to give man and beast a chance, yes.

On the fifth day Dugald brought his cattle down to the lochside road at the Inverbeg Inn (by the side of Loch Lomond). Here was a stance opposite the inn which had formerly been used when the ferry sailed across the loch to Rowardennan, taking the Argyllshire cattle on the shortest route to the Tryst. Sometimes they were swum across, with two experienced cattle which were kept by the inn to lead them.[5]

Some of the drove roads are ancient tracks used, no doubt, for centuries before droving as a recognised profession was established. The great pass of Drumochter from Atholl to Badenoch is often referred to as 'Drumochter of the Cows', probably an age-old name, and there are similar place names elsewhere. It is important to remember that the drove roads ran through Highlands and Lowlands alike. In this brief account it will be sufficient to give a sketch of the two main roads from the Southern Highlands to the North and West.[6]

One, a highway, ran from Stirling by Crieff, Amulree, Aberfeldy, Weem, Tummel Bridge and Trinafour to Dalnacardoch. The last name contains the word *ceàrdach*, Gaelic for 'smithy'. Here cattle were shod, with shoes of metal plates and leather.

At Dalnacardoch it was joined by another more primitive road, not a highway, which ran from Perth by Dunkeld and Blair Atholl. From Dalnacardoch the way continued to Dalwhinnie where it separated again with two main roads, one leading to the north-west through Garvamore and over the mountain pass of Corryarick to Fort Augustus; thence to Glenmoriston and on to the West and the Islands. From Dalwhinnie the other road struck northwards to Badenoch, Carrbridge, Dalnagarry and Inverness.

Farther north again the main drove road ran by Ardersier and Fortrose, through the Black Isle to Dingwall and Tain to Bonar Bridge. This route served the drovers of Sutherland and Caithness, for it continued to the Ord of Caithness and to Wick and John o' Groats.

There were, of course, many tributary roads and tracks all over the country, north, south, east and west, Highland and Lowland, and into England.

The profession of Droving in the Highlands and the drovers' lore, with Gaelic song and anecdote and legend all intertwined, makes a fascinating story that involves centuries of history. As the nineteenth century moved to a close that story was virtually over.[7]

Essays on Literature, Song and Dance

The Gaelic Literary Tradition

I believe it is still possible in Scotland to leave school without hearing anything, or at least anything of interest, about Gaelic. Those children who hear about the Picts and the Scots, and the rest, are most unlikely to learn that the Scots, quite simply, were the Gaels; that their language, which spread throughout the country, is still a living tongue; and that it has been used by generations of major Scottish writers, some of whom are living at the present time.

The importance of Gaelic and its literature as a distinctive element within the greater unit of Scotland needs no stressing, but it may be useful to indicate the extent to which Gaelic impinges upon the rest of Scotland, or at a certain stage of history pervades it. Modern scholarship is becoming aware that even in Lothian, Gaelic settlement began very much earlier and by that token was very much denser than has hitherto been thought. Historical evidence can of course connect with literature in different ways: it must surely add immediacy to the most cursory study of Gaelic if it is realised, for instance, that Gaelic place names extend down to and even beyond the English border.

The history of the Gaelic people and their language in Scotland covers over six centuries of expansion and development followed by a slightly longer period of slow decline. When Gaelic was first spoken in what is now Scotland is not certain; some historians argue for pre-Roman settlements of Gaels. About the beginning of the sixth century Gaelic speakers in Argyll and Antrim were connected via the kingdom of Dál Riata which spanned Scotland and Ireland, the older Scotia. By the early part of the eleventh century King Duncan – the gentle Duncan of Shakespeare's *Macbeth* – had become ruler of the mainland of modern Scotland. The authority of these early Gaelic Kings over a large portion of their realm was merely nominal: the Hebrides, for instance, and sizable tracts of the North and West were under Norse domination.

Nevertheless, the existence of a Gaelic-speaking court, with its attendant patronage, was of great importance to Gaelic literature, the exponents of which were organised in what practically amounted to a caste system. When the court became Anglicised under the sons of Malcolm Canmore and Queen Margaret, the setback was profound and permanent. No longer the *sermo regius* of Scotland, Gaelic was now fated never to fulfil what had seemed to be its destiny: to become the language of cultured society throughout the kingdom and the medium of expression in its leading institutions. Instead there began the process which ultimately banished it to the remote and inaccessible parts of the land; and although development did not by any means cease, Gaelic literature became largely cut off from the influence of the great innovating movements of post-medieval Europe.

Meanwhile in the lowlands of Scotland the northern English dialect was being developed as the national language. This, and the evolution of a distinctive Lowland literature, meant that Scotland became a country of two literary cultures. Down to the sixteenth century the term 'Scots' was used to describe Gaelic, and what we now call Scots was then called 'Inglis'. Later, Gaelic was frequently referred to as 'Irish' or 'Erse' – different forms of the same word. This change in nomenclature serves to illustrate the shift in cultural orientation which the development of the Lowland tongue produced in Gaelic society. Ireland now reassumes a dominant role; in relation to it Scotland becomes something of a cultural periphery.

In that redefined situation the principal focus of Gaelic political and cultural organisation was the confederation known as the Lordship of the Isles. This semi-independent state, which exercised influence, if not always authority, over a considerable part of the North-West mainland was not finally destroyed until the mid-16th century and some of its cultural resonances linger in Gaelic tradition to the present day. Partly because of these facts of history we normally associate Gaelic with the north-west and tend to forget that it was spoken in Galloway, in the extreme south west, until well on in the seventeenth century, and possibly later; or that on the east, Aberdeenshire Gaelic died out only in the 1970s; or, indeed, that only some fifty miles from Edinburgh it was spoken in Perthshire into the 1990s.

The special relationship with Ireland remained intact until the seventeenth century. In spite of differences, political or religious, Ireland and Gaelic Scotland continued to be one cultural area. As the vernacular dialects of the two countries continued to diverge, the mandarin class who cultivated the arts standardised a common language, a flexible, classical form of Gaelic. These learned men moved freely throughout the lands of 'the sea-divided Gael' enjoying a kind of diplomatic immunity. Inevitably they promoted a sense of cultural solidarity, within Scotland as well as between Scotland and Ireland.

In this way Scots Gaelic participates in one of the great literatures of medieval Europe. It is essentially an aristocratic tradition, developed from an ancient native stock under the influence of medieval European rhetoric. In the Dark Ages, poets of the highest caste specialised in historical and mythological lore. Such a poem is the 'Scottish Lay' composed in the reign of Malcolm Canmore and addressed to the poet's peers, the aristocracy of birth as well as the aristocracy of learning:

> O all ye learned ones of Alba
> O stately yellow-haired company[1]

Later reorganisations, perhaps due to the Anglo-Norman invasions of Ireland and Scotland, modified their role to that of panegyrists who wrote to celebrate great men, wherever patrons who were willing to pay for a poem could be found. They remained a professional intelligentsia, justifying a highly stratified society, advising and exhorting their patrons freely, but also on occasion expressing adverse criticism.

But they did not confine themselves to praise-poetry, nor was all poetry written by professionals. Among the aristocracy there were men and women who were sufficiently conversant with Classical Gaelic and skilled enough in the conventions of its court poetry to write subtle, elegant and passionate poems, even if they did not observe the purists' rules of consonantal and vowel rhyme, or all the other ornaments demanded by the poetic schools. Thus we find Isobel, first Countess of Argyll, composing a charming little love-poem in the fifteenth century:

> There is a youth comes wooing me;
> oh King of Kings, may he succeed!
> would he were stretched upon my breast,
> with his body against my skin.
>
> If every thing were as I wish it,
> never should we be far divided,
> though it is all too little to declare,
> since he does not see how the case is.

It cannot be, till his ship comes home,
a thing most pitiful for us both;
he in the east and I in the west,
so that our desires are not fulfilled.[2]

In the same manuscript there is an elegy by the widow of the chief of
the MacNeills. She addresses the rosary, remembering the hand that
had held it until that night. The poem draws upon conventional
images of praise, but it is nonetheless poignant and tender.

Rosary that has roused my tear,
dear the finger that was wont to be upon you;
dear the heart, hospitable and generous,
that owned you ever until tonight [. . .]

A mouth whose winning speech
would wile the hearts of all in every land;
lion of white-walled Mull,
hawk of Islay of smooth plains [. . .]

Mary Mother, who did nurse the King,
may she guard me on every path,
and her Son who created each creature,
rosary that has roused my tear.[3]

In the seventeenth century we find Niall Mór MacMhuirich (c.
1550–post 1613) in South Uist writing elegantly in the *amour courtois*
tradition. His 'Message of the Eyes' is in the same convention as the
Countess of Argyll's poem. The great scholar Robin Flower described
that genre succinctly:

The subject is love, and not the direct passion of the folk-singers or the high
vision of the great poets, but the learned and fantastic love of European
tradition, the *Amour Courtois*, which was first shaped into art for modern
Europe in Provence and found a home in all the languages of Christendom
wherever a refined society and the practice of poetry met together. In Irish,
too, it is clearly the poetry of society. To prove this, we need only point to the
names of some of the authors [. . .] in Scotland, the Earl and Countess of
Argyll and Duncan Campbell of Glenorquhy, "the good knight", who died
at Flodden.[4]

Professor Jackson has given us this rendering of the poem in
English:

A long farewell to yesternight!
soon or late though it passed away.
Though I were doomed to be hanged for it,
would that it were this coming night!

There are two in this house tonight
from whom the eye does not hide their secret;
though they are not lip to lip,
keen, keen is the glancing of their eyes.

Silence gives meaning
to the swift glancing of the eyes;
what avails the silence of the mouth
when the eye makes a story of its secret?

Och, the hypocrites
won't allow a word to cross my lips, O slow eye!
Learn then what my eye declares,
you in the corner over there:–

'Keep this night for us tonight;
alas that we are not like this for ever!
Do not let the morning in,
get up and put the day outside.'

Ah, Mary, graceful mother,
Thou who art chief over all poets,
help me, take my hand –
a long farewell to yesternight!⁵

As a contrast to these, we can quote verses from a panegyric composed by a member of the same family, Cathal MacMhuirich. They are from an elegy for four chiefs of Clanranald who all died in 1636.

Our rivers are without abundance of fishing,
there is no hunting in the devious glens,
there is little crop in every tilth,
the wave has gnawed to the very base of the peaks.

For their sake the fury of the ocean never ceases,
every sea lacks jetsam on its shore;
drinking wine at the time of carousal,
the warriors grieve more than the women. [. . .]

Their survivors are gloomy and wrathful;
the song of the cuckoos is not heard,
the wind has taken on a senseless violence,
the stream washes away its banks over the heather.

Because the men of Clanranald have gone from us
we poets cannot pursue our studies;
it is time for the chief bard to depart after them,
now that presents to poets will be abolished.[6]

The hyperbole of this and similar elegies is rooted in the ancient and universal belief that connects the life of a ruler with the fertility of his land. Earlier still, in the last quarter of the fifteenth century, when the Lordship of the Isles, from which Clanranald sprang, was under attack, we find the anxiety expressed that if Clan Donald, 'the brilliant pillars of green Alba', is destroyed, learning will be destroyed also.

It is no joy without Clan Donald;
it is no strength to be without them;
the best race in the round world;
to them belongs every good man. [. . .]

In the van of Clan Donald
learning was commanded,
and in their rear
were service and honour and self-respect.[7]

The anxiety was well founded, as history was to prove. Yet in spite of wholesale destruction of manuscripts when these learned orders were destroyed, enough has survived of their work, not only in poetry and history and romance, but also in law, medicine, astronomy – not to mention other more arcane pursuits – to show what a rich and varied world existed behind the clouds of political and military turbulence that for most people represents the 'history' of Gaelic Scotland.

Long before that world came to an end, however, the poets who composed in vernacular Gaelic had inherited its basic social and political attitudes and were able to draw freely on the resources of imagery developed by their classical brethren. In the late sixteenth and early seventeenth centuries the upper social reaches of vernacular poetry are inhabited by professional bards and members of leading clan families alike. Its range is quite unrestricted and eventually represents all grades of society, who expressed themselves in a wide variety of stanzaic and metrical patterns. Even the Latin-derived, syllable-counting measures of the classical poets are used with subtlety and ease as early as the sixteenth century: the Ossianic ballads upon which James Macpherson based his *Ossian* belong formally to this sector and they too carry on a Classical Gaelic inheritance into oral tradition, where they are now on the verge of extinction. But hundreds of thousands of lines, in both Classical and colloquial Gaelic, have been preserved.

The classical inheritance thus gives modern Gaelic poetry metrical resources, in the subtle blend of stressed and syllabic verse, comparable to that produced by the fusion of French and Anglo-Saxon measures in English poetry. A demotic syllable-counting verse, with its quiet, tentative movement, is often used for religious and elegiac poetry. The emphasis, however, ought not to be laid so much on choice of subject associated with a particular metrical form as on the relationship between form and its associated rhetorical technique. Some have a rhythmic exuberance, some are exploratory and unhurried, others are abrupt and declamatory. Almost all of this poetry is sung; and in that connection it is relevant to recall W. P. Ker's dictum: 'The difference is in the tune, and it is a difference of thought as well.'

Especially declamatory are the ancient rhythmical metres which antedate the introduction of Christianity and Latin learning and which survived in a modified form though still patently native. The primary function of these particular forms lies in clan panegyric, where the stress is on survival of the group of aristocratic warrior hunters at the top of society. The diction is codified in sets of conventional images, most densely concentrated in the heroic elegy composed at the point of crisis brought about by the death of a leader – in other words, when it is most necessary to reaffirm the traditional values of the community.

One of the stock conventions of this praise-poetry is to rehearse the allies – real or ideal – of a clan. This is developed in poems associated with the eighteenth-century Jacobite Risings. For instance, a poem of 1715 opens by referring to a prophecy (attributed to Thomas the Rhymer) that the Gaels will come into their own again in Scotland: this messianic hope of the disinherited is here firmly pinned on the Jacobite cause, and the poet draws up a formidable list of clans, including those who could not possibly be expected to support Jacobitism. But it is appropriate to note that the bards of Hanoverian

clans were pro-Jacobite, clearly unaffected by the political and religious motives that put their chiefs on the Government side. And in
view of the popular identification made between Jacobitism and
Roman Catholicism, it is worth pointing out that it is a Protestant
poet – Aonghus mac Alasdair Ruaidh – who puts forward the
strongest arguments on behalf of the movement to restore the Stuart
dynasty.

The attempts on the part of poets to preserve at least a conceptual
Gaelic unity, a sense of nationhood, were successful up to a point,
but at a price. The conventions of panegyric became a pervasive
style. The style in turn reflects an attitude towards the world, which
is regarded intellectually in terms of praise versus dispraise.
Through genealogy it works into love poetry; it extends also to
nature poetry, evoking a sense of friendly or unfriendly territory; in
short, it bears the Gaelic sense of social psychology, of history, of
geography. Although 'panegyric' in this context is only a framework, which allows the imagination a great deal of freedom, it seeks
to institutionalise the creative mind and in the end became a
straitjacket.

Through clan poems the social and political values of Gaelic society
find expression. This strand is the Apollonian poetry of Gaelic,
discoursing in a highly deliberate and intellectually controlled manner
on issues that affect the clan or the nation: an example is the poem
against the Union of the Parliaments in 1707.[8]

At the other end of the poetic spectrum we find the Dionysian
poetry that has survived largely in songs used to accompany various
forms of communal labour. The majority were composed by women
and transmitted in a predominantly female environment: more than
one strain in the tradition seems to derive from an exclusively female
sub-culture not necessarily connected with work – accompaniment to
dance is a possibility. Indeed, their strong, almost hypnotic rhythms
give the impression of belonging to an ecstatic ceremony. Their poetry
unfolds, not in a smooth linear movement, but unevenly, with quite
unpredictable changes in focus. But however disconcerting this may at
times be, it is precisely these abrupt transitions from image to image,
governed only by the nature of the situation expressed in the poem,
that release the creative energy. These songs use language according to
a principle which is at the farthest extreme from that of the logical,
ordered sequences of prose. Out of this kaleidoscope of images, fusing
and separating in oral transmission, certain more permanent forms

were from time to time created – for example, the great anonymous poem by a girl to her dead lover Seathan. It ends thus:

But Seathan is tonight in the upper homestead
Neither gold nor tears will win him
Neither drink nor music will tempt him
Neither slaughter nor violence will bring him from his doom [. . .]
Dear Seathan, dear Seathan,
I would not give you to law or king
I would not give you to mild Mary
I would not give you to the Holy Rood
I would not give you to Jesus Christ
For fear I would not get you myself.
O Seathan, my brightness of the sun!
Alas! despite me death has seized you,
And that has left me sad and tearful,
Lamenting bitterly that you are gone;
And if all the clerics say is true,
That there is a Hell and a Heaven,
My share of Heaven – it is my welcome to death –
For a night with my darling
With my companion, brown-haired Seathan.[9]

These tender, intensely passionate songs with their elemental themes provide the main lyrical impulse of Gaelic poetry. They have sometimes been compared with the Scots ballads, for the Ballad starkness is there, often enough. But they lack the supernatural element of the ballads: they are very much poems of this world, and their measure is the measure of a man.

The seventeenth century, to which most of the vernacular poetry we have touched on belongs, is exceedingly rich in various traditional forms. When we come to the eighteenth century, we enter an age of innovation and individual achievement. Alexander MacDonald, the great poet of the '45, was the first person to have a volume of secular poetry published – in 1751. MacDonald was a university man, aware of the wider political and literary issues of the mid-eighteenth century, and he deliberately extended the scope of Gaelic poetry. This he achieved partly by structural means, partly by borrowing from James Thomson and Allan Ramsay and allowing the grafts to take up the vitality of an old Gaelic stock; for instance, in nature poetry. But it is his own native intellectual power and exuberance that gives his genius its force. Of no other Scottish poet can it be said with greater truth that he was possessed by *perfervidum ingenium Scottorum*. His influence was immense. His innovations were rapidly assimilated by contemporaries and successors, some of them illiterate; but so sophisticated is their art that MacDonald's formal learning gives him no advantage over non-literate poets like Duncan Ban Macintyre in Argyll or Rob Donn in Sutherland.

Rob Donn is on the northern boundary of the Gaelic world, psychologically as well as geographically removed from the influence of the Lordship of the Isles and from the panegyric tradition. For that and other reasons, among them the influence of Alexander Pope in Gaelic translation, his poetry of censure is not in the tradition of splendid invective but has the true, and very rare, satirical humour.

Duncan Macintyre, doubtless following MacDonald's example, had his poetry written down for him and published in book form. His masterpiece, 'The Praise of Ben Dorain', is a poem of extraordinary sophistication and sensibility, realising physical nature with a bold sweep of perception but also with a minute, precise, sensual delicateness: the lines of the landscape, the movement of deer, the qualities of the vegetation of the moor. It is a visual documentary, invented before the camera. Duncan Ban is buried in Greyfriars Churchyard in Edinburgh, but he is still remembered in Highland oral tradition: an invariably genial, easy-going man.

Tradition also preserves, perhaps as a counter-weight, the memory of William Ross as the poet who became so anguished and obsessed with a love affair that he wasted away physically to the dimensions of a child. He did in fact die at 28, apparently from tuberculosis, and his love poems are among the finest in all Gaelic.

Finally, in the eighteenth century, Dugald Buchanan of Perthshire is regarded as the most powerful religious poet. His poetry has a terrible austerity: the flame of his compassion barely perceptible in the blinding light of the justice of God. He was a Presbyterian but his 'Day of Judgment' is in the great European tradition of the 'Dies Irae'. These poems are early documents of the Evangelical Revival that was soon to sweep through the entire Highlands and Islands.

Religious poets of the eighteenth century were the first to protest forcefully against the tyranny of landlords. The next century was the bitter century of the Clearances, when the chaos that the break-up of any traditional society produces was intensified beyond endurance in the bewilderment of a people attacked by their own natural leaders.

This broken community eagerly accepted the demands of a passionate and uncompromising faith. It was a new dialectic, powerful enough to replace the deep loyalties of the traditional order, in which not religion but genealogy had been the opiate of the people. Predictably, the Evangelical Revival is bound up with social protest, but since the religion was other-worldly, essentially recluse although practised in open society, it could scarcely yield an adequate strategy from the full range of human experience.

And so Gaelic poetry in the nineteenth and early twentieth centuries is a strange amalgam: the unsettled complex of a transitional age. Partly for that very reason, it is much less dull and trivial than it has often been represented as being. It is sometimes nostalgic and anachronistic, still limited by the stereotype of panegyric. It goes off in false directions that could lead to nothing but sentimentality, as when it borrows from English or Scots and reproduces weak and prettified aspects of Romanticism. (This is not the only stage of Scottish history at which parallels can be drawn between Gaelic and Lowland traditions, but here the parallel is very obvious.)

Yet it is still instinct with the old, splendid craftsmanship and there is a palpable widening and deepening of human sympathy. There are contrasts and oppositions almost at every turn, and they serve to remind us that we are dealing not with one simple strand but with what is still the art of a nation, no matter how attenuated. One vivid contrast, one that might be made a symbol of that age, is provided by the poetry of two MacLeod brothers from Skye: Neil, the reputable author of a highly popular book of poems, a fine, if limited, craftsman whose work almost always tended toward the pretty and sentimental; John, composer of songs in an oral tradition, a sailor and wanderer all his life, a poet of strong, realistic, compassionate poetry, the polarities of which are rooted in the life of Skye and the brutality of life in the sailing ships. John MacLeod was a bohemian trickster, who apparently had strong hypnotic powers; Neil MacLeod was a respectable gentleman and an honoured member of his community.

Contrasts of a different kind emerge in the poetry of Mary MacPherson, the poetess of the radical Land League agitation. In a dialogue poem composed after the flood-tide of the Evangelical Revival had reached Skye and all the pleasures of this world had become vanity, she makes a friend say:

'The people have become so strange
That sorrow to them is wheat
And if you will not go into a whelk-shell for them
You will not be able to stay alive.'

Her own reply comes abruptly:

'We will not go into a whelk-shell for them
And we will be able to stay alive:
Although we will not wear long faces
Nor cause our appearance to change.'

She thanks her friend for her good advice and adds:

'Since vanity is a plant that satisfies the flesh,
it sticks to me as closely as the thong does to the shoe.'[10]

In that climate she could not escape conscience searching. But she had come to terms with herself and had elected to remain robustly of this world, albeit with a strong religious sense of ultimate justice. Her introspection borrows from religion but never turns morbid. She had undergone a harrowing experience of unjust conviction and imprisonment for theft; it was this 'that brought my poetry into being', and the anguish of it remained ardent in her until the end of her life. She had, too, an intense affection for her native community.

All these elements combine in her work, resolved and integrated and given a major dimension by being set in the context of nineteenth-century Radicalism. She had indeed a perverse strain of panegyric (for instance, a 'Song for the Duke of Sutherland'!) which a fuller criticism would take into account. Yet her best work gives the sharp feel of immediate experience while at the same time conveying the pressure of contemporary events. And when she exults that 'We have seen the horizon breaking, the clouds of serfdom dispelled' she is inaugurating a new vision of Gaelic society.

From the nineteenth century onwards the outside world was invading the Gaelic consciousness with cataclysmic effect. The Clearances are usually taken as the prime symbol, but equally destructive in its devastating psychological impact was the imposition of compulsory English education. The 1872 Act abolished the literacy that Gaelic schools had provided, often for monoglot Gaelic speakers. In these circumstances, it is extraordinary that any serious or sophisticated literature survives at all – or rather it would be, were it not for the maintenance of an intellectual tradition and the sense of cultural identity that poetry, very largely circulating orally, kept alive.

The twentieth century witnessed an extraordinary revival. Once again, the parallel with the Lowlands may be noted. John Munro, a university graduate, killed in action in 1918 would certainly, on the promise of the few poems that survived from the trenches of France, have emerged as a major figure. But Sorley Maclean and George Campbell Hay in the Thirties, and Derick Thomson in the Fifties, were the major figures of the movement, and there are a number of other writers, in prose as well as poetry, who are currently extending the tradition. If one were to look for poetic ancestors for the trio mentioned, Munro would have a place in Thomson's genealogy and Mary MacPherson in Maclean's while Campbell Hay's ancestry stretches back to the poets of Classical Gaelic. But that of course is only one aspect: these are contemporary twentieth-century poets whose best poetry is of European stature.

The foregoing account scarcely traces even the salient features of the tradition that they have inherited. It omits, for example, the great collection of charms and incantations and verse prayers that have been published under the title of *Carmina Gadelica*. Most of them are an extraordinary blend of paganism and Christianity: in some, 'paganism' is no more than an academic term, as in these prayers to the sun and moon.

> Greetings to you, sun of the seasons,
> as you travel the skies on high,
> with your strong steps on the wing of the heights;
> you are the happy mother of the stars.
>
> You sink down in the perilous ocean
> without harm and without hurt,
> you rise up on the quiet wave
> like a young queen in flower.[11]

And:

> Greeting to you, new moon,
> kindly jewel of guidance!
> I bend my knees to you,
> I offer you my love.

I bend my knees to you,
I raise my hands to you,
I lift up my eyes to you,
new moon of the seasons. [. . .]

You journey on your course,
you steer the flood-tides,
you light up your face for us,
new moon of the seasons.

Queen of guidance,
queen of good luck,
queen of my love,
new moon of the seasons.[12]

Nor is there space to discuss the epigrams and verse adages that are sometimes reminiscent of the Greek Anthology:

Better is weariness of the legs after a splendid deed
than apathy and weariness of spirit;
weariness of the legs lasts only an hour,
weariness of the spirit lasts for ever.[13]

Frequently verses of such a kind appear in the margins of manuscripts: Gaelic scribes were incorrigibly human. It may be the briefest of comments, like this 'paradigm of a sigh', as it has been aptly described: 'Och, uch, ach, Olivia, it's all right for you!' jotted down when the writer should have been concentrating his attention elsewhere. So, too, as it were in the margins of oral traditions there are stray stanzas, fragments perhaps of longer poems: they wander in the mind, seeking fresh contexts:

I saw a phantom ship last night
A light of death and dread at her mast
And I knew that my young and only son
Was dead beneath the paw of yonder sea.[14]

Or by a woman:

I gave love of such a kind
As would bind the stone without lime
As would send the great ship on the sea
To the heather's crest before she'd stop.[15]

Indicating the main lines of a tradition of necessity turns the attention away from so much of the individual genius: Anna Campbell's lament, for instance, for her drowned lover. It is of the late eighteenth century, but in her distracted grief she calls up an image of a practice that Edmund Spenser mentions in Ireland.

I would drink a drink in spite of my kinsfolk
Not of the red wine of Spain
But the blood of your body – to me a better drink.[16]

We have also to set aside the idiosyncratic, the unexpected quirk of sensibility, the unique quality of imagination such as we find, for example, in the poetry of the obscure Donald of the Lays, son of Finlay who lived in about the year 1600. To him is ascribed a long poem (perhaps a cycle of poems) known as 'The Song of the Owl of Strone',[17] set in the landscape round Ben Nevis. It celebrates mountains and deer-hunting with hounds. It is also concerned with great men, the passage of time, old age, and with many other topics besides. To use Auden's terms, it is full of Sacred Events; and because that ultimate reach of the imagination has been attained, it is simultaneously mundane, vibrant, unmystical, and limitless. The observation in it is a kind of obsessive regard, which at times finds expression in a curious understatement: what emerges has a powerful, disturbing eloquence. But it is much too complex and mysterious to summarise here.

In the twentieth century, and particularly since the 1950s, a tradition of drama has begun to flourish. An annual Gaelic Drama Festival is held in Glasgow, where the movement had its beginnings; significantly, more plays in Gaelic are now being performed at local festivals within the Gaelic-speaking area. The lack of an indigenous dramatic tradition has often been commented on. To some extent, this reflects the rural nature of Gaelic society, the lack of urban centres which might have fostered it. Thus we have no record of mystery and miracle plays. In the period of the Evangelical Revival, the Church itself, particularly in its great open-air communion festivals, satisfied a need for drama.

But there did exist ancient traditions of mumming, associated with Hallowe'en, Christmas, Easter, and with festivals of saints such as St. Bride and St. Michael. They had been given a Christian dress, but they are clearly founded on fertility ceremonies. In the usual manner of such activities, from being performed by adults they developed into children's entertainment. There is one other scrap of information. In 1764 the minister of Glenelg tells that

> The Highlanders, at their festivals and other public meetings, acted the poems of Ossian. Rude and simple as their manner of acting was, yet any brave or generous action, any injury or distress, exhibited in the representation, had a surprising effect towards raising in them corresponding passions and sentiments.

Such evidence as we have, then, suggests strongly that only accidents of history prevented these rudimentary forms from developing. (Interestingly enough the late Professor W. L. Renwick found what might have been the last vestige of dramatic production of Scots ballads in his own Border tradition.)

At all events it is true to say that the main thrust of Gaelic genius has been in poetry, not in drama nor in prose. There is, of course, a prose tradition, and although it has its disjunctions, a case could be made out for its continuity from Classical Gaelic on substantially the same grounds as those advanced by R. W. Chambers for English. In other words, the ecclesiastical influence is paramount: the church is the only public, social institution in which Gaelic is used. The finest prose of all has been lost beyond recall, for it consisted of the extempore sermons and prayers of the Evangelical Revival. Most eighteenth- and nineteenth-century written prose showed ecclesiastical influences of a more moderate and constricting nature; only since the latter half of the twentieth century do we see the steady growth of a more demotic kind. There is one large exception to that, however, in the folktales that have been written down from oral recitation.

For our purposes, we may discount short stories, essays, novels, etc., for the simple reason that they are not available in translation, whereas there are several collections of tales, with English summaries or full translations, dating from the 1860s onwards. This sector of Gaelic literature shares some features with that of poetry. There are an appreciable number of medieval romances which through being read aloud to a semi-literate or completely non-literate audience passed into and survived in oral, colloquial Gaelic. These tales have many of the characteristics of general European medieval romance: there are quests and perilous journeys to strange lands, supernatural adversaries, and the like. A large section consists of 'Fenian' stories, concerned with the exploits of Fionn mac Cumhaill ('Finn mac Cool') and his warriors; Oisean, from which Macpherson's *Ossian* is derived, is the son of Fionn and the poet of this warrior band in the tales and ballads.

One category of stories is known the world over – the 'International Tales' as folklorists call them. Versions of these may be found in Greek mythology, in Sanskrit literature, in collections of popular tales throughout the world, or in English literature, e.g. in Chaucer or Shakespeare. One may still hear the story of the Taming of the Shrew, for instance, in Gaelic, or come across the judgement of Portia and the pound of flesh. 'Three strips of flesh from his back and not one drop of blood to be spilt' as the Gaelic has it. Or it may be the tale more widely known as the story of William Tell, or the Legend of Faust. Professor Kenneth Jackson writes about a visit to a storyteller in Uist:

> listening to the story with the sound of the Atlantic in my ears and the crest of St. Kilda on the horizon it was hard to believe that the first episode occurs in the pseudo-Homer, the main body is in an early Icelandic saga, and the last motif has affinities with an episode in Herodotus.[18]

The story in question was a Novella: these are realistic narratives which quite often introduce the theme of 'poor boy marries rich girl'. They have a wide range, and may borrow from unexpected sources; one very long novella from Benbecula is obviously indebted to *Robinson Crusoe*!

Finally there is one group, and a large one, which is at the farthest remove from the 'Fairytale' type of story and which in certain respects stands alone. These are the historical legends, or more precisely, clan sagas; they are short, many of them no more than anecdotes, and deal with the exploits of the leaders of that society and with feuds between different clans. They sometimes contain elements of the supernatural, not of the extravagant fairytale kind but drawn from the store of traditional belief in second sight and other eerie manifestations and portents. They are certainly founded on historical events and may contain factual information unknown elsewhere; even when they do not, they throw an incidental light on Gaelic attitudes. Almost invariably they are strong, vivid, dramatic narratives reminding us often of the qualities that make the Icelandic sagas so memorable. This extends even to dialogue. We read how the Icelandic warrior, thrust through the body by a spear in the doorway, turns round and observes: 'These broad-bladed spears are becoming fashionable', and it comes vividly before our minds when we hear of an incident in a feud between MacIain of Ardnamurchan and the Camerons.

MacIain raised his helmet then and uncovered his forehead. There were two men of the Camerons opposite him, on the other side of a small stream.

'How nicely an arrow would alight on MacIain's brow!' said one of them.

'That is true', said the other, 'but it is not your wavering eye nor your unsteady hand that could do it.'

The first man was nettled at that. He took careful aim and slipped the arrow. It struck MacIain between the two eyes. MacIain seized the arrow and tore it out of the wound. As it came out the barb of the arrow ripped the artery and the blood gushed forth.

'Was that a cleg that bit me?' he asked. Then he fell to the ground and died.

There is frequently an incident, a mannerism, a physical peculiarity, that identifies a person while he is still far off. Usually it acts as a pivot in the development of the action.

Paul of the Thong in North Uist was given that name because he helped to kill Donald of Harris. Donald's brothers knew that they could not kill Donald except by treachery. They arranged to meet to engage in feats of strength and agility. One of the feats involved leaping through the door of a barn where Paul had been positioned. When Donald of Harris tried the feat, Paul flung a noose round his neck and hanged him in the doorway.

Donald's wife was pregnant and fled to Skye where she bore a son. This became known in Uist. One autumn day, many years later, when Paul and some other men were harvesting, a figure appeared on the skyline. Paul asked at once who it was; they watched him approach but nobody recognised him. Then Paul asked: 'Which way is the wind today?' They told him. Suddenly Paul said: 'If I am not mistaken that is the bouncing step of Angus, son of Donald of Harris!' and he fled, making for the nearest church sanctuary. The stranger, who was indeed Angus, pursued him, overtook him before he got to the sanctuary boundary, and there he killed Paul of the Thong.

That is the barest summary. It is given merely to indicate the tacit power of such legends. Here we have depicted a doomed man who for some twenty years has lived in constant fear, knowing that some day or some night the avenger of blood will appear. His ultimate fate is certain. When nobody can identify the stranger immediately for him, he asks about the wind. What he is concerned with is whether a ship could have sailed from Skye. And he has clearly taken the trouble to find out in detail about the man who is honour bound to take up the blood feud on behalf of his murdered father. He is able thus to identify him himself, from a peculiarity of gait. All this is transmitted with absolute clarity in a few brief phrases.

There is another story which illustrates much the same point but adds a sinister touch. It concerns the avenging of the Heirs of Keppoch. The story is quite long and involved, with a number of dramatic incidents.

A party of Clanranald MacDonalds had come from Uist to Lochaber in order to kill the men who had murdered the rightful heirs of Keppoch. The murderers only came occasionally to Keppoch House since they too knew that the law of the vendetta was inexorable. When the Clanranald men arrived they seized the cowherd but spared his life on condition that he would betray the murderers' presence whenever they came. The signal was to be a cattle-call from a nearby knoll. When the murderers eventually appeared, the cowherd waited until the evening milking, grabbed one of the girls and would let her go only if she promised that she would call a certain cow by name from the knoll.

> 'Why?' asked the girl.
>
> 'Because when I hear you calling that cow Blàrag it seems to me that you have the loveliest head-voice that ever I heard.'
>
> Then he let her go. The girl stood on top of the knoll. 'Blàrag! Blàrag! Blàrag!' she would call. And then she would laugh.

That doom-laden, innocent laugh is hard to forget. From this point the story moves relentlessly towards its foreordained conclusion.

I stated earlier that Gaelic literature had been cut off from the great innovating movements of post-medieval Europe. That this is largely true, at least until the twentieth century, will now be clear. Equally it ought to be clear that Scottish Gaelic literature is not completely a local growth but has direct and indirect links with a much greater world. A close study of its rhetorical structures would demonstrate that beyond possibility of doubt, but it must suffice to draw attention to one figure. There is no more characteristic image of the literatures of medieval Europe than that of the Wheel of Fortune, fixed in the imagination of succeeding generations by Boethius in *De Consolatione Philosophiae*. That this image is a commonplace also of Gaelic poetry, and that it may appear in a song composed in a Hebridean township today, makes an eloquent comment. The continuing neglect of such a fascinating literature is a sad phenomenon of Scottish education.

Sgeul air Cù Chulainn

Nuair a dh'ainmich Domhnall Chaluim Bàin Cù Chulainn an toiseach, bha an naidheachd aige mar a shaoilte a bhitheadh; seadh, mharbh Cù Chulainn a mhac Conlaoch gun fhios aige gura h-e a mhac fhéin a bha ann.

Ach mar a thuirt Domhnall cha robh aige ach bloighean dan eachdraidh agus cha do chlàir e sìon an turas sin. Man àm a thug e dhomh an cunntas seo, bha an aois air laighe air agus a' chuimhne làidir a bh'aige a' fàs fann. Chithear gu bheil e a' ràdh an dara h-uair gun do mharbh Cù Chulainn a mhac; uair eile gura h-e Cù Chulainn am mac agus gun do mharbh athair e.

A thuilleadh air fìor bheagan ann am beulaithris Shléite san Eilean Sgitheanach, is gann gu bheil iomradh an-diugh idir air Cù Chulainn ann an Gàidhlig.[1]

Tha na 'bloighean' aig Domhnall Chaluim Bàin a' cur mìr eile ris an eachdraidh.

'Se 'Cù Chuilinn' an cruth a bha aig Domhnall; chan e 'Cù Chulainn'. Ma bha buaidh aig a' Bheurla air an ainm – is dòcha o ghinealach no dhà air n-ais – chan aithnichte a leithid o sheanchas Dhomhnaill fhéin.

. . . .

'S e Sgitheanach a bh'ann an Cù Chuilinn. Bha mac aige ann an Éirinn agus roghnaich e gu folbhadh e. Bha e ri mhac fhaicinn. Agus thachair a mhac ris agus bha a mhac na b'fhearr na e. Mharbh Cù Chuilinn, mharbh e mhac.

. . . .

Thug iad leotha corp an fhir òig – thug e leis e – agus chaidh e leis fo bhonn craoibheadh ann an Éirinn, Cù Chuilinn. Agus bhàsaich e comh ri corp a mhic fon chraoibh ann an Éirinn. Cha rachadh duine dha choir: bha an t-eagal aca roimhe. 'Sann nuair a chunnaic iad eòin a' laighe man chraoibh, 'sann a thuig iad gu robh Cù Chuilinn marbh. Agus tha e fhé' agus a mhac – a bh'aige an Éirinn – air an tiodhlacadh ann a sin aig bonn na craoibheadh.

. . . .

Bha athair ann an Éirinn is bhiodh am balach òg ag obair air a mhàthair daonnan, Cù Chuilinn, gu dé seorsa duine a bha 'na athair.

'Nach iongantach nach eil e tighinn far a bheil mi na cà faic mi m'athair?'

'Tha e ann an Éirinn', ors ise, ' ' na leithid seo da dh'àite.'

'Well', thuirt esan, 'théid mi agus chì mi m'athair.'

Agus tha e coltach gun robh athair Cù Chuilinn, gur e duine treun a bh'ann fhéi' – fìor dhuine treun – agus nach robh duine an Cóig Cóigeamh na h-Éireann cho calma ris.

Ach chunnaic iad an gaisgeach seo tighinn. Agus 'se an t-athair a chaidh a chur a' chath ris an fhear òg a chunnacas a' tighinn. Agus dh'fhaodadh a' fear òg athair a mharbhadh air a' cheud chaitheadh dan t-sleagh nan do thoilich e fhé'. Ach cha robh e airson athair a mharbhadh. Ach cha robh fhios aig athair có esan air an t-saoghal ach gur e gaisgeach a bh'ann. Agus dh'amais athair, dh'amais e 'm fear òg agus thuit a' fear òg. Is thuirt a' fear òg is e bàsachadh:

Nach b'olc an aithne rinn thu orm
Athair uasail uaibhrich ghràdhaich
Is nach tilginn-s' ach fiar cam
An t-sleagh ann an ceann a h-eàrraich.

'S e an ceann cearr dan t-sleagh a bha a' fear òg a' caitheadh eagal is gu marbhadh e athair.

Well, nuair a chunnaic am bodach gur e mhac a bh'ann, thog e leis a mhac agus thug e go bonn craoibheadh e agus shuidh e fhé' comh ris. Agus cod aige bha 'chridhe tighinn a chòir na craoibheadh? Agus fhuair iad e: nuair a chunnaic iad eunlaith a' laighe air a' chraoibh, thuig iad gu robh gnothaichean sàmhach. Fhuair iad am bodach agus e marbh agus greim aige air a mhac.

English Summary

Folklore about Cù Chulainn is rare in Scotland, and these items, recorded from Donald Sinclair in Tiree, are worth preserving for that reason alone. Although his telling of the tale was originally in its canonical form, by the time he was recorded Donald's memory had become frail with age and he had inverted the roles of Cù Chulainn and his son, Conlaoch.

Twentieth-century Recordings
of Scottish Gaelic Heroic Ballads

The ballads[1] that we call 'Fenian' or 'Ossianic' make their first appearance in literature in Ireland in the twelfth century. Some eight hundred years later a number of these heroic ballads or lays (as well as a couple of ballads on non-Fenian themes) survived in the repertoire of traditional singers in Gaelic Scotland. Since the 1950s the ballads and their melodies have been fairly exhaustively recorded by some members of the staff of the University of Edinburgh's School of Scottish Studies, and are preserved in the School's archives.[2] The second album in the Scottish Tradition series, *Music from the Western Isles*,[3] contains a Fenian ballad 'Latha dh'an Fhinn am Beinn Iongnaidh' ('A day when the Fenians were in the Mountain of Marvels'), sung by a notable singer from South Uist, the late Mrs Archie MacDonald.

I shall give a representative sample of the ballads in our archives.[4] I do not intend, however, to comment in detail on each individual item nor, with one or two exceptions, to discuss the textual relationships of our recorded versions with those to be found in earlier collections. The main interest and value of the recordings lie in the music and in the performance of individual singers. From a purely literary point of view, even our most complete texts add little of interest to what we can find in print; whereas earlier transcriptions of the music of the ballads are much rarer and apparently less accurate or more difficult to interpret. This makes these melodies from the living tradition of unique value but I am not competent to deal with problems of musicology.

Certainly the texts in general are of great interest from both historical and anthropological points of view, showing what did survive and in what form they are preserved. How full or how fragmentary are they? How pure or how corrupt is the transmission? Why did they survive in some communities and not in others? There are also some questions that, I fear, can never be answered now. For instance, when we are dealing with what we call a corrupt text, what did the singers themselves make of it? While the main lines of the narrative may be clear enough, there are frequently obscure words and phrases upon which the singers might have provided their own gloss, whether their personal interpretation would have solved any literary cruces for us or not. This applies particularly to recordings made in the early 1950s by singers who are now dead.

In view of all these things, I shall on the whole confine my remarks to a sketch of the background – the specifically Scottish cultural setting – for although this is a literary inheritance in which Scots and Irish Gaels share, the differing historical circumstance of the two countries tended to produce, as one might predict, certain divergent features. Indeed, the most obvious of these is the survival in Scottish Gaelic oral tradition of the heroic lay as a sung form – whereas in Ireland the practice of singing the ballads has now apparently come to an end.

Now if the Fenian ballads appear as early as the twelfth century in literary form, the fact that oral versions exist at all in a living tradition at the present time is undeniably a remarkable instance of cultural continuity and survival. Yet, whatever may be true of the melodies, so far as textual transmission goes, this is true only in a broad, general sense. None of the ballads in the archives, some of which appear to be purely Scottish compositions, can be traced to such remote origins. On the whole, the later medieval period is probably as early as we can go.

Duain na Féinne(adh) 'the poems of the Fenian-band' is the commonest term now in circulation for the Fenian lays. Fionn and his warriors are not known collectively in colloquial Gaelic as *Fian(n)a* but as *Féinn, Fèinn* or *Fìnn*, depending on dialect: with the article *An Fhéinn*, etc. An individual member is *Fiantaiche*; the plural *Na Fiantaichean* is to be heard side by side with *An Fhéinn*. In some areas *fiantaiche* denotes a wild, uncouth person, more commonly applied to a male than a female, but the feminine *banfhiantaiche* is also known. In some of the strict Presbyterian communities 'fiantaiche' may have the connotation of 'anti-ecclesiastical' or be applied to non-churchgoing members of that society. Indeed, in certain contexts 'fiantaiche' can quite happily be translated as 'heathen' or even 'pagan'. This is no doubt connected with the debates in which Oisein is made the opponent of St Patrick; but the ascetic evangelicalism of relatively modern times clearly plays a major part in this particular semantic development. All over the Gaelic-speaking area, the phrase 'cothrom na Féinne(adh)' – the chance of a fair fight, traditionally offered by the Fenians to their opponents in battle – is still used in the sense of 'fair play'. But not everyone who uses that phrase is aware of the historical or linguistic connections with 'fiantaiche'.

There is no Gaelic word for 'ballad' in the sense of 'narrative poem'. A heroic lay may be 'dàn', 'duan' or 'laoidh'.[5] More precisely, in present day usage, these three terms are used in titles by which singers and listeners alike identify a ballad, e.g. 'Dàn na h-Inghinne', 'Duan na Ceardaich', 'Laoidh a' Choin Duibh'. Using 'poem' as a convenient term for the moment, these are respectively 'The Poem of the Maiden', 'The Poem of the Smithy' and 'The Poem of the Black Hound'. Occasionally *òran*, the unmarked term in modern spoken Gaelic for song-poem, has also been used, to judge from titles in collections. The one ballad from the Isle of Skye in our archives, recorded by myself in 1953, was known to the reciter, Donald Robertson, as 'Òran-mór na Féinne'. He could trace it back in his family to the middle of the nineteenth century but there was no melody for it. The term 'òran-mór', where it exists in genuine oral tradition, does not seem to denote any particular verse structure – in contrast to 'ceòl-mór' and 'port-mór' in piping. Of the examples I know, two are choral refrain compositions (of the waulking song type). The phrase is qualitative, with an aura of dignity, even grandness.

Of the other terms, *dàn* is not now used in the ordinary registers of spoken Gaelic. *Duan* ranges from 'song, rhymed composition, ditty' to 'recitation'; like *iorram* 'rowing-song', it is extended to mean 'harping on, being excessively repetitive', etc. Specifically it is used of certain compositions: Christmas carols, Hogmanay rhymes, and other miscellaneous poems, recited not sung.

In some respects the most interesting term is *laoidh*. Hector Maclean, who was one of J. F. Campbell's fellow-workers, has a note: 'Laoidh, lay, ode, lyric; it differs from dàn a poem, in being more melodious and capable of being sung. It narrates rapidly a few events ending tragically, almost invariably the death of a hero.'[6] As to the last, Maclean no doubt had in mind the Fenian 'Laoidh Dhiarmaid' and the non-Fenian 'Laoidh Fhraoich': these two heroes, Diarmad and Fraoch, both die tragically.

Most modern tradition-bearers imply that all the ballads were at least 'capable of being sung'; where they were not, it was because the melody had been lost in transmission. None the less, it may be the case that some ballads were always recited rather than sung.[7] One of my best informants, the late Domhnall Chaluim Bàin (Donald Sinclair) of Tiree certainly thought that this might be so. He also endorsed, without any prompting by me, the judgement expressed by Hector Maclean to the effect that 'laoidh' was 'more melodious'.

I may add that in everyday Gaelic usage, the generic sense of 'laoidh' is 'hymn, spiritual song'. There is no doubt a continuity of meaning here from early times: the word was used *inter alia* in the sense of a 'poem as medium for legal, historical, religious and didactive lore'. But our easy acceptance in Gaelic of the use of 'laoidh' in sacred and secular contexts alike is surely striking.

Fionn and his men were regarded as historical characters. They were also accorded what practically amounted to a religious veneration. It is told traditionally that one of the nineteenth-century collectors, the Rev. Dr John MacDonald of Ferintosh, a minister of the Free Church of Scotland, once asked an old man in Kintail whether he believed in the historical existence of the Féinn. The man apparently was shocked that the minister should even ask such a question and retorted: 'Do I believe in Christ!' Modern scholars' theories that Fionn originally belonged more to the realm of mythology than of history were anticipated by Dr Alexander MacBain. On one occasion he is said to have roused an audience of Gaelic speakers in Glasgow to intense anger by expressing these ideas. To such people, Fionn and Gráinne had virtually the status of Biblical characters; in that respect not so different in popular imagination from Adam and Eve, who, of course, were regarded as historical characters also. People who would never deny the truth of the Scriptures believed equally strongly in the Gaelic messianic tradition that puts Fionn, lying in Tom na h-Iubhraich, near Inverness, in the role of Sleeping Warrior who will one day reappear to restore the Gaels of Scotland to their former greatness. They also had the evidence of place names to remind them of the names and exploits of these gigantic warriors of song and legend. Not surprisingly a very substantial body of Fenian folktales has been recorded direct from the storytellers by the collectors of the School of Scottish Studies. From the wealth of textual material in collections of the past, taken down from the mouths of the people, we know that the ballads too were immensely popular.

Viewed against that background, then, what is curious is not so much that the ballads survived into the twentieth century but rather that so few of them should have survived. Discounting variants, rerecordings, and odd fragments, and counting titles only, the total of sung ballads in the School's collection amounts to no more than half-a-dozen, to which we can add the two non-Fenian heroic lays. There are, however, in addition to that, genuine oral versions without melodies, as already indicated, and there are others in manuscript which may be genuine enough texts but have come from printed sources.

In terms of contemporary Gaelic oral culture, Fenian tales and heroic ballads alike (Fenian or not) are now little more than curiosities but the quantitative difference is none the less striking. Progressive anglicisation, the devastation of the Clearances, emigration in general, changes in literary fashion: all these are well-known contributory factors in the over-all decline. But perhaps because the ballad-singers were specialists in a more demanding craft, they were fewer in number from the beginning.

Nevertheless, most of Gaelic Scotland is represented in the early manuscript collections. Galloway alone, in the extreme south-west of the country, where Gaelic survived until 1700 or later, is blank. Since Manx Gaelic ballads are mentioned in the eighteenth century,[8] we may assume that the seanchaidhs and singers of Galloway knew them too.

Setting aside the *Book of the Dean of Lismore*,[9] substantial collecting begins about 1739 with the work of the Rev. Alexander Pope – 'Alasdair Pàp', as he was still remembered in Sutherland in my boyhood – minister of the parish of Reay in Caithness. Before 1760 the Rev. James Maclagan in Perthshire had made 'a good collection'; Rev. Donald MacNicol, an Argyll minister, was a contemporary collector; and the work continued well into the nineteenth century, with Presbyterian clergymen prominent throughout.[10] With one or two exceptions, these were ministers of the Established Church of Scotland, whose attitudes towards the secular arts were markedly different from those of the equally Gaelic evangelicals of the nineteenth century, most of whom severed themselves from the Established Church at the Disruption of 1846. This has some relevance to the distribution of ballads in the twentieth century.

The areas from which our recordings come are as follows: on the Scottish mainland, Sutherland and Ross-shire; in the islands, Skye, Mull, Tiree, North and South Uist, Benbecula, and Barra.

The bulk of our recordings – in fact, all the 'titles' alluded to above, given in more or less close variants by a number of singers – come from the Catholic communities of Benbecula, South Uist and Barra, in the Outer Hebrides. From the same communities we also have manuscript versions of texts without melodies. The other areas I have named are each represented by one singer only: these are Presbyterian communities. The breakdown for the latter is as follows: on the mainland of Scotland, one from Lairg in the South of Sutherland; one from Lochalsh, four from Kintail: both on the western coast of Ross-shire; in the islands, one from Mull, four from Tiree: both in the Southern Hebrides; one from the Isle of Skye (without melody). I shall have some further comments to make on these later.

This distribution does not reflect simply a religious divide in Gaelic culture. Distance from centres of anglicising influence has clearly played a crucial part for there are no ballads to be found now, nor since the 1960s, in the Roman Catholic communities of mainland Scotland. Nevertheless, religion has played its own part. Beginning towards the end of the eighteenth century, and continuing into the twentieth century, a popular movement of radical dissent developed within Gaelic Presbyterianism. It was essentially a form of recluse religion practised in, and attempting to dominate, open society; the great majority of its converts came to regard the arts as *vanitas vanitatis*. Fenian ballads may have become a special target because of their 'heathenish' associations: symbols, as it were, of a competing faith. Certainly other types of song (e.g. waulking songs) continued to flourish in the heartland of Evangelical Presbyterianism. But even as early as 1763 the Rev. Alexander Pope notes that 'many of [the ballads] are lost, partly owing to our clergy, who were declared enemies to these poems.'

I want now to make some comments on a number of individual ballads. The first, 'Duan na Ceardaich', is confined to the North Uist to Barra group of islands.[11] Throughout that area it was, within the period of the School's collecting work, and for a considerable length of time before that, the best known of all lays. This is largely due to the fact that it was put to use as one of the *Duain Challainn* 'Hogmanay Rhymes' recited by bands of guisers during their circuit of the township.[12] So far as I know, it is the only example of a heroic lay in that repertoire. It was sometimes sung by the guisers; this, too, is unusual, if not unique: Duain Challainn were normally recited or declaimed.

The oldest literary version is in the seventeenth-century Irish anthology *Duanaire Finn*;[13] the editor dates it to about 1400. The ballad recounts how Fionn and some of his warriors had weapons forged for them by Lon mac Líomhtha, the supernatural smith, and how Caoilte got his name.

The argument of the ballad, as set out by the editor of *Duanaire*

Finn, runs thus:

> Eight of the Fiana, including Fionn and Daolghus, find themselves on Sliabh Luachra [in Kerry]. A monstrous warrior approaches them. He says that he is Lon, chief smith of Norway, and that he has come to race the Fiana. Thereupon he leaps from them. The eight Fian warriors follow him. Lon takes them from Kerry by Limerick through Clare, Galway and Roscommon to the hill of Keshcorran [in South East Sligo]. Lon enters the cave of Keshcoran. In the cave is a smithy with smiths at work. Lon sets about making a sword. Daolghus assists him. Daolghus grows warm till his face glows like a lighted coal. The smiths present ask who this man can be, using the compound adjective *Caoilte* 'slender and hot' to describe him. Fionn fixing on the adjective decides that Daolghus shall be for ever known as Caoilte. Lon offers the Fian hospitality and presents them with spears and swords, the names of which are given. At sun-rise next morning the Fian, having slept soundly, find themselves once more on Sliabh Luachra.

The phrase 'chief smith of Norway' requires elucidation. *Lochlann*, translated 'Norway' above, and in many contexts in modern Gaelic meaning just that, is in earlier, medieval Gaelic a fabulous land which later came to be associated with the Vikings and their homeland. But in other contexts, as here, it remains 'the wonderland of Norway, hovering between geography and romance', as one scholar neatly puts it. In Lochlann there is 'one fixed point', *Beirbhe*, translated Bergen.

In order to show something of the relationship between the literary ballad of c.1400 and the oral versions in Scotland, I shall quote the English translation of the older literary text given in *Duanaire Finn* and then translate the oral version,[14] paraphrasing where a detailed commentary would otherwise be required. I take the *Duanaire Finn* text to be the original of the oral versions: comparison of the Gaelic texts leave little doubt that they are ultimately derived from it.

> Write it, Brogán, a writing,
> in truly pleasant wise speech,
> something of the adventures of the son of Cumhall
> who endured many hard trials.
>
> Let us listen to what Oisín says
> in very mild most pure speech;
> I have not heard from the valiant troop
> a tale it were more fitting to write.

Tell, son of the prince,
in clear voice of little falsehood:
recount for us sweetly and gently
the true tales of the Fian.

Tell us, without omitting it
(let it be no heedless answer),
why the breaker up of combats
was called Caoilte.

We arrive one day on Luachair Deadhadh;
our company was eight brave men,
seven of us about the high king:
dear was that noble and gentle warlike band

I and Daolghus and Diarmaid,
three who obtained roasting in hunting booth,
the three sons of the One Craftsman of Beare,
Fionn himself and Mac Lughach.

We were but a short while on the hill
(long will that tale be remembered)
till there came to us on the fair-sodden plain
a hugely tall warrior with a single foot.

Wonderful was the appearance of the warrior:
we take up arms on seeing him:
he had three arms swinging:
his face was the colour of coal.

One foot supported him on the mountain
as he approached us from peak to peak:
he had one eye in his forehead,
and his gaze was on the son of Cumhall.

One leap sufficed to carry him
over each fair-sodden wild glen.
Hardly did the edge of his garment
reach over his buttocks.

He wore a shirt of twisted waxed thread,
a gray tunic and a red mantle
and a great jet-black waxed hooded cloak of deerskin
on the upper portion of his body.

His big straight dark-blue foot
was more than each warrior's hand could hold:
longer than the shaft of each spear
was the distance from his knee to his ankle.

A headgear for the same cloak was about his head,
which had the appearance of (?) coal.
The shadow of his hand and his gloom
were sufficient danger for us.

When he had come upon the hill,
having approached us, he said,
'May the gods bless thee,
son of Cumhall.'

'May they bless thee too (?)', said Fionn the warrior;
'Who art thou, single man whom I know not?
Tell us thy true name,
O man with the skin garment.'

'Lon son of Líomhtha is the name I have been given;
I have mastered the nature of every craft;
it is I who am teacher of smiths
to the king of Lochlann in Bergen.

'Líomhthach the young, daughter of Bolcán,
she had no ill fortune in her children:
no object of pity is the man who won my mother,
who bore me and my other brother.

'To seek an even race
I have come to you from Bergen:
they say that you are swift,
O people skilled in craft:

'A *geas* and the pangs of a woman in travail (?) be upon you,
ye leaders in every strait,
if the eight of you do not follow me
to the door of my smithy.'

He leaps from us
like a spring wind going over mountain tops.
We followed him forthwith,
a few of the nobles of the Fian.

By the side of Luachair Deadhaidh,
past the gate of Bealach Luimnigh,
over Sliabh Oidhidh, over Eachtghe,
we go in four bands.

The smith formed one of those bands:
everyone was far behind him;
he had a big advantage over Daolghus:
Fionn came after them unaccompanied.

Diarmaid and Mac Lughach
were three hills' length behind them:
I and the three sons of the Craftsman
formed a brave band of four.

Through Magh Maoin, through Magh Maine did we go
(they were far from us after our journey),
into great Magh Meadhbha
across Áth Bearbha, over Mucais

Close by the grave of Fraoch son of Fiodhach
(it was no easy going),
over Gleann Cuilt and over Cruachain:
there Daolghus quickened his pace.

From Magh Luirg down to Seaghais,
indeed, we catch up on one another:
the smith and Daolghus went from us
into the bare hill of Ceann Sléibhe.

We come right up to the Cave of Corann:
'He has gone before us,' said Daolghus:
'Wait awhile, smith:
thou shalt not go in alone.'

They go together into the cavern,
Fionn pressing upon them manfully:
they found bellows a-blowing:
they found earth and a forge,

Anvils and sledgehammers being smitten
and a swift strong blast of flame,
seven swords too stretched out
in straight and lovely masses (?).

Lon himself said, beseeching them (?),
to the grim and mighty gathering,
'This alone is my portion
of the weapons yet unmade.'

He put a tongs into the hearth
and lifted a stone with four ridges:
the smith and Daolghus carried out
some keen and nimble hammering.

The smith had two great sledgehammers
and a strong gray-sided tongs:
he had three hands attending to his tools:
Daolghus responded well.

They make a hard sharp sparkling blade
of good success (?) in striking:
for a hilt's length it lacked two edges,
a fair gray shoot of steel.

Daolghus grew warm beside the forge
(stout were his combats):
redder than glowing coal
was his complexion after the work.

The smiths, who were full rough and surly, said,
'Who is the slender warm man
without weakness who is stretching
the bar of steel?'

Fionn, who made every problem easy,
said answering them,
'That shall be his name always:
Daolghus shall be called Caoilte.'

There you have the manner of his naming
(Good were his valour and his deeds),
Caoilte who was not wont to refuse,
it is fitting to write his tidings.

'Let the soldiery who have come to us
be attended to', said Lon the strong:
'Let a rich bed-chamber be made ready
which will befit the son of Cumhall.

'Give them to keep, to each man
the price of his journey,
to do battle and combat,
a spear and a blue blade of true fierceness.

'Leave steadfast Fionn to me:
I shall give him a pair for battle,
a straight spear, a very straight spear,
and a truly lovely long sword.'

They give us the charmed weapons thereupon
when they had been made,
seven swords and nine spears
from which came many wounds out of harsh fierceness.

Mac an Luin was the name of Cumhall's sword
which caused the flesh of men to suffer:
Diarmaid of the poems had the Drithlinn:
the Créchtach was Caoilte's hard blade.

Fead and Fí and Fosgadh
(many victories have they won me),
these were the swords of the Craftsman's three sons
(they broke up many hard situations).

Here in my hand is Gearr na gColann
which used to be girt on me in fights:
Mac Lughach had the Échtach:
he was happy as he went to victory.

Good was our dark-brown clothing
and our music of brown-plumaged hooded birds:
at rising time next day
we had had sufficient sleep.

When the sun rose next day
on pure Sliabh Luachra
our long swords were good
and our thick strong spears.

It is hard that there should be a complete end
to the fair-haired truly pure host:
O white-penned writer of Patrick,
woe for him who has attained the days when men write about them.

And now the translation of the oral version:

On a day when the Féinn were on Luachair Leodhair,
four young men (warriors) in the company:
myself and Osgar and Daorghlas,
and Fionn himself, the son of Cumhall.

We saw coming from the mountains
a tall dark, one-legged man
with a cloak of dark-grey skin
and an apron of the same dress.

Fionn spoke there on the mountainside
to him as he was passing them,
'To what land is your journey,
man with the skin cloak?'

'Lon son of Líobhann is my name –
if you are bent on hearing my story –
I was for a time tending goats
for the King of Lochlann in Gailbhinn.

'I am of the line of MacAsgaill's daughter
who was good in charge of children:
happy the woman who was mother
to me and my other brother.

'If you mean to attend at the smithy,
then I bind you to go to a dark glen
at the west of the world
far from its door.'

'Smith, where is your smithy:
would we be the better for seeing it?'
'If I could help it, you would not be the better for seeing it –
why should you be?'

Then they set off on their journey,
[through] the Province of Luimneach;
they reached the green Knoll of Dreathaibh
and there divided into four companies.

One band was the Smith's,
another was the band of Daorghlas,
another was the band of Dearg mac Dreathaibh;
Fionn was the last, he was by himself.

The Smith took but one stride
to cross each wild glen:
we could scarcely see
a corner of his cloak on his buttocks.

'Open, open!' said the Smith,
'Don't shut the door before me,' said Daorghlas.
'I would not leave you in the doorway of my smithy,
all alone in a perilous place!'

There they got bellows for blowing,
there they got gear for the smithy;
then there came four smiths:
repulsive, misshapen men.

Four arms on each smith;
tools for gripping, tongs of iron;
the smith who attended them spoke:
no less well did Daorghlas answer.

It was Daorghlas who was heating the forge
(the man who stays standing):
redder than oak charcoal
was his face from the fruit of his labour.

Then one of the smiths spoke,
fearfully and angrily:
'The right hand of that thin one who has no fear in him
has ruined my steel anvil.'

Fionn spoke, he was there beside them,
for it was he who was holding the tongs:
'Daorghlas being called "Caoilte" –
that will make it a widespread name!'

They got there beaten out
the straight, bright swords –
a band fully armed
with the magic swords of the green.

'Fead' and 'Faoidh' and 'Eigheach'
and 'Conalach son of the Smithy';
the twelve swords of Diarmaid –
many a man they killed.

I had 'Geard na Colann',
useful in time of battle;
'Mac a' Luin' in the hand of the son of Cumhall,
it never left unsevered a shred of mortal flesh.

Do you remember the day of the tongue
in the smithy of the Clan of MacLiobhann?
Tonight I lament my condition
after counting the company.

It is interesting to note what changes have occurred in the course of transmission. First, the oral version omits the preamble (four quatrains), the coda (one quatrain), and any reference not only to St Patrick's scribe Brogán but also to Oisín, though the latter is of course known as the poet of the Féinn in Gaelic Scotland. Second, practically the entire litany of Irish place names is dropped: this is natural enough. Of those that remain 'Luachair Deadhadh' becomes 'Luachair Leodhain / Leothaid[17] / Leothair'. For 'Eachtghe' the oral lay substitutes either 'Breitheamh' or 'Dreathaibh'. 'Bealach Luimnigh' (the 'Pass of Luimneach', i.e. Limerick), however, is discernible in the phrase which has been transcribed hitherto as 'buidheann choige(amh) luimneach' and translated as 'five bands'. The word for a 'fifth' (i.e. a province) of Ireland appears elsewhere in Scots Gaelic e.g. 'Cóigeamh Mhumha na h-Éireann' (the Province of Munster); earlier versions of our lay have 'Air Choige Mhumha' and 'Mar chuige mugha na luimedheirg' in the corresponding quatrain. 'Lochlann' remains but 'Beirbhe' ('Bergen'), becomes 'Gailbhinn' ('Galway') here; although 'Beirbhe' remains in earlier variants. It is found also in the poetry of Màiri nighean Alasdair Ruaidh.[18] Third, the names of the swords are little changed: even within the group of very close variants on which the translation is based, we get 'Geur nan Calg' ('Sharp of Swords') as an alternative to 'Geard na Colann' ('Guard of Body'). 'Fasgadh' appears in an earlier printed version.

Finally, two diverting corruptions, 'Ollamh gabhonn' ('teacher of smiths') becomes 'uallach ghabhar' ('tending goats'): the correspondence is clear, visually and aurally, even if the option taken is not. It is, presumably, a recent change: earlier variants from oral tradition keep the original sense. Similarly, 'na teangann' ('of the tongue') is 'na teannruith' ('of the hard running'), in earlier variants.

The ballad in oral tradition has been stripped down to the essential narrative. Just enough is kept to preserve the weird, surrealistic atmosphere: the vivid description of the Supernatural Smith and his helpers is unimpaired; at the same time, the scene in the smithy is naturalistic in its detail: Caoilte red in the face from blowing the bellows; Fionn standing up because he has to hold the red-hot iron on the anvil with the great pincers. The warriors of the Féinn are brought into a familiar, everyday setting.

The next ballad is 'Duan na Muilgheartaich / Muirgheartaich' (the name exists in a number of variants), the lay that tells of the monstrous, one-eyed hag (a small minority of earlier versions make her a male) who comes across the sea to fight the Féinn. It is now known only in South Uist and Barra though it once had a wide distribution. The name is still remembered in Tiree and no doubt elsewhere.

The Muilgheartach, to construct a composite picture, is a horrible apparition: bald, red, thick-maned; her forehead is dark-grey, charcoal-coloured, her teeth red and slanting; she is one-eyed and the darting glance of her eye is keener than a winter star. The great bristles of her head are like withered brushwood covered with hoarfrost. She carries a rusty sword, etc. She is associated with the Ocean Smith; when she is killed by the Féinn, the Smith informs the High King, his father; this king in some variants is the King of Lochlann and, in related stories, the Muilgheartach his (foster-)mother. She herself is first seen 'coming on the tops of the waves'; she attacks the Féinn 'like the sea against the stones of a shingle beach'; after her death, the king swears that he will kick the sea into storm, lift it from its walls of waves and drag the land with curved crooks out of the ocean.

Nineteenth-century collectors and scholars, apparently in line with theories then current concerning Nature gods and Nature myths, explained the Muilgheartach as a personification of the sea. The Rev. J. G. Campbell of Tiree, a noted collector and interpreter of Gaelic oral tradition, calls her 'the ocean itself in the flesh'.[19] Donald Sinclair, son of one of Campbell's informants, told me that his father, Calum Bàn, a fisherman, would glance out when the sea looked threatening and remark, 'Tha droch coltas air a' Mhuilgheartaich an-diugh.' ('The Muilgheartach has a bad appearance today.') This raises the interesting question: is the idea of 'the ocean itself in the flesh' a concept of native Gaelic tradition? Or did the learned minister of Tiree impart the notion to Calum Bàn?

At all events, the Muilgheartach is always closely connected with the sea. The same scholars and collectors interpreted her name as a compound of 'muir' ('sea') and 'iar' ('west') or 'ear' ('east'), with an adjectival suffix. The name may contain 'muir' (with the not uncommon 'l' / 'r' interchange); the rest of the proposed etymology is not possible. Reidar Thoralf Christiansen is inclined to think that, while as she appears in the ballads she seems to belong to Gaelic tradition [. . . she has a] parallel in certain old stories of gigantic females living in the Northern seas [. . .] there are accounts in old Norse sources, as in more recent tradition, of beings that seem to bear a resemblance to the Muireartach. The márgygr of the Speculum regale belongs to this class, she was seen on the Greenland coast, was of tremendous size, and had thick heavy hair which fell all around her head and neck. She was web-footed and used to appear before great storms.[20]

Christiansen's suggestion of a Norse origin makes good sense and better sense if we regard 'margýgr' as a slip for 'margýgr' ('sea-ogress'). Neither 'Muirgheartach' nor any of its variant forms, however, can be derived directly from 'margýgr'. It may be instructive to consider the Lowlands Scots *Gyre-carlin(g)* 'an ogress', whose name is Norse 'gýgr' and 'kerling' ('woman') but many of those attributes are those of the Cailleach, the great Hag of Gaelic tradition, associated with wild weather, the wilderness, the deer, etc. The Gyrecarlin appears to be a composite figure; the Muilgheartach may be likewise. Her name, also, to extend these speculations, may be a contamination product of Norse and Gaelic elements. In this connection, the personal name Muircheartach can hardly be irrelevant.[21]

The next ballad is 'Laoidh Dhiarmaid' ('The Lay of Diarmad').[22] Once widely distributed, it has been recorded as a sung ballad only in South Uist and Barra, and in Kintail. I myself heard a part of it recited in Skye in my boyhood; Domhnall Chaluim Bàin in Tiree knew of it; and snatches of it are still quoted here and there throughout the Highlands and Islands.

The oldest literary version is in the *Book of the Dean of Lismore*.

Fionn has never forgiven his sister's son Diarmaid [. . .] for eloping with Fionn's unloving wife, Gráinne [. . .] A formal reconciliation has been made, but Fionn is bent on revenge [. . .] Fionn prevailed on Diarmaid to go to hunt the venomous magic boar and is himself unscathed. Disappointed at this, Fionn asks Diarmaid to measure and remeasure the boar. The venomous bristles pierce Diarmaid's sole and he dies [. . .]

In Scotland, the scene of the boar-hunt and Diarmaid's death is located in Sutherland, in Kintail, in Brae Lochaber, in Knapdale, in Skye, in Tiree, and most firmly in Perthshire [. . .] This poem, which is not found in Ireland, we are probably safe in regarding as not only purely Scottish, but of Perthshire origin.[23]

Nowadays the lay is invariably known as 'Laoidh Dhiarmaid'; the first line of verse 3 in the Dean's book is 'Èisdidh beag madh ail Libh Laoidh' ('Listen a little, if you would have a lay'); our sung versions begin at that line. In earlier collections, 'Dàn', 'Duan', 'Cumha' ('Elegy, Lament'), and 'Bàs' ('Death'), all appear in the title. The Rev. Alexander Pope has a celebrated account of the singing of this lay:

> There is an excellent poem, called Duan Dearmot, it is an elegy on the death of that warrior, and breathes the sublime very much. This poem is in esteem among a tribe of Campbells that live in this country [the parish of Reay in Caithness], and would derive their pedigree from that hero [. . .] There is an old fellow in this parish that very gravely takes off his bonnet as often as he sings Duan Dearmot: I was extremely fond to try if the case was so, and getting him to my house I gave him a bottle of ale, and begged the favour of him to sing Duan Dearmot; after some nicety, he told me that to oblige his parish minister he would do so, but to my surprise he took off his bonnet. I caused him stop, and would put on his bonnet; he made some excuses; however as soon as he began, he took off his bonnet, I rose and put it on; he took it off, I put it on. At last he was like to swear most horribly he would sing none, unless I allowed him to be uncovered; I gave him his freedom, and so he sung with great spirit. I asked him the reason; he told me it was out of regard to the memory of that hero. I asked him if he thought that the spirit of that hero was present; he said not; but he thought it well became them who descended from him to honour his memory [. . .][24]

Of the ballads in general Pope observes: 'The greatest number are called Duans [. . .] others have different names, but the Duans are generally set to some tunes *different from the rest*.' (My emphasis.) In view of the use of 'Laoidh' in the actual text of this ballad, does Pope's comment have any connection with Hector MacLean's remark, quoted above, that laoidh is 'more melodious' than dàn? Since Pope says that the 'greatest number are called Duans', it seems unlikely; but there may be something here to be investigated.

'Laoidh a' Choin Duibh' ('The Lay of the Black Hound'), is my next example. It is known in Benbecula, South Uist, and Lochalsh – the last, however, a mere fragment recorded from the late Mary Stewart, a member of a family of 'travelling-folk'.

The ballad tells of the fight between Bran, Fionn's famous hound, and the Black Hound, belonging to a stranger. The Black Hound kills a hundred and fifty (the numbers vary) of the hounds of the Féinn before Fionn looses Bran, who kills the Black Hound. 'Laoidh a'

Choin Duibh' is one of a group of ballads that exists in another verse form. I shall comment on these later, taking them together.

The next ballad, 'Laoidh Chaoilte' ('The Lay of Caoilte') appears on the School of Scottish Studies album *Music from the Western Isles* under the title 'Latha dh'an Fhinn am Beinn Iongnaidh'. This is actually the first line of the lay, which is also known as 'Caoilte and the Giant', etc. Here is the English translation which is given in the booklet that accompanies the album:

A day when the Fenians were in the Mountain of Marvels
All of the Fenians, the fierce men
They sent Caoilte, because of his swiftness
Ahead of them to act as guide.

They saw a house far off
With its two doors open
A lovely maid stood on its floor
And a big fire burning steadily
She gave me, as it seemed to me,
Two-thirds of her food and two-thirds of her attire.

Who loomed over me obscuring the light
In the rough doorway but a great giant,
'Keep well clear of me
It wasn't you I came for
But for a sweetheart I had long ago
A honey-sweet girl with beguiling eyes
Seven years have I waited for her
And today I have met you to your misfortune.'

He cast with all his venom
The great spear that was in his hand.

I made a sudden, stabbing cast
And struck his five heads off his neck.

I rested my elbow on the ground
And my wounds bled heavily.

We now come to two non-Fenian heroic ballads, the first of which is 'Laoidh Fhraoich' ('The Lay of Fraoch'). It has been recorded in

Skye, South Uist, Tiree, and Mull. To this may be added a version made up of a text (without melody) from Skye and a tune from South Uist.

This distribution suggests a popularity which tradition corroborates. The scene of the ballad's events is localised in three places: Rannoch, in Perthshire; Loch Awe-side in Argyll; the island of Mull.[25] The oldest literary version, ascribed to an author whose name has been variously interpreted, is in the *Book of the Dean of Lismore*. The editor Neil Ross dates it to the fourteenth century, summarises the story, and gives a brief account of its relationship with the early Irish tale *Táin Bó Fraích*:

> Fraoch son of Fiodhach and of the fairy Be Fhionn, a prince of Connacht and the fairest of the men of Ireland and Scotland, comes to the house of Ailill and Meadhbh, king and queen of Connacht, to woo their daughter Fionnabhair. He refuses, however, to pay such a bride-price as they ask. To prevent his carrying off Fionnabhair, Ailill plans his death. He gets him to swim in a pool in which is a deadly monster. By asking him to fetch a rowan branch from the far side of the pool, Ailill keeps Fraoch in the water until the monster seizes him. With a knife thrown to him by Fionnabhair, Fraoch, though wounded, slays the monster [. . . Fraoch] is removed by fairies and shortly healed [. . .] in the end Fionnabhair is betrothed to him [. . .]

> In the poem it is Meadhbh, who in anger at Fraoch's refusal to be her lover, compasses Fraoch's death. She sends him to fetch magic rowans guarded by a monster in the loch at the root of the tree. With the knife thrown by Fionnabhair he fights the beast, but as he kills it he dies himself [. . .][26]

I do not intend to comment on this further as the whole question of the relationship of ballad to tale, etc. has been meticulously examined by Dr Donald Meek.[27]

'Laoidh Fhraoich', as all the singers call it, appears also, in earlier collections, as 'Duan Fhraoich' or 'Bàs Fhraoich'. This last is the title in the collection made by Jerome Stone (1727-56). In 1756, the year of his death, Stone contributed an English poem of 20 ten-line stanzas, entitled 'Albin and the Daughter of Mey', to the *Scots Magazine*. It purports to be a translation of 'The Death of Fraoch'; in reality it is no more than loosely based on the original Gaelic ballad. A stanza from the middle of the poem gives an impression of the style:

Amidst Lochney, at distance from the shore,
On a green island, grew a stately tree,
With precious fruit each season cover'd o'er,
Delightful to the taste and fair to see:
This fruit, more sweet than virgin honey found,
Serv'd both alike for physic and for food;
It cur'd diseases, heal'd the bleeding wound,
And hunger's rage for three long days withstood,
But precious things are purchas'd still with pain
And thousands try'd to pluck it, but in vain.

The importance of this 'translation' is two-fold: first, it brought to the attention of a non-Gaelic public the existence of heroic ballads in the Gaelic language; and, secondly, it was known to James Macpherson and almost certainly encouraged him in his career as an author.[28] 'Laoidh Fhraoich', therefore, in addition to its interest within Gaelic tradition, has a significant place in Scottish literature generally – indeed, in the development of European Romanticism.

The second non-Fenian ballad is 'Am Bròn Binn' ('The Melodious Sorrow' or, as it is commonly translated, 'The Sweet Sorrow'). Our recordings come from the islands of Benbecula and South Uist, and from Lairg in Sutherland on the mainland. It has no literary original and appears to be a purely Scots Gaelic composition.[29]

The fullest versions (in earlier collections from oral tradition) tell how the King of Britain has Sir Balbha (variants Sior Falaich, Fios Falaich, etc.) sail across the ocean to seek a beautiful maiden he has seen in a dream. He finds her seated on a throne in a castle; the hostile 'Great Man' of the castle is lulled to sleep by the maiden's harp-music and song; Sir Balbha beheads him with his own (the Great Man's) sword and sails off with the maiden.

In only one of our sung versions (recorded from Alasdair Stewart in Sutherland) does this 'Great Man' appear; in all the others it is Fios Falaich who is lulled to sleep and treacherously put to death by the maiden. Instead of 'King of Britain' we may have (though not in our contemporary versions) 'Rìgh Artair' ('King Arthur'). The name 'Fios Falaich', too, is Arthurian: it has been shown ultimately to derive from 'Sir Gawain' or variant forms of his name.

Professor Gillies has conducted a wide-ranging investigation of Arthurian material in Gaelic, which examines the Arthurian affinities of 'Am Bròn Binn'.[30] This makes it unnecessary for me to comment further on this aspect, except to say it is the only ballad in current Gaelic tradition that may be called 'Arthurian'. The name, however, requires a word or two. 'The Melodious Sorrow', with its apparently romantic over-tones is, I think, unique in Gaelic oral tradition. While it is not inconceivable, given the background, that it is modelled on a title or phrase from the Romances, I believe we should consider an alternative possibility. The Arthurian Round Table – 'Am Bord Cruinn' – appears in two earlier versions of our ballad. (It is known in other contexts also, oral and literary.) 'Bord Cruinn' and 'Bròn Binn' stand in the same place – the end phrase – in the text. I suggest 'Bròn Binn' is a garbling of 'Bord Cruinn'.

Finally, I shall comment briefly on a number of fragments I recorded in the island of Tiree from the late Donald Sinclair – Domhnall Chaluim Bàin. In the course of my fieldwork with him, extending over ten years and more, I was able to elicit from him that he had heard heroic ballads in his boyhood. It is important to emphasise that he was not an active ballad singer and that by the time he consented to record these fragments, old age and infirmity had greatly affected his remarkable powers of intellect and memory. His best remembered ballad was 'Laoidh Fhraoich', of which he knew several more verses than those recorded. He had heard and could recall a·verse or two of the ballad of Mànus (Magnus) King of Lochlann, the Death of Osgar, both Fenian ballads, and the non-Fenian Death of Conlaoch the son of Cù Chulainn. He himself did not know the name 'Conlaoch' and, as he reconstructed the story, it was Cù Chulainn who was slain by his own father. By the time he made the recordings he had begun to jumble these fragments in his memory.

A quite different problem arises with regard to the recordings from Kintail. The singer, the late James C. M. Campbell was a noted concert artist who also knew a number of traditional Gaelic songs. He probably heard Fenian lays in Kintail in his boyhood but it is not clear to what extent both words and melodies were affected by written sources. His style of singing also is non-traditional.

The two ballads recorded from Mary Stewart in Lochalsh and from Alasdair (Aili) Stewart in Sutherland might well have come from Island tradition; both Stewarts belonged to the travelling tinsmith class whose circuit included the islands.

The majority of ballad singers in our archives are women. One sometimes gets the impression even from genuine tradition-bearers that the preservation and transmission of heroic ballads was something of a male preserve. But obviously this was not the case. Both men and women were singers and reciters of lays. James Cumming tells of Christina Sutherland and Isabella MacKay (Iseabail Bhàn) in the parish of Reay in Caithness sitting up a whole winter night reciting poems of every description, each in turn and sometimes together repeating them. 'When under 12 years of age she [Christina] would sooner commit to memory a long Duan than most if not any of her acquaintances who were come to maturity. She would go three miles and more to hear a poem not previously recited in her hearing.' Christina Sutherland's two brothers also 'excelled as reciters'.[31]

Christina was born in 1775. Twelve years earlier, Rev. Alexander Pope discusses a ballad which 'some old women repeat with great spirit'. This testimony takes us back into the seventeenth century. Pope also has this to say about the singers (though not specifically women) and ballad melodies: 'The music is soft and simple; but when these airs are sung by two or three or more good voices, they are far from disagreeable.'[32]

I have no evidence from the Gaelic communities of the present that ballads in their 'normal' verse form (but see below) were sung by several singers together. Perhaps something of this kind, however, is implied in the Rev. Donald Macleod of Glenelg's letter of 1764 where he states that the 'Highlanders, at their festivals and other public meeting, acted the poems of Ossian.'[33] When Donald Robertson in Skye recited his version of 'Dàn na h-Inghinne' he inserted 'Esan' ('He') and 'Ise' ('She') before each verse of the dialogue between Fionn and the Maiden in that lay. Debate poems, such as 'Caraid is Namhaid an Uisge-bheatha' ('Friend and Enemy of Whisky') were 'acted' as a dialogue in North Uist until about the end of the nineteenth century: something of the same kind, then, might have been done with ballads.

At any rate, singing by several voices could have an important implication. A number of lays are constructed with repeated couplets: the second couplet of the quatrain being repeated to form the first couplet of the next quatrain. This is characteristic of one category of songs that are said to have been choral;[34] moreover, this is a category that is very strongly associated with women and the compositions of women poets. There are indeed compositions of male authorship within it but so close is the connection of the form with women's poetry that one song, obviously of male authorship, has been fitted out with a circumstantially detailed account of how it was really composed by a woman.

Occasionally such choral songs, sung in quatrains with repeated couplets, may be found in close variants in the waulking song tradition.[35] The latter has preserved songs once used for other communal tasks and furthermore has attracted to it a number of songs, usually lyrical songs that belong, loosely speaking, to the choral tradition of which waulking songs are now the central strand. A few ballads have also been drawn into the corpus of waulking songs. One of these, 'Latha bha an Ridire ag òl' ('One day when the knight was drinking') appears only in the form of a waulking song, complete with a normal chorus of vocables such as we get with these work songs. The versions we have recorded introduce the 'Black Hound', and Bran, no doubt from 'Laoidh a' Choin Duibh' ('The Lay of the Black Hound', mentioned above). One fragmentary printed version of 'Latha bha an Ridire ag òl' prefixes a couplet from 'Laoidh Fhraoich'.[36] Frances Tolmie remarks: 'Several narrative songs, such as 'The Melodious Sorrow', or 'Dream of the King of Britain' and 'The Lay of the Black Dog' [. . .] were sung to the same air with similar refrain.'[37]

In Frances Tolmie's collection there are two songs on the death of Diarmad. The first, without a vocable refrain, is recognisably a variant of 'Laoidh Dhiarmaid' ('The Lay of Diarmad'), and is so titled. The other, in waulking song form, with vocables, is given the title of 'Cumha Dhiarmaid', and is really another song rather than a variant of the Laoidh. Finally, in a number of collections, Oisein's song to his mother appears with vocable refrains: it seems to have been sung only in that form, not in quatrains. It does not follow, however, that ballads which were sung with vocable refrains were necessarily or exclusively used as waulking songs or work songs of any kind. There were other choral refrain songs that were preserved and transmitted outside the work song culture.

How are we to interpret all this? The evidence is exiguous and perhaps insufficient to lead to any certain conclusion; all the possible interpretations will contain an element of speculation. I would suggest, somewhat tentatively, that first the distinctive roles of men and women in preserving and transmitting Fenian and other heroic lays is an old and well-established tradition and that, secondly, this has left a structural impress on the corpus of surviving ballads.

There are also differences, though not readily assignable to male and female roles, in the traditional manner of singing the ballads. The 'prosody' of traditional Gaelic singing, except in the domain of work song, clearly aims at maintaining a conversational rhythm: as older singers used to insist, a song should be 'told'. As a general observation, this applies not only to the so-called 'syllabic' metres[38] but to other metrical forms as well. The technique, however, is not crudely mechanical for it allows subtle modifications of quantity (invariably preserving phonemic distinctions) while syllables that are unstressed in ordinary speech may be given a certain amount of stress.

In contrast to this, a few singers, all from South Uist, employ a different prosody in singing ballads. Certain unstressed syllables are here given a prominent stress, and in highly unusual, probably even unique, positions; as, for instance, when the second syllable of a dissyllabic word is stressed at the end of a line.[39] Such stressing does not occur even in waulking songs. An example of this type of singing can be heard on *Music from the Western Isles*, where Mrs Archie MacDonald sings 'Latha dh'an Fhinn am Beinn Iongnaidh'. In the notes to the ballad, I have drawn attention to this 'tendency to regularise the tempo, which may point to a break with tradition in the twentieth century'. This is a problem which demands rigorous examination by a Gaelic-speaking musicologist who has also an adequate training in linguistics. It is worth noting that although other Uist singers, older than Mrs Archie MacDonald, have a similar style, the singing of her aunt, Mrs Peggy MacDonald, shows a much closer observance of ordinary speech stress, while that of her mother, Mrs Marion Campbell, exhibits even more conspicuously the same characteristics as the daughter's. Yet mother and aunt were near each other in age – and both were born in the 1860s.[40]

While we have noted the survival of these Fenian ballad in the periphery of the Scottish Gàidhealtachd long after they disappeared in Ireland, it is worth mentioning that one ballad, 'Teanntachd Mhór na Féinne' ('The Great Difficulty of the Fiann'), has only been recorded in Nova Scotia. Dr J. L. Campbell recorded it there in 1953 from Angus MacIssac, who seems to have inherited it from the mainland tradition of Moidart.[41]

Although all of the singers who contributed to the archives of the School of Scottish Studies are now no longer with us, over the years a small number of men and women have interested themselves sufficiently in the tradition to learn several ballads. The Rev. William Matheson learnt the melody of 'Laoidh Fhraoich' from Duncan MacDonald, South Uist, and combined it with a text learnt from his uncle-by-marriage, Donald Morrison, Skye.[42] Professor Neil

MacCormick of Edinburgh University learnt the same lay from his grand-uncle Capt. Dugall MacCormick of Glasgow and Mull. Mrs Catriona Garbutt learnt 'Am Bròn Binn' from Mrs Kate MacCormick, Benbecula; and Miss Ishabel T. MacDonald learnt 'Duan na Ceardaich' from Mrs Archie MacDonald, South Uist. By such means, the tradition of singing heroic lays in Gaelic Scotland will continue for at least another generation.

The Choral Tradition
in Scottish Gaelic Songs

I shall concern myself here to a fairly large extent with features that are characteristic of the type of song that most Gaels readily recognise as *òrain-luaidh*. Not to enter too minutely on a detailed description, they are songs of a single line or couplet structure, with a refrain of words or meaningless vocables. I have used the terms 'Òrain-luaidh' or 'Waulking-songs' in the title, however, and there are reasons for this.

It is evident enough that this tradition of song has survived in Gaelic Scotland because of its functional role. But I am not myself entirely persuaded that the origins of the tradition are to be quite so narrowly determined. Moreover, it is the structure and quality of the poetry that concerns me, and the affinity of these with other traditions of Gaelic poetry, rather than the function of the òrain-luaidh as labour songs – although, of course, that aspect is not to be ignored. To make a convenient distinction, I propose to use the Gaelic term 'òrain-luaidh' when I denote the structural type; when I wish to stress the function, I shall use the English term 'waulking-song(s)'.

What exactly is meant by the term 'choral'? The essential idea is that it involves group participation – usually, though not perhaps necessarily, the singing by a group of a refrain, long or short. In this basic sense, choral singing is a very striking feature of the Scottish Gaelic song tradition. Indeed, the whole problem of the chorus, in all its manifestations, in Gaelic song is one of fundamental importance and is well worth an exhaustive study.

A song may be said to be choral if in practice a number of people join in singing it. This is, of course, not quite the same as claiming that it is choral in its nature: that a group *must* be involved – which would be true, for instance, of a part-song. In the course of discussion, we shall have occasion to look at the two concepts.

We all know how audiences join in singing refrains at a modern *céilidh* – or, to take a more traditional setting, at a wedding. In both of these situations we may hear recently composed songs whose connection with the mainstream of Gaelic tradition is often tenuous enough. But the notion of a chorus is by no means new, as a look at our oldest collection of printed Gaelic verse will show. Here I am thinking not of the òrain-luaidh type so much as other structures for which a refrain is indicated.

From the end of the eighteenth century to the end of the nineteenth, these choral songs enjoyed a considerable growth in popularity – a fact which may be checked by comparing Ranald MacDonald's 'Eigg Collection' of 1776 with Archibald Sinclair's *Òranaiche* of 1879. The increase in vogue may imply an increase in actual composition of this kind of song; or it may mean simply that later collectors paid more attention to the genre; or it may mean both of these things.

At this stage I shall simply assume that these refrains are intended primarily for group and not solo performance: the point will be discussed in greater detail later. But to simplify matters I shall from now on, for the most part, use 'refrain' as a generic term.

At this point I feel that a word of explanation is needed concerning the kind of analysis used here. It will deal with the structure of the verse as written down on a page. The reality, however, is not the written text but the song; and we must at all times try to envisage the song as it is sung. The plain implication, of course, is that a study such as this should only be undertaken by a trained musicologist who was properly equipped in Gaelic. Since I have no competence in the field of music, I can only hope to suggest the existence of various connections which subsequent investigation will either confirm or deny.

The refrains of Gaelic song as a whole can be divided in several ways and into several categories, but basically they are of two sorts: those that form an integral part of the verbal structure and those that do not. Let us begin with songs composed in quatrains. To find examples of the first, we may take two well-known songs 'Ged tha mi gun chrodh gun aighean' and 'Och mar tha mi is mi 'nam aonar'. In each case the refrain is simply the opening verse. It is true that in both songs the tone of the opening verse is different from that of the other verses: its function is to set the scene which subsequent verses will explore in greater detail. By the same token, in virtue of the fact that it strikes the keynote, the first verse in its role as refrain reinforces the total statement that the poem makes. This is, indeed, a constant pattern in thousands of Gaelic songs.

In contrast to these we find refrains composed entirely of meaningless vocables: an example is 'Mac Òg an Iarla Ruaidh'. Quite often

– in this section of Gaelic song, probably more often than not – words and phrases are inserted among the vocables. Sometimes the phrase may comment directly upon the matter of the song, e.g. 'A fhleasgaich dhuinn nach ann dhuinn a dh'éirich'; or it may be more or less detached; or it may express a general comment in tune with the mood of the song, e.g. Ailean Dall's 'Gun togainn fonn gu h-aighearach'. All these examples have a quatrain structure both in the verse and in the refrain.

Let us now look at the refrains of òrain-luaidh. In the òrain-luaidh the disposition of refrains appears to present an exact parallel to those we have just been examining. That is to say, we have refrains composed purely of meaningless vocables, refrains of vocables interspersed with words, and refrains that consist solely of words. Let us examine this resemblance more closely.

If we take first a song with a purely vocable refrain we may look at 'Tàladh Dhomhnaill Ghuirm'. The version printed in Watson's *Bàrdachd Ghàidhlig* is a conflate version,[1] and the refrain is not quite identical with that of the version still sung in South Uist. Nevertheless, it serves to illustrate my point.

Even as a text on a page, it strikes us immediately that there is a curious imbalance between verse and refrain compared with the equipoise of the quatrain verse and quatrain refrain of 'Mac Òg an Iarla Ruaidh'.[2] So much is demonstrable. In actual experience – in the reality that the song creates when it is sung – the qualitative difference between the two types is immense. This is in great measure due, it seems to me, to the peculiar relationship between the verse and the refrain, and I shall discuss it in general terms later.

What is true of the impact of the sung refrain of 'Tàladh Dhomhnaill Ghuirm' is true of the vocable refrains of the òrain-luaidh as a whole. Although they are semantically empty, they seem to have an identity of their own, distinct from that of the verse. Mechanically, the verse and refrain may be said to be complementary to each other; aesthetically, the verse actually depends on the refrain. It is noticeable that Gaelic singers feel a close association between the vocable refrain and the melody of the song – as if the vocables had a definite mnemonic function so far as the music is concerned. Admittedly this is true of any Gaelic refrain, though the association is perhaps closest in the òrain-luaidh.

In a song like 'Mac Òg an Iarla Ruaidh' (verse quatrain plus quatrain of vocables) there is certainly contrast and complementarity;

but qualitatively there is not at all the same degree of dependence upon the refrain. This, however, is a value judgment, about which no two people will have exactly the same point of view. For my own part, I feel that there are various degrees of qualitative or aesthetic relationship between verse and refrain in different structures.

For example, the dynamism of the òran-luaidh vocable refrain is weakened, though still palpable, when a meaningful phrase is interposed, as in the song:

> *An turas thug mi chon na Galldachd*
> *Bha mi call 's cha robh mi buinnig*

with its refrain of:

> *hì lì hó leò*
> *hó gi ó mo ghaol a' chruinneag*
> *hì lì hó leò*

But the fact that the phrase has no direct connection with the matter of the song, but suggests, indeed, a quite different dimension of experience – this as verse and refrain in turn come before the listener, generates an energy, in this instance a liveliness, in the complex of the poetry.

When the meaningful element occupies a more prominent place, the power of the relationship between refrain and verse cannot be dissociated from the emotional depth of the theme that is being sung about; but where there is anything like a direct connection between the statement of the verse and the comment of the refrain, it will also depend, very subtly, upon the achievement of a sort of emotional counterpoint. In practice one finds that a song that is great in the poetry of its theme will have this relationship to its refrain, e.g. 'Ailein Duinn o hì shiubhlainn leat'.

In that song the phrase 'Ailein Duinn o hì shiubhlainn leat' opens and closes the three line refrain. In songs like 'Mo nighean donn à Cornaig', the refrain, also of three lines, is composed entirely of words, the third line being a repeat of the first. This is identical with a refrain type which we sometimes find associated with songs whose verses are in quatrains. There may be one or two vocables, but they are not significant; an example is 'Hùgaibh air nighean donn nam meallshuil'. Some of those songs were apparently used at waulkings: a version of the well-known 'O mo nighean donn bhòidheach nan gormshuil meallach' is printed by Craig,[3] as is also the rarer song 'Uallach mo cheum go Bràighe Gharaidh'. It would seem that the quatrain form was retained. We may note in passing that *functionally* these two songs could be classed as waulking-songs.

My point in citing them, however, is to draw attention to the fact that, in contrast to the other quatrain songs we have noticed, these are demonstrably dependent on the refrain. It is not simply an external ornament. When this type of song is sung, the singer does not conclude the stanza at the end of the quatrain but carries on to the fifth line, i.e. the first line of the refrain. To my own mind, such a song has a qualitative link with its refrain which is at least as strong as the link between verse and refrain in an òran-luaidh composed of couplets plus a three line verbal refrain, e.g. 'A nìonag a' chùl-duinn nach fhan thu'. To put it in another way: the poetic statement is partly created by the refrain.

The underlying causes for all this must finally be sought in the music, but the structure of the text itself suggests an explanation. The ratio between stanza and refrain is 4:3, whereas in the other quatrain songs we have mentioned the ratio is 4:4. I spoke earlier of the imbalance between verse and refrain in 'Tàladh Dhomhnaill Ghuirm'. Here, then, we have the same principle illustrated: the difference is merely one of degree. It seems as if a certain structural asymmetry characterises the types of Gaelic song that are closely linked with a refrain. It is only when they are sung that their essential, vital equilibrium is displayed.

Since both òrain-luaidh and this group of quatrain songs with a three-line refrain share the characteristic, are we to argue also that they share a common ancestry? And ought we to attach any significance to the fact that songs like 'O mo nighean donn bhòidheach nan gormshuil meallach' were drawn into the waulking-song culture? The answer is that, at this level of investigation, we cannot tell. These problems may never be solved; they will certainly not be solved until the whole tradition of Gaelic music – Scottish and Irish – has been subjected to a rigorous musicological analysis.

Meantime, however, we can pose some of the questions that we should like to have answered if such a musicological survey is ever undertaken. Is it possible, for instance, to distinguish between songs that are intrinsically choral and those that are not? I ask this for two reasons. First, the conventions of singing suggest that the distinction may be a fundamental one, and secondly, the nature of a vocable refrain – especially a long vocable refrain – seems more in keeping with choral than with individual performance.

But let us begin with the individual. It is noteworthy that when a singer has no group to join in the refrains, he will usually omit, except at the beginning and end of the song, a refrain such as 'Och och mar tha mis is mi 'nam aonar' or 'Air failirinn ìlirinn ùilirinn ó'. For convenience, let us call these Type A. In contrast to that, a song of the type of 'An turas thug mi chon na Galldachd' or 'A nìonag a' chùl-duinn nach fhan thu', which we shall call Type B, will have each verse followed by at least the first line of the vocable or verbal refrain. To isolate a line in this manner is impossible in Type A: their refrains are of a piece. The singer, therefore, has two alternatives when he comes to the end of the verse: he must sing the refrain in full or he must omit it altogether. The former choice is sometimes taken, but the latter is the norm. This again is an illustration of the 'balance' I have talked about. It is created by the refrain in the one case; it pre-exists in the other.

When a singer sings a Type A song in company, the normal convention is for the company to sing the refrain after each verse. But when a type B song – at least one with a vocable refrain – is sung at a waulking, there is almost always a division between solo and chorus refrains. The solo refrain will correspond in this case to the part of the refrain which the individual singer invariably sings. Anyone who wishes to examine this further will find that Frances Tolmie's Collection[4] sets out the divisions clearly.

And there is still another group – 'Tàladh Dhomhnaill Ghuirm' belongs to it – which does not have its refrains divided by the individual singer though at a waulking there *is* a division between solo and chorus refrains. If such a song is sung at all the individual singer will sing the full refrain.

Briefly, the implication of all this is that the conventions of Gaelic singing show that a division is felt to exist between songs that are essentially refrain songs and songs which are only, in the logical sense, 'accidentally' so.

The nature of a vocable refrain has to be considered next. A verbal refrain commenting on and reinforcing the theme of a song, is intelligible in terms of individual creation – whatever the pre-existing models may have been. As an example of this we may note that in the 'strophic metre' songs – the kind of metre in which Màiri nighean Alasdair Ruaidh and Iain Lom composed a number of their songs – we sometimes find repetition of lines. In the simplest variety, two double-stressed lines followed by a triple-stressed line, e.g. Iain Lom's

Mi 'n so air m'uilinn
An ard ghleann munaidh
'S mór fàth mo shulas ri gàire

Turner's Collection prescribes that each verse should be sung twice. There is evidence that in the past, in some places at least, a soloist sang the verse first, whereupon it was repeated by the whole audience.[5] The few singers who still sing these songs do not do this, and there is no evident reason why they should: the verse as it stands seems to be self-contained. This would seem to be no more than a fashion, then, a further development of the 'accidental refrain'; we can understand how it could come into being in a society in which the notion of choral singing already existed. But in the case of a vocable refrain we cannot reconstruct any such process. It is difficult to associate these vocables with individual creation: they give a curious impression of being static and ageless. That may be a highly subjective way of looking at verse structure, but it is very significant that these vocable refrains are considerably more stable than the verse they support. Meaningless sounds of this kind are by no means unknown in other cultures: they are the ideal vehicle for group performance for they allow the minimum of individual choice. They cannot be 'interpreted' as meaningful words can. And we have already seen that when an individual singer is confronted with a vocable refrain, he almost invariably shortens it, unless the song is completely dependent on the refrain. These latter are all songs with a short, two-stressed line – probably a very ancient form indeed.

I would suggest, then, that here we are at the centre of the choral tradition of Scottish Gaelic.

What I have up to this point called òrain-luaidh appear to have been known as *luinneagan* in an earlier age. In the dissertation entitled 'Of the Influence of Poetry and Music upon the Highlanders' published in the Rev. Patrick MacDonald's *Collection of Highland Vocal Airs* – the first printed collection of Gaelic music – we have the following statement:

Over all the Highlands, there are various songs, which are sung to airs suited to the nature of the subject. But on the western coast, benorth middle Lorn, and in all the Hebrides, *luinigs* are most in request. These are in general very short, and of a plaintive cast, analogous to their best poetry: and they are sung by the women, not only at their diversions, but also during almost every kind of work, where more than one person is employed, as milking cows, and watching the folds, fulling of cloth, grinding of grain with the *quern*, or hand-mill, hay-making, and cutting down corn. The men too have *iorrums*, or songs for rowing, to which they keep time with their oars, as the women likewise do in their operations, whenever their work admits of it. When the same airs are sung in their hours of relaxation, the time is marked by the motions of a napkin, which all the performers lay hold of. In singing, one person leads the band; but in a certain part of the tune he stops to take breath, while the rest strike in and complete the air, pronouncing to it a chorus of words and syllables generally of no signification.

These songs greatly animate every person present; and hence, when labourers appear to flag, a luinig is called for, which makes them for a time forget their toil, and work with redoubled ardour. In travelling through the remote Highlands in harvest, the sound of those little bands on every side, 'warbling their native wood-notes wild,' joined to a most romantic scenery, has a very pleasing effect on the mind of a stranger.

The writer of this, who was John Ramsay of Ochtertyre,[6] implies that *iorram* and *luinneag* belong to the same broad category. Of the two terms, luinneag may always have covered a wider range of songs used in communal activities. In our older collections of Gaelic verse, 'luinneag', as a title, without any qualifying epithet, always denotes a song of the òran-luaidh type. With an epithet, however, it is much more likely to denote a different structural type, e.g. 'Luinneag Chaluim a' Ghlinne' or 'Luinneag MhicLeòid'. But it never, so far as I know, applies to a song which has no refrain; and it is frequently used simply for 'refrain' – what is later, and still, referred to as *fonn* or *séis(d)*. Since these last two terms connote both music and vocables or words, we are probably justified in inferring that 'luinneag' did the same: the separate concepts of words and music of a song did not exist.

If my suggestion that the central strand of the Gaelic tradition is found in the òrain-luaidh is valid, and that this class of songs was originally known by the generic name of 'luinneag', we may infer that the use of 'luinneag' for 'refrain' demonstrates the spread of the choral idea to other types of song.

Can we trace any of the stages in this development? Here again we must await the results of musicological investigation. As before, I can only draw attention to certain areas of the subject where the verse structure suggests an articular connection.

There is a class of songs – not very well represented in modern oral tradition – which are sung in quatrains, the second and subsequent quatrains being formed by repeating the last couplet of the preceding one to the tune of the first couplet.

One of these is 'Mac Griogair à Ruadhshruth'; others are 'A Mhic Dhubhghaill mhic Ruairi', 'A Mhic Neachdainn an Dùin', and that other superb MacGregor song 'Is mi suidhe an seo m' ònar'. All these, incidentally, are sung to variants of the same tune. With one exception they have no refrain. To this group may also be added a song still, or until recently, current in oral tradition ''S daor a cheannaich mi 'n t-iasgach'.

In 1862 Donald Campbell, 'late Lieut. 57th Regiment', published a book *The Language, Poetry and Music of the Highland Clans*. Whatever his interpretative competence may have been, Campbell was by family connections, as well as personal inclination, in a position to know a good deal about Gaelic poetry and music. In this book he discusses 'Mac Griogair à Ruadhshruth'; before quoting the text he states as a straightforward fact:

> Two lines of every verse in the following measure, and all similar songs, were sung as a chorus by the audience which had a most pleasing and pathetic effect; hence their repetition in the succeeding verse of two lines of the former verse.[7]

I have no corroborative evidence whatsoever for this practice; but the description makes good sense and I am prepared, at least for the present, to accept it. It poses some questions of fundamental importance, e.g., Is this essentially a choral tradition, or an artistic and social fashion? If it is the former, is the tradition derived from, or independent of, the ancient luinneag?

Before attempting to answer this, we must note the existence of another group. There is another group of quatrain songs which show the same kind of couplet repetition in forming the quatrain. Apart from the melody, what distinguishes them from the 'Mac Griogair à Ruadhshruth' group is that they appear to be indissolubly linked to a vocable refrain. Possibly the distinction is not essential. In modern oral tradition they, too, are rare: some examples are 'Mi am shuidh air an fhaoilinn' and 'Seall a-mach an e latha e' (two of the Iain Garbh laments), 'Bràighe Loch Iall', 'Gura muladach sgìth mi', and 'Gur e m' anam is m' eudail'. It hardly needs saying that our perspective might be altered if we had a wider choice.

Finally, in addition to these quatrain songs there are also eight-lined stanza songs with vocable refrains: a convenient example is Màiri nighean Alasdair Ruaidh's 'Luinneag MhicLeòid'. 'Luinneag Mhi-cLeòid' – note the use of 'luinneag' here – takes up the last couplet of the first verse as the first couplet of the second verse, and so on to the end. But this is not true of another of Màiri's songs 'Òran do Iain mac Shir Tormoid', although it, too, has a vocable refrain.

Is any connection to be traced among all these forms? Without a definite principle to guide us, the pattern of hypothetical relationships could become tediously intricate. In the present state of our knowl-edge, I believe that it would be a waste of time to do more than indicate the main paths that future research might investigate.

Structurally, the couplet would seem to be the common factor. Now, at least since the advent of rhyme in poetry, the couplet has counted as one of the principal units of versification in European literatures. One can go further indeed: it is clear from ethnographic descriptions that it is one of the fundamental forms of song.

Hence, one can scarcely try to establish directly a sequence from the single line through the couplet to the quatrain. In other words, the repeated couplets of 'Mac Griogair à Ruadhshruth' and 'Gur e m' anam is m' eudail' might well represent an independent choral tradi-tion from that of the òrain-luaidh. It is equally possible, of course that these groups represent two lines of descent from a very old common source with development perhaps at different levels of society. Re-petition of a single line to an identical or a different musical phrase is common in òrain-luaidh; similarly the second line of a couplet which is linked only with end rhyme may become the first line of the succeeding couplet. But these couplets that do have internal rhyme and not end rhyme between the couplet lines – the main rhyme of the song being carried by the ending of each second line – never proliferate in this way. An example is 'A nìonag a' chùl-duinn nach fhan thu'. The quatrain songs I have cited also have internal rhyme. This link of internal rhyme is, of course, well-known in other types of Gaelic verse, vernacular and classical.

The possibility should therefore be considered that influences have travelled in two directions, i.e. the idea of repetition came from the òrain-luaidh, while the idea of internal rhyme came from the quatrain songs. The hypothetical course of development would run something like this: on the model of previously existing quatrain structures,[8] couplets from the òrain-luaidh become repeated; on the model of those, other songs are composed and internal rhyme is introduced into some of them; finally, these are re-modelled to fit the metrical conditions of the òrain-luaidh. It is certainly to be noted that òrain-luaidh with internal rhyme seem, on the whole, to be older than those that lack it.

Whatever the history of the development of the refrainless songs might have been, the presence of vocable refrains in quatrain songs of the type of 'Bràighe Loch Iall' and 'Gur e m' anam is m' eudail' can only be explained as deriving immediately from the òran-luaidh choral tradition or from the same common stock. In one of the Iain Garbh laments, in 'Bràighe Loch Iall', and in 'Gura muladach sgìth mi', there is even a suggestion of solo and choral refrains; and the same may hold true, although this is more difficult to decide, of 'Gur e m' anam is m' eudail'.

One of the songs in the 'Mac Griogair à Ruadhshruth' group also has a refrain – three phrases of vocables and one of words. This is the Lewis variant of the song which is known in Uist, and in Benbecula (where, according to the tradition of that island, it was composed) as 'A Mhic Dhubhghaill 'ic Ruairi'.[9] It is never, so far as I know, sung with a refrain.

The question, then, is this: are the refrains of quatrain songs of this kind later accretions or are they original, but have in some cases been lost? That is to say: do the two groups really belong together, and in the presence or absence of the refrain of any essential significance?

Although 'Gur e m' anam is m' eudail' is a song of Perthshire provenance, it is known nowadays only in the oral tradition of the Hebrides. And for some generations back, the Hebrides are the only area where the òrain-luaidh have continued to flourish. On these grounds it might be argued that the choral tradition of the òrain-luaidh was sufficiently dominant in this milieu to extend itself into another sector of poetry. Against this, however, we must set two points. First, in Gillies's collection[10] 'Gur e m' anam is m' eudail' and 'Bràighe Loch Iall' are both printed with a refrain of vocables: 'Mac Griogair à Ruadhshruth' and numerous others, structurally of the same type – they are found in various printed sources – are not. Secondly, although the Lewis song which has become known as 'Milleadh nam Bràithrean' is followed by a refrain, its variant 'A Mhic Dhubhghaill 'ic Ruairi', from one of the central areas of the òran-luaidh culture, has no refrain at all.

So far as the omission or inclusion of vocable refrains in early printed sources is concerned, we must bear in mind that a singer's dictation of the text, or a collector's whim, might determine the issue. We have already seen that a vocable refrain may function as a mnemonic for the melody; consequently some collectors may have regarded it as pertaining more to the melody than to the poetic text – which was, after all, what they were collecting.

We should, perhaps, consider the possibility that some mainland songs, e.g. a Perthshire song like 'Mac Griogair à Ruadhshruth', had lost their refrains before they came into Hebridean oral tradition; while others, e.g. 'Gur e m' anam is m' eudail', were introduced before that had happened. There is some evidence that the luinneag or òran-luaidh type – I am using these terms interchangeably – were falling into disuse in the eastern and far southern parts of the Highlands perhaps as early as the beginning of the eighteenth century. This at any rate is the testimony of John Ramsay of Ochtertyre. Writing in the first years of the nineteenth century, he says: 'The people of Breadalbane, Rannoch, Atholl, and the southern parts of Argyllshire, seldom sing luinneags at their work, though, little past memory of man, their forefathers practised it as constantly as the north-west Highlanders do at present.'[11]

It is conceivable that this recession might have had an effect upon related forms of singing.

But if 'A Mhic Dhubhghaill 'ic Ruairi' is indeed a Hebridean composition, it is difficult to see why *its* refrain should have been lost. And the same thing applies to the song 'Is daor a cheannaich mi 'n t-iasgach' which, by internal evidence, is a song composed in the Islands: it seems to have some connection with Islay. Until recently, it was known in Skye and Uist, but in neither place was it sung with a refrain – nor, for what it is worth, is it printed with a refrain in the two collections, where it appears, Gillies's and MacFarlane's.[12]

The point is worth making that if a refrain becomes ignored somewhere in the line of a song's transmission, it cannot be an organic element in the composition, but a supplement, a decorative adjunct. Thus, singers will feel that the statement of the song is adequately expressed within the compass of the verse alone.

Even so, some singers might retain the refrain as an optional bonus; or, for the same reason, a refrain might, in transmission, get added to a song originally composed without it. This would explain that differ-ence between variants such as 'Milleadh nam Bràithrean' and 'A Mhic Dhubhghaill 'ic Ruairi'. (A parallel might be cited in the singing of strophic metres. Here any repetition which is structurally intrinsic is retained, but the repetition of the whole verse, described by Donald Campbell, is not now practised by the few remaining singers of these songs. Yet, as I am informed by the Rev. William Matheson, the late Duncan MacDonald of South Uist did exactly this.)

But the link between verse and refrain in certain songs was much stronger: the refrain, or part of it, was felt to be essential. This is the group that is represented in oral tradition by 'Bràighe Loch Iall', 'Gur e m' anam is m' eudail', etc. One small point may be noted in connection with this. In Gillies's Collection, refrains are usually written after the verse; 'Bràighe Loch Iall' is printed with one phrase of the vocable refrain on the same line as the end of the verse: it looks as if the editor(s) felt that the verse line and the refrain phrase belong together – which is precisely what contemporary Gaelic singers feel too.

In the last decade or so, 'Gura muladach sgìth mi' has circulated among a relatively wide group of Gaelic singers. It is striking that though a short phrase of the vocable refrain is invariably kept, the full refrain is unknown except to a minority, while one or two seem to keep the full refrain after each stanza. In the case of 'Bràighe Loch Iall', which has enjoyed a rather similar vogue, the full refrain is always sung. Although most of the singers would not call themselves 'traditional', these songs appear, in the main, to have circulated orally, and the pattern of transmission no doubt reflects something of the same process as has happened in the past within the 'traditional' Gaelic community.

All this evidence is in the end rather meagre and it is only too easy to offer over-ingenious explanations. It is fairly certain that these quatrain songs are closely related, but that the distinction between intrinsic and extrinsic refrains divides them into sub-groups. At one time there may have been a convention according to which an audience sang the repeated couplet and the vocable refrain. I would suggest tentatively that the balance of probability is slightly in favour of a growth of the 'Mac Griogair à Ruadhshruth' type of song from the 'Gur e m'anam is m'eudail' type, which in turn *may* have developed from the òrain-luaidh. But as I suggested earlier when I mentioned internal rhyme, influences are not likely to have travelled in one direction.

What influence other strands and other elements in the Gaelic song tradition played in shaping the òrain-luaidh as they survive today is a very difficult question to answer. For, in their function as labour songs at any rate, the òrain-luaidh have shown a remarkable capacity for attracting and remodelling forms that were certainly not in this tradition originally – among them Ossianic ballads. We do not know how old this process may be nor what the effects of the borrowing were upon the borrower.

There appears to be an affinity, as I showed earlier, between the òrain-luaidh and songs such as 'O mo nighean donn bhòidheach nan gormshuil meallach'. These have a quatrain structure, but that is not the same kind of quatrain structure as that of the 'Mac Griogair à Ruadhshruth' or 'Bràighe Loch Iall' groups: in fact, the only point of contact is in their dependence upon a refrain, a feature which they share with 'Bràighe Loch Iall', etc. Beyond that I should not, at the moment, like to commit myself.

With respect to 'Luinneag MhicLeòid' and other eight-lined stanza songs followed by vocable refrains, we might suggest that once the stage of quatrain songs, with repeated couplets and vocable refrains have been reached, more extended forms would follow. 'Luinneag MhicLeòid' we saw had repeated lines, but not 'Òran do Iain, Mac Shir Tormoid'. In such songs we probably have to take account of some of the external influences that helped to shape Gaelic poetry. The new poetry which begins in Europe, and particularly in France, in the early twelfth century is undoubtedly one of these. Professor Kenneth Jackson pointed out that:

> The new poetry appears in English towards the close of the thirteenth century [. . .] It reached Ireland about the same time through French and English and must have been adopted early into Irish, but this kind of poetry does not appear in manuscripts until the rise of the popular *amhrán* metres in the seventeenth century.[13]

Through the centuries during which Ireland and Gaelic Scotland shared in a common culture, such forces could not fail to impinge upon Scottish Gaelic poetry. But Scotland, lying on the periphery of the Gaelic world, of which Ireland was the centre, was affected indirectly: the new fashions would have penetrated by slow degrees and hence could more easily merge with (and, of course, modify) indigenous forms.

The òrain-luaidh tradition, which I have suggested is one of the sources – if not indeed the fountainhead – of the choral style in Scottish Gaelic song, may itself have been affected by extraneous influences to a greater degree than appears at first sight. But in the last analysis, the nucleus of the tradition – and doubtless much more besides – cannot, I believe, be shown to be other than native.

It is therefore all the more regrettable that our earliest collectors should have so largely ignored these songs.[14] In fact, it was not until 1911, with the publication of *The MacDonald Collection of Gaelic Poetry* by the Rev. Archibald and the Rev. Angus MacDonald, that the Gaelic reader had access even to a modest corpus of the poetry of the òrain-luaidh. Since then, in 1949, a valuable contribution has been made by K. C. Craig's *Òrain Luaidh Màiri nighean Alasdair*. It is no accident that these two books draw upon the òrain-luaidh tradition of Uist. In this century these songs had apparently lost their vogue – even in places where waulkings continued to be held – outside Skye and the Outer Hebrides. At the present time, South Uist is probably the area where they are still best remembered.

The eighteenth-century collectors, who almost entirely neglected these luinneagan, were concerned – as a study of their collections proves – with the 'official' poetry of Gaelic society, with poems that embodied the social and political virtues of society in coherent forms.

If we study the texts in Craig's collection, we are immediately struck by the absence of this very quality of coherence. The intensity of statement and the vividness of imagery are overwhelming, but the rapid shifts and leaps of the text can be frankly disconcerting. And we soon discover that the same, or virtually the same, passages appear in different songs. It is as if poems were being created by a process analogous to the nuclear physicist's fission-fusion-fission. Yet not all texts in all sources are incoherent, and so we may surmise that some singers were prone to confusing their songs.

A good knowledge of the whole òran-luaidh tradition, however, will soon show that this 'incoherence' is intrinsic. The quality of transmission will, of course, vary, and, in many cases, the desire to lengthen a song used as an accompaniment to labour is a sufficient reason for adding verses and even sections. But the real explanation must lie deeper. To my mind, it belongs to the essential form. Looking at the extant body of texts, one gets the impression that this is a kaleidoscope of poetic images out of which certain more permanent forms are from time to time created. Some at least of these could be termed 'art' versions – I am not using the word in the 'art' versus 'folk' sense. These, and even short sections in songs of highly irregular pattern, can posses an astonishing power to re-create a situation or a mood: they function as organic poems, not as mere random collocations of images.

If we take a song such as the one called 'Cumha Peathar' in the *MacDonald Collection* and compare its variant in Craig, we may disagree about which is the better of the two poetically, but we can scarcely dismiss either as insignificant. Two or three other variants are known from Skye – the song is doubtless an Island composition, slightly modified in different communities. In all its variants – and they are clearly recognisable – the poem unfolds, not in a smooth linear movement but unevenly, sometimes with quite unexpected changes in focus. As the variant versions show, it is possible, within limits, to rearrange the separate utterances that make up the poem without impairing the power of the whole statement – because here logical progression is only a principle of secondary importance. It is precisely these abrupt transitions from image to image, governed only by the nature of the situation that the poem expresses, that release the creative energy. And the same observation applies to a greater or lesser degree, I believe, throughout the entire corpus.

These songs in fact use language according to a principle which is diametrically opposed to that of the logical, ordered sequences of prose. They body forth a vision which is perhaps necessary in some measure to all artistic creation; but they express it in a primary form – a form which, in its lack of continuity of 'thought', is characteristic of much so-called primitive poetry. This mode of apprehension, of poetic organisation, is by no means rare throughout Gaelic poetry, though outside the òrain-luaidh it is present in a much less extreme form. I shall suggest shortly that we can, indeed, establish a polarity in which the òrain-luaidh stand opposed to certain other structural types.

Before we do this, it remains to ask whether we are to regard the òrain-luaidh as purely labour songs or whether there may be a connection with other traditions of communal activity. I must, in all fairness, declare a prejudice here. It was the writings of W. P. Ker on English and French medieval lyrical poetry which first suggested to me, in undergraduate days, that we had, in these òrain-luaidh, a close parallel to the kind of poetry he was concerned with. Ker, like other scholars of his generation, believed that European lyrical poetry of the twelfth and subsequent centuries spread from France, where it began as popular dance-song connected with seasonal festivals. On first impressions, I was amenable to the idea that the òrain-luaidh were part of a much wider European – and ultimately French – movement. But a little reflexion made it clear that this could not be. Since then, an Irish scholar, Dr Seán Ó Tuama, has presented a very convincing case for the immense French influence on Irish Gaelic popular love songs.[15] Ó Tuama's work has important implications for Scottish Gaelic poetry. Some of the òrain-luaidh structures are known in Irish, where their ambience is rather different from that of their Scottish counterparts.

The theory that European lyrical and ballad poetry originated in the primitive communal dance-songs of seasonal festivals has long ago been rejected. The reaction against it may nevertheless have gone too far; the theory would explain some of the (apparently old) features of the òrain-luaidh poetry which are, to my mind at least, difficult to reconcile with a tradition which is simply and entirely that of labour songs. This, of course, is not to deny that songs with vocable refrains may not from time immemorial have been associated with labour.

An interesting anecdote is given in the *MacDonald Collection* of the genesis of a quern-song. The famous Domhnall mac Iain 'ic Sheumais, who is said there to be the author, is supposed to have come across two women grinding with the quern but not accompanying themselves with a song – their excuse being that they knew no suitable one. 'MacDonald [. . .] told the women to raise the chorus and that he would give them a song.'[16] The tradition would seem to imply that he composed it on the spot. This is obviously very thin evidence indeed; but, taken at face value, it could imply the existence of freely circulating vocable refrains to which a text was fitted whenever the need arose. It may be that texts with a more explicit labour-song content have, in the course of time, been almost entirely displaced by newer creations.

But before leaving this aspect of the subject, let me draw attention to a possible line of descent for at least one element in the tradition. In the Irish Metrical Dindshenchas – the *dindshenchas* being, as Robin Flower neatly and wittily put it, 'a kind of Dictionary of National Topography, which fitted the famous sites of Ireland each with its appropriate legend' – there is a unique description of a famous *oenach* 'assembly': the Oenach of Carmain. Miss Máirín O Daly observes that 'as the poet who wrote it between 1033 and 1079 (and probably in this last year) must himself have attended this fair we can accept his testimony'.[17] Among the activities the poet describes were funeral games and keening for the dead (*cluichi caínte*) – the site, like that of other similar assemblies, was an ancient burial place – recital of tales, playing of music and so forth. In the assembly the women had a gathering of their own – *cluche ban* – from which men were banned, just as women were banned from the men's gathering: 'No men to go into an assembly of women, no women into an assembly of fair, pure men.'[18]

The oenach was held 'on the Kalends of August' which was the *Lugnasad*, the feast of the god Lug. It is evident from this poem that the fertility of the province was bound up with these observances. As we may learn from a wide range of ethnographical literature, such fertility rites are universal, and enclosed gatherings of men into which women may not enter and vice versa, are commonplace. Miss Máire Mac-Néill, in her book *The Festival of Lughnasa* shows us that in modern gatherings which have descended from the ancient pagan assemblies, dancing and match-making were constant elements.[19]

The òrain-luaidh are almost entirely the composition of women, and at every luadh the match-making songs were an important item. Indeed, the sociological function of the luadh, or the subsequent dance or other entertainment, as a meeting-place for young people of opposite sexes, is extremely important. But at one time men were firmly excluded from the luadh itself; the first male to enter the room was often rolled in the material being waulked – a process which was regarded as conferring good luck on the cloth. On one occasion I was assured unequivocally that this 'good luck' meant precisely human fertility.

The òran-luaidh tradition also contains a large number of laments. Do they go back ultimately to the cluichi caínte?

Whatever their origin, and whatever may be the forces that have shaped them, the òrain-luaidh still carry what, for lack of a better term, I can only call the fundamental lyrical urge of Gaelic poetry. I suggest that this lyricism is inseparable from the mode in which experience is apprehended and articulated, and that the mode is in turn created by the conditions of the choral refrain functioning in a sort of dramatic opposition to the words. From this matrix a lyrical impulse has spread into other sectors of Gaelic poetry. We need not expect a qualitative influence such as this to be absolutely bound up with structural types; but I should hazard the opinion that wherever we find the notion of a chorus – particularly a chorus integral to the structure of a Gaelic song – we also find some degree of the lyric quality. I do not deny that extraneous influences may have played a part – perhaps in the case of medieval French lyrical poetry, conveyed to us through Irish, an influence which has its ultimate origins in a similar choral tradition. Nor do I deny that the lyrical quality may degenerate into sentimentality; but that, of course, depends upon a vast complication of factors.

Diametrically opposed to the òrain-luaidh structurally and qualitatively – within the terms of Gaelic poetry – stands the verse composed in strophic metres. One of the primary functions of this form, historically, was to support a social order. I stress that the opposition is to be seen within the framework of Gaelic poetry: seen from without, the whole of Gaelic poetry might seem to lack sustained thematic treatment. At all events, this is the point of the Gaelic spectrum at which we find the largest demonstrable element of non-lyrical exposition. What is expounded are political and social virtues, and the tone of the public poetry is naturally at the farthest remove from that of the intense, intimate utterances of the lyric.

To describe any tradition of poetry in these terms is merely to set up a theoretical model. The reality is very much more complex and ragged, with an indeterminate area of debatable ground. But Scottish Gaelic poetry is extensive enough, and developed enough, to have its Apollonian and Dionysian antimony, however we may explain its workings.

The Oral Tradition
in Scottish Gaelic Poetry

The term 'oral poetry' has gained considerable currency among literary historians. Research on the poetry and song of preliterate communities in various parts of the world has produced its own crop of theories and dogmas to add to an older body of scholarship based on the study of the ballad and the folksong.

For this reason alone, it might be of interest to examine at some length a poetic tradition – such as we have in Gaelic – in the shaping of which oral composition and transmission have at all stages played an important part. In an essay which is meant to be no more than a general review, however, I cannot afford to subject even the most egregious current dogma to a detailed examination. Still, I hope to demonstrate that the Gaelic oral tradition has its own distinctive features; and that, by implication, propositions which may be valid in respect of one tradition are not necessarily so for oral poetry in general.

I propose to use the term 'oral poetry' here as no more than a convenient label to describe both composition by unlettered poets and transmission by unlettered singers – even if some of what is so transmitted may actually have its genesis in writing. The fact of the matter is that in any society in which the art of writing is securely established, the purely oral is a very elusive creature indeed.

Naturally this makes it extremely difficult to define the area of discussion. In some sectors of it, the apparent opposition of 'oral' and 'written' may indeed be quite meaningless: a literate poet may, deliberately or not, produce poetry which is undistinguishable from the compositions of his unlettered brethren. What we can say, however, is that in Scottish Gaelic a body of poems exists which, as a matter of historical fact, has taken the form in which we know it in an environment in which oral poetry (as I have defined it) is at least the norm – and it is with this *shaping* of the tradition that I shall mostly concern myself.

But it may help to illustrate the entanglement of 'oral' and 'written' if I cite the poetry of Duncan Ban Macintyre, who lived from 1724 to 1812. Macintyre, who was illiterate, dictated his poems to the Rev. Donald MacNicol, an Argyllshire minister who was himself a noted collector of poetry. This formed the basis of printed editions of the poet's work, of which Duncan Ban saw three in his own lifetime.

But meantime these same poems, or at least some of them, were circulating as songs in the Highlands and Islands, perhaps already developing variants. It is possible that there were other songs – there were certainly some impromptu compositions – also in circulation, which never found their way into the editions, either because the bard did not dictate them, or because his editors rejected them.

We are still able to record certain of Duncan Ban's songs, but when we come to examine the texts of these we find that while some are considerably developed variants, others follow the book with extra-ordinary fidelity. What has happened there, of course, is that the printed text has stabilised the oral version.

Yet we would be completely unjustified in grounding a general proposition on that, for it is also possible to cite songs of which there are twentieth-century oral versions and eighteenth-century manuscript versions that are almost identical. Even at this level of analysis, then, we can trace more than one current in the stream of oral verse. Nor is it only the actual poetry which is influenced by the written tradition. Duncan Ban is frequently cited as the most popular Gaelic poet – cited, that is to say, by contemporary singers. Yet the number of the songs that have had the quality to survive, out of the total that were once known, is comparatively small. It would seem as if the unlettered singers are to some extent expressing a value judgment formed outside the tradition and communicated to them with the authority of the written word behind it. Much the same could be said of other 'names' that people quote. I think it is true to say that unless we exercise caution we may be in danger both of seeing Gaelic oral poetry as more homogeneous than it in fact is, and of seeing it in terms of the predilections of eighteenth-century collectors, most of whom belonged to the upper stratum of Gaelic society, and all of whom collected selectively.

With the eighteenth century, our materials for the study of Gaelic oral poetry really emerge. Setting aside two very interesting but rather special collections – the Book of the Dean of Lismore (from the early part of the sixteenth century) and Duncan MacRae's *Dorlach Laoid-*

hean – known as the Fernaig MS (from the end of the seventeenth) – our sources go back no further than the eighteenth century, and the bulk of the material is from mid-century, or later.

Of these, the first to be printed is Ranald MacDonald's anthology of 1776, commonly known nowadays as the Eigg Collection. Ranald was a son of Alasdair mac Mhaighstir Alasdair, the poet whose name is always linked with the Rising of 1745, and as such was a scion of the MacDonalds of Clanranald. I select this anthology not only because it affords evidence of the tastes of an eighteenth-century gentleman, but because the introduction, which is in English, gives us an insight to the motives which inspired the work.

'The Gaelic language', it begins, 'now struggling for existence in a narrow corner, was once the mother tongue of the principal states of Europe. It was in particular, and for a considerable length of time, the only language spoken by our ancestors, the ancient Caledonians.'

MacDonald then goes on to trace the decline in the fortunes of the language, and the political causes behind this, until it was at last 'in danger of being entirely obliterated'. But

at this critical period a fortunate event happened. [. . .] Some individuals, animated with the love of their native language, regretted the danger to which they saw it exposed. Compositions of great merit in the language were known to exist. Inquiry was made after these, with a view to publish them; and this was esteemed the best method of preserving the language itself. The inquiry was attended with considerable success; and a few years ago, some fragments of the best and most ancient Gaelic Poetry were offered to the public in an English translation, inspired with a considerable share of the majesty, simplicity, and elegance of the original composition.

The appearance of these Poems excited universal attention. The Highlanders, perhaps, were the only people in Europe whom they did not astonish. Independent of the beauty of their composition, they served to exhibit a picture of human manners so exalted and refined, that some persons, judging from their own depravity, could not believe the existence of the state it described. The general voice, however, declared in favour of the authenticity of the Poems; and the general voice has been supported by the opinions of men of genius and extensive learning. The delineation of Caledonian manners, exhibited in these poems, while it gratified the curiosity, commanded likewise the admiration of Europe. Men of taste and genius, in all parts have coveted an acquaintance with a language which could boast of the name of Ossian; and could triumph, almost unrivaled, in the exalted character of Fingal. Thus the love of the Gaelic has been revived; and a taste for Gaelic compositions has become general.

The Editor, moved by these considerations, and desirous to preserve his mother tongue, has bestowed much labour and expence, during the course of two years, in collecting the poems now offered to the public.[1]

Such an explicit declaration needs no analysis. We may, in passing, note the importance of the Ossianic controversy as a stimulus to further collecting, and go on to observe that the urge to prove to the world at large – in the first instance, no doubt to the English-speaking world – that Gaelic possessed an ancient and civilised poetic tradition may be read in, or from, other contemporary writings. It is, in fact, a manifestation, in the special circumstances of a minority culture, of one of the aspects of European Romanticism.

MacDonald intended his second volume, which never appeared, to demonstrate the antiquity of the tradition. 'Most of the pieces in the first volume', he writes, 'have been composed within the last two hundred years.'

There are 106 poems in all in the book, and not all of them are oral compositions. Some which are not may have entered oral tradition; others, which are, may have come to Ranald in writing. It would be tedious, and I hope unnecessary for our present purpose, to stop to prove that most of them, however, derive ultimately from oral sources of one kind or another. All in all – and including the uncertainties – one may claim that the contents of the Eigg Collection are not unrepresentative of the poetry gathered in that epoch.

The social ambience of much of the verse may be illustrated by a few titles taken almost at random from the first page of the Table of Contents: An Elegy to Sir James MacDonald; an Elegy to MacDougall of Dunolly; a Song to MacDonald of Clanranald who was killed in 1715; a song to Sir Lachlan Maclean of Duart – and so on.

This is clearly a poetic tradition firmly set in the upper echelons of Gaelic society. It is to some extent what we might call a bardic tradition – a tradition of encomia: MacDonald himself expressly mentions 'the elegies on the deaths of prominent men'. But although authors are named who probably held bardic offices under clan chiefs, the focus of the verse as a whole is not so much on the relationship between bard and patron as on the *set* of relationships which constitute the *fine* – the relatively small aristocratic group which forms the upper stratum of Gaelic society in the later Middle Ages and down to the eighteenth century. This invests even the narrower bardic poetry with a certain humanity; but in any case the bardic is only one strain among many, and by the eighteenth century it is already on the decline. Indeed, it is only by emphasising – perhaps over-emphasising – a superficial stylistic uniformity, little greater than persists in many a written tradition over the same length of time, that I am at all able to present this body of poetry as belonging to one category. Divisions could be made in numerous ways, but here I shall merely indicate the scope of the verse by observing that the commonplace kinds – religious or moralistic, satirical, political, convivial, amatory, etc. – are all represented. One may add, however, metrical range as a factor in the variety, and that astonishing rhythmical subtlety that confers an individual distinction on poems composed in the same basic form, for this too is part of the total statement that a poem makes.

From the eighteenth century to the present day, this poetry that we are considering can be seen filling a double role in Gaelic society. One the one hand, simply by having them written down on a page, and by neglecting the musical component of the tradition – for all these poems were sung or chanted – because of these accidents of history, we can regard them as the first phase of our written, vernacular literature. (But the part they play there does not, of course, concern us now.)

On the other hand, they continue in oral circulation – although the tradition is a progressively diminishing one – down to our own time. These examples from modern tradition vary a great deal textually, depending on the lines and circumstances of transmission. While Gaelic society remained stratified, what we may call 'primary transmission' would probably be largely confined to a well-knit group of native aristocracy and minor gentry, and to their immediate dependants, who sat in the *sreath* 'circle' with them. Transmission among the common people would no doubt vary, but one might expect a freer growth of variant versions at that level. One can certainly cite modern variants that show a high degree of mutation which seem to have had a long transmission in that form, e.g. a composite text based on a eulogy by Iain Lom to MacDonald of Sleat, composed perhaps in the 1660s, and an elegy by Niall MhacMhuirich to Alan of Clanranald, who was killed at Sheriffmuir, in 1715. Yet one may also recover texts that are strikingly conservative, although it is not bookish influence that accounts for that, but the fact that the singers are descendants of bards, or of the gentry, or have had access to sources controlled by such people. The situation, however, is so complicated that no short formula can sum it up.

The staple of the major collections, then, is a vernacular, oral, but 'official' poetry. And from internal evidence, from attributions of authorship – which are transmitted concurrently – and from an appeal to records, public and private, against which these facts can be checked, we can plot its history back into the sixteenth century. Very interestingly even our earliest poems display all the security of established practice. The tradition is clearly very much older than the sixteenth century. Sheer lack of evidence makes it improbable that we shall ever solve this question to our entire satisfaction; nevertheless, it is possible to lay down some guiding lines.

It can hardly be irrelevant to the issue that Classical Gaelic bardic poetry is much less strongly attested in Scotland than it is in Ireland. It is possible to think of several reasons for this.[2]

Whatever orders of poet practised their art in very early Gaelic Scotland, the turbulence of events contingent on the founding of the early kingdom of Scotia, the long conflict with the Norsemen, and the aggressive Anglicising policy of the sons of Malcolm III can hardly have provided the ideal milieu for the high caste *filidh*. It is perhaps worth noting here that Anglicisation, or partial Anglicisation, of the eastern and north-eastern areas of the kingdom is reflected also in the distribution of later vernacular poetry.

Be that as it may, full court patronage must have been at least an uncertain thing as early as the twelfth century. We have one glimpse of what may well have been the last official appearance of a seanchaidh at the Scottish court – at the inauguration of the boy king Alexander III, in 1249.[3] It is true that some of the Scottish authors named in the Book of Dean of Lismore may be descendants of families who flourished under court patronage, or under that of the great magnates of the kingdom, at an earlier date. But of the three families of professional composers of *dán díreach* who are most prominent in Scotland, and who survived longest, two – the MacMhuirichs and the Ó Muirgheasáins – are in the nature of reinforcements from Ireland. And the late Professor Angus Matheson has shown that the ancestry of the third – the MacEwens – may be Irish as well.[4]

The emergence of the clan system as we know it in the later Middle Ages included a considerable number of units whose economic power was extremely limited. A clan chief who could not maintain a filidh might well be able, however, to maintain a bard – a representative of a lower and less demanding order. And we know that there *were* clan bards who composed in vernacular Gaelic.

But they were not necessarily all of the same order. Just as 'clan' does not always and everywhere in Scotland denote the same territorial and social unit, neither, one may suggest, does 'bard' always imply the same status. I think it is a reasonable inference that clan bards varied both in their functions and in the kinds of verse in which they specialised.

Where a bard acted as a reciter to a filidh he would be in a particularly advantageous position to fill the role of middle-man between the classical and vernacular traditions. His métier was in the vernacular; but he would be sufficiently conversant with Classical Gaelic poetry to draw on some of its resources and employ them in his own craft.

These resources would naturally include the rhetorical techniques, and the imagery, of encomiastic verse; but just as important is the establishment of a syllabic metric in vernacular Gaelic. By the sixteenth century Gaelic poets were already using syllabic metres in the vernacular with subtlety and ease.

In talking of syllabic metres, one ought perhaps to add that the multiplicity of syllabic forms in Gaelic is not necessarily to be derived direct from dán díreach. There are songs that probably derive from other sources, which are nevertheless sung with the same speech rhythm as dán is: a pattern that derives ultimately from Classical Gaelic poetry having perhaps been imposed upon them. The point is, however, that a feel for speech rhythm in verse is a very marked feature of Gaelic poetry – this constitutes, in fact, one of its major and most sensitive graces.

To return to the bard. I am not suggesting that only professionals cultivated these and other forms. Indeed, it could be argued that it was only when they were taken up generally by lay poets of the fine that they developed their full potential. But the bard as intermediary between classical and vernacular must be given his own place. Other bards, free of the tutelage of any filidh, would have practised other forms, of which one was no doubt the metre that lies closest to the centre of the panegyric tradition – the unequivocally stressed verse that W. J. Watson called 'strophic'.[5]

In an article about the songs of Mary MacLeod I speculated on a formal connection between the strophic poems and passages of *rosg* such as we find in *Scéla Mucce Meic Dathó* and in *Serglige Con*

Culainn,[6] a possibility first suggested by Donald Mackintosh.[7] Such a connection would accord well with the facts on other grounds. Professor Calvert Watkins has shown in his paper on Indo-European metrics and Archaic Irish verse that short-lined verse of this kind tended to be used for more popular types of composition; and such is what we would *a priori* associate with some of the lower orders of bard.[8]

Recently the Rev. William Matheson has drawn my attention to the verses on Brigit in the *Book of Leinster* illustrating the metre called 'dían brecta centronun'.

> *Brigit buadach*
> *buaid na fine*
> *siúr Ríg nime*
> *nar in duine*
> *eslind luige*
>   *lethan breo*
>
> *rosiacht naemnem*
> *mumi Gaedel*
> *riar na n-aiged*
> *aebel ecnae*
> *ingen Dubthaig*
> *duine uallach*
> *Brigit buadach*
>   *bethad beo.*[9]

It is significant that the two stanzas given here are of different lengths: this is a feature of strophic poetry. Moreover, Mr Matheson also points out, the Irish poem can be sung to one of the known Scottish melodies. I consider this an important link in the chain of evidence: we can claim, I think, that we have at least a *prima facie* case for regarding strophic poetry as a peripheral survival of a very ancient form.

It is not, I believe, any longer used by traditional bards. It was closely connected with clan panegyric, which helps to explain its disappearance. It is rather interesting to observe how seldom it was employed for occasional verse – love poetry, for instance; and most religious poets, of whatever persuasion, took good care to avoid it.

The strolling bards, *A' Chliar Sheanchain*, as they are still known in the many anecdotes, printable and otherwise, that circulate about them, survived as an institution in Scotland at least as late as the seventeenth century, and probably in certain areas well into the eighteenth.[10] In oral tradition they appear simply as a degenerate rabble, but here again there was variation in status. Some of their store of poetry seems to have been drawn on by the Dean of Lismore, and we may glance briefly now at the form in which this poetry appears.

The transliteration of the contents of the Book of the Dean by editors such as Watson and Ross show that the verse is dán díreach, though of varying degrees of strictness. But editorial reconstructions perhaps slightly obscure the fact that the verse, as presented by the Dean, is demotic dán díreach, considerably influenced by the vernacular. If Watson is correct in his view that the Dean's poet brother Duncan MacGregor had a good knowledge of the classical tradition, it is difficult to see why he and his brother should have so altered his poetry, unless they were bringing it into line with an existing tradition of 'vernacularised' verse. I realise, of course, that other points of view are possible on this, but the problem is far too complex to tackle here. We can at least suggest that the Book of the Dean represents the confluence of two streams of tradition, oral and written, and that, in the form in which we have it, it looks almost like an early precursor of the popular paperback.

I should like to turn now to consider other aspects of the oral tradition, of which the early major collections give us little or no account. It is quite clear that at least in the last two hundred years a great deal of ephemeral verse was composed – it was designed as such, and filled the need that was later provided for by mass media. One may believe that such a need always existed, even in heroic societies. We know from what Martin Martin has to say in the seventeenth century that the common people of the Isles were greatly given to composing – they had, as he puts it, 'a quick vein of poesy' in them.[11]

But of all the kinds of song that the early collectors neglected or paid only little attention to, by far the biggest and the most interesting from any viewpoint is the category which nowadays appears to be centred on work. The connection with work, however, is almost wholly a functional one: very few pieces indeed would require from the evidence of their content to be classified as work-songs.

I shall call them here, generically, *choral songs*: the refrain, which is a distinctive feature, and which may consist of words (at least in the more modern examples) or of semantically meaningless vocables, or of a mixture of both, demands participation by a group. We have evidence that communal labour, of more than one kind, was in the past accompanied by choral song; in our own time, it is as an accompaniment to the task of 'waulking' or fulling cloth that they have best survived.

But we have evidence that they were used as entertainment as well. 'When the same airs are sung in their hours of relaxation', writes the Rev. Patrick MacDonald in the preface to his *Collection of Highland Vocal Airs* of 1781, '[. . .] one person leads the band; the rest strike in and complete the air to a chorus of words and syllables generally of no signification.'[12]

Both men and women joined in this; and although MacDonald distinguished between songs used for male and female occupations, it is clear that he is thinking in terms of one broad category. These choral songs are all short lyrics composed mostly by women.

The refrains, especially the meaningless vocable refrains, may well be the most primitive part of them – they are certainly a relatively stable element in a very unstable body of texts. At any rate, we seem to have here an obscure core of song round which there have gathered various crusts of accretion. Indeed, one may even find Ossianic ballads broken up into the requisite metrical units, interrupted by refrains.

Mr James Ross has discussed some of the peculiarities of this tradition, distinguishing between the poetic metre and the song metre[13] and is concerned to show that the song metres simply deploy literary metres in a different arrangement. Without going into the various permutations, one may say that the literary metres appear in song as couplets, single lines, or even half-lines.

The most arresting literary form which this study reconstructs is an irregular stanzaic form; when it is written out without the refrains, one could describe it as a paragraphic structure. Mr Ross draws a comparison between this and the structure of the 'Gododdin', and adds: 'This relationship between Welsh medieval poetry and Scottish Gaelic folk poetry is made more striking by the fact that the [. . .] metre [. . .] seems to be unknown in Ireland.'

This most interesting suggestion deserves to be taken out of the realm of conjecture; but my concern at the moment is with the structure of the songs as they are sung. There are doubtless a variety of ways in which the introduction of refrains into poetic metres could be accounted for – in the Eigg Collection there is an example of a syllabic quatrain poem with a refrain of vocables inserted where there may originally have been an instrumental accompaniment[14] – but in the present context, we must surely posit the existence of presumably autonomous metrical units, which are prior to the division of literary structures and which provide the informative principle on which that division is made.

In other words, where we find a line of poem broken up into, say, half-lines for singing, we must posit a prior song form with self-contained metrical units which correspond syllabically or in stress timing with half the line of the literary poem. It is, of course, rather intriguing and suggestive of a certain involution so far as origins are concerned, that some of the literary forms can be divided precisely in this way; in some instances, it is clearly possible because of a caesura in the line; but it must be added that some lines can be divided only by violating the syntax. Each of these half lines either contains two stresses or is capable of bearing two metrical accents. It is tempting, therefore, to see behind this form, too, what Professor Watkins calls the 'Indo-European shorter line' – what I have already alluded to in connection with the strophic metres. To suggest an ultimate connection between fairly humble work songs and socially much higher praise poems may seem incongruous, but in fact certain sophisticated, bardic compositions involving descriptions of travel by sea are actually called *iorram* – 'rowing-song'. It is unthinkable, to my mind, that these panegyrics actually functioned as rowing-songs, but the use of the term *iorram* may reflect an earlier function of the metre or metres on which they are based.

Interestingly enough, one instance of the 'IE shorter line', which Professor Watkins cites, to show its association with an informal style of composition, is a work song – a song no doubt based upon mundane usage, though in the saga context attributed to the *áes-síde*.

We know that rowing was *the* male occupation accompanied by choral song. In fact, the word *iorram* is occasionally used as a generic name for choral song.

This theory, that one strain in the choral songs may be connected formally with vernacular panegyrics, and that both go back to a common origin, may always remain conjectural; but so far as the bard's part in shaping the tradition is concerned, we have still one more fragment of evidence. In a poem traditionally ascribed to one MacBeathaig, piper and bard – a low grade, clearly – to MacDonald of Sleat, there occurs a passage in short double-stressed lines, the content of which is exactly the kind of informal praise poetry in which the choral songs abound.[15]

We may now look beyond the work-song ambience, and ask if there is evidence of any other function for choral songs.

The oral tradition of Uist has preserved the memory of a small clan battle fought in North Uist in 1601. In the battle, Domhnall mac Iain 'ic Sheumais, the leader of the victorious side, was wounded. His foster-mother, so it is said, gathered a band of girls and set off for the scene of the battle, composing a panegyric on the way. This she sang to the wounded man, while the girls sang the refrain. (There are slight variations in tradition – I have given only an outline here.) The song which she is said to have composed is still known and it is a choral song.[16]

This isolated fragment of tradition, transmitted merely as an incidental item in the account of a clan battle, would seem to be the only circumstantial description we have in Scottish Gaelic of the widespread practice of women singing a praise song to a victorious warrior. But from Ireland we seem to have in the tantalisingly brief reference to the *cepóc* mentioned in *Scéla Mucce Meic Dathó* an allusion to the same type of composition. We may also notice here an interesting entry in the Wardrobe Accounts of Edward I of England, detailing a payment made to seven women in Strathearn during the King's journey through Scotland in 1296. These women, who 'came out to meet the king [. . .] and sang before him, as they used to do according to the custom of the time of the Lord Alexander, late King of Scotland',[17] were almost certainly the same kind of *bannal* – the band of girls – as sang for Domhnull mac Iain 'ic Sheumais in Uist 300 years later. The word 'cepóc' survives in at least one dialect of Scottish Gaelic in the form *ceapag* 'an improvised song, a ditty'; such panegyrics might well have been partly improvised. It is interesting that, as O'Curry pointed out long ago, the cepóc may indeed have been regarded at one time as specifically Scottish. However that may be, the singing of such groups would naturally be choral. Is it a complete coincidence that the line of the cepóc quoted in *Scéla Mucce* – 'Fer Loga mo lennan-sa' – can be fitted quite easily into the metrical scheme of Gaelic choral songs?

The erotic strain in the choral tradition is so dominant as to demand some attention. Now, a connection between erotic, lyrical songs and the dance is a very old and well canvassed one, although the theory is nowadays largely out of fashion. The reaction against the 'danced-song seasonal festival' theories which culminates in Louise Pound's *Poetic Origins and the Ballad* has influenced areas of scholarship far beyond the scope of Miss Pound's thesis, which is concerned primarily with the origins of the medieval and later narrative ballad in the

Germanic languages. It would be idle to deny – and Louise Pound herself never attempted to deny it – the connection between dance and song: it is a widely distributed, and perfectly authenticated phenomenon. But so far as Gaelic is concerned there are two problems to be faced.

1. There is no evidence of native choral songs accompanying indigenous dances; for instance, seasonal or fertility dances such as 'Cailleach an Dùdain' appears to be.

2. There is no native word for 'dance'.

The second objection can partly be countered simply by pointing to the existence of a dance like 'Cailleach an Dùdain' or of solo dances like 'Mac Iain Dhìrich'. If these were borrowed, where were they borrowed from? Certainly not from England or France.

Dancing is a fundamental human activity and it seems unlikely that the one or two indigenous dances that we have comprise the sum total of all that existed. It is much more reasonable to suppose that old forms were displaced by new, and that 'dannsa' supplanted the native word or caused it to shift in meaning.

If there really was a tradition of danced song in Gaelic, we would expect it – at least if we follow the old theory – to be connected with seasonal and other festivals. It is significant in this connection that the material gathered by Máire MacNéill in *The Festival of Lughnasa* shows us that dancing and match-making were constants of these festivals, at least in modern times. Even if the forms of dance that are described are modern, can anyone believe that this is not a very ancient practice?

Match-making choral songs, as it happens, are of central importance in the modern luadh. It could be argued that this is, as it were, their proper environment, but it seems to me more natural to explain them as one of the accretions.

Dr Ó Tuama in his brilliant book *An Grá in Amhráin na nDaoine* doubts if the idea of a chorus is native to Gaelic. For Irish he points out that only in Ulster is there a Gaelic word that expresses 'burden' or 'chorus' – the word *luinneog*, Scottish Gaelic 'luinneag'.[18]

In Scotland 'luinneag' nowadays means little more than 'a ditty, a light song'; but it is clear that earlier it did denote a refrain, and particularly a refrain involving meaningless vocables, which points to a choral refrain. And the Rev. Patrick MacDonald in the preface to his *Highland Airs* uses 'luinneag' as the generic term for women's choral songs. All this shows that for Scotland at least the idea of chorus is deep rooted and suggests that it may indeed be a native one. At all events, the alternative theory raises more problems than it solves. I would like to suggest, very tentatively, that 'luinneag' is to be connected with *luinne* – vehemence, ferocity, etc. – and as such could conceivably denote the performance of a song in a situation such as the dance would provide. Professor Jackson has argued that, in the early Welsh *englyn*, incremental repetition can best be explained by the old dance theory, or at least by a theory such as improvisation between two individuals or groups.[19] Verse contests, which feature in Gaelic choral song and are explained as improvisations at an actual luadh, are much more likely to have been composed outside the work-song tradition altogether.

In one or two places, one finds that a chorus of vocables is called *tuireadh* 'lamenting', which suggests perhaps that keening, or some form of keening, employed choral refrains. A large number of choral songs are laments: many of them, as is natural in maritime communities, laments for men lost at sea. But both the evidence about professional keening in the past and the apparently spontaneous performances of a more recent time force one to put keening, if only provisionally, in a separate class. (Where keening has survived until recent times, the word, incidentally, is not *caoineadh*, but *caoidh*.)

Are the love themes, one may now ask, derived from early French in the manner that Dr Ó Tuama has argued so persuasively for Irish popular love poetry? Personally, I am inclined to think not, on the whole, and that any influence from medieval French – or English – lyric poetry is secondary.

W. P. Ker, writing on the Danish ballads at a time when it was believed that the carole was the only progenitor of lyrical poetry and narrative ballad alike in the whole of north-western Europe, was slightly puzzled. The ballads, he says, have discovered a form of poetry which is alive.

> It is a lyrical form, and, though it was a borrowed form from France, it seems to have taken up, like a graft rose on a briar, the strength of an obscure primitive stock of life, so that the English and the Danes and their kindred were able to sing their own native thoughts and fancies to the French tunes. This may sound mysterious, but it cannot be helped. A mystery may be a positive fact, like any other.[20]

It seems to me more than likely that these Scottish Gaelic songs present us with at least part of that stock on to which the French rose was grafted.

I must now turn to consider a less delicate flower. There are in Gaelic verse two distinct strains of bawdry. One, curiously enough, is associated with the words of dance tunes, and though the melodic forms are modern, one wonders if this is not an old tradition of erotica, but one which exists now in caricature. If so, we do not know what the models were.

Although there are numerous declarations and prohibitions by the Church all over Europe against *cantilenae* and the like, we seldom or never have any evidence of what the actual songs were. For instance, in 1596 the Kirk Session of Elgin records that 'Magie Tailzeour [. . .] Elspet Beig [. . .] Magie Thomsoune [. . .] confessit thame to be in ane dance callit gillatrype, singing a foull hieland sang.'[21] But, naturally enough, it is not transcribed.

The other repository of bawdry is the verse contest, sometimes represented as being between the *Cliar Sheanchain* and a known poet, sometimes between two named poets. This can hardly be unconnected with the literary 'flyghtings' of Lowland Scots, of which the most famous is the 'Flyghting of Dunbar and Kennedy'. And Kennedy, it should be noted, is regarded in the flyghting as a Gaelic speaker, which he probably was, being a native of Carrick in Ayrshire.

The contests are also examples of spoken, not sung poetry, and traditionally they are said to be *ex tempore* compositions. No bard was worth his salt who could not improvise at least a quatrain. But it is important to stress, particularly in view of the oral formulaic theory, that Gaelic oral poetry is not markedly formulaic and that what is represented as *ex tempore* composition is perhaps the least formulaic of all. This is not to deny the existence of rhetorical techniques that employ an inherited store of imagery – but that is another matter. I suggest that a good deal of work still needs to be done on the oral formula; and, in this connection, I welcome the severely sceptical approach adopted by Dr Douglas Young.[22] Any modern unlettered bard will very quickly point out the short-comings of the theory to an interested listener, either by precept or example. A colleague and I once had the somewhat startling experience of being addressed for the best part of twenty minutes in impromptu song by a man at whose home we had both called unexpectedly, and for the first time. Yet even this composition was not conspicuously formulaic, let alone made up of formulas.

The ability to improvise verse in this manner is explained by the composers themselves simply as a hereditary gift. The belief that a poet is born, not made, is extremely strong, and a curious aspect of the belief is that very often a bard will stress the fact that his gift comes to him from his mother, or from his mother's people, sometimes even when his father's family seems also to have included bards. The instances of this that I have noted may, of course, be of no special significance; on the other hand they may be related to the belief that transmission of charms, and possibly occult knowledge in general, ought not to be transmitted by the initiate to a person of his or her own sex.

Apart from this possible mystique, however, there is nothing particularly esoteric about transmission. But there is one curious and well-established belief which may be worth mentioning: that is, that a bard cannot be sued for slander or libel uttered in his poetry, provided his name is in *Leabhar nam Bard* 'the Book of the Bards'. This term, however, has no denotation. The idea is simply that the bard must have been officially recognised as a poet: for example, if he had been charged with some crime, and had had his profession entered in court records as 'Poet', he would from then on enjoy a kind of diplomatic immunity. There are numerous anecdotes told in connection with this – always involving the composition of satires, frequently addressed to girls who had spurned the bard's advances. One of these stories relates how a bard from the island of Mull, hearing that he was about to be served with a summons, came to Edinburgh and proclaimed himself publicly at the Mercat Cross as a poet. As soon as this news reached Mull the case was dropped.

This notion of immunity in regard to satire is probably the last reflection in Scottish oral tradition of the privileges of the poets. At least, if there are other beliefs still current that invest the bard with powers other than those of skill in language, we have not so far recovered them, with perhaps one possible exception. Among a number of outstanding poetesses in Gaelic, there are two, both of whom were born in the seventeenth century and died in the eighteenth, in whose legends there seems to be a slightly sinister element. One is Màiri nighean Alasdair Ruaidh, the other is Maighread Ni Lachainn. Màiri never married; nor, according to some traditions, did Maighread. This in itself is at least eccentric in that kind of society. Both of them, it is said, went around accompanied by a woman who seems to have acted as an assistant, one of whose functions was to make up choruses of vocables or to set her mistress's song to a melody. Both women, it is said, too, were buried face downwards.

These are the legends, but no contemporary seanchaidh, so far as I know, can explain them further. There is, however, another tradition which may have a bearing on the matter. Long ago in the Islands, it is said, if a boat went missing, a wise woman was consulted. She was of mature years, unmarried, strong-minded, and she, too, had an assistant. The woman went to sleep, and while she slept, her spirit went out to search for the missing boat. But, if the wind changed while she was asleep, she lost her reason.

This seems to me to be a fairly straightforward description of shamanistic trance and the recovery of hidden knowledge. May it be that some vestige of the poet-seer's practices lingered on in Scotland into the eighteenth century?

I cannot dismiss Maighread Ni Lachainn without mentioning the circumstances in which she composed her poems. Not with eyes covered, and a stone on the belly, as the filidh (according to Martin Martin) composed, but indoors, nonetheless – she simply could not compose out of doors. And at the proper moment, she *saw* her poems running along the green turves that formed the intersection of wall and roof. The phrase used by the seanchaidh who supplied me with this information was 'A' feitheamh na bardachd a' ruith air na glasfhadan'.

The oral tradition covers all this, and much more. In this brief survey, the actual poetry itself has rather been lost sight of. It would take a great deal of time to demonstrate its qualities, for it enshrines the experience of a whole people. One would like to show that even bardic poetry is not necessarily dull, no matter how circumscribed its basic themes may be. It can sometimes have a laconic arrogance that is quite delightful.

> From Diarmad have all of you come –
> An ancient line:
> A clan who are most deserving of praise
> That *we* have heard of.[23]

Almost at the opposite pole stands the beautiful death-bed hymn of Duncan MacRury, the piety of which is not diminished by its delicate nostalgia for the flesh-pots.

> Forgive us our sins –
> We shall not be committing any more.[24]

There is a good deal of what may, broadly speaking, be called satirical poetry in Scottish Gaelic. At one end of the scale there are flights of passionate invective; at the other one finds the true satiric humour of Rob Donn's elegy for the respectable misers, two brothers who died in the same week, a few days after turning away a poor person from their door, and who were laid in the same grave.

> They were men who caused no dissension –
> So far as anyone knew –
> Not did they perform one act
> That the world calls grace:
> But they were conceived and born
> They were reared and they grew
> A swathe of life passed over them
> And in the end they died.[25]

But these are qualities that are to be distinguished by terms to which in the last analysis labels such as 'written' and 'oral' are irrelevant.

Gaelic Song and the Dance

In my essays 'The Choral Tradition in Scottish Gaelic Songs' and 'The Oral Tradition in Scottish Gaelic Poetry', I suggested that one of the strains in the corpus of song that has survived, generally speaking, as *òrain-luaidh* 'waulking-songs', could be connected with the dance. In this essay, I should like to go over some of this ground again in the light of my subsequent researches. I cannot claim that I have proved the case conclusively, but I believe there is further evidence to be considered in addition to what I have already adduced. I would like to emphasise that it is very much a survey of work in progress.

First, however, let me draw attention to what might be criticised as the weakest link in the chain of argument. As I admitted in 'The Choral Tradition', there seemed to be little or no evidence from Gaelic tradition of the existence of a dance-song complex which we could tie directly to the waulking-songs. There are, of course, other connections between song and dance, as in the *puirt-à-beul* ('mouth-music'), and I shall discuss these later.

The idea that the waulking-songs, which are essentially choral in structure, might be linked with dance was in fact derived from reading nineteenth- and early twentieth-century scholars who subscribed to the theory that the ballad – Scottish, English, German, Scandinavian, and so on – came ultimately from the medieval French carole. The outline of that theory can be stated somewhat as follows. This term *carole*, from which we have English 'carol', signified a dance-song and such dance-songs were supposed to have functioned in the celebration of seasonal festivals, which were of unknown antiquity. The survival of carols at Christmas, and to some extent at Easter, is explained by the fact that pagan festivals were Christianised by the early Church. Even so, there were forms of 'carolling' that persisted well into the Middle Ages; and if we may judge from the violent denunciations of the Catholic clergy, these were regarded as pagan survivals, at best dangerous in leading men's minds away from the Gospel, at worst simply wicked and sinful in themselves. The seasonal festivals from which they originally sprang were connected with fertility and fertility rites. Hence the highly erotic nature of many of the older specimens, including those that were written down by scribes in a Christian society.

The relatively short narrative song that goes under the general title of 'ballad', comes also, according to a similar theory, from a complex of dance and song. In the ancestral from of carol and ballad alike, the stanza was probably sung by the leader of the dance, the burden or refrain by the chorus of dancers. ('Chorus' itself, incidentally, is via Latin from Greek *khoros* 'dance'.) This choral refrain has been described as 'an exultation irrelevant to the progress of the story'. An example of such an 'exultation' would be 'Hey the rose and the lindsay, O' in the Scots ballad of 'The Cruel Mother' or in a Faroese version, 'The rose and the lily are growing well'. In our waulking-songs, the equivalent refrains are the choruses of meaningless syllables or *vocables*, or a combination of vocables and words, the latter group found mostly in songs composed from the 1740s onward.

Behind those theories of ballad and carol origins lie the speculations of eighteenth-century Romantic writers, particularly in Germany, on the origins of poetry itself. According to this, all poetry begins in the singing-and-dancing primeval throng: the Folk sing; the Folk dance. These Romantic theories continue to inform the work of certain outstanding ballad scholars, who became known as Communalists (e.g. F. B. Gummere, W. M. Hart and G. L. Kittredge), well into the twentieth century. There were of course those who were severely critical of their ideas but these movements of criticism and counter-criticism need not detain us now. It is sufficient to note the main theoretical stance.

Among British writers of the early twentieth century who accepted the theories of French scholars such as Gaston Paris and Jeanroy on the carole and the origins of lyrical verse, W.P. Ker, in his studies of English medieval poetry and in particular his essays on the Danish ballads, is outstanding in erudition and balance of judgment. There is no question, so far as he is concerned, of the ultimate origin in France: 'The French lyrical dancing game appears to have conquered the north'; 'the ballad refrains of Denmark, like those of the Icelandic *danz*, are after a French original'; 'in English [. . .] this fashion of refrain, all but absolutely universal in the Danish ballads, is the plainest mark of French origin.' But he also notes that 'Refrains, burdens, were known in the ancient northern poetry, as in Anglo-Saxon; it would be strange if this common thing were lacking in any age'. And again, 'Interpolated refrains are found in the popular poetry of all the world.'[1]

When I first came across W. P. Ker's work, as an undergraduate, it struck me forcibly that we might have in Gaelic a parallel to all this. The waulking-songs are of course work-songs and may always have been just that, basically, no matter what other elements have been drawn into their powerful lyrical orbit. But even if we accept the existence of an age-old tradition of songs that accompanied work, that does not mean that there were not both melodic and verbal structures whose origins lie elsewhere. In view of the ballad scholars' theories, it seemed that what Ker called the 'lyrical dancing game' was at least a possible source. Dance, in one form or another, solo or communal, is a fundamental art form in human society.

However, in ballad scholarship the 'danced-song seasonal festival' theory received a severe setback with the publication of Louise Pound's *Poetic Origins and the Ballad* in 1928. Her well argued case had an effect that went far beyond the confines of ballad origin theory. Pound's thesis was concerned primarily with the origins of the medieval and later ballad in the Germanic languages. But Louise Pound did not attempt to deny – for it would be futile to do so – that 'danced song' never existed. Indeed, within the field of ballad performance itself – and in a Germanic language – the ballads are still danced in the Faroe Islands. The problem of ultimate origins is simply another matter.

The question of French and Anglo-French influences on Gaelic poetry was settled long ago by T. F. O'Rahilly and Robin Flower with regard to Classical Irish and Scottish verse and more recently, with regard to popular love poetry, by Prof. Sean Ó Tuama.[2] In fact, Professor Ó Tuama's brilliant and thorough examination raises an important issue. If the French or Anglo-French influence on popular Irish song is as profound and pervasive as he shows it to be, what existed before? Was there in Irish Gaelic, for instance, a tradition of popular song comparable with, say, the Scottish òrain-luaidh with its not inconsiderable component of erotic poetry? If so, we might quote W. P. Ker again, still on the matter of origins and the ballads:

> They [the ballads] have somehow or other discovered for themselves a form of poetry which is alive [. . .] it is a lyrical form, and, though it was a borrowed form from France, it seems to have taken up, like a graft rose on a briar, the strength of an obscure primitive stock of life.

It is obvious enough that the Gaelic choral songs, and particularly the waulking-songs, have an astonishingly intense stock of life. How 'primitive' they are, chronologically speaking, no one can say. For my own part, I am quite prepared to accept the possibility of some waulking-song *melodies* being older by many centuries than the arrival of the Gaels in Alba, or indeed older than the advent of the first speakers of a Celtic language in this part of the world. (I might in passing draw the attention of musicologists to what I think are melodic resemblances to certain songs recorded in Siberia and among the American Indians. But that may be no more than mere chance.)

On this 'primitive' Scottish Gaelic stock, there are possibly one or two French grafts. In a song which opens 'Latha dhomh 's mi falbh an t-sléibhe' or 'an fhraoich / an fhàsaich', we have what appears to be a pastourelle. In its Old French typical form, the author / narrator, who is usually identified as a man of high rank, sometimes a knight, recounts his meeting with a girl of lower social status and his attempt to seduce her. One cannot be certain, however, that this is not a native motif where it appears in Gaelic. We are probably on firmer ground with the song sometimes known as 'A' Bhean Iadaich', which is either a version of, or related to, the ballad of 'The Cruel Sister' and hence more easily categorisable as either migratory or international. But whatever their origins, both of those compositions are securely established within the corpus of òrain-luaidh. In addition to that, there are motifs (not necessarily restricted to the choral tradition) which can be paralleled in songs of French or Anglo-French provenance.

We have always assumed, I think, that such influences, where they can be established, would have reached the Gàidhealtachd primarily from Ireland or percolated northwards from the Lowlands of Scotland, which we know were visited by Gaelic bards and musicians. This is perfectly acceptable, but French and Anglo-French connections can be traced by a more direct route also. A number of great kindreds, Grants, Frasers, Gordons and Chisholms among them, and not least, in the earlier period, the Comyns, are all originally of French ancestry. All became Gaelicised, much as the Anglo-Norman families became Gaelicised in Ireland. It is surely probable that the houses of these magnates would be centres of patronage likely to attract, from the earliest period of their establishment in the Highlands, travelling singers and minstrels and other entertainers of similar linguistic and cultural background. They would also, in the process of establishing themselves in the Gàidhealtachd, presumably bestow patronage on native Gaelic poets and musicians. It would seem very likely, therefore, that here we have dominating centres of cultural influence and exchange in all the arts – poetry and music, song and dance. If strathspeys, reels, jigs and other forms of 'Scottish music' connected with dance are importations (as they are generally agreed to be) then these same centres, though perhaps at a later stage than the first settlement, must have had some function in their introduction to the Gaelic world.

Historians of music can tell us little about the state of the art in Scotland before 1500. Similarly with dance. 'Little is known about the pre-Renaissance dancing of Scotland, although there are indications that many current steps and figures have their origin in both the medieval Lowlands and Highlands' sums up the situation.[3] Most of us would regard 'Dannsa a' Chlaidhimh' as an indigenous Gaelic solo dance. But what of its associated tune 'Gille Caluim', and the port-à-beul: is the measure equally ancient, or is it an imported form? We have a similar problem with 'An Dannsa Mór', said to have been brought from Strath in Skye to the island of Eigg, where it survived in the repertoire of the late Hugh MacKinnon. One of the two puirt-à-beul to which it was danced is basically in reel time, with irregular stressing in all but one of the verses (and hence syncopated if sung properly) although the refrain of vocables with one verbal phrase is in strict tempo. But this song is also known in a more regular variant.

An Dannsa Mór is a ring dance performed by twelve men or more, two of whom move with a formalised 'walk' inside the ring, singing alternate lines of song, then taking their places in the ring as all the dancers join in the chorus. During the chorus the dancers hop around on the left foot, with their legs straight and the right foot about eighteen inches from the floor. The second port-à-beul refers to 'sadach na muilne', while a variant mentions 'Ruidhle nam Pòg', well known as the dance almost invariably performed as the last dance of the evening, particularly at weddings, and the dance in which women chose their men partners. Ruidhle nam Pòg is in all its essentials simply the popular and widely distributed kissing dance known in the Lowlands under a variety of names: 'Babbity Bowster', 'Blue Bonnets', 'The White Cockade', and so on.

An Dannsa Mór appears to be unique in Gaelic tradition. But references to Ruidhle nam Pòg and 'sadach na muilne' may link it to other dances about which we know rather more. In which case, it may have been developed through the ages and drawn on a number of elements, native and foreign.

We do know that, during the centuries in which the Anglo-Norman families were moving into the Gàidhealtachd, the 'French lyrical dancing game' was still flourishing in France and similar ring dancing was enormously popular in England. Do we then have, perhaps in all our dances, a merging of native and foreign forms? Gille Caluim, for instance, may have been a native warrior's dance which was conjoined with a tune that came from outside the Gàidhealtachd. An Dannsa Mór does have parallels in the ring dances of continental western Europe but some kind of 'dancing game' may have been fitted into an existing native frame.

The phrase 'sadach na muilne' of course reminds us of the dance 'Cailleach an Dùdain',[4] where *dùdan* is simply the same as *sadach na muilne*: 'mill dust'. (There are, however, the variants Cailleach an *Dùrdain / Dòrdain* 'humming'.)

(Dannsa) Cailleach an Dùdain is a dramatic performance connected with seasonal and presumably fertility rites. It was performed by two people, in male and female roles, to a tune of the same name played on the pipes or fiddle or sung as a port-à-beul, either by a third person or by the performers themselves. The characters enact a primitive drama in which the man kills the woman, becomes overcome with grief and then resuscitates her, limb by limb, until finally he touches her hair and restores her to life. In some versions both characters are armed with sticks; in others the man holds a 'magic wand' (*slachdan draoidheachd / geasachd*). This death-and-resurrection drama was danced by adults at the great Autumn festival of Michaelmas, *Latha na Féill Mìcheil*, 29th September. After the ceremony fell into disuse among adults, it became a children's game played not at Michaelmas (so far as we know) but on May Day, *Latha Bealltain*, which may indicate it was once enacted then also by adult performers.

This dramatic dance has every appearance of being a ritual of immense antiquity, parallel perhaps to similar practices in other societies but not imported from the Lowlands or from England or France. Yet the tune 'Cailleach an Dùdain' gives no such impression of great age. Alexander Carmichael says: 'The air is quaint and irregular and the words are curious and archaic.' But the tune as we have it is a jig (6/8 time) and much less irregular than a number of puirt-à-beul which have no connection in tradition with ancient ceremonies. Nor are the words, which begin 'A Chailleach an Dùdain cum do dheireadh rium', archaic. The phrase has, of course, a hint of bawdiness, though nothing like the explicit bawdiness of so many puirt. (In this connection, I have pointed out in 'The Oral Tradition in Scottish Gaelic Poetry' that one of the strains of bawdry in Gaelic is particularly associated with the words of dance-tunes; that this may be an old tradition of erotica, possibly going back to fertility rites; but, if this is so, that it is now expressed in caricature.)

If 'Cailleach an Dùdain' as drama is ancient while the tune is relatively modern, do we have to conclude that here we have a cultural merger, a confluence of native and foreign traditions? As we noted earlier, 'strathspey reels' as they were once called, jigs and the customary reels, and the like, are not supposed to be ancient Gaelic forms of music, but musicologists have still to examine this question in depth. Perhaps the roots are deep in native tradition and perhaps *ceòl-beag* borrowed initially from vocal music, whatever influences subsequently modified its genres. There could be a parallel here with the development of strophic metres in Gaelic verse. Almost certainly ancient in origin, these metres must have been modified, with regularisation of metre and introduction of rhyme (the latter pervasive in Gaelic anyway) to produce what emerges in the late sixteenth century in Scotland.

From a linguistic point of view, the problem can be brought into sharp focus by asking: what is the Gaelic word for 'dance'? 'Dannsa' is ultimately from French either direct (through the influence of the Anglo-Norman families in the Gàidhealtachd) or through English. Since there are no other words with an unassailable claim – 'ruidhle', said by some to be Gaelic, is almost certainly of Lowland or Northern English origin – does that mean that the Gaels did not dance at all before their contact with the English and French fashion? If the answer is no, then we can argue that neither did the English dance until they learned to do so from the French, for there is no native English word either. But if dancing is, as we have suggested, a fundamental human activity, this would be a rather odd conclusion to come to with regard to both peoples. It is really much more likely that new fashions displaced the old, driving them out entirely or allowing them to survive in a diminished form in another environment. Alexander Carmichael again:

> Another dance is called *Cath nan coileach*, the combat of the cocks; another, *Turraban nan tunnag*, waddling of the ducks; another, *ruidhleadh nan*

coileach dubha, reeling of the black-cocks; another, *cath nan curaidh*, contest of the warriors [. . .] Many dances now lost were danced at the St. Michael ball.

Some of the names mentioned by Carmichael appear in other sources. According to Skye tradition, 'Dannsa nan Tunnag' was performed at wakes and was one of those practices that came with changing attitudes to be regarded as obscene. Here 'Turraban' may well be the original term, displaced by 'Dannsa'; 'ruidhleadh' in turn may have displaced a native Gaelic word also. Incidentally, the port-à-beul 'Ruidhleadh na Coilich Dhubha, Dhannsadh na Tunnagan' (a reel) uses both these titles, but, according to good tradition-bearers, was not otherwise closely connected with the dances in question.

At all events, we can now suggest that there is enough evidence, fragmentary as it may be, to prove beyond reasonable doubt that there was a native tradition of dance performed at seasonal festivals and in rites of passage in Gaelic society, however different its figures and movements may have been from what we nowadays regard as 'Highland' or 'Scottish' dancing. But ought we to look elsewhere, too, within the corpus of Gaelic song and music?

As I argued in 'The Choral Tradition', òrain-luaidh are essentially 'choral': the refrains are part of their structure and demand participation by a group. Although they were sung outside the work situation, communal labour supplied the basic requisites for strong choral support. In John Ramsay of Ochtertyre's frequently quoted description: '*luinigs* [Gaelic *luinneagan*] were sung by the women [. . .] during almost every kind of work, where more than one person is employed [. . .] The men too have *iorrums* [Gaelic *iorraman*], or songs for rowing, to which they keep time with their oars.' Both had vocable choruses: 'syllables generally of no signification'.[5] A few of the latter were drawn into the repertory of òrain-luaidh. But so were a variety of other structural types (Fenian ballads among them), refashioned for the purpose and demonstrably in some instances fitted with vocable choruses in their new setting. And so we have this large corpus of song – love-songs, laments, panegyrics, and so on – which in *content* make no comment on the work in hand. Ramsay goes on to say, 'When labourers appear to flag, a *luinig* is called for, which makes them for a time forget their toil, and work with redoubled ardour.' We could reasonably argue from this, that it is the very contrast between poetry and toil that makes these songs so efficient in lightening labour. These are songs that accompany work rather than songs *about* work, although there are also a few of the latter, e.g. 'Clò nan gillean iomair o hò | Iomair chuimir iomair o hò', etc.

According to one of the leading authorities in this field, Dr John Lorne Campbell, the majority of òrain-luaidh were composed at the actual waulking, 'extemporised at the waulking board by gifted singers'.[6] He was, of course, aware of the accretions also: 'There are certainly songs sung as waulking songs which were not composed as waulking songs in the first place.' Campbell adds: 'After around 1700 the improvisation of waulking songs at the waulking board died out';[7] in the main a well grounded judgment. (We can accept that, with the slight proviso that improvisation continued in a small way into our own times: this is detectable even when a single singer, out of the waulking environment, recorded a song on more than one occasion.) He also points out that after 1745 the nature of the songs changed: 'the songs tended to become stereotyped in couplets with internal rhyme [. . .] such songs could be used for other forms of labour besides waulking, or even for social entertainment.'

There are two sets of implications here that deserve comment. The rich stock of formulas on which the composers drew have always existed, it would appear, within the limits of the work situation. Origins otherwise are not discussed. (To which one may add that the problem of ultimate origins of formulas is not resolved by positing the existence of sources outside the work-song ambit either.) The other implication is related. When waulking-songs were used for social entertainment, this represents a secondary and very late development, given that, as Dr Campbell himself says, it only developed after 1745 although 'cloth must have been waulked in the Highlands and Islands for hundreds of years before 1600'. Ramsay of Ochthertyre tells that when the luinneagan 'are sung in their hours of relaxation, the time is marked by the motions of a napkin, which all the performers lay hold of'. Holding a handkerchief or some other piece of cloth while singing survived into our own day and is known elsewhere, for instance, in the 'band-dance' of the Faroese and in English Morris dancing.

Just as descriptions of carole and ballad laid emphasis on the roles of leader and chorus, so, in Ramsay's account: 'In singing, one person leads the band [. . .] while the rest strike in and complete the air, pronouncing to it a chorus.' But, of course, in communal work leader and chorus are similarly co-ordinated. It seems then, to sum up the argument so far, that a good case can be made for regarding the òrain-luaidh as a work song tradition and leaving it at that.

If we do try to take the discussion further, the next step is to ask whether musicological analysis tells us anything. Unfortunately, the entire field of Gaelic music is virtually unexamined with regard to such questions. I ought to mention, however, that one musicologist with whom I discussed this particular problem gave as his opinion that some waulking-song tunes seemed to him, from comparative analysis, to be essentially music associated with labour while others gave the impression of being music associated with dance. One example which he singled out as possibly a dance tune in origin is the Lewis version of 'Hè man du'. But, he added, there are dangers in being puristic in making these distinctions until all the material has been analysed.

We can now turn to the evidence of contemporary, or at least recent, tradition, and that can be summarised as follows. In a number of places in Scotland and more generally in Cape Breton Island, Nova Scotia, still, it was customary to sing songs with refrains while standing up, holding hands. Sometimes the singers did not move much from their individual stances but swung their arms rhythmically to the tempo of the song. More often, as enthusiasm increased, so did the singers move, in a line, semi-circle or full circle, the movement being largely dependent on the space available. At weddings, when love-songs formed the greater part of the repertoire, an òran-luaidh with a love-theme, sung by a leader and chorus of guests, was felt to be necessary for the proper celebration of the *bainis*. One informant stressed that when buildings were small, as was usually the case, the singers kept their stance or moved minimally; but when a larger house or barn was available they circled slowly sunwise. (There were, however, no actual dance-steps involved, as there are for example in the Faroese dances.) I suggest that this piece of evidence is sufficient as a basis for discussion: does this singing of choral songs with movement derive from an ancient form of dance?

The *luadh-chas* 'fulling of cloth with the feet' was not, of course, a dance. But the practice might facilitate the process whereby work-songs could develop a secondary role at weddings or other entertainments where people stood up to sing. When singers sang the òrain-luaidh sitting down, in a circle, holding each other's hands or a handkerchief, Necker de Sassure was told in 1807 in Iona that 'such a movement *imitates* the operation of waulking the cloth' (my italics).

Nevertheless, on the whole, I am inclined to think that the work-song and the work-and-movement represent two originally distinct traditions of 'chorality'.

There is a formula of 'climbing the mountain', which is found in different types of Gaelic song. Although it has more than one function, it is conspicuous in songs of lamentation for the dead, e.g. 'Dìreadh na beinne 's ga teàrnadh'. When it is combined with the formula that expresses the dishevelling of hair by a woman, as in 'Cumha Ghriogoir' ('Dhìrich mi a' bheinn mhòr gun anail | Dhìrich agus thèarn | Chuir mi falt mo chinn ri talamh | Basaibh mo dha làmh'), it describes an act of ritual mourning. Could it also have involved ritual procession? If so, were the movements formalised? Were they accompanied by songs of lamentation? We simply lack the answers to these questions.

What we do know, however, is that mourners danced at funerals. The *Oxford Companion to Music* claims, indeed, that the practice survived into nineteenth century. Citing comparative evidence, the writer states: 'It seems probable that the custom of dancing before the dead, which survived in the Highlands of Scotland up to at least the opening of the nineteenth century, had a religious origin.'[8] Religion in this context could take us back a very long time before the coming of Christianity. In the Christian era itself, the carole was frequently danced in or round churchyards, well into the Middle Ages, and Christian churches were often built near ancient pagan burial grounds, where age-old funeral rites had been practised.[9]

The references to dancing at wakes and funerals in Gaelic society are scattered throughout a variety of sources. Anne Grant of Laggan refers briefly to the practice as:

> a custom, indeed, which was not extinct till after 1745, for people to dance at late wakes. It was a mournful kind of movement, but still it was dancing. The nearest relation of the deceased, often begun the ceremony weeping, but did, however, begin it, to give the example of fortitude and resignation. This man, on other occasions, had been quite unequal to the performance of this duty; but at this time, he immediately on coming in, ordered music to begin, and danced the solitary measure appropriate to such occasions.[10]

Instrumental music or song, or both, it would seem, functioned as the accompaniment. The testimony of Thomas Garnett, published in the same year as that of Anne Grant, is also significant. His use of the term 'lament' does not make it clear whether instrumental music or choral song accompanied the dance, but it seems likely that this 'strain' originally derived from vocal music:

In some parts of the country, the funeral dances are still kept up. These commence on the evening of the death. All the neighbours attend the summons; and the dance, accompanied by a solemn melancholy strain called a lament, is begun by the nearest relatives, who are joined by most of those present: this is repeated every evening till the internment. These dances may perhaps be intended as an expression of joy that their friend is removed from this vale of tears and misery, to a better state of existence.[11]

The dance is directly connected with song in the testimony of John Smith three decades earlier. Although he was a devotee of Macpherson's *Ossian*, his antiquarian writings do contain genuine Gaelic material:

In some of the Highlands of Scotland, and in some parts of Ireland, this custom has been very lately practised, and is hardly yet extinct. In the Highlands, the nearest relation is the first to lead, on these occasions, the dance and the song. These, however, have always been of a graver and more solemn kind than what have been used on their ordinary merry meetings. From the air and style of some of these compositions, which are not unfrequent in the poems of Ossian, we may form some opinion of what they have been from their earliest era.[12]

I suspect, but cannot yet prove, that one of the types of song was of the kind described in 'The Choral Tradition': those sung in quatrains, the second and subsequent quatrains being formed by repeating the last couplet of the preceding one to the tune of the first couplet. There I quote Donald Campbell writing in 1862: 'Two lines of every verse in the following measure, and all similar songs, were sung as a chorus by the audience.' Some of these are fitted with a long refrain of vocables; others are not. As Campbell observes, the repetition itself can act as the choral refrain. A number of such songs (though not all) are laments, e.g. the song to MacGregor of Roro who was hanged in 1602.

In other, quite different, environments a few descriptions refer to singing and dancing, without making it clear whether the song actually accompanied the dance or not. Martin Martin tells how after the offering to the 'sea-god called Shony', the people first went to church, then 'all of them went to the fields, where they fell a-drinking their ale and spent the remainder of the night in dancing and singing, etc.'. The 'etc.' may cover activities that are alluded to in the numerous declarations and prohibitions of the medieval Church all over Europe against the cantilenae associated with danced song. And, after the Reformation, we have, for instance, in the records of the Kirk Session of Elgin in 1596, a statement that three women 'confessit thame to be in ane dance callit gillatrype, singing a foull hieland sang'. The song, whatever its precise relationship to the dance, was presumably erotic or perhaps bawdy as well. It might well have been a port-à-beul.

We also have a tradition that when MacDonald returned to the Isle of Skye after some period of absence, girls danced and sang before him. But again, there is no unequivocal declaration that the dance and song was one complex form.

There are descriptions in ethnographic writings of women coming out to greet strangers or visitors with singing and dancing combined; or, for example, when victorious warriors return from battle. There is an interesting entry that refers to Gaelic Scotland long ago and that might be interpreted in that context. In 1296, Edward I of England made a triumphal progress through part of Scotland. In Strathearn seven women (a canonical number, perhaps) 'came out to meet the king [. . .] and sang before him, as they used to do according to the custom of the time of the Lord Alexander, late King of Scotland'.[13]

Three centuries later, in 1601, Domhnall mac Iain mhic Sheumais was wounded at the Battle of Carinish in Uist. According to tradition his foster-mother gathered a group of girls who sang to him while she improvised the famous celebratory song 'A mhic Iain mhic Sheumais | Tha do sgeul air m' aire'.[14] It was choral; it was used as a waulking-song; but it was composed outside the work situation. According to one variant, the girls stood round the wounded warrior to divert his attention while an arrow was being removed. Another variant adds that it was to drown the warrior's cries. Dancing is not mentioned in any version of the story that I know, simply that the girls raised the chorus. Although the detail is unique, there are vestigial traditions of women coming out to greet a warrior which were to be heard among Gaelic speakers I met in Perthshire.

I think it is reasonable to connect the record of the women of Strathearn, the Uist story and the fragments of Perthshire tradition, and to seek parallels in other cultures. In the Old Irish saga of *Scéla Mucce meic Dathó* 'The Story of mac Dathó's Pig', dating from the early 9th century, we seem to have a tantalisingly brief glimpse of a similar kind of composition: a song of greeting and praise addressed to a warrior. Only one line is quoted in the saga; the scribe adds *et reliqua*, i.e. the remainder of the song; as if to say, 'everybody knows how it would go on'. The implication is either that this kind of composition was too unimportant to bother with (which is not the impression the context gives) or it was a very well known form indeed. It is, I believe, significant that the line – 'Fer Loga mo lennan-sa' – fits quite easily in the metrical scheme of a section of our òrain-luaidh. In Old Irish the song is classed as a *cepóc*, a word which has survived in Scottish Gaelic as *ceapag* 'an improvised song, a ditty'. Nora K. Chadwick, in a short discussion of the term gives it as her opinion that '*cepóc* refers to choral singing by a number of girls, and probably to a panegyric, possibly of an erotic character.'[15]

She also quotes from Eugene O'Curry, who commented on the word *aidhbhse*, explained as 'the music or the murmur which [. . .] the men of Ireland used to make'. Chadwick says: 'The *cepóc*, according to [O'Curry . . .] was merely the Scottish name for the Irish performance known as the *aidhbhse*, or *crònan*.' We all know the words attributed to Màiri nighean Alasdair Ruaidh when MacLeod censured her for making songs: 'Chan eil annta ach crònain' ('they were only harmless croons'). She was also accused of praising the children of the household – regarded as hubristic in Gaelic society and in cultures other than Gaelic. 'Aidhbhse' is glossed in the *Dictionary of the Irish Language* as 'used of some kind of singing or chanting'.[16]

There is plainly an area here still to be explored: terms, functions and relationships. But 'aidhbhse' can certainly not be dissociated from the Scottish *aidhbhsich / aidhbhseachadh* (Old Irish *aidbsiu, aidbsiu-gad*). It generally involves praise or at least does not suggest dispraise in an expression such as 'aidhbhseachadh mór aig daoine mu dheidhinn'. It can, indeed, mean simply 'praise', especially praise of a person, though not limited to that. In an almost technical sense it signifies exaggerated praise, which of course might bring nemesis, usually through the Evil Eye. If 'aidhbhse' and 'cepóc' in Old Irish can be equated, as Nora Chadwick suggests, as terms that subsume notions of panegyric, choral singing and content of an erotic nature, then processes of semantic dissimilation which cannot now be traced must have occurred over many centuries. This is a linguistic and cultural jigsaw puzzle most of whose pieces are missing.

'Cepóc' (because of the 'p') is presumably not Q-Celtic (Irish, Gaelic, Manx) in origin at all. Is it a British, or even Pictish, word? Is it related to Latin *capere* 'to take, catch'? In which case we might for the sense compare English 'catch', a variety of the musical 'Round', connected with the Round Dance. 'Crònan', wide as its connotation may be, can be applied to vocables without words, in lullabies for instance, or, in a couple of stories about grinding with the quern, on occasions when one or two singers were merely humming vocables. 'Luinneag', like 'ceapag', is in ordinary spoken Gaelic 'a ditty, a lyric, a light song'. (Dwelly s.v. *ceapag* has 'catch, verse or verses composed impromptu; carelessly sung song'.)

But as we have seen, in eighteenth-century usage, according to John Ramsay, 'luinneag' has a specific denotation: a choral song with vocable refrains. In numerous song collections, from the same century onwards, 'luinneag' is often used for 'refrain' only, and essentially a vocable refrain, in contrast to 'fonn'. (This distinction no longer obtains, so far as I know, in spoken Gaelic.) Occasionally in the collections 'tuireadh' is the term for vocable refrain, which makes a link with songs of lamentation for the dead. Vocable refrains were apparently used in the keening ceremony.[17] And certain of the choral songs (with repeated couplet, discussed above) that may have been sung at funerals and wakes have vocable refrains also.

In the essay 'The Oral Tradition in Scottish Gaelic Poetry' I suggested that 'luinneag' could be connected with *luinne* 'vehemence, ferocity', etc., and might denote the ecstatic performance of dance. Throughout Western Europe in the Middle ages, there are accounts of the 'dancing mania', and stories such as 'The Dancers of Kölbeck', who were cursed to dance day and night forever, and the origins of the disease known as 'St. Vitus' Dance' are among the legends associated with the enormous popularity of these medieval 'raves'.

Just as 'carol', or 'carole' included both dance and song, and 'ballad' is derived from Late Latin *ballare* 'to dance', so, conversely, *danz* in Icelandic came to mean the words rather than the dance in which they were sung. Is it then beyond possibility that 'luinne(ag)' at one time signified both song and dance? But whether this is the word that French-English 'dance' displaced, or whether some other native Gaelic term, if indeed such existed, has completely vanished from the language, we cannot say. When a new fashion and a word for it enters a language, it is not uncommon for the name of the older, native object, practice, or institution to continue in existence, but now in a new context.

Although 'luadh' to us is quite specific, it is noteworthy that Alexander MacBain, a century ago, took it to be 'a side-form of the root of *luath*', and compares 'Irish *luadh*, motion, moving', with further connections with *luaisg* and *lùth*. The *Dictionary of the Irish*

Language gives *luadh* (s.v. 'lúad') as 1 (a) 'act of moving, setting in motion, performing, promoting, etc.'; 1 (b) 'act of mentioning, telling of, discussing'; and 2 'act of fulling (cloth)'.[18] MacBain gives as the root of luinneag '*lundo* – root *lud*, as in *laoidh*, Eng. lay?'. He makes no mention of Latin *ludus* 'play', but the late Prof. Kenneth Jackson expressed his opinion that the connection was by no means impossible.[19]

It is intriguing that the Germanic languages have, from a common root *laiko-*, words beginning with 'l', signifying 'play, sport', etc. In Gothic and in Old High German respectively, the reflexes of the root can mean 'dance' and 'song or melody'. In medieval English *lake* is 'play, sport, glee'; the corresponding verb means 'to exert oneself, to move quickly, leap, spring; hence, to fight'.

There may be a great deal of coincidence here. None the less we seem to have a complex of ideas, perhaps social practices and institutions, too, involving movement, play, melody and dance, distributed throughout a number of languages and cultures. But to attempt further analysis of that aspect is beyond the scope of this paper.

Finally, there are two forms of song to be found within the ambit of the luadh which deserve mention. The first is the verse-debate in which one woman praises her own clan territory and dispraises that of her rival in the dispute. These songs very obviously belong to a genre (or, as some scholars would say, a heterogeneous collection of genres), the poetic contest, found all over the world. They are usually rooted in oral tradition but enjoyed great popularity throughout medieval Europe in courtly as well as in popular or non-literate societies. (The Lowland 'flytings' are well known examples of Poetic Contest.) Two or more protagonists may take part, face to face or in a public setting before an audience.

Most of the recognised modes of expression of verse debate are to be found in Gaelic: in other words, they are not at all confined to the choral tradition or to the luadh. One of the choral songs, however – 'Òran Arabhaig' ('Song of Strife') – is classified by Frances Tolmie as a reaping song.[20] Tolmie gives the following anecdote, set c. 1750: 'On a day in harvest [. . .] a party of reapers [. . .] divided themselves into two rival bands representing the poetesses who had originally sung the words of strife.' She then gives the legend regarding the original, dated to the early years of the seventeenth century. 'Two women hailed one another from each side of the Snizort River which formed a boundary between the territories of MacLeod and Macdonald, and gave expression to their sentiments.' The legend gives the impression that this was a ritual exchange of insults – a custom also practised at weddings, admittedly in a rather different atmosphere. Such origins are to my mind more likely than improvisation at the luadh, although Dr John Lorne Campbell singles out 'especially the flytings' as songs improvised on the spot during the work.

Songs that *were* improvised, though within a given framework, are represented by, for example 'O có bheir mi liom? | Air an luing Éireanna[i]ch? | o có bheir mi liom? | Gur h-e X bheir mi liom' where X is a man's name. These match-making songs were certainly of central importance to the luadh and added gaiety to the proceedings. Yet again extraneous origins ought at least to be considered. Match-making and liaisons of various kinds were associated with seasonal festivals. Máire MacNéill in her classic work *The Festival of Lughnasa* shows that for Ireland dancing and match-making were constants of seasonal festivals there into modern times. And even if the forms of dance are modern, it is impossible to doubt that this is a very ancient practice.

I shall not attempt to sum up the points I have raised in the foregoing survey. The argument, so far as there is one, could only lead to a verdict of not proven. It is difficult at this stage to do more than suggest there is material for much further discussion.

The Panegyric Code in Gaelic Poetry and its Historical Background

In Gaelic one of the highest compliments in our critical vocabulary is expressed in terms such as, 'Nach ann aige tha a' bhardachd; nach math a' bhardachd a th'air an òran sin.' At the simplest level, even in these contexts, it may be sufficient to translate *bardachd* as 'poetry'; but it does not take a great deal of enquiry to realise that something more specific is intended. But is it definable?

For many years this question of what we mean, or imply, when we use the term almost in a technical sense in colloquial Gaelic has interested me.[1] From the outset of my enquiry it was clear to me that songs devoted to the praise of an individual were central to the concept of bardachd. But it was equally clear that there was a special rhetoric of praise which bards and singers regarded as an inheritance. My purpose in this essay is to explore the nature and function of this pervasive system of rhetoric and connect it with the historical experience of the Gaelic nation in Scotland. But although I believe the influence of history in shaping what is very loosely called 'traditional' Gaelic poetry can scarcely be over-estimated, this is not primarily an historical study. My main concern, rather, is to view the rhetoric synchronically and show how it forms a highly complex but coherent network.

If I may take the liberty of beginning with some of my conclusions, it may help to clarify the direction of my argument a little. The primary function of bardachd is to be found in clan panegyric, where the stress is on the survival of the group of warrior-hunters at the top of society. The diction is codified in sets of conventional images, most densely concentrated in the heroic elegy composed at the point of crisis brought about by the death of a leader – in other words, when it was most necessary to reaffirm the traditional values of the community. One of the stock conventions is to rehearse the allies – real or ideal – of a clan. This reaches its height in 'The Song of the Clans', composed at the time of the Jacobite Rising of 1715.[2] The poem is a piece of bardic propaganda for Gaelic nationalism.

The attempts on the part of poets to preserve at least a conceptual Gaelic unity were successful up to a point, but at the price of developing panegyric not only as a form but as a pervasive style. The style in turn reflects an attitude to the world, which is regarded intellectually in terms of praise versus dispraise. It extends to love poetry and to nature poetry, in the latter evoking a sense of friendly or unfriendly territory: in short, it bears the Gaelic sense of social psychology, of history, of geography. One can trace its workings even in a post-1745 poem such as Donnchadh Bàn Macintyre's 'Praise of Ben Dorain' – a panegyric to a mountain, couched in terms of visual documentary. Although 'panegyric' in this sense is only a framework, which allows the imagination a good deal of freedom, in the end it became a strait-jacket.

I am not of course suggesting that Donnchadh Bàn's great poem marks the end of this rhetorical tradition. On the contrary, as I see it, the style is traceable to the present day. It is simply that as one of the best-known monuments of Gaelic poetry, 'Moladh Beinn Dobhrain' is an excellent example to cite of the remarkable development and application of this panegyric code.

I have used the terms 'Gaelic nation' and 'Gaelic nationalism'. The concept of a nation may be interpreted in different ways: some historians would no doubt object to its use in this context, but I know of no more adequate word to express the particular sense of identity possessed by the Gaels throughout the vicissitudes of Gaelic history. Yet there are complexities in the use of the term. During the last two and a half centuries the processes of decline have produced what can only be regarded now as the detritus of a nation. Earlier than that, mostly in the later Middle Ages, internecine strife, often fomented by the policies of the crown and parliament in Edinburgh, made the 'nation' an exceedingly fragmented one. There is in addition to such facts the complication that if we are to speak of a *Scottish* nation, we must fit into that notion this 'nationhood' of the Gaelic part of the Kingdom, and admit that Gaelic Scots (if we are to be regarded as Scots rather than Gaels in Scotland) were at least in a very special relationship with Ireland; Gaelic Scotland and Ireland forming one cultural and linguistic province, if not exactly a unity, until the seventeenth century.[3] But while this is so, the Scots Gaels never denied that they owed allegiance to the King of Scots as their own sovereign, no matter how much they might at any given time disagree with the attitudes and policies of a particular monarch. This in the end became for much of Gaelic society a suicidal loyalty when the flight of James VII and the succession of William of Orange gave it new dimensions.

The historical experience of which all this is part, and which according to my argument forced Gaelic poetry to develop its characteristic rhetoric, cannot be described in any detail in this short essay. Nonetheless it is impossible to understand the processes which brought this about unless we bear constantly in mind the fact that Scottish history may be seen through Gaelic eyes. Within this view, as in any historical assessment, there are differences of interpretation, some of which are relevant to the interpretation of Gaelic poetry. Most of what I have to say on the historical side will perhaps appear commonplace to some people, but I know from experience that my view is by no means always acceptable either to professional historians or to politically conscious individuals who would see Scotland as one homogeneous country and nation, though with of course important regional variations.

From our point of view then, I think it is true to say that at various levels of Gaelic tradition there is to be found an awareness (I shall not put it more strongly than that) of a time when 'all Scotland was a Gàidhealtachd'.[4] In the early part of the eighteenth century, Burt tells us that there is among the Gaels

> a tradition, that the Lowlands, in old times were the possession of their ancestors [. . .] When I mentioned this tradition, [formerly] I had only in view the middling and ordinary Highlanders; [. . . now] I would be understood that it is very probable such a Notion was formerly entertained by some, at least, among those of the highest rank.[5]

We do not have to invoke the political unity of early Gaelic Scotland to account for the persistence of this idea. It is sufficient that there was a strong sense of cultural unity from, say, the eleventh century. Wherever a patron was to be found, there the men of learning would make their way, travelling as freely in Argyll or Moray as they did in Galloway or Lothian. The maintenance of the tradition would naturally be secured in the first instance by the mandarin poets and historians who were associated with the King and Court. The seanchaidh who recited in Gaelic the lineage of Alexander III at the boy King's inauguration in 1249[6] was performing the same kind of *seanchas* 'historical lore' as appears in the 'Duan Albanach', a court poem composed during, or immediately after, the reign of Malcolm Canmore.[7] Although the inauguration of Alexander III may have witnessed the last official appearance of a seanchaidh at the royal Scottish Court, descendants of such poets and historians, or descendants of families of filidh in the service of great magnates of the early Gaelic kingdom, must nevertheless have survived in Scotland long enough to contribute to the stock of knowledge and craft used by later 'bardic poets'. It is interesting to find Donnchadh mac Dubhghaill Mhaoil, brother of the Dean of Lismore, addressing the chief of Clan Gregor (1461–1519) in the formulas of seanchas, reminiscent of the 'Duan Albanach'.

Id chineadh nach críon ré fóir
is é a líon do ghabh coróin
dá fhichead agus triúr ríogh:
dlighthear a n-iúl san airdríomh.

Trí tuaithir, trí deisir dhóibh
i ndiaidh Mhaoil Choluim Cheannmhóir;
dá chóigear choróin a chín
ó Mhaol Choluim go hAilpín

O Ailpín suas is é a mheas
ceithre fir dhéag go Fearghus:
cá líon do sheanchas mar sin?
ríomh go Fearghus is féidir.[8]

Some three and a half centuries after the date of this poem, from the same area of Perthshire, we have an interesting testimony to the state and content of oral tradition. Duncan Campbell, a native of Kerrumore in Glenlyon, tells how his aged grandmother and those of her generation discussed Queen Victoria's coronation, in 1838, enjoying

> the liberty this occasion gave them for going [. . .] to the history of Scottish Kings as far as Kenneth Macalpin, which had come down by oral tradition. Long afterwards when I read the 'Duan Albanach', I was much surprised to discover that the substance of it was retained to a remarkable extent in the oral and local traditions which our aged people recalled and told at the time of Queen Victoria's coronation. As for the later Kings from the days of Wallace and Bruce [. . .] there was nothing very strange in the fact that the traditions were fairly strong and unbroken.[9]

This sense of continuity and historical perspective still exists, though in a very diminished form, in modern Gaelic tradition. We may well doubt, however, whether this would be the case if Gaelic and its culture had suffered a steady and unrelenting decline from the time of the sons of Malcolm III and Queen Margaret. But, as we know, in the reorganisation of Gaelic society after the dynasty had become Anglicised, a new focus of Gaelic culture emerged. This is of course the Lordship of the Isles.

The Gaelic reaction to the aggressive Anglicising policy of the sons of Malcolm and Margaret was at first expressed in large-scale rebellions (in which the MacHeths especially are prominent) organised mainly in the eastern and south-western parts of Scotland.[10] After these had been crushed the main, certainly the successful, sources of rebellion were in the west. In this process, the anti-Scottish inheritance of the Norsemen played a part. As a Gallghaidheal, Somerled himself, though represented in tradition as a leader of the Gaels against the Norsemen, presumably drew upon these attitudes: there is no reason why they should have disappeared as the Isles became progressively Gaelicised. Malcolm MacHeth's 'dynastic' marriage to Somerled's sister points to a community of interest; it may have been this alliance that brought Somerled into conflict with Malcolm IV: 'perhaps for the same reason that Macbeth rebelled against Duncan succession to the Crown by direct descent from the preceding Sovereign, which had not hitherto occurred in the House of Atholl'.[11] This casts MacHeths and Somerled alike in the role of champions of the older order, with the cultural allegiances that that implies.

Given such a framework, attitudes would certainly be strengthened by a process of displacement and dispersal of leaders of Gaelic society from east to west such as is indicated in the statement that 'King Malcolm (IV) transported the men of Moray' in 1162,[12] the year before Somerled met his death. If the Macleans and MacKenzies are of common origin,[13] of the line of Old Dugall of Scone, in Gowrie; and if there was a movement of people from Gowrie to Moray and from Moray to the west; ancient traditions of the Cenél nGabráin, going back to the foundation of the Scoto-Pictish Kingdom, would naturally become compounded with those of the Gallghaidheal, providing an added historical justification in any conflict with the central authorities. The close links of the MacDonalds with Ireland and their acquisition of extensive territories in Antrim are facts that need no elaboration. Yet, as we shall see later, when the poets assert the rights of Clan Donald, their major claim is to possession of half of Scotland, and the spot that symbolises this claim is located, significantly, not even within the confines of the Lordship of the Isles, but in the heart of

Scoto-Pictish Alba, in the ancient province of Fotla, which appears later as Atholl with Gowrie.

The Lords of the Isles as leaders of a semi-independent Gaelic state claimed *ceannas nan Gàidheal* 'the headship of the Gael'. Moreover, they were in a state of fundamental hostility to the 'realme of Scotland':[14]

> Whereby it may be gathered that the name dignitie and race of the MacDonells hath been allways most hatefull to the Princes of Scotland, as usurpers of the patrymonie of their crowne, and also very odious to the house of Argeile, whose risinge grewe by theire ruyne.[15]

By the fifteenth century, the Campbells had secured for themselves the leadership of one of the two provinces originally held by the line of Somerled[16] and they, too, claimed ceannas nan Gàidheal. The long hostility between the Campbells and Clan Donald is an ideological struggle in which the ideologies enshrine the options that presented themselves to the Gael after the royal dynasty of Scotland had become Anglicised: resistance or collaboration. In addition, however, to the historical reality of MacDonald-Campbell warfare (which did not preclude personal friendships), there is an element of historical mythology not only in the general popular conception of the 'feud' but even in genuine Gaelic tradition. In an historical study, the role of clans such as the Frasers or the Gordons, neither of which was accepted as fully Gaelic, and of a clan such as the MacKenzies who were Gaelic but yet frequently played a part in the north comparable to that of the Campbells elsewhere, would all have to be analysed in detail. From time to time, collaboration with Scottish Government policies informed the actions of all the clans, the MacDonalds included, if only, for some of them, to gain a brief respite or a limited tactical advantage. We really ought to regard these manoeuvrings in terms of a Clan Donald versus Campbell 'idea' of Gaelic history rather than concentrate on the 'feud'; seeing the two groups in the role of symbolic as much as real historical protagonists. If the Campbells had not existed we should have to invent them.

In a basic sense the Campbells were as Gaelic as any other kindred, and they, too, inherited ancient traditions deriving from the Scoto-Pictish kingdom which would justify the course they took. Because of their involvement in official Scottish policies, they might be said to be more truly *Scottish* Gaels than their opponents. W. J. Watson makes the interesting point 'that while the MacDonalds vaunted descent from Conn Cétchathach [. . .] and Colla Uais [. . .] Mac Cailin's bards disclaimed Irish connection, and traced the line of MacCailin up to Arthur of the Round Table, emphasising British origin'.[17] All the learned poets were of course aware of the 'British history', and the chief of Clan Gregor is similarly connected with Arthur by the Dean of Lismore's brother, in the poem already quoted. But the Campbells do indeed seem to have developed this pretension as a point of propaganda.[18]

It is interesting also that apparently the only extant poem which has been interpreted as an exhortation to a chief to join in a military campaign undertaken by the realm of Scotland rather than by the Gaelic nation, is the poem addressed to the Earl of Argyll before Flodden. Watson remarks on 'its fierce national spirit' and observes that 'there must no doubt have been many such poems, now lost to us, in connection with the Wars of Independence; one other, composed in 1310 [. . .] is found in the Dean's book';[19] and this judgment may be valid. But even allowing for the distance in time, and the consequently greater chances of loss of manuscripts, it is remarkable that nothing of the kind has been preserved, for instance among MacMhuirich remains. This other poem mentioned by Watson is by no means an unequivocal example of pan-Scottish propaganda (it is, incidentally, from the anti-Bruce side); one may venture to suggest that if Gaelic poems ever existed which gave primacy to the concept of Scottish nationhood (at least from the mid-thirteenth century on), they would be exceptional in attitude, very much in the minority, and except perhaps for the Campbells, something of an aberration. Mr Francis Collinson has observed that:

> It is remarkable for instance that there are no songs or ballads [in Gaelic] on the Scottish War of Independence, with its heroic leaders Wallace and Bruce, and its epic victories of Stirling Bridge and Bannockburn, in which the Highlanders played a brave part. Nor, to look forward a couple of hundred years or so, are there any Gaelic songs about Mary Queen of Scots, whose glamour was surely of the essence of song, and whose impact upon the Highland clans was far from negligible.[20]

The MacDonalds were indeed deeply involved in the Wars of Independence, to a large extent through the personal contacts maintained between Robert the Bruce and Angus Òg of Islay. But there is nothing to suggest in the entire history of Somerled's line, in its various dealings with the Kings of Scotland, that its poet-spokesmen would ever celebrate any great venture in which Clan Donald was involved as other than a primarily MacDonald and Gaelic event. The 'Scottish dimension' might be there, but it is of secondary importance. In this connection one may cite the reference in the Book of Clanranald to these stirring times of the Wars of Independence: the writer merely notes that the MacDougalls took Balliol's side and the line of Raghnall son of Somhuirle took that of Bruce.[21] Even the Campbell poem to the Earl of Argyll which may have been written before his going to Flodden is very much in the conventional terms of Gaelic panegyric. In spite of the 'British origin' which Watson underlines, the poet draws on the commonplaces of Irish mythology and cites Ireland as an example to follow. Even within the Campbell sphere of action the poets kept alive an awareness of the relationship of Irish and Scots Gaels. It is probably true to say, however, that the attitudes of the Classical Gaelic poetic order, partly because it was a conservative, mandarin caste, were not always identical with those of its patrons, who were continuously involved in the rough-and-tumble of Scottish workaday politics.

This highly simplified model of the background to Gaelic poetry emphasises the feeling of continuity from a Gaelic kingdom of Scotland, and a tradition of loyalty to the true dynastic line of Malcolm Canmore. On the other hand, it suggests that the pressure of historical events reduced the possibilities of action to sharply contrasting alternatives: existence as a Gaelic community in collaboration with the central authorities or existence as a Gaelic community in resistance to these authorities.

This is a dialectic of history. The thesis is implicit in the fundamental attitudes of the Lordship of the Isles, their vassals, allies and successors; the antithesis in those of their opponents. There is no synthesis. Gaelic history remained in a dialectical opposition until the whole organisation of society finally broke after 1745. What we have is an ideal synthesis, which must have been taking shape for a long period, perhaps from the time when the issues of the Wars of Independence had been determined, before it emerged in explicit form in the eighteenth century. The development and certain overt expressions of this we owe to the vernacular bards. It was they, amidst all the complexities and vicissitudes of Gaelic history, especially after the downfall of the Lordship of the Isles and the reduction of Gaelic society to a multiplicity of 'clans', who preserved a conceptual unity for the Gaels of Scotland. To concentrate thus on the vernacular poetry is not at all to discount the contribution of the poets of Classical Gaelic, in whose works much of the rhetoric was formulated. Moreover, these poets' high social status almost inevitably ensured a downward and outward propagation of literary influences extending over centuries. Also, there is some evidence of a reverse flow of influence. We could, indeed, be in danger of making too much in Scots Gaelic of the disjunction, in language and literature, between the classical and vernacular traditions: at various points they complement rather than exclude each other; and by the time our vernacular poetry emerges strongly from its prehistoric darkness – in the late sixteenth and early seventeenth centuries – the rhetorical affinities are clear. Nonetheless, the classical poets were relatively an enclosed order; the vernacular bards, with their demotic language, had a much wider social reach.

Bard and Bardachd

At this stage it is necessary to distinguish between two senses of 'bard'. There is the general sense, in which the word is roughly equivalent to 'poet', as when we say that Donnchadh Bàn was a bard. The other sense is technical. In medieval Gaelic society the bards constituted a lower order than the learned *filidh*; they were divided by the jurists into two main classes of *saorbhaird* and *daorbhaird*, each of these being further subdivided. As a generic term, 'bard' here obviously covers a large range and variety of poets, songsters, and other entertainers. It is commonly accepted, however, that one important function of the bard was the making and reciting of praise-poetry.[22]

The semantic development of 'bard' obviously reflects the underlying developments in literature and society. In my opening remarks I claimed that panegyric is a pervasive mode in Gaelic poetry. If the professional bards had always a specific duty to make praise-poems, and if in their various subdivisions they spread over the greater part of Gaelic society, their influence must have impinged throughout, and they are clearly the most important figures in the development of the rhetoric of praise. But as I hinted above there were also cross-currents of influence.

To take an example, what I see as the panegyric commonplaces of 'Òran na Comhachaig'[23] may be parallel to, as much as directly derived from, those of the professional bards. Discussion of these and other problems associated with the bards need not, however, delay us now. It is enough to appreciate that in the form which W. J. Watson called 'strophic metre'[24] we have a tradition of what we may term specifically bardic panegyric which displays the greatest density of the topics of praise. Hence we can analyse the rhetorical system, simply for convenience of description, as if, for instance, the commonplaces of a waulking song, which may well be older than a given poem in strophic metre, were chronologically derivative from the latter.

There are two poems in a simple strophic metre composed by MacGregor bards in the early seventeenth century: the poem on the Rout of Glen Fruin, in 1603,[25] and the poem known as 'Saighdean Ghlinn Lìobhann';[26] both of them compositions associated with battles. These two early anonymous texts differ from each other in that there is more direct passion in the former, and simpler, poem; greater elegance and subtlety of craft in the latter. But they resemble each other in that they both give the impression, on the one hand, that the authors were less concerned with direct personal feelings about the man or men who fell than with the social order to which all of them belonged; on the other, that there is nevertheless enough personal feeling to make us think that the poet is constrained to speak this way because it is the proper convention to follow. Individual emotion may be present but must not obtrude. We also feel that the poems are not so much a lament for the passing of this style of life (not 'the end of the world') as devices for reinforcing it by a recital of its virtues: almost as if the authors might have felt that this bardic rehearsal would help to avert the threat.

These two poems between them display the essential features of the tradition. A subject is eulogised: he is addressed by traditional title and patronymic; his generosity and the magnificence of his household are praised; his prowess as a warrior and hunter celebrated. If the poem is an elegy the loss to the bard and the *fine* 'kin' is emphasised. But in the bardic panegyrics composed by the famous authors of this tradition – Màiri nighean Alasdair Ruaidh, Iain Lom, Eachann Bacach and others – the focus is much wider, the imagery more elaborate. It is possible that in the MacGregor poems we have examples of the professional bard's art, representative of a stage in the development of this tradition before it became greatly involved in celebrating *inter*-clan relationships as well, and before it had taken over and assimilated the imagery of classical Gaelic poetry to the extent that we find it, for instance, in the work of Màiri nighean Alasdair Ruaidh, the prime exemplar of the developed panegyric which nevertheless is still securely set within the confines of one *fine*.

It would be tedious to present detailed lists of rhetorical topics from Màiri's poems; but anyone who cares to look at J. C. Watson's edition[27] will see immediately that all her bardic panegyrics consist of complicated permutations of the same commonplaces. It will also be clear that they do not follow any particular order. The poetess will reintroduce the subject's descent, generosity (especially to men of art), personal beauty, and so on, several times, producing a densely woven texture of imagery in which every phrase, indeed almost every word, is significant. Even the shortest utterance sets off a train of memories of linked epithets. A word such as 'Sìol' will link itself with the name of a man, of a patronymic, of a kin; this in turn leads the mind on to epithets such as 'nan long, nam bratach, na féile, nan corn 's nam pìos', etc. All these evoke different sets of new images interlocking with each other in the same way.

Once these conventions were established, even an oblique reference would be intelligible in the very same terms. The commonplaces work thus for anyone who through song has known the rhetoric from childhood; they work with similar effect upon the imagination of a critic who does no more than familiarise himself with the written texts; and we can take it for granted that the audience in the chief's hall was able to respond, though not necessarily in this self-conscious, analytic manner, to all the nuances of each statement. What the bards have produced here is therefore a coherent system of rhetoric of great resonance and evocative power. Nor is it designed to be merely an enclosed universe of poetic discourse. Every commonplace of the system focuses upon a particular facet of aristocratic life, including relationships to those who provide imaginative, spiritual, and economic support for the aristocracy. As we shall see, the ramifications of the system eventually extend throughout society.

Although it is not easy to unpick this dense fabric, I shall now suggest a number of headings under which some of the points made above can be discussed in greater detail. The first topic I shall call the Allies.

Allies

The MacGregor poems I cited contain no references to other clans. But in 'An Crònan' we find Màiri nighean Alasdair Ruaidh introducing a different convention:

Tha na Gàidheil gu léir
Cho cairdeach dhuit féin

which leads to 'Sir Domhnall à Sléit'. Thereupon she introduces a list
of allies of the MacLeods: Clan Ranald, Glen Garry, the men of
Knoydart, Frasers, MacKenzies and Macleans. How old this convention may be it is impossible to say: it is found in Classical Gaelic
panegyric, and certain vernacular bards, or bards of certain clans, may
always have tried to reinforce the sense of security of the fine in such a
manner. It would be natural that the mutual loyalties of the Lords of
the Isles and their vassals would be thus expressed. But we also find it
used by the Campbell poets. In the sixteenth-century classical poem
'Maith an chairt ceannas na nGaoidheal'[28] which asserts of that
'headship' that 'It is the noblest title in Scotland', the Earl of Argyll's
allies (and vassals) are Clan Donald, Macleans, MacLeods, Mac-
Kinnons and MacNeills. Argyll is called 'airdb(h)reitheamh ós Albain'
– the first Earl was appointed Lord High Chancellor of Scotland in
1483; in another poem he is described as 'iarla Gall is Gaoidheal'.
'Gall' here either refers to the Islesmen of *Innsi Gall* 'the Hebrides' or
possibly, in view of Campbell policy, to the Scots of the Lowlands.[29]
    In her song to MacDhomhnaill Màiri as it were returns the Camp-
bell compliment: the Earl of Argyll heads the list. Then follow
MacKenzies, the various branches of Clan Donald, MacLeods, Mac-
Kinnons, Frasers, Grants, Munros; and before the Irish allies are
listed, the Douglases are mentioned, for this MacDonald's mother was
Lady Mary Douglas, daughter of the Earl of Morton.
    Here then we have an epitome of the competing claims of Campbells
and MacDonalds. J. Carmichael Watson says of the allies that Màiri
nighean Alasdair Ruaidh claims for her own clan, 'Some of them would
have done less [. . .] than Mary would have us believe.' But this is
precisely the point. These are propagandist appeals, not a direct reflection
of political and military realities. The convention can, of course, accommodate that also, and there is no essential difference made between
relatives and allies. In many cases a blood kinship could in fact be traced.
    Màiri closes her poem to MacDhomhnaill with a statement of the
claim that might well be taken as a rhetorical topic in its own right: the
claim of the Lords of the Isles, and of Clan Donald, to 'a house and
half of Scotland'. Traditionally this 'house' is Taigh nan Teud in
Perthshire, which is supposed to mark the centre of Scotland.
Although there are some problems of interpretation, it seems to me

likely that the claim involves a sacral centre, possession of which conferred a title to the entire territory; as I mentioned earlier, it is highly significant that the Lords of the Isles should have thus symbolised their territorial rights, focusing on a point outside the Lordship and in the heartland of the ancient Scoto-Pictish kingdom.

The commonplace of Allies shows clearly how historical circumstances impinge upon, and are reflected in, the rhetoric of Gaelic poetry. It also demonstrates the network through which the bards constantly present an ideal unity of the Gaels.

Address to Subject

In bardic tradition the individual exists in a similar network of relationships: family, ancestors, and allies. And in the manner of classical bardic panegyric, some poems contain a complimentary reference to the subject's wife also. The normal place for this is towards the close of the poem: it is a touch of urbanity (comparable with references to non-warlike qualities in the hero, such as an ability to write, or piety) which involves the community more fully in the poetry. But the wife's ancestry is valued and her kindred celebrated:

Fhuair thu gibht bho Shìol Leòid
Nam brataichean sròil . . .

This complex of topics can be summed up under the heading of Address to subject. He is invariably addressed by name, patronymic, or traditional style and title, which may involve the name of his dùthchas, a territorial style. As this is the traditional patrimony of the fine, we may include in the topic the use of place names in that territory. When Màiri nighean Alasdair Ruaidh says of Iain Garbh 'Is nach faicear gu bràth an Ratharsaidh' there is an emphasis, strengthened by the fall of the stress, on the place name: it suddenly leaps into focus and the loss to the territory and the fine is driven home. Some of the epithets are fixed traditional phrases, so that if certain chiefs' names come to mind their territorial styles come to mind also, in the manner of patronymics, e.g. 'Mac Mhic Ailein à Mùideart, Mac Mhic Alasdair Chnòideart, MacLeòid às na Hearadh', and so on.

The patronymics link naturally with illustrious ancestors and the established lines of descent: this is so prominent a feature that it, too, could stand as a rhetorical category on its own: 'Sìol Airt is Chuinn is Chormaic'; 'Lochlannaich threun'; 'Sìol nan Rìghrean o'n Spàinnt'.

Pride in blood is quite explicit. It is not 'blue blood' but *fionfhuil* 'wine-blood', a term which doubtless carries a hint of the aristocratic drink as well. Nobility of blood is very frequently associated with quick temper, pride, sense of honour, courage and hauteur.

The warriors of the clan may be styled collectively, e.g. 'Fir a' Bhràighe' ('men of the Brae of Lochaber'), 'Fir Mhuile'. The chief's style may involve the name of his homestead combined with an epithet, e.g. 'MacGriogair o Ruadhshruth chnò'; or the homestead or territory may appear without the chief's name: 'Cill Ma-Ruibhe fo sgéith a' Chuain'; 'Uibhist bheag riabhach nan cràgheadh'; or the chief place of the clan may be given its emotional charge by the context:

> 'S goirt an naidheachd so chualas
> O'n là chruinnich do shluagh ann an Àros.

All these stylistic devices are obviously involved in each other. We may link them also with names of battles: Latha Allt Éireann; Raon Ruairidh; Inbhir Chéitein. Such names have an evocative power of the same order as Thermopylae or Trafalgar or Ratisbon or Wounded Knee in other ethnic, national or imperial contexts; but in Gaelic this power has been drawn into the central stream of poetry.

The style of address to the subject in eulogistic verse, carrying with it overtones of all these epithets, may be extended to non-Gaels who have been involved in battle on the Gaelic side. Thus John Graham of Claverhouse 'Bonnie Dundee', is addressed as 'A shàr Chléibhears nan each' and known popularly as 'Iain Dubh nan Cath', and a Stewart woman from Strathspey calls Prince Charles Edward 'Prionnsa Tearlach nam baiteal'. In this manner, non-Gaelic heroes are drawn into the native system of naming and celebrating: the process mediates between an alien, hostile world and an intelligible order, endowing their names with potency in its own terms.

Through the interweaving of these topics of Address with the convention of Allies, there is generated in tradition a sense not only of the friendly territory of the kindred to which the bard belongs, but also a sense of a more extended territory which at the least is potentially friendly; or if it is potentially hostile, according to the circumstances of a given time, its hostility is capable of being subdued by a rehearsal of great deeds enacted in alliance. The poetic 'map' which the bards draw with place names is comparable with the 'map' of Gaelic political unity; less dominating, perhaps, less vividly and precisely drawn, but the function is the same.

The native Gael who is instructed in this poetry carries in his imagination not so much a landscape, not a sense of geography alone, nor of history alone, but a formal order of experience in which these are all merged. The native sensibility responds not to landscape but to dùthchas. And just as 'landscape', with its romantic aura, cannot be translated directly into Gaelic, so 'dùthchas' and, indeed, 'dùthaich' cannot be translated into English without robbing the terms of their emotional energy. The complexity involved can be appreciated by reflecting on the range of meaning: *dùthchas* is ancestral or family land; it is also family tradition; and, equally, it is the hereditary qualities of an individual. A name such as 'Dùthaich MhicLeòid', for instance, is but poorly represented by 'The Land of MacLeod' or 'MacLeod's Country'.

Nonetheless, the purpose and style of the bardic tradition which we are looking at now ensures that place names are kept in their proper, functional place: it is in other verse traditions that they are allowed to achieve their full potential.

Social Roles

The next topic that falls to be mentioned is that of Social Roles (which here include arts of war). The subject of a praise-poem has clearly defined obligations and accomplishments which enable him to discharge his duties to his people. He is a warrior, ruthless to his enemies and tenacious in pursuit but mild to his friends and kinsfolk. He is generous in dispensing gifts and liberal in supplying drink to warriors and men of art. He is a hunter of specific animals and birds. He is a horseman and seaman. He is a wise counsellor, he may be a courtier at the royal court; he is, like his ancestors, a Royalist.

All these topics, like the others we have been considering, appear in so many different contexts that certain aspects of them could as easily be taken under the other headings. For instance, the subject's prowess as a horseman may be expressed in epithets applied in addressing him and rehearsing his noble descent, for like other virtues, this too is hereditary.

> *Sliochd nan Rìgh 's nan long siubhlach*
> *Nan ceannbheairt 's nan each crùidheach.*

Possession of fine horses ready for battle is indicated by Niall MacMhuirich, making a contrast between Clanranald's aristocratic war-horses and the plebeian ponies that are only fit for the churl's occupation of agriculture. The aristocratic disdain for manual work appears more than once.

> *Bhith fo bhinn aig na bodaich*
> *Dh'am bu chosnadh cas-chrom*

and in an extreme form in the bardic elegy composed by his mother to Iain Ruadh mac Dhubhghaill, a famous MacAulay hunter of Ùig, Lewis, in the early seventeenth century:

> *Cas a shiubhal nam fuar bheann*
> *Ghabh thu roghainn bha uasal*
> *'S tu gun treobhadh no buailtean air dòigh*[30]

This praiseworthy neglect not only of ploughing but even of cattle-folds leads one to observe that despite the central place that cattle occupied both in the economy and in the aristocratic war-game of *togail chreach* 'cattle-raiding', possession of cattle is not a topic of rhetorical importance in the strictly bardic tradition.

The seamanship of the subject is an ancestral virtue:

> *Sìol nan Colla bha treun*
> *Stiùireadh loingeas fo bhréid*

We may have a double image:

> *Agus marcaich nan stuagh*
> *Ri là frionasach fuar*

But in the poetry of strophic metres, generally speaking there is not the same direct praise of the individual as seaman as there is, for instance, of him as hunter. It is in fact usual to have the subject presented as a warrior in charge of a ship rather than as a seaman himself. So when an t-Aos-dàna MacMhathain addresses the chief of the MacKenzies on the occasion of a voyage it is the skill of his crew that is celebrated.[31] Much the same applies to Iain Lom's songs. This may be because the subjects are of a high social status and the poems reflect the reality of their behaviour: but it must also be due to the conventions of bardic praise: other traditions of verse tend to give the role greater prominence. Convention also seems to circumscribe somewhat the descriptions of the hunter's role. In other metrical forms one finds the kinds of animals and birds named that are fit for aristocratic sport. In the strophic metres one may find

Bu tu sealgair a' gheòidh [. . .]
Bu tu sealgair an fhéidh

but it is essentially as an arms-bearing warrior-hunter that the hero appears. He is accompanied by his hounds, attended by his retinue, and carries the weapons that are equally the weapons of battle. Once again the descriptions are juxtaposed or delineate him as warrior and hunter in the same highly formalised vignette. Even in a poem such as Iain Lom's 'Tùirneal a' Chnatain', which is certainly not a detached or stylised panegyric in motivation, the hunter's role is felt to be relevant to the statement. Or Eachann Bacach, concerned with Maclean's prowess in battle, moves easily into:

Nàile, chunnaic mi aimsir
Is tu ri siubhal na sealga

Hunting is but another aspect of the martial life as that is understood in the Gaelic context. In contrast to these aspects, however, we find sometimes a more sociable role. The subject is noble in nature and trustworthy, even-tempered, meek and gentle, mild as a maiden, and companiable. His ability to write may be celebrated. This is the urbane side of the tradition. It is undoubtedly important in that it extends the social reach of bardic verse and balances the descriptions of ruthlessness towards the enemy. But it remains, taking the tradition as a whole, in a secondary position, and is, I think, to be viewed as an accretion.

The role of the warrior, protector of fine and tuath, great in body, with immense physical strength, is both centre and apex. Through epithets, references to battles, ancestry, physical strength, weapons, loyalty, and so on, and taking these in all their direct and oblique references, and in all possible permutations, the bards produce a glorification of the warrior that permeates these poems of a brief, late manifestation of an heroic age.

He is 'ceannard nan gaisgeach', the leader of a body of picked fighting men. The loyalty of this comitatus is a key topic. It is interesting to find it as late as 1812 in an elegy to a man who was killed, not in battle, but by an accidental shot.[32] The motif of revenge of the leader's death is here also (as are the majority of the topics of bardic poetry). The relationship between ceannard and luchd-taighe, sliochd an taighe, na h-òganaich, is throughout a focus of loyalty; working once more through the convention of Allies, this focus is widened to encompass the ideal loyalty which all the clans bear to one another.

There are, naturally, hundreds of vignettes of the weapon-bearing warrior. He may be clad in mail or wear a breast-plate; the list of weapons includes Spanish blade, lance; speckled shield, embossed targe; bow of yew, gun, dagger, pistols. The items are not of course listed in such inert sequences but presented in contextual images that are themselves charged with the vitality of the rhetorical system and that of the society which it reflects. But even in their barest form these set pieces have a hard lustre that gives the appropriate impression of metallic tableaux. When the *breacan* 'tartan' is mentioned it is clearly the warrior's dress of battle: in the bardic depiction of this loyal, closely organised fighting unit, dress and weapons alike both function as symbols that command society's highest respect and approval.

The whole concept of leadership and loyalty is given an extra dimension by Royalism, from the Montrose Wars to the Forty-Five. The subject is always *rìoghail*, loyal to the true king but also participating in kingly virtues. We might say that from the time of James VII's deposition, Jacobitism is one of the architectonic influences on Gaelic poetry, exercising a real if usually somewhat distant control – an exact reflection of its control upon the order of society.

Household

The subjects of bardic praise are under a constant obligation to show generosity. Leaders are, typically:

> *Luchd a dh'iomairt an òir*
> *'S iad a dhìoladh an t-òl*

Like other commonplaces this appears throughout the poetry, but there is a natural tendency to concentrate upon it in what I shall call the topic of the Household. A set piece describing the chief's household is not, however, obligatory and there is a shading of emphasis in descriptions of the chief's or leader's generosity and hospitality at the table. Some bardic poems pay greater attention to the drinking and music and tàileasg, etc. Others develop, with greater sophistication, the domestic scene and the less warlike aspects of the hero in his hall, 'talla nam pìos' with its music of violins and harps, tàileasg, bagpipes, drinking, wax candles blazing, bardic contests, dispensing of gold, and minstrels gathered from all the Gaelic lands, from Tara to Iona and north to the Chanonry of Ross. Some poems introduce the piety of the subject and reading of the Scriptures in his household.

But in general the centre of the stage is kept for the carousal of the warriors; and there is no doubt that it is the sharply cut scenes of conviviality, with the blaze of light and the gold and silver vessels, that remain in the memory. This is particularly so when the 'short line' which appears in some of the strophic metres is used. The vivid perfection of this art, still undimmed through the passage of centuries, is an index of the rhetorical energy which lies in the bardic poetry and which cannot have failed to make it a most efficient vehicle in spreading its message.

The personal beauty of the subject is a leading topic. As this is a poetry addressed to men we might expect specifically masculine qualities to be praised. In fact, apart from epithets like 'tréine is lùth', the physical attributes are of the kind that could fit either sex. Good figure, chalk-white teeth, blue eyes, golden hair are the stock conventions. The verse is full of epithets such as: 'sùil ghorm'; 'gruaidh mar am fìon': 'gruaidh dhearg mar an caorann'; 'cùl bachlach (nan dual glan)'; 'ciabhfhalt cleachdach (gu làr)'; 'cùl nan clannfhalt teudbhuidhe'; 'snuadh glan'; 'deud chailc'; 'corp glégheal'.

These are all designed to project an image of 'gentlemen that labouris nocht'. The aristocrat may be a ruthless warrior but there is nothing harsh or rugged about his physical appearance. These qualities belong to the peasantry: the subject of the bardic panegyric is a cynosure of fashion: 'sgàthan sambuill na h-uaisle'. It is noteworthy that men praise and describe other men in warm, intimate terms.

Obsequies

Finally there is the topic of Obsequies. What seems an excessive preoccupation with the death of the hero and the imagery of the grave functions as a harsh reminder of the loss to the clan. But it also serves to remind us of the social importance of the rites of death in a society where ceremonial occasions were associated with elemental issues.

This is, superficially at least, a Christian society, and Christian burial was important. But one senses also in Gaelic tradition (and in Gaelic society to the present day) an enduring pagan concern with the body as almost a sentient thing. Failure to recover the body makes the loss even greater, e.g. 'Thu bhith an innis nan ròn is nach faighear thu.' There is a concentration on the act of sealing the coffin. Sometimes the finality of that act is emphasised so that the carpenters' preparation become an isolated and almost sinister image of it.

From one point of view the preoccupation with death expresses the negative aspect of the intensity and vividness of life as the bards present it. But because this is altogether a celebratory tradition death also is due its proper formalities – in poetry as in the society which the poetry reflects – and through such celebrations the solidarity of the group is reaffirmed.

Kennings

I turn now to a slightly different aspect. The heroic virtues are expressed in a variety of kennings for the warrior. He is a tree: 'bile', 'crann', 'craobh' (especially 'abhall farsaing / freumhach', 'darach', and other 'noble' woods); 'craobh chosgair / chomhraig / as airde 'san doire / shìochaint'; 'fiùran', 'gasan', 'fleasgach', 'slat'. He is a battle-post: 'ursann-chatha', 'sonn'. He may have a bird of prey kenning: 'seabhag fhìrinneach / shuairc / uasal', 'an t-seabhag threun', 'seabhag an t-sluaigh'; 'òg rìoghail na h-ealtain\n'. He is often 'leòghann / leòmhann', 'ard leòmhann'; 'leòmhann fireachail / garg clisgeant'.

The kenning most commonly involved is that of the tree or forest; and the image of the wounded sapling or of the tree or forest stripped of its foliage occurs throughout the elegiac poetry. The power of the tree kenning is ultimately derived from the great legendary trees of Gaelic tradition: 'the five great trees' of ancient Ireland, for instance. There is evidence of the same cult in Scotland, the great yew tree in Fortingall being probably the best-known individual tree. The cult is not only in Gaelic, however, but has a world-wide distribution; the local tree symbolises the mythological cosmic tree, and may be associated with a sacral centre (such as I suggested the bards of the Lords of the Isles claimed) at which, according to Gaelic tradition, rulers were inaugurated.

The unprotected people are frequently likened to bees from a plundered hive, a wounded bird separated from the bird-flock, or a bird that has lost its brood, or motherless lambs, or combinations of these figures. A favourite metaphor is the ship caught in a storm. All these images are drawn from experiences that were known intimately: the behaviour of disturbed or stricken creatures, the flourishing or withered tree, the crop lodged by rough weather; winds, floods, tempests.

But the songs that describe a ship under way (for instance, in some of Iain Lom's splendid *iorram* verse) and the topical references to seamanship give the metaphorical descriptions of a ship at the mercy of wind and tide an added resonance. Once again, this is an example of the inter-connectedness of the rhetoric. When Màiri nighean Alasdair Ruaidh describes Iain Garbh's fate, all these dimensions are present.

The idea of 'the ship of State' has a peculiar force, therefore, in Gaelic. Iain Lom's 'Dia 'na fhear-stiùiridh air t' ardraich' in his poem to the newly-crowned Charles II is the same basic image as An t-Aos-dàna MacMhathain's 'Bidh Dia man cuairt dad' sheòl', in a song composed to the Earl of Seaforth on the occasion of an actual voyage. In the panegyric tradition the ship, with its crew and complement of warriors, is in reality a microcosm of society in its martial, and even convivial, aspect. All this gives added depth and complexity to the image when it is used in the summing up of a bardic elegy to enjoin the heir to maintain ancestral customs. A good example is Eachann Bacach's 'A' Chnò Shamhna' composed on the death of Sir Lachlan Maclean of Duart in 1648. It ends, with a slight echo of the Gaelic 'Ship Blessings':

Ge bu lìonmhor ort frasachd
Chum thu dìreach do mhacaomh
Do bhréid rìomhach gun sracadh;
Cha do dhìobair ceann-slaite thu,
On 's e Crìosda b'fhear-beairt dhuit:
Is sin an Tì a leig leat an taod-sgòid.

A mhic, ma ghlacas tu an stiùir so,
Cha bu fhlathas gun dùthchas
Dhuit bhith grathann air t'urnaigh;
Cuir d'a caitheamh an Triùir oirre:
Cuir an t-Athair an tùs oirre,
Biodh am Mac 'na fhear-iùil oirre
An Spiorad naomh ga giùlan gu nòs.

Metres and Themes

What we have seen thus far is essentially a poetry of chief and fine, which I have presented as an intricate panegyric mode involving the whole dominant social order. The period c. 1600–1745 is the high age of the tradition. Within that period our bardic verse is formally restricted to panegyric:[33] there is no religious, moralistic, nature or love poetry composed in strophic metres; although images and sentiments that carry a hint of them all may be used.

Much the same is true of satire (if we make a distinction between *aoir* as satire and *aoir* as invective). The metrical form itself is probably not the most effective vehicle for satire. But in addition satiric humour requires a special sophistication and detachment, sometimes even a lightness of touch which the constraints of the strophic tradition inhibit. It is as if this rhetoric precludes satire much in the same way as the rhetoric of religion precludes blasphemy: both are specifically designed to justify a given order. But serious invective is quite proper to both.

What we do have is a very complex system of transformations in which the linked rhetorical figures occupy a whole range of constantly shifting positions. In the simplest analysis we may say that they function positively and negatively.[34] Any topic can have its obverse while still retaining its panegyric force. In perhaps the most poignant example of this in Gaelic poetry, the topic of the Allies is used 'negatively' by John Roy Stewart in 'O gur mis' th'air mo chràdh',[35] composed after Culloden, where he names those who failed to come to the Prince's aid in his hour of need.

When we leave the high age of the tradition we find the bardic measures put to different uses; as when Ailean Dall, for instance, towards the end of the eighteenth century employs them for love poetry. This may have been something of a deliberate aberration or at least experiment. It is true, nevertheless, that from a relatively early stage there are off-shoots from the main bardic stem (especially in the simplest, three-lined strophic form), an example being 'Mìle mollachd do'n òl', attributed to Domhnall Donn, mac Fhir Bhoth Fhionntain. Although this song is somewhat on the periphery of the 'universe of discourse' that we have been discussing, the topics of bardic tradition do colour the verse. It is a personal, lyrical poem, as is Murchadh Mór's famous 'An Làir Dhonn', in the same metre, a panegyric to the 'brown mare', his ship – an obvious development of topics we have examined. These are seventeenth-century songs.

In the first half of the nineteenth century the three-lined metre was used in that splendid love song 'Duanag a' Chìobair'. In contrast to Ailean Dall's love poetry, this form gives no impression of forcing the content into the wrong mould; and the same judgment applies to the older love song which probably supplied the model:

> 'S mór mo mhulad 's chan àicheam
> Mu'n sgeul ùr tha mi clàistinn
> 'S mi tearnadh stigh bràigh Uisge Spé.[36]

Yet a poem with which both of these are closely connected, and from which they may, indeed, derive their melodies, is equally eloquent, but in the rhetoric of the bardic tradition. This is Iain Lom's 'Glacadh Morair Hunndaidh':

> Mhuire 's muladach tha mi
> Mu gach sgeul tha mi clàistinn
> 'S mi bhith tearnadh le bràigh Uisge Dhé.[37]

Whatever restrictions the intrinsic demands of the strophic metre may impose, it is clearly the extrinsic conventions that operate in such cases. At all events, the existence of flexible forms of this kind helps to explain the processes by which distinct traditions of verse begin to merge into one another.

This process, as I have already indicated, must have been exceedingly involved, with different strands of poetry mutually influencing each other, so that not only did classical panegyric help to form vernacular panegyric, but the converse also must hold good. We have to beware of reducing to a simple linear progression activities that were going on in many dimensions; equally, we must realise that the bard filled, by precept and example, an essential and formative role in the development of the whole rhetorical system.

From what I have shown already about the conventions, commonplaces, or topics (using the terms interchangeably) of bardic panegyric, it will be obvious to anyone who knows the corpus of verse that these commonplaces are reproduced in the same basic form throughout Gaelic poetry. It is the surface manifestations that are different. I propose now to look at some of them, however superficially, beginning with the topics of *Òran*,[38] not in its generic sense of 'song' but as the technical term for a particular metrical class.[39] For our present purposes, it is sufficient simply to assume the existence of such a category, allowing its relevant characteristics to emerge as we proceed.

In Ireland, òran was formally distinguished from the metres of higher caste poets from at least as early as the fourteenth century.[40] One such poet in that century expresses his contempt for the songs of the strolling minstrels: 'the long haired *abhrán*-singers'. In Scotland, however, there is no indication even in our earliest sources that among the vernacular forms òran was in any way socially unacceptable: by the seventeenth century it was already drawn into the panegyric orbit. But its range throughout is much wider than that of the strophic metres: it may at one time have had a particular formal association with love-poetry; the òran tradition as a whole certainly includes a very large proportion of love-songs, extending in time from our pioneer collections to the present day.

Its high age, to some extent comparable with that of bardic verse, is from c.1600 to the end of the eighteenth century. In this period the form shows considerable variation from sixteen lines (at least as printed) to a simple quatrain, sometimes accompanied by a vocable refrain, with occasional examples which do not fall metrically into multiples of four lines, e.g. 'Tàladh Iain Mhùideartaich'. Òran as a whole has a typical symmetry of design; this quality in the ampler verse structures gives a distinctive tone to the panegyric conventions. There may be a movement away from an opening common in bardic elegy, e.g.

> *Rinn mi suidh' aig a' charn*
> *Ghabh mi mulad nach gann*

in the Marbhrann for Rob Roy.[41] Màiri nighean Alasdair Ruaidh opens her 'Luinneag MhicLeòid':

> *Is mi am shuidhe air an tulaich*
> *Fo mhulad 's fo imcheist*

but she immediately introduces a personal reflection before going on to the eulogistic commonplaces. In bardic verse the development is almost always more abrupt, the personal utterance more circumscribed. The more fluid rhythm of òran, and the change of balance from one line to another, either demands, or gives an opportunity for, a more leisurely exposition. In strophic metres one line follows another in a declamatory sequence: we expect (though we do not invariably find) each line to make a self-contained statement. In òran the natural phrase, no doubt following the musical structure, appears to require two lines and may run over into others. It is only a tendency, but it gives the rhetoric of òran its own distinctive quality.

There are several directions in which these rhythms can lead the discourse. They can give a gentle tone, or a tone of resignation to a poem; they may be subtle and sinuous; used with a richness of vowel sounds to produce a grave eloquence; or they may give an impression of firm statement without the peremptoriness of the bardic metres. In other words, òran is capable of a range of expression, of depth and of freshness; when the developed imagery of the bardic tradition is assimilated to this form, a sophisticated art emerges.

The very fact that òran allows greater freedom is perhaps a limitation in some set pieces of description. There is less immediacy and vividness, for instance in evocations of the festive hall in òran metres, where at least in the best bardic songs the physical scene is presented with such wonderful directness. This may be tested by comparing Iain Lom's 'Cumha Mhorair Hunndaidh', in which the topic is presented with a reflective detachment, with the same bard's 'Marbhrann do Shir Seumas MacDhomhnaill', where it is a static image, charged with sensuous delight. But if we take the Clàrsair Dall's so-called 'Òran Mór MhicLeòid',[42] with its amplitude of form and its rotund diction, we can see that same reflective detachment combining with the other qualities to produce a variety of effects in the measured criticisms of a chief who has failed his people. Not least of these is the retrospect of the household: the pace and dignity of the statement give perfect expression to regret for a vanished age. It is one of the great examples of the 'negative' use of a rhetorical topic in Gaelic poetry.

The same poet has a very fine image which combines the board games, so often mentioned in descriptions of the chief's hall, with reminiscences of battle and the council table.

> fir ag cnapraich mu'n chlàr
> is cath air a ghnàth chur leò;
> dà chomhairleach ghearr
> gun labhairt, ge b'ard an glòir,
> 'S a rìgh, bu tìtheach an guin
> do dhaoine gun fhuil, gun fheòil.

The Blind Harper meets and converses with 'Echo' who has deserted MacLeod's hall now that the clamour of feasting has been banished by a niggardly chief. Similarly Lachlan MacKinnon meets and converses with 'Iochd is Gràdh is Fiùghantas' ('Mercy, Generosity and Love') who are also homeless wanderers on the moor under the new dispensation.[43]

These rhetorical topics, which are clearly related, are handled with great skill and with a sophistication all of their own: in one sense they represent a further move away from the topical norms of bardic poetry, but panegyric òran celebrates the same order of society as the bardic panegyric is concerned to uphold. Its convention is to do so from a more sharply individual point of view, exercising a greater amount of individual freedom and expressing more personal emotion.

A third member of the 'Talisker circle' to which these poets belonged was John Maclean of Mull. In a poem to MacLeod of Talisker, composed in the òran metre popularly known through 'Moladh Chabar Féidh', he pays graceful compliments to the family, drawing upon the conventions of bardic panegyric in very general terms, e.g. praise of generosity, drink, compliments to the lady of the house, a prediction that the little son will be an outstanding man. Although these are by now familiar topics, this is a special development. The entire tone of the poem is 'unbardic' and unmilitary: in fact, a charming expression of thanks in verse to a man's host and hostess. It begins with a rather high-flown and slightly exotic expression:

> *Air sgéith na maidne 's luaithe*
> *Gu tuath thoir mo bheannachd bhuam*
> *A dh'ionnsaigh 'n fhir nach fuath*
> *Gu Uaisle, Fear Thalasgair*

and celebrates, as the central theme, the atmosphere of domestic elegance and goodwill.

Somewhat in contrast to these, there is one rhetorical topic which finds its ultimate and logical development in òran. This is the convention of listing allies. In 1715 Iain Dubh mac Iain mhic Ailein, a MacDonald, makes the topic the whole framework of his 'Òran nam Fineachan Gàidhealach'. The poem opens with a reference to 'the prophecy', which I shall discuss later; celebrates the impetuous mettle of the men of Alba as they go to serve the Crown; then predicts that the great men of the Lowlands will rally eagerly to support the cause: the English (Sasannaich) will be vanquished and the French will pursue them closely. This takes up two stanzas; of the remaining seventeen, sixteen are devoted to a roll-call of Gaelic clans, with appropriate panegyric markers and epithets; the last asserts that if each individual upholds his fellow warriors, and all are of one undeviating mind, victory over the 'Dubhghall' is assured. This is certainly a statement on behalf of the Gaelic nation and represents, to my mind, the explicit form of that ideal synthesis which I said we owed to the bards. Here we have the conceptual unity of the Gaels of Scotland. But is it also an expression of total Scottish unity? I think myself that Iain Dubh meant it to be. *Fir Albann* – mentioned in the opening lines – are given pride of place because they are just that, 'the men of Scotland', Lowland and Highland. The second stanza begins:

> *Théid maithe na Galldachd*
> *Glé shanntach 'sa' chùis*

Iain Dubh places the 'nobles of the Lowlands' there by way of compliment, giving the French allies the closing phrase of the stanza. But having done this the poet in effect then forgets about them. In short, the Scottish dimension is there – seen from the Gaelic point of view. I do not believe, however, that W. J. Watson can be right in glossing *Dubhghaill* here as 'Lowlanders'.[44] If he is, even the complimentary reference to *maithe na Galldachd* has to be taken as no more than an empty formula.

In 1745 Alasdair mac Mhaighstir Alasdair, too, composed an 'Òran nam Fineachan', consciously modelling himself on Iain Dubh's work, and, like him, including the Campbells in his eulogistic list but with an even more elaborate address:

> *An Diùc Earraghaidhealach mar cheann orr'*
> *Gu móralach, mear, prionnsail*[45]

Alasdair gives them the second highest place, immediately after Clan Donald; and he does this with full awareness of what the political and military strategy of the House of Argyll had been and was likely to be, at least in the near future. It is true that in 1715 the Glenorchy, Breadalbane and Glenlyon Campbells declared for the Stuarts and in 1745 more than one Campbell supported the Jacobite cause. This might be taken as a sufficient basis for making realistic overtures to Clan Campbell, but when Alasdair mac Mhaighstir Alasdair deliberately names the Duke of Argyll in this way, he is operating on an entirely different stage.

Love Poetry and Female Poets

There are various stylistic mediations between such highly conscious political verse and the use of òran for more intimate and informal purposes. A good example of a recurring personal note, expressed through original imagery, is to be found in Mairghread Ni Lachainn's lament for Alan Maclean of Brolas.[46] Like any other òran in the panegyric mode, it presents a paradigm of the topics, but here and there a flash of personal emotion injects fresh energy into this poetess's never less than elegant craftsmanship. (As a matter of fact, this is characteristic of Ni Lachainn's poetry, no matter which mode of composition she uses.) The opening statement of this poem has an implicit tenderness:

Chunnaic mise thu Ailein
'S tu gu h-aimideach gòrach
Mun do ghlac thu 'n gnìomh fearail
Na mun d'rinneadh dhiot Còirneal

In a most vivid image she celebrates the warrior company to which Ailein belonged:

Mac samhailt nan daoine
Chan fhaodar am faighinn
Mach o ghathan na gréine
Ann an speuraibh an adhair

And she ends with an equally vivid and highly personal metaphor:

Chan eil fiacaill am dheudach
Nach do leum as mo chlaigeann
A' sìor iargain nan daoine
Ris an glaoidhte na gaisgich.

There is probably as much intensity of feeling here as we are likely to meet in most of the love poems in òran mode. Naturally there are examples of passionate poetry, but as a whole the tradition is romantic and celebratory. There is a certain detached idealisation of the loved one, as well as tenderness, amatory fervour, jealousy, nostalgia, and the rest of the predictable emotions.

What we have in Gaelic is really a compound tradition in which qualities of a general European love poetry, including the so-called 'courtly love' tradition, have been grafted on to an older stock, although that stock was itself perhaps not pure native brier. At all events, what is most significant from our point of view is that native and borrowed fashions both (and we cannot always distinguish them) can be connected with the Gaelic panegyric code. It is of course true that any love poetry contains a panegyric element and lists of accomplishments and especially physical attributes are *de rigeur*. But even if some similarities are 'natural' and therefore ambiguous – for example, between descriptions of a man's handsomeness in bardic panegyrics and those of love songs to men, and indeed to women also (where there is a demonstrable overlap of imagery) – the very recurrence of certain topics cannot have failed to make nodal intersections of a psychological as well as a literary kind. Even the use of a single word. To take an instance: in the following verse the 'greenwood' is a reflection of a common European setting; the lover's protecting plaid is native; yet in both images native and foreign elements may be inextricably fused (cf. 'O wert thou i' the cauld blast'). But with the word 'breacan' there is an immediate arousal in memory of the matrix in which the bards praise the warrior and his dress.

> ’S truagh nach robh mi ’s mo leannan
> Anns a’ ghleannan an uaigneas
> No ’sa’ bhadan bheag choille
> Far an goireadh na cuachan
> Thu sìnt’ ann am bhreacan
> Dlùth paisgt’ ann am shuanaich[47]

Lovers are 'dìleas'; so are the dìlsean of the comitatus: 'dìlseachd' and 'foill' are positive and negative poles. In bardic panegyric the topic of 'luchd mìoruin' may appear as the negative aspect of loyalty to the subject or as a contrast to the ideal solidarity of the fine(achan). 'Luchd mìorun / foille'; 'luchd nam breug' are the lovers' ill-wishers or his (jealous) enemies: it is one of the commonplaces of courtly love, outside Gaelic, also. The camaraderie of warriors and the intimacy of lovers are both 'caidreabh'. A girl may be referred to not only as 'gealach', 'reul', 'canach', etc. but in the tree kennings used of the warrior: 'bile', 'craobh', 'geug', 'slat de'n abhall', with variations and extensions.

In bardic elegy the physician is 'helpless', a topic which may be used exultantly over the slaughter of enemies. Love is a sickness, an unnatural disease, a great, high fever in the presence of which the physician is similarly helpless. Love also deals a wound that will not heal; it bruises the kidneys as the arrow or the sword 'pierces to the kidneys' in bardic verse. This imagery of stricken warrior and stricken lover lies behind William Ross's:

Tha mise ri osnaich 'na déidh
Mar ghaisgeach an déis a leòn

We may note in passing that a large proportion of romantic òrain are compositions inspired by lack of success in the suit or by the absence of the beloved, betrothed or married to another. One might perhaps draw a faint rhetorical parallel between this and the eulogistic tradition in which a praise poem is so often an elegy or is inspired by the absence of the subject from his territory.

We are, however, on surer ground with songs of female authorship, in which the lover is presented in essentially the terms of praise that the eulogists employ, but modified to fit the romantic circumstances. 'Fìonfhuil' or 'fìorfhuil' is important. While the lover is not usually praised overtly as a warrior, this is often implied. He is a horseman, hunter, seaman; he can drink copiously and pays freely for others; he is great, well-shaped with tressed hair. His physical beauty is dwelt on in terms that are sometimes identical with those used for women e.g. 'gormshuilean meallach'; 'caoin mhala'; 'mar chanach an t-sléibhe'. Both men and women walk with a light step 'nach lùbadh am feòirnein'. A girl's aristocratic descent also is celebrated; sometimes her warrior ancestry:

'S tu air do bhuain à freumh nam buadh
do'n treunfhuil uasail steudail

and in the older songs she may play tàileasg with her lover. Women's clothes, often in the context of 'Dol dh'an chlachan Di-Domhnaich', are not so much described as simply named, and translated into symbols of femininity: except for a greater vividness and intensity, this is comparable with the symbol of the breacan.

Throughout this species of love-song the poet, even if infatuated, obviously works to rule. One lover at least states this with an engagingly blunt efficiency: 'Tòisichidh mi aig do chasan'.[48] That the same rhetoric may be extended beyond love-poetry may be seen in a song addressed to Marian MacMarcus, a minister's wife in South Kintyre.[49] It is a complimentary address which draws with great freedom on the catalogue of feminine graces and accomplishments and adds:

Is cinneadh do mhàthar uile
Curaidhean do Chlann Domhnaill
Làidir, duineil, creuchdach, fuilteach
Is furachail mar leòghain

It should be clear from this brief review that in Gaelic poetry there is a distinctive 'panegyric of love' which by no means obscures the universal characteristics but rather orders them in a framework of society and art. This framework is in part identical with the panegyric framework we have analysed in general eulogy, both bardic and òran. In part it is an analogous system, particularly in love songs to women, where we have accomplishments and social roles complementary to those of the male ideal. The ramifications and interactions are virtually endless, and can be traced into the finest capillaries of the whole rhetorical system.

There are, however, social gradations: a girl may be 'banarach na buaile'; a man's social roles may be those of athlete, swimmer, card-player, fiddler, dancer, but may also be those of an expert worker on the harvest field. Towards one end of the social scale, the aristocratic toper is praised; towards the other end, the man who shuns the tavern. But this is related to chronology as well: abstinence is not celebrated in the older songs.

Dàn

We noticed how the structure of òran allows an ampler exposition than the declamatory sequences of the strophic metres. The structural peculiarities of 'dàn' offer similar though not at all identical opportunities. In the context of this study, *dàn* of course is the formal equivalent in demotic terms, vernacular in language and freed from the constraints of the strict rules of composition, of Classical Gaelic poetry. It may not be immediately recognisable as such in written form, for the distinctive isosyllabism of classical dàn is a contingent quality in the vernacular. What it does posses is an irregularity of rhythm (when measured by the criteria of 'ordinary' accentual verse), which has the effect of creating a slow and deliberate pace even when the irregularity is minimal. The characteristic structural unit is the quatrain. But another form, of considerable importance in Scots Gaelic verse, also appears: an eight-lined stanza, the origin of which is obscure. This latter form gives the impression of being brisker. The themes of dàn are on the whole restricted to fairly easily defined categories: primarily encomia, love, religion, and nature. There is a reflection here of the preoccupations of the classical Gaelic poets, acting in both public and private roles.

There are two interesting dàin to different Earls of Argyll, both in a
metre which alternates long and short lines. The first is 'An Duanag
Ullamh', composed in the sixteenth century by Maclean's bard.[50]
Beyond that we know nothing about the author. But on internal
evidence he was a considerable artist, working apparently in the
security of an established tradition. It is tempting, indeed, to think
that he might have belonged to the family of Ó Muirgheasáin who
were professional makers of Classical Gaelic poetry under Maclean
patronage; and that here we have an example of a file composing in
the vernacular some two centuries before Niall MacMhuirich did the
same. At all events, the author must have been in close contact with
the classical tradition, conceivably as a saorbhard of relatively high
standing.

The poem opens with an address to the subject, but not the direct
address of the bardic tradition in strophic metres: this is third person
address; emotionally more formal and mannered. Thereafter a series
of kennings is introduced:

> *Seabhag as uaisle théid 'sna neulta*
> *Crann air chrannaibh [. . .]*
> *Abhall uasal farsaing frèimheach [. . .]*
> *Crann as ùire dh'fhàs troimh thalamh [. . .]*
> *Dias abaich chruithneachd 's i lomlàn*

These are qualified by supporting phrases such as 'Do'n cù'idh
moladh': ''S as mò maitheas': formal, dignified expressions which
with the third person 'address' immediately set the tone of the poem.
In the third stanza there is introduced the couplet:

> *Mac rath do chum Dia gu h-ullamh*
> *Do'n chléir ealamh*

It reminds us at once of the involvement of the House of Argyll in the
politics of the Scottish state-established religion: this is not a direct
parallel with the convention of the piety of a chief's household.

The next sequence of verses, however, consists of the 'ship' topic:
MacCailein has a loingeas laden with warriors. The set piece describing the raising of sails and securing of stays is reminiscent of folktale
runs and foreshadows a similar passage in Alasdair mac Mhaighstir
Alasdair's 'Birlinn'; but although it cannot but convey the vitality of
all realisations of this topic:

An steud ro-luath, sruth ga sàiltibh
'S muir ga bualadh

it is, with due propriety, subdued to the over-all measured dignity of the poem.

Then comes the list of Allies, not a detailed list but summing up 'Uaisle Innse Gall an coimhlion', and extending the formula not only to cover Alba but even to include 'dewy France'. The men of Alba and of Tìr Chonaill loyally and submissively yield tribute. This is the national Gaelic unity from the Campbell point of view; or, more precisely, as Maclean's bard conceived that to be. The poem ends with a pious invocation: may the Holy Trinity protect the King of Loch Fyne.

This poem is clearly, then, exactly of the same thematic and topical order as we have seen in other verse traditions. What gives it a different nature as a work of art is fundamentally its formal detachment. This is one potential function of the measure and here we have an artist who can realise it with a fine sense of propriety. As we have observed, the distancing device of the address gives us our bearings immediately. Concordant with that is the absence of the warriors' (and lovers') emotion of caidreabh. To point the contrast we have only to think of such a phrase as we get in the MacGregor poem on the Rout of Glen Fruin: 'maidhm [. . .] aig mo ghaoil 's aig mo dhìslibh'. A statement of that kind in the context of 'An Duanag Ullamh' would sound vulgarly intimate.

The second poem is that composed by an t-Aos-dàna MacShithich on the occasion of the execution of the ninth Earl of Argyll in 1685.[51] We first notice the kennings: 'Garg an leòmhann'; 'an crann dligheach treun talmhaidh'; the topical allusions: 'taigheadas greadhnach'; 'fine [. . .] nan steud meara'; 'brugh fo thùirse'; 'bhàsaich luchd ciùil'; 'ghluais (a' ghaoth) an fhiùghaidh'. Again, the panegyric framework is demonstrable; and as with 'An Duanag Ullamh' the form confers dignity and gravity. Apart from these stylistic considerations, however, the resemblances are to be qualified. The present elegy is a discourse to an audience: it has a strong religious emotion, which sometimes intensifies to fervour, in some places bringing to mind an English oratorical style of radical, non-conformist politics. Given the evangelical Presbyterian background, the comparison is not perhaps too far-fetched.

Roghainn nan Albannach uile,
De'n àrd fhine;

A dhaoine, nam biodh spéis do dhuine,
Is beud a mhilleadh. [. . .]

Dhaoine ge do fhuair sibh àite
Os cionn Cùirte
Is olc a chuir sibh gliocas Alba
Gu sùrd millte

A veiled minatory *obiter dictum*

Theagamh gun tig là nach fhasa
Dhuibh d'a dhìoladh

is followed by:

Fhuair an fhuil uasal a ceusadh.
Mar fhuair Ìosa:
Ge nach coimeas sud ri chéile
Feudar innseadh.

The poet can clearly become intimate in tone, but it is the intimacy of the preacher. The blend of political and religious homily achieves an arresting eloquence.

Nonetheless, this elegy rallies the Campbells as strongly as any bardic song, and in the same manner:

A dhream Dhuibhneach
Dhream bheadarrach bhuadhach bhàdhach
Mheadhrach mhùirneach

using also the evocative power of dùthchas and place name:

'S nach tadhail an t-Iarla Duibhneach
'S an Dùn Adhrach.

But these profoundly impressive panegyric markers are set in an intellectual and historical grid of 'Alba' very different from that of the 'Taigh is leth Alba' of Clan Donald. Although the state has perpetrated an outrage against MacCailein and against Sliochd Dhiarmaid Mhic Ua Duibhne, and thereby brought peril upon all, the security of the Campbell involvement in the real affairs of Scotland is expressed all the more eloquently because of it. The entire poem is filled with examples of the obverse use of rhetorical devices in order to create a sense of peril, promote the values of this society, and impress upon the audience the duty of rallying to its defence. (In the following lines, where the central concern is ecclesiastical, it is just possible that *na borbaibh* – the barbarous heathen who live in spiritual darkness – may also carry a hint of 'Wild Scots', as John of Fordun and later writers characterised the Gaels in contrast to the 'domesticated' Scots of the low-lying regions.)

> Có chumas còir ris an anfhann
> Is e 'na chruadhaig,
> No chumas casg air gach anghnàth
> Tha teachd nuadh oirnn?
>
> Có chumas còir ris an Eaglais?
> Dh'fhàs i dorcha;
> No chumas suas ar luchd teasgaisg
> Ris na borbaibh?
>
> Có chumas an creideamh cathardha
> Suas gu treòrach,
> Is nach d'fhuair Gille-easbuig cead éisdeachd
> An taic còrach.

It is impossible to conceive of an expository declaration being made with a similar inevitability in any other form but dàn, and perhaps only in a form of dàn in which metrical freedom is conspicuously bounded. In these balancing contrapuntal statements, the short line acts on verbosity like a sudden jerk on a horse's reins.

As a complete contrast in spirit we may cite briefly another poem in the same metre, the anonymous dàn to Alasdair mac Colla.[52] It is a short praise-poem but within its compass the predictable topical points are made. The poet draws on the lore of the Fiann, making comparisons between the hero and Fionn, Goll and Oscar. Alasdair's allies are listed briefly. This is triumphant, warrior panegyric which shows that there are other potentialities of dàn that a good poet can exploit.

> Do mhac-samhail mar ealtainn o dhubhbheinn
> Dol trìd choille dharaich,
> No mar fhrois mhóir a' reubadh tuinne
> Air druim cuain mara.

In the elegiac use of dàn there are poems rather like Dunbar's 'Lament for the Makaris': Donnchadh MacRaoiridh's plaint, left alone after the deaths of great men; MacLeod of Raasay's lament for the 'generous hands' that are gone; or Alasdair mac Mhurchaidh's poem with a somewhat similar theme. The latter loved ships, and women, and wine; now he is left without these and without any of his high-born friends: 'Iomadh duine uasal an Ros [. . .] Is mise 'nan déidh gun phrìs.'

In the quieter tones of elegiac dàn there is less involvement with the fine, and the whole network of relationships in a 'clan and country' political setting, than we find in the other metrical traditions we have surveyed. The poets give the impression that they are less spokesmen for the fine, and less concerned to ensure the continuation of the traditional order through a rehearsal of its virtues; their elegies disclose rather the strength of the personal relationship, though this is set, quite explicitly, in the context of the same order of society. It is partly a matter of epoch; but certainly in the seventeenth century, ascriptions lead us to believe that dàn is definitely linked with high social status, and the authors may have felt that the overt political propaganda of the bardic (and eulogistic òran) traditions was slightly beneath their dignity. It is more befitting to adopt a tone of *sic transit gloria mundi*, even though this is the world that constituted their support. In that sense, dàn discloses something of the luxury of personal poetry by a leisured class. If any conventions drawn from the practice of Classical Gaelic poetry operate here, they are likely to be those that governed the writing of classical poetry in private rather than public roles.

We can see the dignity and profundity of feeling that dàn is capable of very clearly in An Ciaran Mabach's elegy to Macdonald of Sleat.[53] It has intense emotion and a poignancy of personal loss. Nevertheless, the conventional topics constitute the whole frame of the poem. They include one which appears in romantic òran as the lover's death-wish:

> *Chan iarrainn tuilleadh de'n t-saoghal*
> *Laighinn le daolaibh an fhòid*
> *Ann an leabaidh chumhaing chaoil*
> *Sìnte ri taobh do chuid bhord.*

The storm has overtaken him at sea: 'an t-anrath cuain', 'gàir thonn nan sìon'. The stricken ship; the household without music, poets, drink, tàileasg; no longer do young men rise early to hunt in the mountains: without these commonplaces the poem would have no fabric; yet they are not clichés here. A living pulse of emotion gives them a singularly different energy from that which they discharge in other traditions. There is, incidentally, no mention of Allies.

The religious poems are conventional enough in their theology and piety, which does not make them less beautiful as poetry; in some instances at least they tend to be expressions of resignation after a life lived among the flesh-pots. Sometimes the figure of the warrior-Christ (known elsewhere, e.g. in Anglo-Saxon poetry) appears, as in Alasdair mac Mhurchaidh's 'Tà cogadh oirnne do ghnàth'.[54] Christ has been sorely wounded in battle. But:

> *Beiridh mo Chaiptean-sa buaidh*
> *Ceannard sluaigh le'm pillear tòir*

and the weapons of Faith, Prayer and Love are given to us to wield. In such instances conventional piety becomes inextricably part of the world that panegyric celebrates.

A very different poem, which is instinct with religious feeling, is the moving elegy by Murdoch MacKenzie to his grandson.[55] It also is full of touches that renew our contact with the images and symbols that map out the world of this society.

> *Gliocas seanar bh'aig mo ghaol [. . .]*
> *Seanchas filidh, subhailc saoi*
> *geamnaidheachd is bàidh ri bochd.*
> *Thuit m' fhiùran, duilleach fo bhlàth*
> *gun fuireach ri fàs a mhios [. . .]*
> *Chraobh a b'àillte bha mo lios*
> *Ùr fo bhlàth gun dol air ghais*
> *Air a dhearcadh 'n clàr fo lic.*

MacShithich's elegy to the ninth Earl of Argyll ends with a statement of faith:

> *Ri uair feuma tha Dia neartmhor*
> *Ceann gach cùise,*
> *Dhèanadh de bhur naimhdibh treuna*
> *Cairdean ciùine.*

In the bardic tradition enemies are nominally converted into friends through the topic of Allies. Opinions may be divided as to the superior efficacy of diplomacy over faith: both, however, serve the same function in strengthening collective morale.

We have noted the evocative use of place names in other traditions. A poem which concentrates on the virtues of a territorial dùthchas is addressed to Tighearna na Leirge in Kintyre who proposed to sell his dùthchas / dùthaich.[56] In it place names – Allt Pàraig in the south and Allt na Sionnach in the north – mark the bounds of An Learg: then the poet adds: 'Is duine tréigte thug dha fuath.' A critical address which combines directness and censure in a degree unknown in other traditions, particularly in that of the strophic metres:

> *Is e am mìorath a dhall do shùil*
> *Dol a reic do dhùthaich air òr*

is followed by verses that list the virtues of the land: smooth plains, heavy crops, abundance of cattle, singing birds, the roar of the waves on its beaches. This is in fact a species of Nature panegyric. Looked at in an evolutionary perspective it is a pre-Romantic[57] mode of description, concerned with the fertility of a territory, but adding details that go beyond that. Its ancestry is shown if we compare it with similar poems in a modified form of Classical Gaelic, e.g. Deirdre's praise of 'Gleann na Suan' or the poem in praise of Arran, to take two that have a Scottish connection.

Another poem on Kintyre,[58] one long adjectival tour de force, is entirely devoted to the mode and incorporates most if not all of the features that a Nature panegyric can celebrate: climate, sea, hills, glens, flocks and herds, abundance of milk and its products, trees, berries, herbs, crops, various animals and birds, birdsong, pure water, trout and salmon, and hunting deer with hounds. The list of animals and birds includes those considered to be an aristocratic hunter's quarry, e.g. deer, seal, otter, swan, goose, duck, moorfowl. Then harbours and ships are mentioned, with their tall masts, cords, rigging, cross-trees, stays, anchors, cables, etc. It closes with the crowning glory of that region: its nobility and splendid courts, 'Clann Domhnaill na féile is an t-suaircis'. The Nature panegyric is thus rounded off with a straightforward reference to the topic of the fine.

There are two poems that develop the topic of hunting in very different but equally remarkable fashion. In 'Cumha Choire an Easa'[59] the Blind Piper remembers with sadness that the corry used to be the scene of great hunting expeditions. Like the Harper's reminiscence of the vanished glory of his patron's hall this poem among other things is designed to draw attention to the plight of a bard without a patron. 'Cumha Choire an Easa' is a complex work (the second part is a fairly typical piece of nature panegyric) which, very interestingly, employs the dialogue device, here between the poet and the Corry, in a manner which reminds us of the poems by Lachlan

MacKinnon and the Blind Harper. The three poets were, in fact. members of what the Rev. William Matheson has aptly called the 'Talisker Circle'.[60] Place names are used very evocatively in 'Cumha Choire an Easa', but it is another poem of the dàn tradition that allows them to develop into an heroic roll-call, the great 'Òran na Comhachaig'.[61]

Chì mi Coire Ratha uam
Chì mi a' Chruach is a' Bheinn Bhreac
Chì mi Srath Oisein nam Fiann
Chì mi a' ghrian air Meall nan Leac

Chì mi Beinn Nibheis gu h-ard
Agus an Carn Dearg r'a bun
Is coire beag eile r'a taobh
Chìte is monadh faoin is muir.

In spite of what I said earlier about the native sensibility to dùthchas, this is practically an evocation of a 'landscape'. Nonetheless it is a territory of straths and mountains that are drenched with memories of the warrior society in its hunting aspect. Here, too, caidreabh is used: 'An caidreabh fhiadh agus earb'. This is another microcosm of society; and the poet (neatly, for our purposes) contrasts the hunt with the ship, which we have already defined as a social microcosm.

Is aoibhinn an obair an t-sealg
Aoibhinn a meanma is a beachd
Gur binne a h-aighear 's a fonn
Na long is i dol fo beairt.

But, once again, positive and negative aspects arouse and set in motion their own intermingling trains of memory.

All the poems hitherto cited in this section are in quatrains. There is also an eight-lined stanza form of dàn which our bards have used for elegy, for celebrations of battles (e.g. Duncan Ban Macintyre's songs on the Battle of Falkirk and Corporal Alexander MacKinnon's 'Blàr na h-Òlaind' and 'Blàr na h-Éiphit'), for satire, and for religious subjects.

It first appears in Sìleas na Ceapaich's lament for Alexander of Glengarry, a poem which has the distinction of containing the longest list of kennings and related images of praise in Scottish Gaelic verse –

in itself a token of the extent to which this dàn form, from its first appearance, has been drawn into the central stream of encomiastic poetry.

> *Bu tu 'n lasair dhearg gan losgadh*
> *Bu tu sgoltadh iad gu'n sàiltibh*
> *Bu tu curaidh cur a' chatha*
> *Bu tu 'n laoch gun athadh làimhe*
> *Bu tu 'm bradan anns an fhìoruisg*
> *Fìrean air an eunlaith 's airde*
> *Bu tu 'n leòmhann thar gach beathach*
> *Bu tu damh leathann na cràice.*
>
> *Bu tu 'n loch nach fhaoite thaomadh*
> *Bu tu tobar faoilidh na slàinte*
> *Bu tu Beinn Nibheis thar gach aonach*
> *Bu tu chreag nach fhaoite thearnadh*
> *Bu tu clach uachdair a' chaisteil*
> *Bu tu leac leathann na sràide*
> *Bu tu leug lòghmhar nam buadhan*
> *Bu tu clach uasal an fhàinne*
>
> *Bu tu 'n t-iubhar thar gach coillidh*
> *Bu tu 'n darach daingean làidir*
> *Bu tu 'n cuileann 's tu 'n draigheann*
> *Bu tu 'n t-abhall molach blàthmhor*
> *Cha robh do dhàimh ris a' chritheann*
> *Na do dhligheadh ris an fhearna*
> *Cha robh bheag ionnad de'n leamhan*
> *Bu tu leannan nam ban àlainn.*

With such a description we have come back full circle to the bardic matrix from which panegyric grows; only the elaborateness of the kennings, developed as set pieces of decorative as well as functional imagery, shows how far we have moved from the constraints of the bardic utterance in strophic metres.

Choral Song

My last category is that of choral song. I mean by this essentially what we now know as 'waulking songs' but taken in the broadest terms as a structural class with its own conventions. The older generic name was *luinneag*: rather like 'òran' it has now lost practically all its technical significance.

There is, however, more than one strain in Gaelic poetry to which the term 'choral' might be applied, provided 'chorus' is properly defined. One of these is represented by 'Pìobaireachd Dhomhnaill Duibh', associated with the first battle of Inverlochy, fought on 23rd June 1429 between James I and the Lord of the Isles. It is thus one of the oldest dateable songs – if not indeed *the* oldest – in vernacular Gaelic. Apart from that interest, and we have to allow for accretions in the course of oral transmission, it is worth citing here because it contains on the one hand a defiant panegyric element while on the other it seems to express that sense of defeat and dispossession which the historical experience of the Gael in Scotland justifies. And this of course is seen here from the viewpoint of Clan Donald. As sung, the first line of the stanza is repeated twice. The refrain runs:

Pìobaireachd Dhomhnaill Duibh, pìobaireachd Dhomhnaill
Tha pìob agus bratach air faich Inbhir Lòchaidh

But there is also a verse:

Chaidh an-diugh, chaidh an-diugh, chaidh an-diugh oirnne
Chaidh an-diugh is chaidh an-dé is chaidh a h-uile là oirnne.

What we have been looking at up to now are verse traditions in which men and women have participated; but the world that their poetry projects is, with certain reservations, as in òran, a man's world. Although there are some compositions of male authorship in the òran-luaidh tradition, these choral songs are essentially the women's contribution to Gaelic literature, and in this poetry we view through their eyes the order of society which we have already seen reflected from somewhat different points of view in the other verse traditions. Yet so pervasive is the panegyric code that we can without any difficulty trace the same rhetorical topics throughout this tradition as well. Generally speaking the songs are anonymous and there are very few attributions to authors of any social status.

In earlier centuries, in the prehistory of these songs (which is longer than for other traditions because the main written sources are twentieth century in date) women of all classes may have participated freely in composing them and there is some slight internal evidence for that; but references to herding cattle, the sheiling life, reaping, etc., give the impression that the settings at any rate are plebeian. In addition, we have songs of complaint by girls of the *tuath* 'the common people' made pregnant or jilted by high-born men. It is possible, too, that the songs of male authorship may have originated in the lower grades of Gaelic society. However that may be, what is important from our point of view is the diffusion of the panegyric code.

There is a strong amatory strain, erotic rather than 'romantic', in the women's songs which may have provided a native stock of erotic poetry on to which those elements we discussed in romantic òran were grafted. There may also be some obscure connection between the 'cepóc' of Old Gaelic which appears to have been some sort of greeting sung by women to a victorious warrior and the erotic element of luinneag. Furthermore, since luinneag is so distinctively a Scottish rather than a Scoto-Irish form, it may be significant that 'cepóc' survives in Sutherland Gaelic 'ceapag' but not in Irish; and also that the 'cepóc' was once held to be a Scottish type of song. 'Tàladh Dhomhnaill Ghuirm'[62] – there are a few such tàlaidhean – may or may not be part of this tradition of greeting a warrior; it is certainly a splendid, vivid panegyric:

> Neart na gile   neart na gréine
> Bhith eadar Domhnall   Gorm 's a léine

Equally vivid is its treatment of the ship topic:

> Long mo rìgh-sa   long nan Eilean [. . .]
> Tha stiùir òir oirr'   trì chroinn sheilich
> Gu bheil tobar fìona   shìos 'na deireadh
> Is tobar fìoruisg   'sa' cheann eile

It introduces what we may term a special development in luinneag of the topic of the Household:

> Ge bè àite   an tàmh thu an Alba
> Bidh sud mar ghnàs ann   ceòl is seanchas
> Pìob is clàrsach   àbhachd 's dannsa

and:

> Ge bè caladh   tàimh no àite
> Gum bi mire   cluiche 's gàire
> Bualadh bhròg   is leòis air dearnaibh
> Bidh siud is iomairt   air an tàileasg
> Air na cairtean   breaca bàna
> Is air na dìsnean   geala chnàmha

This tàladh is attributed to Domhnall Gorm's foster-mother. Similarly the song to Donald of Eriskay composed just after the battle of Càirinis in 1601 (a rare example of a dateable luinneag) is attributed to Donald's foster-mother.[63] This is certainly a panegyric to a victorious warrior. It begins with the address to the subject:

A mhic Iain mhic Sheumais
Tha do sgeul air m'aire [. . .]
'S cha do ghabh thu 'm bristeadh
Làmh ligeadh na fala.

There follows a series of conceits of a kind found in Classical Gaelic dàn.

Bho'n là thug thu 'n cuan ort
Bha gruaim air na beannaibh
Bha snigh' air na speuran
'S bha na reultan galach
Bha'n raineach a' ruadhadh
'S bha 'n luachair gun bharrach
Mu mhac Iain mhic Sheumais
Duine treubhach smearail

It closes with a statement emphasising nobility:

'S cairdeach a Rìgh Leódhuis
Mo leòghann glan uasal [. . .]
'S cairdeach tha mo leanabh
Shìol Ailein mhic Ruairi.

The patronymic address, sometimes with a territorial style, is typical here as elsewhere in Gaelic poetry. Or it may be 'Òganaich òig'; 'A fhleasgaich a' ghunna'. The style is frequently intimate and affectionate: 'Ailein Duinn a chiall 's a thasgaidh'; 'M'eudail mór Mac Mhic Ailein'.

Allies as such are rarely mentioned. In these choral songs the stress is on the kin and blood-relationship; the subject may be a lover or a child, often a child born out of wedlock. If the father is of noble blood the mother may boast of his descent and connections.

Chan ann le balach mo throm
Ach leis a' lasgaire dheas dhonn

Toiseach bainne tighinn am chìochan
O'n òg as glan sìoladh fala

'S car thu a dh'Iarla Ìle
Bheir a' chìs às na batail
'S car thu Chloinn Domhnaill
Nan ròiseol 's nam bratach
'S car thu MhacDhubhghaill
O thùr nan clach snaighte
Gura cairdeach mo leanabh / leannan
Dha na falannan uasal
Do MhacLeòid anns na Hearadh
'S do Mhac Alasdair Ruaidh thu [. . .]

Car thu a Dhomhnall Gorm Sléiteach
Làmh a reubadh nan cuantan

In the negative aspect we find:

Tha dhìth orm cairdean
Mo chinneadh mór rìoghail
Nan sìneadh 's na blàraibh.

The focus on the personal relationship rather than on any political implications (in the widest sense) is characteristic of all the topics in this tradition. The figure of the warrior, his bearing and appearance are still important:

Ort a thig na h-airm gu deiseil
Sgiath bhreac nan dual air do leathtaobh
Claidheamh chinn òir ann ad dheaslaimh

But his role as an actual fighter is more often than not merely implied:

Mhic an fhir bu mhath 'sa' chruadal
Thilleadh dhachaidh crodh na tuatha

He is usually lover as well and is presented as hunter, horseman and seaman in a clarity of passion. But there are some songs in which the warrior is celebrated as such; predictably Alasdair mac Colla, who is in a sense the Achilleus of Gaelic poetry, figures in one of the best known of them:

Alasdair mhic Colla ghasda
Às do làimh-sa dh'earbainn tapadh

The song ends with almost the identical words that Iain Lom uses in one of his addresses to him:

> *Alasdair mhic Colla ghasda*
> *Làimh dheas a sgoltadh nan caisteal*

The luinneag, with vocables, says:

> *Alasdair 'ic ò hò*
> *Cholla ghasda hò hò*
> *Làimh sgoltadh na hò hò*
> *'N tùr 's nan caisteal chall éile*

The lover is usually addressed or spoken of with frank intensity, or with a lyrical delicateness which extends to the setting.

> *Coisich a rùin, lùb nan geallamh*
> *'S minig a laigh mi fo t'earradh*
> *Ma laigh cha b'ann aig a' bhaile*
> *Mullach nam beann fad o'n t-sealladh [. . .]*

> *Ri solus nan reul is soills' na gealaich*
> *Sìoban nam beann sìor dhol farainn [. . .]*
> *A lorg an fhéidh a nì a' langan*
> *'S minig a laigh mi fo t'earradh*

> *Alasdair òig, mhic 'ac Neacail*
> *B'fhearr liom fhìn gum beirinn mac dhut*
> *Cóigear no sianar no seachdnar [. . .]*
> *Bheirinn cìoch is glùn an asgaidh*
> *Thogainn suas air barraibh bas iad*
> *Air mo ghualainn fhìn gu faict' iad*
> *'S rachainn leotha a Leódhus dhachaidh*
> *Gu baile bòidheach a' chlachain*
> *Do thaigh ùr an urlair fharsainn*
> *Dh'òlte fion aig bord a' bhaistidh*
> *Dh'òlte fion dearg is fion datht' ann*

This is altogether a different mode of address from what we have seen in romantic òran. The last example and the following show a characteristic movement to a topic that emphasises the lover's aristocratic qualities: he drinks wine; he dances on a floor of wood not on the bare earth of a humble dwelling.

> *Tha mi torrach dumhail trom*
> *Leis an lasgaire dheas dhonn*
> *Nach danns air an urlar lom*

Gun an lobhta làir fo bhonn
Truagh nach fhaicinn fhìn do long
Air a luchdachadh gu trom
Le òr dearg, le airgead pronn
Bu liom fhìn an luchd 's an long.

Through such capillaries of the rhetorical system our attention is drawn back to the central topics. We have seen repeatedly how the panegyric commonplaces are introduced and re-introduced in other verse traditions. In choral song this process is carried to such an extreme that the entire corpus appears to be a kaleidoscope of images, forming new patterns – which are variant, or different, songs – with every movement.

It is unnecessary to quote from the many descriptions of the aristocratic lover as hunter of wild goose, seal, red deer and roe, otter, moorfowl and white swan. But it should be noted that mere mention of a man in this role invests him with 'aristocracy'. It is not so much a matter of class as of caste behaviour. There are also extended descriptions of the seaman. The choral tradition, however, casts the subject in the part of an active seaman rather than that of a leader of a warrior crew.

Bha mo leannan air a' stiùir [. . .]
Às do làimh gun earbainn m'anam
Dol timcheall rubha ri gaillinn
Fhad 's a mhaireadh bith 'na darach
No buill chaola ri crainn gheala
No giuthas os cionn na mara

Formalised, economical descriptions of ships are the rule:

Chì mi am bàta seach a' rubha
Is i 'na siubhal fo làn éideadh

As always in Gaelic verse these are full of energy. There may be a positive and explicit joy:

Is ait liom am bàta 'na gabhail
A' toirt a cinn dh'an t-seann chuan domhain

Descriptions of personal beauty are of the same order as in romantic *òran*, but considerably less elaborate; this tradition does not often use strings of descriptive adjectives: it is the personal emotion which is important: phrases such as 'Se mo ghràdh do chùl ceutach' are much more common than 'Gruag leadanach theudach dhuilleach'.

The lover's literacy is sometimes referred to, as elsewhere; place names mark out territory; there are passages which celebrate the fertility of a territory: we have here, in fact, the same basic code. But there is one development of the topic of Obsequies which is worth noting. In songs that lament death by drowning we find an image such as:

> 'S duilich liom do chùl clannach
> Bhith 'san fheamain ga luadh
> 'S duilich liom do gheal dheudan
> Bhith ga reubadh 'sa' chuan.

Or there is the arresting image of the bodies at the wake:

> Chuala mi gun deach sibh fairis
> 'S gum bu chluasag dhuibh an fheamain
> Gum b'e na ròin ur luchd-faire
> Gum b'e na staimh ur coinnlean geala
> Is ur ceòl fidhle gaoir na mara

Màiri nighean Alasdair Ruaidh would no doubt have known such images when she laments that Iain Garbh is 'an innis nan ròn'. Or when she laments the death of the Laird of Applecross and says:

> Chaidh do bhuidheann an òrdugh
> Cha b'ann mu aighear do phòsaidh
> Le nighean Iarla Chlann Domhnaill [. . .]
> Is ann chaidh do thasgadh 'san t-sròl fo d'léine

she may have been aware of what seems to the modern reader or listener the profounder emotion of this, for instance:

> Chì mi luingeas air Caol Ìle
> Tighinn a dh'iarraidh Cairistìona
> Chan ann gu bainis a dhèanamh
> Ach a cur 'san talamh ìseal
> Fo leacan troma gu dìleann

But the currents run in both directions. It is the intensity of utterance, and the abrupt changes in the emotional focussing, that makes the choral songs so different, even when the topics can be said to be identical. They do, however, have another dimension also: a passionate jealousy and hostility:

'S truagh, a Rìgh! nach fhaicinn ise,
A taobh leòinte 's a glùn briste,
'S gun aon léigh fo'n ghréin ach mise!
Chuirinn creuchd am beul gach niosgaid
Air mo làimh gun dearbhainn misneach!
Bhristinn cnàimh 's gun tàirninn silteach,
Chuirinn ùir air bruaich do lice.
Gus an càirinn thu 'san islig
'S gus an dùininn thu 'sa' chiste.

The images of that fierce poetry are drawn from battle and burial.
The 'léigh' is the physician who is powerless when the great man's
hour of death comes or when a hapless lover is in love's fever: his
role is given a strange, sinister meaning here, as is the warrior's
'misneach'.

Finally, there is the topic of Household. The generosity and magnificence of the household are seen as if through less sophisticated eyes
than those of the bards who celebrate their warrior-patron's generosity with drink and gold. But the aristocrat is still the man 'A bheir air
an togsaid ligeadh' and this may be in:

Taigh mór farsuinn, urlar sguabte
Teine mór air bheagan luatha
Ruithleadh ubhla sìos is suas air [. . .]
Seòmbraichean am biodh daoin'-uaisle
'G òl à cupannan 's à cuachan
Nìonagan glana ri fuaigheal
Cur an t-sìoda dhuinn 'na dhualaibh

There is one particular realisation of the topic which brings out the
vividness and joyousness of the art of these songs. During the
festivities of 'the mild spring evening' the innocent eye sees the old
renew their youth:

Dhomhsa b'aithne beus do thalla
'S an fheasgar chiùin fhiathail earraich –
Muc ga ròsladh, bó ga feannadh,
Lòmhnaichean òir air coin sheanga;
Fiamh an duin' òig air an t-seannduin'.

Modern Gaelic Poetry

The quotations that illustrate the argument of the foregoing sections are drawn from the poetry of the past. Obviously there are certain areas where this is inevitable, beginning with the direct poem of praise by a professional bard to a patron. But one has only to reflect for a moment on the repertoire of song composed by modern 'traditional' poets – songs, for instance, that celebrate or satirise people or events; describe egregious animals, a township bull or a dead whale washed ashore; praise the poet's homeland; and so on – to realise that even contemporary poetry employs a system of rhetoric which involves panegyric topics in both their positive and negative aspects. It is not possible of course to demonstrate here what I believe are the historical continuities, I can only indicate certain links.

To begin with the role of the warrior, in terms of military tradition there was a transference of loyalty from the context of the fine and the Gaelic nation to the British Army. The Disarming Act of 1746, which presumably recognised the status of the breacan as a warrior's dress, had a profound effect on morale. Only in the Independent Companies, the precursors of the Highland Regiments, was the dress allowed. The anonymous song 'Soraidh leis a' Bhreacan Ùr' shows one of the effects:

> *Soraidh leis a' bhreacan ùr*
> *O 's ann dha thug mi mo rùn*
> *B'ait liom e an cùl nan glùn*
> *Ann am pleatadh dlùth mun cuairt*
>
> *Chuir mi bhriogais ghlas fo m'cheann*
> *An àite 'n éilidh bhig a bh'ann*
> *Gos bhith coltach ris a' Ghall*
> *Tha an taobh thall do dh'Uisge Chluaidh*

The young man laments that no girl will look at him: he remembers the associations of the kilt with hunting; but he knows how he can regain dress and morale.

> *Nuair a théid mi fhìn dh'an arm*
> *Gheibh mi éileadh 's sporan garbh*
> *Boineid bhiorach mholach ghorm*
> *Slat do ribein stoirm m'am chluais*

The scores of songs that celebrate 'Gillean an Éilidh' down to the Second World War canalise the emotions developed in the poetry we have analysed.

The sense of dùthchas, in its military aspects, is also drawn upon in these songs:

> *Seinneam cliù na dh'fhàg Port-rìgh* [. . .]
> *Seinneam cliù na dh'fhalbh à Sléit*

Their dress is 'Éideadh sunndach nan gaisgeach'.

Bards still sing the praise of their native parish or island, celebrating in strings of adjectives the fertility of the soil and the abundance of crops and the heroes who have been reared there. There are songs that single out and develop elements in the topic of hunting: praise of the red deer and its free life is notable. The panegyric art of 'Moladh Beinn Dobhrain', as I implied above, is certainly one of the great culminations of the tradition. At one level the poem gives an impression of innocence of vision; at another level great sophistication as it assembles, redeploys, and recreates, in the framework given by Alasdair mac Mhaighstir Alasdair's panegyric of love, 'Moladh Móraig'. These topics that we can now see belong to the very essence of our poetry.

The topics of sailing and seamanship are still evident in Gaelic song. Over and over again we have noted the importance of the warrior-lover as seaman and the existence of the ship as the microcosm of society. The ship survives as a remarkable figure to the present day in romantic òran. It may have heroic overtones: 'long ard nan trì chrannaibh', but it may also be introduced in an invitation to elopement. A ship under sail is 'fo bhréid' – like a woman. Love-songs composed by sailors, for instance at the wheel, during the night-watch, continue though the sailing ships have gone. A ship herself may be the 'girl' of the love-song, e.g. 'Dhèanainn sùgradh ris an nighinn duibh' or 'Mo rùn-sa mhaighdeann', to name two well known examples.

We have moladh and diomoladh of the bagpipes in the past; similarly whisky is praised and dispraised, sometimes in dialogue form: 'Caraid agus Nàmhaid an Uisge-Bheatha'. Nowadays, so far as drink is concerned, only dispraise survives. In Gaelic the verse dialogue is a form of fundamental importance. The verse debate, in flytings, for instance, is often a vehicle for the panegyric code. However, since such genres are widely distributed throughout other literary cultures I need not explore them further at the moment.

It is arguable that even if all these devices and systems of imagery can be shown to form a network of rhetoric which persists to the present day, the reason is that we are dealing with a society which was enclosed in itself, cut off from the influence of the greater world, and therefore, inevitably, one that produced an in-bred literature. To some extent this must be so. It may also be true that the categories of praise and dispraise can be applied to poetry generally and that there is consequently a danger of reading too much into the Gaelic evidence, elevating a common situation to special status. But I also believe that unless we see these rhetorical codes (of which panegyric is only one, though in my view the dominant one) in the setting of Gaelic history, we get a very limited picture.

We discussed already the two compositions in which the topic of Allies becomes the framework of the entire poem. The 1715 'Òran nam Fineachan Gàidhealach' opens:

> 'S i so an aimsir an dearbhar
> An tairgeanachd dhuinn

The 'prophecy' can only refer to the prophecy of Thomas the Rhymer, cited by a number of poets from the seventeenth century onwards, and still current in oral tradition, that one day the Gaels of Scotland will come into their own again. This formulation of the messianic hope of Gaelic nationalism, here firmly identified with Jacobitism, must have been already well-known before the Montrose wars gave it a new dynamic – Iain Lom refers to it casually as an established tradition. Although the Lords of the Isles themselves never advanced a claim to the whole of Scotland so far as I am aware, such a concept – a *de jure* right, which, as we have seen, Burt mentions – must have existed in the background. We find it hinted at in a Classical Gaelic poem to Alasdair mac Colla:

> Cíos is cána ar urleith Alban
> Aimsir oile
> Biaidh sin ag an droing mar dhlighe
> Nó an rionn riomhe.[64]

This is the voice of Clan Donald, and in 1745 one of the poetesses of Keppoch says:

> Nuair théid gach cinne ri chéile
> Eadar Sléite 's a' Cheapach
> Eadar Uibhist is Mùideart

> 'S Mac Iain Stiubhart na h-Apuinn
> Bidh a' Ghàidhealtachd uile
> Gu treun fuileach 'sa' bhaiteal
> 'S ged nach tigeadh na Guimhnich
> 'S beag ar suim do na phac ud.[65]

There is, as I suggested earlier, a continuity in Gaelic history. Because the Lordship of the Isles is a reaffirmation within narrower territorial limits of the Gaelic Kingdom of Scotland (or, if that is ambiguous, of the Kingdom of Alba) we have to give the Clan Donald view its due place. So far as the study of vernacular panegyric is concerned, the patronage of the Lordship and the diffusion of its cultural resonances can hardly be over-stressed. I find it difficult to believe, for instance, that the peculiar cast of Rob Donn's poetry is unconnected with the peripheral situation, so far as the Lordship of the Isles and Clan Donald were concerned, of Dùthaich MhicAoidh.

Equally, there is a noticeable absence of true bardic vernacular panegyric in Campbell poetry. There is, of course, as we have seen, Classical Gaelic panegyric; and it is interesting to find what may be an alternative formulation of the Gaelic messianic hope in one of these classical poems:

> Ceannas Ghaoidheal 'na chéim cleachtuidh
> Ag aoinfhear d'fhéin Breatuin bhíos[66]

This may derive ultimately from the prophecies attributed to Merlin;[67] if that is so we have here another link with the 'British history'. But without the voice of the vernacular bard the idea could not develop as it did under the patronage of Clan Donald. One result of this is that even in genuine oral tradition (let alone popular Scottish antiquarianism) it is the MacDonald view that has prevailed and it still moulds our historical conceptions.

At the same time it is true that Gaelic society in its entirety has been for centuries under pressure, indeed fighting for survival. In this process, the serf class, which survived in Lewis until the late sixteenth century, lost its exemption from conscription for warfare. Economic stratification, we know, remained; but the new weapon-bearing class would necessarily participate in 'heroic' values and loyalties previously reserved to the aristocracy and their immediate followers. Gaelic poetry reflects both the stratification and the shared values. Bardachd begins in direct praise of patron; develops by a kind of historical selection to express the solidarity of a nation; and finally extends its rhetorical control far enough for it to become the generic term for 'poetry'. Naturally this extension is uneven and in the present study I have simply avoided these areas in which the code has left faint traces or none at all.

Conclusions

Gaelic panegyric is not merely the direct celebration of great men in life and death, although it is of course that. It is also a system which reflects the entire Gaelic experience in Scotland and the siege mentality which that experience created as the Gaelic nation strove to maintain an identity. The historical realities of this precarious situation ensured that an artist was honoured in proportion as he celebrated those qualities and those values that were necessary for the survival of the nation. That is the reason why the warrior's role is the apex of the panegyric code. We can see how the system works with centripetal compulsion, ever bringing us back to this central symbol: the warrior who is protector and rewarder. All else is made ancillary to this, each role taking its own part in the hierarchy. Religion, too, can be subordinated to the main principle, serving to support the household of the protector.

It may be true to say that the sets of imagery are ornamental, but they are much more than 'decorative' or even 'literary'. They find their origin and evocative power in the network of relationships in a society in which status and function and role, male and female, were clearly defined and yet interacted upon each other to a high degree. It could be at times a society in which relationships might be savage, but there is no evidence that they were cold or aloof. This makes it all the more important to investigate those aspects of life in which the gentler emotions are predictable, and to relate the treatment of them to other modes of literary expression. The aesthetic ideology which the panegyric code imposes does allow love poetry, sometimes of great intensity, to emerge; but that is because the elemental passions cannot be stifled. Love is subordinated to the social demands to a certain degree, but its divisive, heretical tendencies are observable: in some instances it has elements of the Greek *ate* – the tragic madness. But they are not the norms of behaviour; these, ideally, are established in a society that does not tolerate cultural anarchism, and the Verbal Icons of the poetry (to borrow Wimsatt's famous terminology) can be used in the equivalent of a diplomatic note, from a high social level in the seventeenth and eighteenth centuries to that of the township bardachd at the present day.

To the extent that poets used and reinforced these verbal icons, their break-up, in the crumbling of the traditional rhetoric of Gaelic poetry, involved a crumbling of Gaelic identity also. In this connection, it is to be observed that, apart from the transference of loyalty to the British Army and Empire which we commented on, the only system which introduced a competing psychology, and therefore offered a new identity, was the intense, evangelical Presbyterianism which took root in most of the Gaelic area only after 1745 – in fact, in the later eighteenth century and throughout the nineteenth – that is to say, when the older social system had been conspicuously broken. Nevertheless, this was too recluse and other-worldly a psychology to provide in literature an adequate strategy for a wide range of human experience. It affected but failed to displace the older intellectual order: indeed, although the panegyric code can be traced even in some of the hymns of the Evangelical Revival, the two systems remained on the whole in mutual hostility.

Gaelic identity, however, has not been eroded; on the contrary, in the poetry of the twentieth-century renaissance it has taken on new dimensions. Even at that level, but more obviously at the 'traditional' level, it has found expression in successive transformations of the code we have been studying. While we all allow that 'traditional' Gaelic verse (a parochial and dismissive label for the poetry of centuries) imposed in the end a fundamentalist tyranny, this is itself a token of its enduring power. In its high age, or in poetry of genius in any age, it is charged with dynamic virtue.

The rhetorical hierarchy of Gaelic poetry is not primarily concerned to explore the eccentricities of the individual imagination – these exist on the margins – nor with exaggeration of the individual perceptions. The utterance is controlled by social norms, and deviations are more likely to be regarded as such than to be valued as an original point of view. But far from weakening poetic expression this confers strength, clarity and classical normality on it. It often concentrates the art so that the mundane takes on an archetypal intensity.

Furthermore, Gaelic rhetoric does not obscure the contribution of the individual genius. Our concern in this study has not been with the individual but with the terms within which he (or so often, in Scots Gaelic poetry, she) has worked. It is perfectly possible to read or listen to the poems as individual works or as the voices of individual authors; but to do so is like reading Spenser's *Faerie Queen* and neglecting the 'Numbers of Time' or reading the *Roman de la Rose* and ignoring the allegory.

Sùil air Bardachd na Gàidhlig

A réir nan seann sgeulachdan, is ann an Éirinn a tha tinnsgeadal nan Gàidheal an Alba ri lorg. Is ann an Éirinn, mar an ceunta, a tha freumh ar litreachais. Tha sinne a' meas gu bheil a cheart uiread de chòir againn, ann an seagh, air an roinn Éireannach dh'ar litreachas is a tha aig na h-Éireannaich air prós is air bardachd Alba. Is e aon sluagh a tha annainn.

> Gaoidhil Éireann ocus Alban
> aimsir oile
> ionann a bfrémha is a bhfine:
> sgéla ar sgoile.[1]

Is ann ri linn Alasdair mhic Colla Chiotaich a rinneadh an ceathramh ach tha iarmad dhen dùthchas a tha e a' cur an céill beò 'nar seanchas chon an latha an-diugh.

Chan ionann sin is a ràdh, ga tà, nach do chuir aomadh nan linn iomadh sgaradh eadar sinne agus na h-Éireannaich. A chionn is gu robh an eachdraidh riamh air feadh an t-saoghail a' cur a dreach fhéin air an ealain, agus a chionns gu bheil eachdraidh Alba ann an caochladh dhòighean aocoltach ri eachdraidh Éirinn, tha e nàdurra gum biodh an uiread sin co-dhiubh de dhealachadh ri fhaotainn eadar an dà dhùthaich. Ach tha adhbhar eile ann cuideachd: thuinich is lìonsgair na Gàidheil am measg nan Cruithneach. Chan fhaod a bhith nach robh buaidh air choireigin aig a' chothlamadh a tha sin. Aig a' cheart àm chan eil fianais againn air na cùisean sin ann, ach tha fianais againn – ged nach biodh ann ach an dàn dìreach fhéin – air a' cheangal a mhair eadar Alba is Éirinn gu ruige an seachdamh ceud deug. Aig an inbhe sin is chon na h-ìre sin, bha an saoghal Gàidhealach slàn. Faodaidh sinne an Alba, ma tha, a bhith tagradh gu bheil sinn co-ionann ri Éirinn ann an aois is ann an urram a thaobh cùrsa ar cànain is ar litreachais. Agus an co-bhuinn sin faodaidh sinn agairt cuideachd gu bheil càileachd a bhoineas do Alba a-mhàin a' gabhail ri ar cuid ealain.

Is ann am bardachd gu h-àraid, ged nach ann idir gu h-iomlan, a nochd na daoine againn cumhachd an aigne. Tha sin, saoilidh mi, fìor co-dhiubh mu litreachas Alba. Gu dé is gnè, ma tha, dhan bhardachd sin?

Mar a thubhairt mi an ceartair, tha an dàn dìreach ri fhaighinn an Alba mar a tha an Éirinn, ged nach eil e ach gann an Alba an taca ri Éirinn, ma leughar an suidheachadh a réir na shàbhail dheth o dhìmeas agus o ainneart. Ach is dòcha nach robh e riamh anabharrach pailt. Cha b'e Albannaich o thùs a bh'ann a dhà dhe na teaghlaichean a b'ainmeala ach Éireannaich: Clann Uí Mhuirgheasáin agus Clann Mhic Mhuirich a shìolaich o Chloinn Uí Dhálaigh; agus a réir coltais faodar Clann Mhic Eoghain a chur ris an àireamh.

Tha riaghailtean fhéin aig an dàn dìreach agus a shealladh fhéin, mar gum b'eadh, air an t-saoghal; rud a tha fìor am modh a' mholaidh gu sonraichte san dà dhùthaich. Thall is a bhos tha dàin anns a faicear na feartan dligheach sin air an toirt gu airde feabhais; gheabhar cuideachd dàin a tha dol a-mach air frithrathad agus cuid dhiubh annasach gu leòr dhuinne an-diugh. Tha dà dhàn aig a' Bhard Mac an t-Saoir an Leabhar Deadhain a' Lios Mhóir, a bhoineas dhan cheud phàirt dhen t-siathamh ceud deug: 'Créad í an long-sa ar Loch Inse' agus 'Tánaig long ar Loch Raithneach'. Té aca le 'a lán do bhantracht na mbéad san sál gan salm gan sáilchreád'; agus an té eile 'long na ndrochbhan.'

Tha an dealbh a tha am bard a' tarraing cho soilleir sgaiteach is nach mór nach mionnaichinn mu na dhà aca – agus ga b'ar bith gu dé am modh-litreachais anns a bheil am bard ag obair – gu bheil an ìomhaigh air a stéidheachadh air rudeigin a chunnaic e le a dhà shùil fhéin. Seadh, mar gu faca e ciomball de bharrach no seann duilleach no murrag chrìon air coireigin eile làn bhiastagan a' sèoladh air na tuinn.

> Buird do sgiathaibh daológ ndubh
> ó a corraibh síos 'na sliosaibh;
> tairngí gan fuamadh 'gá fuaim
> ar an bhuachain aird ionnfhuair.[2]

agus:

> Reanga láir do luachair chrín
> totaí coiseóga cláirmhín
> ráimh do sgealbaibh raithnigh ruaidh
> ré gráin na fairge fionnfhuair.

Crann siúil do chuilcnibh calma
ré muir dúrdha danarra [. . .]

Cáblaí do chaithibh eórna
ar srothaibh 'gá sírsheóladh;
seól sreabhainn ris an chairbh dhuibh,
deabhaidh searbh ag na srothaibh.[3]

Ma tha comh-cheangal aig na longan sin, le an luchd dhroch
mhnathan, ris an *Narrenschiff* aig Sebastian Brand, a thàinig a-mach
an 1494, a chuireadh an Laideann an 1497 agus am Beurla an 1509,
nach luath fhéin a ràinig an duan Gearmailteach cho fada an iar ri
Gàidhealtachd Alba? Ach chan eil an comh-cheangal cinnteach ann.

Mhair an dàn dìreach an Alba chon an ochdamh ceud deug. Fada
roimhe sin bha dàin is duain is òrain air an cumadh an Gàidhlig an t-
sluaigh. Chan e nach robh buaidh aig Gàidhlig fhoghlaimte an dàin
dìrich orra, is gheabhar a chomhtharra sin thall is a bhos. Bha
sgoilearan de ghinealach a thàinig romhainn dhen bheachd gun dàinig
ath-leasachadh bunaideach mu thoiseach an t-siathamh ceud deug air
bardachd na Gàidhlig. Dhen dithis a fhuair urram an inntreachdainn
sin, Màiri nighean Alasdair Ruaidh agus Iain Lom, is ann do Mhàiri a
thugadh am prìomh àite. A réir Iain MhicCoinnich a chuir a-mach *Sàr
Obair nam Bàrd Gàelach* ann an 1841, cha robh Màiri an eisimeil aon
duine riamh, an darna cuid an cruth no an susbaint a bardachd. Ach
chaidh a shealltainn on uairsin gu robh obair Iain Luim pailt na bu
tràithe is a thuilleadh air sin gur h-ann o na baird fhoghlaimte a
thainig samhlaidhean a' mholaidh agus theagamh modhannan ealain
eile cuideachd g'a h-ionnsaigh.

Anns an aiste 'The Oral Tradition in Scottish Gaelic Poetry' rinn mi
fhìn oidheirp air cruthan nan òran aice a cheangal ri fìor sheann
bhardachd Éireannaich. Is e Domhnall Mac an Tòisich a' cheud
sgoilear a chuir an céill am beachd gu robh ceangal air choireigineach
ri lorg eadar an t-seann bhardachd ris an cainte 'Rosg' agus a'
mheadarachd a nochd mar gu robh i ùr nodha san t-seachdamh ceud
deug. Is fheudar dhomh aideachadh nach robh mise ach a' leantainn
Mhic an Tòisich: is esan a chuir an gnothach air shùilean dhuinn air
tùs.[4]

An-diugh is ann a tha sinn buailteach, is dòcha, air cus a dhèanamh
dhen t-sinnsireachd agus air dìmeas a dhèanamh air an annas. Co-
dhiubh, is e mo bheachd-sa nise gun dàinig da-rìribh blàth is adhartas
air bardachd, gu h-àraid sa chruth sin air an dug MacBhatair an t-

ainm *strophic*,[5] ri linn Màiri nighean Alasdair Ruaidh agus Iain Luim. Bha an cruth ann am bith gun teagamh man do rugadh iadsan, ach dh'fhàg iad le chéile a' bhardachd deàrrsach toirteil seach mar a fhuair iad i, gu ìre is gu faodar am facal 'athleasachadh' a chleachdadh gun mhearachd. Their cuid nach eil cinnt nach robh baird eile a bha cheart cho cumhachdach riutha beò rompa is nach eil ann ach nach do mhair an cuid obrach-san air bilean an t-sluaigh, air neo nach deach a cur air pàipear nuair a bha seinneadairean is luchd seanchais beò aig a robh eòlas air a leithid.

Nise faodaidh sin a bhith ceart. Thòisicheadh air bardachd neo-sgrìobhte a chruinneachadh san t-seachdamh ceud deug (gun a bhith a' cunntas Leabhar an Deadhain) ach is ann eadar meadhon an ath cheud agus toiseach an naoidheamh ceud deug a rinneadh na comh-chruinneachaidhean móra. Rinn na h-ughdairean uile cnuasach is rannsachadh air feadh na Gàidhealtachd, fad is farsaing, agus cair-dean is luchd-cuideachaidh ag obair an co-bhuinn riutha. Saoilidh mise, nam b'e is gu robh baird cho toirteil ann, gum biodh fear seach fear dhe na daoine sin air amas air an cuid òran. Ach cha d'amais. Is urrainn dhuinn an-diugh fhéin òran no dhà le Iain Lom no le Màiri nighean Alasdair Ruaidh a thrusadh, is iad air an gabhail gu dùth-chasach, corr math is trì ceud bliadhna an déidh an ama. A réir sin bu chòr gu robh cuimhne san ochdamh ceud deug air òrain a rinneadh corr is trì ceud bliadhna roimhe sin a-rithist. Agus, mar a thubhairt mi, cha robh cion rannsachaidh ann. Chanainnsa nach robh rian gu seachnadh bardachd dhen inbhe air a bheil mi a-mach air trusaichean cho ealanta is cho mionaideach ri mac Mhaighstir Alasdair no ri Raghnall Dubh a mhac, a chuir an comh-chruinneachadh a-mach an 1776 – a' cheud leabhar a nochd dha sheòrsa. Is bha gu leòr eile ann: MacGillAdhagain is MacNeacail, dithis mhinisteirean; an Dotair Eachann MacGillEathain; Pàdraig Mac an Tuairneir a bha 'na shaighdear is 'na cheannaiche-siubhail; agus an dithis bhràithrean Domhnall agus Alasdair Stiùbhart.

Ged a tha grunnan math againn de dhàin is de òrain a tha nas sine na linn Iain Luim agus Màiri, chan eil na th'ann am meadarachd *strophic* dhiubh ach simplidh an taca ris na h-òrain aca-san.

Is e an t-òran is sine a th'againn air a faodar bliadhna a chur – seadh, dhe na h-òrain a tha air an gabhail fhathast – 'Pìobaireachd Dhomhnaill Duibh'. Cha rachainn an urras nach eil dàin is òrain eile ann a tha nas sine, agus cuid dhiubh sin cuideachd ri an cluinntinn fhathast air an seinn, ach mu chuspair an fhir seo tha de fhiosrachadh againn ann an sgrìobhadh na nì ceangal dearbhte eadar tachartas na h-eachdraidh agus briathran a' bhaird.

> Pìobaireachd Dhomhnaill Duibh
> Pìobaireachd Dhomhnaill
> Tha pìob agus bratach air faich Inbhir Lòchaidh.[6]

Sa bhliadhna 1429, air an treas latha deug dhen Òg-mhios, choinnich feachd Rìgh Seumas a h-Aon ri arm Gàidhealach mu Inbhir Lòchaidh an Loch Abar. Bha Clann an Tòisich agus Clann Mhuirich, is iad de Chloinn Chatain le chéile, san fheachd Ghàidhealach. Ach nuair a nochd arm an rìgh, theich iad chon an taobh-sin.

> Theich is gun do theich
> Is gun do theich Clann an Tòisich
> Dh'fhalbh Clann Mhuirich
> Ach dh'fhuirich Clann Domhnaill.

Chuala Bhatar Scott an t-òran agus is ann às a rinn e 'Pibroch o' Donal Dhu'.

Is e port-mór a th'ann am 'Pìobaireachd Dhomhnaill Duibh': is e sin, òran a bhoineas a thaobh an fhuinn do phuirt-mhóra na pìoba – dhan Cheòl-mhór, a' phìobaireachd *par excellence*. Tha grunn dhe na h-òrain sin a dh' fhaodar a cheangal ris a' cheòl-mhór: 'A Cholla mo rùin', 'Maol Donn', 'A Mhnathan a' Ghlinne-sa' agus mar sin. Ach air a shon sin tha móran dhiubh aig nach eil dàimh sam bith ri puirt-phìoba is aithne dhuinn an-diugh: co-dhiubh is e nach robh riamh dàimh ann air neo nach do mhair iad am measg nam pìobairean is adhbhar dha. Agus ceist eile: an ann o cheòl na pìoba a thàinig na h-òrain no an deach an ceòl-mór a stéidheachadh air puirt a bhathar a' seinn am measg an t-sluaigh? Is dòcha nach fuasglar a' cheist sin a feasda; ma dh'fhuasglar is e sgoilearan ciùil a nì an gnothach air a' chùis.

Tha ceathramh ann am fear dhe na puirt-mhóra:

> Dhìrich mi a' bheinn mhór gun anail
> Dhìrich agus thearn
> Chuir mi falt mo chinn ri talamh
> Basaibh mo dhà làmh.

Is e ceathramh fuadain a tha ann: tha e ri fhaighinn an òran eile.

Tha dìreadh is tearnadh na beinne, 'dìreadh na beinne is ga tearnadh', riaghailteach cumanta ann an òrain mhulaid agus caoidh

– is chan e mhàin òrain anns am bidhear a' caoidh nam marbh. Ged a gheabhar an dearbh mhodh-labhairt ann an òrain le cuspairean eile, saoil an e faileas de dheasghnath caoidh a th' againn an seo? Chan eil teagamh nach e deasghnath mulaid a th' ann an sgaoileadh na gruaige: boinidh e do chaitheamh nam mnathan-tuiridh. Tha an ceathramh a chaidh aithris cheana: 'dhìrich mi [. . .] chuir mi falt mo chinn', ann an òran a rinn bana-Chaimbeulach an déidh dha cuideachd an duine aice, Griogair MacGriogair, a dhicheannadh aig Caisteal a' Bhealaich an Siorrachd Pheairt sa bliadhna 1570.[7] Agus tha deasghnath eile air ainmneachadh san aon òran:

> Chuir iad a cheann air ploc daraich,
> Is dhòirt iad fhuil mu làr:
> Nam biodh agam-sa an sin cupan
> Dh' òlainn dith mo shàth.

Tha iomradh air òl na fala ann an lethdusan òran no man tuairmse sin, fear aca san ochdamh ceud deug. Is e sin an t-òran a rinn Anna Chaimbeul, nighean Fir Scalpaigh na Hearadh, ris an fhonn 'Ailein Duinn ó hi shiubhlainn leat'. Bha Ailean Moireasdan air an t-slighe a' seòladh à Leódhus a' tighinn a choimhead oirre-se, is iad suas ri chéile, nuair a chaidh a bhàthadh. Seo mar a thubhairt i:

> Dh'òlainn deoch ga b'oil lem chairdean
> Cha b'ann de fhìon dearg na Spàinne
> Ach fuil do chuim an déidh do bhàthadh.[8]

Man ìre sin – an t-ochdamh ceud deug – is dòcha nach robh ann ach agalladh bròin a bha an imis a dhol 'na chuthach. Air an làimh eile tha naidheachd againn on aon linn mu Bheathag Mhór san Eilean Sgitheanach, a' bhean-dìolain a bh'aig Martainn a' Bhealaich, ag innse mar a dh' imlich ise an fhuil mu bheul a leannain an uair a bhàis.

Cha do rinn Beathag cumha no marbhrann do Mhartainn Mór, cho fads is aithne dhuinn, ach rinn i òrain eile is tha iad beò fhathast an dùthchas an Eilein. Is e fear dhiubh sin an t-òran air a bheil an t-séist:

> B'e siod e an cùl
> Seo e an cùl bachlach
> B'e siod e an cùl.

Mar bu dual, tha maise an fhuilt air ainmeachadh le uaill:

B'e siod e an cùl bachlach dualach
Òr-bhuidhe cuachach cas-bhuidhe.

Cha ghabh e bhith nach eil na mìltean de òrain is de dhàin ann a tha a'
dol a-mach air cuspair na gruaige: o fhalt sgaoilte a' bhròin is an
tuirimh gu ruige clannagan bòidheach na maighdinn is cùl snìomhain
a' ghaisgich agus gruag rèidh air a cheangal fon bhréid phòsda.

   Tha cuimhne air ainm Beathaig fhathast agus air ainm iomadach té
eile ged a dhìochuimhnicheadh o chionn fhada ainmeannan nam
boireannach gun àireamh a rinn feadhainn dhe na h-òrain is drùitiche
a tha againn an Alba. Ach ged a thachair sin, mhair dhe na h-òrain
fhéin na leigeas leinn a ràdh gur h-e crùn air ar n-ealain a tha san
dìleab a dh'fhàg iad.

   Cha mhór nach gabh roinn a dhèanamh ann an Gàidhlig eadar
bardachd nam fear agus bardachd nam ban, gu sonraichte sna
sreathan uachdrach dhen t-sluagh. Moladh nan ceann-cinnidh is
nan gaisgeach, 'nam beatha is 'nam bàs, agus a' moladh na fine is
a' cumail cuimhne air dìlseachd is air na beusan is na buadhan a bha
daingneachadh neart an t-sluaigh Ghàidhealaich – sin a bha iomchaidh is dligheach os cionn gach nì ann am bardachd nam fear. Gun
teagamh, mas e riochd no cruth an t-slat-tomhais, chan eil mi a' ràdh
gum biodh e cho furasda an roinn sin a dhèanamh an déidh an
ochdamh ceud deug, nuair a bha modh beatha nan uaislean a'
teannadh ri crìonadh. Agus o thùs, is dòcha, ann an sreathan ioch-
drach an t-sluaigh, cha bhiodh an roinn eadar na cruthan-òrain a
bhoineadh dha na fir is an fheadhainn a bhoineadh dha na boireannaich cho faicsinneach. Chan eil an sin ach tuairim. Is e th'agam san
amharc seo: chan eil fianais ann gu robh cruth air leth ann an òrain-
obrach ged a bha an òrain fhéin aig na fir agus na mnathan. Ach mara
robh a' chrìoch glan gearrte aig àm sam bith dh'ar n-eachdraidh, aig
mithean no aig maithean, is coma: tha aomadh dhen t-seòrsa a
dh'ainmich mi léirsinneach gu leòr an cruth agus am faireachadh le
chéile. Dh'fhaoite a ràdh gum boin an 'luinneag' – no a' bhardachd
'luinneagach' – agus sin a' toirt leis séist (lididhean, chan e briathran:
'faill i eo ho' agus a leithid) cho math ri brìgh dhian, lasarra; géiread is
cumhachd; dearrsadh ann an dealbh nam facal – gum boin an
luinneag do aigne nam ban.

   Nuair a gheabhar nas leòr dhe na feartan sin comhlamh ann an dàn
no ann an òran a rinneadh le fireannach, tha – no bha – e doirbh
dhuinne a chreidsinn gur h-e fireannach da-rìribh a rinn e. Tha òran

ainmeil ann, 'Clann Ghriogair air fògradh' (timcheall air 1600, is dòcha) agus tha na sreathan seo ann:

Ann am Bothan na Dìge
Ghabh sibh dìon air an rathad;
Far an d'fhàg sibh mo bhiodag
Agus crios mo bhuilg-shaighead.[9]

Leis an arm sin air a ghiùlain, òran a rinn fireannach, nach e? A dh'ainneoin sin, ma tha, chan eil air feadh Gàidhealtachd Alba ach an aona mhìneachadh: is e sin gur h-e *boireannach* a rinn e nuair a bha an tòir a' teannadh dlùth air a' bhothan aice agus comhlan ghaisgeach de Chloinn Griogair a' gabhail dìon ann. (Is e ainm àite, faodaidh mi a ràdh, a th'am 'Bothan na Dìge': faisg air Dail Mhàilidh.) Chan eil séist air an òran seo idir no air grunnd òran eile dhen aona chruth; ach tha àireamh againn dhen ghnè cheunta is tha séist de lididhean riutha-san. Is d'fhiach a thoirt fa-near gun cainte uaireannan 'luinneag' ri séist dhen t-seòrsa: gu dearbha, ri séist de sheòrsa sam bith.

Chuir Màiri nighean Alasdair Ruaidh (no té eile a bhiodh a' falbh 'na cois, mar a bha cuid de na seanchaidhean a' cumail a-mach) séist ri òrain nach sùilichte, is dòcha, gum biodh séist riutha. A bheil comh-cheangail aig sin ris an agalladh a rinn i nach robh sna h-òrain aice-se ach 'crònain'? Agus an ann a' cur an céill a bha i nach robh ise a' gabhail gnothach ri saoghal nam fear no ri òrain-mholadh nan gaisgeach, mas e is gun do thogadh sin 'na h-aghaidh?

Ga b'e ar bith gu dé a thubhairt i, is ann gu cinnteach do mholadh a' chinn-chinnidh is do shaoghal na gaisge a bhoineas a h-obair-ealain. Ma bha sin an aghaidh nàduir, mar gum b'eadh, do bhoireannach – chan e buileach am moladh ann fhéin idir ach cruthan àraid agus modhannan a' mholaidh a bha dùthchasach dha na cruthan sin a chur an cleachdadh – cha robh Màiri 'na h-aonar. Tha bardachd Mairghread Ni Lachainn is Sìleas na Ceapaich is bardachd bhoireannach eile 'na dhearbhadh air sin. Ach ma dhùisg casaid is gamhlas 'nan aghaidh 'nan linn fhéin, cha do chuir sin bacadh air na sgoilearan a chruinnich na h-òrain aca no air na seinneadairean a chum na h-òrain beò.

Mu dheireadh an ochdamh ceud deug is dòcha nach robh na Gàidheil san aon inntinn is a bha iad roimhe sin. Air neo is dòcha gu bheil an suidheachadh gu math nas achrannaiche na tha sinne a' tuigsinn. Gu dearbha, cha rachainn fhìn an urras, nan robh eòlas mionaideach againn air cor Alba agus a h-ealain mus do lìonsgair na Gàidheil am measg nan Cruithneach, nach digeadh iomadach rud

annasach air uachdar dhuinn. Am faodadh e bhith, an-dràsta, gu robh
inbhe aig banabhaird am measg nan Cruithneach is gun do lean
reumhag dhen dùthchas a tha sin ri caitheamh-beatha nan Gàidheal
Albannach? Air neo an e a tha ann gun do mhair cleachdadhnan an
Alba a bha an Éirinn cuideachd aig aon àm? No an e cothlamadh dhe
na dhà a th' againn? San *Táin* fhéin, tha iomradh air bainfhilidh a bha
air tilleadh a dh'Éirinn an déis a bhith foghlam filidheachd an Alba. Is
ged nach ionann 'Alba' an uairsin agus Alba an-diugh, chan eil sin,
saoilidh mi, gu móran mudha.

Dhen triùir bhanabhard a dh'ainmich mi, Màiri is Mairghread is
Sìleas, thar liom gu bheil Mairghread Ni Lachainn a' filleadh 'na chéile
aignidhean is samhlaidhean à bardachd nam fear is nam ban is gur h-e
sin trian dhen tàladh a tha 'na bardachd-se. Co-dhiubh, tha lìonm-
horachd nam banabhard an Alba an taca ri Éirinn 'na adhbhar
iongantais do luchd-rannsachaidh.

Tha car dhen aon duatharachd fuaite ri tinnsgeadal nan òran
luaidh. Cha b'e an luadh an aon obair a bhathar ag aodramachadh
leis na h-òrain sin: bhite a' gabhail an dearbh sheòrsa an co-bhuinn ri
iomradh is buain is eile. Tha na h-òrain-luaidh cho fìor Albannach an-
diugh, ach is e a' cheist an ann mar sin a bha iad o thùs? A robh iad an
Éirinn cuideachd uair dhe robh an saoghal? Mar a thubhairt mi, chan
eil a' cheist uile gu léir aocoltach ris a' cheist a thog mi mu na
banabhaird. A thuilleadh air corr òran-iomraidh no iorram, is e òrain
bhoireannach a tha sna h-òrain-luaidh.

Seo criomag de òran Leódhusach, iorram a réir na sgeòil, agus
iorram a bhoineas do dheireadh an t-siathamh ceud deug. Chan eil mi
sàr chinnteach nach do chuireadh ris on uairsin – ach is e òran
fireannaich a tha ann, theirinn, gun teagamh:

> Iomair thusa Choinnich chridhe,
> Néill a mhic is na hù a hó [. . .]
> Iomairidh mise fear mu dhithis
> Is nam b'éiginn e fear mu thrithir [. . .]
> Cha dàinig mi riamh an cuan seo
> Gun bhall taobh is gun taod guailne
> Is gun an rac a bhith sa bhuaraich
> Cupaill ann am bord an fhuaraidh[10]

Agus seo a nise òran a theirte anns an Eilean Sgitheanach gur h-e
iorram a bh' ann.

Eile na hùraibh o ho
Eile na hùraibh a ho
Is fliuch an oidhche
O hù a hó
Eile na hùraibh o ho
Nochd is gur fuar i
O hùraibh o ho
Thug an iubhrach
Ùr an cuan oirr'[11]

Tha na h-uimhir de òrain le cuspair dhen t-seòrsa sin cumanta am mesag nan òran-luaidh: thòisich iad, bidh e coltach, 'nan iorram is chaidh an cur an sàs san luadh, mar a thachair do òrain eile, fiù is gu ruige cuid de laoidhean is de dhuain na Féinne. Ach ma dh' fhaodhar 'òrain-luaidh o thùs' ainmeachadh (rud a tha a' seachnadh ceist), is e an gaol – chan e obair – is cuspair na tromalaich dhiubh sin: gràdh a tha dian agus uaibhreach, glé thric, is chan eilear a' cleith inntinn no faireachadh. A bheil gnothach aig na h-òrain sin ris an ealain ris an cainte o shean *cepóc*, agus a bheil stéidh aig a' bheachd gu robh ceangal àraid aig an ealain sin ri Alba? Am faodadh e bhith gur h-e facal a thàinig o na Cruithnich no o na Breatannaich a th'ann; air tùs on Laideann, is dòcha? Tha am facal 'ceapag' an Gàidhlig Alba fhathast: duanag no luinneag – san t-seagh 'òran beag aodram' – is ciall da. A réir teist a th'againn on ochdamh ceud deug is e 'luinneag' an t-ainm dòigheil a bh' air an t-seòrsa ris an can sinne nise 'òran luaidh'.

Tha moladh a' ghaisgich follaiseach gu leòr sna luinneagan. Is dòcha gum biodh na boireannaich – bannal chaileag – a' cur fàilte air a' ghaisgeach, an déidh dha tilleadh às a' bhlàr is e air cur às dha naimhdean, no aig àm freagarrach eile. Tha cunntas ann gun do sheinn bannal de sheachdnar bhan do Eideard a h-Aon, Rìgh Shasainn, nuair a thàinig e dh'Alba, dìreach mar a bhiodh iad a' dèanamh air beulaibh 'an Tighearna Alasdair nach maireann', Rìgh Alba.

Corr is trì ceud bliadhna as déidh sin, chruinnich muime Dhomhnaill mhic Iain mhic Sheumais bannal ghruagach a sheinn timcheall air a' ghaisgeach mhór sin, fear de Chloinn Domhnaill, an déidh dha bhith air a leòn aig Blàr Chàirinis an Uibhist, an 1601: ise a' dèanamh an òrain is iadsan a' togail an fhuinn. Mas e 'luinneag', san t-seann chiall, a tha san òran a rinn iad comhlamh: 'A mhic Iain mhic Sheumais | Tha do sgeul air m'aire',[12] nach dòcha gur h-e 'ceapag' a th'ann cuideachd, ach ann an seann bhrìgh an fhacail sin. Oir an-diugh chan eil mi an dùil gun cainte 'ceapag' ri leithid an òrain seo: tha e tuilleadh is domhain, tuilleadh is toirteil.

An latha thug thu an cuan ort
Laigh gruaim air na beannaibh
Bha snighe air na speuran
Is bha na reultan galach
Mu mhac Iain mhic Sheumais
Duine treubhach smearail.

Mar a chuir mi an céill mar tha, tha feabhas mór am bardachd nam ban: aon de sheachd mìorbhailtean na h-Alba, ma thograr a chur mar sin. Seo màthair a' caoidh a cuid mac; is ann ri h-ighinn a tha i a' tòiseachadh is an nighean air cur as a leth nach do chaoin i na mairbh cho math agus a dh'fhaodadh i. Thuirt an nighean:

'Gur truagh nach fhaicinn fhéin mo mhàthair
A' ruith bho àite gu àite
Gun fhasgadh gun àite tàmh
Aig olcas is a chaoidh i na bràithrean.'

'Uist, a bhean gun chiall gun tuigse
Is mic dhomh fhéin mas bràithrean dhut-s' iad
À ìochdar mo chuim a thuit iad
Is i mo ghlùn fhéin a dh'fhurtaich
Bainne mo dhà chìch a shluig iad.'

Thog mi an gàrradh is lìon mi an iodhlann
Chan ann dhan eòrna ghlan, thioram
No de choirce geal na mìne
Ach a dh'ògradh òg mo chinnidh.[13]

Agus seo sreathan à toiseach 'Cumha Sheathain' – Seathan, mac Rìgh Éireann, mar a theireadh feadhainn ris.

Is mairg a chuala e nach d'innis e
Go robh mo leannan-sa am Minginis
Nam bitheadh a ghaoil, is fhad o thilleadh tu [. . .]

Ach tha Seathan a-nochd 'na mharbhan
Sgeul is bochd le fearaibh Alba
Sgeul is goirt le luchd a leanmhainn
Sgeul is moit le luchd a sheilge [. . .]

A Sheathain duinn, a shaoi na mìne
Is beag an t-àite an cuirinn fhìn thu
Chuirinn am barr mullach mo chinn thu
Chuirinn an tarr mo dhà chìch thu
Eadar Brighde is a bréid mìn thu
Eadar maighdean òg is a stìom thu
Eadar òigh ghil is a brat sìod thu
Eadar mi fhìn is mo léine lìn thu.[14]

An déidh àireamh cheathramhnan:

Ach tha Seathan san t-seòmar uaigneach
Gun òl cupa, gun òl cuaiche
Gun òl fìon à pìosan uaibhreach
Gun òl beòir le eòil is le uaislean
Gun òl ceòil, gun phòg bean buairidh
Gun cheòl cruite, gun cheòl cluaise
Ceanglaichean teann air a ghualainn
Ceanglaichean dul air na fuaintean.

Agus na ceathramhnan a tha ga dhùnadh: briathran cumhachdach anns a bheil a' bhanabhard – bean-dìolain Sheathain, mar a tha seanchas ag aithris – a' cur an céill déinead a gràidh:

A Sheathain chridhe, a Sheathain chridhe
Cha doirinn do lagh no rìgh thu
Cha doirinn dhan Mhoire mhìn thu
Cha tiodhlaicinn dhan Chrò Naomh thu
Cha doirinn do Ìosa Crìosd thu
Air eagal is nach fhaighinn fhìn thu
A Sheathain, mo ghile gréine
Och dha m'aindeoin ghlac an t-eug thu
Is dh'fhàg siod mise dubhach deurach
Is iargain ghointeach orm ad dhéidh-sa.
Is masa fìor na their na cléirich
Gu bheil Irinn is gu bheil Nèamh ann
Mo chuid-sa Nèamh, di-beath an éig e
Air son oidhche mar ris an eudail
Mar ri Seathann donn mo chéile.[15]

Tha òran goirid drùiteach ann a thàinig a-nuas ann an dùthchas an teaghlaich againn fhìn. Tha atharrach againn dheth à Bearnaraigh na

Hearadh: bha e aig Ceit an Tàilleir nach maireann (Mrs. Dix) anns an eilean sin. Tha an dealbh a tha am bard no a' bhanabhard (chan urrainnear a ràdh a thaobh an òrain seo có aca) a' tarraing, agus am faireachadh a tha an dealbh sin a' leigeil ris, cho cùmhnach sgiolta cinnteach agus is aithne dhomh ann am bardachd ann an cànan sam bith.

> Dh'éirich mi moch madainn earraich
> Madainn dhuanaidh fhuarraidh earraich
> Ghabh mi suas ri guala a' bheannain
> Shuidh mi air cnoc is leig mi m'anail
> Dh' amhairc mi bhuam fad mo sheallaidh
> Chunna mi long sa Chuan Chanach
> Chuala mo chluas fuaim a daraich
> Fuaim a cuid seòl is iad a' crathadh
> Is i a' strì ri sgrìoban geala
> Is i a' sìor-ruith dh'ionnsaigh cala
> Chunnaic mo shùil i dol farais
> Socrachadh sìos anns a' ghainimh
> Lùb mi mo ghlùn, dh'iarr mi sìth dhaibh
> Sìth do Eoghain, sìth do Ailein
> An dà bhràthair tàmh biodh agaibh.

Tha a' mhocheirigh – 'dh'éirich mi ro bheul an latha' is a leithid – agus tric gu leòr mocheirigh earraich, a' toirt caismeachd dhuinn gu bheil gnothach annasach air choireigin no cudromach ri a nochdadh: sealladh iongantach no sgeul aoibhneis no cràidh. Tha seòl-tomhais aig na baird Ghàidhealach a bhios a' cur an sàs ràithean na bliadhna: cinneachadh an earraich; fàs an t-samhraidh – 'samhradh a' bhainne'; abaichead an fhoghmhair; crìonadh na dùlachd gheamhraidh. Is tha lathaichean fa leth – 'a' cheud Di-Luain dhen ràithe', 'Di-hAoine an aghaidh na seachdain' agus mar sin, 'nan comhtharran chan ann a-mhàin air aimsir no air ùine ach air tachartas an fhreasdail. Tha feadhainn de lathaichean sealbhach is feadhainn mishealbhach. Tha car dhen aon chàileachd fuaite ri lathaichean féille: an Fhéill Bhrighde; an Fhéill Phàdraig; an Fhéill Mhìcheil air an fheadhainn is ainmeala. Is iadsan gu sonraichte a bha a' comhtharrachadh roinnean na bliadhna ach tha bheag no mhór de bhuaidh eile a' gabhail riutha cuideachd. Aig inbhe na h-ealain boinidh iad do sheòl-beatha an t-samhlachaidh.

Agus tha na monaidhean is na beanntan agus eileanan a' chuain 'nan samhlachas air seòl-beatha eile. Tha am baile – na taighean comhnaidh is an talamh àitich is na bhoineas dhan treabhaire – air an riaghladh mar is dual do mhórchuid de luchd-tuinichidh an domhain. Tha fiadhaire glas an fhàsaich saor o leithid sin de riaghailt. Tha a' Choill Uaine agus an t-eilean uaigneach dhen aon ghnè. Is e na h-àiteachan fiadhaich sin ionadan a' ghaoil fhalaich: àiteachan coinnimh nan leannan san uaigneas.

> Is truagh nach robh mise is tusa, fhleasgaich
> Aig bun nan craobh fo bharr nam preasan
> Is truagh nach robh mi is an t-òg gasda
> Am mullach beinne guirme caise
> Gun duine beò bhith 'nar n-aisge
> Ach dall is bodhar is bacach
> Is thigeamaid a-màireach dhachaigh
> Mar gum pòsamaid on altair.
>
> Is truagh nach robh mise is tusa, ghràidhein
> An eilean mara nach tràghadh
> Gun sgoth gun bhirlinn gun bhàta
> Ach coite beag is dà ràmh air.[16]

No, a-rithist an t-òran seo:

> Coisich a rùin, lùb nan geallamh
> Is minig a laigh mi fo t' earradh
> Ma laigh cha b'ann aig a' bhaile
> Ach mullach nam beann fad on t-sealladh
> Do làmh fom cheann, an té eile tharam
> Do bheul rim bheul, breug nach gealladh.
> Is mi suaint an cirb do bhreacain bhallaich
> Sìoban nam beann a' sìor dhol tharainn
> Uisge fìorghlan fuarain fallain
> Fo shoillse nan reul, solus na gealaich
> An lorg an fhéidh a nì an langan
> Is minig a laigh mi fo t'earradh.

Tha am fàsach agus am baile a' tighinn ann an samhlachas fa chomhair a chéile san òran Ghriogaireach air an dug mi tarraing mar tha an co-cheangal ri bhith ag òl na fala. San dala h-atharrach dheth tha a bhanabhard a' ràdh:

> Ràinig mise rèidhlean Bhealaich
> Is cha d'fhuair mi ann tàmh

> Cha d'fhàg mi ròin de m'fhalt gun tarraing
> No craiceann air mo làimh.

San fhear eile:

> Dhìrich mi a' bheinn mhór gun anail
> Treis man d'ghlas an là
> Chuir mi falt mo chinn ri talamh
> Is craiceann mo dhà làmh.

A réir a' mhìneachaidh sin, cha robh fois no cobhair dhi air taobh seach taobh dhen chruinne Ghàidhealach.

Tha na beanntan is na fàsaichean agus na féidh 'nan cuspairean iongantach anns an dàn fhada ris an canar 'Òran na Comhachaig'.[17] Is ann mu dheireadh an t-siathamh ceud deug a rinneadh e, le fear Domhnall mac Fhionnlaigh nan Dàn an Loch Abar. Is e sealgair a bha ann agus bard; bha e a nise air fàs sean agus, mar a tha an naidheachd ag innse, thugadh dha peata comhachaig. Is ann eadar e fhéin is a' chomhachag sin a tha comhradh an dàin. Tha a' chomhachag aosda is glic an dùthchas nan Gàidheal dìreach mar a thathar ga meas ann an uirsgeulan dhaoine eile. Tha am bard a' tòiseachadh:

> A Chomhachag bhochd na Sròine
> A-nochd is brònach do leaba
> Ma bha thu ann ri linn Donnghail
> Chan iongnadh ge trom leat t'aigne.

Agus tha ise ga fhreagairt:

> Is comhaois mise don daraig
> Bha 'na faillean anns a' mhòintich
> Is iomadh linn a chuir mi romham
> Is mi comhachag bhochd na Sròine.

Tha aois anabharrach an eòin air a dèanamh 'na luim gus a faodar ainmeannan nan sealgairean uasal, gaisgeil air a bheil cuimhne aice-se a chur san rann:

> Chunnaic mi Alasdair Carrach
> An duine b'allaile bha an Albainn
> Is minig a bha mi ga éisdeachd
> Is e a' réiteach nan tom-sealga.

An déidh tuilleadh comhraidh tha i a' sìneadh air maise na dùthcha a mholadh agus os cinn nan uile Creag Uanach.

> Creag mo chridhe-sa Creag Uanach
> Creag an d'fhuair mi greis de m'àrach
> Creag nan aighean is nan damh siubhlach
> A' chreag aighearach ùrail eunach
>
> A' chreag mu'n iadhadh an fhaghaid
> Bu mhiann liom a bhith ga tadhal
> Nuair bu bhinn guth galain gadhair
> A' cur greigh gu gabhail chumhaing.

Tha moladh dhaoine-uaisle, agus ionndrainn nam marbh, moladh nam beann le an grianain is le an cuid fhuaran fìoruisge, moladh sealg nam fiadh le coin-mhóra is leis a' bhogha-shaighead, uile fillte 'na chéile sa bhardachd; sin agus caoidh laige na h-aoise. Tha an aois air comas na seilge is na bardachd a thoirt o Dhomhnall mac Fhionnlaigh agus air comas ruith agus tabhainn a thoirt on t-seann chù. Tha rithim nan rann iomaghluasadach: a' carachadh is ag atharrachadh o cheathramh gu ceathramh – agus tha atharrachadh brìgh a' cinneachadh san dàn a réir sin. Dha – no – trì rainn dheth: chan ann as leathoir a chéile a tha iad.

> Is truagh an-diugh nach beò an fheadhainn
> Gun ann ach an ceò den bhuidhinn
> Leis am bu mhiannach glòir nan gadhar
> Gun mheadhair gun òl gun bhruidhinn.
>
> Chì mi bràigh Bhidein nan Dos
> An taobh so bhos de Sgurra Lìth
> Sgurr a' Chòinnich nan damh seang
> Ionmhainn liom an-diugh na chì.
>
> Cha mhi fhìn a sgaoil an comunn
> A bha eadar mi is Creag Uanach
> Ach an aois gar toirt o chéile
> Gur goirid a' chéilidh fhuaras.
>
> Is ann a bha an comunn bristeach
> Eadar mise is a' Chreag Sheilich
> Mise gu bràth cha dìrich
> Ise gu dìlinn cha teirinn.

Tha na rainn a leannas a' tighinn as leathoir a chéile:

> Cead as truaighe ghabhas riamh
> Don fhiadhach bu mhór mo thoil
> Chan fhalbh mi le bogha fom sgéith
> Is gu là bhràth cha leig mi coin.

> Mise is tusa, ghadhair bhàin
> is tùirseach ar turus don eilean
> Chaill sinn an tabhann is an dàn
> Ged bha sinn grathann ri ceanal.

> Thug a' choille dhiot-sa an earb
> Thug an t-ard dhiom-sa na féidh
> Chan eil nàire dhuinn, a laoich
> On laigh an aois oirnn le chéil'.

An déidh sin tha iomradh aige air an aois a chromas 'an duine dìreach | a dh'fhàs gu mìleanta gasda'. Agus anns a' chomhradh a tha aige a nise ris an aois, mar a bha aige roimhe ris a' chomhachaig, tha e a' ràdh: 'Cuime leiginn leat, a lobhair | Mo bhogha thoirt dhiom air éiginn':

> On is mi fhìn a b'fhearr an airidh
> Air mo bhogha ra-mhath iubhair
> Na thusa, aois bhodhar sgallach
> Bhios aig an teallach 'ad shuidhe.

Ach ged a tha am bard a' feuchainn ri toirt air an aois iomlaid a dhèanamh ris air chor is gun gabhadh ise am bata uaidhe-san is gun doireadh i am bogha air n-ais dha, cha ghabh sin a bhith: tha an rann mu dheireadh aice-se.

> Is iomadh laoch a b'fhearr na thusa
> Dh'fhàg mise gu tuisleach anfhann
> An déidh fhaobhach as a sheasamh
> Bha roimhe 'na fhleasgach meanmnach.

Chan aithne dhomh gu bheil leithid de thuigse air móralachd agus air laigead is giorrad na beatha seo air an cothlamadh 'na chéile san aon dealbhachadh an àite sam bith eile 'nar n-ealain. Gu dearbha, theirinn-sa gu robh 'Òran na Comhachaig' cho mìorailteach ri dad sam bith a chaidh riamh a dhèanamh ann an Gàidhlig. Tha e achrannach ann an rithim is achrannach ann an aignidhean agus tha e soilleir gearrte:

drùiteach le iargain, mórail le moladh is le miann – meas air daoine is air dùthaich; aoibhneas ga dhèanamh is uaill às a bhith beò. Chan eil mi fhìn a' creidsinn gun d'fhuair Domhnall mac Fhionnlaoigh nan Dàn fhathast a àite dligheach am measg baird Alba.

Cha d'fhuair co-dhiubh an taca ri Donnachadh Bàn Mac an t-Saoir a dh'fhàg Beinn Dobhrainn cho ainmeil. 'An tusa a rinn Beinn Dobhrain?' arsa fear òg air choireigin ris is e 'na shean duine air chuairt feadh na Gàidhealtachd. 'Cha mhì', arsa Donnchadh Bàn: 'Dia a rinn Beinn Dobhrain ach mhol mise i.' Tha bliadhnaichean móra o chuir mi an toiseach air shùilean do dhaoine nach b'e an Dr John Grierson idir a chuir an cruth air an ealain ris an can iad *documentary film* ann am Beurla ach Donnchadh Bàn Mac an t-Saoir anns an dearbh mholadh sin. Bha sùil a' chamara aig Donnchadh Bàn fada man dàinig innleachd a' chamara fhéin agus gu sonraichte an dealbh-gluasaideach.

Dh'fhaoite briathran 'Moladh Beinn Dobhrain' a ghabhail 'nan sgrìobt, gun aona lideadh a chur riutha no a thoirt uapa; agus cha bhiodh aon fhacal de chunntas no mìneachadh a dhìth air an dealbh. Tha e caimhlionta is tha e coilionta. Is soilleir sin ri fhaicinn, co-dhiubh leughar ann am Beurla no an Gàidhlig e.

Air neo dh'fhaoite a thagairt nach eile feum fiù is air na faclan fhéin aithris idir, fhads a rachadh a h-uile sreath a leanalt gu mionaideach. Uaireannan is ann air astar a tha am fradharc: nuair a tha am bard a' faicinn, abair, imireachadh nam fiadh a-mach ri guala beinne; uair-eannan is ann meanbh, dlùth a tha e, is dòcha a' dealbhachadh gunna-snaip no dìtheinean is lusan a' mhonaidh, no ceann eilid. Tha fàire an aonaich, aomadh is dìreadh a' mhonaidh, dathan an t-sléibh, ràsan nan allt, luisreadh na frìthe, cruth is dreach is gluasad fhiadh, coltas eòin an fhraoich is an fhirich, iasgach a' bhric is sealg an fhéidh le mìolchoin; tha a h-uile nì dhe sin is barrachd air an toirt fa chomhair na sùla ann an òrdugh cho innleachdach, cho ealanta, is gu faodar a ràdh gu bheil 'Moladh Beinn Dobhrain', dhe sheòrsa, gun mheang is gun chomadh.

A dh'ainneoin sin, tha e ri aithris, le fear dham b'aithne Donnchadh Bàn, nach robh beachd mór sam bith aig a' bhard fhéin, a réir coltais, air a chuid òran. Agus tha luchd sgrùdaidh ann chon an latha an-diugh nach diùltadh uile gu léir an aonta. Air an làimh eile tha feadhainn ann a tha a' toirt an urram is airde dha. Ged a tha aona phrìomh fhacal sa h-uile cànan – 'bardachd', 'filíocht', is mar sin – tha e mar is trice a' toirt leis iomad gnè ealain. Is ged a chuirinn-sa, mi fhìn, Domhnall mac Fhionnlaigh nas airde na Donnchadh Bàn a thaobh aona ghnè, dh'aidichinn gu saor gu bheil àite aig Donnchadh dha fhéin, mar a dh'fheuch mi ri mìneachadh. Ged a tha a' chainnt am 'Moladh Beinn Dobhrain' dumhail, toirteil tha an dealbh, ga meas a réir léirsinn, agus a réir claisneachd cuideachd, rèidh soilleir. 'Soilleir-eachd an t-sléibh | Bha mi sonrachadh': tha an t-soillse sin a' sgaoileadh air feadh an òrain.

Tha iomadach dàn is òran eile a dh'iarradh duine tarraing a thoirt orra nan robh rèidhleach ann. Tha de shaidhbhreas am bardachd na Gàidhlig an Alba gur ann ainneamh a gheabhar fear-sgrùdaidh dhan urrainn breith chothromach a thoirt air a h-uile roinn is dual dhi. Aon eiseimpleir: tha dàn aig a' Phìobaire Dhall (1656–1754) dhan Mhormhaire Shléiteach a tha a' cur an céill an t-seann dàimh a bha eadar am fear-ealain is am fear-taic aige. Mara tuigear cumhachd an dàimh sin, ged is ann do latha a dh'aom o chionn fhada a bhoineas e; mar bheil brìgh beò leinne sa bhardachd a tha cinntinn às; tha móran nach tuigear leinn, agus nach déid againn a mheas, am bardachd Ghàidhlig air fad.

Tha am Pìobaire Dall a' ràdh mu theaghlach nan Domhnallach:

> Is gach aon diubh gam àrach cluth
> Thuigeadh iad uam guth nam meur.

agus:

> Is gach aon diubh le cridhe mór
> Toirt domh airgeid is òir riamh.

Tha e ag ainmeachadh nan ceann-cinnidh, sinnsirean Sior Alasdair, am Mormhaire, mar seo:

> B'aithne dhomh Sior Seumas Mór
> Is b'eòl dhomh Domhnall a mhac
> B'eòl dhomh Domhnall eile a rìs
> Chumadh fo chìs na slòigh ceart.
>
> B'eòl dhomh Domhnall nan trì Domhnall
> Is ge b'òg e bu mhór a chliù
> Bidh fearaibh Alba agus Éirinn
> Ag éirigh leis anns gach cùis.
>
> B'eòl dhomh Sior Seumas na rùin
> T'athair-sa, mhic chliùitich féin,
> Is tusa nis an sèathamh glùn
> Dh'òrdaich Rìgh nan dùl 'nan déidh.

Nan tuiteadh m'aois cho fada mach
Is do mhac-sa theachd air mo thìm
B'e sin dhomh-sa an seachdamh glùn
Thàinig air an Dùn rim linn.[18]

Ged a tha buillsgean ar bardachd-ne ri fhaotainn anns an dàimh a bha eadar am bard is am fear-taic, is ged a tha aonachd an t-sluaigh Ghàidhealaich 'na balla-crìche air cuspairean nam bard air chor is nach eil na h-aignidhean pearsanta cho saor is a dh'iarramaide; a dh'ainneoin sin is 'na dheaghaidh tha seachd seallaidhean, mar a theirte, o rubha na bardachd. Teanntachd eachdraidh ann no às, tha an daonnachd ga nochdadh fhéin mar a dh'imireas i a dhèanamh. Mara dig faireachadh a' chridhe am barr anns an teis meadhoin thig e am barr anns na h-iomaill.

Agus tha sin a' tachairt ann am bardachd Ghàidhlig cuideachd. Ann an seagh, tha buannachd is call le chéile ri an tomhas air feadh réis ar n-eachdraidh, ged nach eil cothrom agam leudachadh air sin ann a sheo. Ach is fheudar a ràdh gu bheil an t-athleasachadh a thàinig air litreachas na Gàidhlig ri ar linn fhìn a' dearbhadh gu bheil draoid-heachd is susbaint 'nar bardachd fhathast.

Baird is Bleidirean

Ann an Gàidhlig Alba, se 'bard' a theirear ri duine sam bith a bhios a' dèanamh òran no a tha an sàs an ealain den t-seòrsa. Ged is aithne dhuinn am facal 'filidh' is ged a bhios sinn ga chleachdadh ann an òrain is a leithid, is gann a ghabhas e a ràdh gu bheil e beò ann an cainnt chumanta an t-sluaigh an-diugh. Agus is gann cuideachd, a thuilleadh air ainmeachas de urram, a tha am facal a' toirt leis sìon a bharrachd is a tha 'bard' fhéin a' toirt leis 'na bhrìgh. Cha b'ann an-dé a thòisich an tàrmachadh sin a dh'fhàg a' Ghàidhlig am freasdal an fhacail 'bard'.

Sa bhliadhna 1800, thug Lachlainn MacMhuirich a chomhdach air a shinnseirean, a bha 'nam filidhean cho ainmeil is a bha idir ann, agus thuirt e:

> gur e fein ant ochda glun deg o Mhuireach a bha leanmhain teaghlaich mhic 'ic Ailein, ceannard chlann Raonail, mar bhardaibh, agus o an am sin gu robh fearan [. . .] aca mar dhuais bardachd o linn gu linn feadh choig ghlun deag [. . .] agus bha e mar fhiachaibh orra, nuair nach biodh mac ag a bhard, gu tugadh e foghlam do mhac a bhrathar, no d'a oighre [. . .] agus is ann areir a chleachdai so fhuair Nial, athair fein, ionnsacha gu leugha agus scriobha eachdrai agus bardachd [. . .]¹

Chan eil am facal 'filidh' air a chleachdadh.

San dearbh bhliadhna, thug Huisdean Domhnallach an Cille Pheadair an Uibhist a Deas a agalladh fhéin. A-rithist, se 'bard' is 'bardachd' a tha aige-san, gun ghuth aige air 'filidh'. Tha e a' ràdh, an lùib rudan eile:

> Bha na tighearnan agus na h-uachdarain tabhairt duais do na bardaibhse. [. . .] Ata codach nas leor gu robh teaghlaichean Gaidhealoch ag cumail bhard. [. . .] Aig teaghlach Mhac Dhonuil be Jain Mac Codrum am bard mo dheridh [. . .] roimhe sin Donnacha Mac Ruairi ag a robh achadh nam bard ann an Troternis mar fhearann oidhreachd, agus tha a shliochd fein agus sliochd a shinnsear ar sloinidh clann a bhaird. [. . .] Nuair a chuir Mac Leoid bhuaidh Mac Ille Riabhich agus a ghabh e fear eile na aite, thug Mac

Dhonuil, ged a bha bard aige fein, fearran dha [. . .] ris an can iad baile mhic Ille Riabhich gus an diudh. [. . .] Ag teaghlach mhic Mhic Ailen bha clann Mhuirich feadh iomadh linn nam baird [. . .][2]

Tha na 'baird' a tha air an ainmeachadh an sin de thrì seòrsaichean: Donnchadh MacRuairi agus MacGilleRiabhaich, dithis a bhuineadh do theaghlaichean dhan robh dreuchd a' bhaird, gu ìre air choreigin, dùthchasach; MacCodrum, fear nach buineadh idir do leithid sin de theaghlach; agus Clann MhicMhuirich, na filidhean. Ann an sealladh Huisdein, b'e 'baird' a bha annta gu léir, gun atharrachadh ga chur eatorra.

Aig deireadh an t-seachdamh ceud deug tha teist againn air na baird is air luchd-ealain eile o làimh Mhgr Iain Friseal, ministeir Easbaigeach. Seo mar a tha esan ga chur:

They had Bardi, poetici, and Seneciones, peculiaire to every family, and symphoniaci; the Bard's office was to rehears what was compiled by the Poets; the poets versified with admirable art, and in such a high and lofty stile, and such exact measures, and variety of measure, as may justly be compared with Homer or Virgil. Ther Bards was sometimes allowed to compose some Rythmi, but not to medle any higher.[3]

Tha e soilleir gura h-e *poetici* na filidhean agus gura h-e na *Bardi* na baird – chan e na baird anns an fharsaingeachd, mar a chleachdadh sinne an-diugh am facal, ach baird ann an dreuchd stéidhte, ord a bha fo smachd aig na filidhean. Tha an tuairisgeal sin a' tighinn a réir aithris nan Éireannach air a' chuspair: ann an Éirinn cuideachd bha am bard de rang na b'isle na bha am filidh. Ach chan eil an 'reacaire' Éireannach ri a lorg idir ann an Alba, nas lugha na tha an t-ainm ann an cothlamadh eile againn sa chruth 'creacaire' no 'sracaire'.[4]

Mu dheireadh an t-seachdamh ceud deug a-rithist tha tuairisgeal nas annasaiche is nas làine againn. Sin litir a chuir James Garden an Colaiste an Rìgh an Obar-Dheathain gu John Aubrey, an sgrìobhadair Sasannach, a' freagairt cheistean a chuir Aubrey air mu chleachdannan nan Gàidheal is eile. Thàinig am fiosrachadh o fhear à Srath Spé: 'by profession a student of Divinity and by birth a gentleman's son in Strathspey'. 'You have', tha Garden a' ràdh ri Aubrey, '[. . .] by the same hand, an account of the Bards such as they are at present in these parts, & such as they were within the memory of my informer's father (who is an aged man of ninetie seaven years) [. . .].'

A chionn is gu bheil an litir an clò cheana agus furasda gu leòr a ruigheachd, agus a chionn is gu bheil àireamh phuingean innte air nach urrainn domh beachd a ghabhail an seo, cha dèan mi ach earrann no dhà a thaghadh aisde. Ach bu chòir a ràdh nach eil an fhianais uile gu léir rèidh comhnard: is dòcha gura h-e as adhbhar dha sin gu bheil an teist a' comhdach an t-suidheachaidh mar a bha e gu math na bu tràithe den cheud, ri cuimhne an athar, cho math ris an t-suidheachadh fa chomhair na h-uarach. Faodar a ràdh cuideachd gu bheil am facal 'Irish', ann an toiseach an t-seanchais, a' ciallachadh Gàidhlig Albannach; cleachdadh a bha cumanta aig an àm.

> A Bard in common Irish signifies a little poet or a rhymer, they use to travel thorow countries and coming into ane house, salute with a rhym called in Irish *Beanacha p baird*, i.e. the Bard's salutation qch is onlie a short verse or rhym touching the praise of the master and mistris of the house. The inferior sort of them are counted amongst the beggers [. . .]
>
> This inferior sort, otherwise called beggers makes few or no verses or rhyms of their own, but onlie makes use of such as hath been composed by others [. . .]
>
> He thats extraordinarie sharp of these bards is named *phili*, i.e. ane excellent poet, these frequent onlie the company of persons of qualitie & each of them hes some particular person whom he owns his master. [. . .] These bards in former times used to travel in companies, sometimes 40, 50, 60 persons between men, wives & childrene, and they were thus ranked, the first were termed *philies*, i.e. poets [. . .] & the 4 [i.e., an ceathramh rang] [. . .] such as proponed enigmaes & othere difficult questions [. . .] that delights to invade others with subtilities & ambiguous questions. The whol caball was called *Chlearheanachi* [. . .][5]

Is fhurasda fhaicinn nach ionann dhan dà dhealbh. A réir an Fhrisealaich, tha aon dreuchd chunbhalach aig a' bhard; a réir an fhir eile, tha na h-uimhir de dhithean a' tighinn fon ainm 'bard'. Theirte o theist Mhgr Iain gu robh am *poeticus* ann an rang ard air leth; ged a tha am filidh air a ainmeachadh is air a shonrachadh aig an Speidheach, thathas a' cur air shùilean duinn nach eil ann, mar gum b'eadh, ach fear eile de na baird: 'He that's extraordinarie sharp of these bards is named *phili*'; agus sin a dh'ainneoin 'A Bard [. . .] signifies a little poet or a rhymer'. Chan fhuilear mar sin nach eileas a' cleachdadh 'bard' ann an dà sheagh ann an seo, seagh farsaing agus seagh cumhang. Chan e idir gu bheil an dithis ughdar a' dol calg dhìreach an aghaidh a chéile; chan eil ann ach gu bheil an dala fear nas achrannaiche na a sheise. Dh'fhaodadh uird fa leth a bhith sna *Bardi* aig Mgr Iain cuideachd, ged nach eil e gan roinn a-mach o chéile, no a' dèanamh leudachadh sam bith air a' phuing.

Sann am Muile a rugadh Iain Friseal, sa bhliadhna 1647. Bhuineadh e mar sin dhan t-seann ord de phearsachan-eaglais, dham b'aithne seòl-beatha agus ealain nan Gàidheal, an àm a bha an saoghal Gàidhealach fhathast gu math slàn. Agus leis gura h-ann à Muile a bha e, chan fhuilear nach robh eòlas aige air dithis dhaoine a bha ri ealain san eilean sin ri a linn fhéin. B'iad sin Maol-Domhnaigh Ó Muirgheasáin, fear den teaghlach a bha 'nam filidhean aig Clainn Ghill-Eathain am Muile agus aig Clainn MhicLeòid an Dùn Bheagain. Chaochail Maol-Domhnaigh sin mun bhliadhna 1660. Car 'na chom-haoise do Mhaol-Domhnaigh, bha Eachann Bacach MacGill-Eathain air fear de na baird a b'ainmeala ann am meadhon an t-seachdamh ceud deug. A réir agalladh fhéin san òran 'A' Chnò Shamhna', am marbhrann a rinn e do Shior Lachlainn, an ceann-cinnidh, bha e 'na eòlach ann an taigh MhicGill-Eathain o bha e 'na naoidhein.

Bha mi tathaich do chùirte
Seal mum b'aithne dhomh an t-urlar a dh'fholbh.[6]

Tha e ri a ràdh gu robh tuarasdal beag aige on cheann-chinnidh. A réir sin uile, bidh e coltach gu robh Eachann Bacach ann an dreuchd baird dìreach mar a bha Maol-Domhnaigh ann an dreuchd filidh.

Ach a bheil e coltach gum biodh leithid Eachainn Bhacaich 'na 'reacaire' – 'na ghille-aithris, mar a dh'fhaodamaid a ràdh – aig an fhilidh? Ma ghabhas sinn ri fianais an Fhrisealaich gu litireil, b'e sin a dhleasdanas. Ach thoireamaid fa near gum b'e gaisgeach agus fear de theaghlach ghaisgeach, a réir an t-seanchais, a bha an Eachann: teaghlach a bha an dàimh ri fine a' chinn-fheadhna fhéin, agus theagamh 'na bhall den léine-chneis aige. Tha naidheachd gun deach seachdnar de a bhràithrean a mharbhadh ann am Blàr Inbhir Chéitein, gu robh fear aca, Niall Buidhe, 'na shàr cheatharnach, agus gura h-e an lot a fhuair Eachann fhéin an latha sin a dh'fhàg bacach ri a bheò e.

Co-dhiubh na co-aca, bha inbhe is urram ga thoirt da os cionn a' chumantais, oir b'esan fear den chóignear bhard air an deach an titeil 'Aos-dàna' a bhuileachadh.[7] Is dòcha nach ann a-mhàin air an t-suidheachadh ann am Muile a bha sùil Mhgr Iain ach air àiteachan eile agus linntean eile a cheart cho math.

Gu dé nise a bha sna *Rhythmi* – na cruthan sin a b'airde dh'fhao-dadh am bard a chur an sàs? Ma bha am bard 'na reacaire chan eil rian nach cuireadh e eòlas air dàn dìreach an fhilidh, ged nach biodh an sin ach nàdar de aithris-bheòlain fhéin. Mar sin dh'fhaodadh e a bhith 'na mheadhon air cruth an dàin a stéidheachadh sa Ghàidhlig chumanta; rud a thachair am pailteas. Tha caochladh sheòrsaichean meadair againn a ghabhas sloinneadh air an dàn gun teagamh, is tha caochladh bhealaichean ann air am faodadh iad tighinn gar n-ionnsaigh.

Air aon bhall-sampaill, tha seòrsa de *shnéadhbhairdne* againn aig a bheil comh-cheangal ri féilleachadh is moladh. Cha rachainn an urras nach eil corr agus aon tinnsgeadal aige, ach air an trò-sa fuilingidh e a chur fon aon cheann. Chithear e anns 'An Duanag Ullamh' a rinn bard MhicGill-Eathain san t-siathamh ceud deug; ann an 1685, se an riochd a tha air a' chumha a rinn an t-Aos-dàna MacShithich do Iarla Arra-Ghàidheal; anns an t-seachdamh ceud deug cuideachd tha e aig MacBeathaig, bard an Domhnallaich san Eilean Sgitheanach; gheabhar a-rithist e ann an duan molaidh gun urrainn do Alasdair mac Colla; agus mar sin air n-adhart. San ath cheud, chuir Donnchadh Bàn Mac an t-Saoir an sàs e ann an 'Rainn gearradh-arm': duan dhan cheann-chinnidh aige fhéin, anns a bheil e a' moladh fine Chlainn an t-Saoir.[8] Ri mo linn fhìn bha seanchaidhean ga mheas 'na mheadar urramach is theirte gura h-e sin adhbhar gun deach 'Duan a' chaisteil' – ealaidh a tha a' cumail togail Chaisteil Armadail ann an Sléite an Eilean Sgitheanaich air chuimhne – a dhealbh air an riochd sin.

Se a' cheist chudromach ach gu dé an ceangal, gu h-ionaigear, a tha eadar na cruthan sin agus ealain a' bhaird 'na dhreuchd stéidhte? An do lean na baird, o linn gu linn, ri meur den t-seann *bhairdne*, no gu dé an casadh eile a tha san eachdraidh; air neo an e dìreach tuiteamas fhéin a th'ann gura h-e gnè de bhairdne co-dhiubh a tha againn sna duain sin?

Tha e cinnteach gu leòr gu robh na baird a bha dlùth dha na cinn-chinnidh, agus an fhuil uasal is dòcha annta fhéin, a' cur an sàs gu suaicheanta a' mheadair air an tug W. J. Watson an t-ainm *strophic*.[9] Tha e comharraichte aig Iain Lom is aig Màiri nighean Alasdair Ruaidh. Tha an dearbh nì ann an tomhas fìor a thaobh Eachainn Bhacaich agus masa h-esan a bha aig Mgr Iain Friseal san amharc, chan eil rian nach e seo an cruth air a bheil e a' toirt an ainm *Rhythmus*.

Is ged nach b'e Eachann Bacach idir an t-eisimpleir ghabhadh na *strophics* an ceangal ri dleasdanas a' bhaird: moladh an duine-uasail is moladh na fine. A réir a' bheachd-sa, b'e sin meadar dùthchasach nam bard o shean, riamh mun d'éirich iad ann an inbhe is mun d'fhuasgail iad na bannan a bha gan cumail fo chuing. Nuair a rinn iad sin, air neo nuair a ghabh na 'baird mhóra' – leithid Iain Luim is Eachainn Bhacaich fhéin – an ealain aca an iasad, cha robh na baird mhóra ach a' leasachadh a' chruth a bha dùthchasach dha na 'baird bheaga' a bha ann rompa.

Tha sin reusanta gu leòr 'nam bharail-sa is co-dhiubh chuireadh an céill cheana e. Ach a' meas an t-suidheachaidh an-diugh, saoilidh mi, gus a' mheidh a chumail cothrom, gum bu chòir dhuinn pailt uiread de àite a thoirt dhan t-seann bheachd gun do rinn Màiri nighean Alasdair Ruaidh, abair, ealain ùr nodha, is a bheir sinn dhan bheachd nach robh innte-se agus 'na comhaoisean sa bhardachd, ach geug den t-seann chraoibh. Se sin a bha innte, theagamh, ach cha ghabh e a bhith nach tàinig lìonsgaradh anabharrach agus tàrmachadh anns an linn sin. Is mar is aithne dha na h-uile, tha Iain Lom nas toiseannaiche. Cluinnear fhathast, chon an latha an-diugh fhéin, dorlach de na h-òrain aig Iain Lom is aig Màiri is aig Eachann Bacach, agus iad air mairsinn corr is trì ceud bliadhna. Nam b'e is gu robh, a' dol air n-ais trì ceud bliadhna eile, leithid de ealain air lorg nuair a bha luchd-tionail cho dian air an tòir san ochdamh ceud deug, nach fhaod a bhith nach biodh iadsan air an cruinneachadh? Se bha ann, is cinnteach, nach robh an seòrsa sin, co-ionann an càileachd ri obair nam 'bard mór', am bith an uair sin fhéin; agus se buil a tha ann nach eil againn an-diugh ach dhà-no-trì de òrain-mholaidh a tha nas sine na a' cheud cheathramh den t-seachdamh ceud deug mum faoidhte a ràdh gura h-e saothair a' bhaird mhuinntireis a tha annta.

A thaobh sin uile, ma tà, tha a thuar gum bi an cnap-starra seo romhainn am feasda: nach eil ach am beagan beag againn de fhianais chinnteach à Gàidhlig fhéin air dreuchd is dleasdanas a' bhaird nuair a bha e 'na dhuine air a fhasdadh air thuarasdal, air a chumail iriosal air a stall, agus ealain aige ri chumadh 'na iomlaid sin. Tha aon rud dearbhte: nach urrainn duinn agairt le cinnt gura h-e aon chruth no aon mheadar a bha aig na baird air tùs. Dh'fhaodadh gu robh roinnean an sin cuideachd, a réir gach breath den ord, eadar shaorbhard, is dòcha, agus dhaorbhard.

Chunnaic sinn mar tha gu robh fear MacBeathaig 'na bhard aig MacDhomhnaill san t-seachdamh ceud deug. Bha e an dreuchd pìobaire aig an aon àm. Nise se port-pìoba an t-òran as sine, cho fad is a ghabhas a leithid a dhèanamh aithnichte, a tha againn an Alba de òrain a thathar a' seinn fhathast. Sin am port 'Pìobaireachd Dhomhnaill Duibh [. . .] Pìob agus bratach air faich Inbhir Lòchaidh'.

Chaidh am port a cheangal ri dà bhlàr is ri dà bhliadhna fa leth:

1427 agus 1431. Se fìor chothlamadh a th'ann, ma ghabhar ri gach ainm a gheabhar anns gach samhail dheth (rud nach buin dhan rannsachadh an-dràsta) ach tha aon cheathramh a tha ga stéidheachadh.

> Theich is gun do theich is gun do theich Clann an Tòisich [. . .]
> Dh'fhalbh Clann Mhuirich ach dh'fhuirich Clann Domhnaill.

Chan e an dala cuid 1427 no 1431 a' bhliadhna, air a shon sin, ach 1429. Sin a' bhliadhna a chomhlaich arm an Rìgh, Seumas a h-Aon, agus feachd Mormhaire nan Eilean aig Inbhir Lòchaidh agus a thréig Clann Chatain na Domhnallaich.[10] A dh'ainneoin an titeil chan eilear ag innse gura h-e pìobaire a rinn e; ach corr agus ceud bliadhna gu leth an déidh sin, air a' chóigeamh latha den Lùnasdal 1596, mharbhadh Lachlainn Mór MacGill-Eathain ann an Ìle agus tha am port a rinn am pìobaire aige ga sheinn againn fhathast.

> Sann aig Ceann Tràigh Ghruineard
> A dh'fhàg mi an curaidh[11]

A bheil sin a' ciallachadh, ma tà, gu robh rang de na baird a bha 'nam pìobairean? Chan eil buileach, oir dh'fhaodadh am bard na facail a chur ris a' cheòl as déidh làimhe. Ach mar a dh'ainmicheadh mar tha, bha MacBeathaig, air aon fhear co-dhiubh, 'na phìobaire agus 'na bhard.

A réir dùthchas nan athraichean, nuair a dhèanadh pìobaire port den t-seòrsa seo, bha de bhuaidh ann an guth na pìoba fhéin na chuireadh an céill na briathran dhan luchd-éisteachd. Cha chanar 'Ceòl-mór' ri ceòl nam port seo idir ach se 'Pìobaireachd' a tha ann. Tha mi fhìn den bheachd gura h-e seo ealain dhùthchasach a' phìobaire an Alba mas do dhealbhadh an Ceòl-mór; seadh, nuair is ann aig a' chlàrsair a bha an inbhe agus am pìobaire ann an rang na b'ìsle, mar a bha am bard fhéin. Tha e a cheart cho dòcha gun do chum cuid de na pìobairean orra leis an t-seòrsa ealain seo linntean an déidh dhan Cheòl-mhór nochdadh anns an riochd anns an aithne dhuinn e.

Ach faodaidh e a bhith nach ann aig na pìobairean a-mhàin a bha i. Tha cuid de na puirt-mhóra sin, mar a theirear riutha an-diugh co-dhiubh, air an sloinneadh a thaobh dealbhachaidh, chan ann air pìobairean ach air boireannaich. Nise tha suaip aig bloigh den bhardachd a tha air a h-ainmeachadh air MacBeathaig ri feadhainn de na h-òrain-luaidh, ann an gnè agus ann am meadar. Se boireannaich a rinn a' mhórchuid de na h-òrain-luaidh ged a tha iarmad ann a

rinneadh le fir: iorram no dhà is a leithid. Is dòcha, ma tà, gu robh fìor
bhardachd nam ban, cuid de ealain nam bard a bu lugha, agus
seòrsaichean sonraichte de òrain-obrach nam fear uile coltach ri a
chéile.

Chan eil agam ach tuairim an sin: chan eil e furasda amas air na
stairean a dh'iarramaid gus ar toirt air n-ais ceum air cheum de ar n-
eachdraidh. Tha an-dràsta an litir aig Garden ag ainmeachadh *Bea-*
nacha p baird mar nach buineadh e ach dhan bhard bheag. Ceart gu
leòr; ach dh'fhaodadh am Beannachadh Baird a bhith fada na bu
ghreadhnaiche na thogamaid à sin – mar a tha am Beannachadh Baird
a rinn am Pìobaire Dall ann an 1730 do MhacCoinnich Ghearrloch
nuair a phòs e. Agus tha teist eile a-rithist aig Martin Martin is e ga
cheangal ri cleachdadh nan urracha-móra.

> Among Persons of Distinction it was reckon'd an Affront put upon any
> Company to broach a Piece of Wine, Ale, or *Aquavitae*, and not to see it all
> drank out at one Meeting. If any Man chance to go out from the Company,
> tho but for a few Minutes, he is oblig'd upon his Return, and before he take
> his Seat, to make an Apology for his Absence in Rhyme; which if he cannot
> perform, he is liable to such a share of the Reckoning as the Company thinks
> fit to impose: which Custom obtains in many places still, and is call'd
> *Beanchiy Bard*, which in their Language signifies the Poet's congratulating
> the Company.[12]

Theagamh gu bheil gach fianais dhiubh urrasach ach feumar gach
teist a mheas a réir an ama agus a réir an t-suidheachaidh. Is cha dèan
math gin aca a ghabhail 'na ònrachd.

Co-dhiubh, bha e 'na chleachdadh againn, ann am fearas-chuideach-
da, ceathramh a dhèanamh an làrach nam bonn. Air na bainnsean o
shean, bhite a' cur timcheall pìos feòla – caob de chnàimh an droma às a'
cheathramh-deiridh – ris an canamaid *an dronn*. Masa h-e feòil-mairt a
bh'ann, theirte dronn no ruinnse, bu choingeis. Se ruinnse na bà am pìos
a tha car eadar bun an earbaill agus na meidheannan. Nise, bha e ri a
ràdh gura h-e an dronn cuid a' bhaird às a' chaoraich; às a' bhoin
cuideachd, is dòcha a réir na h-inbhe a bhiodh aige. Air na bainnsean
thuiteadh e gun tigeadh an dronn air fear sam bith, co-dhiubh bu bhard e
gus nach b'eadh – ach nam b'e is gu robh bard an làthair, sin a b'fhearr
buileach. An duine air an tigeadh an dronn, dh'fheumadh esan rann a
dhèanamh as an t-seasamh. Mura dèanadh, chuirte an 'Dubhchapall'
air. (Eadar-dhà-sheanchas, thugadh an cleachdadh seo gu ruige Eileanan Fàro: sann o 'dhronn' a thàinig am facal *drunnur* aca-san.[13])

Tha iomradh air cleachdadh eile a tha glé dhlùth an gnè dha seo.
Sann air na bainnsean a-rithist a bu bhitheanta a chleachte e, a réir is
mar a chuala mise, ach theagamh gu robh e aig daoine ann an
cuideachda cheòlmhor sam bith. Fon fhacal 'struileag' tha Dwelly
ga mhìneachadh mar seo:

> An imaginary boat used in a contest of wit or singing at a marriage or other
> gathering. When one has sung or otherwise contributed to the amusement of
> the party, he says 'Cuiream struileag seachad orm gu——', naming some
> other person, who makes the same remark when he has finished his share of
> entertaining.[14]

Chan e bàta (no a shamhla) a chuala mise a bh'ann ach pìos maide
agus se 'struilleag' (*l* chaol, làidir) chan e 'struileag' (*l* chaol, lag) a
theirinn ann an gearradh an fhacail. Ann an *Carmina Gadelica*, fon
cheannfhacal 'struilleag', chan e conaltradh nam bard no fearas-
chuideachda a tha fillte sa bhrìgh ach iomairt geasachd.[15] Ach tha
'Òran a' bhàta do'm b'ainm *Struileag*'[16] againn is chan aithnichte gu
robh sìon sonraichte a' gabhail ris seach òran eile mu bhàta, ach gu
bheil na fir-dheasachaidh iad fhéin a' toirt iomradh air 'an imaginary
boat which was sent from one person to another accompanied by a
rhyme'. Faodaidh gu bheil aoireadh am falach ann am briathran an
òrain.

Bha fear de mo shinnsre fhìn, Lachlainn mac Thearlaich Òig à Srath
an Eilean Sgitheanaich, turas air banais an Loch Aillse, mu choinneamh an t-Sratha, air tìr-mór. Bhiodh seo a-nise mu dheireadh an t-
seachdamh ceud deug no toiseach an ath cheud. Nuair a bhathar a'
riaghladh a' bhidhe, chuireadh ruinnse bà air beulaibh Lachlainn. Se
bard ainmeil a bha ann agus is fheudar gun do smaoinich e gura h-e
tàmailt a bha na h-Aillsich a' toirt da, a' tabhann na ruinnse air a
leithid-san – a' dèanamh a' bhaird bhig dheth, mar gum b'eadh. Thog
e an ruinnse is thuirt e:

> Chuir sibh chugam air an truinnsear
>   cuid a' bhaird de fheòil na bainnse
> ach mar tha an seanfhocal ag innse–
>   ceann na ruinnse taobh Loch Aillse.[17]

Bha seo mar gum biodh e a' tomhadh na tòine ris an dùthaich is ri a
cuid sluaigh. Bha an tuasaid air a bonn air ball air chor is gum bu
ghann a thug Lachlainn e fhéin às le a bheatha.

Bhiodh Lachlainn mac Thearlaich agus a sheòrsa a' dol air chuairt mar a bha dùthchasach dha na baird. Ach air a shon sin dh'fheumte a inbhe fhéin a thoirt da. Sin mar a bha an Clàrsair Dall a réir coltais cuideachd. Mar a chithear san litir aig Garden, bhiodh na baird, eadar bheag is mhór, uaireannan co-dhiubh, a' siubhal comhla. Tha an Clàrsair a' ràdh:

ghabh mi tearbadh o'n treud sin
far an robh mi am mheanbhghair
an toiseach aimsir mo chéitein[18]

– bha sin ann mas d'fhuair e inbhe aig MacLeòid an Dùn Bheagain.

Se an 'treud' a' Chliar Sheanchain.[19] Nise chan e 'Cliar Sheanchain' – o ainm Sheanchain, am filidh mór – a their sinne idir, ach 'A' Chliar Sheanchain', agus tha sin fhéin a' seall.tainn nach robhar a' tuigsinn tinnsgeadal an ainme. A thuilleadh air sin, ma bha urram fuaighte ris an t-sloinneadh air tùs cha do mhair e. Chan ionann brìgh an fhacail 'cliar' ann an abairt 'talla nan cliar' agus a leithid sin agus anns a' 'Chliar Sheanchain'. O chionn àireamh mhath ghinealach cha robh sa Chléir Sheanchain leinne ach gràisg lìonmhor, shanntach, ladarna. Tha e soilleir gura h-e na baird bheaga air a bheilear a' cuimseachadh anns gach seanchas a tha againn umpa. Thigeadh iad gu dàna, danarra a dh'ionnsaigh taighe sam bith – is iad acrach, pàiteach – is neart air cheart dh'fhuiricheadh iad an sin gus an tilleadh cuideigin iad le aoir no le gearradh-cainnte. Is minig a chuala mi o bha mi beag: 'Cho leisg ris a' Chléir Sheanchain'; 'cho lìonmhor ris a' Chléir Sheanchain'; 'cho mìomhodhail ris a' Chléir Sheanchain'. Bha urnas dhiubh da-rìribh.

Thàinig iad an turas a bha seo, uair de robh an saoghal, gu taigh san Eilean Sgitheanach is bha iad an imis muinntir an taighe a chreachadh. Gu ruige seo, dh'fhaillich air gach duine a chuireadh gan coinnea-chadh an tilleadh. Ach a' mhadainn-sa thàinig fear an taighe orra a-muigh is iad uile air an tom air cùl gàrraidh.

'Tha e coltach gura h-ann air an aon latha', arsa esan, 'a chaidh na h-éisgean a dhàir.'

'Masa h-ann', arsa fear aca-san, 'tog thusa leat na laoigh.'

'Cha do thog mise riamh laogh', arsa esan, 'gus an d'imlich a mhàthair fhéin an toiseach e.'

Dh'fhoghain sin daibh is thog iad ri glas.[20]

Tha gnè na naidheachd sin a' cur an céill mar a bha an sluagh gam meas.

Bha e riamh 'na chleachdadh aca a bhith a' cur cheistean dorcha is a' freagairt ann an dubhchainnt. Dìreach mar a tha an litir a' toirt fianais: '[they] proposed enigmaes & othere difficult questions' agus a-rithist 'one that delights to invade others with subtilities & ambiguous questions'. Ach cha robh an sin ach an rang a b'ìsle. Ann an dùthchas an t-sluaigh, b'e an dubhchainnt rogha is taghadh ceirde na Cléir Sheanchain air fad.

Tha Mgr Domhnall MacNeacail ag aithris gura h-e an 'thesis [which] James the Sixth gave to some poets as a trial of skill in their profession', na sreathan seo:

> SUBJECT
> Snamhaid an Lach is an Fhaoilin
> Da chois chapail chaolin chorr
>   ANSWER
> 'D fhuaras Deoch a Laimh Ri Alba
> A Cup Airgid agus Oir;
> An Aite nach do shaoil mi fhetin –
> 'S da chois chapail chaoilin chorr.

> The poet who performed best was to get one cupful of wine from the king's own hand, and another cupful of gold as his reward.[21]

Bha an rann sin, anns na dearbh bhriathran gu beagnaich, air a aithris san Eilean Sgitheanach; ach cha b'ann an dala cuid air rìgh no air baird urramach a bhathas ga fhàgail ach air a' Chléir Sheanchain. Agus bha seo gus a shealltainn nach tuigeadh duine cneasda sam bith gu dé fon ghréin ghil a bha dubhfhacail na gràisge ud a' ciallachadh.

Bha an fhaighdhe 'na cleachdadh dùthchasach am measg nan Gàidheal, is cha b'ann aig na baird a-mhàin. Tha dealbh eirmseach shoilleir air a tarraing air luchd na faighdhe ann an Leabhar an Deadhain:[22] 'Mór an feidhm freagairt na bhfaighdheach | Thig fá seach'. Agus tha dealbh eile san aon leabhar a' toirt cunntas air na 'lorgánaigh'. Ach atharrachadh beag a thoirt asda thall is a bhos, cha toir iad sìon an cuimhne duine a bha eòlach air a leithid ach an Luchd-siubhail, mar a their iad fhéin – na Ceardannan, Ceardaidhean, Ceaoird, etc., mar a their muinntir na tuatha riutha – nuair a bha iad 'nan luchd-siubhail da-rìribh is a chromadh iad air baile.

Sna linntean a dh'aom bha na h-uimhir sheòrsaichean de luchd-siubhail a' falbh air feadh na Gàidhealtachd, eadar cheannaichean-siubhail is bhaigearan, is iad a' toirt am beòthachd às mar sin. Tha Garden a' ràdh mu na baird: 'The inferior sort of them are counted amongst the beggars'; agus a-rithist: 'This inferior sort, otherwise called beggars [. . .]'.

Ann an àiteachan, ged is aithne do dhaoine am facal 'Ceard', tha ainm eile air an luchd-siubhail sin: na Bleidirean. Tha 'bleid' a' toirt leis beul-brèagha is brosgal, agus sann mar sin as trice a mhìnichear e; ach tha e a' toirt leis cuideachd, a bheag no a mhór, sìor iarraidh is cnuasach, le moladh-meallta 'na chois, ladarnas, gearradh-cainnte is freagairt ullamh, agus ainmeachas de bhuaireadh air an cùl. A thuilleadh air sin uile, tha 'cladhaire' ga chur mu choinneamh an fhacail 'bleidir(e)' sna faclairean. Tha a' cheud lideadh ann am 'bleid', is anns na facail a bhuineas dha, daonnan goirid.

Tha rann againn a tha air fhàgail air Màiri nighean Alasdair Ruaidh:

> Cha diochd fhad 's tha mi 'g éisdeachd
> Ri bléidrich mo mhàthar
> A' sìor mholadh Sir Ailein
> Ceann-alla nam meairleach

Tha sin air a thionntadh ann an *Carmina Gadelica*: 'More than long am I listening to the wheedling of my mother, ever praising Sir Allan, very chief of the thieves.'[23]

Ged a tha *bléidirich, pléidirich* 'a' sìor iarraidh', etc. againn, saoilidh mi nach e 'wheedling' an seo an seagh buileach ach caran a' cumail air an aon iorram, an aon duan, mu chuspair sam bith; agus an seo 'sìor mholadh labharra' no a leithid sin, ged a dh'fhaodadh 'moladh-meallta' a bhith a' ruith fodha. Tha a' cheud lideadh fada.

Tha an uairsin dorlach beag fhacal ann air am bu chòir beachd a ghabhail; is iad sin 'blad', 'bladair(e)', 'bladaireachd', 'bladar', agus eile. Tha brosgal, ceilg, coiteachas, cainnt gun diù agus cladhaireachd air cuid de na tha fillte annta. Tha suaip aca ri facail ann am Beurla Shasainn is ann am Beurla na Galldachd is dh'fhaodadh gu bheil dàimh diamhair aca riutha; is comh-cheangal eile, ma dh'fhaoidhte, ri Laideann is ri cànan nan Lochlannach: se na facail Bheurla *blather, blether, blatter, bladry* is a leithid sin; agus facal mar a tha *bladzean* air cùl-fraoin.

Tha a-nise aon fhacal eile ann a dh'fhaodadh e a bhith riatanach sùil a thoirt air: se sin 'pléid'. Ann am *Bàrdachd Ghàidhlig*, tha W. J. Watson a' radh: '*pléid* [. . .] spite. wrangle; Ir. *pléid*, spite'. Ach ann an eadar-theangachadh an dàin 'Cia don phléid as ceann uidhe?'[24] se a tha aige ach 'Whom does begging make its goal?' agus mar sin air feadh an dàin; fiù is gu ruige 'cia ar gceann pléide is fanámhad : who now is our chief beggar and our chief butt?' – seagh nach eil uile gu léir sùmhail, thar liom, san t-suidheachadh.

Chaidh an dàn a dheasachadh as ùr le William Gillies; tha esan a' dèanamh 'disputation' den fhacal 'pléid' agus a' ràdh ann an nota: 'For the meaning of *pléid* which Watson took as 'begging', v. RIA Contrib., Dineen, etc.'[25] Tha sin cho cothromach is a ghabhas. Ach tha e dearbhte on fhaclair ann am *Bàrdachd Ghàidhlig* nach b'ann air amas ach a dh'aon ghnothach a rinn Watson 'begging' de 'phléid', ged nach do rinn e soilleir ciamar a thàinig e chuige.

Tha 'pléid' aig Iain MacCodrum dà uair is tha dà chiall mu choinneamh san eadar-theangachadh aig William Matheson: 'spite' san dala h-àite agus 'adulation' san àite eile; 'ionadail cairdeil gun phléid : approachable and friendly without adulation';[26] rud a tha caran den aon ghnè ri 'fàilte gun phléid' aig Eoghan MacLachlainn ged nach e sin an seagh a tha Watson a' toirt às san fhaclair ann am *Bàrdachd Ghàidhlig.*[27]

Ma ghabhas sinn ri beachd nan urracha sin, gun an corr eadar-sgaraidh a dhèanamh, tha rèidhleach cuibheasach farsaing againn le 'begging, wrangle, spite, disputation, adulation'. Chan eil e 'nam ruigheachd-sa breith chothromach a thoirt eatorra a thoradh is nach eil e riatanach an sgrùdadh seach sin an-dràsta; ach tha e aithnichte gu bheil an t-sreath mhìneachaidh a' thathar a' toirt do 'phléid' a' tighinn air àrainn na crìche aig 'bleid' a thaobh brìgh, le brosgal is faighdhe is buaireadh car 'nan caitcheann aca eatorra.

Anns an fhaclair aig Maclennan[28] gheibhear dà fhacal: 'pléid'. Tha an toiseach '*pléid* [. . .] spite, wrangle'; an uairsin '*pléid* [. . .] solicitation, imposing on good nature. See *bleid*.' Tha e annasach gu bheil '*pleid*, solicitation; see *bleid*' aig MacBain[29] cuideachd: is ma dh'fhaoidhte gu robh buaidh aig sin air Maclennan. Co-dhiubh, tha an eadar-iomlaid b~p cumanta gu leòr, gu sonraichte sna fa-cail-iasaid: Bìobla~Pìobla, briogais~priogais, is mar sin air n-adhart.

Nise, anns na litrichean aig Edmund Burt, san ochdamh ceud deug – thòisich e orra ann an 1726 – tha cunntas air luchd-taic ceann-cinnidh 'nam measg:

```
. . . Bard      His Poet
Bladier    His Spokesman . . .³⁰
```

Ann an 1831 tha ion is an aon chunntas aig James Logan ach gu bheil neoni de leasachadh air:

The Bladair, or spokesman
The Bard . . .[31]

Gu dé an cruth a bhiodh air *bladier* / *bladair* ann an Gàidhlig? Nas lugha na se iomrall a tha san *-ier* aig Burt, dh'fhaodadh *bladier* a bhith 'na riochd Beurla air 'bleidir' no air 'bléidir'. Ach a chionn is nach eil *bléidir, cho fad is fiosrach mi, ri a fhaighinn sa chànan, dh'fheuma-maid a dhealbh on fhacal 'bléidrich', le 'pléid: 2' aig Maclennan a' toirt taic dha; is chan eil an stéidh sin ach cugallach.

Tha an clàr-ainm anns a bheil 'bladair' aig Logan a' cur air shùilean duinn gu bheil e an eisimeil a' chunntais aig Burt. Ma tha, carson a rinn Logan 'bladair' den fhacal? An do thog e cearr e? No an robh fiosrachadh eile aige fhéin gu pearsanta gura h-e 'bladair(e)' a theirte ri a leithid seo de fhear-dreuchd ann an Gàidhlig; air neo – rud a tha car a-cosail – an e oidhirp air 'bleidir' a chur an céill a th'ann? Tha Dwelly a' toirt duinn s. v. 'bladair: 8, One of the followers of a Highland chief'; se as ughdar dha sin faclair Armstrong, a nochd an 1825, sia bliadhna mun tàinig an leabhar aig Logan a-mach, is e air a stéid-heachadh gu ìre bhig air Gàidhlig Siorrachd Pheairt. Ach chan eil cinnt co-dhiubh sann à Gàidhlig na dùthcha sin no à Gàidhlig eile a thug Armstrong an seagh sonraichte a tha an seo.

San àite mu dheireadh tha 'bleidein' againn. Ann an dhà-no-trì de na h-òrain-luaidh tha iomairt aig dithis bhan air a chéile, a' moladh is a' diomoladh, gach té a' bruidhinn as leth na fine aice fhéin; agus gheabhar ràdh 'thàinig bleidein' san rann. Mar seo: 'Thàinig bleidein bleidein bòsdail | Le mheilibheid 's le spuir 's bòtainn'[32] air neo, ann an samhail eile: 'Thàinig bleidein | bleidein leòmach'.[33]

Tha iad sin air an eadar-theangachadh: 'There came a pleading, boastful blether | Wearing velvet, spurred and booted'; agus 'Came a wheedler, a saucy wheedler'.

Tha am bleidein a' cur ceist: 'Ciod e bu bheus . . . ? Gu dé b'fhasan . . . ?' (do na Leòdaich no do Chlann Domhnaill) a tha a' toirt cothrom dhan duine eile teannadh air a' mholadh.

A réir éideadh a' bhleidein, far a bheil sin air a ainmeachadh, chan e duine cumanta a tha ann ach fear de na h-urracha-móra. (Ann an cuid de na h-òrain se té – 'i' air a ghabhail oirre – a tha sa bhleidein; chan eil an sin ach atharrachadh, tha mi a' dèanamh dheth, a thugadh às anns na h-òrain-luaidh is iad fuaighte ri saoghal nam ban.) Ma tà, an e duine-uasal a th'ann, is e ri bleid? Dh'fhaodadh e bhith. Ach gu dé masa h-e a dhreuchd a tha a' toirt na h-inbhe dha is gura h-e am 'bladier', mar a tha aig Burt air, aig a' cheann-chinnidh a th'ann? Nan gabhamaid ris an tuairmse sin, chuireamaid 'spokesman' no a leithid an àite 'blether/wheedler' san eadar-theangachadh; dhèanamaid 'proud, conceited' de 'leòmach' agus 'swaggering, vaunting' is mar sin de 'bhleideil, bòsdail'.

A-nise, suim an rannsachaidh. Tha 'Bleidirean' 'na leasainm air na Ceardannan a bha gus o chionn grunnan bhliadhnaichean a' dol air chuairt; bha 'bleidir' no 'bladair' (no is docha 'bléidir' fhéin) 'na fhear-dreuchd aig na cinn-chinnidh; tha 'bleidein', an uchd moladh is diomoladh fine, a' tighinn an làthair anns na h-òrain-luaidh.

Seallamaid air an t-suidheachadh mar seo. Bha na baird o thùs air an roinn 'nan rangan. Mar a bha sochairean an fhilidh a' cnàmh às, bha tàrmachadh a' tighinn sna rangan a b'airde; agus, gu ìre co-dhiubh, dh'oighrich na baird sin air dìleab an fhilidh. Tha sin uile riaghailteach stéidhte. Chan fhuilear nach robh buaidh aig a' ghlua-sad seo air an ord air fad. Ri linn gach caisleachadh a bha ann an uairsin, no fada roimhe sin, rinneadh ainm tàireil de 'Chléir Shean-chain'.

Bha breath de na 'baird bheaga' ris an cainte Bleidirean; gu h-àraid san Iar thuath, is dòcha, ma tha dual Lochlannach san amaladh a tha ann.[34] Ach dh'fhaoidhte 'bard' a ràdh ris a h-uile rang dhiubh, on fhear a b'uachdraiche chon an fhir a b'ìochdraiche, mar a chunnaic sinn.

Bhiodh na Bleidirean a' dol air chuairt cuide ri luchd-ceirde is ri baigearan; bhiodh iad air earrainn den Chléir Sheanchain air a bheil na h-eachdraidhean againn a' cumail cuimhne bheò; air neo bha a' Chliar Sheanchain agus na Bleidirean co-ionnan. Nuair a chaidh a' Chliar Sheanchain mu sgaoil, mhair an t-ainm 'na Bleidirean', ach mhair e 'na fharainm air companaich nam bard, na Ceardannan.

Ann an caochladh àiteachan is aig caochladh àmannan, dh'éirich am bleidir ann an inbhe, cleas mar a dh'éirich rangan uachdrach nam bard. An iomall a deas na Gàidhealtachd, mura h-e 'bleidir' (no 'bléidir') an titeil, se 'bladair' an t-ainm dòigheil. Chan eil sa bhleidein ach am bleidir ann an riochd eile. Las is gu bheil an ceangal, tha failbheag eadar na h-òrain-luaidh (an seòrsa òran anns am faighear am bleidein an lùib a' mholaidh is an diomolaidh) agus mìr den bhardachd a rinn Bard-is-pìobaire MhicDhomhnaill is e a' moladh Dhomhnaill Ghuirm agus beus na cùrtach aige.

Ged a tha seagh cho tàireil aig 'bleidir(e)', 'bleidein' agus 'bladair(e)' an-diugh, chan airde na sin cliù na Cléir Sheanchain.

Aon phuing eile; tha seanfhacal againn: 'urram a' bhleidire dhan t-sràcaire', air a bheil an tionntadh Beurla: 'The sneak's deference to the swaggerer'. Ach am faod e bhith gu bheil ciall nas eagarra air a chùl?

Tha am facal 'sracaire' stéidhte sa chànan is tha e againn, a réir coltais, ann an 'Duanaire na Sracaire' ann an Leabhar an Deadhain.[35] Am faodadh e bhith, ga tà, gura h-e 's(t)ràcaire' a th'ann? An co-bhuinn ri sin, thigeadh e dhuinn a' cheist seo a chur: uair de robh an saoghal, am buineadh an s(t)ràcaire e fhéin do ord muinntir nan dàn is nan òran?

Is gann a ruigear a leas a ràdh nach eil anns a' chuid-mhór de na sgrìobh mi an seo ach cothlamadh de cheistean is de thuairim. Sann a dh'aon ghnothach a sheachain mi na tha ri fhaotainn agus ri mheas sa Ghàidhlig Éireannaich ged a tha ruith de na h-aon fhacail – pléid, bleid, bladaire – an sin cuideachd.

Fàgam a' cheist sin aig an fhear as eòlaiche agus as ealanta a tha ann, an rannsachadh cainnte is faclaireachd. An cois a bhith a' cur meal an naidheachd air, bu cheart a ràdh nach urrainnear urram nas airde a chur air faclairiche sam bith na snaidhm-gruaimein den t-seòrsa seo a shìneadh dha, le cinnt ma tha fuasgladh air gura h-esan am fear as fhearr dhan aithne sin a dhèanamh de na tha an sàs san obair air 'feadh an ghormfhuinn Ghaoidhealaigh'.

English Summary by the Editor

This essay explores a number of related Gaelic words (*bleid, bleidir-ean, bléidirich, blad, bladair, bladaireachd*) and their usages in regards to the terms for and functions of poets. These terms resemble, and seem to be ultimately related to, English words such as 'blather', 'blether', 'blatter' and 'bladry'.

MacInnes posits a chain of social and linguistic developments to account for the evidence as we have it. The poetic order was always a hierarchical one, with poets arranged in ranks of degree. According to some early sources, chieftains had in his retinue a spokesman called *bleidir*(or a variation of this term), presumably engaged in praise and dispraise. In some circumstances (especially on the margins of Gael-dom, and during the decline of the formally trained poetic order), distinctions between ranks of poets were muddled, and some bleidir-ean may have achieved a degree of prestige and recognition. The legendary travelling band A' Chliar Sheanchain seems to have been constituted in part or sometimes entirely of bleidirean and they frequently kept company with the travelling people and with beggars. After A' Chliar Sheanchain disbanded, the term bleidirean became associated most strongly with the travelling people.

Gaelic Poetry in the Nineteenth Century

The poets of the nineteenth century inherited a broken world. A new world was meantime emerging, often with cataclysmic effect, all around them. They composed poetry, of course, as individuals, out of individual sensibilities, and the Gaelic reader will evaluate them individually, poets and poems alike. But in such a study as this we have to pay attention also to the sociology of the poetry, where failure is as interesting as success. We must ask what structures these poets inherited from the past; which among these was adaptable, and which had already reached an unrepeatable perfection. What strategies could Gaelic poets now adopt if they were to cope with the demands of their age?

Literacy in vernacular Gaelic – the adaptation, in the eighteenth century, of Classical Gaelic orthography – is obviously a very important factor. In the nineteenth century there is a dramatic increase in the number of books of Gaelic poetry in print. But even literate poets may use traditional styles, and Gaelic poets certainly did so. There were still current, particularly before the Clearances, vast repertoires of oral song-poetry, aristocratic as well as plebeian, much of it exhibiting stylistic features that worked semiotically, revealing the ancient landmarks of the Gaelic cosmos. The forces that shaped Gaelic society had also ordained that poets came to occupy a role as the acknowledged spokesmen of society – custodians of its identity – sustaining and celebrating a conservative social order through the development of bardic praise-poetry.

In the eighteenth century that order was destroyed; its bardic conventions, expressing the customary expectations of Gaelic society, were now anachronistic; yet the panegyric code of the bards had long since become a pervasive style in Gaelic poetry. The result was that the more nineteenth-century poets confined themselves to the security of established practice, the less likely were they to be able to cope realistically with the problems of their contemporary situation. The farther they moved away, on the other hand, from these stylistic codes that gave Gaelic poetry such a distinctive flavour, the less likely was their acceptance as poets in what was still, in the main, a traditional society. Those who did experiment were first and foremost those who had been formally educated in English or who had educated themselves. It is important to remember that the 'university of art' – *univers na h-ealadhna*: the courses of instruction in colleges of poetry and rhetoric – was long gone. In the nineteenth century there was no rounded, let alone liberal, education possible in Gaelic. It is very much the century of the Gaelic autodidact.

Writing in 1918, W J Watson, with characteristic clarity and directness, has this to say:

> The poetry of the nineteenth century, with some exceptions [. . .] shows increasing English influence in style, thought, and metre. Much of this later poetry is pretty and witty, but it has little of the old fire and virility; often, not without reason, it expresses the wail of a dejected and harassed people. It is at this stage, and at no other, that the famous 'Celtic Gloom' is to be found in the literature, when the Gaelic people were left dependent, intellectually and economically, on what was to them a foreign and distasteful culture. The poetry that was inspired by the infamies of Culloden and the Clearances could not be other than gloomy.

Watson's own criteria are clear. As a classicist, he notes that in the older Gaelic world the qualities which go to make Gaelic poets *Gaelic*

> are very different from what English-speaking people of the present day are accustomed to. In fact, the poets' outlook on things and the qualities that appealed to them – race, physical beauty, manly accomplishments, free-handed generosity, wisdom in council – are more akin to what is found in Homer and Pindar.[1]

If such are our criteria, these judgements are perfectly defensible. Later writers, as one might expect, have not all taken such an unequivocal stance. Nonetheless, in what literary criticism we have (most of it written in English and perhaps subtly conditioned by that) the main thrust of Watson's argument has not been turned.[2] We still measure nineteenth-century poetry against the great triumphs of our past. We still agree, however reluctantly, that the social conditions of the age and the poetry that reflects them mark our lowest point. We find the poetry nostalgic and anachronistic, still limited by the stereotype of panegyric or going off in false directions that could lead to nothing but sentimentality, as when it borrows from English or Scots and reproduces weak and prettified aspects of Romanticism.

Yet the fact of the matter is that this poetry is much less dull and trivial than that would suggest. Watson himself noted, in his sweeping judgement, that there were 'exceptions': they are the poets whose imaginative world is still that of heroic society and its praise-singers. Their poetry is still instinct with the old, splendid craftsmanship; and they are not alone in that respect. But equally conspicuous to the historian are the writers of 'Heroic' poetry which even in its own time was held by some to be bogus. The question of authenticity has been decided long since in favour of the sceptics, but the poetry is none the less nineteenth-century Gaelic poetry; and its acceptance by Gaels – partial acceptance, it may be, by a minority of readers – demands our consideration accordingly. Under the influence of Romanticism and other movements, some of them in religion (and there is a vast corpus of religious poetry deriving from this century) sensibilities were being extended. There is a palpable widening and deepening of human sympathies. We may deplore dependence on 'a foreign and distasteful culture' and deprecate the 'increasing English influence in style, thought, and metre'. More trenchantly, we have to go on to ask whether it is these influences, in themselves, that are to be deplored; or is it the circumstances, the denial of cultural opportunity, that pre-vented poets from drawing upon an even wider range of influences, from absorbing them, from turning them to their own advantage, in the creation of a contemporary poetry?

A similar question must arise in a political context. There are some poets who are realistic enough in their political observations without apparently being able to place these observations in a sufficiently wide frame of reference. We may, of course, if we wish, see the poetry of the century as a strange amalgam: the unsettled complex of a transitional age. But if we view it, as indeed we must, from within Gaelic society itself, we shall find it at least as rich and rewarding as that of any other period in Gaelic history. In geographical distribution it spans the Gàidhealtachd, literally *o Hirt gu Peairt* ('between Perth and St Kilda'), as the traditional phrase has it, from Aberdeenshire to Dunbartonshire, from Sutherland to Argyll, and south to the Island of Arran. In its diversity of aims and levels of writing, it serves to remind us that we are dealing not with one simple tradition but with what is still the art of a nation. Parochial limitations there may be but there are also European dimensions.

From the events that cluster round the end of the eighteenth century and the beginning of the nineteenth, we can without difficulty select a number that signal for us some of the activities that characterise the history of the century and the themes we shall encounter in the poetry. In 1785, the first large-scale Clearances were carried out on the Glengarry estates; the following year there were extensive emigrations to Canada, from the same lands. In 1800, the first Clearances occurred in Sutherland. In 1807, publication of the Gaelic Bible (New Testament, 1767; Old Testament, completed in 1801) concluded a process that leads back into the seventeenth century; although only from 1767 onwards was the sacred text made linguistically accessible to all.

In 1807 also there appeared the 'official text' of *The Poems of Ossian in the original Gaelic*. (The 1818 'Ossian' was published 'for the general good of the people of the Gàidhealtachd'; it was distributed free throughout the Highlands and a copy sent to every parish school where Gaelic was taught.) In 1804, the brothers Alexander and Donald Stewart published a celebrated anthology of poems 'collected in the Highlands and Isles': one of the primary sources for the study of Gaelic poetry, it continues a cultural campaign which began in the eighteenth century and goes on throughout the nineteenth. Finally, in 1801 the British Expeditionary Force under General Sir Ralph Abercromby landed at Abukir Bay in Egypt and won a decisive victory, although Abercromby himself was killed, at Alexandria. The loyalty of his Highland Regiments and Abercromby's appreciation of their gallantry are duly recorded: 'My brave Highlanders, remember your country, remember your forefathers.'[3]

All of these events, one way or another, are diagnostic. The themes they suggest: military glory in the service of the expanding British Empire; celebration of the religious life, set in the context of a Protestant Evangelicalism; emigration and concern with conditions of life in the New World, its attractions or its hardships; all are woven into the fabric of the verse. There also runs through it, as a terrible *leitmotif*, the theme of dispossession. And almost everywhere, variously expressed, we can sense a continuing Gaelic identity. Poets are still the spokesmen of society.

Initially at any rate the Gaelic response to military service was direct, naive, and enthusiastic. As in other parts of the Empire, a warrior tradition was given a new setting, with enough in the way of military trappings and emblems to maintain a feeling of continuity. The kilt and the bagpipes, both allowed in the Army after they were otherwise proscribed in 1746, were of course the egregious symbols.

An anonymous song, composed apparently between 1746 and the rescinding of the Disarming Act in 1782, makes a vivid and revealing comment. A young Gael complains that since the tartan dress has been taken away, no girl will look at him. He has put on the grey trousers, like the Lowlander who lives on the far side of the Clyde. Then he continues:

Tha mi màireach dol dhan Arm
Gheibh me eibhleadh 's còta dearg
Bonaid bhiorach mholach ghorm
Slat de ribein stoirm mam chluais[4]

Tomorrow I am going to the army
I shall get a kilt and a red coat
A shaggy, cocked, blue bonnet
A yard of ribbon storming about my ears.

That new identity was securely established by 1800. The Cameron Highlanders, for instance, were raised in 1793, the Gordon Highlanders, the 92nd Regiment, in 1794.

Alexander MacKinnon from Arisaig (1770–1814) enlisted in the 92nd Regiment when he was twenty-four years of age. He fought with Abercromby in Egypt in 1801 (where he was severely wounded and left for dead on the field) as previously he had fought with Abercromby and Moore in the Netherlands campaign in 1779. He celebrated both experiences in songs entitled 'The Battle of Holland' and 'The Battle of Egypt'; these paeans earned him lasting fame. MacKinnon is one of two exceptional poets who W. J. Watson singles out as being unaffected by increasing English influence in style, thought and metre. In spirit at least his war-songs are the celebrations of a Gaelic warrior in a British imperial setting. In 'The Battle of Egypt' he retails the tactical moves of the action in detail: this is description by an involved professional observer. But he has his bardic models to guide him and the campaign 'well deserved a bard to sing it'. Abercromby is 'ar n-ard cheannfeadhna' ('our high chief'); 'commander-in-chief' but, more precisely, the leader of band of picked warriors, a comitatus: this is a commander 'who could inspire us to action like Fionn rousing the host'.

Such songs run like a continuous thread through the nineteenth century, as campaign follows campaign, to the Crimean and Boer Wars. (They are found, indeed, as late as the Second World War.) In their realism of observation they have a strong and authentic voice. They also carry, and modify, the traditional formulas of panegyric: these signals that give the poets, and us, our bearings. To a foreign reader they are probably on the whole tedious, their value lying in their historical testimony to a successful transference of loyalties and the forging of identity in a novel setting. But from within Gaelic society they are charters that reflect and endorse a new security. Their aesthetic power is inextricably bound up with the assertions they make.

They exist, however, on a different literary level from certain other songs that touch on war and service in the British Army. From an anonymous song, probably by a woman, come these verses about the same 'Battle of Egypt':

Och, alas, brown-haired lad
Handsome brown-haired lad
Och, alas, brown-haired lad

That battle they fought in Egypt
(After it) they did not rise together [. . .]

Stretched out in the rushes
Blood pouring about their shoulders

Stretched out without a pillow
And gold will not ransom them

Many a gentleman's daughter
Will now lie alone[5]

or this, from 'Òran an t-Saighdeir' ('The Soldier's Song'):

One day when I was out strolling
High on the Brae of Edinburgh
Who should I meet but a soldier
And he asked me what was my news.

He said: 'Enlist in the Army
It's the best profession under the sun
You'll have silver in your pockets
And gold you'll never need!'

The young man is talked into enlisting and given a musket (feminine in Gaelic):

They gave me to carry
A grey-faced female who won't wash my shirt for me
One they call Janet, Daughter of King George,
And little do I care for her.

A pity they haven't got her locked up
In the great Castle of Edinburgh
Long might she live there
Before I'd ask how she was.

Songs of this type, however, are practically non-existent in the collections of the nineteenth century although that 'Soldier's Song', for example, is one of the most popular in oral tradition to the present day. But absence from the written record of soldiers' protest songs should not delude us into thinking there was a strong underground anti-military tradition.

At any rate, the songs that have survived to be collected in the twentieth century express no more than the common soldier's complaint the world over with his lot. From 'The Soldier's Song' again:

My curse upon the French
Mustering their camps
And my curse upon the Colonel
He didn't even give us furlough
The girls all getting married
And I can't have one of them.

At least as common, even in oral tradition, are statements such as this, from a song with the refrain:

O light we thought the journey, leaving happily
with little sorrow, going to meet Bonaparte,
because he threatens King George.

Though only the Gaels should be there,
manly, handsome, strong, they would put the fear of death
into every enemy alive [. . .]

Hearty lads, let us be merry,
Let us uphold our country's honour [. . .]
Scotland, Ireland and England, at present
joined together: they are of one mind,
like the sound between flint and hammer.[6]

The modern reader may well feel there is an ironic ring to that neat metaphor that expresses British unanimity but none is intended. Neither is there any emotion but pride in the words of the Skye soldier who hopes to return to the 'Land of MacLeod' – even if the last phrase might suggest otherwise.

> *Nuair a chuir iad sinn air bord*
> *Anns an ordugh bu ghrinne*
> *Bha gach fear is bean a' ràdh*
> *'Cha dean pàirt aca tilleadh' [. . .]*
>
> *Nuair a chuir iad sinn air tìr*
> *Am measg sìoban is muran*
> *Thug sinn batal air an tràigh*
> *Is gun d'rinn pàirt againn fuireach [. . .]*
>
> *Thainig esan, mac an Rìgh,*
> *Is mar aon dhinn 'sa chuideachd:*
> *'An iad seo Gàidheil an Taobh Tuath?*
> *Bha iad bhuam is fhuair mi uil' iad.'*[7]

When they put us on board
in finest order
every man and woman was saying
'Some of them will never return' [. . .]

When they put us ashore
amongst the spume and the bent-grass
we fought a battle on the shore
and some of us stayed there [. . .]

He himself came– the King's son –
he was as one of ourselves in the company:
'Are these the Gaels of the north?
I needed them, and I have got them all.'

If it is true to say that the British Empire and the Highland Regiments recreated the Gaelic view of the world, so that now the enemies of the Empire were the enemies of the Gael also, it is even truer that religion brought a new identity. The mediating process here is what is sometimes known as the 'Evangelical Movement', sometimes as the 'Evangelical Revival'. It was a Protestant movement (the greater part of the Highlands and Islands had been Protestant since the

Reformation) manifesting itself among Presbyterians, Baptists, Congregationalists, etc, and bound up with social protest. Evangelicalism was a highly complex, asymmetrical movement which did not affect all communities equally, and certainly not all individuals in any community. Nevertheless, it is not an exaggeration to say that overall it produced something like a cosmological revolution in Gaelic society. For that reason it is necessary to look in some detail at the background to the religious poetry of the nineteenth century.

The immediate setting is that of Gaelic society midway through the first period of major Clearances (1782–1846). Chiefs and tacksmen had turned against their own tenantry: the tenants were by now developing their own hostility against landlords. In a traditional, hierarchical society, in which there were no social mechanisms to organise expression of 'untraditional' emotions, the hostility demanded formulation by a circuitous route. Religion provided just that.

The process had began in the eighteenth century when religious poets were the first to protest against the tyrannical exactions of landlordism; when Dugald Buchanan, for instance, in his poem 'An Gaisgeach' ('hero, warrior', etc) displaces the hero of tradition and bardic praise with the hero of Christian life and belief. And in 'An Claigeann' ('The Skull'), his attack on contemporary rack-renting is charged with anger and contempt. Buchanan's influence was enormous; his poetry, printed, but very soon also circulating orally (controlled by the written text), set and sung to traditional secular melodies, spread throughout the Gàidhealtachd. His own conversion, from what he and his kind would call nominal Christianity to an austere and passionate faith, occurred when the Gaelic world, a relatively fixed social order, had already been shattered in the aftermath of the Forty-Five, and the ancient cultural landmarks were being uprooted.

These changes of course continued; the exactions of the landlords intensified; the attitudes of the tenantry changed in reaction to them. Even those who did not personally experience a radical conversion could hardly fail to be affected by a religious movement which so unflinchingly acknowledged the misery of human existence. It squared only too well with contemporary Gaelic experience. The world was essentially a place of suffering, a vale of tears. Nor was there any comfort to be found, if people were realistic, in nostalgia. A Golden Age was mere sentimentality.

In a poem that opens with a traditional formula 'Mìle marbhphaisg ort a shaoghail' ('World, a thousand shrouds[8] upon you!'), Mrs Mary Clark, 'Bean Thorra Dhamh', in Badenoch (*c. 1740–c.* 1815), is one of the earliest poets to comment on that. The formulaic opening would be immediately recognisable; the reference to the pre-Forty-Five law of pit and gallows and the rule of chiefs is startlingly new:

Chuir iad cas air reachd na fìrinn
Is ghluais iad dìchiollach 'san droch-bheart
Claoidh nam bochd 's gan lot le mìorùn
Banntraich 's dilleachdain gun choiseachd
B'uamhasach an cleachdadh tìre
Croich is binn air aird gach cnocain
Cùirt nan spleadh gun lagh gun fhìrinn
Is tric a dhìt an tì bha neo-chiont'.[9]

They placed their foot on the rule of truth
and they proceeded diligently in mischief
harassing the poor and wounding them with malice –
widows and orphans without the power of walking:
fearful was the custom of the country –
a gallows and sentence on the summit of every hillock:
the court of make-believe, without law, without truth –
often did it condemn the innocent.

The Gaels now had the Bible in Gaelic. It is true the translation was in a 'high' register of the language (derived, though at one or two removes, from Classical Gaelic), but as Gaelic literacy was founded on Bible reading, through the narrow, religious curriculum of the Gaelic schools, and at home through the innovation of family worship, this soon ceased to be a barrier to understanding. Biblical diction presently became an important part of the fabric of spiritual songs, creating a new rhetoric of exposition, providing a new reservoir of imagery; and used with the same ease, and to much the same good effect, as Marxist jargon elsewhere in political argumentation.

An even more alarming consequence was that the laity were now able to interpret the Scriptures for themselves, without relying on the clergy: worst still, they began to judge the faith and works of their ministers in the light of Biblical standards. What one landlord described as 'the peasant religion' had clearly arrived. To the ordinary people it was *An Creideamh Mór* 'The Great Faith', from whose subversive influence, according to Skye tradition, ministers prayed to be delivered.

The popular conception of the Established Church minister is that of a man of levity, given to hunting and shooting, highly convivial ('as good a drinker [. . .] as the laird' – a severe standard), violinist and piper, the best dancer in the parish, a fine judge of horseflesh, and much concerned with good husbandry and agricultural development. Some of the descriptions may be slightly exaggerated but there is plenty of contemporary evidence to make it plain they are on the whole true. The Rev. Roderick MacLeod of Skye (1794–1868) – the famous Maighstir Ruairi, who himself later became one of the leaders of the Evangelicals – confessed that at the beginning of his ministry 'his mind was occupied with his barge, and steed, and gun, and such-like amusements': he was frequently the violinist who played at the dances that followed upon funerals. When MacLeod was settled in Skye in 1823, one of his first duties was to assist his fellow-presbyters in finding their beds after a clerical gathering. 'Presbyteries are for the most part held at public houses [. . .]', another writer comments, and 'The holy fathers stand in no need of Paul's advice to Timothy respecting his weak stomach.'[10]

It was against these 'Moderates', as they were called, that the Evangelical 'Men' (*na Daoine*, that is to say, the laymen) and an emergent clergy, drawn from the lower classes of society, set their faces and the poets their songs. Traditionally the clergy of the Established Church in the Highlands were drawn from the upper classes; in addition to aristocratic lineage, which many of them could claim, they formed an 'aristocracy of learning' – as the learned orders of medieval and later Gaelic society have been described. The Presbyterian ministers in fact continued the significant role and function of the earlier Gaelic literati: throughout the nineteenth century they are among the foremost collectors of the song-poetry of oral tradition. Highly educated, well-versed in the Classics, they were gentlemen farmers, sometimes on a very large scale. In the 1840s, John Matheson of Uist in his 'Òran na h-Eaglais' ('The Song of the Church'), expresses the Evangelical view of them in a parody of the Creed:

Creideam an crodh is an caoraich
Creideam an stìopainibh mór
Creideam 'san duais tha mi faotainn
An t-airgead, an glìob, is an t-òr
Creideam 'san uachdaran thìmeil
An aghaidh an nì a deir Pol.

Creideam an cumhnanta gnìomha
Creideam am dhèanadas féin
Creideam 'sa' Phatronage bhreugaich
A dh'èalaidh a-staigh air a' chléir
A dh'fhògar na teachdairean diadhaidh
Nuair chunnaic iad ìomhaigh na béist.[11]

I believe in cattle and sheep
I believe in great stipends
I believe in the rewards I receive
silver and glebe and gold
I believe in the temporal lord
In the face of what Paul declares.

I believe in the covenant of works
I believe in my own achievement
I believe in the lying Patronage
that has crept in upon the clergy
which the godly messengers drove out
when they saw the image of the beast.

Matheson is said to have 'made a bolt for freedom' and deserted the Evangelicals – but he made his mark while he was there. The new faith had allowed him to express the common opinion, shared by converted and unconverted alike.

It is well to emphasise again the grass-roots nature of this social and religious upheaval. The ordinary tenantry, turning against their land-lords, turned also against their clergy, who belonged to the same social stratum. The clergy, for their part, regarded religious enthusiasm with grave suspicion as a parochial variety of a wider subversive move-ment, which threatened Church and State alike. They themselves were loyal members of a State church and their sermons were often said to contain news of British imperial victories. In some instances, indeed, these topics apparently formed the staple of the address. By such means, the role of the Gael in a military context would have been bolstered. The Evangelicals, ironically, did not extend their opposition to that aspect of clerical instruction. Instead, they tended to align themselves with the view that British imperialism was a civilising influence in the world. Foxe's *Book of Martyrs*, with its sense of England's divine mission, was known; it was an acceptable document in certain Evangelical circles and contributed still further to security

within a universal social order. Very occasionally, we may find a hint
of another view:

> *Is fhad on thòisich an aimhreit*
> *Is an ainneart tha mór*
> *Dhùisg an cogadh an Càin*
> *Mharbh e bhràthair gu h-òg*
> *Bha an claidheamh 's gach linn*
> *A' cur nam mìltean fo 'n fhòid*
> *Dhòirteadh aibhnichean fala*
> *Tre shannt, an-iochd is pròis.*[12]

> Long ago did disagreement begin
> and excessive force
> warfare awoke in Cain
> he killed his brother when he was young
> the sword in every age
> has put thousands beneath the sod
> spilling rivers of blood
> through greed, cruelty and pride.

But these statements from John MacLean's 'An Cogadh Naomh' ('The
Holy War'), even if that 'War' is spiritual, do not actually recommend
pacifism. Such poems draw on the bardic images of the warrior, still
asserting cultural continuities. Side by side with them, we have poems
in tribute to colonial missionaries, such as Peter Grant's 'Òran nam
Misionaraidh' ('The Song of the Missionaries') or another of Mac-
Lean's poems 'Craobh-sgaoileadh an t-Soisgeil' ('The spreading of the
Gospel'):

> *Luchd-teagaisg diadhaidh truacant*
> *Tha dol thar na stuadhan ard*
> *Tha sluagh cur cùl ri ìomhaighean*
> *'S a' tighinn gu Ìos le gràdh.*[13]

> Compassionate, godly instructors
> who go across the high sea billows
> the people turn their backs on images
> and come to Jesus with love.

This is simply the standard British view expressed in Gaelic. The
poetry that carries it is often pedestrian but it is not parochial. Behind
it lies a coherent theory of history: God's will is at work in the

historical process; the Gaels have their own place in that scheme; and finally, at the end of time, universal peace will descend upon all.

Psychologically, the price the Gaels paid for this world-view was that they came to regard the Gàidhealtachd itself as a heathen mission-field. It was not, of course, an entirely new attitude: Alcuin's famous question with regard to the singing of English heroic ballads: 'What has Ingeld to do with Christ?' had been echoed by clergymen who regarded the Gaelic heroic ballads as myths of a competing faith. But while Gaelic society was relatively whole, the clergy in general gave the secular arts encouragement and respect. Now, however, when so much of the distinctive social order lay in ruins, anything that symbolised the traditional Gaelic arts came under attack as 'vanity'.

Chan noimheachd air Oisean nam Fiann
No gaisgeach bha riamh am feachd
Cha noimheachd air creachadh nan Gall
Le ceatharn nan gleann 's nan stùchd
No idir air siubhal nan gleann
An éideadh nach ceangladh glùn.
Chan noimheachd air fineachan treun
A chogadh 's nach géilleadh beò
Clann Ghriogair bha aineolach treun
Clann Domhnaill le'm b'aiteas làmh dhearg
Clann Chamshroin bha calma gun chéill
Ach noimheachd air soisgeul nan gràs
Bhi sgaoileadh 's gach aird mu'n cuairt.[14]

Not a tale of Ossian of the Fian
nor any hero in a host
not a tale of plundering the Lowlanders
by the caterans of the glens and the mountains
nor any tale of roaming the glens in the dress that does not impede the knees
nor a tale of brave clans
who would fight and never surrender till death
Clan Gregor who were strong, and ignorant
Clan Donald whose delight was the Red Hand
Clan Cameron who were bold, without sense
none of these but the news of the gospel of grace
spreading in every airt all around.

So James MacGregor, in 1825. Peter Grant (1783–1867), a Baptist minister and one of the most renowned writers of Gaelic spiritual songs, attacks the singing of secular songs, gatherings in houses of music, and levity in general; and lists them beside Sabbath-breaking, drunkenness, swearing, and all manner of superstition.

Peter Grant of Strathspey is the type of one kind of Evangelical; the Rev. Dr John MacDonald (1779–1849), minister of Ferintosh, and known as the 'Apostle of the North', is of another, and very different, kind. MacDonald was not an ascetic at all: he was robust and convivial, a piper all his life, and interested enough in Gaelic secular poetry to have made a valuable collection from oral tradition of Fenian ballads. His own poetry, all of it religious, consists for the most part of versified exposition and exhortation but without the extraordinary eloquence which is said to have marked his extempore preaching. The elegy on his father, the saintly catechist of Reay, presenting him as an ideal of Christian life, contains some of his vivider remarks: he stresses how he hated hypocrisy:

> 'S an eudan mhùgach, bhalbh
> 'S na h-osnaidh chneadach, chiùchranach
> Gun sùgh annt' ach an dealbh.[15]

and a sullen, dumb face
groans and plaintive sighings
that have no substance in them beyond the appearance.

We shall see how another poet applied these lines later. In the same poem, he takes a palpable hit at some of the assertive laymen who moved from parish to parish, as itinerant preachers, sometimes sporting a distinctive, eccentric style of dress, and were fast becoming so anti-clerical that even the Evangelical ministers grew uneasy. The poet's father, he says, would not perplex and weary his listeners 'with hard, high questions'. This is precisely one of the charges levelled in the seventeenth century at the wandering poets, the 'inferior rhymers' who moved from place to place, quartering themselves on their unwilling hosts. It is one example of the many continuities that run beneath the surface of Gaelic cultural history.

A very great deal of the religious poetry of the nineteenth century can be characterised by a remark made by a Mull poet in 1850. He thinks his poems 'may be defective in poetry but is confident [they] are founded on the Scriptures'. Within a considerable section of Gaelic society, however, and over a very wide area of the Gàidhealtachd, they clearly had an aesthetic power. Sung to traditional melodies, dignified with formulaic passages that sometimes echoed secular poetry but more often embodied Biblical imagery, they had much the same effect in creating the sense of solidarity that bardic poetry, classical and vernacular, had in earlier ages.

We can sense in the traditions of the nineteenth century not only bewilderment with the loss of a way of life, with Clearance and emigration, but also an intellectual and spiritual hunger accompanying the physical hunger of economic poverty. Theological exposition in verse, carried by traditional music, supplied some of the needed pabulum. But this must be seen in context. Lacking alternative sources of liberal and philosophical learning, lacking, too, political and social institutions which an autonomous community would have provided, this movement developed what was essentially a recluse religion, practised in open society and seeking to dominate it. It had neither the resources nor the strategies to cope with more than a limited range of human experience.

Yet it was a movement which was full of intellectual passion and dissenting fervour and which attracted men and women of powerful mind and personality. It helped to create a spirit which was anti-authority in general, anti-ecclesiastical in particular. Rather remarkably, the energies thus engendered were spent more in theological and denominational dispute, on the one hand, and in direct action (during the years of the Land Agitation campaign[16]), on the other, than in the creation of what detached critics would call 'memorable' poetry. Religious poems of the nineteenth century stand primarily as endorsements of a state of grace – charters of Gaelic identity within that context – and their aesthetic and spiritual power derive from an undivided substance. As a matter of fact, traditional Gaelic verse, still closely tied to the recurrent melody of its stanzaic organisation, was formally too rigid to contain the passionate eloquence that found a place in the extempore prayer and the extempore sermon. They are the real art-forms of the Evangelical Revival.

There is one poet, however, whose work displays the originality and eloquence of direct experience: John Morrison (1790–1852), Iain Gobha na Hearadh 'the Harris blacksmith'. His most often quoted poem is the subtle psychological study of the Old Man and the New Man – the old Adam and the regenerate Christian. But there is much of the same freshness running through all of his poetry.

I am drowned in the 'old' man's sea
in sharp cold dew and winter's coldness
the glorious 'new' man comes to his temple
and he sets my feet a-dancing
It is the 'old' man who has made me gloomy
the 'new' man is my blazing lantern.[17]

Earlier than our period (but not published until 1816) Donald Matheson (1719–1782) in Sutherland recognised the disintegration of the old Gaelic social order and realised that God had ordained a deliverance from the hand of the oppressor.

I see a wonder
happening at this time;
we have but to listen
to what He is telling us.

I see a reflection
of what happened long ago,
when the Israelites were
in Egypt in distress.

He brought them
with a strong hand
away from Pharaoh himself
when he pursued them.

I see a wonder
happening at this time;
it is the fulfillment of a truth
revealed to us long since.

There would be a vacant land,
and people would be sent there;
there they would settle
with their cattle and their children.[18]

In the apportionment of blame for eviction and emigration, this Evangelical vision of the Promised Land – a promise of a new earthly world rather than a spiritual other world – has apparently escaped censure. Most of the enticements to emigrate were put in more mundane terms and the poems composed by emigrants in the New World, Nova Scotia in particular, show sharp contrasts between acceptance or optimism and a sense of loss and betrayal. This Christian hope, a novel variation on the old messianic theme of Gaelic tradition, was undoubtedly diffused throughout society and cannot have failed to exercise an influence.

In the poetry of Clearance and Land Agitation, landlords are the main targets. Even when we find references to ill-gotten gains, as in 'A Song for Sportsmen' by John Smith (1848–1881) – 'Some of them trafficked in opium | they gathered a great deal of riches'[19] – and the rapacity is clearly seen in a context of imperialism, there is still no suggestion that the Empire, under which the Gaels lived, was, in itself, an alien polity. In the work of other poets, there is a recurrent plea which can be summed up in the formula: 'Do not replace people with sheep for sheep will not defend Britain in the face of the enemy.' These poets were political realists but their strain of realism does not make for great, or even stirring, poetry.

There are no more than a handful of statements that overtly criticise the clergy on the specific issue of eviction: nothing comparable for instance, with the denominational violence expressed against the Established Church. Nor does the composite portrait of the 'Calvinist minister' of popular, English-language accounts ever make an appearance: the grim, pro-landlord ascetic, opposed to music and song, who at best acquiesced, preaching that such suffering was sent in retribution for the sins of the people. This last doctrine, straight or distorted in growth, has of course its roots in universal Christian teaching; but there is nothing in Scottish Gaelic verse that parallels an Irish Catholic poet's expression of it at the time of the Plantation of Ulster.

Moreover, the 'Calvinist' label, equally applicable as it is (with different sets of reservations) to both main groups, Evangelicals and Moderates, simply obscures the divisive social and cultural hostilities of the age. In actual fact, many ministers, especially among the Evangelicals – most of whom became Free Churchmen at the Disruption of 1843 – supported the crofters. One of the two greatest champions of the crofters' cause, the Rev. Roderick Macleod, Maighstir Ruairi, was Free Church, and a notorious ascetic; the other, decidedly not puritanical, was the Rev. Donald MacCallum. MacCallum was arrested and imprisoned for inciting the lieges to subversion. There are many paradoxes in all this. One of the most greatly loved clergymen of the entire Gàidhealtachd was Dr John MacDonald, mentioned above, who was certainly not a grim ascetic. Yet, whatever he may have said in his sermons, he never refers to Clearances in his poetry.

Mary MacPherson (1821–1898), Màiri Mhór nan Òran 'Big Mary of the Songs', often invokes the name of Maighstir Ruairi poignantly in her poetry and is eloquent in celebration of the Rev. Donald MacCallum. She is also the most eloquent opponent of the clergy who remained aloof.

> Preachers have so little concern
> Seeing the plight of my people –
> As dumb on the subject in the pulpit
> As though their listeners were of the brute creation.

John Smith's analysis of the issues of the time is much more intellectual than Mary MacPherson's; Smith was a university educated writer, Mary an oral poet. Each of them attacks the pharisaic aspect of Evangelicalism, each characteristically, in modes that make a fine stylistic contrast. The attack is very conspicuous in two of Smith's major poems ('The Spirit of Pride' and 'The Spirit of Kindliness'); e.g. this from the former:

> I'm certain I'm a child of grace,
>   numbered forever with the elect;
>   my belief is firm and strong,
>   and I loathe the name of pride.
> I am conscious of that love;
>   my new nature's Spirit-given,
> I praise the One who quenched my hauteur
> I'll find favour, being a lamb.[20]

Then Mary MacPherson:

> The people have become so strange
> that sorrow to them is wheat
> and if you don't go into a whelk-shell for them
> you cannot stay alive.
>
> We will not go into a whelk-shell for them
> and we can stay alive
> although we shall not put on long faces
> or wear a look of gloom
>
> with groans and plaintive sighing
> that have no substance in them but vapour
> so the world may believe
> that a Change has come upon us.

The poem ends with an eloquent rejection of the Evangelical attitude to the vanity of earthly life – including music and song:

> But because vanity is a plant
> that satisfies the flesh
> it clings to me as firmly
> as the thong does to the shoe.

The gloomy, long-faced hypocrisy which she rejects, however, is the gloomy hypocrisy that the Rev. Dr John MacDonald also inveighs against, almost in identical words, in the lines quoted above from the elegy on his own father. Given the fame of the Apostle of the North, and the people's familiarity with his spiritual songs, the connection is no doubt consciously and deliberately made.

In that climate of opinion, Màiri Mhór could hardly escape conscience-searching. But she had come to terms with herself and elected to remain robustly of this world, albeit with a strong religious sense of ultimate justice. Her introspection borrows from religion but never turns morbid. She had herself undergone a harrowing experience of unjust conviction and imprisonment for theft; it was this 'that brought my poetry into being', and the anguish of it remained ardent in her until the end of her life. But it also gave authority to her words of comfort to the Skyemen who were imprisoned in Edinburgh in 1883: 'Prison is a good college | I myself got to know that, long ago.' Mary had an intense, passionate affection for her native Skye, its community and its way of life in her own youth.

All these elements combine in her work, resolved and integrated and given a major dimension by being set in the context of nineteenth-century radicalism. She is representative of many traditional strains of Gaelic poetry, and sometimes limited by them, but her best work gives the sharp feel of immediate experience while at the same time conveying the pressure of contemporary events. Because she possesses such abundant emotional vitality and because she is not a self-conscious analyst of historical processes, the Gaelic world of the later nineteenth century, with its varied and sometimes antipathetic movements, is more vividly and intimately realised in her poetry than in that of any other poet of the age.

Among the hundreds of poets who deal with similar – and different – themes, Neil MacLeod (1843–1924) and Dr John MacLachlan (1804–1874), for example, William Livingstone (1808–1870) stands out as the self-taught man of learning, with the strengths and weaknesses of autodidactism. (In passing, one may contrast John Smith again: the formally educated writer who can construct a successful modern heroic ballad, taking some details from 'Ossian', but is never in danger of being overwhelmed by the influence of his sources or led astray by them.) Livingstone's 'Fios thun a' Bhaird' ('A Message to the Poet'), is dignified but full of anger at the desolation brought about in Islay. It is a beautiful and moving poem, in its marriage of craftsmanship and artistic sincerity.

But what a literary historian must find astonishing, especially in a writer who was so aware of contemporary issues, are his long poems: for instance, the poems set in the days of the Norsemen (two poems each running to over a thousand lines) and during the Wars of Independence. None of Livingstone's longer poems can be said to lack energy; what they are singularly lacking in is architectonic power, and for the most part they simply do not succeed. But it is the grand ambition more than the false directions that concerns us here. Livingstone, a Nationalist, Gaelic as well as Scottish, self-taught in Latin, French and Welsh, with some Greek and Hebrew, and well-read in the history of his country, is a failed epic poet. In his attempts to write 'heroic' verse, the influence of Sir Walter Scott is faintly detectable.

Within Gaelic, and easily accessible as a source of malign influences, there was 'Ossian', especially the Gaelic verse translations of James Macpherson's 'translation' from Gaelic. It is at such points as these that a vagueness of conception in design and imagery can be seen entering Gaelic poetry. This is largely a phenomenon of acculturation. Emigration to the cities, which increased in volume throughout the century, brought Gaels more and more in contact with Scots and English, and with the popular, rather than the learned, cultures of these languages. Gaelic poets in their new milieu naturally tried to 'modernise' their tradition; what they produced all too often are song-poems, sometimes composed to Lowland melodies, on sentimental subjects, where pathos is produced to order, as in poems on the death of children or other tragic losses, e.g. Neil MacLeod's 'The Death of the Widow's Child' or 'The Death of Màiri' by Evan MacColl (1808–1898):

> She died at the beginning of her beauty;
> Heaven would not spare its own;
> she died, oh Màiri died,
> like the sun quenched at its rising.[21]

Many of these compositions are by no means lacking in tenderness and compassion but the expression of the emotion often strikes us as facile. The same defects of sentimentality and simulated emotion are also conspicuous in the numerous songs that gaze nostalgically back at the lost homeland of the Highlands.

But here a note of caution is necessary and the observation is applicable also to what may seem to be romantic evocations, of a lost Golden Age, in the poetry of the Clearances. There are recurrent formulas of the type of 'Land of Bens and Glens and Heroes' to be met with almost in every poem. These are not mere romantic clichés but semiotic markers drawn from the established panegyric code of Gaelic poetry and still functioning as such. The signal they give is that the Gàidhealtachd is still, culturally and geographically, a 'territorial' unity.

By the later nineteenth century, cheap Gaelic books, anthologies and individual poetry collections among them, were easily available and a variety of periodicals which included Gaelic verse enjoyed wide circulation. Among the poems which appear in these sources and which illustrate the effects of 'Twilight', 'pathetic fallacy' and contrived sentiment, few can have been more popular than 'MacCrimmon's Lament', published in 1836. As has recently been shown, it is in fact based on Sir Walter Scott's English 'MacKrimmon's Lament' of 1818.[22]

But in all these movements, William Livingstone stands out from the common run of his contemporaries. For one thing, his longer works are poems, not songs: they have no musical component, actual or potential. What he is apparently trying to do, in successive efforts, is to provide the Gaelic nation with its own Heroic Poem, that uniquely European literary institution, without which a European nation has not really achieved maturity. That any poet in a culture so reduced as Gaelic was by the mid-nineteenth century should even think of such a scheme is remarkable. But the Gaelic sense of identity was still strong enough, in spite of the appearances. There is a perverse, if not downright lunatic, expenditure of energy in the venture, but it is, of course, perfectly understandable. For if we seek to isolate one unifying principle in the poetry of the nineteenth century, it is to be found in a continuing consciousness of a Gaelic cosmos which tries to assert, and reclaim, an identity in non-parochial terms, and in spiritual as well as temporal contexts.

To modern critics, it seems that what is 'parochial' in the poetry of that age is by the same token not only more immediate and realistic but also more successful in achieving universality than the poetry which was consciously designed to enlarge Gaelic horizons. But clearly for many who formed the Gaelic readership of the century, and who were neither academics nor tradition-bearers, this cannot have been the perspective in which they viewed their poetry.

There is, indeed, one academic who articulates what must have been a common view. Donald MacKinnon, first incumbent of the Chair of Celtic at Edinburgh, time and time again in his literary criticism (written in Gaelic) expresses a reaction against the merely verbal virtues of traditional poetry, developed, in his opinion, at the expense of intellectual range and grasp. To MacKinnon, the eighteenth-century religious poet Dugald Buchanan has a unique intellectual quality but the yardstick of excellence is Oisean ('Ossian'). MacKinnon was not a great critic, his views on Ossian particularly seem muddled, and his opinions were opposed by other Gaelic scholars of his own time. But if we fail to see that his testimony is representative of the feelings of nineteenth-century Gaels trying to come to terms with the modern world, we shall also fail to understand a whole dimension of the history of Gaelic poetry.

A Radically Traditional Voice

Sorley Maclean and the Evangelical Background

In the late 1930s an Appin man gave as his opinion that the poetry of Sorley Maclean and his contemporaries was 'the last glimmer of the Gaelic sun before it goes down for ever'.[1] The pessimism of that judgment in regard to the future was no bleaker than the poet's own. The fifty-fifth poem of *Dàin do Eimhir* reads in translation:

> I do not see the sense of my toil, putting thoughts in a dying tongue, now when the whoredom of Europe is murder erect and agony: but we have been given a million years, a fragment of a sad, growing portion, the courage and patience of the many and the marvel of a beautiful face.

Why then did Sorley Maclean write in Gaelic at all? A writer who enjoys the freedom of more than one language is not forced to write in his first. Conrad did not write in Polish; nor does William Heinesen write in Faroese. And Maclean's chosen medium was not, after all, a developed 'modern' language. Vis-a-vis English its status was little more than that of a dialect; its literature long cut off from the influence of the great innovating movements of post-medieval Europe.

Confronted with such a situation, a writer whose horizons were anything but parochial and whose formal education had been in English might well be expected to choose the language of authority and the dominant culture. In fact, Sorley Maclean did write poetry in English, from his teens into his early twenties. Normally writers who elect to use a minority language are motivated by patriotism, cultural or political, or both. Maclean's motives were different. It was the simple realisation that his Gaelic poetry was far superior to his English poetry – and far less self-conscious – that made him confine himself to the former. How much loss or gain that decision involved we shall probably never know.

In any event, what is of much greater critical significance is the fact that he was not so much the chooser as the chosen. And equally relevant is the fact that only an inheritance of immense strength and potential could have compelled Sorley Maclean to follow a path which sober and restrained critics might quite fairly have warned him to avoid. The processes that led to it, that made him put his modern, contemporary 'thoughts in a dying tongue', were ones in which free-will appears to have played singularly little part. I believe deeply that his achievement as a poet is connected with that, and connected at more than one level. To say this does not of course make any denial whatsoever of individual genius. Nor does it set aside the deliberate exercise, the avid exploration of tradition, by which a writer con-sciously prepares himself for his role. In that connection, and bearing in mind these two words 'tradition' and 'inheritance', Eliot's famous essay on 'Tradition and the Individual Talent' makes an important point:

> Tradition [. . .] cannot be inherited, and if you want it you must obtain it by great labour. It involves, in the first place, the historical sense [. . . which] involves a perception, not only of the pastness of the past, but of its presence; the historical sense compels a man to write not merely with his own generation in his bones, but with a feeling that the whole of the literature of Europe from Homer and within it the whole of the literature of his own country has a simultaneous existence and composes a simultaneous order. This historical sense, which is a sense of the timeless as well as of the temporal and of the timeless and of the temporal together, is what makes a writer traditional. And it is at the same time what makes a writer most acutely conscious of his place in time, of his own contemporaneity.

I do not apologise for quoting the passage at such length. Eliot's words have always seemed to me almost as if they had been designed with Sorley Maclean in mind. And yet when *Dàin do Eimhir* appeared, it was not any traditional quality, as that is more usually defined, which seized the imagination of his Gaelic readers. There were some who criticised the poetry for its strangeness; others for its difficulty. The editor of the Gaelic supplement to the Church of Scotland's *Life and Work*, one Malcolm MacLeod, drew attention to what he attacked as crudeness and bad taste. This was perhaps predictable ecclesiastical cant; either that or the reverend gentleman was signally devoid of critical sense and perhaps ignorant of the healthy Rabelaisian strains in Gaelic literature. Another criticism was to be heard also: more than one learned man declared that these poems did not even scan. (So far as that point is concerned, they were not, alas, learned enough).

But to those Gaels who enjoy being pharisaic, thanking God that they are not as other men are, the poetry of Sorley Maclean was like newly minted coin. Probably few of us, even at that, could have told what mines its ore had come from. But we recognised the quality of the metal and we knew that here was the currency of our own times and of our own land. Certainly, the poetry could be difficult. Some poems, it is true, were as transparent as the simplest song. But others were dense, with a baffling vocabulary, an impenetrable weave of thought, and what seemed to be a positively Shakespearean excess of language.

And yet the same voice could be heard so clearly throughout them all that one had the strangest feelings about these 'difficulties'. It was as if terms such as 'difficult' and 'simple' would have made no sense to the owner of this voice: he was merely using Gaelic in what was to him the most perfectly natural and direct way. It was an object lesson in practical criticism. One realised with the force of a personal revelation that in poetry no two things are as far from each other as difficulty and obscurity. I suppose, however, that by any reasonable canon of educational theory, the experience of reading Sorley Maclean's poetry ought to have unhinged the minds of young native speakers of Gaelic who had received not so much as one formal lesson in their own tongue. But it did not. So compellingly vivid was the poetry, so living and passionate was the language, that some Gaels of that generation actually became literate in Gaelic through reading *Dàin do Eimhir*. When Iain Crichton Smith says that with the publication of *Dàin do Eimhir* a new kind of 'Highlander' emerged, we know exactly what he means. (For 'Highlander', however, read Gael.)

Nowadays, when so many new poets are writing – so many 'Joshuas to command the Gaelic sun to stop in the heavens', to quote the gloss that Maclean himself makes on the Appin man's comment – when so much new verse is appearing, some of it brilliant, some of it bad, most of it adventurous, Sorley Maclean is beginning to look, and actually to be called, 'traditional'. Although his poetry is still new and vital, it is easier now to see his links with the past. The judgments complement each other.

To what extent does this single him out? To what extent can we trace in Sorley Maclean that 'historical sense which [. . .] makes a writer traditional'? This is a question that is well worth asking if only because there are a number of distinct lines of descent to be traced in modern Gaelic poetry. From that point of view, some of our contemporary poets are only distantly related to each other. For example, George Campbell Hay, the other doyen, has a very different poetic lineage; and so have Derick Thomson, Donald MacAulay and Iain Crichton Smith, to mention only the best known of the older writers.

To deal with this matter of formative influences and literary ancestry takes us back to the potential of this 'undeveloped' language which nevertheless is capable of giving serious and ambitious writers so many options, so many opportunities for diversity.

Gaelic is not only not a dialect; it is not even a minor language. Its literary continuities stretch back into the Dark Ages; its linguistic resources – from colloquial Gaelic in its rich regional variations to the more or less standardised registers – involve us in the same perspective; and throughout history, Gaelic oral and literary traditions have been almost inextricably intertwined, to the enrichment of both. But although Gaelic still has an extraordinary range of active working vocabulary (an astonishing fact in view of the circumstances of the past few centuries) its uses have not been diversified through the intellectual activities of the modern scientific world. It can indeed cope with these, as Professor Rankin has shown in Mathematics or Professor Thomson in Biology. Only accidents of history, which include the deliberate acts and policies of individual men, have forced it into parochialism.

There is a comparison to be drawn here between linguistic and social structure. Just as it is misleading to analyse modern Gaelic society entirely in terms of class structure, neglecting the hierarchies of caste, so it is misleading to analyse the Gaelic language entirely in terms of its status as dialect in the linguistic hierarchies of the United Kingdom, and leave it at that. It seems to me that we shall be guilty of a grave distortion of the facts unless we accept the paradox that modern Gaelic is really a major medieval European language. If we do accept this, we can the more easily understand how its uses may be extended in all sorts of directions.

Let us look at one among the more important resources that Sorley Maclean as an aspiring poet had at his disposal. There is one public social institution, and nowadays only one, in which Gaelic is used not as a dialect but as a language: confident, mature, and on a par with any other. This is the Church. The continuity of Gaelic prose is due to the Church, in much the same way as in England a prose tradition was maintained from Old to Middle English. In Gaelic, partly through the translation of the Bible and works of devotion, which drew upon the dignified classical language which Scottish and Irish Gaels used as a common medium (until it died out in Scotland in the eighteenth century), the clergy evolved their vernacular medium of instruction. In the absence of secular institutions of education, all Gaelic writers naturally enough were strongly influenced by this background. The standard prose styles which developed from such homiletic origins achieved a supreme clarity in formal registers of the language but tended until recently to carry into creative writing an expository and even didactic tone. Among Gaelic prose writers the name of the Rev. Dr Norman MacLeod 'Caraid nan Gàidheal' is famous.

In case anyone thinks that all this is irrelevant to the poetry of Sorley Maclean, let me quote his own words:

> In those years [1780–1870] most of the real spiritual quality of the Gaelic-speaking people was expressed in the almost wholly extempore and un-recorded sermons and prayers of ministers and 'men' to whom all poetry and song except the Psalms of David was one of the more seductive vanities of this vale of tears. If only a moderate fraction of those sermons and prayers had been recorded, however, Scottish Gaelic would have a great 19th-century prose. Even as late as the 1920s it was quite common to hear some minister or elder quoting richly, by oral tradition, from sermons or prayers delivered 70 or 100 years before. Such quotations made it quite plain that in frankness, sincerity and psychological insight, expressed with an astonishing wealth of imagery and illustration, sometimes sonorously eloquent with the incomparable resonances of the Gaelic language and sometimes racily colloquial, Gaelic once had a great prose. If a man of imagination is convinced of the rags of human righteousness and of the desperate wicked-ness of the human heart, the expression of his conviction cannot fail to be powerful. Even to this day there may be heard Gaelic sermons in which the thought is essentially that of St Augustine, Calvin or even Pascal, and the prose one of great tension and variety. I fully believe that I have never heard or read as great a Gaelic prose as I have heard in the unrecorded sermons of Ewan MacQueen.
>
> I do believe that this almost lost prose had far more impact on modern Gaelic poets than the prose, for instance, of Norman MacLeod, who was regarded until recently as the 'greatest' Gaelic prose-writer.[2]

Readers who are ignorant of Scottish Church history may be par-doned for wondering what constitutes this great gulf between two authors who surely are both equally representative of Gaelic, Calvinist Presbyterianism. The difference is that the ministers and laymen to whom Maclean pays such a memorable tribute are the heirs of the Evangelical Movement which swept through the Highlands in the late eighteenth and early nineteenth centuries and wrought a fundamental transformation in the life of the tolerant, structurally Calvinist, spiritually lax Established Church of Scotland in the Gàidhealtachd. Those were the bitter years of the Clearances when the chaos that the break-up of any traditional society produces was intensified beyond endurance in the bewilderment of a people attacked by its own natural leaders.

This broken community eagerly accepted the demands of a passionate and uncompromising faith. Here was a new dialectic, powerful enough to replace the deep loyalties of the traditional order. It was theology that now supplied an identity, and a world view of history, partly in millenarian terms. Predictably, therefore, the movement is bound up with social protest. We owe to its poets, for instance, the first powerful attack on the injustices perpetrated by the landlord class, one of whom opprobiously described this Calvinist Revival as 'the peasant religion'. Since the Established Church drew its ministers from that class, it is hardly surprising that the Calvinists viewed ministers and landlords alike with equal hostility. This radical movement, with its intellectual tumult and dissenting fervour, bred an anti-Establishment attitude which is apparent to the present day even *within* the denominations that still profess its principles. There are thus anti-ecclesiastical songs still being composed by adherents of the strictest persuasion; and one of the authors was a relative of Sorley Maclean. But this strain derives in part, too, from those sections of the community who resisted the Evangelicals' attacks on all secular culture: these are the men and women who ensured the continuance of the rich oral tradition of Gaelic song and story in the strict Presbyterian areas.

Significantly, it is from these same areas and from that complex background that our leading contemporary writers come. But the most powerful element in their heritage was also the most puritanical – in effect a recluse religion practised in open society and trying to dominate it – and it could not on its own produce an adequate strategy to deal with the full range of human experience. Even within its own limits it has given us neither a Gaelic John Bunyan nor a James Hogg. Modern Gaelic writers, provoked into reaction by the austerity of ascetic evangelical Presbyterianism, have on the whole gained little of positive value from it.

In this respect, Sorley Maclean is unique. When he writes about this 'almost lost prose' and its 'impact on modern Gaelic poets', he is really making a claim on his own behalf. It is perfectly clear that he would not be the kind of poet that he is, if he had ignored the impassioned

eloquence of the Church; it is almost as certain that he would be a
different kind of poet if he had rejected the conscience-searching that
the teachings of the Church invite. Yet he does make his rejections,
and he makes them with the same evangelical conviction. Poems such
as 'Calvary' and 'The Black Tree' are well known. Less well known is
the following *jeu d'esprit*, the poem called 'Scotus Erigena'. Johannes
Scotus Erigena or Eriugena ('John the Irish Gael') was a ninth-century
Christian theologian who was dangerously witty as well as dangerously heretical. He was in fact one of the most original thinkers of the
Middle Ages.

> Have you heard the story of Scotus Erigena, who spoke against Predestina-
> tion, tirelessly, for two days; and who annihilated Hell also, and Sin, with his
> persistent, accurate words – before he was silenced in the cause of peace?
> Alas that no one like him has been heard attacking the Seceders.

The Seceders is the nickname (since no sect is ever a sect but always the
True Church) of the Free Presbyterian denomination in which Sorley
Maclean was brought up. In the most general terms, Maclean's debt to
the Church is in confidence of language; the unconfined deployment of
an enormous range of vocabulary, abstract and concrete. The sermons
of the gentlemen ministers of the old Established Church – the Auld
Kirk of Lowland Scotland – were bland, if lucid and elegant, homilies.
The surviving examples at any rate have little sap in them.

The sermons of the Evangelicals, on the other hand, whose ministers
and lay members came almost entirely from the common people, were
enormously vital and passionate and drew on every available linguistic
register of Gaelic. The 'sometimes racily colloquial' speech could move
imperceptibly into the arcane language of theological disputation. Or
it could move with disconcerting abruptness from the flamboyant to
the austere. It was a theatrical display (the diabolic lure of this did not
go unexamined, from time to time) in which groundlings and initiates
were equally catered for by preachers whose social origins were the
same as their hearers', and who never assumed that the congregation
could possibly contain linguistic defectives. The Evangelicals were
never guilty, in this sense at least, of talking down to their audiences.
The point made earlier about difficulty and obscurity is equally
applicable here. And of course there was no 'folksiness' in that deadly
serious performance.

But most important of all, these great riches of language were not
amassed with any motive of cultural patriotism but with one single

objective: saving souls. I suppose that when we talk of prose we subsume several distinct categories of verbal activity, just as we do when we talk of poetry. At any rate this eloquent prose, or poetry, or whatever it is, settled easily into the patterns of Maclean's verse. It is demonstrably there in 'Prayer', with the authentic pyrotechnics. And in the verse:

> Young Cornford had this in his heroism
> The fear of the thought of his love being near him
> When Spain was a fast-day for him:
> Fear of his loss in the man,
> Fear of fear in the hero

the Gaelic word for 'this' – incredible as it may appear to some – is in fact a technical term borrowed from ecclesiastical usage. These rich quotations that came by oral tradition, 'even as late as the 1920s [. . .] from sermons or prayers delivered seventy or a hundred years before', were almost invariably introduced with the formula 'X had *this*' or 'X always used to have *this*'. It often prefaced some dictum or maxim enshrining a basic truth of the spiritual life. Such clues are easy to miss. (I think that may be an understatement.)

The poem opens abruptly, as extempore prayers frequently do, with a conclusive statement: 'Because there is no refuge | and because my desire | is only the vain reflection of a story' – as if it had been preceded by vehement but silent spiritual wrestlings. 'Prayer' moves in an indirect way which is peculiar to the genre it imitates. This is a genuine prayer of the unconverted, no less authentic for being a sceptic's prayer, which constantly turns aside and returns as obsessively in a hopeless search for one fixed point of human experience. At one level it is incoherent, deliberately so, for the argument cannot have a conclusion; belief in the eternal truths is impossible: they cannot be accepted, but neither can they be rejected, in this

> blasphemous, imperfect prayer,
> the crooked perverted prayer that turns back
> the prayer that I may pray
> without praying to reach the substance.

The theme is thus refracted throughout the poem, sometimes into prognostications of terror and famine and disintegrating personal identity, sometimes into gnomic asides which are also mimetic. Extempore prayers use gnomic statements and biblical quotations to give structural strength.

Anyone who knows the nature of Sorley Maclean's poetry will immediately recognise that the 'real' theme of 'Prayer' is the conflict between a love affair and the poet's 'political passion' as he himself has called it. But although it is a multi-dimensional poem the form which I have sketchily traced here is unmistakable. Something of the same kind may be said of 'The Woods of Raasay'. I mean by this that although both form and symbolism are different from those of 'Prayer', one of the themes, too, of 'The Woods of Raasay' is the quest for perfectibility. John Herdman pointed out that the heart of that poem is to be found in the passage which contains the stanza 'What is the meaning of giving a woman | Love like the growing blue of the skies',[3] and this is undoubtedly true. The previous stanza reads:

> To believe with flesh,
> with brain and heart,
> that one thing was complete,
> beautiful, accessible:
> a thing that would avoid the travail
> of the flesh and hardship,
> that would not be spoiled by the bedragglement
> of time and temptation.

No doubt this is a fundamental quest in all human experience, but we know what the mediating institution was for Sorley Maclean. We know too that other forces have moulded him as a poet. What I have given here is only a superficial treatment of one influence. To do justice even to this would require an analysis of the connection, and disjunction, between the Marxist view of history and the world view, in the Gaelic Evangelical context, of history and its meaning, as that has been interpreted in Christian thought. From childhood Maclean was accustomed to hearing discussions on these subjects – and he heard them in his native Gaelic. It is impossible to overemphasise the unparochial nature of such views, even when they involve a tunnel-vision of history. Sorley Maclean was not the only Free Presbyterian Marxist in Raasay.

We should also have to analyse the ideas of a long poem, only published in part which takes the theme of the Gaelic legend of the piper who enters the Cave of Gold (*Uamh an Òir*) and disappears; Maclean gives it a remarkable interpretation. In the legend the notes of the piper's melody are heard as words of song (a commonplace of such stories): he laments that he has but two hands when he needs three –

two for the pipes and one for the sword – as he is being attacked by 'the green bitch'. The green bitch is the fairy hound; the fairies themselves are, among other things, the malevolent dead.

In the poem, Maclean asks: Why did the piper leave the beautiful earth and the sun to meet his death in the darkness? The answer is implied in the line: 'For the green bitch is death'.

In Maclean's poem, not the legend, a second man, a blind man, goes into the cave also. The blindness works on more than one level of symbolism. On one of these levels the second man has an affinity with Blind Donald Munro, a fiddler-catechist under the dispensation of the Established Church, who became an ascetic and one of the leading figures of the Evangelical Movement in the Isle of Skye when the intense new faith was introduced there early in the nineteenth century. 'An Dall Mun-rotha' ('The Blind Munro') gave up the pleasures of this world, including the fiddle, whose music had now become for him profane vanity. What is the nature of this compulsion that draws piper and blind man both into subterranean darkness and death?

In this connection, it is appropriate to quote from Mary MacPherson, 'Big Mary of the Songs', the great poet of the Land League in Skye in the nineteenth century, when Presbyterianism was being transformed throughout the Gàidhealtachd and transforming the Gaelic community in the process.

> The people have become so strange
> That sorrow to them is wheat
> And if you will not go into a whelk-shell for them
> You cannot stay alive.
>
> We will not go into a whelk-shell for them
> And we *can* stay alive
> Although we will not wear long faces
> Nor cause our appearance to change.

And then she adds: 'Since vanity is a plant that satisfies the flesh, it clings to me as closely as the thong does to the shoe.'

In that climate she could not escape conscience-searching. But she had come to terms with herself and elected to remain robustly of this world, albeit with a strong religious sense of ultimate justice. Mary's introspection, too, borrows from religion but it never becomes morbid in the process. She had undergone a harrowing experience of unjust conviction and imprisonment for theft: it was this 'that brought my poetry into being', and the anguish of it remained with her. It can be sensed throughout her poetry even when it does not break surface. She had also an intense affection for her native community, the common people. All these elements combine in her work, resolved and integrated and given a major dimension by being set in the context of nineteenth-century Radicalism. Her best work gives the sharp feel of immediate experience while at the same time conveying the pressure of contemporary history. And when she exults that 'We have seen the horizon breaking, the clouds of serfdom dispelled', she is, it seems to me, inaugurating a new vision of Gaelic society.

In their kinship of spirit and background there is more than one link between Mary MacPherson and Sorley Maclean. For instance, in Mary's poetry, Maclean has pointed out, 'echoes of the old songs are heard far oftener and more authentically than in any other nineteenth-century Gaelic poet'.[4] In Maclean we find the same echoes, especially in the poem 'The Cuillin'.

But there are also important differences between these two major poets. Mary MacPherson, obviously, did not enter the darkness of the 'Cave of Gold'. Very probably Mary would have understood the question that Maclean poses in that poem. But she would not, I believe, have thought of asking it herself. The much more palpable spiritual concern of Maclean's poetry, and the strains of pessimism and remorse that appear in it, cannot but lead us to this surmise: if Sorley Maclean had been born in 1811 instead of 1911, would he have become not a Gaelic poet but one of the leading figures in the Evangelical Movement? Would the tremendous passion and anguish of his poetry have flowed instead into the channels of 'the peasant religion'? And if so, what kind of prayers and sermons would he have delivered? Like Mary MacPherson and the two MacCallum brothers, ministers (and, be it noted, ministers of the Established Church) as well as leaders in the Land League agitation movement, he would certainly have rejected the quietism of the Evangelicals. Although Evangelicals were not necessarily quietists, Maclean's comment in 'A Highland Woman' is fair:

> And Thy gentle church has spoken
> about the lost state of her miserable soul
> and the unremitting toil has lowered
> her body to a black peace in a grave.

It may be a frivolous exercise of the imagination to ask whether we might now be mentioning the name of Sorley Maclean alongside those of John MacRae of Kintail and John MacDonald of Ferintosh, the 'Apostle of the North'. It is doubtless equally frivolous to ask, but hard to avoid wondering, had the past been different, what kind of poetry MacRae or MacDonald would have composed. For these men were lords of language. In the judgment of one who was well qualified to know, John MacDonald of Ferintosh was a superbly greater orator than all the leading Parliamentarians of England in the age of Disraeli and Gladstone. They were artists. They were spokesmen of a spiritual movement which, I would argue, in spite of many tokens to the contrary, was related to the European Romantic Revival. How passionately they themselves would have rejected that interpretation.

Language, Metre and Diction
in the Poetry of Sorley Maclean

In the history of Gaelic poetry no voice is more distinctive than that of Somhairle MacGill-Eain ('Sorley Maclean'). Although readers who have some knowledge of Gaelic poetry in translation may well give an immediate assent to that, realism demands that we base the judgement on a knowledge of the Gaelic poetic tradition in its entirety and in the original language. This is no doubt as much of a commonplace as it is to observe that thematic power, brilliance of imagery, and the various other qualities that distinguish a writer, can and do make their own impact even in translation. But it becomes something more than a mere truism when the original language and the language of translation are as far removed from each other as are Gaelic and English, in nature, in history, and in status. It is not merely that English and Gaelic are inherently, both structurally and phonologically, so very different. There is also the question of cultural and historical perspective. Somhairle MacGill-Eain restored to Gaelic poetry the scope and amplitude of a mature, adult voice. His work is not only the product of his own genius but is shaped, controlled and energised by tradition.

Gaelic literature has developed over some fifteen centuries: a rich, dominating, hierarchical literature which expresses the manifold experience of a people who eventually, between Ireland and Scotland, divided into two nations. It has its aristocratic and plebeian aspects; its literary, sub-literary and non-literate streams. As a living language with an immensely large working vocabulary, rich and flexible in the usages of its oral verse-making and story-telling, supported by vigorous traditions of expository prose in writing and extempore eloquence in the Church, Gaelic had by no means lost contact with its former greatness during Somhairle MacGill-Eain's formative years. It is true that by that time Gaelic poetry had in some respects become attenuated, but the language could still cope with an astonishingly wide range of human experience. In none of its registers could it be called a 'peasant language', no matter how poor many of its speakers may have been in terms of this world's goods.

A large part of Somhairle MacGill-Eain's greatness as a poet lies in his restorative work: this can properly be celebrated as a triumph of regeneration. His poetry is intensely Gaelic even when it is so different from anything else in Gaelic; his art, even at its most personal, draws upon so much of the inherited wealth of immemorial generations. What is perhaps more difficult to convey to a non-Gaelic reader is that this sense of the restoration of our heritage to its proper place plays a fundamental part in our assessment of his poetry. We experience a shock of excitement as we read him. Naturally this cannot be separated from his art and craft, or from the pain and joy of his poetry, from its subtlety and passion. Yet it is logically, and, perhaps more important, psychologically distinct. There is pessimism in Mac-Gill-Eain's poetry: much of it, indeed, is tragic. But his voice, in my sense of the term, is at the same time optimistic and resurgent and these sentiments are conveyed to at least the same degree as his pessimism. If that is a paradox or a mystery it cannot be helped. The point is that it is true.

How does Somhairle MacGill-Eain achieve this? How did he revolutionise Gaelic poetry? What resources did he have at his disposal in native Gaelic? What did he borrow? What were his strategies? How colloquial or dialectal, literary or artificial, is his language? How different are the formal structures of his verse from those of the poets who preceded him? To deal with any of these questions adequately would require much greater scope than that of a short essay. All I can hope to do here is to indicate some of the answers and warn non-Gaelic readers of certain pitfalls.

To begin with a general point. Simply by reading an English translation, no one could ever guess at the nature of MacGill-Eain's Gaelic diction. There is nothing very difficult – nor, in purely linguistic terms, anything very egregious – in the English. By contrast the original Gaelic exhibits virtually an entire spectrum of language. Transparent simplicity is to be found side by side with a formidable density of verbal texture. A full linguistic commentary must await another occasion; for the moment it is enough to say that practically all the available registers of Gaelic, ranging in quality from the demotic to the arcane, are included at some point or another. There are times, naturally, when the ordinary reader requires industry combined with ingenuity to unravel the meaning. This fact alone would give added value to the poet's authoritative translations. Personally, and in spite of the author's modest disclaimer, I regard these translations as poems in their own right. Of course they make a very different impression from their originals. Perhaps because in English they do not administer quite the same shock of modernity, or because they are easier, or for some other related reason, bilingual readers may occasionally prefer the translation. MacGill-Eain may be the 'Bard of his people', as he has been described, but one must understand that this is a specialized use of the word 'bard'. In medieval and later Gaelic society the bard was a fairly simple praise-singer.

There are undoubtedly misconceptions held about some aspects of his work. I have heard him referred to as a Romantic who consistently uses strict Classical forms. This is at best a partial judgement. I have heard it said also that his originality is restricted to the content of his poetry: that he has not brought to Gaelic verse much in the way of metrical innovation. His art has been described as essentially that of a maker of songs, with the corollary that their true quality could only emerge with the support of a musical setting. This last point may display a confusion concerning 'lyricism' or it may be connected with the fact that in Gaelic tradition almost all poetry, including non-lyrical poetry – what we, from a modern Western European point of view, would certainly call poems not songs – was linked with melody or performed in chant.

It is only fair to add that none of these observations have appeared in print, in serious criticism. Rather they are all the kind of comment which one may hear in discussion, made by people who have at best an imperfect knowledge of Gaelic or who have failed to read the poems very closely. One can often see what gives rise to such judgements but there is not a great deal of substance in any of those I have cited. In what follows, I am keenly aware that much of what I say about MacGill-Eain, especially on the subject of his technical achievement, cannot be demonstrated to a non-Gaelic reader. This is unsatisfactory but unavoidable. Matters of technique, and rhythm in particular, require direct knowledge of a language, or an unconscionable amount of space. But a good deal of the argument is really concerned with cultural background and that at least can be checked.

It is obvious from the content of his poetry that MacGill-Eain is a contemporary European poet. What then are the resources that are available to a modern Gaelic writer whose horizons are as wide as that, and what are their limitations?

First, Gaelic is a major European language, drawing as it does on the oldest literary tradition in Europe outside Latin and Greek. But it is not a 'modern' language in the sense that English, French or German are modern languages. The processes of history – which for us have been also processes of ethnocide – have disposed that the terminology of the modern sciences, for instance, is not represented in the Gaelic vocabulary. To put it succinctly: there is a word for 'atom' but only a recent coinage for 'molecule'. On the other hand, largely because of a continuing theological tradition, it is possible, without creating an unduly large number of neologisms, to discuss philosophy, literary criticism and the arts in general.

But the major Gaelic contribution to scientific enquiry is in the field of language. In Europe in the Middle Ages, Gaelic poets and men of letters were unique in the analysis of their own language. Their approach was not based on the model supplied by the grammatical categories of Latin alone, and using a fresh and independent eye, they developed attitudes that are strikingly similar to those of modern linguistic science. The potential of the language for coping with linguistic analysis is therefore clear enough; how easily it can be used in other fields of intellectual and cultural activity has been demonstrated in the twentieth century. Irish Gaelic, which has a roughly similar history, is used in all the disciplines of university curricula; in Scotland, too, Gaelic has been shown to be perfectly adequate for dealing, for instance, with mathematics and biology. But these contemporary experiments apart, the learned vocabulary of Scots Gaelic has on the whole remained substantially that of a medieval European language.

Secondly, the Gaelic poetic tradition is one that takes us back almost 1,500 years, and this literary tradition does not divide, at any rate in its higher reaches, into its distinctively Scots and Irish streams until the seventeenth century. Throughout the stages and vicissitudes of that long history, formal characteristics of structure and rhythm, alliteration, rhyme, elision, and all the other properties that can be an integral part of the statement of a poem, engrossed the attention of Gaelic poets and linguistic scholars alike.

For instance, rhyme, when it emerges in the poetry of the seventh century, is carried not only by the vowels and diphthongs of the language but also by the consonants, which were analysed phonetically and organised in distinct categories for that purpose in the schools of rhetoric. So strong is the Gaelic fascination with the

refinements of literary form (and the fascination still exists) that in the
'Dark' Ages high-class men of letters, as a leading Irish scholar,
Professor James Carney, has argued, not only concentrated on the
most difficult and impressive metres: in the early period these élitists
went so far as to avoid vowel rhyme altogether, preferring the subtler
and more sensitive, but much more demanding, consonantal rhyme.
Such craft could only exist in a sophisticated written literature. At a
lower level, so to speak, oral poetry and song followed their own
ways, from time to time borrowing, as elsewhere in the world, from
the writers.

To take one example, although Gaelic is a 'stress-timed' language,
the Gaelic literati of the Middle Ages evolved a metrical system in
which symmetry is achieved not on the basis of the heavy stresses of
the verse line but on the number of syllables within it – no matter
where the stresses fall. The visual pattern of such strictly 'syllabic' lines
is, however, disrupted in speech or song by the inherent rhythm of the
language itself, since regularity of stress predominates. What emerges
in this kind of poetry then is an overall symmetry which may involve
varying degrees of light and heavy stress, wrenched accents, or even
silent stresses. Any tendency to preciosity in these 'Strict Metres' was
removed when oral poets took over and modified the exacting
syllable-count of the writers. Indeed, what are faults from a scholastic
point of view seem to me, from the viewpoint of modern Gaelic
sensibility, often to be positive virtues. The verse becomes loosened
but the subtle rhythmic complexities remain and are still conspicuous
in certain areas of Gaelic poetry.

Although the *quasi parlando* style characteristic of some traditional
Gaelic singing may be of different or diverse origins, its subtleties are
comparable with those just described. Even in the songs that accompanied communal labour (such as the well-known waulking-songs)
there are similar variations in movement, although they can hardly
have developed from written poetry. The fact of the matter is that a
feel for complexity of rhythm – for the freedom of speech-rhythm, for
instance, pitted against the demands of strict form – is one of the most
special and sensitive graces of Gaelic verse in general. At one extreme
it can be found in dance-songs, particularly the older *puirt-à-beul*,
which preserve their regularly accented dance rhythms over against a
variably stressed text. The result is a form of syncopation.

But from about the mid-nineteenth century the mainstream of
Gaelic poetry failed to draw upon this astonishing rhythmical abun-

dance. For the most part the rhythms commonly used by poets whose work was published tended to be regular, and rather mechanical, stressed patterns. Paradoxically, the technical resources of Gaelic verse had become much more depleted in what was then appearing in print, and in the songs that enjoyed a vogue among the *émigré* Gaels of Lowland cities, than in the still vigorous oral poetry of the Gàidhealtachd itself. MacGill-Eain had free access to this area of poetry – it was a living tradition within his own family – just as much as he had to the entire body of published Gaelic verse. Because he had these advantages, both sides of the Gaelic poetic inheritance contributed to his own metrical restorations and innovations. In that process MacGill-Eain may be said to have slowed down the pace of Gaelic poetry, enlarged its metrical scope and created verse techniques that were capable of coping with the demands of a modern sensibility.

In this connection it is interesting to note that one or two earlier poets, notably the Lewisman John Munro, a young graduate of Aberdeen who was killed in action in 1918, had also felt the need to break the constraints of traditional form. It is evident that Munro was influenced by English metrics. MacGill-Eain, of course, also had the freedom to choose from English metrics, but his strategy was different. In essence most of MacGill-Eain's metrical patterns are derived from Gaelic or are a very subtle compound of English and Gaelic forms. The latter offers a range that stretches from the free verse of charms and incantations to the strict metres of the learned poems.

While MacGill-Eain has not cultivated these 'Strict Metres' in the way that George Campbell Hay has done, his technical virtuosity is based on his awareness of what non-literate poets have done in the development of these same forms. Writing about the great anonymous songs of sixteenth, seventeenth and eighteenth centuries, he himself has this to say: 'Technically they are simple but adequate, their metrical basis being the old syllabic structure modified by speech stress'; and significantly he adds: 'I think that is the most permanently satisfying basis for Gaelic metrics.'[1]

Technically, MacGill-Eain's own verse is anything but simple. It is true that he is not averse to the use of couplets, quatrains and other well-established traditional forms. It is true, too, that some poems can appear to traditionalist readers to be more complex technically than they really are. The syntactical patterns may be unexpected, and grammatical inflection much more strictly imposed than in any variety of colloquial Gaelic; but the stanza-forms and rhymes will remain quite regular. And it is probable also that the brilliant, novel imagery combined with traditional form can give the impression of a new technique. But these are not the poems in which MacGill-Eain's technical originality best manifests itself.

While, as I have suggested, he may have restored a slower pace to Gaelic poetry, MacGill-Eain also writes in metres that stride and surge and alter speed in much the same way as he changes the shape of the stanza and the trajectory of his rhythms from one section of a poem to another. In 'Coilltean Ratharsair' this protean quality is obvious to anyone whether he reads Gaelic or not. In 'Cumha Chaluim Iain MhicGill-Eain', which has a unique structure in Gaelic poetry, the stanzas vary from four to twelve lines; and the rhyming lines vary more or less in the same unpredictable way. There is a long poem, 'Craobh nan Teud', the elements of which may, technically speaking, all be derived from Gaelic tradition but which are combined in new relationships. (The title 'Tree of Harpstrings' – or of any stringed instrument – is taken from the pibroch 'The Lament for the Tree of Harpstrings'. It may be a corruptly transmitted name, but even if it is a corruption, it is still a remarkable metaphor. MacGill-Eain uses it as a kenning: it is 'the tree of poetry', 'the tree of art', and I shall refer to it briefly in another connection at a later stage.)

'Craobh nan Teud' opens with a section of short-lined octaves:

Air cruas nan creag
tha eagar smuaine
air lom nam beann
tha 'n rann gun chluaine:
air mullach beò
tha treòir nam buadhan:
air airde ghil
tha 'n lios gun luaidh air.

On the hardness of the crags
there is precision of thought;
on the bareness of the mountains
there is an undeviating verse;
on a living summit
the energy of [mental] gifts;
on a shining height
is the garden that is not spoken of.

After eight declamatory stanzas in which both rhymes and rhythms vary their pattern, there comes a section of ten quatrains of longer lines.

> *Chunnacas fo sgàil craobh na dòrainn*
> *ag coiseachd sràidean Pharais gu lòghmhor*
> *na seann siùrsaichean beaga breòite*
> *a chunnaic Baudelaire 'na ònrachd.*

> Beneath the shadow of the tree of agony,
> walking the streets of Paris radiantly,
> I saw the little, old, infirm harlots
> whom Baudelaire saw in his loneliness.

Between the fourth and fifth quatrains, an octave, in basically the same metre as the first section, interrupts the progression; the last two stanzas of the second section are also octaves which again reflect the metres of the first section. Each of these has its own individual properties of rhythm and rhyme. These permutations are repeated (though never identically) with an extraordinary exuberance and virtuosity, in diction as well as metre, until we come to the end of the poem.

The sensuous effects which the poet achieves here through rhymes and contrasts of sound, through sustained and cumulative rhythms, and through alternating and contrastive rhythms, are of course utterly impossible to reproduce in translation. I can only offer the suggestion that the intensity and complexity of emotion which are evident even in translation find a counterpart in these 'formal' aspects of the original.

Earlier I drew attention to the fascination that Gaelic poets had, right from the beginnings of our literary history, with the very substance of language and the ways in which its strength and richness and delicateness may be exploited to make an impact upon the senses. MacGill-Eain's concern with the auditory properties of his medium puts him securely in that tradition: it is partly what makes him a Gaelic poet. Yet although at times there is almost an excess in this side of his writing, he can just as easily compose in other styles.

Most of MacGill-Eain's poems have an abundance of traditional rhymes, both internal as well as end-rhymes. A few have only minimal or unconventional rhyme. Many poems are in traditional rhymed quatrains; others are in irregular paragraphs. There is no definite linear development to be traced from any one of these positions to another. His two earliest published poems 'A' Chorra-Ghridheach' and 'A Chiall 's a Ghràidh' are in markedly different styles: the first in rhyming quatrains, of strong but varied rhythm, which shows a number of departures from strict conventions of rhyme; the second in an unusually bare and sensuously meagre *vers libre*, the lines of which are grouped in threes. Certain features of the design of both these poems appear and develop throughout his work.

MacGill-Eain employs the traditional Gaelic system of internal as well as final rhyme very freely. Technically, this ornamenting device, as I shall call it for the moment, is perhaps his most conspicuous link with the traditional past. The internal rhyme is the most distinctive marker of what the modern Gaelic speaker regards as 'traditional' technique (end-rhyme is of course taken for granted) and it remained the leading ornament in the diminished verse tradition of the late nineteenth and twentieth centuries which I alluded to earlier. It is sometimes implied that this cross-rhyming is a difficult art. It is not. The fact of the matter is that the Gaelic imagination is so dominated by the design that it is almost impossible to avoid it.

Connected with that fallacy is another. We sometimes hear it said that unless we bring a conscious awareness of these aural patterns to bear upon the poems or songs that contain them, our appreciation of the poetry is limited. This is almost the reverse of the truth. If the ornamentation obtrudes, the poem remains no more than an artefact – either that or we ourselves are guilty of focussing on the craft at the expense of the poetry. It is only when we take the craft for granted, and the aural sensuousness works upon us subliminally, that total communication takes place. Furthermore, because of the tyranny of mechanical rhythm and predictable rhyme, it is a more difficult art to break the hold of these metres than to follow their rules. But perhaps even more difficult is to combine old and new in such a way that neither neutralizes the other. This poetry never lets us forget that it is extending the tradition in which it is so obviously rooted.

If Somhairle MacGill-Eain's poetry were subjected to a mechanical analysis in terms of all its rhetorical techniques, we could show that its author is a master in the use of traditional ornament. But the 'ornament' is an integral part of a dense fabric of speech. At other times the senses are jolted because the reinforcement of an expected rhyme is suddenly withheld. The effect is physical and the meaning is altered as well. Those who care to test any of these statements can find the proof almost anywhere in his poetry.

One good example is the beautifully designed, wistful poem 'Gleann Aoighre'. It is a sad, exquisite poem of great rhythmic poise and delicateness, with rich textures of vowel contrasts and harmonies, none of which is external to the meaning. Later poems, 'Aig Uaigh Yeats' to take an example at random, on the whole tend towards a looser weave of sound; in this poem the lack of rhyme in expected places and the sudden occurrence of rhyme, as well as the asymmetry of its three stanzas (8 lines; 9 lines; 8 lines), are quite as much part of the meaning as the aural tapestry of 'Gleann Aoighre'. Another late poem 'Creagan Beaga' has a completely different design: three quatrains with regular 'ab' end-rhyme and no internal rhymes.

Tha mi dol troimh Chreagan Beaga
anns an dorchadas liom fhìn
agus an rod air Camus Alba
'na shian air a' mhol mhìn.

I am going through Creagan Beaga
in the darkness alone
and the surf on Camus Alba
is a sough on smooth shingle.

The use of 'agus' ('and') at the beginning of a line (where traditionally Gaelic would nearly always use the connective ''s') has a strangely unsettling effect. It checks movement and gives the scene a kind of stillness – unremarkable as the word 'and' may seem in translation. The word 'agus', however, is used in various other places in MacGill-Eain's poems in a normal colloquial way but none the less not in the way of colloquial Gaelic in poetry. On each occasion it makes a special impact. The last line of the verse ' 'na shian air a' mhol mhìn' has a magical effect, achieved by the vowel contrast, of realising the sound of the surf on a shingle beach, and the effect is made intensely real and intensely local by the use of the word 'rod' which is localised in the Gaelic of Raasay and parts of Skye.

Of course one can find in various areas of Gaelic poetry manifestations of a comparable art. In some verse forms the full panoply of rhyme and other devices is mandatory and if the pattern is broken the art is flawed. Other forms allow considerably more freedom. MacGill-Eain uses all the possibilities and uses them together. No other Gaelic poet has produced an art which gives the impression in such a remarkable way of playing constantly fluctuating movement against stable forms. No Gaelic poet has a richer or more delicate or more varied auditory imagination. Yet at no time are we in danger of being seduced by that. It is what he says, not how he says it, that arrests the attention. The reasons why the labels of 'romantic' and 'classical' have been applied respectively to the content and form of his poetry are easy to see but like any other major artist he is not to be restricted by them. Integrity, not formalism, is the distinguishing feature of his poetry. Thus he will introduce stanzas in different metres, or alter their lengths or their rhyme-schemes, according to the demand of the moment and still create a sense not of formal ineptitude but of artistic inevitability.

It ought to be clear even from the brief sketch I have given of the metrical resources of Gaelic that the modern poet has almost an embarrassment of riches to draw on. But because MacGill-Eain's complex music is verbal, not melodic; since the great bulk of what he has written is poetry and not song and has a self-contained existence in speech or on the printed page; it is undoubtedly different in kind from the music-and-verse that precedes him. Does this difference in kind then mean that he has borrowed from English or other metrical traditions? One of the problems in tackling that formidable question is that although Gaelic has unique metrical forms, it also shares a common Western European literary heritage. Specifically with regard to Somhairle MacGill-Eain, one may single out a given structure and find its parallels easily enough in other literatures; sometimes, however, one can more easily find them in earlier Gaelic. Take an example: the fundamental metric of 'A' Bhuaile Ghréine'

> *Do m' shùilean-sa bu tu Deirdre*
> *'S i bòidheach 's a' bhuaile ghréine*

> To my eyes you were Deirdre
> beautiful in the sunny cattle-fold

is the same as W.B. Yeats' 'To Ireland in the Coming Times'

> Know that I would accounted be
> True brother of a company

Of course each poet realises the metre in his own individual way. The young Yeats (of the 1890s) lacks the sophistication, the varied pace, of the young MacGill-Eain (of the 1930s); Yeats' later rhythms often remind one, quite irresistibly, of the movement of MacGill-Eain's poetry. Even the sequences of rhyme used by both poets have sometimes a good deal in common. MacGill-Eain tells us (although the statement is not necessarily about metrics) that he 'did not know the middle and later poetry of Yeats until well on in the thirties, but from then on it affected me considerably'.[2] He has also declared, in a completely different context, that 'metrically Gaelic can do anything English has done, but the metric of the great bulk of Gaelic poetry is impossible in English'.[3] We must guard against facile comparisons and facile inferences alike.

In any event, there are in Gaelic more than one species of metric in what may generically be called choral songs (waulking-songs and the like) which yield a pattern not unlike that of 'A' Bhuaile Ghréine', 'An t-Eilean', 'Coin is Madaidhean-Allaidh', 'Nighean is Seann Òrain' and one or two others.

To put it in the simplest terms, waulking-songs are sung in couplets or single lines. When these are written down without their choruses of vocables, we find in some of them a paragraphic structure of irregular lengths, each paragraph division being indicated by change of rhyme. The change usually marks a change in thematic treatment or in subject-matter. There are a few songs (I cannot think of more than half-a-dozen in the whole of Gaelic literature) which appear to have been sung in these irregular paragraphs, not in the lines or couplets of the waulking-song tradition. One of the best known in print is an address to the famous seventeenth-century warrior, Alasdair mac Colla (Alexander Colkitto), 'Alasdair a laoigh mo chéille | Có chunnaic no dh'fhàg thu 'n Éirinn'.[4]

The poems I have cited – 'A' Bhuaile Ghréine', etc. – are certainly not replicas: they all tend toward couplet rhyme, here and there extended beyond the couplet, but they do give the same sense of rhythmic drive and energy. This traditional paragraphic structure probably affords one of the best starting points for adapting a Gaelic metre to what we may call, for brevity's sake, a non-traditional sensibility. This opens up an interesting line of speculation, seeing that the metre is native and ancient and that some of the poetry composed in it has a positively surrealistic character. For MacGill-Eain has his own vein of surrealism: 'Coin is Madaidhean-Allaidh', among other poems, exemplifies it. Almost at every turn, the critic is forced to adopt a Janus attitude. Furthermore, Gaelic poetry, in which the oral element is so strong, frequently displays the paratactic style associated with oral poetry throughout the world. The stanza, or even the line, is usually self-contained, in sense as in syntax.

In MacGill-Eain's work in general what we find is the normal thematic development of literary poetry. This is not a matter of adding one idea to another, line after line. But when there is a tendency to make the line or couplet autonomous in meaning, the reader frequently has a sense of being poised between the old Gaelic poetry and the new. That feeling is inescapable even if the explanation suggested here is wrong. At all events, the modern revolution in Gaelic poetry is to a large extent centred on thematic development. A new concept of poetic structure has been introduced to Gaelic literature and English poetry certainly provides a wide enough field in which to seek its source. Yet when all background influences on MacGill-Eain's poetry come to be investigated, these vivid, passionate songs, with their flexible paragraphic structure, cannot be left out of account. They have their own kind of thematic sequences which use an antithetical, cumulative or climactic mode of expression.

How did Somhairle MacGill-Eain solve the problem of creating a 'modern' diction from the resources of his native language? First, so far as I am aware, there is not a single neologism, strictly speaking, in the whole of his poetry. 'An ceathramh seòl-tomhais' (the fourth dimension), might seem to qualify for the label of neologism but 'seòl-tomhais' (a mode of measurement), is colloquial enough: 'seòl' in such compounds is still productive in Gaelic. An English reader, finding the word 'synthesis' in the translation, might well suspect that the original is a modern coinage. But 'co-chur' (better 'cochur': it is stressed on the first syllable) is a well-established item in the vocabulary of Presbyterian theology and preaching. In that context it has a slightly different meaning: its elements nevertheless are precisely equivalent to the Greek elements which form the word 'synthesis'. The fact that the poet can find what he needs in the working vocabulary of the language is a comment on the extraordinary wealth of Gaelic and its capacity for survival in spite of the ethnocidal policies of centuries. MacGill-Eain draws on every area of Scots Gaelic, sometimes using obscure and little-known words, whether from literature or from the living language. It may be that certain of the 'literary' words are now obsolete in speech but it is dangerous to dogmatise about obsolescence in Gaelic, as anyone who has devoted a reasonable amount of time to the study of dialects and oral tradition will appreciate.

A rare, if not obsolete, word is 'drithleann' ('sparkle, gleam', etc.), which occurs, for instance, in the very early 'A' Chorra-Ghridheach': 'luasgan is cadal gun drithleann' ('unrest and sleep without a gleam');

'ciùrrte, aon-drithleannach' ('wounded, with but one sparkle'). The adjective 'drithleannach' is used in a striking image of a piper's fingering in a seventeenth-century song by the Blind Harper at Dunvegan. Noun and adjective alike, however, are rare even in literature. Another very rare word is 'diùchd' ('appear, manifest (oneself)'). So far as I know, only two poets have used it before MacGill-Eain: Uilleam Ros and his maternal grandfather Am Pìobaire Dall, from whose poetry Ros possibly learnt it. If it is short – 'diuchd' and not 'diùchd' – it may still be known in speech, though in a somewhat different sense. There is actually some doubt as to the quantity of the word: MacGill-Eain writes it with a long vowel.

Interestingly enough, a number of words exist in Gaelic which certain writers, from about the second half of the eighteenth century, have lengthened unhistorically. Some of these are part of the same Presbyterian and theological vocabulary as 'cochur'. For instance, MacGill-Eain takes 'éire' ('burden') from established ecclesiastical usage: it occurs in 'Coilltean Ratharsair':

'S e gu bheil iad ag éirigh
às an doimhne thruaigh reubte
tha cur air beanntan an éire

It is that they rise
from the miserable torn depths
that puts their burden on mountains

We know from the song tradition, however, that the word is short (e.g. 'Och a Rìgh gur trom m' eire | Nochd 's mi 'n eilean a' chaoil', where rhyme fixes the quantity). Although some academic critics may feel that words like these are solecisms, and that it is an aesthetic and linguistic lapse to prolong their existence, this is surely far too austere a view. MacGill-Eain is perfectly justified in choosing words from this particular literary register of Gaelic just as he is justified in taking words from any area of living Gaelic speech.

Words are public but far from impersonal entities and frequently have a private life in individual imagination. When an author (who is perhaps more likely to be a writer rather than a non-literate composer) succeeds in transmitting his individual perception of a word – its sound, its appearance on a page, or a latent meaning – to the public context of his work, a hitherto unrealised potential is made available. In that creative process a writer puts his own impress on a word: it can never be quite the 'same' word again. Its position in the language has shifted; its status has been enhanced and its meaning extended. A major writer alters the language itself.

MacGill-Eain uses the Gaelic lexicon in such a way that literary Gaelic will never be the same again. The context of his poetry gives the common currency of Gaelic, as well as the antique and unusual words, the quality of newly-minted coin. Recurrent words – among them words that express degrees of brightness, unrest, unattainableness, transience, suffering, pride – form his unmistakable signature. An individual reader will, of course, have his own predilections in choosing the words that sign a poet's style. Some readers may agree that the word 'lì' ('sheen, tinge' in spoken Gaelic) has a distinctive place in the group: normally in MacGill-Eain's poetry it is the sheen of beauty or just 'beauty' itself. 'Ardan', another key-word, is in common usage 'pride' in a pejorative sense, a tendency to take offence easily. MacGill-Eain emphasises rather its sense of 'proper pride, fierce pride, proud anger'.

Of the various words for 'jewel' in Gaelic, he chooses the interesting and fairly rare 'leug'; adj, 'leugach'. Historically it is interesting, if only for the fact that it has been described as 'a false "literary", "southern" [Highland] restoration'.[5] Although this judgement is unduly dismissive, the word is probably to be regarded as a literary coinage. It is certainly one of the lexical markers of MacGill-Eain's poetry: 'Mo leug camhanaich is oidhche' ('My jewel of dawn and night'); 'Agus fodham eilean leugach' ('And under me a jewel-like island'); 'Ciamar a smaoinichinn gun glacainn | An rionnag leugach òir' ('How should I think I would seize the radiant golden star'); 'Agus fo reultan Africa | 's iad leugach àlainn' ('And under the stars of Africa, | jewelled and beautiful'). A few poets have used 'leug' in the past but it now exists in a wholly new dimension.

From the poet's own translations it is evident that he sometimes focusses sharply and individualistically on a particular point in the semantic range of a word. 'Labhar', for instance, in its general import 'loud', is almost always translated 'eloquent'. This meaning is known neither in literature nor in contemporary spoken Gaelic. But it may have been used in that sense in certain contexts in the past: Dwelly's Dictionary gives 'eloquent' as the fourth sense of the word. This development, too, may have come from ecclesiastical usage. Wherever such extensions of meaning may have their source, they are to be regarded as an enrichment of the language. Even if Somhairle Mac-

Gill-Eain is only making accessible what is already latent in Gaelic, his claim to originality is high in this sphere also. No doubt if this poetry were written in Lowland Scots, it would have been celebrated or criticised long before now for its 'synthetic' diction. But if there is any parallel, on a purely linguistic level, between MacDiarmid's treatment of Scots and MacGill-Eain's treatment of Gaelic, the cultural perspectives of Gaelic makes for a fundamental difference of approach on the part of Gaelic readers from that of the critics of 'synthetic Scots'.

Gaelic poets of the past, literate or non-literate, were frequently eclectic. The non-literate Màiri nighean Alasdair Ruaidh in the seventeenth century, composing in the vernacular, borrows directly or at one or more removes from Classical Gaelic poetry. In the eighteenth century the highly literate Uilleam Ros sought what he required in the living dialects. And there are many other examples. As a general observation, one may say that in Gaelic tradition (where fame and linguistic versatility are closely allied) no poet of note has been, in the strict senses, a 'dialect poet'. Even with this background, however, the linguistic authority and arbiter of usage that MacGill-Eain constantly cites is the Church – in his case the Free Presbyterian Church, of which his family were adherents. Time and time again I have heard MacGill-Eain back up his discussion of linguistic usage with the phrases: 'Chuala mi 'san eaglais e' or 'Dh'fhaodainn a bhith air a chluinntinn 'san eaglais' ('I (could have) heard it in church').

If English translation cannot possibly transmit a sense of the variety and luxuriance of MacGill-Eain's Gaelic or convey the impact of a rare word in a new and contemporary setting, much less can it suggest the 'ambiguity' which a complex of associations creates. The following lines occur in 'Aithreachas': 'A Dhia, 'se bòidhche a' ghàrraidh: [. . .] nach fhan ri buidheachas an fhoghair' ('O God, the beauty of the garden: [. . .] which will not stay for the yellow gratitude of autumn'). 'Buidheachas' is gratitude; 'buidhe' is yellow. These words are unrelated and are not normally linked in the mind of a native speaker of Gaelic. The present context, however, inevitably evokes the image of ripening corn. At a deeper level of analysis, still another word 'buidhe', which belongs with 'gratitude' not with 'yellow', and survives in some stereotyped phrases, where it is in fact linked with 'yellow', would also come under scrutiny. This is the 'buidhe' of the line 'bu bhuidhe dhomh na do na h-eòin' ('the springtide is more golden to me than to the birds') in 'Reothairt'.

Another example of ambiguity may be found in the opening line of

'Am Mùr Gorm': 'Mur b'e thusa bhiodh an Cuilithionn | 'na mhùr eagarra gorm'. Here the two words, again unrelated, are 'eagarra' ('precise') and 'eag(ach)' ('notch(ed)'). The translation, 'But for you the Cullin would be | an exact and serrated blue rampart', has perforce to put the two elements on the same semantic footing. The original Gaelic allows the primary sense to remain dominant. In his English translations of each of these citations the poet has succeeded in conveying the scope of the images by making them fully explicit. Even if some subtlety is lost they are still powerful.

Occasionally an image or a statement seems, indeed, to make as great an impact in English as in Gaelic. One of these is the marvellous line in 'Hallaig': 'Anns a' chamhanaich bhalbh bheò', translated 'in the dumb living twilight'. 'Balbh' is primarily 'dumb, without speech', but is also the normal colloquial Gaelic for 'still, hushed'. In Gaelic 'beò' ('living') is as unexpected as 'dumb' is in the brilliant translation which selects the primary meaning of 'balbh'. When the native element is combined with a concept that is Romantic (in the sense that Wordsworth's 'living air' is Romantic), the resulting compound image is a microcosm of the blend of sensibilities that makes MacGill-Eain the kind of poet that he is: modern, sophisticated and Gaelic.

I am therefore not implying in anything that I have written that the non-Gaelic reader is cut off from his poetry. What I am emphasising is the need to assess his work against the background, and within the perspectives, of Gaelic literature as a whole, if those aspects to which translation gives us access are to be understood in all their richness. A number of topics which still require to be interpreted in that light come to mind. For instance, an entire essay could be devoted to his use of place names; another to the sea as a source of imagery. Place names occupy a central place in Gaelic literature. The sea is one of the great themes of Gaelic poetry, particularly the song-poetry of the Hebrides and the North Western seaboard. In MacGill-Eain's poetry these and other themes make comparisons and contrasts with the poetry of the past.

The wonderful celebration of mountains in 'Ceann Loch Aoineart' is unique as a nature poem in Gaelic in the way it brings together visual, aural and tactile images in a multi-dimensional style. This can certainly be said to be a poem of Romantic sensibility; it is also a poem which is probably quite as effective in English translation as it is in Gaelic. For all that, a Gaelic reader recalls other celebrations of famous mountains: Donnchadh Bàn Mac an t-Saoir's panegyric to

'Beinn Dobhrain', for instance, or Domhnall mac Fhionnlaigh nan Dàn's passionate evocation of the mountains of Lochaber. Certainly a contrast of sensibilities exists between 'Ceann Loch Aoineart' and 'Beinn Dobhrain', whatever terms we may find to express it.

Curiously enough, there is more of a bond between the Romantic in MacGill-Eain and the sixteenth-century hunter-poet Domhnall Mac Fhionnlaigh nan Dàn as he views the mountain he shall never climb again while it 'will not descend until doom'. More than a gap of centuries, however, separates Domhnall Mac Fhionnlaigh's unclimbable mountain and 'the mountain that may not be climbed' of MacGill-Eain's 'Nighean is Seann Òrain'. And yet at a much deeper and more obscure level one can sense a relationship between, say, 'the full, bare mountain' ('a' bheinn làn lom') in 'Craobh nan Teud' and the mountains of the wilderness that appear in Gaelic song more than once under the name of 'A' Bheinn Mhór'. Symbolically, the mountain is a place of ritual mourning: 'ascending and descending the mountain'. It is also equivalent to the Greenwood of Love: 'on the peaks of the mountains [. . .] in the track of the bellowing deer'. The mountain and the wild moor symbolise the anarchic energies and activities of human life set in contrast with the regulated life of the settled community. At times one feels that this is an archetypal image: that the 'great mountain', the 'forbidding mountain', the 'mountain of mist', and so forth, are all partly a reflection, no matter how faint, of the cosmic mountain which features in art and culture throughout the world. How much of that is directly relevant to the mountain symbol in MacGill-Eain's poetry ('A' Bheinn air Chall', for example; or 'the shifting mountain of time') must be left in the realms of conjecture. The point is, once again, that the Gaelic reader is aware of the tradition no matter what the sources of the poet's inspiration may have been.

Something of the same kind is true of the image of the tree. Gaelic poetry is full of kennings and metaphors of trees. They are to be found in love poetry and in eulogies composed for the warrior, the 'tree of battle', the 'tree of slaughter'. In a mid-seventeenth-century poem Gaelic warriors are described as 'trees of good lineage from fairy hills'. The fairy mound or *sìdhein*, the abode of the ancestral dead, is also the local focus of the Otherworld in pagan Gaelic cosmology. An image such as that continues to draw upon a primitive source of energy. The seventeenth-century poet was no doubt well versed in the ancient lore of the great sacred trees of Gaelic mythology which are themselves

representatives of the tree that grows at the axis of the world. For
those who know that lore and the kennings of Gaelic poetry, 'Craobh
nan Teud', with its 'tree of poetry'; 'the beautiful heroic tree'; 'tree of
ecstasy'; 'the love-tree'; the 'great tree of the high mountains' develops
a familiar rhetoric even if the development is new and extraordinary.
Nevertheless, these particular metaphors actually lead us away from
the mythopoeic universe. We return to it in 'Hallaig':

> 's tha mo ghaol aig Allt Hallaig
> 'na craoibh bheithe, 's bha i riamh
> eadar an t-Inbhir 's Poll a' Bhainne,
> thall 's a bhos mu Bhaile-Chùirn:
> tha i 'na beithe, 'na calltuinn,
> 'na caorunn dhìreach sheang ùir [. . .]
> Chunnacas na mairbh beò [. . .]
> na h-igheanan 'nan coille bheithe,
> dìreach an druim, crom an ceann.

> and my love is at the Burn of Hallaig,
> a birch tree, and she has always been
> between Inver and Milk Hollow,
> here and there about Baile Chùirn:
> she is a birch, a hazel,
> a straight, slender young rowan [. . .]
> The dead have been seen alive [. . .]
> the girls a wood of birches,
> straight their backs, bent their heads.

'Hallaig' is a twentieth-century poem and contains images of its time.
Setting these aside, I have the feeling it is also a poem that would have
been understood a thousand years ago and more. The mandarin caste
of medieval society who were the keepers of ancient wisdom and
learning, and whose name *file* originally meant 'seer', might not find
'Hallaig' as mysterious as some modern readers do. 'Coilltean Ratharsair' would be far more baffling.

   These of course are opinions that depend upon a knowledge of Gaelic
poetry throughout history. Much more accessible are the synchronic
aspects of MacGill-Eain's poetry: the inner relationships that exist
between individual poems and the deployment of certain leitmotifs.
Within the limits of this essay I can only draw attention to one or two
examples of what I mean. In spite of the fundamental difference between

the symbolism of 'Craobh nan Teud' and 'Coilltean Ratharsair', we can sense here and there an underlying connection in imagery, as if parts of each poem had the same matrix. 'Craobh nan Teud' has:

Gealach is dubhar uaine choilltean,
Cùirneanan an driùchd 'na boillsgeadh,
brìodal sùgraidh nan òg aoibhneach,
'nan leugan òirdhearc 'na loinn ghil.
Suaimhneas sneachda nam beann grian-laist'

Moon and green shadowiness of woods,
Beads of dew shining in its light,
Tender love-talk of the happy young,
Splendid jewels in its bright elegance.
Snowy tranquillity of sun-lit mountains

Compare that from 'Craobh nan Teud' with this from 'Coilltean Ratharsair':

[. . .] sàmhchair choilltean,
ceilearadh shruthan is suaineadh aibhnean,
ciùine reultan buidhe a' boillsgeadh,
lainnir a' chuain, coille-bionain na h-oidhche.
Nuair dhòirt a' ghealach na crùin shoilleir
air clàr dùghorm na linne doilleir [. . .]
[. . .] Sgurr nan Gillean [. . .]
[. . .] sgiamhach le ghile,
le ghile sneachda 'na dhrithleann,
ciùin agus stòlda 'na shitheadh [. . .]
Coille uaine [. . .]

[. . .] the peace of the woodlands,
the bird-song of rivulets and the winding of burns,
the mildness of yellow stars shining,
the glitter of the sea, the phosphorescence of night.
When the moon poured the bright crown pieces
on the dark blue board of the sea at night [. . .]
Sgurr nan Gillean [. . .]
[. . .] in its whiteness,
in its snow whiteness sparkling,
calm and steadfast in its thrust [. . .]
Green wood [. . .]

It is only a trace and I have to mutilate the verse in order to focus on it. The next example is somewhat different. *Dàin do Eimhir* LII reads:

> Do m' dhùr-amharc bha thu 'nad reul
> 's tu leat fhéin 's an iarmailt:
> is thugadh dhut an dà leus
> le m' aigne thorrach 's m' iargain.
>
> 'S an uair sin bhoillsg thu le trì
> an aon leus dìreach trianaid;
> ach cha robh 'nam leòis dhian fhìn
> ach clann do lithe 'n iargain.
>
> Bha mi feitheamh ris a' bheum
> a mhilleadh do réim le chrìonadh;
> ach thug mi dhut na trì dhut fhéin
> an ceann réis deich bliadhna.
>
> Oir nam b' iad mo leòis gin fhìn
> a bheòthaich lì 'nad lias-sa
> bu chinnt gun cailleadh iad am brìgh
> le glasadh tìm deich bliadhna.
>
> A shuilbhireachd 's a chridhe chòir
> 's sibh lòghmhor ann an aodann:
> a mheallaidh cridhe 's a mheallaidh sùla
> ur n-ìomhaigh rùin a h-aogas!
>
> Cha b' ann fada bha an tòir
> a thug corr 's deich bliadhna
> an uair a bha an fhaodail corr
> 's na dh'fhoghnadh dòchas sìorruidh.

To my steady gaze you were a star
all alone in the skies,
and you were given two rays of light
by my fertile mind and my longing.

Then you shone forth with three
in a single direct effulgent trinity,
but in my intense rays of light
there were only the children of your beauty yearning.

I waited for the stroke
that would impair your power and wither it;
but I gave you the three for yourself
at the end of a space of ten years.

For had they been of my own begetting,
those rays that kindled beauty in your brightness,
they would surely have lost their power
through ten years of time's greying.

Affable nature and kind heart,
you are radiant in one face –
beguiling the heart and beguiling the eyes –
beloved image of her appearance.

It was not long, the pursuit
that took longer than ten years,
when the treasure-trove
was more than enough for eternal hope.

If this is compared with 'An Sgian', it is clear that both are metaphysical poems, twin poems though not identical; and both immediately recognisable as the offspring of one intellect. Finally, from 'Craobh nan Teud' again come these images:

Éibhneach anns a' mheangach bhlàthmhor
suaimhneas geal an aodainn àluinn,
leugach anns a' chumadh-fàire
fiamh ulaidhe an rainn neo-bhàsmhoir.

Mar a reachadh i na b'fhaide
's ann a theannadh i na b'fhaisge,
's mar a thrialladh i am fadal
's ann a mhiadaicheadh a h-aiteal.

Joyful in the flowering branches
White tranquility of a beautiful face,
Jewelled in the horizon's shape
The precious gleam of immortal verse.

The farther it moved away
The nearer it approached,
As it travelled into the distance
So would its light increase.

In passing we may note the resemblance of the first verse to the last stanza of 'Am Mùr Gorm':

Agus air creachainn chéin fhàsmhoir
chinn blàthmhor Craobh nan Teud
'na meangach duillich t' aodann,
mo chiall is aogas réil.

And on a distant luxuriant summit
there blossomed the Tree of Strings,
among its leafy branches your face,
my reason and the likeness of a star.

There are other connections, some simple and some complex, between 'Coilltean Ratharsair', 'Craobh nan Teud' and the short poem 'An té dh'an tug mi [. . .]', with its images of 'dim wood', 'slender branching' and 'her beauty like a horizon opening the door to day'. The second verse contains precisely the same kind of metaphysical conceit as we find in the fifth stanza of 'An Sgian':

Mar a rachadh i an àireamh
nam bruan gearrte prann,
's ann a ghabhadh i aonachd
'na h-aonar cruaidh teann.

As it increased in number
of cut and brittle fragments,
so it took unity,
alone hard and taut.

The intellectual groundwork of 'Craobh nan Teud' is quite different from that of *Dàin do Eimhir* LII and of 'An Sgian', yet both display quite clearly a leitmotif of MacGill-Eain's metaphysical poetry. There are naturally very many finer threads of connection, through the themes of time's destructiveness, for instance, or the unattainability of human desire. But to demonstrate these connections would require a much closer examination of MacGill-Eain's vocabulary.

My register of techniques and formal relationships would not be complete without some illustration of the way in which rhythmic patterns become a vital part of the meaning. I shall take two examples. In 'Hallaig', 'The girls a wood of birches | [. . .] in silent bands | go to Clachan as in the beginning | and return from Clachan | from Suisnish and the land of the living; | each one young and light-stepping, | without the heartbreak of the tale':

> *O Allt na Fearnaibh gus an fhaoilinn*
> *tha soilleir an dìomhaireachd nam beann*
> *chan eil ach coimhthional nan nighean*
> *ag cumail na coiseachd gun cheann.*

> From the Burn of Fearns to the raised beach
> that is clear in the mystery of the hills,
> there is only the congregation of the girls
> keeping up the endless walk.

In the last line two conflicting rhythms, one the natural speech rhythm of the phrase, the other the rhythm dictated by the verse form, operate at the same time, each inhibiting the other. The result is that the line seems to be suspended: metrically it is in absolute accord with the meaning of the words. The other example comes from 'Cumha Chaluim Iain MhicGill-Eain'. If we read the last line of the sixth stanza 'Nan tigeadh tu a nall' ('If you were to come over') with elision of the 'obscure' vowel written 'a' – in other words, according to the normal pattern of Gaelic speech – a remarkable metrical effect is produced:

> *Nan robh thu anns a' Chlachan eile*
> *Tha bhos ann an Loch Aills,*
> *Bhiodh am fear treun ud dhe do shinnsre,*
> *Ruairi Beag a' chlogaid dhrilsich*
> *Moiteil 's e dèanamh gluasaid*
> *Gu do leigeil-sa ri ghualainn –*
> *Nan tigeadh tu (a) nall.*

> If you were in the other Clachan
> that is over here in Lochalsh,
> that brave man of your ancestors
> Ruairi Beag of the glittering helmet,
> would be proud to move
> to let you to his shoulder –
> if you were to come over.

The verse has overall a dominating, progressive movement which builds up over six lines. In the last statement that flow is suddenly checked. This gives the impression of a counter-current starting up against the main stream. The effect on the meaning is that the affirmation of the preceding lines is abruptly nullified. There are other examples of equal metrical delicateness but none of greater poignancy in the whole of MacGill-Eain's poetry.

If this is a revolution in Gaelic poetry we might reasonably expect that the architect of the revolution had a plan of campaign. Yet this does not appear to be the case. We can, of course, infer the strategy from the evidence of the poetry itself; but nothing that MacGill-Eain has said or written allows us to state that he set out deliberately to change the course of Gaelic poetry. It was the realisation, during his undergraduate years (when he was still writing English as well as Gaelic verse) that the latter was far superior, that made him confine himself to Gaelic. This does not mean that he had not prepared himself: from his teens, according to his own account, he had been reading Gaelic poetry obsessively. In 'A Radically Traditional Voice' I have drawn attention to the relevance of T. S. Eliot's 'Tradition and the Individual Talent':

> Tradition [. . .] cannot be inherited, and if you want it you must obtain it by great labour. It involves, in the first place, the historical sense [. . . which] involves a perception, not only of the pastness of the past, but of its presence [. . .] And it is at the same time what makes a writer most acutely conscious of his place in time, of his own contemporaneity.

Few people know the corpus of Gaelic poetry, published and unpublished, as intimately as MacGill-Eain knows it. Yet he hardly ever draws directly on the highly developed, involuted and sophisticated verbal code which constitutes the traditional diction of Gaelic poetry. In one of the sub-codes of that diction there is a phrase 'thall 's a bhos' ('here and there'), usually followed by 'mu' ('around, about'). In itself no more than one of the inconspicuous pinning-stones of speech, it is used in lyrical poetry with overtones of tragedy, loss and grief. In a famous seventeenth-century song, a party of the hapless Clan Gregor are apparently scattered as fugitives 'here and there around Loch Fyne'; in the lament of Campbell of Glen Faochain's widow in 1645 (after Inverlochy): 'Here and there about Inveraray women wring their hands, their hair dishevelled.' It is as if Auden's 'altogether elsewhere' had the backing of centuries of usage. When MacGill-Eain writes in 'Hallaig': 'Here and there about Baile Chùirn' these resonances are unmistakeably there. But this type of borrowing is very rare indeed.

MacGill-Eain has invented his own diction. As a poet who is secure in his tradition, 'acutely conscious of his own contemporaneity', he has, pre-eminently, a sense of the presence of the past. He is a magisterial writer who is totally in charge of his language and the techniques of his poetry; he is never controlled by them. There are times when he appears to be pushing Gaelic to its limits. There are times, indeed, when he gives the impression of being positively cavalier in his attitude towards the language. At any event he makes no concession to his readers. From that point of view it is perfectly legitimate to call his poetry élitist. Or rather, since the term may be taken to imply conscious intention, the poetry would qualify for that description were it not for the fact that, as he says himself, 'I was not one who could write poetry if it did not come to me in spite of myself, and if it came, it had to come in Gaelic.' And it comes, one may add, in spite of what the poetry declares of a division between heart and intellect, as the utterance of an entire person. In other words it has artistic sincerity.

The poetry registers such a range and intensity of emotion that even when its language is most literary and most elevated, it still speaks with affective directness and a simple passionate immediacy. There is no artifice. There are simplicities and difficulties; tenderness, delicateness and a rough-hewn quality; exquisite purity, and here and there an almost stumbling innocence; and immense sophistication. It is truly astonishing that only Gaelic, when it had already been driven so much into decline, could have provided a poet with the passionate eloquence to express that integrity. Somhairle MacGill-Eain needed Gaelic and Gaelic needed Somhairle MacGill-Eain.

Sorley Maclean's 'Hallaig': a note

In 1846 John MacLeod, the chief of the MacLeods of Raasay (styled in Gaelic 'Mac Gille Chaluim') sold the island to a pious gentleman from Edinburgh whose name was George Rainy. Rainy in effect introduced the Clearances to Raasay. Between 1852 and 1854 the entire population of twelve townships, ninety-four families in all, were driven from their homes, the majority of them being forced to emigrate to the Colonies. One of these townships was Hallaig.

Hallaig lies on the eastern side of Raasay, overlooked by Dùn Cana, the highest hill on the island. From the Dùn Cana ridge the land falls dramatically in great terraces of rock and sweeping green plateaus down to the sea. It is a heroic landscape, in some ways reminiscent of the east of Skye, round the Stoer rock, but different in scale and line, a remote place of haunting stillness and emptiness that was once full of the sound of human voices.

The memories that cling to the very name of Hallaig cannot but have a special poignancy for Sorley Maclean, for in these townships of Raasay untold generations of his own people lived and died. Interestingly enough, one of the Maclean families of that area (probably Screapadal) makes a brief appearance in the pages of James Boswell's *Journal of a Tour to the Hebrides with Samuel Johnson in 1773*. Boswell's account of his visit to the homestead is the merest vignette but is vivid enough to give us a fleeting glimpse of what this modestly prosperous Gaelic community of small farms was like. By a curious coincidence, it was exactly a hundred years after the final destruction of that community that Sorley Maclean composed 'Hallaig'.

The rubric 'Time, the deer, is in the wood of Hallaig' is not a quotation from another poem but a separate line composed at the same time as 'Hallaig'. It is clear that the deer that is killed by love's bullet is Time itself. This reminds us at once of another poem, Edwin Muir's 'The Road'.

There is a road that turning always
Cuts off the country of Again.
Arches stand there on every side
And as it runs Time's deer is slain,
And lies where it has lain.

Sorley Maclean's poetry is often preoccupied with the nature of time, as may be seen most clearly in the great metaphysical love poem 'A face haunts me', translated by Iain Crichton Smith in *Poems to Eimhir* (No. LVII). The concern with time is manifest in 'Hallaig' also, and not only in the final statement. The entire poem projects a vision which is tragic and redemptive. Tragic in that the reality of time, of history, what actually happened in that particular place, Hallaig, 'the heartbreak of the tale', is inescapable. Redemptive in that destructive time is itself destroyed in the vision of love that transmutes experience into the timelessness of art; but tragic, too, in that this transcendence is bounded by mortality. While the poet lives, it is implied in the last verse, the vision will remain; time will be arrested; but only for a measure of time.

This dialectical movement, so very characteristic of Maclean's mind, can be followed throughout the structure of the poem, at different levels of analysis. In the most general terms, it expresses that intersection of time with the timeless already mentioned. And so, while the sabbath of the dead reigns in Hallaig, the dead live again. So, also, 'the endless walk'. These antitheses can be multiplied. For instance, two types of tree stand in contrastive roles – the great pines of the south-western sector of Raasay and the deciduous woods that are simply part of the island's natural features. But although the birch and rowan and hazel – especially the birch – are the prime symbols of the poem, and at one level symbol only, they also, at another level, have their existence in an organic landscape. It is this organic nature that puts them as symbols at the farthest possible remove from allegory. To add one more paradox, that fact undermines the poet's fear that his vision is limited by his mortality.

For the landscape is a Gaelic landscape. A feeling for landscape, for nature in general, is very old in Gaelic poetry, stretching back beyond the Scottish vernacular to the Scoto-Irish literary traditions of the early Middle Ages. In one of the Scottish developments, landscape, delineated through its place names, and community, delineated through the personal names of its heroes, are both celebrated in one complex whole. In the erosion of Gaelic society and identity this framework was virtually destroyed and nature poetry, in common with other kinds, became increasingly open to outside influences. Broadly speaking, the dominant influence in the process was English Romanticism, especially from 1872 when compulsory education (in English only) was imposed, and an 'educated' Gael was more likely than not to be illiterate in his own tongue. In such depressed social and cultural circumstances, the inevitable result was a poetry that always tended to sentimentality.

Nevertheless, something of that traditional apperception that links people and landscape in one humanised environment remained alive in the Gaelic view of the world, and from it 'Hallaig' draws part of its strength and its poignancy. Yet equally palpable is the Romantic sensibility of the poem. What Sorley Maclean has done here, as elsewhere in his poetry, is to fuse these disparate elements of two cultures in an utterly new statement which is emotionally subtle and powerful, unsentimental, and wholly Gaelic. Through his genius, both the Gaelic sense of landscape, idealised in terms of society, and the Romantic sense of communion with Nature, merge in a single vision, a unified sensibility.

In noting these exterior relationships the focus, of course, must always be on the finished product itself. 'Hallaig' is a living Gaelic poem – a true and realistic poem – because it synthesises the manifold variety of the modern Gaelic mind. Moreover, the final distillate of this compound experience is so pure that although 'Hallaig' is obviously a poem of great sophistication, it can also, because it completely avoids the esoteric, be described as a poem of great simplicity and innocence.

This could not be achieved without a superb technical accomplishment, but the technique is so effortless, so much part of the total statement of the poem, that even to call it brilliant seems incongruous. Beneath that even surface, variegated but indivisible as water, the Gaelic reader is aware of a profound depth of pathos and yearning: such a sense of completion at the symbolic level, such a sense of incompletion at the level of history. 'Hallaig' is a strange compound of dialectic and dream.

How much of all this is conveyed in translation, each English reader must judge for himself. He will at least be able to trace the different levels of the poem and the complications of its imagery. It is these demonstrable complexities that make 'Hallaig' a most remarkable artefact. It is its undemonstrable complexities that make it a great poem.

Postscript

This was originally written in support of Prof. Geoffrey Dutton's proposal to award Maclean an honorary doctorate from the University of Dundee.

Essays on Belief Systems and World View

Religion in Gaelic Society

Religion is certainly one of the most important constituents of any society and Gaelic society is no exception. Almost at any point in our history from the introduction of Christianity to the present day, it would be possible to test the truth of that statement. Although 'religion' here is to be equated with Christianity, a detailed investigation could not limit itself to what we might call the 'official' religion of Gaelic society but would also take cognisance of certain beliefs that anthropologists (if not theologians) would recognise as ingredients of the larger complex of Gaelic religious consciousness. That is, to be exhaustive, we should have to examine at least the social role of what we so often tend to dismiss as 'superstition'. But of course in this short essay I cannot even analyse the developments within Christianity itself in any but the most superficial way. I hope, nevertheless, from time to time to glance at some of the interactions in Gaelic society between certain 'superstitions' and the faith of the Church. But in overall terms my intention is really no more than to indicate what I think are areas in which students of religion, social anthropologists, sociologists, and indeed historians also have still a good deal of work to do.

We are all by nature inclined to adopt without much questioning the historical perspectives that are transmitted to us as part of our own cultural heritage. All history or rather all historiography is in a certain sense propaganda. Writers of history, consciously or otherwise, assess motives and events according to a system of values which, crudely speaking – and I emphasise that – are 'tribal'. The 'tribe' may be an empire or a nation, a linguistic group or a religious tradition. Or it may contain elements of all of these at one and the same time. Most of what has been written, it seems to me, about the history of the Highlands is governed, often quite subtly, by an 'imperial' idea. Nor is this confined to the period in which the Gaels served the British Empire. As we all know, there has been some reaction to that kind of historiography. But the reaction is still largely against economic imperialism, much less against cultural imperialism and the erosion of our identity as a distinctive people.

On any reading of history, it is clear that the Church, in all its branches, has contributed something of importance to the culture, and cultural identity, of the Gaels. It is so also in the case of other nations. No one denies, for instance, the importance in English of the Authorised Version of the Bible or, in an earlier age, the importance of the homiletic literature that ensured the continuity of English prose from late Old English through Middle English into the early modern language.[1] In Gaelic we owe much the same debts to the Church, for example with regard to the formal continuity of written Gaelic prose. But at the present day what is perhaps the most important fact of all is that only in the Church, among major social institutions, is Gaelic used, not as if it were dialect but as a language, and used as a medium of exposition on a par with any other language in that context.

At the other end of the historical scale we have some fascinating examples of how the old and new faiths, the Christian and the pagan, became blended in what we, quite properly, regard as poetry but which the authors, quite as properly, no doubt regarded as prayers or spells. One of these is the so-called 'Breastplate of St Patrick', a composition now believed to be of the eighth century, some three hundred years after Patrick's time. 'Breastplate', of course, is metaphorical: the armour of faith. It will be known to most of us in the form in which it appears in the Hymnary: 'I bind unto myself today | The strong Name of the Trinity.' A more literal rendering of the original Gaelic is this:

> Today I gird myself
> With a mighty power
> Invocation of the Trinity,
> Belief in the Threeness,
> Affirmation of the Oneness,
> In the Creator's presence.
>
> Today I gird myself
> With the power of Christ's birth together with his baptism,
> With the power of his crucifixion together with his burial,
> With the power of his resurrection together with his ascension,
> With the power of his descent to pronounce the judgment of Doomsday.

Shortly after that there comes a stanza:

> Today I gird myself
> With the strength of heaven,

Light of the sun,
Brightness of the moon,
Brilliance of fire,
Speed of lightning,
Swiftness of wind,
Depth of sea,
Firmness of earth,
Stability of rock.

After an intervening verse we have:

Today I interpose all these powers between myself
And every harsh pitiless power which may come against my body and my
  soul,
Against the predictions of false prophets,
Against the black laws of paganism,
Against the crooked laws of heretics,
Against the encirclement of idolatry,
Against the spells of women and smiths and druids,
Against every knowledge which harms a man's body and soul.[2]

Some further stanzas and this poetic prayer ends with the words in
which it opens. This is obviously a Christian composition and in its
main statement perfectly orthodox. But compare the following, which
is also a Breastplate.

I invoke the seven daughters of the sea
Who form the threads of the long-lived youths.
May three deaths be taken from me,
May three life-times be granted me.
May seven waves of luck be poured out for me.
May spectres not harm me upon my rounds
In the breastplate of Laisrén, without injury.
My fame is not bound to perish.
May long life come to me,
May death not come to me
Until I am old.

I invoke my silver warrior
Who has not died, who will not die.
May time be granted me
With the virtue of *findruine*.

May my shape be made golden,
May my rank be ennobled,
May my strength be magnified.
May my burial not be swift,
May death not come to me upon the road,
May my journey be confirmed.
May the senseless snake not seize me,
Nor the harsh grey worm,
Nor the senseless beetle.
May no thief destroy me,
Nor a company of women,
Nor a company of warriors.
May an extension of time be granted me
By the King of all things.

I invoke Senach of the seven ages,
Whom fairy women fostered
On the breasts of inspiration.
May my seven candles not be quenched.
I am an impregnable fortress,
I am an immovable rock,
I am a precious stone,
I am a weekly blessing.
May I live a hundred times a hundred years,
Each hundred of them in turn.
I summon their benefits to me;
May the grace of the Holy Spirit be upon me.[3]

Only a couple of references and the closing phrase allows us to identify this as Christian at all; it has the appearance of a pagan invocation, still powerful in its imagery, even now when the precise sense of the allusions is lost to us. There is in Gaelic tradition a complex synthesis of pagan past and Christian present, as suggested by recent discussion of this genre: 'it provides unique and fascinating evidence of the complicated interrelationship between native tradition and Christian spirituality at the highest levels of the early Irish ecclesiastical hierarchy.'[4] The vivid images we find in the charms and incantations of Gaelic tradition, a few of which have survived into our own time, continue in varying proportions the same diversity. There is indeed a charm which contains the term *fàth-fith* (also *fìth-fàth*), explained as an 'occult power which rendered a person invisible to mortal eyes'.[5] This is undoubtedly to be connected with *Fáeth Fiadha* ('Cry of the Deer'), which is interestingly the alternative title of 'St Patrick's Breastplate'.

What do the statements 'I am an impregnable fortress | I am an immovable rock | I am a precious stone' remind us of? Surely some of the images from Sìleas na Ceapaich's elegy to Alasdair of Glengarry who died in 1721. Her hero is an undrainable loch, a genial well of health, an unscalable cliff, the topmost stone of the castle, a brilliant jewel of virtues, the noble stone in the ring. There is a space of a thousand years between Sìleas's elegy and the anonymous eighth-century breastplate but the same stock of imagery was available to the authors of both compositions.

There is also, I believe, a continuity of tradition to be found in another area of our literature. As we have seen, 'St Patrick's Breast-plate' contains the sequence: 'With the strength of heaven [. . .] Stability of rock'. There are other medieval breastplate poems which employ essentially the same imagery.[6] In their invocatory sequences they are strongly reminiscent of the seventeenth-century 'Tàladh Dhomhnaill Ghuirm'. The poet asks that Domhnall Gorm be pro-tected by the strength of the sun, of the young corn in May; by the power of the roaring tempest and the terrible thunderbolt; by the strength of the bull and the leaping salmon; by the strength of the warriors of myth and legend. This magnificent song may not strike the reader or listener (it is still sung) as religious in a conventional sense but the invocation of elemental powers puts it on a par with the 'paganistic' breastplate; and, in some versions, the sequence is rounded off in a similar way with a prayer that the strength of the Son of God may give protection.

In the more conventional pieties of Christian poetry there are, predictably, connections with the rest of Christendom besides those within the Gaelic tradition itself. Dugald Buchanan's 'Latha a' Bhreitheanais' is in the tradition of the great Latin poem 'Dies Irae'. The terrors of the last judgement are almost a mandatory theme in medieval Christian poetry, Gaelic poetry included. In the century before Buchanan, Cathal MacMhuirich dwells on them in a poem composed in the Classical Gaelic that unites Scottish and Irish litera-tures. If we do not over-emphasise the disjunction between Classical Gaelic and vernacular Gaelic, we can trace all sorts of continuities in the religious poetry of some thirteen hundred years. Here in English translation is a verse from a poem in praise of Calum Cille, St

Columba, composed probably within a hundred years of the saint's death in Iona, in 597:

> He took to Godly love – its strength a support –
> Often travelling;
> After his time, when all was done,
> He was the Christian who God loved.[7]

That would pass without comment in any Gaelic obituary poem or song composed on a man of piety in our own day.

Admittedly many of the most conspicuous links are merely the expression of basic Christian doctrines. Nevertheless there are curious and interesting relationships between ancient and modern compositions, the steps of which have still to be worked out. One example is the Old Irish 'Cáin Domnaig' ('Law of the Lord's Day')[8] and the Scots 'Duan an Domhnaich' ('Poem of the Lord's Day') which is published in *Carmina Gadelica*[9] and still survives in oral tradition.

Published in the same work, and still surviving traditionally, are what we may call genuine Christmas carols, some of the most interesting of them from the Presbyterian island of Lewis.[10] In the same island I myself recorded what I believe is the only version recorded in Scottish Gaelic of the tale of the man who left the Church after discovering that the minister is a thief. Afterwards he meets a stranger who accompanies him along the side of a stream. The man becomes thirsty and drinks from the stream. Having praised the purity of the water, the two of them keep on until suddenly they find the carcass of a dead horse in the stream. The man is disgusted but the stranger explains that the water remains unpolluted just as the Word of God cannot be defiled no matter who conveys it. He then disappears; the man realises that the stranger was an angel sent to rebuke him and comes back to the faith.

This story, which is rare as a folktale, is one of the exempla or moral tales of the medieval preaching friars and comes from the *Gesta Romanorum* ('Deeds of the Romans'), a Latin collection of tales and anecdotes, compiled in England about 1300.[11] Exempla are still used by Gaelic preachers, at least in some of the Presbyterian denominations. A few of these anecdotes may have survived in fact from pre-Reformation days. In this connection, it is worth observing that the more conservative, evangelical denominations retain distinct medieval qualities in styles of preaching; for instance, in allegorical interpretations of Scripture. This is only one aspect of Gaelic anti-modernist tradition and while it deserves to be investigated as a rich seam in our cultural heritage, the subject is far too big to deal with now.

It is not only religious literature which has roots in the past. In the Gàidhealtachd, as elsewhere throughout the world, an official religion can exist, comfortably or otherwise, side by side with a variety of esoteric beliefs. One example is the *sìdhichean*, of which 'fairies' is not a very adequate translation. The belief is of complex origins but can be traced back, at least in outline, through many centuries. It has important links with a pre-Christian cult of the dead but was adapted to the Christian view of the universe by transmogrifying the fairies into a species of angel.[12] They were those who remained neutral, according to one medieval legend, when Lucifer rebelled against God and was cast out of heaven. The neutral angels were thereafter condemned to live in the hills and rocks of the earth. Yet vestiges of the belief in its earlier, pre-Christian form still remain. Nowadays we either dismiss such beliefs altogether or we try to find an explanation in acceptable modern terms. The fairies are therefore held to be the people who built underground houses and made the stone arrowheads which are uncovered from time to time. Or some other rationalisation may be used.

Much more resistant to modern scepticism are second sight and clairvoyance in general. There are, of course, everywhere individuals who are agnostic or even hostile. Otherwise this category of belief is apparently distributed with fine impartiality across the entire denominational spectrum. There is naturally quite a gradation between, say, omens and portents on the one hand, and the evil eye or the like on the other; but so far as the former is concerned, many people are able to accommodate them without undue discomfort in a Christian cosmology. Casual experience of omens is different from possession of second sight, which is never represented as anything but a burden. Carrying a Bible, however, may prevent the vision; or someone's snapping a Bible shut so that the seer feels the gust of air ('gaoth a' Bhìobaill') may banish it. This suggests that second sight is regarded as a sinister visitation. It is true that what we call preternatural phenomena were not necessarily regarded as such by our ancestors. But it is also true that all such experience has tended, throughout history, to attract the Church's obloquy. This feeling, then, about second sight may be old. But my information comes from Presbyterian areas, which could mean it is of comparatively recent growth. Once again, all this requires to be investigated. The fact of the matter is that we tend to hold stereotyped views with regard to denominational attitudes, whether these pertain to conventional theology or to secular affairs.

In the twentieth century a clergyman was asked what his flock really believed. His reply was that, first, they believed in the teachings of the Church and in reward and punishment after death. Secondly, they believed that when a human being dies, he dies as an animal dies, and that is that. Thirdly, they believed that the dead remained in the churchyard, malevolently watching the living. The clergyman in question was a priest in the Irish Gàidhealtachd. We know, however, that the idea of the *faire-chlaidh* 'the graveyard watch', according to which the person last buried must watch over the community of the dead until relief comes with the next burial, was a common Gaelic belief (known elsewhere in the world, also) and the following idiosyncratic variant of it comes from Presbyterian Skye. There a middle-aged woman, some fifty years ago, confided to a neighbour that she often thought of the first human being to be buried in a certain churchyard, waiting with longing for the last burial of all. 'Nach ann air a' cheud duine a chaidh dh'an talamh a dh'fheumas an fhadachd a bhith gos an déid an duine mu dheireadh ann.'

There are scores of similar stories from the same areas: stories of fetches of the living, for instance, appearing in a place where their 'owners' longed to be, or stories of a *taidhbhse*, whose appearance presaged the death of the mortal whom he represented. It is probably the case that most of these are now told merely as stories, with little or no belief in their actuality but this is due as much to the influence of modern scientific scepticism as it is to the influence of religious teaching. For one thing, throughout the history of Christianity, a basic acceptance of miracles could extend itself to precognition and related experience. There could thus be a sanctified foreknowledge as well as forms of clairvoyance which were held to be connected with the powers of darkness. Naturally there were shifting and ambivalent areas: on the whole, as with quicksands, it was safer to avoid the entire locality.

If we are to draw any distinction with regard to acceptance or rejection of what we now call the preternatural, and draw that distinction along denominational or sectarian lines, the evidence of tradition suggests that, for most of the Gàidhealtachd, we begin no earlier than the eighteenth century. And the same applies, *a fortiori*, to ecclesiastical attitudes to Gaelic secular culture in general. Popular commentators, as opposed to serious historians, appear to have been conditioned beyond recall to make a simple equation between Protestantism and Calvinism and between Calvinism and the Presbyterian denominations as we know them from the early nineteenth century. 'Calvinism', for example, becomes a factitious term, bandied about with a remarkable lack of discrimination by those who apparently know little history and less theology.

It ought to be stressed that we ourselves, the native Gaels, have been affected by the same process of conditioning. This has created a 'folklore' which is full of false syntheses and equally false antitheses. Thus, Protestant and Jacobite *must* be mutually exclusive terms; the 'Church in the Highlands' is synonymous with the main development of Presbyterianism post-1843 (with the implication that there is one smooth, unbroken flow from the Reformation to the present day); Gaelic Protestants and Gaelic Catholics *must* always have been in clear-cut opposition to each other. Or, to make further refinements: the Established Church of Scotland, being 'Moderate', was to all intents and purposes, identical with the Church of Rome; Calum Cille (St Columba) was a Presbyterian; the Presbyterian clergy were always anti-Gaelic or opposed to the arts; the MacDonalds of Glencoe could not possibly have been Protestant. These are not, I should add, fabricated examples but have all been noted in discussion. Indeed, the last in the list is a notion to which some historians have given their assent.[13]

However naive or bizarre these judgements may be it is not difficult to see how they come into existence. We only need one fragment of evidence, taken in isolation, and generalise from that. The conclusions after all are scarcely more extravagant or preposterous than those which express the popular notion of 'clan society'. In either case reality is vastly more complicated and considerably more interesting.

In this short essay I am not concerned with theological issues as such. I suspect, however, that a certain amount of clarification is necessary in that field also if we are to understand relationships between different areas of the Gàidhealtachd from the Reformation onwards. It would be of inestimable value if we were to have studies, preferably written in Gaelic, made from within each branch of the Church.[14] Just as in literary criticism, where the critical perspective is liable to shift, sometimes grossly, at other times almost imperceptibly, when the language of criticism differs from that of the literature, so, also, I believe, with our assessments of other cultural institutions. If that is the case, we might expect Gaelic studies of religious traditions to be less dominated by the 'imperial idea' which I mentioned at the beginning of this essay. That is to say, we should be more likely to see our separate denominations and their mutual relationships working within the framework of Gaelic society itself.

To take one example, it appears to me that the 'Men' of the Evangelical Movement have been assigned a position which they do not seem to occupy when we view them from within Gaelic tradition. There they do not form the homogeneous social institution that the English appellation connotes. In actual fact *na Daoine*, originally at any rate, simply denotes 'the laymen', usually 'the laymen of the common people', in contrast to the clergy of the Established Church, who on the whole were drawn from the upper strata of Gaelic society and whom these evangelical laymen almost invariably opposed.

Naturally one can use different levels of analysis and different criteria. Broadly speaking, it should be possible to draw distinctions between theological, personal and social relationships. Between Episcopalians and Roman Catholics, for instance, theological differences are clear. Yet in political alignments (which for our purpose at the moment we can lump together in one 'Social' category) Episcopalian Protestants and Roman Catholics stand together over against Presbyterian Whigs. It should be noted, however, that not all Presbyterians were Whigs: there were Presbyterians before the last quarter of the seventeenth century! And throughout our history, personal relationships cut across the boundaries of the other categories: one thinks of Colin of Glenure and Alasdair mac Mhaighstir Alasdair among a great multitude of such friends. It should be put on record that, for example, in Presbyterian Skye, in quite recent times, the most esteemed family of the landlord class were Roman Catholics.

To a remarkable degree personal relations could remain good even in the face of blatant economic discrimination. It would be useful for all sorts of reasons if comparative studies were made in order to assess the limits of religious and economic polarities in different areas. A possible area for investigation for the Scottish Gàidhealtachd exists in the Outer Hebrides. Traditionally Catholic South Uist and Barra would seem to have had Presbyterian economic ascendancies which lasted into the twentieth century. Did it make any difference that tacksmen and tenantry alike were equally Gaelic? On the evidence at our disposal, it would seem that within the bonds of a shared culture, a common Gaelic identity, warm personal relationships, social inequality, and theological disparity could all co-exist. But only a minute sociological investigation would disclose the various forces at work in this cultural symbiosis. A comparison might then be drawn, through equally searching enquiries, with purely Protestant areas, where the same social and economic stratification obtained.

The Gaelic adage 'Sannt nan seachd sagart, fear gun mhac gun nighean' ('a childless man is as grasping as seven priests') expresses, among other things, the ancient, anti-clerical tradition of Christendom. There is also an abundant anti-clerical lore among Protestants. A distinction can be drawn here between genuine Gaelic oral tradition and the assessments of English-speaking commentators. I think Gaelic tradition, generally speaking, distinguishes between economic avarice and religious austerity. The part played by the Presbyterian clergy during the period of the Clearances has often been described and possibly as often distorted. If it has been distorted, this has come about by lumping together a heterogeneous group, composed in reality of men who were frequently of diametrically opposed views and style of life, and representing them under the figure of 'the Calvinist minister'. In the popular scenario this grim figure is firmly on the side of the landlord and at the same time virulent in his opposition to the secular arts, even to the Gaelic language itself. What is the historical background to this?

The clergy of the Established Church in the Highlands were traditionally drawn from the tacksman class; in addition to aristocratic lineage, which many of them could claim, they formed an 'aristocracy of learning', to borrow the description that W. J. Watson applied to the learned classes of medieval and later Gaelic society, whose significant role and function, indeed, the Protestant clergy continued, particularly in the cultural transformations of the eighteenth century. Calvinist in theology, they numbered in their ranks those whom even later, and generally hostile, Presbyterian commentators regarded as men of genuine piety. But puritanical they most decidedly were not. There is a body of folklore which depicts them as careless pastors, sometimes even as dissolutes. Rob Donn's satiric comment that they were men of outstanding ability: shrewd farmers, capable cattle-dealers, thrifty stewards of estates – able in fact in every profession except the calling in which they had taken their ordination vows – is re-echoed in tradition. As a class they were worldly 'squarsons'.

A minister who is still remembered, not for his worldliness, however, but rather for his goodness and piety, is the Rev. Murdoch MacDonald of Durness 'Maighstir Morchadh', the friend and mentor of Rob Donn. Joseph MacDonald of the *Compleat Theory of the Bagpipe* and Rev. Patrick MacDonald who published, in 1784, the first printed collection of Gaelic airs ever to appear in Scotland, were his sons. These famous sons received their first musical instruction in the Manse of Durness, from their father. The Rev. Murdoch Mac-Donald was by no means the only talented violinist and piper among the Presbyterian clergy. And in the first half of the eighteenth century, in nearby Reay, the Rev. Alexander Pope made a valuable collection of Ossianic ballads. The name 'Alasdair Pàp' also is still remembered in the oral tradition of Sutherland.

Two of the great, fundamental collections of Gaelic poetry, repre-senting almost every genre of Gaelic verse, were made by the Rev. James Maclagan and the Rev. Donald MacNicol. The roll-call of names – men of the calibre of Rev. Dr Irvine, Rev. Thomas Sinton, Rev. J. Gregorson Campbell, the Rev. Drs Archibald and Angus MacDonald – would take several pages if we were to make a list of the Presbyterian ministers without whose labours we should have virtually no Gaelic literature preserved at all. (In an interdenomina-tional list Father Allan MacDonald of Eriskay would, of course, have an honoured place.)

But the point I am making here is that the figure of the puritanical Calvinist minister, hostile to Gaelic and its culture, has no place within this clerical class. While Gaelic society was still relatively unbroken, even clergymen of intense personal devotion, such as Maighstir Morchadh in Durness, gave the secular arts encouragement and respect. And this, incidentally, is in conformity with Calvin's teaching. The extent of the confusion that exists with regard to these matters may be illustrated by a remark I heard recently which took Bishop Carswell's often quoted denunciation of the 'lying' romances as an epitome of the attitude of the 'Church in the Highlands' towards Gaelic literature. Such denunciations could be paralleled a hundred times over in the history of the Christian church, from the Patristic writers onwards. One example, from a letter written by Alcuin of York to the Bishop of Lindisfarne, will suffice.

> Let the word of God be read when priests sit together. The lector should be heard there, not the harper; sermons of the fathers, not songs of the pagans. What has Ingeld to do with Christ? The house is narrow: it will not be able to

hold them both. The heavenly King wants nothing to do with the lost kings of the pagans, kings in name alone: for the eternal King reigns in heaven, while the lost pagan king groans in hell. Listen to the voices of lectors in your houses, not to the laughter of the crowd in the market-place.[15]

Neither the great Catholic scholar in the eighth century nor the learned Knoxian bishop in the sixteenth was aiming at extirpating secular literature: they were both much too wise to attempt such an impossibility. Both men had the same object, seen according to their own lights, namely, to ensure that God's word was given its proper place. Probably the most important difference between them was that Alcuin was a man of profound and somewhat austere faith; Carswell was a worldly prelate.

The reaction against the Established clergy, which we know as the Evangelical Revival[16] needs no recapitulation here, except perhaps to emphasise how much a movement of the common people it was. The movement was both social and religious: it would have been strange if the ordinary tenantry, turning against their landlords, did not also turn against their clergy, who belonged to the same social stratum. The religious leaders of the revival were to a large extent laymen: the so-called 'Men'. In due course the movement produced its own ministers: on the whole men of the lower ranks of Gaelic society. There was, however, one notable exception, the Rev. Roderick MacLeod, Established Church minister of Bracadale and later of Snizort in Skye: the famous Maighstir Ruairi. Roderick MacLeod was an aristocrat – a grandson of MacLeod of Raasay – and when he cast his lot in with the Evangelicals, he was regarded by his peers as a traitor to his own class.

This particular development in Gaelic Presbyterianism did undoubtedly bring an intense puritanism into the life of the church. It was at this stage in history that the people become 'so strange that sorrow to them is wheat', as Màiri Mhór nan Òran puts it. The revival came to her native Skye at the beginning of the nineteenth century, and among early converts was Blind Donald Munro, a catechist who carried his fiddle around with him on his religious visitations. More than one catechist is known to tradition in an accepted role of storyteller or singer or instrumentalist. Not infrequently they were blind men who, like blind musicians in other parts of the world, developed compensatory talents. But after his conversion Donald Munro forsook his secular music along with the other seductive vanities of this world.

Not every Evangelical layman or minister was equally puritanical, however. At one end of the scale stands the Rev. Dr John MacDonald of Ferintosh, the 'Apostle of the North', a man of warm personality and according to tradition a preacher of unsurpassed eloquence – a greater orator, on the evidence of Duncan Campbell of Glenlyon,[17] who had heard the leading parliamentarians in the age of Disraeli and Gladstone, than any of these – and one of the important collectors of Ossianic ballads. At the other end stands Maighstir Ruairi. Roderick MacLeod was indeed a severe ascetic. But he was also a champion of the common tenantry and both these facts are recalled in the traditions of Skye where he is still remembered with honour.

The Evangelical Movement, as we know, coincided with the social upheavals stretching from the later eighteenth century to near the end of the nineteenth. How much did the 'Calvinist minister' really contribute towards the economic and, even more important, the psychological despair which the Clearances brought? The ministers stand accused of having comforted their flocks with the doctrine that their sufferings were simply the consequence of their sinfulness. Might they have used words such as these which follow? The original is, of course, in Gaelic.

> We have witnessed egregious changes [. . .] Heavy is the shame [. . .] the oppressiveness of the judgments passed upon them [i.e. the Gaels], it steals away their souls from them [. . .] they most resemble half-dead corpses [. . .] The expulsion of the Gaels [. . .] although its vaunt is claimed for a foreign battalion, it is the wrath of God scourging them before all – that is the (real) cause of their expulsion. They are not the only ones to have been destroyed; many's the race for whom there was decreed ill, as a result of the wrath of God in Heaven, whereat the shafts of His wrath burst. The sons of Israel of the bright weapons, when His wrath was kindled against them, many's the plague with which he visited his fury (upon them) to chastise them in the midst of all [. . .] However far each of these people progressed towards meriting the wrath of the King on High, pure repentance for their sins procured forgiveness for them thereafter. Repentance now, after that fashion – alas that the sons of [the Gael] do not do that, to cast off from them His anger, to remove the true anger of the King on High. The stock of the Gaels of the bitter conflicts, till they may reach the virtuous state of repentance, (let) their protection be placed in (the hands of) the Creator of the Elements, in order to avert the wrath of the Lord.
>
> The vengeance of God is the reason [. . .] Where have the Gaels gone?[18]

The quotation, however, is from a poem by an Irish Gael, a Catholic poet, and his subject is the Plantation of Ulster, when the indigenous Gaelic population were being driven off their lands and replaced with Scots and English Protestants. If the Gaelic clergy preached the same doctrine they were certainly not exceptional in that. There is nothing Calvinist in the Irish Catholic poet's theology!

Nor is it the case, if the worldly, anti-puritanical ministers of the Established Church employed the same orthodox Christian arguments, that they were motivated by the theology of Calvin. They were probably much more concerned with the loss of their own good lands. But even here one must be careful not to make too sweeping a denunciation. There were ministers even in the Established Church who were prepared to speak publicly on behalf of the crofting tenantry.[19] And indeed the two clergymen who stand head and shoulders over most of their clerical brethren in any branch of the Church, Catholic, Episcopalian, Baptist or Presbyterian, were in the Established Church. They were the brothers Malcolm and Donald MacCallum. The Rev. Donald MacCallum was in fact arrested and jailed. The names of these two men are still recalled with admiration and pride throughout the Gàidhealtachd of Scotland.

There are other counter-currents, too, in this perplexed situation. The growth of literacy, giving the people the ability to read the Bible for themselves, is held to have played a significant part in the transformation of religious life. This was for the most part achieved, very ironically, in the schools set up by the Scottish Society for the Propagation of Christian Knowledge in order to root out papistry and the Gaelic language. (There were other schools too but the SSPCK gives the dominant tone.) The Society's ruthless attack on the Gaelic language was carried out with evangelical zeal. It only compounds the offence that the Society was also dedicated to rooting out papistry, with which Gaelic was associated in the minds of the proponents of the policy, no matter what faith any particular Gaelic-speaking community happened actually to profess. For in all of this, and in their deliberate refusal to bring the Scriptures to the common people in their own tongue, the directors of this strategy, ostensibly heirs of the Reformation, were sinning against one of the cardinal principles of the Reformed faith. Eventually tactics were altered; the Scriptures were translated; Gaelic literacy increased.

Literacy, whether in English or Gaelic, did not perhaps so much widen people's horizons, although it must have done that to some degree, as increase their desire for knowledge, especially for the certainties of some creed or philosophy that would explain the cataclysmic break-up of their traditional world. We can sense in the traditions of the terrible century or so of the Clearances not only bewilderment but an intellectual and spiritual hunger accompanying the physical hunger of economic poverty. But that grass-roots movement, which found the homilies of the Established clergy so inadequate, and replaced them with the *Sturm und Drang* of great extempore sermons, was nonetheless limited.

Lacking alternative sources of liberal and philosophical learning, lacking, too, the political and social institutions which an autonomous society would have provided, this considerable section of the Gaelic nation developed what was essentially a recluse religion. That it was practised in open community, that it attracted men and women of imagination and intellect, equipped to be natural leaders, did not soften the ascetic rigour which is always part of a faith that turns its back on the world. For in this situation we have a recluse religion, not only turning away from the seductions of this world, but actually seeking at the same time to dominate ordinary, open society. The grave, divisive consequences of that are still with us.

Yet it was a movement which was full of intellectual passion and dissenting fervour which affected, within the Presbyterian communities themselves, even those areas, or for that matter, those individuals, who resisted its ecclesiastical demands. It also helped to create a spirit which was anti-authority in general and it fostered, from within, the growth of anti-ecclesiastical poetry. And not least, the years of the Evangelical Revival witnessed the growth and development of congregational and familial psalm-singing. That great tumult of heterophony is still capable of reducing even humanist composers and musicologists to awe-stricken silence. In certain areas it is a richly ornamented style, which some consider to have developed from the plain-song of the pre-Reformation church. Whether that is so or not, it is profoundly liturgical and charged with the dramatic emotions of great elemental art.

The dramatic element in the worship of the evangelicals can probably be paralleled elsewhere. So no doubt can the extreme rigour of their theological analysis and exposition. Rarely, however, can both have come together to make such a powerful compound given verbal expression as it was by men who were the inheritors of the rich and varied traditions of Gaelic oral literature. The result was that they added a new dimension to the Gaelic language.[20] As Sorley Maclean, discussing these sermons and prayers, puts it:

> in frankness, sincerity and psychological insight, expressed with an astonishing wealth of imagery and illustration, sometimes sonorously eloquent with the incomparable resonances of the Gaelic language and sometimes racily colloquial, Gaelic once had a great prose. If a man of imagination is convinced of the rags of human righteousness and of the desperate wickedness of the human heart, the expression of his conviction cannot fail to be powerful.[21]

As the people more and more deserted the Parish Church, the practice grew of holding Communion services out of doors. To these services vast concourses of men and women gathered, often travelling long distances, usually on foot. Eventually no church building would have been capable of holding such immense congregations. Even if we had not heard about these gatherings of the people, it would be easy to imagine the scene. With the mountains in the background and the sea never far away, the human voices blend with the sound of the wind and running water, as the music of the psalms rise from thousands of worshippers meeting together, and affirming their togetherness, much as their remote ancestors must have met in tribal gatherings in sacred places to renew the spiritual vigour and fertility of the community at large. But the solidarity was now in terms of a very different loyalty. When they sang the forty-sixth psalm, 'God is our refuge and strength, a very present help in trouble. Therefore we will not fear, although the earth be removed', they could hardly be unaware that that was literally what was happening.

Is it simply a coincidence that in several areas the sites chosen for Communions are also sites with strong pagan associations? In some instances the physical configuration of the terrain make the choice obvious. In others one wonders if there was not some vestige of memory that these were traditionally gathering-places; latterly perhaps for a clan muster or the like. At any rate, the natural amphitheatre of Leaba na Bà Bàine ('the Bed of the White Cow') in Gairloch – the cow goddess of Gaelic tradition – was one of the famous sites; another was Beul Àtha nan Trì Allt ('The Ford of the Three Streams') in Skye. This location has associations with the 'fairies', the ancestral dead; tribal gatherings were normally held at or near immemorial burial grounds. Interestingly enough, open-air meetings of the Land League were also held at this place where three streams meet. Màiri Mhór nan Òran's song:

Nuair a sheas MacCaluim làmh rinn
Aig Beul Àtha nan Trì Allt

commemorates that. And 'MacCaluim' is the Rev. Donald MacCallum whom I have already mentioned as a champion of the crofters.

I am very much aware that what I have presented here is only a superficial survey which has neglected to discuss many large issues not to mention the more intricate details that each point of the argument calls forth. I am also aware that I have spent perhaps a disproportionate time on the Evangelical Movement – on what one of the more notable landlords, Evander MacIver of Gress in Lewis, called 'the peasant religion', which he and his kind saw as a subversive influence. But I would argue that the processes of this profound change in outlook, though not, I think, in the Gaelic temperament (using that simply as a portmanteau word) amounted to a cultural revolution, which went some way at least towards forging a new Gaelic identity.

The break-up of traditional loyalties inevitably released enormous energies: given the historical and cultural situation of the time and the hierarchical structure of Gaelic society, no other form of revolution was thinkable. From this point of view the Evangelical Movement is an expression of social cataclysm, at one and the same time giving direction to and imposing limitations on the energies which it generates. But this may be a facile interpretation. It may give too great a priority to social dissension which religious unrest sometimes concealed (even from those engaged in it) and sometimes openly manifested. I can only try to stimulate others to attack these problems from quite different points of view.

Note

Translations of the Breastplates in the original essay were drawn from *A Golden Treasury of Irish Poetry* AD *600 to 1200*, edited and translated by David Greene and Frank O'Connor. Texts and translations on pp. 27–35. The first of these, they point out, 'is a Christian breast-plate with druid ornamentation, while the other is a druid breastplate with Christian ornamentation'.

The Seer in Gaelic Tradition

One of the words for 'poet' in Gaelic is *fili*.[1] According to accepted opinion, it is connected with the root of a verb 'to see': the *fili* was originally a seer. From this one might be led to suppose that poetry and prophecy, or divination in general, are closely linked in Gaelic tradition; the more so as romantic notions still persist in some quarters, of the Gaelic bard with his 'eye in a fine frenzy rolling'. In actual fact, the figure of the 'seer-poet' has very little place either in the historical record or in the oral tradition of Gaelic. In Scots Gaelic, to which this short account is restricted, there is indeed a very important prophecy which is ascribed to a particular poet and alluded to by other poets and I shall deal with it at the end of this essay. There are also occasional stray verses, some of which can be regarded as a sub-class of the lore of names, that presage death or disaster at a certain place, as in the following stanza from the Isle of Skye, which I give in translation. Tobar Tà is a well in the parish of Strath:

> Tobar Tà, that well Tobar Tà
> A well at which a battle will be fought
> Lachlan of the three Lachlans will be slain
> Early, early at Tobar Tà.

'Lachlan' is a common personal name among the MacKinnons in whose traditional territory the well of Tobar Tà lies. But there is a variant which substitutes the personal name 'Torcall', traditionally a MacLeod name and in particular the eponym of Sìol Torcaill ('the Seed of Torcall'), who are the MacLeods of Lewis and their derivative kindreds. It has been suggested that this variant refers to the death of Torcall who was the third Torcall of the Lewis line; his sister married Lachlan MacKinnon of Strath and Torcall MacLeod may have met his death in MacKinnon territory through having come to Skye for refuge or aid.[2]

Such prophecies are on this analysis all *ex post facto*. But even to the present day they are not so regarded in Gaelic tradition. Like most prophecies they are ambiguous with a fine protean quality – a third version declares that 'torc nan trì lochan' ('the boar of the three lochs') will be killed at Tobar Tà – and their fulfilment is still awaited by some people.

It may be that such rhymes are vestiges of a tradition of poetic prophecy, but to go beyond that would be most unsafe in the light of the evidence at our disposal. It would also be inappropriate, in my opinion, in the present context, to enquire whether any of these predictions, so-called, are the expression of anything that might be described as genuine precognition. We do better to accept them here as cultural items which have their place in the social construction of reality. Traditional Gaelic culture in Scotland presents us with a strong sense of territory in which place names are charged with historical and legendary associations in a timeless order in which geography and history are merged. On such a plane, our modern divisions of time into past, present and future may not, for the makers of these 'prophetic' rhymes, have had the relevance that we are so much inclined to take for granted. However that may be, the prophecies themselves have survived in Gaelic into the modern age where such temporal divisions do obtain. And in modern Gaelic there exist other beliefs also that clearly are tied to the notion of linear time, the most conspicuous being the concept of second sight. In fact it is not too much to say that in contemporary Gaelic society, the very idea of divination is centred on the belief in second sight.

In earlier times there was a greater range of techniques at people's disposal both for revealing future events and for describing present events happening at a distance. We can still hear in tradition about some of the mechanisms of these arts just as we can hear, more immediately, of isolated visions, waking or dreaming, that fall in our own day and involve precognition and detection. These latter experiences may not always be classed as instances of second sight but in so far as people actually give them credence, it is because they relate them to this pivotal phenomenon of second sight. Gaelic society accepts, if one may put it that way, that certain individuals exist who have peculiar clairvoyant powers which are not subject to the control of the will. It is accepted too that any of us may have premonitions or similar experiences – perhaps only once in a lifetime – and, equally, that any of us may be misled as to the nature of such experiences. It is in fact not unusual to hear it said that So-and-So, who claimed to have had a precognitive vision, was more likely to have been day-dreaming or had succumbed to some form of self-indulgent fantasy. But that is very different from denying the existence of second sight itself.

Second sight is not a form of self-indulgence; more often than not it is regarded as an affliction; and, moreover, it is a faculty whose existence is endorsed by the two great forces of authority that validate experience in a traditional society: the powers of the non-mortal world and the testimony of the ancestors. And so, if we do accept someone's claim regarding an isolated vision or premonition, it is because at the centre of this cosmology, the idea of second sight is so firmly established.

Within the same frame of reference, we explain other phenomena. For instance, I have on several occasions heard discussions on belief in the existence of fairies summed up by the observation that the capacity to see the fairies must have been a form of second sight now lost to us.

With regard to all these matters there are of course sceptics or at least those who profess scepticism. But overall I think one might say that such sceptics are no more than agnostic. At the same time we must not assume we can measure degree of belief by the popularity of stories about second sight. Many of these stories survive simply because they are vivid narratives and those who keep them in circulation may well be the most sceptical, while those who are held to have second sight themselves are often the most reticent. But there is evidence that that was not always so.

The English term 'second sight' is on record from the seventeenth century, all the early references being in Highland contexts. Nevertheless, 'second sight' is not a direct translation from Gaelic: the Gaelic term is *An Dà Shealladh* (literally 'the two sights'); or, much less commonly, *An Dà Fhradharc* ('the two visions'). (The first is the object of sight; the second is the power of sight.) By the beginning of the eighteenth century the term 'second sight' is well established in English usage in ethnographic writings about the Highlands and Islands. These accounts provide a remarkable range of data which makes it plain that the seers of the past were much less inhibited in describing their experiences than their modern counterparts.

It would at all events be impossible, in my estimation, to record such astonishing abundance of first-hand reports nowadays. One can think of several reasons for this. In the period to which these testimonies belong, and perhaps in most places until the early years of the twentieth century, the modern sceptical intellect had scarcely begun to impinge on traditional Gaelic society. Even if certain of the writers who took down the evidence profess their own scepticism – few in fact do – their attitudes would not in themselves have had much effect on their informants. The reticence of contemporary seers, on the other hand, is in some degree at any rate due to a fear of being regarded as 'primitive' or 'superstitious'.

But it may also be true that the contemporary second-sighted individual actually has less to tell. If we allow that an element of creative imagination is an essential component of divination, we might suggest that certain of the functions of the seer in older, traditional society have been taken over by the creative writers of modern society. I am implying, then, that the seer is an artist and that the products of his vision are art-forms (whatever else they may or may not be) shaped by the expectations of society and its aesthetic needs. Even some of the eighteenth-century writers declare that the visionary faculty is already in decay. Similar statements are, it is true, made about the decay of the traditional arts of Gaelic society in general in the same period, but we cannot use the one set of judgments to invalidate the others.

A parallel can be drawn with the history of Gaelic song. On the verge of extinction in the eighteenth century, according to certain writers of the time, it is still, as modern collectors point out, enjoying an apparently undiminished vigour. But, in fact, the range has diminished; certain metrical and melodic categories have disappeared, displaced in popularity by other forms, and even within the last fifty years individual repertoires have shrunk drastically. The true oral song-maker has virtually gone while the song-writer and the literate poet have taken his place. And much the same could be said of Gaelic story-telling. These are processes of decay but they are also processes of substitution and adaptation. In all of these fields we can reconstruct the main lines of the tradition from our contemporary evidence and in some cases even supplement the data from the past. What we cannot do is readily assemble a comparably rich and varied body of material or recover the authoritative tone of these informants of long ago. But so far as accounts of second sight are concerned, I know of nothing from one period that absolutely contradicts our information from the other.

As in contemporary Gaelic society, occasional experiences were fitted into a frame of reference organised by the concepts of second sight and the uniquely endowed seer. Both in past and present accounts there is some uncertainty as to whether the faculty is hereditary or may be learned. Before I comment on that and other points, let me quote from a celebrated description written by Martin Martin (c.1660–1719), a native of the Isle of Skye. A number of the observations he makes can be compared with the testimony of modern tradition. Martin, a graduate in medicine of Edinburgh and Leyden, was a keen and intelligent observer of his Gaelic community and no sceptic in regard to the existence of second sight:

THE Second Sight is a singular faculty of seeing an otherwise invisible object, without any previous means used by the person that sees it for that end; the vision makes such a lively impression upon the Seers, that they neither see nor think of any thing else, except the vision, as long as it continues: and then they appear pensive or jovial, according to the object which was represented to them.

At the sight of a vision, the eye-lids of the person are erected, and the eyes continue staring until the object vanish. This is obvious to others who are by, when the persons happen to see a vision, and occurred more than once to my own observation, and to others that were with me.

There is one in Sky, of whom his acquaintance observed, that when he sees a vision, the inner part of his eyelids turn so far upwards, that after the object disappears, he must draw them down with his fingers, and sometimes employs others to draw them down, which he finds to be the much easier way.

This faculty of the Second Sight does not lineally descend in a family, as some imagine, for I know several parents who are endowed with it, but their children not, *et vice versa*: neither is it acquired by any previous compact. And after a strict inquiry, I could never learn from any among them, that this faculty was communicable any way whatsoever.

The Seer knows neither the object, time, nor place of a vision, before it appears [. . .]

One instance was lately foretold by a Seer that was a novice, concerning the death of one of my acquaintance; this was communicated to a few only, and with great confidence: I being one of the number, did not in the least regard it, until the death of the person about the time foretold, did confirm me of the certainty of the prediction. The novice mentioned above, is now a skilful Seer [. . .]

Children, horses, and cows, see the Second Sight, as well as men and women advanced in years [. . .]

That horses see it, is likewise plain from their violent and sudden starting, when the rider or Seer in company with him sees a vision of any kind, night or day. It is observable of the horse, that he will not go forward that way, until he be led about at some distance from the common road, and then he is in a sweat.[3]

Some of the detail in that account finds corroboration in modern tradition, some does not. I have heard references to the staring eyes of the seer but nothing about the turning inwards of the eyelids. There is no longer a belief that children *qua* children 'see the Second Sight', as Martin puts it; nor are cows regarded as being especially sensitive.

It is perhaps curious that Martin does not mention dogs: in modern Gaelic society, as in some other cultures, dogs are held to be particularly quick to react to atmosphere, and especially to psychic phenomena. But the horse is unique. Only certain humans are second-sighted; all horses have the faculty. The horse is the seer of the animal kingdom. Moreover, a horse sees living people in a unique perspective: seven times their real size. If they were not constrained by this peculiar vision, it is said, they would not submit to human domination.

Martin has several references to novice seers, and to one 'that was a novice [. . .] and [. . .] is now a skilful Seer'. This implies that the skill develops, though it is not explained what the process of development entails. He provides no information about, for example, initiation or tuition of novices by master seers, for the faculty itself, so far as he could discover, is not 'communicable any way whatsoever'. Nor is it (necessarily) hereditary.

But other witnesses differ somewhat on certain of these points. For instance, in a letter to John Aubrey, dated 1694, the writer declares, 'I am informed, that in the Isle of Sky [. . .] several families had it by succession, descending from parents to children, and as yet there be many there that have it that way.' And in the same letter Aubrey's correspondent tells of a meeting between his own father and one John MacGrigor, a seer:

> My father [. . .] being very intimate with the man, told him he would fain learn it [i.e. second sight]: to which he answered, that indeed he could in three days time teach him if he pleased; but yet he would not advise him nor any man to learn it; for had he once learned, he would never be a minute of his life but he would see innumerable men and women night and day round about him; which perhaps he would think wearisome and unpleasant, for which reason my father would not have it [. . .] I am also informed by one who came last summer from the Isle of Sky, that any person that pleases will get it taught him for a pound or two of tobacco.[4]

Modern tradition has something to say about both points of view. First, the faculty of foreseeing is on the whole hereditary but does not necessarily manifest itself in every individual in a family nor even in every generation. Secondly, it is communicable, temporarily or permanently. The essential element in communication is physical contact.[5] We hear of a seer in the act of seeing, inadvertently or deliberately touching, or being touched by, another person who then shares in the experience. When the contact is broken, participation in the vision ceases immediately. A more elaborate device requires the would-be participant to hold the seer's hand while placing a foot on his foot and looking over his shoulder. There are variants of this stance but in most of the descriptions the left hand or foot or shoulder is involved. In that sense alone, it is a 'sinister' ritual. In some instances this ritual confers only a temporary power, more or less brief; in other instances the faculty remains, although apparently only for the lifetime of the initiated person. In other words, from an evolutionary point of view, it is only an acquired characteristic.

The emphasis on heredity is exceedingly strong in Gaelic society and is used to explain personal qualities, artistic abilities, mannerisms and the like. The possession of second sight is fitted into this framework and validated by the concept of hereditary transmission just as the concept of second sight itself validates other phenomena. When Martin Martin says 'several parents are endowed with it, but their children not, *et vice versa*' this would only mean to us that the talent does not manifest itself in every generation. Martin's ideas of heredity are in fact more rigorous than those to which modern Gaelic society subscribes.

There is an anecdote which makes an interesting comment on the relevance of hereditary powers. There were two men working together, the older of whom was a seer. For a long time the younger man pestered his companion to make him a seer too but the older man refused. Eventually, however, he agreed and the younger man became a seer himself. But because second sight was not hereditary in his family, he was unable to cope with his experiences and in the end lost his reason.

This suggests that the seer's visions are normally of a tragic nature. In modern tradition this is certainly the case, although one hears of visions that were taken to presage disaster but in the event (which was interpreted as the fulfilment of the vision) produced a happier outcome. None the less, the typical modern vision is the funeral procession. As for times past, our commentators are not unanimous. John Aubrey's informant declares that

> the objects of this knowledge, are not only sad and dismal; but also joyful and prosperous: thus they foretell of happy marriages, good children, what kind of life men shall live, and in what condition they shall die: and riches, honour, preferment, peace, plenty and good weather.[6]

On premonitions in general, Martin observes that

> Things also are foretold by smelling, sometimes as follows. Fish or flesh is frequently smelled in a fire. [. . .] This smell several people have, who are not endowed with the Second Sight, and it is always accomplished soon after.[7]

There is nothing sinister here: merely a foretoken of a certain kind of food. Such prognostications are still believed in and have their own terminology: 'manadh', 'meanmhain', 'sgrìob', etc. They may involve any of the senses (smell, curiously enough, least of all, so far as my information goes) and have specific interpretations: an itchy palm signifies one is to get money; the sensation of wispy material in the mouth means drink, and so on. *Manadh* is a more serious portent, generally speaking, and its commonest form is some kind of light. Second-sighted people are held to experience these more frequently than others; and although the seer by definition *sees*, habitual experiences of a non-visual kind may set a person apart from the rest of society. There is perhaps one exception to this in the case of *seinn-bàis*, the 'death-music', a high-pitched humming which portends the death of someone known personally or connected with the family or local community or sometimes even an individual of national standing but who is not an acquaintance. Apparently one can hear the *seinn-bàis* very frequently without acquiring the reputation of a seer.

Dreams are an important vehicle of divination as they are in other cultures. I shall only touch on one aspect of dream interpretation here: the significance of animals in dreams. There was apparently a system in which certain animals represented clans or clan names. Thus a dog represented a MacDonald, a bull a Maclean and a deer a MacKenzie. Sometimes the animal is the same as the animal represented in the clan crest: for instance, the boar for the Campbells. But at least as often, the emblematic animal is different from the dream animal: the crest of the MacLeods shows a bull's head; in dream lore the MacLeods are represented by a horse. It is of great interest that in some Gaelic songs (the examples are seventeenth-century MacDonald compositions and hostile to the MacLeods) the MacLeods are referred to as the 'Seed of the Mare'. These references to the equine ancestry of the MacLeods were taken by themselves as highly insulting, and the choice of another animal, the bull, as their emblem was no doubt deliberate. Behind all this may lie an ancient totemic system.

Stories of dreamers being able to locate a missing person, more often than not a dead person, are well known. Sometimes the dreamer hears a voice, perhaps the voice of the missing person, with or without the appearance of the person, directing the searchers to a particular location. This form of divination, in which events not of the future but of the present, and happening at a distance, could be described, was practised through formal rituals. In the Hebrides the term for this – the word is still known – is *frith* and it can be used in the expression 'a' deanamh frìth' ('making a frìth'). Alexander Carmichael has the following note:

> The 'frìth', augury, was a species of divination enabling the 'frìthir', augurer, to see into the unseen. This divination was made to ascertain the position and condition of the absent and the lost, and was applied to man and beast. The augury was made on the first Monday of the quarter and immediately before sunrise. The augurer, fasting, and with bare feet, bare head, and closed eyes, went to the doorstep and placed a hand on each jamb. Mentally beseeching the God of the unseen to show him his quest and to grant him his augury, the augurer opened his eyes and looked steadfastly straight in front of him. From the nature and position of the objects within his sight, he drew his conclusions.[8]

To this I would add, from my own knowledge, that frìth normally involved bird augury, 'a' leughadh nan eun' ('reading / interpreting the birds'). In some Hebridean dialects, *ealta* 'bird flock', with an interesting semantic shift, seems to be involved in a phrase such as 'Tha droch coltas air an ealtainn' ('The sky looks ominous'). In fact, 'ealtainn' can be used in these dialects, without any particular connotation, simply for 'sky'. If my etymology is valid, the link would seem to be provided by the practice of taking auguries from the flight of birds. Another tradition, which I cannot explore here, involves learning of future events from the speech of birds.[9] This happens usually not by design but by chance or good fortune.

Divination by means of the shoulder-blade, the scapula, was widespread throughout the whole Gaelic area and known, of course, in other parts of the world also. There are numerous references to it in our ethnographic literature. Alexander Carmichael again: 'It required highly specialised gifts on the part of the diviner.' In the eighteenth century, John Ramsay of Ochtertyre tells us that

> The scapula or shoulder-blade of a black one-year old sheep is commonly preferred. [. . .] The moon must not change between the death of the creature and the making this use of its shoulder-blade. [. . .] In later [*sic*] times a certain proportion of the shoulder-blade was appropriated to every clan.[10]

This last observation reminds us of the representation of clan names in dreams; while in connection with the scapula again another writer talks of the 'death of some remarkable person in a particular tribe or family'. The ritual was used both for prognosticating the future and for detecting events at a distance. Used for foretelling, it could apparently be fraught with danger for the diviner. At any rate I have heard it said myself that divination from the scapula could put a soul in mortal peril: at a certain point the diviner had to go 'glé fhaisg air fiacaill an Diabhail' ('very near the Devil's tooth').

There is another and rather obscure tradition about locating missing persons. My information can be summarised as follows. Long ago, if a ship failed to return, a certain ritual was carried out. A specially selected woman, who was a virgin, went to sleep and while she slept her spirit left her body and searched for the ship. The woman had to be of strong mind. If the wind changed while her spirit was absent from her body, she was in peril of losing her reason: hence the necessity of having a woman of strong mind. When her spirit returned to her body she woke up and reported where the ship, or its wreckage, was to be found and what had happened to the people aboard. (The changing of the wind may be compared with the detail about divination from the scapula during one phase of the moon.) The description of the search for the ship by the sleeping woman's spirit is suggestive of shamanic trance.

There are several accounts of the progress of a battle being seen in the sky. One of these tells how some women, standing on the Bridge of Inveraray, witnessed the Battle of Ticonderoga, on 10th May 1773, during the American War of Independence, and were able to tell who had been killed or wounded of the soldiers from Argyll, long before the news came by a more conventional route.

The term An Dà Shealladh does not nowadays in the North-West Highlands and in the Isles embrace the idea of detection of things at a physical distance. But in the central Highlands, at least from Lochaber to Perthshire, An Dà Shealladh includes both precognition and tele-cognition. Returning to Martin Martin in the Isle of Skye, however, it would appear that the connotation of second sight was not so restricted there at the end of the seventeenth century as it is now. At all events, Martin says:

> I have been seen thus myself by Seers of both sexes at some hundred miles distance; some that saw me in this manner, had never seen me personally, and it happened according to their visions, without any previous design of mine to go to those places, my coming there being purely accidental.

Such manifestations are explained rather differently by modern exponents of the matter. There is a widely distributed belief (which is known also in the Gaelic community of Cape Breton in Canada) that holds that anyone, seer or not, may see the fetch or 'resemblance' of a living person, especially, though not necessarily, if that person feels or expresses an intense desire to visit a particular place or company. What may be an extension or refinement of this is the belief in the existence of a co-walker, a doppelgänger. If there is a difference between the two notions, it centres on the belief that the co-walker is apt at any given time to be roaming around unknown to its 'owner', creeping up on people in order to frighten them, and generally behaving in a disorderly manner. To that degree, the co-walker is not so much an exact replica of a person as an alternative personality of a much more anarchic nature. Just as a seer may see himself or herself (normally a presage of the seer's death), so anyone may see his or her own co-walker, who is recognisable even at a distance because it moves as a mirror-image of the watcher. But there are further variations on this theme. Martin tells of a Lewisman who

> is much haunted by a spirit, appearing in all points like to himself; and he asks many impertinent questions of the man when in the fields, but speaks not a word to him at home, though he seldom misses to appear to him every night in the house, but to no other person. He told this to one of his neighbours, who advised him to cast a live coal at the face of the vision the next time he appeared: the man did so next night, and all the family saw the action; but the following day the same spirit appeared to him in the fields, and beat him severely, so as to oblige him to keep his bed for the space of fourteen days after.[11]

Before I comment on that, I must look very briefly at some Gaelic terms. The basic word for a 'phantasm' is *taidhbhse*: it is used also for the faculty of seeing phantasms. Etymologically it means something revealed, an appearance or vision. A person with second sight is a *taidhbhsear* or, in some dialects, *taidhbhseadar*; *taidhbhsearachd* is the activity and craft of a seer. In the older English-language accounts of second sight, these are the terms that are used should there be any reference to Gaelic terminology.

A fetch or double in the sense of 'astral body' is *samhla* 'likeness, resemblance'; the doppelgänger is *co-choisiche*, literally 'co-walker'. In some areas samhla not 'taidhbhse' is the word in common use for what might in English be called a ghost, while in others the word 'co-choisiche' does not appear to be known at all. 'Ghost' in the sense of 'revenant' does not have much part – certainly not a central part – in the cosmology of second sight. Yet there is an adage that both living and dead have a taidhbhse. This, however, exists side by side with an adage that only the living has a taidhbhse.

In some instances my evidence may be rather fragmentary but my impression is that we are dealing not with one static system of belief but with several dynamic systems. There is certainly no reason to doubt the possibility that change and adaptation have been, and still are, occurring. I am myself inclined to think that the terms An Dà Shealladh and An Dà Fhradharc are both relatively modern coinages although their exact linguistic relationship with 'second sight' presents a difficult problem. 'Co-choisiche' has all the appearance of a calque and, indeed, translates 'doppelgänger'. Yet the essential idea of doppelgänger is already present in our specific sense of *samhla*, unequivocally a native term. As I have said earlier, the co-choisiche is not so much a replica as an anarchic alternative personality. This is taken a step further (though not chronologically) in the seventeenth-century story of the Lewisman who was confronted with his own hostile alter ego. In these connections, one cannot but think of Jekyll and Hyde or of Gilmartin[12] in James Hogg's novel *Confessions of a Justified Sinner*.

Looking at the problem from another angle, it is noteworthy that although Irish and Scots Gaelic culture are fundamentally so similar, neither the terminology of the 'Two Sights' and the 'co-walker' nor the idea of the alternative personality are to be found, so far as I have been able to discover, in genuine Irish Gaelic tradition. It would seem that we are dealing here with a distinctively Scottish concept.

The Lewisman's 'double', you will remember, asked him 'impertinent questions'. Dialogue between a seer and a taidhbhse is not unknown although it must be said that modern taidhbhsean seem to be notably taciturn. Yet one informant told me of a famous seer in the Hebrides who died around the turn of the century and who was so well acquainted with his taidhbhsean, and they with him, that they habitually came into whatever house he happened to be visiting after dark and plucked at his sleeve. He would thereupon rise and go outside to talk to them. (Again, one may compare the Lewisman's spirit who spoke to him 'in the fields'.) But this Hebridean seer always spoke to his ghostly visitants lying prone on the ground: without that contact with the earth he would be in danger.

In the majority of cases, the seer's visions simply fade from perception. I have heard, however, of one seer in Skye in the late nineteenth century who maintained that the figures disappeared from the ends. Perhaps a variant of the latter mode of seeing is implicit in the account of the death of Donald MacCrimmon the piper during the Jacobite Rising of 1745, when a seer reported 'that, after the said Donald, a goodly person, six feet high, parted with him [. . .] he saw him all at once contracted to the bigness of a boy of five or six years old, and immediately with the next look, resume his former size'.

Assuming that there has been continuity as well as innovation in what we call second sight, it would seem reasonable to suggest that the influence of Christianity would have caused structural changes in the system of belief. During some periods the clergy were fairly lax in their attitudes towards these matters. Still, any system of divination is bound to attract the attention of theologians; in Gaelic society there has clearly been an ambivalent relationship between the Church, in all its branches, and the second-sighted. Some of the early accounts stress the piety of certain seers; others tell of those

that have a sense of God and religion, and may be presumed to be godly, [who] are known to have this faculty. This evidently appears, in that they are troubled for having it, judging it a sin, that it came from the devil, and not from God; earnestly desiring and wishing to be rid of it, if possible; and to that effect, have made application to their minister, to pray to God for them that they might be exonerated from that burden. They have supplicated the presbytery, who judicially appointed public prayers to be made in several churches, and a sermon preached to that purpose, in their own parish church, by their minister; and they have compeared before the pulpit, after sermon, making confession openly of that sin, with deep sense on their knees; renounced any such gift or faculty which they had to God's dishonour, and earnestly desired the minister to pray for them; and this their recantation recorded; and after this, they were never troubled with such a sight any more.[13]

Modern tradition corroborates this to some extent, telling of the loss of the faculty due to religious conversion, or how seers will only go out at night if they carry a Bible, or how the act of seeing can be terminated by 'gaoth a' Bhìobaill' ('the wind of the Bible'): the draught of air caused by snapping a Bible shut behind the seer's head. At the same time, there is sanctified precognition: the Rev. John Morrison (1701–1774), the 'Seer of Petty' (a parish near Inverness), and the Rev. Lachlan MacKenzie of Lochcarron (1754–1819) were two of the most celebrated clergymen-seers.

Gaelic oral tradition has also preserved the names of several seers who are not second-sighted men and women gifted or burdened with that particular faculty, but are represented as individuals who deliberately sought to possess occult powers or had them conferred upon them in a special set of circumstances. Certain sinister rituals, like raising the Devil in the form of a monstrous cat, are also alluded to, both in written and oral accounts; although not, so far as I am aware, in genuine oral tradition, in connection with any of these notable people. A seer in this category is not so much a taidhbhsear as a *fiosaiche* 'augur, soothsayer'; his or her occult knowledge is *fiosachd*; (*fios* 'knowledge': the two terms have the appropriate agental and abstract endings). Two of the most celebrated of them were the Lady of Lawers in Perthshire and the Fiosaiche Ìleach 'the Islay Seer'.

But the archetypal seer of Gaelic tradition is Coinneach Odhar ('Sallow Kenneth'), known in English as the 'Brahan Seer' since 1896, when a book of his 'Prophecies' was published. This name comes from Brahan Castle, a MacKenzie stronghold in Ross-shire. According to one version of the legend, his mother was given a diviner's stone for him, when he was a baby, by the ghost of a Norse princess in Lewis. In an outstanding piece of historical detective work,[14] the Rev. William Matheson has shown that Coinneach Odhar was an historical character, though not, as had hitherto been supposed, a MacKenzie, who flourished in the 1570s and was probably put to death for sorcery. The legend of Coinneach Odhar was brought from Ross-shire to Lewis, where his birthplace became fixed: it was carried to the Hebrides, Matheson thinks, through the MacKenzies' conquest of Lewis in the early seventeenth century; and round his name has gathered almost every species of prophecy in Gaelic tradition. Among these are variants of the widespread Signs of the Last Days: women will lose their modesty and ministers will be without Grace.

There is still a lively interest in interpreting the prophecies ascribed to him; his prediction of the coming of the 'black rain', for example, is taken to mean either North Sea oil or alternatively acid rain. And clearly, new prophecies are still being constructed. Quite recently I was told that Coinneach Odhar had predicted that when two women rule this land the kingdom is approaching its end. Some of his older prophecies, about the Clearances, for instance, are ascribed in variant form to other seers also, among them Thomas the Rhymer.

Tómas Reumair, as he is known in Gaelic, has a unique status as prophet of the messianic hope of the Gaels: one day we will regain our rightful place in Scotland. By the mid-seventeenth century it was already well known, judging from allusions to it in Gaelic poetry; in the songs of the Jacobite campaign of 1715 it had a prominent place. One of them begins with the words: 'This is the time when the Prophecy shall be fulfilled'. This messianic theme has always appeared to me to be an important element in the cultural life of Gaelic Scotland and psychologically important in the Jacobitism of the eighteenth century. Conventional historians disregard it.[15]

Within the scope of this essay I could only touch on a number of the more prominent aspects of Divination and the Seer. My bias overall would be to emphasise the aesthetic interest of stories and verses that are claimed to be the vehicles of divination. There are alternative ways of analysing the data, of course; but in this field, it seems to me, it is possible to see the creative imagination as strongly and as subtly at work as in other areas of what we call imaginative literature. Does this 'literature', however, have any other social function? Native ethnographers of the past have been at pains to point out that Gaelic 'second sight' is only a local variety of a global phenomenon. Nowadays, we tend more to stress our prerogative right to the 'gift'. That is to say, we use it positively in defining ourselves as Gaels over against the dominant cultures of Lowland Scotland and England. There is even a belief, presumably connected with the retreat of Gaelic into the North and West, that no one who is born far from the sea can possess second sight.

Finally, there is an interesting contrast between present and past accounts in what they imply is the relationship of precognition with the nature of fate. It is generally believed now that it is pointless for a seer to warn those who have been seen and recognised in a vision of disaster. (Portents and premonitions give room for manoeuvre.) The event has been preordained and fate cannot be averted. But it was not always so. Seers of the past had a duty to warn of approaching danger; evasive action was possible; fate was not fixed to that degree. A social anthropologist might see in this a reflection of the Gaelic sense of history. For many centuries Gaelic society has been subjected to a process of ethnocide. We once had some command over our destiny; now we have none. But whether this is what Gaelic seers, unconsciously it may be, have to tell us, I must leave to others to judge.

Looking at Legends of the Supernatural

Scholars of folklore use the term 'supernatural' in a very wide sense, covering practically everything in a society that can be labelled as religion or dismissed as superstition. It is not altogether surprising, therefore, that some who have commented on this folkloristic usage have argued that a more precise terminology is required. Social anthropologists, for example, would deal with these beliefs in terms of social function and the like while theologians would distinguish between concepts of the supernatural and the preternatural. Psychologists who study folktales or traditional beliefs have still other sets of categories. Professional folklorists are of course well aware of all these distinctions but regard the label of 'supernatural' as a convenient generic term.

Within a given society it may often be the case that what analysts call supernatural or preternatural, or whatever, is in fact regarded by members of that society as part of the order of nature itself. In Gaelic the term *anaghnàthaichte* – in reality not much more than 'unusual' – was sometimes applied to phenomena that could be interpreted as omens and portents. That in turn raises the question of what a society's concepts of 'nature' and 'natural' actually are; and what may be the status of different beliefs at different times throughout history: here specifically throughout that of Gaelic society. We certainly ought to take all that into account in looking at these 'legends of the supernatural'.

In our contemporary Gaelic community, now almost entirely bilingual and to a very large extent bicultural, the situation is very complex. For instance, only a few native Gaels, in my experience, are prepared to express without reservation a belief in the existence of fairies. Some of those who do, while denying the existence of such beings nowadays, are none the less prepared to assert that they must – or may – have existed in the past. There must surely have been *some* substance, they will say, in the scores of tales that they themselves heard from parents and grandparents. Others again will circumscribe their assent in a different way. Fairies still exist, but people have lost the power of seeing them. It is we who have changed not they. And, as with a general approach to all such 'supernatural' phenomena, this may be tied in with the attitude that the Gaelic world has suffered, and continues to suffer, a reduction in 'the natural emotions'. People nowadays are less hospitable, less kind to each other, less generous, more materialistic, and altogether less 'spiritual'. 'Tha gràdh nàdarra fhéin a' falbh' is one of the expressions used of the process. In certain contexts, a connection may be made with 'the signs of the latter days' – *na lathaichean deireannach*. These eschatological statements have a very long history throughout Christendom.

Many of the attitudes I have touched on are difficult to elicit, I believe, unless the enquirer is himself or herself a member of the Gaelic community or at the least is regarded as someone who subscribes to the systems of belief under discussion. But obviously that limitation does not apply when storytellers confine themselves to their actual narrative, without adding much in the way of commentary, or when they are able to reserve their position with regard to their own personal beliefs. It is also noticeable that stories about omens and portents, warnings given in dreams, for instance, are more readily shared with visitors to a community than are, say, stories of encounters with the fairies. By this I mean not only first-person accounts but stories involving named contemporaries or individuals of the recent past. It seems to be assumed, no doubt correctly on the whole, that some degree of belief in premonition is more widely shared by the greater world. Discussion of such matters leads very easily to the belief in second sight.

Although it is very rare indeed, at any rate in our own times, to find, within Gaelic society, a person who will openly declare that he or she has second sight, the belief itself is seldom treated with complete scepticism. I shall return to second sight; but let me say at this point that in certain respects belief in this faculty acts as an organising principle, colouring people's opinions about other phenomena. For instance, a person who denies the existence of the fairy-folk in our age will argue that people of the past must have had a faculty of 'seeing', comparable with second sight, that allowed them to perceive those beings about which so many tales are told. And a few tradition bearers will insist that what they tell is no more than sober truth. It hardly needs saying that the data assembled from storytellers and tradition bearers can lend themselves to a range of interpretations.

Depending on whom he or she is talking to, an informant can offer rather dissimilar testimonies, as I have already indicated. The language used in field-work may have a bearing on this. For instance, the English term 'second sight' can cover much more than the Gaelic term *An Dà Shealladh* denotes. In addition to that, genuine tradition itself may present divergent or even contradictory accounts of belief. In one area of the Gàidhealtachd we hear that all apparitions are appearances of the living only: there are no apparitions of the dead. In another it is said that both the living and the dead can appear to mortal eyes: there are fetches and there are revenants. To that may be added further a variety of rationalisations, most of them dismissive of all 'supernatural' or 'preternatural' experience as containing nothing more than figments of the imagination. Or again one person may assert that second sight is hereditary, another that it can be learnt but does not last, while yet a third witness is equally certain that it can be learned and then last for a lifetime. This indeed constituted a problem for enquirers of the seventeenth and eighteenth centuries.

Obviously the process of reducing these conflicting views throughout the tradition to a workable model would be complex and difficult. In this short essay I do not intend to embark on any such hazardous venture. All I aim at is to select a few examples of the material that forms the corpus of supernatural legends and indicate some of the approaches that have been taken in an attempt to elucidate the 'true' meaning of these folktales.

We may conveniently begin with legends of the fairies. Although I shall employ both the English and Gaelic terms here, I should observe that, for a number of reasons, the word 'fairy' is a rather misleading translation of *sìdhiche* or *sìdheanach* or the various other forms we have in Gaelic. *Na sìdhichean* are not diminutive creatures with wings, although on occasion they may appear as shrunken or wizened, but are generally of human dimensions and appearance. Nor are their clothes markedly different from ours. With perhaps a few exceptions, the colours they normally wear are restricted to muted shades of grey, green, blue and brown. (Because the Gaelic spectrum expresses varying intensities of light within one 'colour' – glas, uaine, liath, gorm, ruadh, donn – the English terms are only rough equivalents.) These are all colours that are easily obtained from natural dyes but it is perhaps significant that the vivider tones are absent. More precisely, the fairies do not appear in bright colours when they are seen outside. This is usually beyond the bounds of the *baile* 'human habitation and arable land', on the moorland, in the glens, and among the mountains. The fairies are creatures of the wild; the colours of their clothes are the colours of the vegetation, in growth and decay, and merge with that of their surroundings, almost like camouflage. There is, however, a group of stories which depicts them inside their own dwelling and there their appearance is quite different.

The various forms of 'sìdhiche' contain the element *sìdh* 'a mound or hill'. We seem to have this in certain mountain names: Beinn t-Sìdh or Sìdh Chailleann, the latter explained as the 'Hill of the Caledonians', perhaps the sacred mountain of that tribal confederation. The fairy knoll is, in the Gaelic of many areas, *Sìdhean, sìdhein* yet we normally write this with -'th'-. Although there is a consensus of opinion among scholars that the sìdhichean are the 'folk of the hill', there is a long tradition that makes them *daoine sìthe* 'the people of peace'. One suggestion is that as *sìdh* 'mound' and *sìth* 'peace' lost their distinctive endings, in the course of development of the language, both coming to be pronounced 'sì', and with 'sìdh' becoming obsolete as a common noun, it was inevitable that the name 'sìdhichean' should be interpreted as 'the peaceful people'. Another view is that the name was given in order to placate them. The fairies could be malevolent towards human beings and it was only prudent to refer to them by a name that did not evoke their hostility. Just so did the Greeks refer to the Furies as the *Eumenides* 'the kindly ones'. There is still another opinion that 'sìdh' and 'sìth' are in fact connected.[1]

Theories about the origin of the sìdhichean abound. We might note first of all the medieval Christian interpretations.[2] According to one of these, the fairies are fallen angels. When Lucifer rebelled against God, was defeated, and cast into the infernal regions, those angels who had sided with him were consigned to perdition also. The angels who refused to take Lucifer's part stayed in Heaven. But there was a third lot who remained neutral. Not good enough for Heaven and not bad enough for Hell, they were banished to this world and sentenced to dwell here in the hills and the hidden places of the earth until the end of time. They are our sìthichean.

This is clearly an attempt to fit a strongly held belief into the framework of Christian cosmology. Certain pagan beliefs, incompatible with Christianity, were as far as possible destroyed by the early Christians; others less dangerous imperceptibly merged in different ways with the faith or simply lingered on in a diminished form: others again were found to be reconcilable with a Christian view of the universe and in that framework remained remarkably distinctive.

Those beliefs that survived in spite of ecclesiastical hostility were often held by people who believed in the teachings of the church as well. For example, there were Gaels alive in the mid-twentieth century who subscribed to the Christian belief in the afterlife and to the concept of reward and punishment after death. Yet they also believed implicitly that the ancestral dead in the churchyard were in some sense all still alive there in another dimension of existence. And they held these apparently mutually exclusive beliefs at the same time – a thing human beings are of course perfectly capable of doing. I am thinking here of people I knew personally. None of them had heard of the Rev. Robert Kirk (1644–92) but their views were basically the same as those of that strange savant as expressed in his fascinating book *The Secret Commonwealth of Elves, Faunes and Fairies*, published in 1691.[3]

I think some people regard Kirk as an isolated phenomenon – and in view of his clerical profession there is some justification for that assessment – but he was only bringing together in a more sophisticated way those apparently incompatible beliefs which I already alluded to and which many of his congregation must also have held. In passing I should add that a minister of the Church of Scotland in the Isle of Skye firmly asserted that he had seen the fairies dancing. He was the Rev. Donald MacLeod (1872–1955) and his experience can be dated to around 1878.[4] He was a native of Torrin (*Na Torran*) and he saw them at A' Chreag Liath. To him this was an objective phenomenon not to be explained away by hallucination, trick of the light, or any other rationalising approach. Very interestingly, the figures he saw were tiny, dancing creatures, clad in green, quite different, it would seem, from the conventional depictions of Gaelic legend where the sìthichean are normally larger.

There was at one time a theory popular among antiquarians, but held by certain scholars, too, that belief in fairies preserves a memory of a 'former people', perhaps the Picts. This theory is by no means dead; it is indeed one of the explanations proffered by native Gaels who have heard the legends, seen ancient ruins, *taighean-fo-thalamh* 'underground houses', and the like, and put two-and-two together. No folklorist takes it very seriously now, it would seem: at all events not as the one and only explanation. For all that, there is no reason to reject it out of hand.

To some scholars, for instance the late Professor Kenneth Jackson, the sìthichean are simply the ancestral dead and the sìthean is in origin a prehistoric burial mound. These fairy knolls that patently are not burial mounds but natural features have quite simply been drawn into the scheme of things at a later date.

It is without any doubt true that sìthichean are sometimes associated with ancient burial places, mounds or no mounds. Prehistoric burial sites may have been sacral centres, just as the older Christian graveyards were, situated round a church. Some of the sìtheanan are in proximity to early Christian sites, presumably because a pagan sacral centre was Christianised. The Rev. Robert Kirk himself tells us that churches are sited near fairy knolls.

In the parish of Strath in Skye, to take one instance, there is a very arresting sequence of names and places to be observed between Kilbride and Broadford. There is a standing stone known as Clach na h-Annaid in Kilbride. Assuming that the stone predates the introduction of Christianity (a reasonable assumption), this area was chosen as a Christian centre – Cille Bhrighde 'the Cell of Bride or Bridget' – at an early date. The rather mysterious word *Annaid* is held to designate a 'mother church'. Not very far away, we have the Church of Cill a' Chrò, the Gaelic name being explained as 'the church of the [cattle]-fold': the 'fold' being the great enclosure of land between Suardail and Beinn na Caillich. This is the traditional explanation, probably a folk etymology, for the Latin name in medieval records is Corpus Christ, whence the modern English 'Kilchrist'. Next in sequence, coming towards Broadford is the famous Sìdhean, where the poet William Ross was born.

How do the theories of origin square with the data provided by the legends? Before we attempt to answer that, we should be aware that we are dealing here, as elsewhere in Gaelic tradition, not with static but with dynamic systems of belief which change through the ages, adjusting to changes in social circumstances. Second, it is unlikely that one single, reductive explanation will ever account for all the phenomena. In the legends themselves there are many complexities and sometimes apparent contradictions.

Generally speaking, the sìdhichean of the legends are never presented as any kind of 'former people'. By definition, they are not and never were mortals at all. Nor are they ever, in direct description, the dead. The dead may be with them, however. There are many stories of how someone who has entered the fairy knoll recognises people who had died or who had suddenly and mysteriously disappeared from human ken. There are stories of how a mortal hears a song coming from beneath a moorland sward (not necessarily a knoll) and recognises the voice of a dead relative or a person who wandered into the hills and never returned.

Yet there are also legends in which there is more than a suggestion that the sìthichean resemble the dead. In some of these the fairies are dumb or they have no music and no mirth. In one of the formulas of Gaelic lament, the dead are characterised as those without speech, without mirth, without music. But to complicate the issue, the fairies are frequently depicted as beings who are in fact full of wonderful music and not at all dumb. Moreover, in a small group of tales (or multiforms of a tale) humans are the dumb ones and the world of mortals is the land of the dead. These extraordinary inversions cannot detain us now but I do believe they have a deep psychological significance.

Stories of the *Sluagh* 'the host' usually imply that this is the fairy host flying through the air. Furthermore, they frequently mention that the person who witnessed this flight recognised one or many people who had long since died, now being carried in the sky by the fairy host. A few legends tell of a living person who was swept away by the Sluagh and deposited elsewhere unharmed.

It is impossible, within the limits of this brief essay, to detail the kinds of encounter which mortals may have with the world of the sìthichean. A brief summary must suffice.

Encounters with the fairies are rarely by choice. Of course, one may wander into the knoll at Hallowe'en or New Year (both of those being important boundaries in time) when the door is open and in some stories the visitor knows that this is a sìdhean. But on the whole it is the fairies who come into the world of humans. A human midwife may be summoned to deliver the queen of the fairies. A mortal may be abducted. Babies are stolen, unbaptised babies being most at risk, and changelings left in their place. The sìdhichean require an infusion of human blood from time to time as if to strengthen the fairy stock. Living mortals abducted by them often act as helpers to later human visitors and help them to escape.

The fairies have their own cattle and hounds and so on. But just as they abduct human beings they steal animals also, or they take the vital substance of the animal, living or dead, leaving only a husk. Fairy cattle appear from time to time and can interbreed with domestic cattle. And deer, red deer, not roe, are, in a particular sense, the cattle of the fairies.

Fairies confer good and bad fortune. They give health or take it away. They have artistic powers in their gift, music most of all and especially the art of piping. The MacCrimmon pipers in Skye are in one legend said to have obtained their wonderful powers from the sìdhichean. This transference may occur when the recipient is wide awake or it may happen after falling asleep on the fairy mound. I know of few legends that credit the fairies with the poetic gift of a named individual, but traditionally people were aware that poetry as well as music could come from the fairy hill. An interesting term is *siubhal-sìdhe* 'fairy motion'. In a general sense this can be used to express smooth, unhindered movement, a glide. Nowadays at any rate the usage tends to be restricted to contexts of heightened or 'poetic' speech. Metaphorically it is applied to 'effortless superiority': success, especially worldly or material success with the minimum expenditure of effort. But it has another side to it. People who have the siubhal-sìdhe are liable to lose their wealth as easily as they have acquired it. This reminds us that fairy gold or other gifts frequently turn into mud or withered leaves or dung.

On the other hand, when good fortune or artistic powers are bestowed these are seldom taken away and much the same applies to health and strength. But the fairies are always capricious. There is the famous legend of the hunchback who pleases the fairies by supplying a tune for their dance – actually a recital of the first few days of the week. His companion then recites the days of the week in full; this makes them dance too fast; and they transfer the hump from the first man to the second. But looking at Gaelic tradition throughout, we seem to have something of a divide between artistic gifts on the one hand and material wealth on the other and this cannot but have some psychological significance.

The sìdhichean then are benevolent and malevolent; they bestow fertility and sterility; they appear to be self-sufficient in a dimension of existence that parallels that of human society, yet they also depend on humans and on domestic animals since from time to time they steal animals and humans alike. The ambivalent nature of the fairies is presented visually in images of great power in one of the multiforms of the legend known as 'Midwife to the Queen of Fairies'. When the human midwife enters the sìthean it is a palatial dwelling with walls of gold and silver and glittering jewels. The men and women are young and beautiful; wine sparkles in exquisite goblets; and the music is the loveliest ever heard. The fairies would have kept the woman there forever but a human helper in the sìthean instructs her to rub soap of a certain colour on her eyes and she does so. Immediately the place is transformed. What she sees now is an ugly great cavern whose walls are grey and brown earth and stone; the creatures who inhabit it are shrunken, gnarled, wizened beings; and the only sounds are those of dripping water and the rush of the mountain winds. This in effect is a mound of the living dead out in the wilds.

From such evidence as we possess of the ancient Celtic pantheon, Donn, the 'Brown One', is the ruler of the kingdom of the dead. He is the dark god from whom all mankind is descended and to whom all return in death. Most scholars would agree that the sìthichean must be connected with this shadowy otherworld. There ordinary time does not hold sway: a mortal who spends a year in the sìthean thinks that no more than a day has passed.

But other elements also must have contributed to the complex of beliefs. Among them may be a belief in the existence of spirits of the wilderness: beings who live in rocks and trees, in hills and solitary places. And if successive waves of invading peoples (long before the arrival of Celts) tended to drive their defeated predecessors into the less hospitable parts of the land, sightings of those survivors, or tales of their timidity, hostility, or unpredictability could have played their own part in the formation of the belief as we have inherited it. If any of us nowadays happens to glimpse, far out in the mountains, a human figure dressed in clothes of muted colours, such as a stalker might wear, we think little of it. If the person seems anxious to avoid contact and quickly disappears, we might assume this was someone engaged in poaching deer or in some similar activity. Our ancestors would be more likely to identify the figure as one of the sìdhichean. And through the centuries all those reports would merge and produce fresh material to validate the belief.

From altogether another point of view we may look for psychological insights.

For example, we could take the fairy knoll as a metaphor of the imagination, perhaps as an equivalent of the modern concept of the Unconscious. From this shadowy realm comes the creative power of mankind. An old friend of mine used to say, when he produced songs or legends that I did not realise he knew: 'Bha mi 's a' Chnoc o chunnaic mi thu' ('I was in the [fairy] Hill since I saw you'). And others had similar vivid expressions. None of them was to be taken literally but there was a system of belief behind the expression.

There is a great area here, as I see it, still to be explored. Let us take one example: the legend of the Sealwoman.[5] In North Uist there were once stories of sealmen as well.[6] (The Orkney and Shetland stories of the Selchie / Selkie / Silkie – who may be a man or a woman – are multiforms of the Gaelic tale.) In outline our Gaelic story runs as follows. A fisherman walking above the beach sees a number of seals coming ashore. They take off their skins, lay them on the strand, and turn into beautiful young women. They begin to romp and play, moving away from the heap of pelts, one of which the man removes. After a while the women come back, each puts on her skin again, turns into a seal and returns to the sea – all but the one whose sealskin is missing. The man captures her and takes her home, where she learns human speech. The man married her and in due course they have a family. Her husband keeps the sealskin hidden in the barn among the corn. One day one of the boys of the family finds it and tells his mother about the beautiful thing his father keeps hidden in the corn in the barn. The mother takes it at once, goes down to the beach, turns into a seal again and swims away. That family and their descendants were for evermore lucky in fishing.

The story has a wide distribution in Norse and Celtic lands. In Scotland it has a particularly close connection with the MacCodrums in North Uist of whom the most famous representative was of course Iain MacFhearchair, John MacCodrum the bard. Although the kindred name MacCodrum no longer exists there the MacCodrums are still remembered as *Sliochd nan Ròn* 'Descendants of the Seals', and the designation Clann MhicCodrum nan Ròn is well enough known to the present day. According to the late Rev. William Matheson:

> It was said [. . .] that a woman of the name of MacCodrum, possibly a relative of the bard, was regularly seized with pains at the time of the annual seal hunt, out of sympathy, as was supposed, with her kith and kin. It was even darkly suggested that the MacCodrums could and did sometimes assume the forms of seals, and that several of them had lost their lives in that way.[7]

There are, it may be said, other families also who are said to be descendants of the seals but nowadays there is a tendency to interpret that as descendants of seal hunters.

Folkloristic studies of the legend trace the distribution and probable origin of the story and some might leave it at that. Dr Dáithí Ó hÓgáin goes further and links it with themes and motifs of the Otherworld

Wife and the Goddess of Sovereignty whom the rightful king takes as mate, for she is the goddess of the land. He suggests that the Seal-woman legend:

> sprang from a specific application of the account [i.e. of a man marrying a spirit-woman] to the marine context in medieval times. We are told that a man once saw a beautiful maiden on a rock by the shore [. . .] The legend, some versions of which describe the lady as a seal-maiden rather than a mermaid, spread to Scotland and to Iceland, probably in the late Middle Ages.[8]

It should be added that a few variants of the story in Scottish Gaelic too make the woman a mermaid.

Does this legend have any other significance? Just as we can take the sìthean as a metaphor of the imagination, we can look at a legend such as that of the seal mate in both sociological and psychological perspectives.

All maritime communities are dependent on the sea, principally as the source of much of the food. Fishing, wild-fowling, whale and seal hunting were in the past all practised off the north-west coast. Travel was to a very large extent by sea; 'cuan sruthach nan ròd' ('the streaming ocean of the roadways'), as Iain Lom calls it. Much more than that, the sea in Gaelic lore takes on mythic proportions. The great sea-hag of the Fenian ballads is one aspect. Whether she is or is not a personification of the wild ocean, there is no such reservation with regard to the belief that the sea itself is a living being, and a female.

In passing, I may observe that the Rev. Dr Kenneth MacLeod's famous essay 'Duatharachd na Mara' is sometimes regarded as being coloured by the author's own romanticisings. But all the essential beliefs he draws upon are still talked about by bearers of Gaelic tradition. And seals in particular have a special status in those contexts as if they most of all represent 'the people of the sea'.[9] To meet a seal on land at any distance above the highest tide line is a portent of ill-fortune: in this situation it is a *droch comhdhalaiche*, someone or something it is unlucky to meet, for the seal's proper place is in the sea or next to it. Yet, essentially of the sea as they are, and not amphibious to the same extent as otters, for instance, seals none the less do come ashore. They bask on rocks, they mate and bring forth their young on land; they do not wholly belong to either element. In that sense they are intermediaries between two worlds that are basically in opposition to one another. This process of mediation is taken further and becomes charged with symbolic power in the marriage of man and seal. The union validates the relationship between mortals and one of the elements on which they depend for food and freedom of movement and the like; at the same time it sets limits on it. In the end, the Seal woman returns to the sea.

Another angle of perception is found in a psychological analysis of the legend. The interpretation I select now is made from a feminist point of view but is also informed, with some significant differences, by principles of Jungian psychology. Clarissa P. Estés[10] sees the story as one

> told across the world, for it is an archetype, a universal knowing about an issue of soul. Sometimes fairy tales and folktales erupt from a sense of place [. . .] This story is told in the cold countries to the north, in any country where there is an icy sea or ocean. Versions of this story are told among the Celts, the Scots, the tribes of north west America, Siberian and Icelandic peoples. The story is commonly called 'The Seal Maiden or Selkie-o, *Pamrauk*, Little Seal; *Eyarlirtaq*, Flesh of Seal' [. . . it] tells about where we truly come from, what we are made of, and how we must all, on a regular basis, use our instincts and find our way back home.

Estés bases her analysis on Inuit versions of the legend. A number of the motifs correspond with those of the Gaelic tale; others show significant divergences. In Inuit the man who captures the Sealwoman is a lonely individual who pleads with the woman to marry him. As in the Gaelic version it is their son (but in the Inuit tale he is an only child) who finds the skin and gives it back to his mother. In an important departure from the Gaelic version, however, the boy accompanies his mother out to sea when she rejoins her own kind. But mother and grandfather bring him back 'because his time is not yet to be here with us'. The boy returns to land and grows up there where in due course he becomes a mighty shaman – a religious leader and 'medicine-man' – 'a singer and a maker of stories, and it was said all this came to be because as a child he had survived being carried out to sea by the great seal spirits'.

The parallel here with the bestowal of artistic and creative powers by the sìdhichean is quite arresting. However, Estés's psychological analysis takes her much further than that. Here I can only indicate some of her approaches, using as far as possible her own words.

First she draws attention to the fact that the legend

has a retrograde motif [. . .] In most fairy tales, a human is enchanted and turned into an animal. But here we have the opposite: a creature led into a human life. The story produces an insight into the structure of the female psyche [. . .] The pelt in this story is not so much an article as the representation of a feeling state and a state of being [. . .] Psychologically, to be without the pelt causes a woman to pursue what she thinks she should do, rather than what she truly wishes. It causes her to follow whoever or whatever impresses her as strongest – whether it is good for her or not.

In Jungian psychology, the ego is often described as a small island of consciousness that floats in a sea of unconsciousness. However, in folklore the ego is portrayed as a creature of appetite often symbolised by a not very bright human or animal surrounded by forces very mystifying to it, and over which it attempts to gain control. Sometimes the ego is able to gain control in a most brutish and destructive manner, but in the end, through the heroine's or hero's progress, it most often loses its bid to reign [. . .] In this spirit, let us consider that the lonely man who steals the sealskin represents the ego of a woman's psyche [. . .] It is a timeless motif in human psyche that the ego and the soul vie to control the life force [. . .] The lonely man in the tale is attempting to participate in the life of the soul. But like the ego, he is not particularly built for it, and tries to grab at the soul rather than develop a relationship with it [. . .] the union of opposites between ego and soul produces something of infinite value, the spirit child [. . .] It is the child who brings the sealskin [. . .] back to his mother. It is the child who enables her to return to her home. This child is a spiritual power that impels us to continue our important work, to push back, change our lives, better the community, join in helping to balance the world [. . .] all by returning home.

These short extracts do no more than signal the approach adopted by an analyst who seeks to interpret folktales with the use of modern psychological insights. Estés has examined many stories worldwide and is of the opinion that 'In some of the greatest tales, such as the Gaelic "Beauty and the Beast", the Mexican "Bruja Milagra" and the Japanese "The Crescent Moon Bear," finding the way back to one's rightful psychic order begins with the feeding of or the caring for a lonely and/or injured woman, man, or beast.'

Professional folklorists are on the whole not very concerned with this kind of interpretation, being inclined to the view that it is all too easy to find in folktales whatever the psychological analyst wants to find in them. This is undoubtedly a danger. Quite different conclusions are drawn by Bruno Bettelheim, for instance, working from a Freudian basis

or even by Marina Warner, from a feminist stance. Nevertheless it seems
to me that folklorists ought to welcome all these approaches. If we say
that the storytellers themselves are completely unaware of those 'meanings' and in some instances would probably be hostile to the psychologists' interpretations, we reduce the undeniable power of the stories to
what is immediately accessible to the conscious mind and the rational
intellect. The strange compulsion that folktales have exercised and
continue to exercise upon untold generations of adults as well as children
is scarcely to be accounted for by a simple positivist approach.

From that point of view we may look briefly at one or two aspects of
second sight. As I said earlier this English term is used rather more loosely
than An Dà Shealladh in Gaelic. In spite of contrary accounts, I think we
have sufficient information from tradition to argue that Gaelic society
observed a division between the 'seer' who possesses a special faculty of
'seeing' and other members of the community who *may* experience
premonitions, which can include visions of human figures, recognisable
to them or not. A further distinction ought to be drawn between a
taidhbhsear – a second-sighted individual, in English parlance – and a
fiosaiche 'augur, soothsayer'. By far the best-known representative of a
fiosaiche is of course 'Coinneach Odhar Fiosaiche', as he was frequently
called. There were probably social states and functions involved here,
but I cannot pursue that at present. What concerns us now is the concept
of the 'samhla' (or in some places *co-choisiche*, 'co-walker') as opposed
to that of the 'taidhbhse'. In some areas of the Gàidhealtachd there is
some overlap in usage, or only one term or the other is known. A number
of other terms exist also but it is not necessary to discuss the full range of
nomenclature in the present context.

The *samhla* can be seen by anybody. It appears as a normal person,
dressed in the normal way. He or she is a replica of a living individual
and cannot be distinguished from that individual. The same *can* apply
to a *taidhbhse* but the seer knows what the import of the vision is. This
apparition is that of a still-living person or of the dead and so of course
may appear in a shroud or is accompanied by certain diagnostic signs
often conveying menace. Essentially the distinction, then, lies not in
the vision itself but in the person who sees the vision – who possesses a
particular faculty. If there is any further proviso to be inserted in this
summary description, it is that *taidhbhsean* (pl.) are only frequently
and consistently seen by the *taidhbhsear* (agent noun).

The samhla on the other hand can be described as a visual
embodiment of telepathy. For example, if someone is concentrating

on a situation at a distance, mentally focusing on another person or group of people, anxious about them, eager to be in their company, strongly desirous of sharing information or emotions of joy or sorrow with them, in general filled with an urge to communicate, then his or her samhla may appear to that individual or company. What is more it can be seen by a number of people at the same time. The theory which Gaels appear to have held is that everyone has a samhla or co-choisiche (a co-walker). There is nothing sinister about that aspect.

There are, however, stories that point to another dimension. If a person is intense or turbulent by nature, possesses a streak of violence, or is stressed by circumstance, that person's samhla can set off on its own and behave mischievously or even wreak havoc. Very significantly, there are people who in themselves appear to be very controlled individuals, of impeccable behaviour, whose samhla is particularly dangerous. The 'normal' self, so to speak, has no control over the unruly self, of whose doings he or she has no knowledge. This is not quite the Jekyll and Hyde scenario but the existence of an anarchic alternative personality which is released in particular circumstances cannot but remind us of R. L. Stevenson's powerful tale. Was Stevenson, who knew a good deal about certain aspects of Gaelic tradition (the evidence is in *Kidnapped* and *Catriona*) aware of these legends?

A person may see his or her own samhla and may indeed be attacked by it.[11] The relationship of Wringhim to Gilmartin in James Hogg's *Confessions of a Justified Sinner* may seem to be rather far removed from that. Yet it is intriguing that Gilmartin, that sinister character, bears the same name as *Gille Màrtainn* in Gaelic. This 'Servant of St Martin' in Gaelic tradition is a bye-name for the fox: the crafty one. In the well-known song which a cousin of Allan MacDonald of Kingsburgh composed against the Martins in Skye – Mac-GilleMhàrtainn is the older form – the poet says:

> *Gum bi Clann MhicGilleMhàrtainn*
> *Fo na carnaibh far robh 'n dùthchas*
> *Cuide ris na sionnaich òga*
> *Dh' itheas an fheòil anns na cùiltean.*[12]

The Martins will be
Under the cairns, where their ancestry comes from,
Along with the young foxes,
Who eat flesh in the nooks and corners.

Like Stevenson, James Hogg, too, had acquired some knowledge of Gaelic and Gaelic lore. Did he get the name Gilmartin from Gaelic?

More important in the present context, is there a psychological explanation for these beliefs in the existence of two personalities? It seems to be established that psychological trauma, especially in childhood experience, may lead to creation of alternative selves. Given that the idea of the doppelgänger – and the word 'co-choisiche' could, linguistically speaking, be a translation of doppelgänger – is an extremely widespread concept, we might posit the following. The potential 'other self' was known in Gaelic as in many other cultures. Gaelic society was under stress for centuries, with its identity constantly threatened on so many levels. Might this have strengthened the idea and led, particularly in certain individuals, to what was virtually a collective neurosis? Or is the phenomenon something else altogether: a safety valve to prevent neurosis?

Related to these notions is an attitude to second sight and fate. In the past, so far as I am aware, a seer's vision or precognition did not imply that the event was predestined and absolutely bound to happen. In fact it was a seer's duty to warn of the approaching danger. The individuals concerned had some freedom to take evasive action. But it is not so now, in the minds of those who believe in such matters and are prepared to discuss them. Fate is now fixed. Is this a reflection of Gaelic historical experience, which is so much an experience of ethnocide?

Although no attempt is made in this paper to present a unified theory on the basis of these selected items from legends of the supernatural, the interconnectedness of the data is easily seen. We have simply to look at the information which Gaelic tradition presents directly, for theoretical models may obscure the connections. At one extreme there are historical and antiquarian interpretations (as has happened on the whole in treating legends of the sìdhichean) and psychological constructs at the other.

Gaelic tradition tells us that an 'Otherworld' exists from which benevolent and malevolent influences emanate. The world of the sìdhean is such; the source of the seer's visions is such also; and the living sea who gives and takes away is yet another.

In a further area of Gaelic tradition, we may note, the wilderness is in oppositional relationship to the *baile* – homestead and settlement, enclosing humans, arable land and domestic stock. This emerges vividly from time to time in Gaelic poetry, especially erotic poetry.

Inaccessible islands in the wilderness of the sea serve a similar purpose in poetic imagery. In such places lovers celebrate their clandestine meetings or their illicit relationships. The baile is governed by social conventions, social control. In the wilderness the conventions are subverted.

So in legends of the supernatural. The human base and centre is the baile; that of the sìdhichean is the wilderness. The baile is where ordinary time – what students of comparative religion call 'profane time' – runs; the sìdhean, where ordinary time is suspended, is the place of 'sacred time'. To vary the image, we have baile versus wilderness; time versus timelessness. In the visions of the seers also, ordinary time is suspended. Serial time can be reversed. And finally, the anarchic self – the samhla in its unruly activities – is, according to some of the stories, most prone to uncontrolled behaviour not when it is within the confines of settled community but when it crosses the boundary that separates civilised society from the wild.

Each area, terrestrial or temporal, has its boundaries: between cultivated and uncultivated, between dry land and sea, between time and timeless. Each of them can be crossed by humans as by 'other-world' beings. There are constant exchanges across the divides. Men and women have fairy lovers; fairies take mortals to ensure that an infusion of human blood and human properties is received by their kind. The descendants of the Sealwoman are not less human than others nor are they artistically gifted. They are simply the most conspicuous in an endless process of mediation between the historical and the non-historical. Yet these two categories are always impinging on each other and overlapping. In a sense 'historical' subsumes 'non-historical'.

None the less, the boundary crossings are always fraught with danger: there are precautions to be observed. One does not engage in conversation with a 'ghost' except under certain conditions. One does not take cloth dyed with crotal (which belongs to the rocks of the land) out to sea. One takes an artefact of iron from the baile to ensure a safe return from the sìdhean.

And all through the legends, the human form is the primary symbol. The human shape is that in which fairies appear to mankind; the seals become humans; and the visions of greatest import involve figures of men and women. It is as if the legends were telling us that although the condition of being human means that men and women are constantly being visited by mysterious powers, the focus is none the less on humanity, on human nature. Humans are ultimately in control. The adage 'Na doir géill do gheas is géillidh geas dhut' ('Do not submit to superstition and superstition will submit to you') may have been created in a Christian cosmology, but its injunction is only an alternative to more complex rules for keeping the unpredictable elements of the imagination, and therefore the human universe, in equilibrium.

A sure sign that harmony and equilibrium are threatened is given when a red deer comes from the wild, crosses the boundary into the cultivated land in broad daylight, and remains happily there. The deer is the wild animal par excellence – *fiadh*, with its congeners 'fiadhaich', 'fiadhaire', 'dol am fiadh', etc. (The hare *gearr*[-*fhiadh*] has its own conspicuous place in legends of witchcraft and shape-shifting.) The deer are fairy cattle, as we have noticed, and they have an enormously important mediating role throughout all Gaelic tradition. But their real place is in the wild.

I remember very vividly, when I was a little boy, seeing a wild hind grazing within the confines of the baile. Those who could read the signs realised that the natural order was being overturned and said 'Se comhtharra cogaidh a tha seo' ('This is an omen of war'). Not very long after that the Second World War began. That sighting, that metaphor of order invaded by the wild, helped those who witnessed it to arrange their experience. The metaphor has a very long history behind it.

New Introduction to
the Carmina Gadelica

For the best part of a hundred years Alexander Carmichael's great collection of Gaelic verse and prose, characterized by archaic charms and incantations, which we know as *Carmina Gadelica*, has dominated its own sector of the field of Gaelic literature. Carmichael's interests, both as collector and littérateur, extended well beyond the sphere of the purely religious, as indeed the six volumes that *Carmina* eventually became were so richly to demonstrate. But there is no doubt that his deepest concern was with hymns and charms and prayers, for this is the kind of material that he selected for the first two volumes of *Carmina Gadelica*, the only ones edited by himself and published in his own lifetime.

These religious texts with their strange blend of pagan and Christian imagery, witnesses to the spirituality of a vanished age, their complement of mysterious words and phrases, apparently unknown outside this repository of incantations, and their dignified, almost liturgical, style, fascinated the reading public, Gaelic and English alike. Here it would seem was a lost lexicon of piety which almost miraculously had survived into modern times. It had been discovered on the verge of extinction, in remote places and in an obscure tongue; it was now, at the last possible moment, being revealed to the world at large. The publication of *Carmina Gadelica* was a signal triumph, an outstanding literary achievement, and an event of the greatest moment to the whole of Gaelic Scotland.

What of the collector and editor? Alexander Carmichael was born in 1832 in the Island of Lismore – *Lios Mór*, the 'Great Garden' – off the coast of Argyll. The kindred from which he sprang had of old held lands in Lismore, the head of the family being known as the Baron of Sguran House. At least as significant, however, was the connection of Clann MhicGilleMhìcheil (the Carmichaels) with the Columban church established in Lismore by St Moluag who died, according to the Annals of Ulster, in 592. Specifically, there was kinship with An t-Easbaig Bàn 'the Fair-Haired Bishop', remembered in Gaelic tradition as the builder of the cathedral of the island. Genealogical claims such as these are commonplace in Gaelic society and central to the construction of its kinship systems. They are not a matter of mere pretentiousness let alone snobbery in its commonly accepted meanings. They have little to do with consciousness of 'class' – though they may convey a vestigial sense of caste – but they function in such a way that they give the individual a place, historically and psychologically, in the vision of his own people. Family tales of an ancestral connection with the church of Columba and its later history cannot have failed to exercise an influence on the young Carmichael and may well have prepared his mind and imagination for what was to be his life's work: the preservation for posterity of the spiritual heritage of the Gaelic church of Columba and its missionaries.

Alexander Carmichael's daily bread, however, came from the more mundane source of the Civil Service of the United Kingdom. After formal education in Greenock Academy and collegiate school in Edinburgh, Alexander was accepted by the Commissioners of the Civil Service for work in Customs and Excise. No better choice could have been made. Carmichael's duties took him, among other places, to Skye, to Uist, to Oban, and then back to Uist again. In these areas, in the middle of the nineteenth century, when Gaelic was still the dominating everyday speech and English for thousand of Gaels simply a foreign language, Alexander Carmichael was introduced to 'Gaelic oral literature', as he tells us, '[. . .] widely diffused, greatly abundant, and excellent in quality.'

From the great abundance, largely between 1855 and 1899 and particularly from 1865 to 1882 when the family's permanent residence was in the Hebrides, Carmichael drew the major texts of his collection. Even as late as 1910, when he was in his late seventies, we have a report of a 'collecting pilgrimage' throughout the northern counties. The enthusiasm was characteristic for, as one of his obituary notices puts it: 'What he failed to get in Uist he searched for in Glengarry; what he lost in Kintyre he tracked in Sutherland.' During all that time he received no financial help from any institution. In the Introduction to *Carmina Gadelica Volume I*, he sums it up himself thus: 'Three sacrifices have been made – the sacrifice of time, the sacrifice of toil, and the sacrifice of means. These I do not regret.'

Alexander Carmichael contributed folk tales, proverbs, and papers on antiquarian and other topics to a variety of journals, and to books such as John Francis Campbell's *Popular Tales of the West Highlands* (1860–62) and Alexander Nicolson's *A Collection of Gaelic Proverbs and Familiar Phrases* (1881). Among those texts are a heroic ballad from the Isle of Skye (still known there in substantially the same form) and an orally transmitted version of the great medieval Gaelic prose epic *Táin Bó Cuailnge* 'The Cattle Raid of Cuailnge'. An oral recension of the ancient tragic story of Deirdre, taken down from a storyteller in Barra, was presented, first in Gaelic, then in English, to the Gaelic Society of Inverness and printed in their *Transactions* 13 and 14 (1886–87; 1887–88); later these were published in book form.

The title *Carmina Gadelica*, Latin for 'Gaelic songs / hymns / incantations, etc.' was not, it would appear, Carmichael's own first choice but was urged upon him by one or more of his friends; the Gaelic title is *Ortha nan Gàidheal* ('Charms / Incantations of the Gaels'); both English and Gaelic have lengthy subtitles. There are six volumes: I and II, as already noted, edited by the collector, with substantial help from others, and published in 1900. In 1928 Volumes I and II were reprinted with minor alterations by his daughter Ella (Mrs W.J. Watson). Volume III (1940) and Volume IV (1941) were edited by her son, Alexander Carmichael's grandson, James Carmichael Watson; Volume V (1954), consisting for the most part of secular poetry, and Volume VI, with comprehensive indexes and bibliographical information (1971) by Angus Matheson. The material in these volumes and in Alexander Carmichael's manuscripts in the University of Edinburgh has been classified in broad terms under the following headings: invocations (e.g. prayers for protection, prayers before going to sleep); addresses to the saints; seasonal hymns, including genuine Christmas carols; blessings for everyday tasks (banking up the fire for the night, reaping, grinding, milking, herding, and hunting); incantations used in healing; prayers to the sun and the moon; rhymes about animals and birds; blessings on cattle and other livestock; miscellaneous songs, e.g. praise-songs, love-songs, milking songs, fairy songs, waulking songs; auguries, with notes on the augurs' methods; and much incidental information on custom and belief in general.

From any point of view that is an extraordinary assemblage consisting as it does of formally structured items, verse and prose, curious and arcane knowledge, and miscellaneous lore of great variety and often unique nature. Here is a fine sweep of the landscape of the Gaelic imagination now apparently for the first time revealing its mysteries.

It was therefore natural that publication of what was really no more than a sample of Carmichael's material (Volumes I and II) earned the collector immediate and unqualified praise. Writing in 1901, Dr Alexander MacBain, one of the leading Gaelic scholars of his day, expressed the view that 'Mr Alexander Carmichael's *Carmina Gadelica / Ortha nan Gàidheal* is one of the most important books ever published in connection with Gaelic.' High praise indeed from a man who was noted for his lack of sentimentality in such matters.

In 1906 Carmichael received jointly with his wife, a Civil List pension; three years later the University of Edinburgh conferred on him the honorary degree of LL.D. These honours were primarily bestowed in recognition of his literary work but it is important to note that that work could and did have a bearing upon the everyday life of the people who had given Carmichael so unstintingly of their own literary inheritance. The writer of the obituary in the *Celtic Review* of October 1912 (presumably the editor, Mrs W. J. Watson, Carmichael's daughter) records the following item of information:

> When Dr Skene was preparing his Celtic Scotland, he asked Mr Carmichael to write the chapter on old Highland land customs. This paper first turned the attention of Lord Napier and Ettrick to the condition of the crofters, and led to Mr Carmichael being asked to write a more elaborate paper of a similar nature for the Crofter Royal Commission Report. Lord Napier used to say that these two papers had more to do with the passing of the Crofters Act than people knew.

The Act in question, passed in 1886, won security of tenure for crofters, who had formerly been only tenants-at-will, liable to be turned off their holdings at a landlord's whim or that of a landlord's servant. Alexander Carmichael knew the economic aspects of life in crofting communities as well as the spiritual and aesthetic aspects (his paper for the Royal Commission is still an authoritative source) and his concern was not limited to the prayers of the people.

According to some of his friends, Carmichael was himself 'one of the folk'. One would think that his profession of Excise Officer can scarcely have endeared him to those who saw no harm in distilling their own whisky (and selling it at a sensible profit) or who considered that divine favour could be measured by the riches of the flotsam cast up on the beaches. Yet Carmichael's success as a collector of arcane spells and the like argues that his informants confided in him as a trusted friend.

One of his intimates and admirers was the Rev. Dr Kenneth MacLeod, composer of the words to 'The Road to the Isles' and collaborator with Marjory Kennedy-Fraser in *The Songs of the Hebrides* (1909). In an appreciation published shortly after Carmichael's death (and reprinted in *Carmina Gadelica Volume IV*), MacLeod has this to say:

> [Others] could get the heroic tales and ballads, the things which were recited in public at the *céilidh*; only Alexander Carmichael could have got the hymns and the incantations, the things which were said when the door was closed, and the lights were out [. . .] Not all of what he learned was written down, or if written down, has been preserved; many curious rites, embodied in unusual language [. . .] were revealed to him under a strict pledge of secrecy [. . .] A characteristic instance is within the writer's knowledge. One evening a venerable Islesman, carried out of himself for the time being, allowed Dr Carmichael to take down from him a singularly beautiful 'going in to sleep' rune; early next morning, the reciter travelled twenty-six miles to exact a pledge that his 'little prayer' should never be allowed to appear in print. 'Proud, indeed, shall I be if it give pleasure to yourself, but I should not like cold eyes to read it in a book.'
>
> In the writer's [i.e. Dr Kenneth MacLeod's] presence, the manuscript was handed over to the reciter, to be burnt there and then – but for days and nights after, the music of that rune haunted two men!

A kind, generous, sensitive man, then, according to all accounts, Carmichael also had, as we have seen, a robust awareness of the everyday life of crofters and the demands of their daily round of work. It was due to his representations that the Inland Revenue was persuaded to abolish the tax on horse-drawn carts in crofting townships and on dogs kept for purposes of herding. These were by no means trivial measures for those whose lives were cast in a harsh environment, bound by the constraints of a subsistence economy. Carmichael's perceptions of Gaelic society certainly were not those of an Ivory Tower artist.

Nevertheless, he obviously had his critics. The Rev. Dr Kenneth MacLeod again:

> It is sometimes said that Dr Carmichael idealized us; not merely our past, which was allowable, being borne out by the beautiful material he had collected, but also our present, which itself contradicts his picture of it; that he idealized, at any rate, such of us as had passed the three score years, and

more particularly such of them as had a tale to tell or a rune to chant. One does not care to deny so pleasant a charge. Every man makes his own world, to the extent, at any rate, of unconsciously reading himself into it; and thus the worse the reality idealized, the better the man who idealizes [. . .]

These last are significant words and to some readers might seem to verge on the casuistical.

Earlier in the same appreciation, Kenneth MacLeod had drawn a highly suggestive contrast between Alexander Carmichael and two of 'our other great ones': Alexander MacBain, about whom 'one could never quite get rid of the feeling that in temperament he was Teutonic rather than Celtic'; and John Francis Campbell of Islay, pioneer collector and scholar in the study of Gaelic folktales. Campbell, Dr MacLeod says, 'was never quite one of us – he could never altogether hide the fact that he had learnt his art with other peoples and in other schools. And though he doubtless loved our tales and our beliefs for their own sake, yet: "The following collection is intended to be a contribution to this new science of Storyology. It is a museum of curious rubbish about to perish, given as it was gathered in the rough.".' Campbell is referring here to his *Popular Tales of the West Highlands*.

Kenneth MacLeod may seem to us unduly sensitive to Campbell's 'curious rubbish' – the science of folklore was in its infancy – for, in another place, as MacLeod well knew, Campbell insists on the *value* of 'this despised old rubbish'. But the telling phrase is 'given as it was gathered in the rough'. Neither Kenneth MacLeod nor Alexander Carmichael, nor the great majority of their kind, would for a moment have agreed with the propriety of doing that. Yet it is this phrase that enshrines the principle by which henceforth the work of all collectors of oral literature would be judged.

It was John Francis Campbell himself, characteristically, who first expressed a disquiet about Alexander Carmichael. In 1861 Carmichael, who was then living in Skye, wrote to Campbell to thank him for printing some of his (Carmichael's) contributions. He continued to send material, including texts of heroic ballads. From such poetry James Macpherson (1736–96) had 'translated' his *Ossian*, which was itself then translated into Gaelic verse as part of the campaign to vindicate Macpherson's claims. For Campbell, as for others who knew the primary sources, authentic and spurious 'Ossianic' ballads were usually not difficult to tell apart. But at least at this stage in his career,

Alexander Carmichael apparently could not or would not draw that crucial distinction. Of his notes to one of the ballads, Campbell observes: 'The remarks of Carmichael are very curious. The Lay which he sends is a genuine ballad [. . .] Nevertheless the collector is so impressed with the authenticity of *Ossian* that he makes game of the genuine ballad.' And of Carmichael's version of a folktale 'A' Chaora Bhòidheach Ghlas' ('The Pretty Grey Sheep'), Campbell remarks: 'It is Ossianic book Gaelic in places, the scribe being a firm believer in Macpherson's *Ossian*.'[1]

Throughout this century more than one Gaelic reader felt some degree of uneasiness as he or she read through the volumes of *Carmina Gadelica*, especially volumes I to IV. Few of these readers, however, were tradition–bearers themselves or, indeed, had ever heard a genuine Gaelic incantation. For those who had, or had access to comparative material in print, there was a sufficient amount of patently genuine material on the pages of *Carmina* to make them conclude that Carmichael, working amidst the abundance of an earlier age, had the good fortune to discover fuller and more elegant versions than the fragmentary variants that they knew themselves. If other collectors had printed specimens of Gaelic charms that lacked the amplitude and dignity of those in *Carmina*, that surely was due to Carmichael's greater skill and assiduity in searching, as well as to the trust which the 'Folk' reposed in him.

Calum Maclean, then a collector at the School of Scottish Studies at the University of Edinburgh, reviewed *Carmina Gadelica Volume V* in the Swedish journal *Arv*. Maclean had worked in Uist and Barra, the communities of which had been Carmichael's richest sources, and was an expert in Gaelic folklore. He writes:

> It has been said that Carmichael's work was vitiated by the romanticism of Mac-Pherson's *Ossian* and the sentimentalism of the Celtic Twilight. *It was, but to a surprisingly small degree* [my italics]. In some instances tradition bearers in the course of common, informal narration appear to use the somewhat florid style of formal heroic narrative and literary manuscript tradition.[2]

Maclean grants that the introductory narrative passages ascribed to informants 'are not, I think, the product of the tradition bearers themselves'; but he argues that 'Carmichael can hardly be accused of taking liberties with the actual texts of lays, songs, hymns, charms, prayers, etc.'. And, while Carmichael's 'texts in verse are remarkable in that they have an almost suspicious polish [. . .] in many cases versions identical with the texts of *Carmina Gadelica* and even superior to them have been recorded within recent years, e.g. Volume V, songs on pp 28, 36'. Songs, however, be it noted; not incantations. Carmichael, he concludes, 'was in a sense more of a littérateur than a student of folk tradition, but his main interest was in the literature of the folk'.

Twenty-one years later, these judgments were to be seriously challenged.

In 1976, Hamish Robertson published an analysis of Carmichael's collection, manuscript and printed, in the journal *Scottish Gaelic Studies*.[3] Here he accused the collector-editor of consistent, large-scale fabrication. Charms and incantations that were 'incomplete' or 'inferior' in Carmichael's estimation were simply re-made. In some instances, 'words are substituted, lines are shortened or lengthened, new lines appear, verses are switched round and what was one poem-piece in the Appendix [to the Royal Commission Report – texts given by Carmichael] can swell to two or three in *Carmina*'. Moreover, Carmichael tried 'and sometimes obviously, to draw a spurious sanctity of age about his collections, [. . .] resurrecting Gaelic words of doubtful provenance'.

According to these arguments, Carmichael was a literary forger and the stylistic elegance that had evoked so much admiration little more than a meretricious gloss. Dr Kenneth MacLeod's anecdote about the venerable Islesman and his 'little prayer' is seen in a new and quite different light by Mr Robertson:

> The man who walked miles to ask Carmichael to destroy a copy of the charm he had just previously given him had more to fear than intrusion into a secret, but also – had he only known – the threat of being labelled father to a pious rigmarole composed by a romantic dilettante.

From a consideration of the volumes edited by Carmichael himself Robertson moves to those edited by James Carmichael Watson and finds the material there suspect also. For instance, several charms in Volumes III and IV 'seem to be full and flowery elaborations of charms or themes of charms evident in Volumes I and II'. Robertson lists a number of points that Carmichael's grandson-editor must have been aware of: 'In spite of these deterrents, he chose to publish. But it is doubtful if he became a happier man for having decided to do so.'

Although Hamish Robertson scores a number of palpable hits in his investigation of Carmichael and *Carmina*, certain of his observations remain speculative. He explains why this is so:

> Our chances of ascertaining the original form of charms in *Carmina* seem remote, for there is no trace of material existing for Volumes I and II among the manuscripts of the Carmichael-Watson collection, except for a few rare passages [. . .] There is also a scarcity of manuscript material for Volume III.

All this makes him raise the possibility of there having been 'something to hide in the event of any posterior scrutiny into the texts'.

A strong rejoinder to many of Robertson's points came from an expert in Gaelic folklore, Dr John Lorne Campbell.[4] While the tone of Mr Robertson's contribution was critical but somewhat hostile, that of Dr Campbell's was critical but rather sympathetic. Campbell makes two very important points, one about editorial methods, the other about motives. He quotes from Carmichael's letters to show how the great collector was driven by intense idealism and concern for his fellow Gaels. To Fr Allan MacDonald of Eriskay, for instance, in June 1905:

> Everything Highland is becoming of interest. Let us try to meet this interest and to show the world that our dearly beloved people were not the rude, barbarous, creedless, godless, ignorant men and women that prejudiced writers have represented them. It is to me heart-breaking to see the spiteful manner in which Highlanders have been spoken of.[5]

Campbell comments that these motives were 'entirely honourable. Contemporary critics of today do not always realize the strong anti-Highland feeling that existed in various "Anglo-Saxon" circles in Victorian times.'[6]

As for the charges of fabrication, it had long been known to Campbell that Carmichael edited the raw materials of his collection; an Irish reviewer of *Carmina Gadelica Volume V*, in fact quotes him on this very point:

> Carmichael's texts often surprise Irish readers [. . .] Their literary excellence as compared with recordings of similar matter by other collectors is probably explained by Mr. John Lorne Campbell's suggestion in his booklet on Fr. Allan McDonald of Eriskay (1954) (p. 29) that Carmichael's practice "seems to have been to dovetail different versions of traditional poems, etc., in order to produce *the best possible literary version*".[7]

This was no more than normal editorial practice of the time. Carmichael had been quite open about his methods. Of a certain song text, for instance, he says:

> I have some ten or twelve versions of that, all differing more or less. How to deal with them all is hard to say. I cannot give all the versions separately. To give all the versions of all poems separately would be ruinous. I must therefore collate them all and give the result alone – not at all an easy matter.

Or on a particular prayer, Robertson comments 'the IV and V verses were not in the first version of this beautiful hymn. I am not sure that they originally formed part of it.'

Robertson declared that this prayer (printed in the Appendix to the Royal Commission Report) 'has been split into two for *Carmina* and the two fragments polished, lines inflated or curtailed according to which of two differing metrical schemes Carmichael saw fit to squeeze them into.' Campbell dismisses this criticism with the tart comment that: 'From the purist point of view, Carmichael did rightly when he separated these verses from the others and printed them separately in *Carmina*.'[8]

But in general John L. Campbell acknowledges that 'much of the first three volumes of *Carmina* must be taken as a literary and not as a literal presentation of Gaelic folklore' and furthermore that 'Carmichael Watson perpetuated a style of editing in the third and fourth volumes of *Carmina*, which by 1940 was out of date'.[9] Campbell also brings to our attention that 'neither Carmichael nor James Carmichael Watson was sufficiently acquainted with Catholic devotional literature to realize that some of the items they were printing were Gaelic versions of well-known Catholic hymns.'[10] Campbell's assessment is that Volumes V and VI alone are adequately edited. In a word, the shortcomings of *Carmina Gadelica* are not due to any kind of literary forgery but to the fact that '[Alexander] Carmichael's love for the Highlands coloured the early volumes of *Carmina* with a sentimentalism which is rather irritating at times' and that James Carmichael Watson 'was handicapped for editing *Carmina* by (1) an excessive *pietas* regarding his grandfather's work, (2) lack of direct acquaintance with the oral tradition of South Uist and Barra, and (3) the fact that he was working under heavy pressure of time'.[11]

But the controversy was not to end there. In 1984 Alan Bruford carried out a comparison of the story of Deirdre as published by Carmichael and a transcript of field notes of the tale as it was told to Carmichael in 1867 by John MacNeill at Buaile nam Bodach in

Barra.[12] The results of Bruford's enquiry into Carmichael's methods here show that 'he revised every sentence, almost as if he were trying to evade copyright restrictions'. *Deirdire* is not part of *Carmina Gadelica*, but Alan Bruford's conclusion has a bearing upon that work: 'There is reason enough here to apply stringent critical standards to everything that Carmichael published or prepared for publication [. . .] we are entitled to accept, if not expect, the possibility of "improvement" or even forgery.'

Readers of *Carmina Gadelica*, whether in English or Gaelic, cannot expect to be given a final answer on the fine detail of this controversy until all the evidence (including Carmichael's missing field notes) is assembled. But some general statements can be made. The texts of non-religious songs, in Volume V for instance, seem to be on the whole free of gross invention though obviously they are sometimes conflated versions of a number of variants, according to Carmichael's own explicit declaration.

To pass judgment on the charms and prayers is more difficult. Gaelic incantations do seem now to be very rare in genuine popular tradition. There are however two papers in the *Transactions of the Gaelic Society of Inverness* which give a good basis for comparison with some of the material in *Carmina*.[13] The charms are drawn from more than one source – Carmichael himself contributed indirectly to each paper, though neither paper is mentioned in *Carmina* – but there is no question here of re-working or collation of texts.

William MacKenzie has a charm of 'The Genealogy of St Bride' which he received from Fr Allan MacDonald of Eriskay, and which he translates as follows:

> St Bridget, the daughter of Dughall Donn,
> son of Hugh, son of Art, son of Conn.
> Each day and each night
> I will mediate on the genealogy of St Bridget
> [whereby] I will not be killed
> I will not be wounded,
> I will not be bewitched;
> Neither will Christ forsake me;
> Satan's fire will not burn me;
> Neither water nor sea shall drown me;
> For I am under the protection of the Virgin Mary,
> And my meek and gentle foster-mother, St Bridget.[14]

Alexander Carmichael's version opens with what is clearly the title though it is printed as two lines of verse and its diction is ornate enough to make it seem a slightly exotic graft:

> The genealogy of the holy maiden[15] Bride,
> Radiant flame of gold, noble foster-mother of Christ.
> Bride the daughter of Dugall the brown,
> Son of Aodh, son of Art, son of Conn,
> Son of Crearar, son of Cis, son of Carmac, son of Carruin.

Carmichael's 'Aodh' and 'Dugall the brown' and MacKenzie's 'Hugh' and 'Dughall Donn' are identical names in the Gaelic text. Some at any rate of the names in line 5 are known in other charms. Carmichael does not seem to have added much here.

Probably the single most famous charm in the whole of *Carmina Gadelica* is 'Ora nam Buadh' ('the Invocation of the Graces') of Volume I which opens:

> I bathe thy palms
> In showers of wine
> In the lustral fire,
> In the seven elements

Hamish Robertson points out that the 'Invocation of the Graces' section in Volume III 'all seem to elaborate on certain themes in the famous *Ora nam Buadh* [. . .] Such a genre of charm probably existed', he writes, and goes on to assert that 'several of the phrases and some of the tone of the *Carmina Gadelica* version [of 'Ora nam Buadh'] could well be genuine'.

Carmichael has a verse in 'Ora nam Buadh' as follows:

> Dark is yonder town,
> Dark are those therein,
> Thou art the brown swan,
> Going in among them.
> Their hearts are under thy control,
> Their tongues are beneath thy sole,
> Nor will they ever utter a word
> To give thee offence.

In William MacKenzie's 'Charm to Obtain Justice',[16] there are related lines. MacKenzie's translation of his charm is as follows:

I go forth in the name of Gods;
In the likeness of iron; in the likeness of the horse;
In the likeness of the serpent; in the likeness of the deer;
Stronger am I than each one [or 'than any one else']
Black to yonder town;
And black to those who reside therein;
[May] Their tongues be under my soles [or 'feet']
Till I again return.
May I be the white swan,
As a queen above them.
I will wash my face
That it may shine like the nine rays of the sun,
As the Virgin Mary washes her Son with boiled milk.
May restraint be on my tongue,
Love on my countenance;
The palm of Mary round my neck,
The palm of Christ on my face,
The tongue of the Mother of Jesus in my mouth,
The eye of the Protector between them;
And may the taste of honey be of every word
I utter till I return.

The much more elaborate invocation in *Carmina Gadelica* Volume
I interprets this section very differently – the swan symbolizes a young
girl, according to Carmichael's conjecture – but it suggests that the
Invocation was put together from a number of shorter charms to
which other elements were added, for instance the name *Eimir*,
glossed in Carmichael's notes[17] as 'the wife of Cuchulainn. She is
the type of beauty in Gaelic story.' The form is however a literary
mistranscription and is most unlikely to have been transmitted in oral
tradition.

Some lines in Carmichael's 'Invocation':

An island art thou at sea,
A fortress art thou on land,
A well art thou in the desert,
Health art thou to the ailing

are paralleled by lines in the 'Charm of Protection':

An island art thou in the sea,
A hill art thou on land,

A well art thou in wilderness,
Health art thou to the ailing

A variant of this charm was recorded by Calum Maclean in South Uist.[18] According to Maclean's informant, Donald Macintyre, this was the charm pronounced over Allan, chief of Clanranald who was killed in 1715.[19]

Donald Macintyre's version runs as follows in translation:

A charm that Brigit set upon Her Fosterling,
A charm that Mary set upon Her Son,
A charm that Michael set upon his shield,
A charm that the Son of God set around the City of Heaven.
A charm against sword,
A charm against arrow,
A charm against fits of anger and of foolishness.
A charm against fairy folk,
A charm against magic folk,
A charm against pitiless folk,
A charm against the peril of drowning.
A charm against the hurt of the red bog-myrtle,
A charm against the wounding of the impetuous Fiann.

The mantle of Columba be with you,
The mantle of Michael the Valiant be about you,
The mantle of Christ, my love, be around you
To protect you behind,
To protect you behind and before,
From the crown of your head to your brow
And to the black sole of your foot.

An island you are in the sea,
A hill you are on land,
A well you are in the waste,
Health are you to the ailing.

Great shall be the danger to him
Who sees the charmed body,
For the aid of Columba is with you,
And the mantle of Michael valiant is about you
And his great shield protecting you.

Compare this with Carmichael's text of the 'Charm of Protection' in *Carmina Gadelica Volume III*. It is immediately obvious that the *Carmina* text and the mid-twentieth-century texts are reasonably close variants and that there is nothing in Carmichael's version to cause us to doubt its genuineness. Furthermore, in both variants Michael, the Archangel, has the epithet *mìl* ('soldier', but given a variety of meanings in the *Carmina* translations). This effectively destroys Mr Robertson's argument that: 'The form *Mìcheal mìl* probably represents an ingenious antiquarian's guess, which is phonetically feasible, but should be treated as one of Carmichael's inventions.'

In spite of many unanswered questions, it is now clear that *Carmina Gadelica* is not a monumental exercise in literary fabrication nor, on the other hand, is it a transcript of ancient poems and spells reproduced exactly in the form in which they survived in oral tradition. There are elements of fabrication undoubtedly: perhaps few texts in *Carmina* are totally free of some editorial repair-work and some, including the 'Invocation of the Graces', may have it to a very high degree. But throughout the collection, the core of the material is the treasure-trove of oral literature that Carmichael discovered in Gaelic Scotland.

He himself tells in his Introduction to Volume I, 'Although these compositions have been rescued chiefly among Roman Catholics and in the islands, they have been equally common among Protestants and on the mainland', for until the Evangelical Movement (c.1800 onwards) there was little or no difference between different religious confessions in their attitude towards the secular arts. The ancestry of some of the invocations and prayers for protection must in some cases link up with the ancient *Loricae*, of which the so-called 'Breastplate of St Patrick' is probably the best-known example. Their perspective is not that of the later medieval, Romanized church: St Andrew, 'patron saint of Scotland' is only mentioned twice: Calum / Colm Cille 'Columba', is still the dominating figure, with *Brìde* 'St Brigit', a complex figure – pagan goddess, Christian saint, and foster-mother of Christ – taking a leading role.

The latest comment on *Carmina Gadelica* comes from Mr Ronald Black of the University of Edinburgh.[20] He is well aware that Alexander Carmichael's writings can lead astray the unwary. Even so, he declares that '*Carmina Gadelica* is by any standards a treasure house [. . .] a marvellous and unrepeatable achievement. There will never be another *Carmina Gadelica*.'

Am Fàsach ann an
Dùthchas nan Gàidheal

Is fheudar dhomh a ràdh aig toiseach tòiseachaidh nach eil agam an seo
ach àireamh phuingean a ghabhas togail mun chuspair: chan e rannsachadh mionaideach a tha ann. Tha grunn bheachdan ann a chaidh a
chur an céill mar-thà is a gheibhear ann an clò thall is a bhos mun roinn a
tha eadar an dachaigh agus an saoghal a-muigh ann an eachdraidh a'
chinne-daonna. A chionn is gu bheil an cunntas a tha againn an-dràsta
air a dhealbh a réir nam beachdan sin, faodar cuid dhiubh ainmeachadh.

(a) Tha Nàdar is Cultar air an roinn agus air am meas mar gum b'
ann an aghaidh a chéile. Tha seo a' toirt leis 'fiadhaich' mu choinneamh 'soitheamh'; is air an aon seòl, fiadhantas is tuineachas; sluagh
fo riaghailt air an dara làimh is fàsach gun cheannsachadh air an
làimh eile; agus na tha fuaite ri eòl agus aineol. Ma tha duine fada bho
dhaoine fhéin, is e aonaranach is uaigneach, their na baird gu bheil e,
mun tuirt té gun ainm 'na h-òran:

> liom fhìn san tìr aineoil
> mi gun phiuthar gun bhràthair
> gun mhàthair gun athair
> mi gun duine dham dhaoine
> ris a faod mi mo ghearain[1]

(b) Tha crìoch chomharraichte a' cuartachadh àite-comhnaidh
dhaoine. Tha gàrradh-crìche, mar gum b' eadh, a' cumail an fhàsaich
a-mach. Tha e a' dìon na dachaigh. Ann an seagh samhlachail, tha e
cumail cumhachdan an fhàsaich fo smachd anns an inntinn.

(c) Tha cunnartan san fhàsach ach tha tarraing ann cuideachd. Tha
buannachd is call ann. Faodaidh an t-uaigneas eagal a chur air duine;
aig a' cheart àm tha feum aig an inntinn air an uaigneas.

(d) Mas ann a dh'aon ghnè a tha na roinnean a tha eadar nàdar is
cultar, chan eil teagamh nach eil iad gan nochdadh fhéin ann an
caochladh dhòighean is chruthan, mar a shùilichte, o dhùthaich gu
dùthaich is o linn gu linn, fad eachdraidh a' chinne-daonna.

(e) Tha feadhainn air am beachd a chur an céill gu bheil an t-eadar-dhealachadh eadar 'baile' agus 'fàsach' ri lorg ann an seann Linn na Cloiche; feadhainn eile dhan bharail gur h-ann le àiteach fearainn (sin a réir luchd-eachdraidh, eadar an t-Seann Linn agus Linn Nodha na Cloiche) a thòisicheadh air 'fàsach' a dhealbh ann an inntinn mac an duine. Co-dhiù an ann gus nach ann, chan eil teagamh nach biodh buaidh aig àiteach, le sìol ga chur is pòr ga bhuain, air sealladh dhaoine air an t-suidheachadh gu léir. Tha an t-àiteach a' ceannsa-chadh earrainn dhan fhiadhaire. Air a' cheann thall, thigte gu bhith meas gun robh clàr nàdarra na dùthcha ann agus clàr air an deach cumadh a chur le làmhan dhaoine. Agus tro na linntean, gu ruige ar latha fhìn, shùilicheamaid gum maireadh reumhag air choireigin de fhìor sheann bheachdan agus iad sin air am filleadh an lùib bheachdan eile a tha gu math nas ùire. Tha alpadh dhan t-seòrsa sin cumanta gu leòr sa h-uile suidheachadh ann an eachdraidh.

Aig an ìre seo, bu chòir a ràdh, a thaobh gach barail a chaidh ainmeachadh, gu bheil cuid dhiubh nas stéidhte na chéile; cuid a tha caran tuaireamach.

Nise, chan eil aon fhacal air leth againn sa Ghàidhlig mu choinneamh *landscape* na Beurla: cruth is cumadh na dùthcha agus an coltas a tha air an tìr. Ach tha am pailteas againn de dh'fhaclan a tha cur gnè is dreach an fhuinn an céill air dà thaobh a' ghàrradh-chrìche. San roinn a-muigh, faclan mar a tha 'fàsach', 'frìth', 'aonach', 'mon-adh' is 'sliabh' is 'beinn', agus an leithid.

Is e 'fàsach' am facal as farsainge 'na ruigheachd: àite 'fàs' – seadh, falamh. Àite gun taighean, gun daoine, àite gun treabhadh gun ruamhar; àite gun chur gun bhuain. Ann an dùthaich no dhà, 's e fearann-am-pàirt a th' ann am 'fàsach': ann am briathran eile, monadh no beinn, coitcheann, sliabh, geàrraidh no cùl-cinn. Nam bite lorg Beurla air (a thuilleadh air na roinnean a tha 'geàrraidh' is 'cùl-cinn' is mar sin a' nochdadh dhuinn) 's e *wilderness* as dlùithe dha. Chan eil fear seach fear dhiubh a' ciallachadh nach eil luisreadh is ionaltradh pailt ann a leithid a dh'àite. Chan e *desert* na Beurla a tha ann idir.

Ach a thaobh na h-eileamaid *wild* am Beurla, 's e 'fiadhair(e)' as dlùithe. Sin talamh gun treabhadh no talamh a chaidh àiteach uair-eigin ach a tha nise air a dhol am fiadh. Agus gabhaidh e càradh cuideachd ri feur cruaidh a' mhonaidh.

Tha 'fireach' air a chleachdadh mu na h-àiteachan monadail; glé thric àiteachan uaigneach, fad às. San òran 'Maol Ruanaidh Ghlinneachain' dh'fhalbh màthair a' ghille bhig, a réir na sgeòil, a dh'fhuireach cuide ris na sìdhichean: 'Dh'fhalbh do mhàthair is thug i a' fireach oirre.'[2] 'S ann sna monaidhean fada muigh a bha sin: cha chainte 'fireach' ris an fhiadhaire a bha faisg air baile ann, anns a' chumantas co-dhiù.

Tha 'frìth' mar is trice muigh sna monaidhean cuideachd oir 's e àite seilge a th' ann – 'frìth nan damh ruadh' is a leithid. 'S ann on Bheurla a thàinig am facal air tùs. Sa chànan sin tha coilltean is preasan is barrach fuaite ris, ach sa Ghàidhlig, ged is e *hunting / deer forest* gu minig a gheibhear air, 's e lombar an fhàsaich, monadh is beinn as ciall dà. Chan eil mi an dùil gu bheilear ga chleachdadh an-diugh – ma tha, 's ann ainneamh – ach ann an òrain is ann an sgeulachdan agus ann an seanchas a bhoineas dhaibh.

Theagamh gun tàinig am facal dhan Ghàidhlig tràth dhar n-eachdraidh. A chionn is gun robh an t-sealg riamh measail aig na huaislean, faodaidh e bhith gun tugadh dhan Ghàidhlig e ri linn Mhaol Chaluim Cheannmhoir agus a chuid mac: seadh, nuair a dh'atharraicheadh cainnt na cùrtach an Alba o Ghàidhlig gu Beurla nan Gall, timcheall air deireadh an aona ceud deug agus an linn as déidh sin.

Tha am facal 'aonach' annasach da-rìribh. Is dòcha gun deach corr is aon fhacal an lùib a chéile. Air neo is dòcha gu bheil fàs is tàrmachadh an fhacail rim mìneachadh fhathast.

Tha an ciall 'féill' no 'faidhear' aig aonach; tha grunn àiteachan ann far an robh margadh ga chumail o shean agus tha Aonach san ainm aca. Ach tha ciall àraid aige, mar a gheibhear san ainm 'An t-Aonach Eagach'. Air feadh na Gàidhealtachd, theirte 'muigh san aonach' ri 'muigh sa mhonadh' no 'sa bheinn', is mar sin. Bha MacBhàtair (W. J. Watson) dhan bheachd gur h-ann o 'aon' a bha an dà sheagh:[3] chan eil e leudachadh seach sin air. Ach ma nì sinn dealbh dhuinn fhìn air an tsuidheachadh mar a bha e o chionn àireamh cheudan bliadhna – no is dòcha mìltean – saoilidh mi gun gabh facal leasachaidh no dhà chur an céill fhathast.

Bhiodh e riamh na bu choltaiche gun cumte aonach no féill chan ann an teis meadhain baile fearainn ach taobh a-muigh nan crìochan agus faisg orra, air àrainn a' bhaile. Bhiodh an stall sin san fhiadhaire, theagamh air rèidhleach comhnard. Dh'fhoghnadh sin fhéin, is dòcha, gus brìgh an fhacail atharrachadh air chor is gur h-e blàr farsaing réisg bu chiall dà air a' cheann thall no cìrean creagach fhéin. Air neo, is dòcha gur h-e bha ann gum biodh aonach mór eadar grunn threubhan air a chumail fada air astar o fhearann sluaigh sam bith; uime sin, ann an àiteachan uaigneach, monadail o thùs. Tuaiream, ga-tà, a tha sna beachdan sin.

Ach chan e tuaiream idir a th' ann a ràdh gu bheil am facal 'monadh' cho suaicheanta is a tha ann sa chomhlan fhacal air a bheil sinn a' gabhail beachd. Bha e aig aon àm nar n-eachdraidh a' comharrachadh no samhlachadh rìoghachd Alba fhéin, tuath air Cluaidh agus Foirthe. Na beanntan ris an canar Na Mórbheanna – *Grampians* am Beurla – b' iadsan 'Am Monadh' seach monadh sam bith eile. B' e 'Dùn Monaidh' suidhe an rìgh agus an riaghaltais is nuair a ghluais rìgh Alba gu deas, dh'fhaoite an t-ainm a chàradh ri Dùn Éideann!

Tha a dh'annas eile air 'monadh' gur h-ann on fhacal *mynydd* sna cànanan Breatannach is Cruithneach a thàinig e. Faodaidh am monadh a bhith riaghailteach comhnard ach tha e a' toirt leis, gu h-àraid o shean, cnuic is beanntan mar a tha Am Monadh Liath, agus Am Monadh Ruadh, seann ainm nam beann anns a bheil An Càrn Gorm.

Dhe na faclan sin a tha a' cur 'fàsalachd' an céill agus a tha a' tomhadh dhuinn an roinn a tha eadar iomairean àitich agus am fàsach, 's e 'monadh' as cumanta. Ach an cearna no dhà gheibhear 'beinn' an àite 'monadh'; ged nach biodh airde ro mhór san fhearann idir.

Tha an uairsin 'mòine' is 'mòinteach' againn. Ged nach ionann mòinteach is monadh, bidh sinn uaireannan gan cleachdadh car an lùib a chéile; ach 's e gnè an fhuinn a tha 'mòinteach' a' dèanamh aithnichte.

'S e monadh is chan e sgurr a tha 'sliabh' a' ciallachadh an Gàidhlig an latha an-diugh: 's e sin, comhnard is leathad seach na mullaichean arda. (Tha Gàidhlig a' Bhìobaill agus cuid de sheann dàin fhoghlaimte a' leantainn cleachdadh na Gàidhlig an Éirinn.) An corra àite, gheibhear 'sliabh' ga ghabhail air an fhiadhaire, far a bheil 'monadh' is 'beinn' aig daoine ann an àiteachan eile. A thuilleadh air sin, ann an iomadach àite, bidh daoine a' cleachdadh 'sliabh' airson an fheòir ris an canar *deer-grass* am Beurla. Mar a dh'ainmicheadh mar tha, tha 'fiadhaire' fhéin air a chur an sàs car san aon dòigh – agus 'riasg' cuideachd, cho math ri gnè an fhuinn – ged nach eil iad air an ceangal cho dlùth ri aon seòrsa sonraichte feòir is a tha 'sliabh'. Ach boinidh iad uile dhan fhàsach: seo am feur a tha dùthchasach dhan fhearann gun àiteach, gun cheannsachadh.

Tha dà fhacal eile ann as dleas dhuinn sùil a thoirt orra san dol seachad: 'dìseart' agus 'dìthreabh'. Chan aithne dhomh gu bheil 'dìseart' (on Laideann *desertum*; *desert* am Beurla) 'na ainmear cumanta againn ach tha e ann an grunnan beag de ainmeannan àiteachan. 'Ann an Clachan an Dìseirt | Ag òl fìon air na maithibh', mar a tha san òran Ghriogarach.[4]

Chan aithne dhomh gur h-e àite gun toradh, gun fhàs-feòir no gun choille a th' ann an 'dìseart' a réir cleachdadh na cainnte – aocoltach ri *desert* na Beurla. 'S e tha ann ach àite a tha falamh de dhaoine is de thuineachadh. Chithear sin cuideachd san fhacal 'dìthreabh', àite anns nach eil 'treabh', 'taigh(ean)-comhnaidh'. Tha MacBhàtair ga chur gu sgiolta: 'the uninhabited and untilled waste'.[5]

Mar a thuirt mi, 's ann an ainmeannan àiteachan a-mhàin a gheibhear e: co-dhiù, cha chuala mise 'na fhacal cleachdte sa Ghàidhlig riamh e. Ann an ceann a tuath na Gàidhealtachd, 's e 'An Dithreibh Mór' air taobh siar Rois an t-ainm as fhearr aithne air. 'S e 'An Diri Mór' a their muinntir an àite ris is iad a' leanailt cleachdadh na cainnte aca fhéin; tha iad an dùil an-diugh gur h-e 'dìthreadh' a tha ann, oir tha an t-àite monadail.

A-nise, faodar gluasad o fhiadhaire an fhearainn a dh'ionnsaigh fàsach a' chuain. Chan e buileach an aon seòrsa roinn a tha eadar talamh-àitich is fàsach an aghaidh a chéile, air an dara làimh, agus fearann an aghaidh muir no cuan air an làimh eile. A dh'aindeoin sin, tha suaib aig na roinnean ri chéile. Chan e nach eil iomadh filleadh sa chainnt a bhios sinn a' cleachdadh agus san dealbh a bhios sinn a' dèanamh air gach roinn is dàimh dhuibh. An-dràsta, a' coimhead on chuan, 's e 'fearann' a tha san tìr; air tìr 's e 'fearann' an talamh-àitich, agus mar sin air adhart mar a chunnaic sin. Ach tha an dà 'fhàsach' air an comharrachadh sa mhac-mheanmhain Ghàidhealach, saoilidh mi, mar gun robh iad, ann an tomhas, an co-ruith a chéile. Tha cunnart is toradh annta le chéile. Ged nach eil na tha gnàthaichte agus ana-ghnàthaichte air an roinn a réir na crìche a tha eadar talamh-àitich is fàsach no eadar muir is tìr – oir ruigidh am monadh teis-meadhain a' bhaile – chuala sinn sna h-uirsgeulan gu bheil manaidhean is taidhbh-sean is eile gu math fuaite ris an fhàsach. 'S e am fàsach an t-àite gàbhaidh, an t-àite àibheiseach gun iùil, far a bheil iomadach tachar-tas uamhalta a' feitheamh air an duine nach eil air uidheamachadh. Ach mar a tha comharran-stiùiridh aig maraichean, tha ceumannan is frith-rathaidean aig luchd siubhail a' mhonaidh. Agus, a réir dùthchas nan Gàidheal bha dòigh air an inntinn ullachadh cuideachd air chor is gun gabhadh cunnart a chronachadh 's gach àite dhiubh. Bha seun is ortha is caochladh mheadhainean eile aig daoine fiosrach.

Bha an sluagh Gàidhealach o shean a' toirt creideas dha na nithean sin air a bheil sinn a-mach. Tha sgoilearachd an latha an-diugh air stall eile uile gu léir, a' rannsachadh nam beachdan a gheibhear anns na seann sgeulachdan chan ann idir gan gabhail gu litireil ach a' sìor chur cheistean man deidhinn: a bheil an 'saobh chreideamh' sin ag innse dad dhuinn mu inntinn mac an duine is mun t-seòl air a bheil am mac-mheanmhain ag obrachadh? Agus theagamh gum bi a bheachd fhéin aig gach neach air a' mhìneachadh cheart.

Thoireamaid sùil aithghearr air fear no dhà dhe na samhlaidhean a tha nochdadh sna naidheachdan. An toiseach, na féidh. Mar a tha an t-ainm a' sealltainn, 's e 'fiadh' am fiadhbheathach os cionn nan ainmhidhean fiadhaich air fad: fìor chreutair an fhiadhaire is an fhàsaich. Agus tha an gearr dhan aon ghnè oir 's e giorrachadh air 'gearrfhiadh', seadh, am 'beathach fiadhaich beag' a tha ann an 'gearr'. Bha an gearr sonraichte am measg nan ainmhidhean leis gum biodh na banabhuidsichean cho tric a' dol an riochd gearr. Tha co-cheangal dlùth aige mar sin ris an t-saoghal ana-ghnàthaichte. Is boinidh an dearbh chàileachd dhan fhiadh mhór cuideachd. Bha, mar gum b' eadh, dà shealladh (chan e an Dà Shealladh fhàistinneach idir) aig na Gàidheil air an fhiadh.

Chan eil san fhiadh ach creutair nàdarrach: ainmhidh a bhite a' sealg. Fo shealladh eile, 's e na féidh spréidh nan sìdhichean is tha na sìdhichean a' comharrachadh air iomadh dòigh cumhachdan is cunnartan an fhàsaich. Tha agus na Cailleachan a bha a' comhnaidh ann an raointean uaigneach a' mhonaidh. Bha té dhiubhsan gu h-àraid, Cailleach Beinne Bhric, a' gabhail nam fiadh air a cùram agus bha e dh'fhasan aice caismeachd a thoirt do shealgairean a bha a' marbhadh cus dhiubh. Tha uirsgeul againn mun t-sealgair a chuimsich air agh féidh. Nuair a chuir e a shùil ris a' ghunna 's e boireannach a bh' aige; leag e an gunna; 's e fiadh a bh' aige. Sin ann am facal an dà shealladh air a bheil mi a-mach. Bhiodh cuid dhe na seanchaidhean a' ràdh gur h-e Cailleach Beinne Bhric i fhéin a bha an sin, ann an riochd a' bhoireannaich; feadhainn eile gur h-e comharradh a bha ann air dà nàdar an fhiadh bheathaich – gnàthaichte agus ana-ghnàthaichte.

Ann am fìor sheann sgeulachdan bha ainmhidh ann a bha gu léir ana-ghnàthaichte: b' ise a' bhò ris an cainnte A' Ghlas Ghaibhleann. Tha na Leapannan aice air an ainmeachadh air feadh na Gàidhealtachd (uaireannan, is dòcha, mar a th' ann an Gearrloch, 'Leaba na Bà Bàine'; no san t-Srath san Eilean Sgitheanach 'Leaba na Bà Uidhre'). San t-Srath cuideachd, tha Leaba na Glais Ghaibhleann, sna Torran, 'na ainm eòlach aig a h-uile duine. Agus bha an rann seo mu na leapannan ri chluinntinn uair dhe robh an saoghal.

> Gleann Dàil an Diùranais
> Gleann Ùige an Tròndarnais
> Gleann sgiamhach Sgàladail
> Gleann àlainn Ròmasdail
> Glacagan Beinn Dìonabhaig
> Is Slaopan mèadhaineach nan Torr

Nan robh gort san àite no éiginn eile ann, thigeadh A' Ghlas Ghaibhleann mar gum b' ann às an fhàsach agus bheathaicheadh i an sluagh. Dh'fhalbhadh i an sin gun fhiosda.

A thaobh fàsach na mara, tha caochladh sheòrsaichean bheò-chreutairean ann a ghabhadh taghadh: crodh mara, sìdhichean na mara, a' mhaighdeann-mhara, is an leithid, ach 's e an ròn as motha tha a' giùlan dhan t-samhlachas. Tha móran naidheachdan ann; an té as suaicheanta dhiubh an sgeulachd a bh' aig muinntir Uibhist a' mìneachadh an t-sloinnidh aig 'Clann MhicOdrum nan Ròn'. Tha na ròin a' tionndadh 'nam boireannaich; tha am fear a chunnaic iad a' glacadh té aca, ga pòsadh, is tha teaghlach aca. Air a' cheann thall, tha am boireannach a' lorg na béin a bh' oirre nuair a bha i 'na ròn, is tha i a' tilleadh dhan chuan. Bha a sliochd riamh fortanach aig an iasgach.

Nise, ma thomhaisear an suidheachadh san fharsaingeachd, agus ma chuirear samhlachas car an darna taobh, tha e soilleir gu bheil toradh a' tighinn dhar n-ionnsaigh on mhuir agus on mhonadh: sealg is sitheann, fraoch, ionaltradh, mòine; air muir, sealg is sitheann a-rithist, iasg, feamainn is muragan. Uime sin, tha dol a-null is a-nall air na crìochan iomchaidh agus cumanta. Agus tha creutairean an fhàsaich a' tighinn dhar n-ionnsaigh-ne o àm gu àm. A dh'aindeoin sin, tha a' chrìoch daingeann; is air an taobh thall tha na beanntan, 'nan àite fhéin agus an cuan 'na àite fhéin.

Tha 'A' Bheinn Naomh' no 'A' Bheinn Choisrigte' a' nochdadh an iomadh cultar. Chan eil buileach sin againne an dùthchas nan Gàidheal (ged is dòcha gur h-e sin a bh' ann an Sìdh Chailleann air aon té). Ach tha sreathan ann an òrain, gu h-àraid sna marbhrannan, a tha a' dùsgadh smaointinn. Leithid: 'Dìreadh na beinne 's ga teàrnadh'. A robh deasghnàth air choireigin ann o shean a' dol a-mach dhan t-sliabh a chaoidh nam marbh? Ma bha aonach ga chumail aig an t-sluagh ann an uaigneas a' mhonaidh, a bheil ceangal aige ri sin? Air neo, is dòcha rud as coltaiche, am biodh daoine dol a-mach leotha fhéin a chumha san fhàsach agus iad iomrallach, uaigneach 'nan aignidh? Chan eil freagairt air na ceistean sin ann, ged nach eil sin a' cur nach bu chòir an togail.

Ann an 'Cumha Ghriogair', gheibhear: 'Dhìrich mi 'bheinn mhór gun anail | Dhìrich agus theàrn' agus ann an seòrsa eile dheth: 'Ràinig mise rèidhlean Bhealaich | Cha d'fhuair mi ann tàmh'.[6] Mar gun robh an té a rinn e a' caoidh san fhàsach agus, anns an atharrach, a' caoidh sa bhaile. Tha na dhà comhla a' dèanamh dealbh iomlan.

Tha òrain eile a tha sealltainn mar a tha am fàsach a' toirt saorsa do dhaoine o smachd agus riaghailt an t-sluaigh.

> 'S minig a laigh mi fo t' earradh
> Ma laigh cha b' ann aig a' bhaile
> Ach mullach nam beann fad on t-sealladh
> [. . .] an lorg an fhéidh a nì langan

Tha an dearbh shaorsa ri faotainn an eileanan a' chuain: ''S truagh gun mise 's mo ghràdh | An eilein mara nach tràigh | man iathadh muir làn' – agus nan robh 'Thigeamaid am màireach dhachaidh | Mar gum pòsamaid on altair'.

'S iad sin na h-eileanan air am bite a' cur dhaoine (boireannaich gu h-àraid) air fògradh cuideachd: 'Chuir iad mise dh'eilein liom fhìn | Eilean mara fada bho thìr'.[7] 'S e fàsalachd a thathas a' tomhadh dhuinn, a cheart cho math ris an t-saorsa, an sin cuideachd.

A réir beachd ar sinnsre, bha 'pearsa' eile aig a h-uile duine, 'samhla' no 'co-choisiche', a dh'fhaoite fhaicinn air astar, can nan robh duine a' miannachadh gu dùrachdach a bhith ann an cuideachd dhaoine fad às no leithid sin de shuidheachadh. Nise, ged a chìte an co-choisiche an àite sam bith 's ann a-muigh san fhàsach a bu mhotha bha de shaorsa aige. Ann an tomhas, bha riaghailtean an t-sluaigh a' cumail smachd air aig baile.

Is e seòrsa de fhaileas a tha sa cho-choisiche ach faileas a bhios uaireannan a' dol bho rian agus air aimhreit. Tha a neart fhéin aig an 'fhaileas'. Agus tha feum air an dà phearsa sin – an neach 'nàdarrach' agus an neach 'mì-nàdarrach' – gus an urra bhith 'na aon agus slàn. Sin co-dhiù barail nan seann Ghàidheal. Chan eil e aocoltach ris an dealbh a bhios feallsanaich an latha againn fhìn a' feuchainn ri tharraing is iad a' 'mìneachadh' gnè na h-inntinn. Tha 'inntinn mhothachail' ann agus inntinn 'neo-mhothachail' – ann am Beurla *conscious* agus *unconscious*. Is ann à doimhne agus uaignes na h-inntinn a thig cumhachd a' mhac-meanmhain – ealain is eile – ach tha riaghailt a' tighinn on chlàr uachdrach agus o sheòl-beatha an t-sluaigh anns a bheil gach duine againn a' comhnaidh. Ma thathas a' meas gu bheil e ro dhàna ràdh gu bheil baile-is-àiteach an coimeas ri fàsach-is-fiadhaire ann an dòighean iongantach 'nan samhlachas, faodar seo agairt: Tha a cheart uiread de 'shaobh chreideamh' ann am beachdan foghlaimte ar latha-ne is a tha ann an uirsgeulan nan Gàidheal.

English Abstract by the Editor

Wilderness is a fundamental concept in Gaelic tradition, as it is in many others. The opposition between wilderness and domesticated space, is expressed in ways specific to Gaelic culture. The English word 'wilderness' overlaps semantically with several in Gaelic, but has no exact equivalent. The distinction between humanised land and non-humanised land is paralleled in the distinction between the land and the sea.

The wilderness, being outside the normal boundaries of convention and order, was associated with the supernatural. The deer was the creature most strongly associated with the wilderness, as is suggested by its common name in Gaelic *fiadh* 'wild'. The deer were believed to be the livestock of the fairies, and the fairies themselves represent in many ways the powers and dangers of the wilderness.

Another important supernatural creature of the wilderness was *A' Ghlas Ghaibhleann*, a white cow which also figures in Irish literature. She would appear in times of famine to feed people and had a number of beds where she rested throughout the Highlands. The sea has its own supernatural inhabitants, but the seal was particularly important in Gaelic tradition.

The wilderness offers both dangers and freedoms. Although a person's *co-choisiche* 'doppelgänger' can be seen anywhere, it is most often seen in the wilderness, where it is unhampered by the restrictions of domesticity. The relationship between a person and his *co-choisiche* is similar to that between the conscious and unconscious as defined by modern psychology, and Gaelic tradition implies that the distinction between wilderness and humanised space is mirrored in the human psyche.

Glossary of Uncommon Gaelic Words

A-cosail: 'likely' in ironic sense, expressing doubt.

Agalladh: declaration, assertion.

Allamh (var. *Eallamh*): speedy, ready, unhesitant.

Ana-ghnàthaichte: the Gaelic means of expressing English 'supernatural'.

Bard muinntearas: bard in formal position of employment.

Caimhlionta: unhampered, unimpaired, typically used of people to mean 'mentally and physically fit'.

Caitean: a rough surface; 'nap' (a surface raised on cloth by finishing process); a variegated surface.

Cèal: cranny; *cùil is cèal* 'nook and cranny'.

Ceum-a'-mhonaidh: the springy step of Highlanders used to walking through moorland, called in Lowland Scots 'the heather loup'.

Comadh: peer, equal.

Co-réir: syntax.

Co-ruith: parallel; *an co-ruith a chèile* 'in parallel with one another'.

Crùibheadh: shoeing.

Cùl-cinn: outrun, the common grazing of a township, between the arable land and the moor; extended to mean 'background'.

Cul-fraoin: far, remote place, 'back of beyond'.

Cumhnach (var. *Caomhnach*): economical, sparing.

Dìth: a layer, stratum.

Glas: referring to the colour of the land that one takes to leave the settled community, between the arable and the moorland; *thog iad ri glas*: 'they sped off on their way'; sometimes expressed as *gorm*.

Inntreachdainn: innovation.

Ion: equivalent of, as good as *ion is a bhith* to the point of, on the verge of.

Ionaigeir: precise.

Las: loose.

Leathoir: *as leathoir a chèile/as a leathoir* in sequence.

Lìonsgair, Lìonsgaradh: spread out, expand.

Reumhag: literally, small root; by extension, a slight connection, as in genealogy or relationships; a vestige.

Snaidhm-gruaimein: a granny knot, i.e., a poorly tied, entangled knot.

Stall: a stance.

Taisealach: substantial, frequently used about cloth.

Tàrmachadh: growth, development.

Tàrmasach:	fussy, particular.
Teibse:	correctness, particularly of speech.
Tinnsgeadal:	origin.
Toiseannach:	advanced, ahead of others.
Tromalach:	the heavier portion of something; extended to mean 'majority of'.
Urnas:	infamy *Bha urnas aig daoine dheth* 'people spoke of him as infamous'.

Bibliography

ALMQVIST, BO, 'Of Mermaids and Marriages. Séamas Heaney's 'Maighdean Mara' and Nuala Ní Dhomnaill's 'An Mhaighdean Mhara' in the light of folk tradition', *Béaloideas* 58 (1990), 1–74.

ANDERSON, ALAN O., *Scottish Annals from English Chroniclers* (London: David Nutt, 1908).

—— *Early Sources of Scottish History, A.D. 500 to 1200*, 2 vols. (Edinburgh: Oliver and Boyd, 1922).

—— 'The Prophecy of Berchan', *Zeitschrift für Celtische Philologie* 18 (1930), 1–56.

ANDERSON, M. O. (ed.), *A Scottish chronicle known as the Chronicle of Holyrood* (Edinburgh: Scottish Historical Society, 1938).

BAIN, JOSEPH (ed.), *Calendar of Documents relating to Scotland preserved in Her Majesty's Public Record Office, London* (Edinburgh: H.M. General Register House, 1881–1888).

BANNERMAN, JOHN W. M., 'The King's Poet and the Inauguration of Alexander III', *The Scottish Historical Review* 68 (1989), 120–49.

BARROW, G. W. S., *The Kingdom of the Scots: Government, Church and Society from the Eleventh to the Fourteenth Century* (London: Edward Arnold, 1973).

BEST, R. I., O. BERGIN AND M. A. O'BRIEN (eds.), *The Book of Leinster* Vol. 1 (Dublin: Dublin Institute for Advanced Studies, 1954).

BINCHY, D. A., 'The Fair of Tailtiu and the Feast of Tara', *Ériu* 18 (1958), 113–38.

BLACK, RONALD, 'The Genius of Cathal MacMhuirich', *Transactions of the Gaelic Society of Inverness* 50 (1977), 327–65.

—— (ed.), *An Lasair / Anthology of 18th Century Scottish Gaelic Verse* (Edinburgh: Birlinn, 2001).

BLANKENHORN, VIRGINIA, 'Traditional and Bogus Elements in "MacCrimmon's Lament"', *Scottish Studies* 22 (1978), 45–67.

BRODERICK, GEORGE, 'Fin as Oshin', *Celtica* 21 (1990), 51–60.

BROUN, DAUVIT, 'Defining Scotland and the Scots before the Wars of Independence', in Dauvit Broun, R.J. Finlay, and Michael Lynch (eds.), *Image and Identity: the Making and Remaking of Scotland through the Ages* (Edinburgh: John Donald, 1998), 4–17.

BRUFORD, ALAN, ' "Deirdre" and Alexander Carmichael's treatment of oral sources', *Scottish Gaelic Studies* 14 (1983), 1–24.

CAMERON, PAUL, 'Perthshire Gaelic Songs', *Transactions of the Gaelic Society of Inverness* 27 (1891), 126–70.

CAMPBELL, DONALD, *A Treatise on the Language, Poetry, and Music of the Highland Clans: with illustrative Traditions* (Edinburgh, 1862).

CAMPBELL, DUNCAN, *Reminiscences and Reflections of an Octogenarian Highlander* (Inverness: Northern Counties Publishing Company, 1910).

CAMPBELL, EWAN, *Saints and Sea-kings: The First Kingdom of the Scots* (Edinburgh: Historic Scotland, 1999).

CAMPBELL, J. F., *Popular Tales of the West Highlands*, 2 vols. (Edinburgh: Birlinn, 1994 [1860–2]).

—— *Leabhar na Féinne* (London: Spottiswoode & Co., 1872).

—— *More West Highland Tales*, ed. W. J. Watson, D. MacLean and H. J. Rose, 2 vols. (Edinburgh: Birlinn, 1994 [1940, 1960]).

CAMPBELL, J. G., *The Fians, Waifs and Strays of Celtic Tradition* 4 (London: David Nutt, 1891).

—— *Superstitions of the Highlands and Islands of Scotland* (Glasgow: MacLehose, 1900).

CAMPBELL, J. L. (ed.), *Òrain Ghàidhealach mu Bhliadhna Theàrlaich / Highland Songs of the Forty-Five*, Scottish Gaelic Texts 15 (Edinburgh: Scottish Gaelic Texts Society, 1984 [1933]).

—— *Gaelic in Scottish Education and Life, Past, Present and Future* (Edinburgh: W. & A. K. Johnston, 1945).

—— (ed.), *Stories from South Uist (told by Angus MacLellan)*, (Edinburgh: Birlinn, 1997 [1961]).

—— 'Notes on Hamish Robertson's "Studies in Carmichael's *Carmina Gadelica*" ', *Scottish Gaelic Studies* 13 (1978), 1–17.

—— (ed.), *Songs Remembered in Exile*, Second edition (Edinburgh: Birlinn, 1999).

—— AND FRANCIS COLLINSON (eds.), *Hebridean Folksongs*, 3 vols. (Oxford: Clarendon Press, 1969–81).

—— AND DERICK S. THOMSON, *Edward Lhuyd in the Scottish Highlands 1699–1700* (Oxford: Claredon Press, 1963).

CAREY, JOHN, *A Single Ray Of The Sun: Religious Speculation In Early Ireland* (Andover: Celtic Studies Publications, 1999).

—— *King of Mysteries: Early Irish Religious Writings* (Dublin: Four Courts Press, 2000).

CARMICHAEL, ALEXANDER, *Carmina Gadelica*, 6 vols. (Edinburgh: Scottish Gaelic Texts Society, 1900–71).

CARNEY, JAMES, *Studies in Irish Literature and History* (Dublin: Dublin Institute for Advanced Studies, 1955).

CHADWICK, NORA K., *The Heroic Age* (Cambridge: Cambridge University Press, 1912).

—— 'The Story of Macbeth', *Scottish Gaelic Studies* 6 (1949), 189–211.

—— 'The Lost Literature of Celtic Scotland', *Scottish Gaelic Studies* 7 (1953), 115–83.

CHAMBERS, R. W., *On the Continuity of English Prose from Alfred to More and his School* (London: Early English Text Society, 1932).

CHRISTIANSEN, REIDAR THORALF, *The Vikings and the Viking Wars in Irish and Gaelic Tradition* (Oslo: Dybwad, 1931).

CLANCY, THOMAS (ed.), *The Triumph Tree: Scotland's Earliest Poetry, 550–1350* (Edinburgh: Canongate Classics, 1998).

CLEMENT, DAVID, 'Gaelic' in Peter Trudgill (ed.), *Language in the British Isles* (Cambridge: Cambridge University Press, 1984), 318–42.

COLLINSON, FRANCIS, *The Traditional and National Music of Scotland* (London: Routledge & Kegan Paul, 1966).

—— *The Bagpipe* (London and Boston: Routledge & Kegan Paul, 1975).

CRAMOND, WILLIAM (ed.), *The Records of Elgin*, Vol. 2 (Aberdeen: New Spalding Club, 1908).

CRAIG, K. C. (ed.), *Òrain Luaidh Màiri nighean Alasdair* (Glasgow: Alasdair Matheson, 1949).

CREGEEN, ERIC, 'Recollections of a Highland Drover', *Scottish Studies* 3 (1959), 143–62.

DAICHES, DAVID, *Scotland and the Union* (London: J. Murray, 1977).

—— (ed.), *The New Companion to Scottish Culture* (Edinburgh: Polygon, 1993).

DILLON, MYLES, *Early Irish Literature* (Chicago: University of Chicago Press, 1948).

—— (ed.), *Irish Sagas* (Dublin: Mercier Press, 1959).

DOMHNALLACH, IAIN, *Marbhrainn a Rinn air Diadhairibh Urramach Nach Maireann agus Dàna Spioradail eile* (Edinburgh: MacLachlan & Stewart, 1885 [1848]).

DONALDSON, GORDON, *Scotland. James V – James VII* (Edinburgh: Edinburgh University Press, 1965).

DRISCOLL, STEPHEN, *Alba: The Gaelic Kingdom of Scotland* (Edinburgh: Historic Scotland, 2002).

DUMVILLE, DAVID, 'Ireland and Britain in *Táin Bó Fraích*', *Études Celtiques* 32 (1996), 174–87.

DWELLY, EDWARD, *The Illustrated Gaelic-English Dictionary* (Glasgow, 5th ed. 1949).

EMMERSON, GEORGE, *A Social History of Scottish Dance* (Montreal: McGill-Queen's University Press, 1972).

ESTÉS, CLARISSA PINKOLA, *Women Who Run With The Wolves* (London: Ballantine, 1992).

FERGUSSON, WILLIAM, 'Religion and the Massacre of Glencoe', *Scottish Historical Review* 46 (1967), 82–7.

—— 'Religion and the Massacre of Glencoe', *Scottish Historical Review* 47 (1968), 203–9.

FLETT, J.F. AND T.M., 'Some Hebridean Folk Dances', *Journal of the English Folk Dance and Song Society* 7 (1953), 113–27.

—— 'Dramatic Jigs in Scotland', *Folk-lore* 67 (1956), 84–96.

FLOWER, ROBIN, *The Irish Tradition* (Oxford: The Claredon Press, 1947).

FRASER, JOHN, 'Varia 2. leug "(precious) stone"', *Scottish Gaelic Studies* 5 (1942), 161.

GARNETT, THOMAS, *Observations on a Tour through the highlands and part of the Western Isles*, 2 vols. (London, 1811).

GILLIES, JOHN (ed.), *Sean dain agus orain Ghàidhealach* (Peairt, 1786).

GILLIES, WILLIAM, 'A Poem on the Downfall of the Gaoidhil', *Éigse* 13 (1969–70), 203–10.

—— 'The Gaelic Poems of Sir Duncan Campbell of Glenorchy (II)' *Scottish Gaelic Studies* 13 (1977), 263–88.

—— 'Some Aspects of Campbell History', *Transactions of the Gaelic Society of Inverness* 50 (1978), 256–95.

—— 'Arthur in Gaelic Tradition Part I: Folktales and Ballads; Part II: Romances and Learned Lore', *Cambridge Medieval Celtic Studies* 2 (1981), 47–72; 3 (1982), 41–75.

—— 'The "British" Genealogy of the Campbells', *Celtica* 23 (1999), 82–95.

GORDON, COSMO, 'Letter to John Aubrey from Professor James Garden', *Scottish Gaelic Studies* 8 (1958), 18–26.

GRANT, ANNE, *Essays on the Superstitions of the Highlanders of Scotland* (New York: Eastburn, Kirk & Co., 1813).

GOWANS, LINDA, *Am Bròn Binn: An Arthurian Ballad in Scottish Gaelic* (Eastbourne: Manor Park Press, 1992).

GUNDERLOCH, ANJA, 'Donnchadh Bàn's *Òran do Bhlàr na h-Eaglaise Brice* – Literary Allusion and Political Commentary', *Scottish Gaelic Studies* 20 (2000), 97–116.

GWYNN, EDWARD (ed.), *The Metrical Dindshenchas* Part III, Royal Irish Academy Todd Lecture Series Vol. X (Dublin: Royal Irish Academy, 1913).

HALDANE, A. R. B., *The Drove Roads of Scotland* (Edinburgh: Birlinn, 1997 [1952]).

HAYES-MCCOY, G. A., *Scots Mercenary Forces in Ireland (1565–1603)* (Dublin: Burns, Oates & Washbourne, 1937).

HERDMAN, JOHN, 'The poetry of Sorley Maclean: a non-Gael's view', *Lines Review* 61 (1977), 25.

HUNTER, MICHAEL, *The Occult Laboratory: Magic, Science and Second Sight in Late Seventeenth-Century Scotland* (Woodbridge: The Boydell Press, 2001).

JACKSON, KENNETH H., *Studies in Early Celtic Nature Poetry* (Cambridge: The University Press, 1935).

—— 'Incremental Repetition in the Early Welsh Englyn', *Speculum* 16 (1941), 304–21.

—— 'More Tales from Port Hood, Nova Scotia', *Scottish Gaelic Studies* 6 (1949), 178–83.

—— ' "Common Gaelic": The Evolution of the Goedelic Languages', *Proceedings of the British Academy* 37 (1951), 71–97.

—— 'The Folktale in Gaelic Scotland', *Proceedings of the Scottish Anthropological and Folklore Society* 4 (1952), 123–40.

—— 'The Duan Albanach', *The Scottish Historical Review* 36 (1957), 125–37.

—— The International Popular Tale and Early Welsh Tradition (Cardiff: University of Wales Press, 1961).

—— 'The Breaking of Original Long ē in Scottish Gaelic', in James Carney and David Greene (eds.), *Celtic Studies: Essays in Memory of Angus Matheson* (London: Routledge & Kegan Paul, 1968), 65–75.

—— A *Celtic Miscellany*, Revised edition (London: Penguin Books, 1971).

—— *Gaelic Notes in the Book of Deer* (Cambridge: Cambridge University Press, 1972).

JARMAN, A. O. H., *The Legend of Merlin* (Cardiff: University of Wales Press, 1960).

KENDRICK, T. D., *British Antiquity* (London: Methuen, 1970).

KER, W. P., *Collected Essays*, ed. Charles Whibley, 2 vols. (London: Macmillan and Co., 1925).

KERMACK, W. R., 'Emblems of the Gael', *Scottish Gaelic Studies* 7 (1953), 184–92.

—— *The Scottish Highlands: A Short History* (Edinburgh: Johnston & Bacon, 1957).

KIRK, JAMES (ed.), *The Church in the Highlands* (Edinburgh: Scottish Church History Society, 1998).

LOCKWOOD, W. B., 'Chr. Matras' Studies on the Gaelic Element in Faroese: Conclusions and Results', *Scottish Gaelic Studies* 13 (1978), 112–26.

—— 'Remarks on Ir. *Inse Orc, Inse Catt*', *Scottish Gaelic Studies* 21 (2003), 247–9.

LOGAN, JAMES, *The Scottish Gaël, or, Celtic manners as preserved among the Highlanders being an historical and descriptive account of the inhabitants, antiquities and national peculiarities of Scotland, more particularly of the northern or Gaëlic parts of the country, where the singular habits of the aboriginal Celts are most tenaciously retained by the late James Logan edited, with memoir and notes by Alex Stewart*, 2 vols. (Edinburgh: John Donald, 1976 [1876]).

LYLE, EMILY B., 'Thomas of Erceldoune: the Prophet and the Prophesied', *Folklore* 79 (1968), 111–21.

MACBAIN, ALEXANDER, 'Gaelic Incantations', *Transactions of the Gaelic Society of Inverness* 17 (1890–91), 222–66.

—— *An Etymological Dictionary of the Gaelic Language* (Inverness: Northern Counties Printing and Publishing Co., 1896).

—— and Revd John Kennedy (eds.), *Reliquiae Celticae: Texts, Papers and Studies in Gaelic Literature and Philology Left by the Late Rev. Alexander Cameron*, 2 vols. (Inverness: Northern Counties Newspaper and Printing and Publishing Co., 1894).

McCAUGHEY, TERENCE, 'The performing of Dán', *Ériu* 35 (1984), 39–57.

—— 'Protestantism and Scottish Highland Culture' in James Mackey (ed.) *An Introduction to Celtic Christianity* (Edinburgh: T&T Clark, 1989), 172–205.

MacCOINNICH, AONGHAS, ' "Kingis Rabellis" to "Cuidich 'n Rìgh"? Clann Choinnich: the emergence of a kindred, *c. 1475–c.1514*' in Steve Boardman and Alasdair Ross (eds.) *The Exercise of Power in Medieval Scotland c.1200–1500* (Dublin: Four Courts Press, 2003), 175–200.

MacDOMHNUILL, RAONUILL (ed.), *Comh-chruinneachidh Orannaigh Gaidhealach* (Duneidinn, 1776).

MacDONALD, ALEXANDER, *Ais-Eiridh na Sean-Chanoin Albannaich* (Edinburgh, 1751).

MacDONALD, A. AND A. (EDS.), *The MacDonald Collection of Gaelic Poetry* (Inverness: Northern Counties Newspaper and Printing and Publishing Co., 1911).

MacDONALD, MÀIRI A., Drovering', *Transactions of the Gaelic Society of Inverness* 49 (1974–76), 189–97.

MacDONALD, NORMAN (ed.), *The Morrison Manuscript: Traditions of the Western Isles* (Stornoway, 1975).

MacDONALD, PATRICK, *A Collection of Highland Vocal Airs* (Skye: Taigh na Teud, 2000 [1784]).

MacDONALD, R. ANDREW, 'Treachery in the Remotest Territories of Scotland: Northern Resistance to the Canmore Dynasty, 1130–1230', *Canadian Journal of History* 33 (August 1999), 161–92.

—— 'Rebels without a Cause? The Relations of Fergus of Galloway and Somerled of Argyll with the Scottish Kings, 1153–1164', in E. J. Cowan and R. Andrew McDonald (eds.) *Alba: Celtic Scotland in the Medieval Era* (East Linton: Tuckwell Press, 2000), 166–86.

MacDONELL, MARGARET (ed.), *The Emigrant Experience* (Toronto: University of Toronto Press, 1982).

MacEOIN, G. S., 'Invocation of the Forces of Nature in the Loricae', *Studia Hibernica* 2 (1962), 212–7.

—— 'Some Icelandic Loricae', *Studia Hibernica* 3 (1963), 143–54.

MacFARLANE, PATRICK (ed.), *Co'-chruinneachadh de dh'òrain agus de luinneagaibh thaghta Ghàe'lach* (Dun-eudainn: T. Stiùbhart, 1813).

MacGILL-EAIN, SOMHAIRLE, *Ris a' Bhruthaich: The Criticism and Prose Writings of Sorley MacLean*, ed. William Gillies (Stornoway: Acair, 1985).

MacGILLEATHAIN, IAIN, *Odusseia Homair* (Glasgow: Gairm, 1976).

MacGREGOR, MARTIN, 'Church and Culture in the Late Medieval Highlands', in James Kirk, *The Church in the Highlands*, 1–36.

—— ' "Surely one of the greatest poems ever made in Britain": the lament for Griogair Ruadh MacGregor of Glen Strae and its historical background', in E. J. Cowan and D. Gifford (eds.), *The Polar Twins* (Edinburgh: John Donald, 1999), 114–53.

—— 'Genealogies of the clans: contributions to the study of MS 1467', *The Innes Review* 51 (2000), 131–46.

MacILLEDHUIBH, RAGHNALL, 'The Trouble with *Carmina*', *West Highland Free Press* 29 May 1992.

MacINNES, REV. JOHN, 'Gaelic Spiritual Verse', *Transactions of the Gaelic Society of Inverness* 46 (1969–70), 308–52.

MacÌomhair, Domhnall Iain, *Coinneach Odhar* (Glasgow: Gairm, 1990).

MacKay, John G.,'Cànain nan Eun', *Scottish Gaelic Studies* 3 no. 2 (1931), 160–87.

MacKechnie, Rev. John (ed.), *The Dewar Manuscripts Volume 1* (Glasgow: William MacLellan, 1964).

MacKenzie, Alexander, *The Prophecies of the Brahan Seer* (Stirling, 1896).

Mackenzie, Annie (ed.), *Òrain Iain Luim / Songs of John MacDonald, Bard of Keppoch*, Scottish Gaelic Texts 8 (Edinburgh: Scottish Gaelic Texts Society, 1964).

MacKenzie, Henry (ed.), *Report of the Committee of the Highland Society of Scotland appointed to inquire into the Nature of the Authenticity of the Poems of Ossian* (Edinburgh: Edinburgh University Press, 1805).

MacKenzie, John (ed.), *Sàr Obair nam Bàrd Gàelach; or, The beauties of Gaelic poetry and lives of the Highland bards* (Glasgow: McGregor, Polson & Co., 1841).

MacKenzie, William, 'Gaelic Incantations, Charms, and Blessings of the Hebrides', *Transactions of the Gaelic Society of Inverness* 18 (1891–92), 97–182.

Maclean, Calum, 'Traditional Songs from Raasay and their value as Folk-Literature', *Transactions of the Gaelic Society of Inverness* 39/40 (1949), 176–92.

—— Review of *Carmina Gadelica Vol. V*, *Arv* 11 (1955), 152–4.

—— 'A Variant of the Charm of the Lasting Life from Uist', *Saga Och Sed* (1959), 75–8.

—— 'A Folk-variant of the Táin Bó Cúailnge from Uist', *Arv* 15 (1959), 160–81.

MacLean, Donald, *The law of the Lord's Day in the Celtic church* (Edinburgh: T. & T. Clark, 1926).

Maclean, Sorley, 'Some Gaelic and Non-Gaelic Influences On Myself', in Robert O'Driscoll (ed.), *The Celtic Consciousness* (Toronto: The Dolmen Press, 1981).

Maclennan, Malcolm, *A Pronouncing and Etymological Dictionary of the Gaelic Language* (Edinburgh: J. Grant, 1925).

MacLeod, Angus (ed.), *Òrain Dhonnchaidh Bhàin / The Songs of Duncan Ban Macintyre*, Scottish Gaelic Texts 4, (Edinburgh: Scottish Gaelic Texts Society, 1952).

McLeod, Wilson, 'Galldachd, Gàidhealtachd, Garbhchriochan', *Scottish Gaelic Studies* 19 (1999), 1–20.

—— 'Anshocair nam Fionnghall: Ainmeachadh agus ath-ainmeachadh Gàidhealtachd na h-Albann', in Colm Ó Baoill and Nancy McGuire (eds.), *Rannsachadh na Gàidhlig 2000* (Aberdeen: An Clò Gàidhealach, 2002), 13–23.

—— 'Rí Innsi Gall, Rí Fionnghall, Ceannas nan Gàidheal: Sovereignty and Rhetoric in the Late Medieval Hebrides', *Cambrian Medieval Celtic Studies* 43 (2002), 25–48.

—— 'Language Politics and Ethnolinguistic Consciousness in Scottish Gaelic Poetry', *Scottish Gaelic Studies* 21 (2003), 91–146.

—— 'Gaelic in the New Scotland: Politics, Rhetoric and Public Discourse', *Journal on Ethnopolitics and Minority Issues in Europe*, http://www.ecmi.de/jemie/.

—— *Divided Gaels: Gaelic Cultural Identities in Scotland and Ireland c. 1200–c.1650* (Oxford: Oxford University Press, 2004).

MacLeod, Roderick, 'Ministearain an Arain', *Transactions of the Gaelic Society of Inverness* 52 (1980–82), 222–42.

MacLeòid, Calum Iain, *Sgial is Eachdraidh* (Glasgow: Gairm, 1977).

MacMhathain, Aonghus, 'Aos Dàna (I)', *Gairm* 8 (1954), 343–7.

MacNéill, Máire, *The Festival of Lughnasa* (Oxford: Oxford University Press, 1962).

M'Nicol, Donald, *Remarks on Dr. Samuel Johnson's Journey to the Hebrides* (New York: Garland Publishing, 1974 [1779]).

Macphail, J. R. N. (ed.), *Highland Papers Vol. I* (Edinburgh: Scottish History Society, 1914).

―― (ed.), *Highland Papers Vol. III* (Edinburgh: Scottish History Society, 1920).

MacPherson, Donald (ed.), *An Duanaire* (Dun-eidin: MacLachluinn, 1868).

Mackintosh, Donald, 'Notes', *Scottish Gaelic Studies* 6 (1949), 21–6.

Martin, Martin, *A Description of the Western Islands of Scotland* (London, 1716).

Matheson, Angus, 'Some proverbs and proverbial expressions from Lewis', *Journal of Celtic Studies* 1, pt. 1 (1949), 105–15.

―― 'Bishop Carswell', *Transactions of the Gaelic Society of Inverness* 42 (1953–59), 182–205.

―― 'Documents connected with the trial of Sir James MacDonald of Islay', *Transactions of the Gaelic Society of Glasgow* 5 (1958), 207–22.

Matheson, John, *Òran na h-Eaglais* (Edinburgh, 1846).

Matheson, William (ed.), *Òrain Iain Mhic Fhearchair a Bha 'n a Bhàrd aig Sir Seumas MacDhomhnaill / The Songs of John MacCodrum: Bard to Sir James MacDonald of Sleat*, Scottish Gaelic Texts 2 (Edinburgh: Scottish Gaelic Texts Society, 1938).

―― 'Traditions of the Mackenzies', *Transactions of the Gaelic Society of Inverness* 39–40 (1949), 193–228.

―― 'Traditions of the Mathesons', *Transactions of the Gaelic Society of Inverness* 42 (1953–59), 153–81.

―― 'The historical Coinneach Odhar and some prophecies attributed to him', *Transactions of the Gaelic Society of Inverness* 46 (1969–70), 66–88.

―― (ed.), *An Clàrsair Dall: Òrain Ruaidhri Mhic Mhuirich agus a Chuid Chiùil / The Blind Harper: The Songs of Roderick Morrison and his Music*, Scottish Gaelic Texts 12 (Edinburgh: Scottish Gaelic Texts Society, 1970).

―― 'The MacLeods of Lewis', *Transactions of the Gaelic Society of Inverness* 51 (1978–80), 320–38.

Meek, Donald, '*Táin Bó Fraích* and other "Fráech" Texts', *Cambridge Medieval Celtic Studies* 7 (1984), 1–37; 8 (1984), 65–85.

―― 'The Death of Diarmaid in Scottish and Irish Tradition', *Celtica* 21 (1990), 335–61.

―― 'The Gaelic Ballads of Scotland: Creativity and Adaptation', in Howard Gaskill (ed.), *Ossian Revisited* (Edinburgh: Edinburgh University Press, 1991), 19–48.

―― 'Place-names and Literature: Evidence from the Gaelic Ballads', in Simon Taylor (ed.), *The Uses of Place-Names* (Edinburgh: Scottish Cultural Press, 1998), 147–68.

―― 'The Reformation and Gaelic culture: perspectives on patronage, language and literature in John Carswell's translation of "The Book of Common Order"', in Kirk, *The Church in the Highlands*, 37–62.

―― (ed.), *Caran an t-Saoghail / The Wiles of the World, Anthology of 19th Century Scottish Gaelic Verse* (Edinburgh: Birlinn, 2003).

―― 'The pulpit and the pen: clergy, orality and print in the Scottsh Gaelic world' in Adam Fox and Daniel Wolf (eds.), *The Spoken Word: Oral Culture in Britain, 1500–1850* (Manchester: Manchester University Press, 2003), 84–118.

Mhàrtainn Cairistìona (ed.), *Òrain an Eilein* (Skye: Taigh na Teud, 2001).

Morrison, Hew (ed.), *Songs and Poems in the Gaelic Language* (Edinburgh: n.p., 1899).

MURCHISON, THOMAS MOFFATT (ED.), *Sgrìobhaidhean Choinnich MhicLeòid / The Gaelic Prose of Kenneth MacLeod*, Scottish Gaelic Texts 16 (Edinburgh: Scottish Gaelic Texts Society, 1988).

MURPHY, GERARD, *Early Irish Metrics* (Dublin: Royal Irish Academy, 1961).

—— Review of *Carmina Gadelica Vol. V*, *Éigse* 8 (1956), 167.

—— and Eoin MacNeill (eds.), *Duanaire Finn*, 3 vols. (Dublin: Irish Texts Society, 1908–53).

NEWTON, MICHAEL, *Bho Chluaidh gu Calasraid / From the Clyde to Callander* (Stornoway: Acair, 1999).

—— *We're Indians Sure Enough: The Legacy of the Scottish Highlanders in the United States* (Richmond: Saorsa Media, 2001).

NÍ ANNRACHÁIN, MÁIRE, *Aisling agus Tóir: an slánú i bhfilíocht Shomhairle MhicGill-Eain* (Magh Nuad, 1992).

NICOLSON, ALEXANDER, *History of Skye: A Record of the Families, The Social Conditions and The Literature of the Island*, ed. Dr Alasdair Maclean (Portree: Maclean Press, 1994 [1930]).

—— *Gaelic Riddles and Enigmas* (Glasgow: A. Sinclair, 1938).

—— *A Collection of Gaelic Proverbs and Familiar Phrases*, ed. Malcolm MacInnes (Edinburgh: Birlinn, 1996 [1951]).

Ó BAOILL, COLM (ed.), *Bàrdachd Shìlis na Ceapaich c.1660–c.1729 / Poems by Sileas MacDonald c.1660–c.1729*, Scottish Gaelic Texts 13 (Edinburgh: Scottish Gaelic Texts Society, 1972).

—— 'Inis Moccu Chein', *Scottish Gaelic Studies* 12 (1976), 267–70.

—— (ed.), *Eachann Bacach agus Bàird Eile de Chloinn Ghill-Eathain / Eachann Bacach and Other MacLean Poets*, Scottish Gaelic Texts 14 (Edinburgh: Scottish Gaelic Texts Society, 1979).

—— (ed.), *Iain Dubh* (Aberdeen: An Clò Gàidhealach, 1994).

—— 'Moving in Gaelic Musical Circles: The root *lu-* in music terminology', *Scottish Gaelic Studies* 19 (1999), 172–94.

—— and Donald MacAulay, *Scottish Gaelic Vernacular Verse to 1730: A Checklist*, Revised edition (Aberdeen: Celtic Department of the University of Aberdeen, 2001).

Ó BUACHALLA, BREANDÁN, *Aisling Ghéar: Na Stíobhartaigh agus an t-Aos Léinn 1603–1788* (Baile Átha Cliath: An Clóchomhar Tta, 1996).

Ó CATHASAIGH, TOMÁS, 'The Semantics of Síd', *Éigse* 17 (1977–9), 137–55.

Ó CUÍV, BRIAN, 'A Poem in Praise of Raghnall, king of Man', *Éigse* 8 (1957), 283–301.

O DALY, MÁIRÍN, 'The Metrical Dindshenchas' in James Carney (ed.), *Early Irish Poetry* (Cork: The Mercier Press, 1965), 59–72.

OFTEDAL, MAGNE, 'On the frequency of Norse loanwords in Scottish Gaelic', *Scottish Gaelic Studies* 9 (1962), 116–27.

Ó HÓGÁIN, DÁITHÍ, 'An e an t-Am fós é?', *Béaloideas* 42–44 (1974), 213–308.

—— *Myth, Legend & Romance: An Encyclopædia of the Irish Folk Tradition* (London: BCA,1990).

O'RAHILLY, THOMAS, *Irish Dialects, Past and Present* (Dublin: Dublin University Press, 1988 [1932]).

Ó TUAMA, SEÁN, *An Grá in Amhráin na nDaoine* (Baile Átha Cliath: An Clóchomhar, 1960).

PARTRIDGE, ANGELA, 'Wild Men and Wailing Women', *Éigse* 18 (1980), 25–37.

POTTLE, FREDERICK A. AND CHARLES H. BENNETT (eds.), *Boswell's journal of a tour to the Hebrides* (London: W. Heinemann, 1936).

QUIN, E. G. (ed.), *Dictionary of the Irish Language* (Dublin: Royal Irish Academy, 1983).

RAMSAY, JOHN, *Scotland and Scotsmen in the eighteenth century / from the mss. of John Ramsay, esq. of Ochtertyre*, ed. Alexander Allardyce, 2 vols. (Edinburgh and London: W. Blackwood and Sons, 1888).

RENWICK, W. L. (ed.), *A View of the Present State of Ireland by Edmund Spenser* (London: Scholartis Press, 1934).

ROBERTSON, HAMISH, 'Studies in Carmichael's *Carmina Gadelica*', *Scottish Gaelic Studies* 12 (1976), 220–65.

ROSS, JAMES, 'The Sub-Literary Tradition in Scottish Gaelic Song-Poetry. Part I. Poetic Metres and Song Metres', *Éigse* 7 (1953–55), 217–39.

ROSS, NEIL (ed.), *Heroic Poetry from the Book of the Dean of Lismore*, Scottish Gaelic Texts Society 3 (Edinburgh: Oliver & Boyd, 1939).

SELLAR, W.D.H., 'The Origins and Ancestry of Somerled', *Scottish Historical Review* 45 (1966), 123–42.

––––––– 'The Earliest Campbells – Norman, Briton or Gael?', *Scottish Studies* 17 (1973), 109–25.

––––––– 'Celtic law and Scots law: survival and integration', *Scottish Studies* 29 (1989), 1–27.

SHAW, MARGARET FAY, *Folksongs and Folklore of South Uist*, 3rd edn. (Aberdeen: Aberdeen University Press, 1986).

SHAW, JOHN, 'Scottish Gaelic Traditions of the Cliar Sheanchain', in C. Byrne, Margaret Harry and P. Ó Siadhail (eds.), *Celtic Languages and Celtic Peoples: Proceedings of the Second North American Congress of Celtic Studies* (Halifax: St Mary's University, 1992), 141–58.

––––––– 'What Alexander Carmichael Did Not Print: The *Cliar Sheanchain*, 'Clanranald's Fool' and Related Traditions', *Béaloideas* 70 (2002), 99–126.

SIMMONS, ANDREW (ed.), *Burt's Letters from the North of Scotland* (Edinburgh: Birlinn, 1998 [1754]).

SINCLAIR, ALEXANDER MACLEAN (ed.), *The Gaelic Bards from 1411 to 1715* (Charlottetown: The Examiner Pub. Co., 1890).

SINCLAIR, ARCHIBALD (ed.), *An t-Òranaiche: comhchruinneachadh de dh'orain Ghàidhealch* (Glasgow: A. Sinclair, 1879).

SINTON, THOMAS (ed.), *The Poetry of Badenoch* (Inverness: Northern Counties Newspaper and Printing and Publishing Co., 1906).

SKENE, WILLIAM, *Celtic Scotland: a history of ancient Alban*, 3 vols. (Edinburgh: D. Douglas, 1886–1890).

––––––– *History of the Highlanders of Scotland*, ed. Alexander MacBain (Stirling: E. Mackay, 1902).

SMITH, JOHN, *Galic antiquities: consisting of a history of the Druids, particularly of those of Caledonia; a dissertation on the authenticity of the poems of Ossian* (Edinburgh: 1780).

STEER, K. A. AND JOHN BANNERMAN, *Late medieval monumental sculpture in the west Highlands* (Edinburgh: Her Majesty's Stationery Office, 1977).

STEVENSON, A., J. STEWART AND T. STEWART (eds.), *Miscellanea Scotica. A collection of tracts relating to the history, antiquities, topography and literature of Scotland*, 4 vols. (Glasgow: J. Wylie & Co., 1818–20).

STEVENSON, DAVID, *Alasdair Mac Colla and the Highland Problem in the Seventeenth Century* (Edinburgh: John Donald, 1980)

STEWART, DAVID, *Sketches of the character, manners, and present state of the Highlanders of Scotland with details of the military service of the Highland regiments*, 2 vols. (Edinburgh, 1822).

THOMSON, DAVID, *The People of the Sea* (Edinburgh: Canongate Books, 2001 [1954]).

THOMSON, DERICK, 'Scottish Gaelic Folk-Poetry Ante 1650', *Scottish Gaelic Studies* 8 (1955), 1–17.
—— 'Bogus Gaelic Literature c. 1750 – c. 1820', *Transactions of the Gaelic Society of Glasgow* 5 (1958), 172–88
—— 'The MacMhuirich Bardic Family', *Transactions of the Gaelic Society of Inverness* 43 (1963), 276–304.
—— *An Introduction to Gaelic Poetry*, 2nd edition (Edinburgh: Edinburgh University Press, 1990).
—— (ed.), *The MacDiarmid MS Anthology*, Scottish Gaelic Texts 17 (Edinburgh: Scottish Gaelic Texts Society, 1992).
—— (ed.), *The Companion to Gaelic Scotland* (Glasgow: Gairm, 1994).
—— 'The Blood-drinking Motif in Scottish Gaelic Tradition', in Roland Bielmeier (ed.), *Indogermanica et Caucasica: Festschrift für Karl Horst Schmidt zum 65. Geburstag* (Berlin: Walter de Gruyter, 1994), 415–24.
—— (ed.), *Alasdair mac Mhaighstir Alasdair / Selected Poems*, Scottish Gaelic Texts, New Series 1 (Edinburgh: Scottish Gaelic Texts Society, 1996).
THOMSON, R. L., *Adtimchiol an Chreidimh: The Gaelic Version of John Calvin's 'Catechismus Ecclesia Genevensis'* (Edinburgh: Scottish Gaelic Texts Society, 1962).
TOLMIE, FRANCES, *Journal of the Folk-song Society*, no. 16 (1911) (reprinted as *One Hundred and Five Songs of Occupation from the Western Isles of Scotland* (Felinfach, Dyfed: Llanerch, 1997)).
TURNER, PATRICK (ed.), *Comhchruinneacha do dh'òrain taghta Ghàidhealach* (Edinburgh, 1813).
WARD, JOHN OWEN (ed.), *The Oxford Companion to Music* 10th edition (Oxford: Oxford University Press, 1970).
WATKINS, CALVERT, 'Indo-European Metrics and Archaic Irish Verse,' *Celtica* 6 (1963), 194–249.
WATSON, JAMES CARMICHAEL (ed.), *Òrain us Luinneagan le Màiri nighean Alasdair Ruaidh / Gaelic Songs of Mary MacLeod*, Scottish Gaelic Texts 9 (Edinburgh: Scottish Gaelic Texts Society, 1934).
WATSON, W. J., 'Classic Gaelic Poetry of Panegyric in Scotland', *Transactions of the Gaelic Society of Inverness* 29 (1914–19), 194–234.
—— 'Cliar Sheanchain', *The Celtic Review* 4 (1919), 80–8.
—— *The History of the Celtic Place-Names of Scotland* (Edinburgh: Birlinn, 1986 [1926]).
—— 'Unpublished Gaelic Poetry – III', *Scottish Gaelic Studies* 2 (1927–8), 75–91.
—— 'Early Irish Influences in Scotland', *Transactions of the Gaelic Society of Inverness* 35 (1929–30), 178–203.
—— (ed.), *Bàrdachd Albannach O Leabhar Deadhan Lios-Móir / Scottish Verse from the Book of the Dean of Lismore*, Scottish Gaelic Texts 1 (Edinburgh: Scottish Gaelic Texts Society, 1937).
—— (ed.), *Bàrdachd Ghàidhlig: Specimens of Gaelic Poetry, 1550–1900*, 3rd edn. (Stirling: An Comunn Gàidhealach, 1959).
WITHERS, CHARLES, *Gaelic in Scotland, 1698–1981* (Edinburgh: John Donald, 1984).
—— *Gaelic Scotland* (London and New York: Routledge, 1988).
WOOLF, ALEX, 'The 'When, Why & Wherefore' of Scotland', *History Scotland* 2 no. 2 (2002), 12–6.
YOUNG, DOUGLAS, 'Was Homer an Illiterate Improviser?', *The Minnesota Review* 5 (1965), 65–75.

Notes

Biographical Sketch

1. The conservative versions are in J. L. Campbell and Francis Collinson (eds.), *Hebridean Folksongs*, 3 vols. (Oxford: Clarendon Press, 1969–81), ii.124.
2. 'The Scottish Gaelic Language' in Glanville Price (ed.), *The Celtic Connection* (Dublin: Gerrard's Cross), 101–30 (at 129).

Gaelic Poetry and Historical Tradition

1. Archibald Sinclair (ed.), *An t-Òranaiche: comhchruinneachadh de dh'orain Ghàidhealach* (Glasgow: A. Sinclair, 1879), 126.
2. Derick Thomson, 'The Blood-drinking Motif in Scottish Gaelic Tradition', in Roland Bielmeier (ed.) *Indogermanica et Caucasica: Festschrift für Karl Horst Schmidt zum 65. Geburtstag* (Berlin: Walter de Gruyter, 1994), 415–24.
3. W. L. Renwick (ed.), *A View of the Present State of Ireland by Edmund Spenser* (London: Scholartis Press, 1934), 62. See also Angela Partridge, 'Wild Men and Wailing Women', *Éigse* 18 (1980), 25–37.
4. A. and A. MacDonald. (eds.), *The MacDonald Collection of Gaelic Poetry* (Inverness: Northern Counties Newspaper and Printing and Publishing Co., 1911), x, 31.
5. W. J. Watson, *The History of the Celtic Place-Names of Scotland* (Edinburgh: Birlinn, 1986 [1926]), 28–30. Though see now W. B. Lockwood, 'Remarks on Ir. *Inse Orc, Inse Catt*', *Scottish Gaelic Studies* 21 (2003), 247–9.
6. A. Sinclair, *An t-Òranaiche*, 131–5.
7. See 'The Choral Tradition in Scottish Gaelic Songs' and 'The Oral Tradition in Scottish Gaelic Poetry' in this volume.
8. David Dumville, 'Ireland and Britain in *Táin Bó Fraích*', *Études Celtiques* 32 (1996), 174–87; Dauvit Broun, 'Defining Scotland and the Scots before the Wars of Independence', in Dauvit Broun, R.J. Finlay, and Michael Lynch (eds.), *Image and Identity: the Making and Remaking of Scotland through the Ages* (Edinburgh: John Donald, 1998), 4–17.
9. Annie Mackenzie (ed.), *Òrain Iain Luim / Songs of John MacDonald, Bard of Keppoch*, Scottish Gaelic Texts 8 (Edinburgh: Scottish Gaelic Texts Society, 1964), 193; Alexander MacBain and Revd John Kennedy (eds.), *Reliquiae Celticae: Texts, Papers and Studies in Gaelic Literature and Philology Left by the Late Rev. Alexander Cameron*, 2 vols. (Inverness: Northern Counties Newspaper and Printing and Publishing Co., 1894), ii. 154–5: 'All the islands from Man to the Orkneys were in the possession of the Norsemen'. Shetland is not mentioned.
10. Wilson McLeod, 'Anshocair nam Fionnghall: Ainmeachadh agus ath-ainmeachadh Gàidhealtachd na h-Albann', in Colm Ó Baoill and Nancy McGuire (eds.), *Rannsachadh na Gàidhlig 2000* (Aberdeen: An Clò Gàidhealach, 2002), 13–23.

11. A. O. Anderson, *Scottish Annals from English Chroniclers* (London: David Nutt, 1908), viii, 202.
12. G. W. S. Barrow, *The Kingdom of the Scots: Government, Church and Society from the Eleventh to the Fourteenth Century* (London: Edward Arnold, 1973), 362 ff.
13. See 'The Gaelic Perception of the Lowlands' in this volume.
14. W. J. Watson (ed.), *Bàrdachd Albannach O Leabhar Deadhan Lios-Móir / Scottish Verse from the Book of the Dean of Lismore*, Scottish Gaelic Texts 1 (Edinburgh: Scottish Gaelic Texts Society, 1937), 214–7.
15. Kenneth Jackson, 'The Duan Albanach', *The Scottish Historical Review* 36 (1957), 125–37.
16. Duncan Campbell, *Reminiscences and Reflections of an Octogenarian Highlander* (Inverness: Northern Counties Publishing Company, 1910), 136–7.
17. Andrew Simmons (ed.), *Burt's Letters from the North of Scotland* (Edinburgh: Birlinn, 1998 [1754]), 192.
18. See the discussion in 'The Panegyric Code in Gaelic Poetry and its Historical Background' in this volume.
19. James Carmichael Watson (ed.), *Òrain us Luinneagan le Màiri nighean Alasdair Ruaidh / Gaelic Songs of Mary MacLeod*, Scottish Gaelic Texts 9 (Edinburgh: Scottish Gaelic Texts Society, 1934), 57–9.
20. W. J. Watson (ed.), *Bàrdachd Ghàidhlig: Specimens of Gaelic Poetry, 1550–1900*, 3rd edn. (Stirling: An Comunn Gàidhealach, 1959), 247.
21. Wilson McLeod, *Divided Gaels: Gaelic Cultural Identities in Scotland and Ireland c. 1200–c.1650* (Oxford: Oxford University Press, 2004), 29–33.
22. James Carmichael Watson, *Òrain us Luinneagan*, 95.
23. William Matheson (ed.), *Òrain Iain Mhic Fhearchair a Bha 'n a Bhàrd aig Sir Seumas MacDhomhnaill / The Songs of John MacCodrum: Bard to Sir James MacDonald of Sleat*, Scottish Gaelic Texts 2 (Edinburgh: Scottish Gaelic Texts Society, 1938), 129–31.
24. Colm Ó Baoill (ed.), *Eachann Bacach agus Bàird Eile de Chloinn Ghill-Eathain / Eachann Bacach and Other MacLean Poets*, Scottish Gaelic Texts 14 (Edinburgh: Scottish Gaelic Texts Society, 1979), 15.
25. J. R. N. Macphail (ed.), *Highland Papers Vol. III* (Edinburgh: Scottish History Society, 1920), 268.
26. K. A. Steer and John Bannerman, *Late medieval monumental sculpture in the west Highlands* (Edinburgh: Her Majesty's Stationery Office, 1977), 201.
27. Wilson McLeod, '*Rí Innsi Gall, Rí Fionnghall, Ceannas nan Gàidheal*: Sovereignty and Rhetoric in the Late Medieval Hebrides', *Cambrian Medieval Celtic Studies* 43 (2002), 25–48.
28. Alexander MacBain and Revd John Kennedy, *Reliquiae Celticae*, ii. 214–5.
29. Ibid., ii. 156–7.
30. Derick Thomson, 'The MacMhuirich Bardic Family', *Transactions of the Gaelic Society of Inverness* 43 (1963), 276–304.
31. Brian Ó Cuív, 'A Poem in Praise of Raghnall, king of Man', *Éigse* 8 (1957), 283–301. Apparently Raghnall's ship was named 'An Eala' ('The Swan'), which according to Skye tradition was also the name of Domhnall mac Iain mhic Sheumais' ship. Domhnall is the subject of the panegyrics mentioned above; notes 4 and 6.
32. K. A. Steer and John Bannerman, *Late Medieval*, 206, f.n. 7.
33. W. J. Watson, *Bàrdachd Albannach*, xviii. But see W. J. Watson, 'Classic Gaelic Poetry of Panegyric in Scotland', *Transactions of the Gaelic Society of Inverness* 29 (1914–19), 194–234 (at 205).

34. E.g., waulking songs. See further discussion in Wilson McLeod, *Divided Gaels*, Chapter Two.
35. K. A. Steer and John Bannerman, *Late Medieval*, 205; see now Martin MacGregor, 'Genealogies of the clans: contributions to the study of MS 1467', *The Innes Review* 51 (2000), 131–46 (esp. 143–5).
36. W. J. Watson, *Bàrdachd Albannach*, 3.
37. Ibid., xvii.
38. Cosmo Innes (ed.), *Collectanea de Rebus Albanicis, consisting of original papers and documents relating to the history of the Highlands and Islands of Scotland* (Edinburgh: Iona Club, 1847), 23–32.
39. W. J. Watson, *Bàrdachd Albannach*, 90–5.
40. A. and A. MacDonald, *The MacDonald Collection of Gaelic Poetry*, 6.
41. W. J. Watson, 'Classic Gaelic Poetry', 214–8.
42. W. J. Watson, *Bàrdachd Ghàidhlig*, 259.
43. Translation from the poem 'Maith an chairt ceannas na nGaoidheal' in W. J. Watson, 'Classic Gaelic Poetry', 217, 222.
44. W. J. Watson, 'Unpublished Gaelic Poetry – III', *Scottish Gaelic Studies* 2 (1927–8), 75–91 (at 77).
45. Annie Mackenzie, *Òrain Iain Luim*, 143.
46. Ronald Black, 'The Genius of Cathal MacMhuirich', *Transactions of the Gaelic Society of Inverness* 50 (1977), 327–65 (at 329–30).
47. William Matheson, 'Traditions of the Mathesons', *Transactions of the Gaelic Society of Inverness* 42 (1953–59), 153–81 (at 160); Aonghas MacCoinnich, ' "Kingis rabellis" to "Cuidich 'n Rìgh"? Clann Choinnich: the emergence of a kindred, *c.* 1475–*c.*1514' in Steve Boardman and Alasdair Ross (eds.), *The Exercise of Power in Medieval Scotland c.1200–1500* (Dublin: Four Courts Press, 2003), 175–200.
48. K. A. Steer and John Bannerman, *Late Medieval*, 210.
49. W. J. Watson, *Bàrdachd Albannach*, 159–61. 'Drive the Saxons back' is perhaps the sense.
50. W. J. Watson, *Bàrdachd Albannach*, 290; but see now Wilson McLeod, *Divided Gaels*, 27–9.
51. Donald Meek, ' "Norsemen and Noble Stewards": The MacSween Poem in the Book of the Dean of Lismore', *Cambrian Medieval Celtic Studies* 34 (1997), 1–49.
52. Alexander MacBain and Revd John Kennedy, *Reliquiae Celticae*, ii. 157.
53. W. D. H. Sellar, 'The Origins and Ancestry of Somerled', *Scottish Historical Review* 45 (1966), 123–42.
54. W. J. Watson, 'Classic Gaelic Poetry', 215–6.
55. William Gillies, 'Some Aspects of Campbell History', *Transactions of the Gaelic Society of Inverness* 50 (1978), 256–95 (esp. 276–85). See also Wilson McLeod, *Divided Gaels*, 214–5; William Gillies, 'The "British" Genealogy of the Campbells', *Celtica* 23 (1999), 82–95.
56. Ronald Black, 'Genius', 330.
57. William Skene, *History of the Highlanders of Scotland*, ed. Alexander MacBain (Stirling: E. Mackay, 1902), 421.
58. W. D. H. Sellar, 'The Earliest Campbells – Norman, Briton or Gael?', *Scottish Studies* 17 (1973), 109–25. In addition to the Galbraiths, the MacArthurs, one of the 'three septs' of the Campbells according to George Black's *Surnames of Scotland*, are worth investigating if only because Gaelic tradition everywhere claims that they are the oldest *fine* in Scotland.
59. J. F. Campbell, *Popular Tales of the West Highlands* 4 volumes (Edinburgh, 1860), iii. 96 note 59.

60. James Carney, *Studies in Irish Literature and History* (Dublin: Dublin Institute for Advanced Studies, 1955), 129 ff., 385 ff.; A. O. H. Jarman, *The Legend of Merlin* (Cardiff: University of Wales Press, 1960). The name 'Merrin / Meirbi / Smerbi', etc may be connected with Gaelic 'Morbán', discussed by Carney, op. cit.

61. A. O. H. Jarman, *The Legend of Merlin*, 28.

62. T. D. Kendrick, *British Antiquity* (London: Methuen, 1970), 35.

63. J. G. Campbell, *Superstitions of the Highlands and Islands of Scotland* (Glasgow: MacLehose, 1900), 271.

64. E. B. Lyle, 'Thomas of Erceldoune: the Prophet and the Prophesied', *Folklore* 79 (1968), 111–21.

65. Classified as 'The Legend of Barbarossa' in Stith Thompson's *Motif-Index of Folk-Literature*.

66. J. F. Campbell, *Popular Tales*, iv. 35.

67. James Carney, 'Cath Maige Muccrime' in Myles Dillon (ed.), *Irish Sagas* (Dublin: Mercier Press, 1959), 152–66 (esp. 160); Breandán Ó Buachalla, *Aisling Ghéar: Na Stíobhartaigh agus an t-Aos Léinn 1603–1788* (Baile Átha Cliath: An Clóchomhar Tta, 1996), 449–52. The deliverer is 'The Red-handed One', etc. Carney remarks on 'the reference most likely being to the bloodshed that will precede the glory of the messianic era.' The colour Red, which symbolises blood and death, recurs remarkably often in Gaelic legends of the Sleeping Warrior: see Dáithí Ó hÓgáin, 'An e an t-Am fós é?', *Béaloideas* 42–44 (1974), 213–308. The 'Red Hall' of King Arthur may involve the same symbolism. Red Knight and Round Table both appear in a story of Ceann Aistear (probably a corruption of 'Cing Arthur') recorded in Nova Scotia: Kenneth Jackson, 'More Tales from Port Hood, Nova Scotia', *Scottish Gaelic Studies* 6 (1949), 178–83 (at 186–7).

68. Alan O. Anderson, *Early Sources of Scottish History, A.D. 500 to 1200*, 2 vols. (Edinburgh: Oliver and Boyd, 1922), i.447–8; 'The Prophecy of Berchan', *Zeitschrift für Celtische Philologie* 18 (1930), 1–56 (at §148–151). The phrase 'go mbuair mbra(i)s' translated as 'with nimble cattle' may mean 'rutting cattle'.

69. Annie Mackenzie, *Òrain Iain Luim*, 29, 53.

70. William Matheson, *Òrain Iain Mhic Fhearchair*, 131.

71. Colm Ó Baoill (ed.), *Bàrdachd Shìlis na Ceapaich c.1660–c.1729 / Poems by Sileas MacDonald c.1660–c.1729*, Scottish Gaelic Texts 13 (Edinburgh: Scottish Gaelic Texts Society, 1972), 43.

72. Colm Ó Baoill (ed.), *Iain Dubh* (Aberdeen: An Clò Gàidhealach, 1994), poem 5.

73. Ibid., poem 6. The song may represent a surfacing of a sub-literary current connected with the Irish Aisling ('Vision') poetry, on which see Gerard Murphy, 'Notes on Irish Aisling Poetry', *Éigse* 1 (1939), 40–50; Breandán Ó Buachalla, *Aisling Ghéar*, Chapter 11.

74. Tomás Ó Cathasaigh, 'The Semantics of Síd', *Éigse* 17 (1977–9), 137–55.

75. W. J. Watson, 'Unpublished Gaelic Poetry – III', 85.

76. Annie Mackenzie, *Orain Iain Luim*, 222–9.

77. Ibid., 146–51.

78. W. J. Watson, *Bàrdachd Ghàidhlig*, 282 note 1987.

79. W. J. Watson, 'Unpublished Gaelic Poetry – III', 77.

80. See discussion Wilson McLeod, *Divided Gaels*, 194–5.

81. The 1802 edition is a reprint of the very rare 1751 edition.

82. Raonuill Macdomhnuill (ed.), *Comh-chruinneachidh Orannaigh Gaidhealach* (Duneidinn, 1776), v.

Notes

517

83. Derick Thomson (ed.), *Alasdair mac Mhaighstir Alasdair / Selected Poems*, Scottish Gaelic Texts, New Series 1 (Edinburgh: Scottish Gaelic Texts Society, 1996), poem 5.
84. Paul-Yves Pezron's *L'Antiquité de la Nation et la langue des Celtes* (1703), translated into English in 1706, is one of the important sources. Macdonald may well have known it. For relevant discussion of the rhetoric in Gaelic poetry praising the Gaelic language, see Wilson McLeod, 'Language Politics and Ethnolinguistic Consciousness in Scottish Gaelic Poetry', *Scottish Gaelic Studies* 21 (2003), 91–146.
85. Derick Thomson, *Alasdair mac Mhaighstir Alasdair*, poem 8.
86. 'Ruith a' chorrain air a' chuinnlein | air na bheil beò dhe na Guibhnich'; K. C. Craig (ed.), *Òrain Luaidh Màiri nighean Alasdair* (Glasgow: Alasdair Matheson, 1949), 108.
87. J. L. Campbell (ed.), *Òrain Ghàidhealach mu Bhliadhna Theàrlaich / Highland Songs of the Forty-Five*, Scottish Gaelic Texts 15 (Edinburgh: Scottish Gaelic Texts Society, 1984 [1933]), 29.
88. Ronald Black, 'The Genius', 330.
89. Colm Ó Baoill and Donald MacAulay, *Scottish Gaelic Vernacular Verse to 1730: A Checklist*, Revised edition (Aberdeen: Celtic Department of the University of Aberdeen, 2001), item 388.
90. See 'The Panegyric Code in Gaelic Poetry and its Historical Background' in this volume.
91. William Skene, *Celtic Scotland: a history of ancient Alban*, 3 vols. (Edinburgh: D. Douglas, 1886–1890), iii. 428 ff.
92. *Celtic Magazine* 2 (1877), 484–5. See also Alexander Maclean Sinclair (ed.), *The Gaelic Bards from 1411 to 1715* (Charlottetown: The Examiner Pub. Co., 1890), 27–8.
93. Colm Ó Baoill and Donald MacAulay, *Scottish Gaelic Vernacular Verse*, item 50.
94. Quoted in G. W. S. Barrow, *The Kingdom of the Scots*, 368.
95. Annie Mackenzie, *Òrain Iain Luim*, xxix-xxx.
96. Traditional text; see W. R. Kermack, 'Emblems of the Gael', *Scottish Gaelic Studies* 7 (1953), 184–192 (esp. 189), for further discussion on the yew, etc.
97. W. J. Watson, *Bàrdachd Ghàidhlig*, xlv-liv.
98. For discussion of some of the questions involved, see John MacInnes, 'Gaelic Songs of Mary Macleod', *Scottish Gaelic Studies* 11 (1966), 3–25.
99. For a recent analysis, see Anja Gunderloch, 'Donnchadh Bàn's "Òran do Bhlàr na h-Eaglaise Brice" – Literary Allusion and Political Commentary', *Scottish Gaelic Studies* 20 (2000), 97–116.
100. Angus MacLeod (ed.), *Òrain Dhonnchaidh Bhàin / The Songs of Duncan Ban Macintyre*, Scottish Gaelic Texts 4, (Edinburgh: Scottish Gaelic Texts Society, 1952), poems 1 and 62.
101. J. L. Campbell, *Òrain Ghàidhlig*, poem 32 (286–91).
102. Dáithí Ó hÓgáin, 'An e an t-Am fós é?', 217, 224.
103. Emily Lyle, 'Thomas of Erceldoune'.
104. Alexander Nicolson, *A Collection of Gaelic Proverbs and Familiar Phrases*, ed. Malcolm MacInnes (Edinburgh: Birlinn, 1996 [1951]), 152.
105. I owe to Mr Matthew P. MacDiarmid the suggestion that the line 'I saw a dead man win a fight' is to be understood in connection with the belief in the Sleeping Warrior and related traditions.
106. W. J. Watson, *Bàrdachd Ghàidhlig*, 283; Michael Newton, *We're Indians Sure Enough: The Legacy of the Scottish Highlanders in the United States* (Richmond: Saorsa Media, 2001), 33–5.

107. William Matheson, 'Traditions of the Mackenzies', *Transactions of the Gaelic Society of Inverness* 39–40 (1949), 193–228.
108. N. K. Chadwick, 'The Lost Literature of Celtic Scotland', *Scottish Gaelic Studies* 7 (1953), 115–83 for general background.
109. Gerard Murphy and Eoin MacNeill (eds.), *Duanaire Finn*, 3 vols. (Dublin: Irish Texts Society, 1908–53), iii. 360, 'Donn': R. A. Breatnach, 'Tóraigheacht Dhiarmada agus Ghráinne' in Myles Dillon, *Irish Sagas*, 138–51 (esp. 149 ff).
110. James Carney, *Studies*, 129 ff, 385 ff.
111. In this connection, see Gerard Murphy, *Duanaire Finn*, iii. Appendix F ('On the use of non-essential resemblance to establish real influence of one story on another').
112. Proinsias MacCana, *Celtic Mythology* (New York: Peter Bedrick Books, 1983 [1968]), 113.

The Gaelic Perception of the Lowlands

1. The most recent discussion is in Wilson McLeod, '*Galldachd, Gàidhealtachd, Garbhchriochan*', *Scottish Gaelic Studies* 19 (1999), 1–20.
2. G. W. S. Barrow, *The Kingdom of the Scots: Government, Church and Society from the Eleventh to the Fourteenth Century* (London: Edward Arnold, 1973), 362.
3. Andrew Simmons (ed.), *Burt's Letters from the North of Scotland* (Edinburgh: Birlinn, 1998 [1754]), 192.
4. W. J. Watson (ed.), *Bàrdachd Ghàidhlig: Specimens of Gaelic Poetry, 1550–1900*, 3rd edn. (Stirling: An Comunn Gàidhealach, 1959). 192–4.
5. A variant from oral tradition. For editions, see Margaret MacDonell (ed.), *The Emigrant Experience* (Toronto: University of Toronto Press, 1982), 42–3; Michael Newton, *We're Indians Sure Enough: The Legacy of the Scottish Highlanders in the United States* (Richmond: Saorsa Media, 2001), 175–8.
6. J. L. Campbell and F. Collinson (eds.), *Hebridean Folksongs*, 3 vols. (Oxford: Clarendon Press, 1969–81), ii. 677–83.
7. W. J. Watson, *Bàrdachd Ghàidhlig*, 93.
8. A. and A. MacDonald (eds.), *The MacDonald Collection of Gaelic Poetry* (Inverness: Northern Counties Newspaper and Printing and Publishing Co., 1911), 78–9.
9. W. J. Watson, *Bàrdachd Ghàidhlig*, 172.
10. Colm Ó Baoill (ed.), *Iain Dubh: Òrain a rinn Iain Dubh mac Iain mhic Ailein (c.1665–c.1725)* (Aberdeen: An Clò Gàidhealach, 1994), song 5.
11. See Wilson McLeod, *Divided Gaels: Gaelic Cultural Identities in Scotland and Ireland c. 1200–c.1650* (Oxford: Oxford University Press, 2004), 27–9, for some discussion.
12. Alexander MacDonald, *Ais-Eiridh na Sean-Chanoin Albannaich* (Edinburgh, 1751).
13. David Stevenson, *Alasdair Mac Colla and the Highland Problem in the Seventeenth Century* (Edinburgh: John Donald, 1980), p. 19.
14. Patrick Turner (ed.), *Comhchruinneacha do dh'òrain taghta Ghàidhealach* (Edinburgh, 1813), 282; Michael Newton, *We're Indians*, 33–5; W. J. Watson, *Bàrdachd Ghàidhlig*, 283.
15. Henry MacKenzie (ed.), *Report of the Committee of the Highland Society of Scotland appointed to inquire into the Nature of the Authenticity of the Poems of Ossian* (Edinburgh: Edinburgh University Press, 1805), 50.

16. Donald MacPherson (ed.), *An Duanaire* (Dun-eidin: MacLachluinn, 1868), 46.
17. Angus Matheson, 'Some proverbs and proverbial expressions from Lewis', *Journal of Celtic Studies*, 1, pt. 1 (1949), 105–15 (at 108). There is a variant of this in the Charles Robertson Collection (National Library of Scotland MS 398:11).

Clan Sagas and Historical Legends

1. Kenneth Jackson, 'The Folktale in Gaelic Scotland', *Proceedings of the Scottish Anthropological and Folklore Society* 4 (1952), 123–40 (at 131).
2. J. F. Campbell, *Popular Tales of the West Highlands*, 2 vols. (Edinburgh: Birlinn, 1994 [1860–2]), i. 24–5, 76–7.
3. See *Transactions of the Gaelic Society of Inverness* 50 (1976–8), 429 quoting from Charles Fraser-Mackintosh who says (*Antiquarian Notes*, 2nd Series, 422) 'In the Commissary Court Records are to be found names of some of the family of John Beg MacAndrew, Dalnahatnich, establishing that this person, regarding whom so many startling traditions, chiefly concerned with Lochaber raiders, existed.'
   A story about Iain Beag appears in *Transactions of the Gaelic Society of Inverness* 50 (1976–8), 430 and a further one in *Transactions of the Gaelic Society of Inverness* 52 (1980–2), 118 along with some information about him.
4. From family tradition.
5. 'Is math a dhannsas tu! Ma dhannsas tu cho math sin air oidhche do bhainnseadh ri nighean dhubh chamadhalach Loch Iall, cha bhi móran aig duine sam bith ri thogail ort.'
6. From family tradition.
7. W. J. Watson (ed.), *Bàrdachd Albannach O Leabhar Deadhan Lios-Móir / Scottish Verse from the Book of the Dean of Lismore*, Scottish Gaelic Texts 1 (Edinburgh: Scottish Gaelic Texts Society, 1937), poem 13.
8. Norman MacDonald (ed.), *The Morrison Manuscript: Traditions of the Western Isles* (Stornoway, 1975), 1–5; see D.S. Thomson (ed.), *The Companion to Gaelic Scotland* (Glasgow: Gairm, 1994), 205, 'Morrison, John'.

Gleanings from Raasay Tradition

1. J. F. Campbell, *More West Highland Tales Volume II*, eds. W. J. Watson, D. MacLean and H. J. Rose (Edinburgh: Birlinn, 1994 [1960]), 22–4.
2. J. G. Campbell, *The Fians*, Waifs and Strays of Celtic Tradition 4 (London: David Nutt, 1891), 258–9.
3. 'Tobar an Fhìon(a)' may be the older form and 'nan Eun' a corruption. See W. J. Watson, *The History of the Celtic Place names of Scotland* (Edinburgh: Birlinn, 1986 [1926]), 436–7 for remarks on wells with this name.
4. I am grateful to Mr Alick Morrison for corroboration of this.
5. Frederick A. Pottle and Charles H. Bennett (eds.), *Boswell's journal of a tour to the Hebrides* (London: W. Heinemann, 1936), 138–9. I am grateful to Mr D. A. MacDonald for checking the reference and providing the bibliographical details.
6. It is printed without attribution in Alexander Nicolson, *Gaelic Riddles and Enigmas* (Glasgow: A. Sinclair, 1938); the source, however, was the same John MacLeod, Raasay, as he himself recorded on tape for the archives of the School of Scottish Studies, University of Edinburgh.

7. J. F. Campbell, *More West Highland Tales Volume II*, 12–14.
8. Calum Maclean, 'Traditional Songs from Raasay and their value as Folk-Literature', *Transactions of the Gaelic Society of Inverness* 39/40 (1949), 176–92.
9. Colm Ó Baoill and Donald MacAulay, *Scottish Gaelic Vernacular Verse to 1730: A Checklist*, Revised edition (Aberdeen: Celtic Department of the University of Aberdeen, 2001), item 494.
10. For a discussion of the background of this song, see John MacInnes, 'Personal Names in a Gaelic Song', *Scottish Studies* 6 (1962), 235–43.
11. K. C. Craig (ed.), *Òrain Luaidh Màiri nighean Alasdair* (Glasgow: Alasdair Matheson, 1949), 66.
12. J. L. Campbell and Francis Collinson (eds.), *Hebridean Folksongs*, 3 vols. (Oxford: Clarendon Press, 1969–81), i.70–3. As my colleague Ms Morag MacLeod points out to me, the melodies are also variants.
13. I recorded a few items from Mrs Beaton when I was a student at Edinburgh University.
14. John MacInnes. 'Personal Names'.
15. K. C. Craig, *Òrain Luaidh*, 20, 98.
16. Place names, too, may be involved in the processes of formulaic composition, sometimes altered or corrupted. In A. and A. MacDonald (eds.), *The MacDonald Collection of Gaelic Poetry* (Inverness: Northern Counties Newspaper and Printing and Publishing Co., 1911), 344, there is a place name 'Caisteal Ròchaidh' rhyming with 'Rònaidh' in the same couplet. This may originally have been 'Caisteal Bhròchaill'. The name 'Crodhlain' (? = 'Crowlin') appears in the same text.
17. Alexander Carmichael, *Carmina Gadelica*, 6 vols. (Edinburgh: Scottish Gaelic Texts Society, 1900–71), i.198ff; iii.138ff.
18. Lady D'Oyly (Elizabeth or Eliza Ross: she seems to have been known by both names) was a granddaughter of James, the 12th chief. She was not only a Gaelic poet but an important link in the history of Ceòl-mór.
19. Colm Ó Baoill, 'Inis Moccu Chein', *Scottish Gaelic Studies* 12 (1976), 267–70.

Family Tradition In The Isle of Skye: Clann Aonghuis – The MacInneses

1. J. R. N. MacPhail (ed.), *Highland Papers Vol. I* (Edinburgh: Scottish History Society, 1914), 5–6.
2. W. D. H. Sellar, 'The Origins and Ancestry of Somerled', *Scottish Historical Review* 45 (1966), 123–142; John W. M. Bannerman and K.H. Steer, *Late Medieval Sculpture in the West Highlands* (Edinburgh: Her Majesty's Stationary Office, 1977), Appendix Two.
3. I owe this information to Mr Alick MacAulay, the leading *seanchaidh* of North Uist.
4. Martin Martin, *A Description of the Western Islands of Scotland* (London, 1716), 142.
5. The term 'Mormhaire' – the mormaer of early Scottish history – is still used colloquially in Skye and other places; written forms such as 'morair', 'mór-fhear', which are in any case unhistorical, are simply not to be heard in ordinary Skye Gaelic. *Bàn* 'fair-haired'.

6. Alexander Nicolson, *History of Skye: A Record of the Families, The Social Conditions and The Literature of the Island,* ed. Dr Alasdair Maclean (Portree: Maclean Press, 1994 [1930]), 160–1.
7. National Library of Scotland MS 3784.

The Scottish Gaelic Language

1. Gordon Donaldson, *Scotland. James V – James VII* (Edinburgh: Edinburgh University Press, 1965), 30.
2. David Daiches, *Scotland and the Union* (London: J. Murray, 1977), 15.
3. Gordon Donaldson, *Scotland*, 259.
4. Derick Thomson (ed.), *The Companion to Gaelic Scotland* (Glasgow: Gairm, 1994), contains a wide range of specialist articles with detailed bibliographies while David Clement, 'Gaelic' in Peter Trudgill (ed.), *Language in the British Isles* (Cambridge: Cambridge University Press, 1984), 318–42, provides a general survey.
5. Alex Woolf, 'The 'When, Why & Wherefore' of Scotland', *History Scotland* 2 no. 2 (2002), 12–6 (at 14).
6. Ewan Campbell, *Saints and Sea-kings: The First Kingdom of the Scots* (Edinburgh: Historic Scotland, 1999), 31–41; Stephen Driscoll, *Alba: The Gaelic Kingdom of Scotland* (Edinburgh: Historic Scotland, 2002), 20–1.
7. W. J. Watson, 'Early Irish Influences in Scotland', *Transactions of the Gaelic Society of Inverness* 35 (1929–30), 178–203 (at 198).
8. Stephen Driscoll, *Alba*, 33–5.
9. W. J. Watson, *The History of the Celtic Place-Names of Scotland* (Edinburgh: Birlinn, 1986 [1926]), 133.
10. W. D. H. Sellar, 'Celtic law and Scots law: survival and integration', *Scottish Studies* 29 (1989), 1–27.
11. R. Andrew MacDonald, 'Treachery in the remotest territories of Scotland: Northern resistance to the Canmore dynasty, 1130–1230', *Canadian Journal of History* 33 (August 1999), 161–92.
12. John W. M. Bannerman, 'The King's Poet and the Inauguration of Alexander III', *The Scottish Historical Review* 68 (1989), 120–49.
13. Wilson McLeod, *Divided Gaels: Gaelic Cultural Identities in Scotland and Ireland c. 1200–c.1650* (Oxford: Oxford University Press, 2004), 29–33.
14. Ibid., Chapter Two.
15. Kenneth Jackson, *Gaelic Notes in the Book of Deer* (Cambridge: Cambridge University Press, 1972), 150.
16. G. W. S. Barrow, *The Kingdom of the Scots: Government, Church and Society from the Eleventh to the Fourteenth Century* (London: Edward Arnold, 1973), 364.
17. Charles Withers, *Gaelic in Scotland, 1698–1981* (Edinburgh: John Donald, 1984), 22.
18. Ibid., 23.
19. Ibid., 22-4.
20. Donald Meek, 'The Reformation and Gaelic culture: perspectives on patronage, language and literature in John Carswell's translation of "The Book of Common Order"', in James Kirk (ed.), *The Church in the Highlands* (Edinburgh: Scottish Church History Society, 1998), 37–62.
21. R. L. Thomson, *Adtimichiol an Chreidimh: The Gaelic Version of John Calvin's 'Catechisms Ecclesia Genevensis'* (Edinburgh: Scottish Gaelic Texts Society, 1962), xxxix.

22. Donald Meek, 'The pulpit and the pen: clergy, orality and print in the Scotish Gaelic World' in Adam Fox and Daniel Wolf (eds.) *The Spoken Word: Oral Culture in Britain 1500–1850* (Manchester: Manchester University Press, 2003), 84–118.

23. Iain MacGilleathain, *Odusseia Homair* (Glasgow: Gairm, 1976), 3–4.

24. John L. Campbell, *Gaelic in Scottish Education and Life, Past, Present and Future* (Edinburgh: W. & A. K. Johnston, 1945), 47.

25. Donald M'Nicol, *Remarks on Dr. Samuel Johnson's Journey to the Hebrides* (New York: Garland Publishing, 1974 [1779]).

26. Cathair Ó Dochartaigh (ed.), *Survey of the Gaelic Dialects of Scotland*, 5 vols. (Dublin: Dublin Institute for Advanced Studies, 1997).

27. Alexander MacBain and Revd John Kennedy (eds.), *Reliquiae Celticae: Texts, Papers and Studies in Gaelic Literature and Philology Left by the Late Rev. Alexander Cameron*, 2 vols. (Inverness: Northern Counties Newspaper and Printing and Publishing Co., 1894), ii. 197.

28. Angus Matheson, 'Documents connected with the trial of Sir James MacDonald of Islay', *Transactions of the Gaelic Society of Glasgow* 5 (1958), 207–22 (at 211–2).

29. Derick Thomson, *The Companion*, 98–9.

30. Ibid., 107.

31. Magne Oftedal, 'On the frequency of Norse loanwords in Scottish Gaelic', *Scottish Gaelic Studies* 9 (1962), 116–27.

32. Charles Withers, *Gaelic Scotland* (London and New York: Routledge, 1988), 336.

33. Wilson McLeod, 'Gaelic in the New Scotland: Politics, Rhetoric and Public Discourse', *Journal on Ethnopolitics and Minority Issues in Europe*, http://www.ecmi.de/jemie/.

34. Myles Dillon, *Early Irish Literature* (Chicago: University of Chicago Press, 1948), xvi.

Cainnt is Cànan

1. Kenneth Jackson, ' "Common Gaelic": The Evolution of the Goedelic Languages', *Proceedings of the British Academy* 37 (1951), 71–97 (aig 92).

2. Thomas O'Rahilly, *Irish Dialects, Past and Present* (Dublin: Dublin University Press, 1988 [1932]), 164.

3. Tha iad a-nis ann an clò: Cathair Ó Dochartaigh (ed.), *Survey of the Gaelic Dialects of Scotland*, 5 vols. (Dublin: Dublin Institute for Advanced Studies, 1997).

4. Bha e dh'fhasan aig K. C. Craig nach maireann an dà 'M' a sgrìobhadh mar a chìthear san leabhar *Òrain Luaidh Màiri nighean Alasdair*.

5. Kenneth Jackson, 'The Breaking of Original Long ē in Scottish Gaelic', in James Carney and David Greene (eds.), *Celtic Studies: Essays in Memory of Angus Matheson* (London: Routledge & Kegan Paul, 1968), 65–75.

Dròbhaireachd

1. Martin Martin, *A Description of the Western Islands of Scotland* (London, 1716), 101–2.

2. A. R. B. Haldane, *The Drove Roads of Scotland* (Edinburgh: Birlinn, 1997 [1952]), 23 (bho 'The Two Drovers').

3. Calum Iain MacLeòid, *Sgial is Eachdraidh* (Glasgow: Gairm, 1977), 48.
4. John MacInnes, 'Òran nan Dròbhairean', *Scottish Studies* 9 (1965), 189–203.
5. A. R. B. Haldane, *The Drove Roads of Scotland*, 24.
6. Colm Ó Baoill and Donald MacAulay, *Scottish Gaelic Vernacular Verse to 1730: A Checklist*, Revised edition (Aberdeen: Celtic Department of the University of Aberdeen, 2001), item 429.
7. Paul Cameron, 'Perthshire Gaelic Songs', *Transactions of the Gaelic Society of Inverness* 17 (1891), 126–70 (at 156).
8. Archibald Sinclair (ed.), *An t-Òranaiche: comhchruinneachadh de dh'orain Ghàidhealach* (Glasgow: A. Sinclair, 1879), 356.
9. Donald MacPherson (ed.), *An Duanaire* (Dun-eidin: MacLachluinn, 1868), 55–7.
10. 'Àiridh Luachrach Uige'; faic Cairistìona Mhàrtainn (ed.), *Òrain an Eilein* (Skye: Taigh na Teud, 2001), 53.
11. Tha cuid dhe na briathran air an toirt sìos cearr ach a chionn is nach eil againn ach sgrìobhadh – chan e teip: chaidh sin a ghlanadh – feumar cur leis an aithris mar a tha i. Tha e soilleir gur e Trithinn a' Phùir an iomall Athaill a tha an 'Taigh na Fùr'. Agus tha puingean eile ann a tha teagmhach. 'S e Calum Mac Gill-Eathain a chlàr agus a sgrìobh an seanchas.

Highland Droving

1. Martin Martin, *A Description of the Western Islands of Scotland* (London, 1716), 101–2.
2. A. R. B. Haldane, *The Drove Roads of Scotland* (Edinburgh: Birlinn, 1997 [1952]), Chapter Eight (133–49).
3. Ibid., 24.
4. Some details in the transcription are wrong, but since the original tape-recording was destroyed, the account has to stand. 'Taigh na Fùr', for instance, is Trinafour – in Gaelic 'Trithinn a' Phùir' – in Atholl, Perthshire.
5. Eric Cregeen, 'Recollections of a Highland Drover', *Scottish Studies* 3 (1959), 143–62. Direct quotations from Dugald MacDougall are indicated.
6. Details of the drove roads are given in A.R.B. Haldane's classic *The Drove Roads of Scotland* (1952, 1968, 1973, 1995).
7. In addition to Haldane's *The Drove Roads of Scotland*, see Màiri A MacDonald, 'Drovering', *Transactions of the Gaelic Society of Inverness* 49 (1974–76), 189–97.

The Gaelic Literary Tradition

1. Kenneth Jackson, 'The Duan Albanach', *The Scottish Historical Review* 36 (1957), 125–37.
2. W. J. Watson, (ed.), *Bàrdachd Albannach O Leabhar Deadhan Lios-Móir / Scottish Verse from the Book of the Dean of Lismore*, Scottish Gaelic Texts 1 (Edinburgh: Scottish Gaelic Texts Society, 1937), 308.
3. Ibid, 60–5.
4. Robin Flower, *The Irish Tradition* (Oxford: The Claredon Press, 1947), 142.
5. Kenneth Jackson, *A Celtic Miscellany*, Revised edition (London: Penguin Books, 1971), 109.
6. Ibid., 239.
7. W. J. Watson, *Bàrdachd Albannach*, 90–3.

8. Annie MacKenzie (ed.), *Òrain Iain Luim / Songs of John MacDonald, Bard of Keppoch*, Scottish Gaelic Texts 8 (Edinburgh: Scottish Gaelic Texts Society, 1964), 222–9.
9. Alexander Carmichael, *Carmina Gadelica* vol. 5 (Edinburgh: Scottish Gaelic Texts Society, 1954), 76–9.
10. Probably the old, home-made shoe in which the thong was part of the upper.
11. Alexander Carmichael, *Carmina Gadelica* vol. 3 (Edinburgh: Scottish Gaelic Texts Society, 1954), 310; Kenneth Jackson, *A Celtic Miscellany*, 85.
12. Alexander Carmichael, *Carmina Gadelica* vol. 3 (Edinburgh: Scottish Gaelic Texts Society, 1954), 284; Kenneth Jackson, *A Celtic Miscellany*, 86.
13. W. J. Watson, *Bàrdachd Albannach*, 250–1.
14. Thomas Moffatt Murchison (ed.), *Sgrìobhaidhean Choinnich MhicLeòid / The Gaelic Prose of Kenneth MacLeod*, Scottish Gaelic Texts 16 (Edinburgh: Scottish Gaelic Texts Society, 1988), 18.
15. From oral tradition.
16. From oral tradition; an early text, and references to other variations, can be found in John L. Campbell and Francis Collinson (eds.), *Hebridean Folksongs* Vol. 1 (Oxford: Clarendon Press, 1969), 44–7, 161.
17. W. J. Watson, (ed.), *Bàrdachd Ghàidhlig: Specimens of Gaelic Poetry, 1550–1900*, 3rd edition. (Stirling: An Comunn Gàidhealach, 1959), 249–59; Colm Ó Baoill and Donald MacAulay, *Scottish Gaelic Vernacular Verse to 1730: A Checklist*, Revised edition (Aberdeen: Celtic Department of the University of Aberdeen, 2001), item 379.
18. Kenneth Jackson, 'The Folktale in Gaelic Scotland', *Proceedings of the Scottish Anthropological and Folklore Society* 4 (1952), 123–40, at 128.

Sgeul air Cù Chulainn

1. Calum Maclean, 'A Folk-variant of the Táin Bó Cúailnge from Uist', *Arv* 15 (1959), 160–81.

Twentieth-Century Recording of Scottish Gaelic Heroic Ballads

1. 'Ballad' and 'lay' are used interchangeably throughout this essay.
2. Notably by C. I. Maclean and D. A. MacDonald. Ballads were recorded from the 1940s onwards by Dr and Mrs J. L. Campbell, the pioneers of wire- and tape-recording of Gaelic song.
3. *Music from the Western Isles (Scottish Tradition 2)*, Greentrax Recordings CDTRAX9002.
4. For reasons of space alone, it has not proved possible to provide transcriptions of these examples.
5. *Rann* 'verse' may be used occasionally; rann is sometimes applied to any composition which is fairly short and not sung.
6. J. F. Campbell, *Popular Tales of the West Highlands*, 2 vols. (Edinburgh: Birlinn, 1994 [1860–2]), ii. 273.
7. Rev. Alexander Pope in a letter dated 15 November 1763 says that 'the greatest number of them have particular tunes to which they are sung'. See Henry MacKenzie (ed.), *Report of the Committee of the Highland Society of*

Scotland appointed to inquire into the Nature of the Authenticity of the Poems of Ossian (Edinburgh: Edinburgh University Press, 1805), 52–5. Quotation on 54.

8. George Broderick, 'Fin as Oshin', *Celtica* 21 (1990), 51–60.
9. Donald Meek, 'The Gaelic Ballads of Scotland: Creativity and Adaptation', in Howard Gaskill (ed.), *Ossian Revisited* (Edinburgh: Edinburgh University Press, 1991), 19–48.
10. J. F. Campbell (ed.), *Leabhar na Féinne* (London: Spottiswoode & Co., 1872).
11. Rev. Alexander Pope, *loc. cit.* Pope was writing in an area – the Whig 'Mackay's Country' (Dùthaich MhicAoidh) – where Evangelicalism was already an established tradition. Even there, however, Evangelical ministers such as the Rev. Murdoch MacDonald of Durness were patrons of the Gaelic arts.
12. John Shaw also recorded a version of it from Joe Allan MacLean of Christmas Island, Cape Breton, on April 7, 1978 (Tape 56 Item 2 of the StFX Gaelic Folklore Project Collection). The original settlers of Christmas Island were from Barra.
13. See Alexander Carmichael, *Carmina Gadelica*, 6 vols. (Edinburgh: Scottish Gaelic Texts Society, 1900–71) i. 126 ff.
14. Gerald Murphy and Eoin MacNeill (eds.), *Duanaire Finn*, 3 vols. (Dublin: Irish Texts Society, 1908–53), ii. vii ('Argument of the Poem'); ii. 2 ff (text and translation).
15. Reidar Thoralf Christiansen, *The Vikings and the Viking Wars in Irish and Gaelic Tradition* (Oslo: Dybwad, 1931), 416, 421.
16. For other translations from recent oral tradition, see Margaret Fay Shaw, *Folksongs and Folklore of South Uist*, 3rd edn. (Aberdeen: Aberdeen University Press, 1986), 31; J. L. Campbell (ed.), *Stories from South Uist (told by Angus MacLellan)*, (Edinburgh: Birlinn, 1997 [1961]), 17–9.
17. genitive of *leathad* 'slope'.
18. See James Carmichael Watson (ed.), *Òrain us Luinneagan le Màiri nighean Alasdair Ruaidh / Gaelic Songs of Mary MacLeod*, Scottish Gaelic Texts 9 (Edinburgh: Scottish Gaelic Texts Society, 1934), 125: 'This is perhaps the only name of a place in Scandinavia which survives in modern Scottish Gaelic [. . .].'
19. J. G. Campbell, *The Fians*, Waifs and Strays of Celtic Tradition 4 (London: David Nutt, 1891), 131.
20. Reidar Christiansen, *The Vikings*, 412.
21. The Irish Muircheartach who was killed in 943, fighting against the Norsemen, had the nickname 'na gcochull gcraiceann' ('of the skin coverings'); an appellation also given to characters of romance and folklore, among them the Supernatural Smith. In a waulking song the phrase 'A Muilgheartach nan cochull craicinn' is used abusively and taken by singers to refer to the Muilgheartach of the ballad. See J. L. Campbell and Francis Collinson (eds.), *Hebridean Folksongs*, 3 vols. (Oxford: Clarendon Press, 1969–81), ii. 128, 237. The Irish 'Laoidh na Mná Móire thar lear' ('The Lay of the Giantess who comes from across the sea') is relevant also.
22. The name 'Diarmad' is usually inflected in genitive case as 'Diarmaid' in Scots Gaelic.
23. Neil Ross (ed.), *Heroic Poetry from the Book of the Dean of Lismore*, Scottish Gaelic Texts Society 3 (Edinburgh: Oliver & Boyd, 1939), 221–2. The poem has been most recently edited in Donald Meek, 'The Death of Diarmaid in Scottish and Irish Tradition', *Celtica* 21 (1990), 335–61.
24. Rev. Alexander Pope, *loc. cit.*
25. Donald Meek, 'Place-names and Literature: Evidence from the Gaelic Ballads',

in Simon Taylor (ed.), *The Uses of Place-Names* (Edinburgh: Scottish Cultural Press, 1998), 147–68 (at 162–5).

26. Neil Ross, *Heroic Poetry*, 250–1.
27. Donald Meek, 'Táin Bó Fraích and other "Fráech" Texts', *Cambridge Medieval Celtic Studies* 7 (1984), 1–37; 8 (1984), 65–85.
28. See Derick Thomson, 'Bogus Gaelic Literature c. 1750 – c. 1820', *Transactions of the Gaelic Society of Glasgow* 5 (1958), 172–88 (see esp. 174–6).
29. Linda Gowans, *Am Bròn Binn: An Arthurian Ballad in Scottish Gaelic* (Eastbourne: Manor Park Press, 1992), is a thorough examination of this ballad, including a list of all known versions and sources.
30. William Gillies, 'Arthur in Gaelic Tradition Part I: Folktales and Ballads; Part II: Romances and Learned Lore', *Cambridge Medieval Celtic Studies* 2 (1981), 47–72; 3 (1982), 41–75.
31. Cited by J. F. Campbell, *Leabhar na Féinne*, xxxii.
32. Rev. Alexander Pope, *loc. cit.*
33. Henry MacKenzie, *Report of the Committee*, 29. See James Logan, *The Scottish Gaël, or, Celtic manners as preserved among the Highlanders being an historical and descriptive account of the inhabitants, antiquities and national peculiarities of Scotland, more particularly of the northern or Gaëlic parts of the country, where the singular habits of the aboriginal Celts are most tenaciously retained* by the late James Logan edited, with memoir and notes by Alex Stewart, 2 vols. (Edinburgh: John Donald, 1976 [1876]), 247.
34. See 'The Choral Tradition in Scottish Gaelic Songs' in this volume.
35. See *Waulking Songs from Barra (Scottish Tradition 3)* Greentrax Recordings CDTRAX9003; See J. L. Campbell and Francis Collinson, *Hebridean Folksongs*, iii. 40–5; 235 ff.
36. K. C. Craig (ed.), *Òrain Luaidh Màiri nighean Alasdair* (Glasgow: Alasdair Matheson, 1949), 46.
37. Frances Tolmie, *Journal of the Folk-song Society*, no. 16 (1911) (reprinted as *One Hundred and Five Songs of Occupation from the Western Isles of Scotland* (Felinfach, Dyfed: Llanerch, 1997)), 254. For 'Group III – Ancient Heroic Lays', see 245–54.
38. Demotic Gaelic versions of heroic lays do not observe, except accidentally, the strict syllabic count of literary originals. The same qualification applies, of course, to lays for which no literary originals exist; and the same is true of other forms of 'syllabic' versification in vernacular Scots Gaelic.

    Murphy argues that the syllabic verse of the literary ballads should be read 'in accordance with natural Irish word-stress'. Irish and Scots Gaelic are both 'stress-timed' languages (to use Pike's terminology) in which, by definition, stress pulses and hence the stressed syllables are isochronous. It therefore follows, if the 'syllabic' verse is performed (spoken or sung) with a pattern of stressing identical with that of speech, that there are no syllabic metres in Gaelic. There is no differentia.

    MacNeill took the view that 'all syllables, in whatsoever position, and however lightly accented in modern pronunciation, must be regarded as equally accented.' The evidence from Scots Gaelic, on the whole, bears out Murphy's theory: the opposition of stressed versus unstressed syllables, as perceived by the native speaker, is maintained. This is not to say, however, that singing 'with speech-rhythm', or *quasi parlando* singing, always exhibits a stress-pattern identical with that of speech.

    For a summary of their views, see Gerald Murphy and Eoin MacNeill (eds.), *Duanaire Finn*, iii. xc–xcii.

39. It is conceivable that a stress such as that on the second syllable of *Éirinn* 'Ireland', might derive from deibhidhe metre. ('The words *sing: liking* are an example of this form of rime in English', Ibid.).

40. Terence McCaughey, 'The performing of *Dán*', *Ériu* 35 (1984), 39–57 goes over this ground, examines the salient problems, and emphasises their implications for our claim that the survival of ballads in Scots Gaelic preserves a medieval style of performance.

41. J. L. Campbell (ed.), *Songs Remembered in Exile*, Second edition (Edinburgh: Birlinn, 1999), 181–4.

42. Text, translation and transcription of melody in *Tocher* 35 (1981), 292–7.

The Choral Tradition in Scottish Gaelic Songs

1. W. J. Watson (ed.), *Bàrdachd Gàidhlig: Specimens of Gaelic Poetry, 1550–1900*, 3rd edition (Stirling: An Comunn Gàidhealach, 1959), 246–9.

2. Archibald Sinclair (ed.), *An t-Òranaiche: comhchruinneachadh de dh'orain Ghàidhealch* (Glasgow: A. Sinclair, 1879), 175–6.

3. K. C. Craig (ed.), *Orain Luaidh Màiri nighean Alasdair* (Glasgow: Alasdair Matheson, 1949), 6–7, 35–6.

4. Francis Tolmie, *Journal of the Folk-song Society*, no. 16 (1911) (reprinted as *One Hundred and Five Songs of Occupation from the Western Isles of Scotland* (Felinfach, Dyfed: Llanerch, 1997)).

5. Donald Campbell, *A Treatise on the Language, Poetry, and Music of the Highland Clans: with illustrative Traditions* (Edinburgh, 1862), 153. 'In the absence of the chorus, which was only the case in triads, or songs of three lines, the verse was first sung by the professional vocalist, or the best amateur singer present, and then by the audience.' I assume that Campbell's 'triads' are strophic metres.

6. John Ramsay, *Scotland and Scotsmen in the eighteenth century / from the mss. of John Ramsay, esq. of Ochtertyre*, ed. Alexander Allardyce, 2 vols. (Edinburgh and London: W. Blackwood and Sons, 1888), ii. 411 fn.

7. Donald Campbell, *A Treatise*, 186.

8. That is, the repeated lines of waulking-songs suggest the further development of repeating couplets; but previously existing quatrain structures supply the teleological cause.

9. It is known to me only in the version sung by the Rev. William Matheson, who learnt it in Uist.

10. John Gillies (ed.), *Sean dain agus orain Ghàidhealach* (Peairt, 1786).

11. John Ramsay, *Scotland and Scotsmen*, ii. 415–6.

12. Patrick MacFarlane (ed.), *Co'-chruinneachadh de dh'òrain agus de luinneagaibh thaghta Ghàe'lach* (Dun-eudainn: T. Stiùbhart, 1813).

13. Kenneth H. Jackson, *Studies in Early Celtic Nature Poetry* (Cambridge: The University Press, 1935), 153.

14. Two important early collections have been discovered and printed since this article was originally published: the Donald MacCormick collection (published as J. L. Campbell and Francis Collinson (eds.), *Hebridean Folksongs Vol. 1* (Oxford: Clarendon Press, 1969)), consisting entirely of waulking-songs, and the Hugh MacDiarmid collection (published as Derick Thomson (ed.), *The MacDiarmid MS Anthology*, Scottish Gaelic Texts 17 (Edinburgh: Scottish Gaelic Texts Society, 1992)), which contains several choral songs.

15. Seán Ó Tuama, *An Grá in Amhráin na nDaoine* (Baile Átha Cliath: An Clóchomhar, 1960).
16. A. and A. MacDonald (eds.), *The MacDonald Collection of Gaelic Poetry* (Inverness: Northern Counties Newspaper and Printing and Publishing Co., 1911), xi-xii.
17. Máirín O Daly, 'The Metrical Dindshenchas' in James Carney (ed.), *Early Irish Poetry* (Cork: The Mercier Press, 1965), 59–72 (at 66).
18. For the whole poem (with English translation), see Edward Gwynn (ed.), *The Metrical Dindshenchas Part III*, Royal Irish Academy Todd Lecture Series Vol. X (Dublin: Royal Irish Academy, 1913), 1–25.
19. A study of fundamental importance is D. A. Binchy, 'The Fair of Tailtiu and the Feast of Tara' *Ériu* 18 (1958), 113–38.

The Oral Tradition in Scottish Gaelic Poetry

1. Raonuill MacDomhnuill (ed.), *Comh-chruinneachidh Orannaigh Gaidhealach* (Duneidinn, 1776), v-viii.
2. See Wilson McLeod, *Divided Gaels: Gaelic Cultural Identities in Scotland and Ireland c. 1200–c.1650* (Oxford: Oxford University Press, 2004), Chapter Two, for the most recent discussion of this issue.
3. John W. M. Bannerman, 'The King's Poet and the Inauguration of Alexander III', *The Scottish Historical Review* 68 (1989), 120–49.
4. Angus Matheson, 'Bishop Carswell', *Transactions of the Gaelic Society of Inverness* 42 (1953–59), 182–205 (at 203); Wilson McLeod, *Divided Gaels*, 69.
5. W. J. Watson (ed.), *Bàrdachd Ghàidhlig: Specimens of Gaelic Poetry, 1550–1900*, 3rd edn. (Stirling: An Comunn Gàidhealach, 1959), xlv-liv.
6. John MacInnes, 'Notes on Mary MacLeod', *Scottish Gaelic Studies* 11 (1966), 3–23 (at 22–3).
7. Donald Mackintosh, 'Notes', *Scottish Gaelic Studies* 6 (1949), 21–6 (at 23–6).
8. Calvert Watkins, 'Indo-European Metrics and Archaic Irish Verse.' *Celtica* 6 (1963), 194–249 (at 238).
9. R. I. Best, O. Bergin and M. A. O'Brien (eds.), *The Book of Leinster* Vol. 1 (Dublin: Dublin Institute for Advanced Studies, 1954), 175–6.
10. 'Baird is Bleidirean' in this volume; John Shaw, 'Scottish Gaelic Traditions of the Cliar Sheanchain', in C. Byrne, Margaret Harry and P. Ó Soadhail (eds.), *Celtic Languages and Celtic Peoples: Proceedings of the Second North American Congress of Celtic Studies* (Halifax: St Mary's University, 1992), 141–58.
11. Martin Martin, *A Description of the Western Islands of Scotland* (London, 1716), 200.
12. Patrick MacDonald, *A Collection of Highland Vocal Airs* (Skye: Taigh na Teud, 2000 [1784]), 10.
13. James Ross, 'The Sub-Literary Tradition in Scottish Gaelic Song-Poetry. Part I. Poetic Metres and Song Metres', *Éigse* 7 (1953–55), 217–39.
14. Raonuill MacDomhnuill, *Comh-chruinneachidh*, 23; W. J. Watson, *Bàrdachd Ghàidhlig*, 221–3.
15. William Matheson (ed.), *Òrain Iain Mhic Fhearchair a Bha 'na Bhàrd aig Sir Seumas MacDhomhnaill / The Songs of John MacCodrum: Bard to Sir James MacDonald of Sleat*, Scottish Gaelic Texts 2 (Edinburgh: Scottish Gaelic Texts Society, 1938), 256–7.
16. Colm Ó Baoill and Donald MacAulay, *Scottish Gaelic Vernacular Verse to*

1730: A Checklist Revised edition (Aberdeen: Celtic Department of the University of Aberdeen), item 382.

17. Joseph Bain (ed.), *Calendar of Documents relating to Scotland preserved in Her Majesty's Public Record Office, London* (Edinburgh: H.M. General Register House, 1881–1888), 475.
18. Seán Ó Tuama, *An Grá in Amhráin na nDaoine* (Baile Átha Cliath: An Clóchomhar, 1960), 215.
19. Kenneth Jackson, 'Incremental Repetition in the Early Welsh Englyn.' *Speculum* 16 (1941), 304–21 (at 315).
20. W. P. Ker, *Collected Essays*, ed. Charles Whibley, 2 vols. (London: Macmillan and Co., 1925), ii. 95.
21. William Cramond (ed.), *The Records of Elgin* Vol. 2 (Aberdeen: New Spalding Club, 1908), 40.
22. Douglas Young, 'Was Homer an Illiterate Improviser?' *The Minnesota Review* 5 (1965), 65–75.
23. W. J. Watson, *Bàrdachd Ghàidhlig*, lines 4696–9.
24. Ibid., lines 6251–2.
25. Hew Morrison (ed.), *Songs and Poems in the Gaelic Language* (Edinburgh: n.p., 1899), 50.

Gaelic Song and the Dance

1. W. P. Ker, *Collected Essays*, ed. Charles Whibley, 2 vols. (London: Macmillan and Co., 1925), 'Danish Ballads'. ii.63–115.
2. Seán Ó Tuama, *An Grá in Amhráin na nDaoine* (Baile Átha Cliath: An Clóchomhar, 1960).
3. David Daiches (ed.), *The New Companion to Scottish Culture* (Edinburgh: Polygon, 1993), 'Dance' by R. N. Goss.
4. Alexander Carmichael, *Carmina Gadelica* Vol. 1 (Edinburgh: Scottish Gaelic Texts Society, 1900), 206–7; J.F. and T.M. Flett, 'Some Hebridean Folk Dances', *Journal of the English Folk Dance and Song Society* 7 (1953), 113–27; J.F. and T.M. Flett, 'Dramatic Jigs in Scotland', *Folk-lore* 67 (1956), 84–96; Francis Collinson, *The Traditional and National Music of Scotland* (London: Routledge & Kegan Paul, 1966), 99; Derick Thomson (ed.), *The Companion to Gaelic Scotland* (Glasgow: Gairm, 1994), 'Dance in Gaelic Society'.
5. Patrick McDonald, *A Collection of Highland Vocal Airs* (Skye: Taigh na Teud, 2000 [1784]), 10.
6. J. L. Campbell and Francis Collinson (eds.), *Hebridean Folksongs*, 3 vols. (Oxford: Clarendon Press, 1969–81), i. 28; iii. 6–7.
7. Ibid., i. 6.
8. John Owen Ward (ed.), *The Oxford Companion to Music* Tenth edition (Oxford: Oxford University Press, 1970), 'Dance'.
9. There is much material from English and Continental European sources to demonstrate this; evidence that similar rites were practiced in graveyards in Scotland can be found in George Emmerson, *A Social History of Scottish Dance* (Montreal: McGill-Queen's University Press, 1972), 19.
10. Anne Grant, *Essays on the Superstitions of the Highlanders of Scotland* (New York: Eastburn, Kirk, & Co., 1813), 98–9. I owe this and the following two references to my friend Dr Michael Newton.
11. Thomas Garnett, *Observations on a Tour through the highlands and part of the Western Isles*, 2 vols. (London, 1811), i.119.

12. Smith, John, *Galic antiquities: consisting of a history of the Druids, particularly of those of Caledonia; a dissertation on the authenticity of the poems of Ossian* (Edinburgh: 1780), 56.

13. Joseph Bain (ed.), *Calendar of Documents relating to Scotland preserved in Her Majesty's Public Record Office, London* (Edinburgh: H.M. General Register House, 1881–1888). Reference to a similar custom appears in the *Chronicles of the Kings of Man and the Isles* describing the arrival of Godred in Dublin in 1144 (1154).

14. Colm Ó Baoill and Donald MacAulay, *Scottish Gaelic Vernacular Verse to 1730: A Checklist* Revised edition (Aberdeen: Celtic Department of the University of Aberdeen), item 382.

15. Nora Chadwick, 'The Story of Macbeth', *Scottish Gaelic Studies* 6 (1949), 189–211.

16. E. G. Quin (ed.), *Dictionary of the Irish Language* (Dublin: Royal Irish Academy, 1983), 'aidbse', 'aidbsiu', 'aidbsiugad'.

17. Calum Johnston provided the melody and syllables of one: it begins 'pill il il iù'. See Frances Collinson, *Traditional and National Music*, 115–6, where the melody is transcribed.

18. See now Colm Ó Baoill, 'Moving in Gaelic Musical Circles: The root *lu-* in music terminology', *Scottish Gaelic Studies* 19 (1999), 172–94.

19. Personal communication.

20. Frances Tolmie, *Journal of the Folk-song Society*, no. 16 (1911) (reprinted as *One Hundred and Five Songs of Occupation from the Western Isles of Scotland* (Felinfach, Dyfed: Llanerch, 1997)), 234–5.

The Panegyric Code in Gaelic Poetry and its Historical Background

1. Some of the results of this enquiry are in a doctoral thesis 'Gaelic Poetry', University of Edinburgh, 1975.

2. Colm Ó Baoill (ed.), *Iain Dubh* (Aberdeen: An Clò Gàidhealach, 1994), poem 5; Ronald Black (ed.), *An Lasair / Anthology of 18th Century Scottish Gaelic Verse* (Edinburgh: Birlinn, 2001), poem 10.

3. Wilson McLeod, *Divided Gaels: Gaelic Cultural Identities in Scotland and Ireland c. 1200–c.1650* (Oxford: Oxford University Press, 2004).

4. I owe this phrase to Prof. John MacQueen.

5. Andrew Simmons (ed.), *Burt's Letters from the North of Scotland* (Edinburgh: Birlinn, 1998 [1754]), 192.

6. John W. M. Bannerman, 'The King's Poet and the Inauguration of Alexander III', *The Scottish Historical Review* 68 (1989), 120–49.

7. Kenneth Jackson, 'The Duan Albanach', *The Scottish Historical Review* 36 (1957), 125–37.

8. W. J. Watson (ed.), *Bàrdachd Albannach O Leabhar Deadhan Lios-Móir / Scottish Verse from the Book of the Dean of Lismore*, Scottish Gaelic Texts 1 (Edinburgh: Scottish Gaelic Texts Society, 1937), 214–6.

9. Duncan Campbell, *Reminiscences and Reflections of an Octogenarian Highlander* (Inverness: Northern Counties Publishing Company, 1910), 136–7.

10. See R. Andrew MacDonald, 'Treachery in the remotest territories of Scotland: Northern resistance to the Canmore dynasty, 1130–1230', *Canadian Journal of History* 33 (August 1999), 161–92; 'Rebels without a Cause? The Relations of

Fergus of Galloway and Somerled of Argyll with the Scottish Kings, 1153–1164', in E. J. Cowan and R. Andrew McDonald (eds.) *Alba: Celtic Scotland in the Medieval Era* (East Linton: Tuckwell Press, 2000), 166–86.

11. W. R. Kermack, *The Scottish Highlands: A Short History* (Edinburgh: Johnston & Bacon, 1957), 47.

12. M. O. Anderson (ed.), *A Scottish chronicle known as the Chronicle of Holyrood* (Edinburgh: Scottish Historical Society, 1938); William Matheson, 'Traditions of the Mackenzies', *Transactions of the Gaelic Society of Inverness* 39–40 (1949), 193–228 (at 215 ff).

13. Ibid.

14. Document of credence given by the Islesmen to the Commissioners empowered to treat with Henry VIII for aid, 1545. Quoted in G. A. Hayes-McCoy, *Scots Mercenary Forces in Ireland (1565–1603)* (Dublin: Burns, Oates & Washbourne, 1937), 1.

15. Ibid., 29.

16. John W. M. Bannerman, 'The Lordship of the Isles' in Jennifer M. Brown (ed.), *Scottish Society in the Fifteenth Century* (London: Edward Arnold, 1977), 209–40.

17. W. J. Watson, 'Classic Gaelic Poetry of Panegyric in Scotland', *Transactions of the Gaelic Society of Inverness* 29 (1914–19), 194–234 (esp. 215).

18. William Gillies, 'Some Aspects of Campbell History', *Transactions of the Gaelic Society of Inverness* 50 (1978), 256–295 (276–85); Wilson McLeod, *Divided Gaels*, 214–15.

19. W. J. Watson, *Bardachd Albannach*, 290. For the texts see 6–13, 158–165. See also Wilson McLeod, *Divided Gaels*, 27–9.

20. Francis Collinson, *The Traditional and National Music of Scotland* (London: Routledge & Kegan Paul, 1966), 50.

21. Alexander MacBain and Revd John Kennedy (eds.), *Reliquiae Celticae: Texts, Papers and Studies in Gaelic Literature and Philology Left by the Late Rev. Alexander Cameron*, 2 vols. (Inverness: Northern Counties Newspaper and Printing and Publishing Co., 1894), ii. 156.

22. Most, though not all, of this evidence is in Irish sources and cannot be applied to the Scottish situation without qualification. The separate development of poetry and orders of poets in the two countries may be seen in the fact that in modern Irish Gaelic the common word for poet is 'file', not 'bard'.

23. W. J. Watson (ed.), *Bàrdachd Ghàidhlig: Specimens of Gaelic Poetry, 1550–1900*, 3rd edn. (Stirling: An Comunn Gàidhealach, 1959), 249–59.

24. Ibid., xlv-liv.

25. Derick Thomson, 'Scottish Gaelic Folk-Poetry Ante 1650', *Scottish Gaelic Studies* 8 (1955), 1–17 (at 17); Michael Newton, *Bho Chluaidh gu Calasraid / From the Clyde to Callander* (Stornoway: Acair, 1999), 212.

26. W. J. Watson, *Bàrdachd Ghàidhlig*, 239–41.

27. James Carmichael Watson (ed.), *Òrain us Luinneagan le Màiri nighean Alasdair Ruaidh / Gaelic Songs of Mary MacLeod*, Scottish Gaelic Texts 9 (Edinburgh: Scottish Gaelic Texts Society, 1934).

28. W. J. Watson, 'Classic Gaelic Poetry', 217.

29. My friend Mr Ronald Black strongly favours the former.

30. *Celtic Magazine* 2 (1877), 484–5. See also Alasdair Maclean Sinclair, (ed.), *The Gaelic Bards from 1411 to 1715* (Charlottetown: The Examiner Pub. Co., 1890), 27–8.

31. Colm Ó Baoill and Donald MacAulay, *Scottish Gaelic Vernacular Verse to*

1730: A Checklist Revised edition (Aberdeen: Celtic Department of the University of Aberdeen), item 344.

32. Patrick Turner (ed.), *Comhchruinneacha do dh'òrain taghta Ghàidhealach* (Edinburgh, 1813), 264 ff.

33. The love song in Raonuill Macdomhnuill (ed.), *Comh-chruinneachidh Orannaigh Gaidhealach* (Duneidinn, 1776), 325–6 is one exception, if it is ante-1745, as it probably is.

34. These functions can be described in formal logical terms but to do so here would introduce quite unnecessary complexities.

35. J. L. Campbell (ed.), *Òrain Ghàidhealach mu Bhliadhna Theàrlaich / Highland Songs of the Forty-Five*, Scottish Gaelic Texts 15 (Edinburgh: Scottish Gaelic Texts Society, 1984 [1933]), 176–85.

36. Thomas Sinton (ed.), *The Poetry of Badenoch* (Inverness: Northern Counties Newspaper and Printing and Publishing Co., 1906), 46.

37. Annie Mackenzie (ed.), *Òrain Iain Luim / Songs of John MacDonald, Bard of Keppoch*, Scottish Gaelic Texts 8 (Edinburgh: Scottish Gaelic Texts Society, 1964), 44–7.

38. Òran, amhrán, abhran, etc. are in effect only variants. In some quarters it seems to be thought that Òran alone is generically 'song'.

39. For remarks on these classes see William Matheson (ed.), *An Clàrsair Dall: Òrain Ruaidhri Mhic Mhuirich agus a Chuid Chiùil / The Blind Harper: The Songs of Roderick Morrison and his Music*, Scottish Gaelic Texts 12 (Edinburgh: Scottish Gaelic Texts Society, 1970), 149–63.

40. Gerard Murphy, *Early Irish Metrics* (Dublin: Royal Irish Academy, 1961), 24.

41. Ronald Black, *An Lasair*, 144–9.

42. William Matheson, *An Clàrsair Dall*, 58–73.

43. Ronald Black, *An Lasair*, 28–37.

44. W. J. Watson, *Bàrdachd Ghàidhlig*, 'Dubhghall' in the glossary.

45. J. L. Campbell, *Òrain Ghàidhealach*, 72–85.

46. Patrick Turner, *Comhchruinneacha do dh'òrain*, 13–18.

47. Raonuill Macdomhnuill, *Comh-chruinneachidh Orannaigh*, 332.

48. From the well-known 'Mo nighean dubh tha bòidheach dubh'; there is a version in Archibald Sinclair (ed.), *An t-Òranaiche: comhchruinneachadh de dh'orain Ghàidhealch* (Glasgow: A. Sinclair, 1879), 230. The same 'rule' is found elsewhere, e.g. in Irish keening.

49. Ibid., 224.

50. Colm Ó Baoill and Donald MacAulay, *Scottish Gaelic Vernacular Verse*, item 391.

51. Ibid., item 338; W. J. Watson, *Bàrdachd Ghàidhlig*, 172–6.

52. Colm Ó Baoill and Donald MacAulay, *Scottish Gaelic Vernacular Verse*, item 442; W. J. Watson, *Bàrdachd Ghàidhlig*, 209–11.

53. Colm Ó Baoill and Donald MacAulay, *Scottish Gaelic Vernacular Verse*, item 51; W. J. Watson, *Bàrdachd Ghàidhlig*, 179–181.

54. Colm Ó Baoill and Donald MacAulay, *Scottish Gaelic Vernacular Verse*, item 171; W. J. Watson, *Bàrdachd Ghàidhlig*, 233–4.

55. Colm Ó Baoill and Donald MacAulay, *Scottish Gaelic Vernacular Verse*, item 184.

56. W. J. Watson, *Bàrdachd Ghàidhlig*, 176–8.

57. 'Pre-Romantic' here is descriptive not evaluative.

58. W. J. Watson, *Bàrdachd Ghàidhlig*, 183–6.

59. Colm Ó Baoill and Donald MacAulay, *Scottish Gaelic Vernacular Verse*, item 167; W. J. Watson, *Bàrdachd Ghàidhlig*, 119–23.

60. William Matheson, *An Clàrsair Dall*, lxv.
61. Colm Ó Baoill and Donald MacAulay, *Scottish Gaelic Vernacular Verse*, item 379; W. J. Watson, *Bàrdachd Ghàidhlig*, 249–59.
62. Colm Ó Baoill and Donald MacAulay, *Scottish Gaelic Vernacular Verse*, item 414; W. J. Watson, *Bàrdachd Ghàidhlig*, 246–9.
63. Colm Ó Baoill and Donald MacAulay, *Scottish Gaelic Vernacular Verse*, item 382.
64. W. J. Watson, 'Unpublished Gaelic Poetry – III', *Scottish Gaelic Studies* 2 (1927–8), 75–91 (at 76).
65. Patrick Turner, *Comhchruinneacha do dh'òrain*, 185.
66. W. J. Watson, 'Classic Gaelic Poetry', 217.
67. A. O. H. Jarman, *The Legend of Merlin* (Cardiff: University of Wales Press, 1960).

Sùil air Bardachd na Gàidhlig

1. W. J. Watson, 'Unpublished Gaelic Poetry – III', *Scottish Gaelic Studies* 2 (1927–8), 75–91 (aig 84).
2. W. J. Watson (ed.), *Bàrdachd Albannach O Leabhar Deadhan Lios-Móir*, Scottish Gaelic Texts 1 (Edinburgh: Scottish Gaelic Texts Society, 1937), 220.
3. Ibid., 226.
4. Donald Mackintosh, 'Notes', *Scottish Gaelic Studies* 6 (1949), 21–6 (aig 23–6).
5. W. J. Watson (ed.), *Bàrdachd Ghàidhlig: Specimens of Gaelic Poetry, 1550–1900*, 3rd edition. (Stirling: An Comunn Gàidhealach, 1959), xlv-liv.
6. Colm Ó Baoill and Donald MacAulay, *Scottish Gaelic Vernacular Verse to 1730: A Checklist,* Revised edition (Aberdeen: Celtic Department of the University of Aberdeen, 2001), òran 388.
7. Martin MacGregor, ' "Surely one of the greatest poems ever made in Britain": the lament for Griogair Ruadh MacGregor of Glen Strae and its historical background', in E. J. Cowan and D. Gifford (eds.), *The Polar Twins* (Edinburgh: John Donald, 1999), 114–53.
8. John L. Campbell and Francis Collinson (eds.), *Hebridean Folksongs* 3 vols. (Oxford: Clarendon Press, 1969–81), i. 44–7, 161.
9. W. J. Watson, *Bàrdachd Ghàidhlig*, 243.
10. Colm Ó Baoill and Donald MacAulay, *Scottish Gaelic Vernacular Verse*, òran 405.
11. Ibid., òran 430.
12. Ibid., òran 382.
13. Alexander Carmichael, *Carmina Gadelica* vol. 5 (Edinburgh: Scottish Gaelic Texts Society, 1954), 12
14. Ibid., 66, 72–4.
15. Ibid., 78.
16. *cf.* K. C. Craig (ed.), *Òrain Luaidh Màiri nighean Alasdair* (Glasgow: Alasdair Matheson, 1949), 10.
17. W. J. Watson, *Bàrdachd Ghàidhlig*, 249–59; Colm Ó Baoill and Donald MacAulay, *Scottish Gaelic Vernacular Verse*, òran 379.
18. John MacKenzie (ed*.), Sàr Obair nam Bàrd Gàelach; or, The beauties of Gaelic poetry and lives of the Highland bards* (Glasgow: McGregor, Polson & Co., 1841), 97.

Baird is Bleidirean

1. Henry MacKenzie (ed.) *Report of the Committee of the Highland Society of Scotland appointed to inquire into the Nature of the Authenticity of the Poems of Ossian* . . . (Edinburgh: Edinburgh University Press, 1805), 275–7.
2. Ibid., 38–43.
3. J. L. Campbell and D. S. Thomson, *Edward Lhuyd in the Scottish Highlands 1699–1700* (Oxford: Claredon Press, 1963), 34.
4. Tha an t-ainm 'creacaire' san litir aig Garden: faic nota 5; a thaobh 'sracaire', faic nota 34.
5. C. A. Gordon, 'Letter to John Aubrey from Professor James Garden', *Scottish Gaelic Studies* 8 (1958), 18–26; Michael Hunter, *The Occult Laboratory: Magic, Science and Second Sight in Late Seventeenth-Century Scotland* (Woodbridge: The Boydell Press, 2001), 125–6.
6. Tha a' bhardachd aig Eachann Bacach agus iomradh coilionta air a' bhard fhéin aig Colm Ó Baoill ann an *Eachann Bacach agus Bàird Eile de Chloinn Ghill-Eathain*, (Edinburgh: Scottish Gaelic Texts Society, 1979).
7. Faic Aonghus MacMhathain, 'Aos Dàna (I)', *Gairm* 8 (1954), 343–7.
8. Faic W. J. Watson (ed.), *Bàrdachd Ghàidhlig: Specimens of Gaelic Poetry, 1550–1900*, 3rd edition. (Stirling: An Comunn Gàidhealach, 1959): 'An duanag ullamh', 259–62; 'Cumha Iarla Earra-Ghàidheal', 172–6; 'Roinn do Alasdair mac Colla', 209–11; 'Rainn gearradh-arm', 61–2 (tha am meadar corrach) faic Angus MacLeod (ed.), *Òrain Dhonnchaidh Bhàin* (Edinburgh: Scottish Gaelic Texts Society, 1952), 234 is 503. Tha a' bhardachd aig MacBeathaig aig William Matheson (ed.), *Òrain Iain Mhic Fhearchair a Bha 'na Bhàrd aig Sir Seumas MacDhomhnaill*, (Edinburgh: Scottish Gaelic Texts Society, 1938), 256–7.
9. W. J. Watson, *Bàrdachd Gàidhlig*, xlv et seq.
10. Am beulaithris. A thaobh 1427 is 1431, faic F. Collinson, *The Bagpipe* (London and Boston: Routledge & Kegan Paul, 1975); a thaobh 1429, faic J. R. N. Macphail (ed.), *Highland Papers Vol. III* (Edinburgh: Scottish History Society, 1920), 11, 19.
11. Am beulaithris.
12. Martin Martin, *A Description of the Western Islands of Scotland* (London, 1716), 106–107.
13. Faic W. B. Lockwood, 'Chr. Matras' Studies on the Gaelic Element in Faroese: Conclusions and Results', *Scottish Gaelic Studies* 13 (1978), 112–26; gu sonraichte 116–7.
14. Edward Dwelly, *The Illustrated Gaelic-English Dictionary* (Glasgow, 5th edition. 1949).
15. Alexander Carmichael, *Carmina Gadelica Vol. VI: Indexes*, ed. Angus Matheson (Edinburgh: Scottish Gaelic Texts Society, 1971), 133.
16. A. and A. MacDonald (ed.), *The MacDonald Collection of Gaelic Poetry* (Inverness: Northern Counties Newspaper and Printing and Publishing Co., 1911), 316–17.
17. À dùthchas an teaghlaich.
18. William Matheson (ed.), *An Clàrsair Dall: Òrain Ruaidhri Mhic Mhuirich agus a Chuid Chiùil* (Edinburgh: Scottish Gaelic Texts Society), xliv.
19. Faic W. J. Watson, 'Cliar Sheanchain', *The Celtic Review* 4 (1919), 80–88 (aig 80). Se 'Clearsheanachi', gun alt, a th'aig Garden, le 'Sheanachis' 'ane historie' air a mheas 'na bhun dha. Tha caochladh mhìneachaidhean aig an t-sluagh chon an latha an-diugh.

20. À dùthchas an teaghlaich; faic cuideachd John Shaw, 'What Alexander Car-michael Did Not Print: The *Cliar Sheanchain*, 'Clanranald's Fool' and Related Traditions', *Béaloideas* 70 (2002), 99–126.

21. Donald M'Nicol, *Remarks on Dr. Samuel Johnson's Journey to the Hebrides* (New York: Garland Publishing, 1974 [1779]), 436.

22. W. J. Watson (ed.), *Bàrdachd Albannach O Leabhar Deadhan Lios-Móir*, Scottish Gaelic Texts 1 (Edinburgh: Scottish Gaelic Texts Society, 1937), 66–81.

23. Alexander Carmichael, *Carmina Gadelica Vol. VI*, 35–6.

24. W. J. Watson, *Bàrdachd Albannach*, 14–21.

25. William Gillies, 'The Gaelic Poems of Sir Duncan Campbell of Glenorchy (II)' *Scottish Gaelic Studies* 13 (1977), 236–88; faic gu sonraichte 267 is 271.

26. William Matheson, *Òrain Iain Mhic Fhearchair*, 188.

27. W. J. Watson, *Bàrdachd Ghàidhlig*, 20.

28. Malcolm Maclennan, *A Pronouncing and Etymological Dictionary of the Gaelic Language* (Edinburgh: J. Grant, 1925).

29. Alexander MacBain, *An Etymological Dictionary of the Gaelic Language* (Inverness: Northern Counties Printing and Publishing Co., 1896).

30. Andrew Simmons, (ed.), *Burt's Letters from the North of Scotland* (Edinburgh: Birlinn, 1998 [1754]), 220.

31. James Logan, *The Scottish Gaël, or, Celtic manners as preserved among the Highlanders being an historical and descriptive account of the inhabitants, antiquities and national peculiarities of Scotland, more particularly of the north-ern or Gaëlic parts of the country, where the singular habits of the aboriginal Celts are most tenaciously retained by the late James Logan edited, with memoir and notes by Alex Stewart*, 2 vols. (Edinburgh: John Donald, 1976 [1876]), i. 180.

32. J. L. Campbell and Francis Collinson (eds.), *Hebridean Folksongs*, 3 vols. (Oxford: Clarendon Press, 1969–81), ii. 156.

33. James Carmichael Watson (ed.), *Òrain us Luinneagan le Màiri nighean Alasdair Ruaidh* (Edinburgh: Scottish Gaelic Texts Society, 1934), 6.

34. Aig MacBain, *An Etymological Dictionary*, gheabhar 'bleideir, coward; from Norse bley?i', cowardice and Sc[ots] blate (?)'.

35. Faic W. J. Watson, *Bàrdachd Albannach*, 2 is xvi.

Gaelic Poetry in the Nineteenth Century

1. W. J. Watson (ed.), *Bàrdachd Ghàidhlig: Specimens of Gaelic Poetry, 1550–1900*, 3rd edn. (Stirling: An Comunn Gàidhealach, 1959), xxxiii, xix.

2. For another reassessment of the poetry of this era, see the Introduction of Donald Meek (ed.) *Caran an t-Saoghail / The Wiles of the World, Anthology of 19th Century Scottish Gaelic Verse* (Edinburgh: Birlinn, 2003).

3. David Stewart, *Sketches of the character, manners, and present state of the Highlanders of Scotland with details of the military service of the Highland regiments*, 2 vols. (Edinburgh, 1822), i. 467.

4. Traditional; there are several variants.

5. Traditional; there are several variants.

6. Margaret Fay Shaw, *Folksongs and Folklore of South Uist*, 3rd edn. (Aberdeen: Aberdeen University Press, 1986), 92–3.

7. Ibid., 94–5.

8. 'plague', 'malison', etc. are conventional renderings.

9. Thomas Sinton (ed.), *The Poetry of Badenoch* (Inverness: Northern Counties Newspaper and Printing and Publishing Co., 1906), 345.

10. See Roderick MacLeod, 'Ministearain an Arain', *Transactions of the Gaelic Society of Inverness* 52 (1980–2), 222–42.
11. John Matheson, *Òran na h-Eaglais* (Edinburgh, 1846).
12. (Rev.) John MacInnes, 'Gaelic Spiritual Verse', *Transactions of the Gaelic Society of Inverness* 46 (1969–70), 308–52 (at 329).
13. Ibid., 330.
14. Ibid., 336.
15. Iain Domhnallach, *Marbhrainn a Rinn air Diadhairibh Urramach Nach Maireann agus Dàna Spioradail eile* (Edinburgh: MacLachlan & Stewart, 1885 [1848]), 124.
16. This became an organised and politicised movement in the 1880s.
17. Derick Thomson, *An Introduction to Gaelic Poetry*, 2nd edition (Edinburgh: Edinburgh University Press, 1990), 222.
18. Margaret MacDonell (ed.), *The Emigrant Experience* (Toronto: University of Toronto Press, 1982), 20–7.
19. Derick Thomson, *An Introduction*, 240.
20. Ibid., 241.
21. Kenneth Jackson, *A Celtic Miscellany*, Revised edition (London: Penguin Books, 1971), 267.
22. Virginia Blankenhorn, 'Traditional and Bogus Elements in "MacCrimmon's Lament"', *Scottish Studies* 22 (1978), 45–67.

A Radically Traditional Voice: Sorley MacLean and the Evangelical Background

1. Somhairle MacGill-eain, *Ris a' Bhruthaich: The Criticism and Prose Writings of Sorley MacLean*, ed. William Gillies (Stornoway: Acair, 1985), 114.
2. Ibid., 108–9.
3. John Herdman, 'The poetry of Sorley Maclean: a non-Gael's view', *Lines Review* 61 (1977), 25.
4. Somhairle MacGill-eain, *Ris a' Bhruthaich*, 111.

Language, Metre and Diction in the Poetry of Sorley MacLean

1. Somhairle MacGill-eain, *Ris a' Bhruthaich: The Criticism and Prose Writings of Sorley MacLean*, ed. William Gillies (Stornoway: Acair, 1985), 76.
2. Sorley MacLean, 'Some Gaelic and Non-Gaelic Influences On Myself', in Robert O'Driscoll (ed.), *The Celtic Consciousness* (Toronto: The Dolmen Press, 1981), 499–501 (at 500).
3. Somhairle MacGill-eain, *Ris a' Bhruthaich*, 75–6.
4. John Mackenzie (ed.), *Sàr Obair nam Bàrd Gàelach; or, The beauties of Gaelic poetry and lives of the Highland bards* (Glasgow: McGregor, Polson & Co., 1841), 56–7.
5. John Fraser, 'Varia 2. leug "(precious) stone"', *Scottish Gaelic Studies* 5 (1942), 161.

Religion in Gaelic Society

1. The arguments are set out in detail in R. W. Chambers, *On the Continuity of English Prose from Alfred to More and his School* (London: Early English Text Society, 1932).
2. John Carey, *King of Mysteries: Early Irish Religious Writings* (Dublin: Four Courts Press, 2000), 130–3.
3. Ibid., 136–8.
4. Ibid., 129.
5. Alexander Carmichael, *Carmina Gadelica*, 6 vols. (Edinburgh: Scottish Gaelic Texts Society, 1900–71), ii. 24–24; v.174–175.
6. G. S. MacEoin, 'Invocation of the Forces of Nature in the Loricae', *Studia Hibernica* 2 (1962), 212–7; 'Some Icelandic Loricae', *Studia Hibernica* 3 (1963), 143–54. MacEoin suggests that the Icelandic loricae ('Breastplates') originated 'among bilingual Christian Norsemen in Ireland or Gaelic Scotland'. In this connection the significance of 'Tàladh Dhomhnaill Ghuirm' is obvious. See also the list of editions of charms in John Carey, *King*, 129 note 8.
7. Thomas Clancy (ed.), *The Triumph Tree: Scotland's Earliest Poetry, 550–1350* (Edinburgh: Canongate Classics, 1998), 109 (slightly adapted).
8. Donald MacLean, *The Law of the Lord's Day in the Celtic Church* (Edinburgh: T. & T. Clark, 1926).
9. Alexander Carmichael, *Carmina*, i.216–23.
10. Ibid., 126–7.
11. Kenneth H. Jackson, *The International Popular Tale and Early Welsh Tradition* (Cardiff: University of Wales Press, 1961), 30–1.
12. John Carey, *A Single Ray Of The Sun: Religious Speculation In Early Ireland* (Andover: Celtic Studies Publications, 1999), Chapter One.
13. William Fergusson, 'Religion and the Massacre of Glencoe', *Scottish Historical Review* 46 (1967), 82–87; 47 (1968), 203–9. This demonstrates that they were Episcopalians as their own tradition asserts also.
14. Several important studies of this sort have since appeared: Terence McCaughey, 'Protestantism and Scottish Highland Culture' in James Mackey (ed.) *An Introduction to Celtic Christianity* (Edinburgh: T&T Clark, 1989), 172–205; Jane Dawson, 'Calvinism and the Gaidhealtachd in Scotland' in Andrew Pettegree, Alastair Duke and Gillian Lewis (eds.) *Calvinism in Europe, 1540–1620* (Cambridge: Cambridge University Press, 1994), 231–251; James Kirk (ed.), *The Church in the Highlands* (Edinburgh: Scottish Church History Society, 1998).
15. John Carey, *A Single Ray*, 2.
16. 'Movement' and 'Revival' are both used.
17. Duncan Campbell, *Reminiscences and Reflections of an Octogenarian Highlander* (Inverness: Northern Counties Publishing Company, 1910), 80.
18. William Gillies, 'A Poem on the Downfall of the Gaoidhil', *Eigse* 13 (1969–70), 203–10.
19. I am indebted to my friend Prof. Donald Meek for this information.
20. See discussion in Donald Meek, 'The pulpit and the pen: clergy, orality and print in the Scottish Gaelic world' in Adam Fox and Daniel Wolf (eds.) *The Spoken Word: Oral Culture in Britain, 1500–1850* (Manchester: Manchester University Press, 2003), 84–118.
21. Somhairle MacGill-eain, *Ris a' Bhruthaich: The Criticism and Prose Writings of Sorley MacLean*, ed. William Gillies (Stornoway: Acair, 1985), 108.

The Seer in Gaelic Tradition

1. This is the older form: Scots Gaelic 'filidh'.
2. William Matheson, 'The MacLeods of Lewis', *Transactions of the Gaelic Society of Inverness* 51 (1978–80), 320–38 (esp. 336).
3. A. Stevenson, J. Stewart and T. Stewart (eds.), *Miscellanea Scotica. A collection of tracts relating to the history, antiquities, topography and literature of Scotland*, 4 vols. (Glasgow: J. Wylie & Co., 1818–20), iii.177–82.
4. Ibid., 222–3; Michael Hunter, *The Occult Laboratory: Magic, Science and Second Sight in Late Seventeenth-Century Scotland* (Woodbridge: The Boydell Press, 2001), 149–50.
5. Martin, like some other writers, is aware of this but does not consider that it 'communicates' the ability except for that occasion.
6. A. Stevenson et al, *Miscellanea Scotica*, 221 note 3.
7. Ibid., 181–2.
8. Alexander Carmichael, *Carmina*, ii.158.
9. See John G. MacKay, 'Cànain nan Eun', *Scottish Gaelic Studies* 3 no. 2 (1931), 160–87.
10. For this and other references to the use of the scapula, see *Transactions of the Gaelic Society of Glasgow* 5 (1958), 92–3.
11. A. Stevenson et al, *Miscellanea Scotica*, 190. In the same place he tells of a twelve-year-old girl haunted by her double.
12. 'Gille-Màrtainn', interestingly, is a bye-name in Gaelic for the fox, conventionally a trickster.
13. A. Stevenson et al, *Miscellanea Scotica*, 216–17 note 3. But another correspondent claims that only the 'vicious' have the sight: 'some say they get it by compact with the devil; some say by converse with these demons we call fairies.'
14. William Matheson, 'The historical Coinneach Odhar and some prophecies attributed to him', *Transactions of the Gaelic Society of Inverness* 46 (1969–70), 66–88. See also Alexander MacKenzie, *The Prophecies of the Brahan Seer* (Stirling, 1896); Domhnall Iain MacÌomhair, *Coinneach Odhar* (Glasgow: Gairm, 1990).
15. This theme is explored extensively in an Irish context in Breandán Ó Buachalla, *Aisling Ghéar: Na Stíobhartaigh agus an t-Aos Léinn 1603–1788* (Baile Átha Cliath: An Clóchomhar Tta, 1996), especially Chapters 9–12.

Looking at Legends of the Supernatural

1. Tomás Ó Cathasaigh, 'The Semantics of Síd', *Éigse* 17 (1977–9), 137–55.
2. John Carey, *A Single Ray Of The Sun: Religious Speculation In Early Ireland* (Andover: Celtic Studies Publications, 1999), Chapter One.
3. Most recently edited in Michael Hunter, *The Occult Laboratory: Magic, Science and Second Sight in Late Seventeenth-Century Scotland* (Woodbridge: The Boydell Press, 2001), 77–106.
4. I heard this from the Rev. Donald MacLeod himself. His daughter, Mrs Mona Smith, refreshed my memory. She adds that there were three children involved: her father, her aunt, and another little boy and all of them had the same vision. They were accompanied by a certain Miss or Mrs MacAllister, who was reported to have second sight. This woman held the children by the hand and it was then they saw the fairies, who were dancing in a ring round a fire.

Next day, they went to look for the ashes of the fire but there was nothing to be seen. The physical contact here between the seer and the children fits into the pattern mentioned elsewhere. I am greatly obliged to Mrs Smith for supplying the information.

The sìdhichean, it should be added, are often described as *daoine beaga* but only 'small' as human beings can be small. They are not usually 'tiny' in the legends.

5. For an exhaustive study of the legend, see Bo Almqvist, 'Of Mermaids and Marriages. Séamas Heaney's 'Maighdean Mara' and Nuala Ní Dhomhnaill's 'An Mhaighdean Mhara' in the light of folk tradition', *Béaloideas* Vol. 58 (1990), 1–74.

6. William Matheson (ed.), *Òrain Iain Mhic Fhearchair a Bha 'na Bhàrd aig Sir Seumas MacDhomhnaill / The Songs of John MacCodrum: Bard to Sir James MacDonald of Sleat*, Scottish Gaelic Texts 2, (Edinburgh: Scottish Gaelic Texts Society, 1938), Introduction, xxxvi ff., esp. xxxix. Matheson says that 'According to other accounts it was the other partner [i.e. the man] of the union who was a seal.'

7. Ibid. Matheson draws upon a variety of printed sources as well as oral tradition – which of course are themselves taken from an earlier stage of that tradition. This particular item comes from *The Highland Monthly* IV, 467. f.

8. Dáithí Ó hÓgáin, *Myth, Legend & Romance: An Encyclopædia of the Irish Folk Tradition* (London: BCA,1990), 187.

9. This is the title of David Thomson's book *The People of the Sea* (Edinburgh: Canongate Books, 2001 [1954]).

10. Clarissa Pinkola Estés, *Women Who Run With The Wolves* (London: Ballantine, 1992). Chapter 9 (256–97), headed 'Homing: Returning to Oneself', is entirely devoted to this legend of the Seal who turns into a human and to its analysis. I am indebted to my daughter Catriona MacInnes for drawing my attention to this book and its treatment of the legend.

11. Taidhbhsean can be physically dangerous like other species of spectres, etc. But my best informants are adamant that attack by one's own samhla is to be distinguished from other hostile encounters. Such an attack upon oneself obviously invites investigation in clinical psychological terms.

12. There are a number of variants.

New Introduction to Carmina Gadelica

1. Rev. John MacKechnie (ed.), *The Dewar Manuscripts Volume 1* (Glasgow: William MacLellan, 1964), 34.

2. Calum Maclean, Review of *Carmina Gadelica Vol. V*, *Arv* 11 (1955), 152–4.

3. Hamish Robertson, 'Studies in Carmichael's Carmina Gadelica', *Scottish Gaelic Studies* 12 (1976), 220–65.

4. J. L. Campbell, 'Notes on Hamish Robertson's "Studies in Carmichael's *Carmina Gadelica*" ', *Scottish Gaelic Studies* 13 (1978), 1–17.

5. Ibid., 1.

6. Ibid., 2.

7. Gerard Murphy, Review of *Carmina Gadelica Vol. V*, *Éigse* 8 (1956), 167.

8. J. L. Campbell, 'Notes', 10.

9. Ibid., 13.

10. Ibid., 3.

11. Ibid., 13–14, 4.

12. Alan Bruford, ' "Deirdre" and Alexander Carmichael's treatment of oral sources', *Scottish Gaelic Studies* 14 (1983), 1–24.

13. Alexander MacBain, 'Gaelic Incantations', *Transactions of the Gaelic Society of Inverness* 17 (1890–91), 222–66; William MacKenzie, 'Gaelic Incantations, Charms, and Blessings of the Hebrides', *Transactions of the Gaelic Society of Inverness* 18 (1891–92), 97–182.

14. William MacKenzie, 'Gaelic Incantations', 121.

15. 'Woman' would be a sufficient translation; there is no suggestion of a 'maiden'.

16. Ibid., 111–12.

17. ii.284.

18. Calum Maclean, 'A Variant of the Charm of the Lasting Life from Uist', *Saga Och Sed* (1959), 75–8.

19. Allan had rendered the charm useless by saying 'If I come back [from battle]' thereby implying doubt in the power of the spell. Carmichael's traditions about Allan are found in the note to *Carmina Gadelica* ii.26.

20. Raghnall MacIlleDhuibh, 'The Trouble with *Carmina*', *West Highland Free Press* 29 May 1992.

Am Fàsach ann an Dùthchas nan Gàidheal

1. Bhon òran 'Gura muladach sgìth mi | 'S mi liom fhìn san tìr aineoil', foillsichte ann an *Tocher* 39 (1985), 122.

2. Frances Tolmie, *Journal of the Folk-song Society*, no. 16 (1911) (reprinted as *One Hundred and Five Songs of Occupation from the Western Isles of Scotland* (Felinfach, Dyfed: Llanerch, 1997)), 184–5.

3. W.J. Watson, *The History of the Celtic Place-Names of Scotland* (Edinburgh: Birlinn, 1986 [1926]), 491.

4. 'Clann Ghriogair air Fògradh', foillsichte ann am W. J. Watson (ed.), *Bàrdachd Ghàidhlig: Specimens of Gaelic Poetry, 1550–1900* 3rd edition (Stirling: An Comunn Gàidhealach, 1959), ss. 6393–6506 (ss. 6403–4).

5. W. J. Watson, *Celtic Place-Names of Scotland*, 357.

6. W. J. Watson, *Bàrdachd Ghàidhlig*, 6471–2.

7. Margaret Fay Shaw, *Folksongs and Folklore of South Uist*, 3rd edition (Aberdeen: Aberdeen University Press, 1986), 136.

General Index

Index of Titles and First Lines

Titles and first lines (in italics) of songs and poems referred to in the text, in so far as it has been possible to identify them.